S0-AFP-493

MCAD/MCSD

Developing XML Web Services and
Server Components with Visual C# .NET
and the .NET Framework

Exam 70-320

Amit Kalani
Priti Kalani

Training Guide

MCAD/MCSD (70-320): DEVELOPING XML WEB SERVICES AND SERVER COMPONENTS WITH VISUAL C# .NET AND THE .NET FRAMEWORK

International Standard Book Number: 0-7897-2824-9

Library of Congress Catalog Card Number: 2003100818

Printed in the United States of America

First Printing: April 2003

06   05   04   6   5   4

Trademarks

Warning and Disclaimer

PUBLISHER
Paul Boger

EXECUTIVE EDITOR
Jeff Riley

DEVELOPMENT EDITOR
Steve Rowe

MANAGING EDITOR
Charlotte Clapp

PROJECT EDITOR
Elizabeth Finney

COPY EDITOR
Margo Catts

INDEXER
Ken Johnson

PROOFREADER
Juli Cook

TECHNICAL EDITORS
Karl Hilsman
Steve Heckler

TEAM COORDINATOR
Sharry Gregory

MULTIMEDIA DEVELOPER
Dan Scherf

INTERIOR DESIGNER
Anne Jones

COVER DESIGNER
Charis Ann Santillie

Que®
CERTIFICATION

Que Certification • 800 East 96th Street • Indianapolis, Indiana 46240

A Note from Series Editor Ed Tittel

Congratulations on your purchase of the 70-320 Training Guide, the finest exam preparation book in the marketplace!

As Series Editor of the highly regarded Training Guide series, I can assure you that you won't be disappointed. You've taken your first step toward passing the 70-320 exam, and we value this opportunity to help you on your way!

As a "Favorite Study Guide Author" finalist in a 2002 poll of CertCities readers, I know the importance of delivering good books. You'll be impressed with Que Certification's stringent review process, which ensures the books are high-quality, relevant, and technically accurate. Rest assured that at least a dozen industry experts have reviewed this material, helping us deliver an excellent solution to your exam preparation needs.

Favorite Study Guide Author

We've also added a preview edition of PrepLogic's powerful, full-featured test engine, which is trusted by certification students throughout the world.

As a 20-year-plus veteran of the computing industry and the original creator and editor of the Exam Cram series, I've brought my IT experience to bear on these books. During my tenure at Novell from 1989 to 1994, I worked with and around its excellent education and certification department. At Novell, I witnessed the growth and development of the first really big, successful IT certification program—one that was to shape the industry forever afterward. This experience helped push my writing and teaching activities heavily in the certification direction. Since then, I've worked on more than 70 certification related books, and I write about certification topics for numerous Web sites and for *Certification* magazine.

In 1997 when Exam Cram was introduced, it quickly became the best-selling computer book series since "...*For Dummies*," and the best-selling certification book series ever. By maintaining an intense focus on the subject matter, tracking errata and updates quickly, and following the certification market closely, Exam Cram was able to establish the dominant position in cert prep books.

You will not be disappointed in your decision to purchase this book. If you are, please contact me at etittel@jump.net. All suggestions, ideas, input, or constructive criticism are welcome!

Ed Tittel

Contents at a Glance

Table of Contents

Part II   Final Review

XVI   MCAD/MCSD TRAINING GUIDE

Part III   Appendixes

ABOUT THE AUTHORS

Amit Kalani is a Microsoft Certified Application Developer (MCAD) and Microsoft Certified Solution Developer (MCSD) for Microsoft .NET. He is an author of *MCAD/MCSD Training Guide: Developing and Implementing Web Applications with Visual C# .NET and Visual Studio .NET (Exam 70-315)* and *MCAD/MCSD Training Guide: Developing and Implementing Windows-based Applications with Visual C# .NET and Visual Studio .NET (Exam 70-316).*

Amit has long been associated with Microsoft certification exams. In an earlier job, he also managed a Microsoft Certified Technical Education Center (CTEC), where he closely worked with students to understand their requirements, and he guided them toward passing the certification exams. You can reach Amit at amit@techcontent.com.

Priti Kalani is a Microsoft Certified Application Developer (MCAD) and Microsoft Certified Solution Developer (MCSD) for Microsoft .NET. Priti has been programming with the .NET Framework since its early beta versions. She has also been a technical reviewer for several popular books about the .NET Framework and related technologies.

Priti works for TechContent, where she divides her time between crafting words and code. She welcomes your comments about the book at her email address, priti@techcontent.com.

Dedication

To our parents.

Acknowledgments

Many people have worked hard to make this book possible. It is our immense pleasure to acknowledge the efforts of these fine people.

We are fortunate to have worked with the talented and dedicated team of publishing professionals at Que Certifications. Special thanks to Jeff Riley for giving us the opportunity and for working patiently with us at every step of the project. Thanks also to Steve Rowe for his focus on quality and for guiding us toward the goal of producing the best possible training guide. Thanks to Sheila Schroeder and Elizabeth Finney for diligently coordinating the review process of this book.

Our thanks also go to Mike Gunderloy, who wrote the Visual Basic .NET version of this book. Mike generously shared his chapter drafts with us and provided us with valuable comments. It was a treat to work with him, as there was so much to learn from his vast experience and expertise.

Thanks to our technical editors, Steve Heckler and Karl Hilsmann, for sharing their technical expertise and reviewing the contents of this book for correctness. Their constructive comments and suggestions also ensured that we did not miss anything that is of importance to the exam.

If this book is readable, the credit must go to Margo Catts. She did the copy editing for this book and did a great job in making sure that the words are correct and the format is consistent.

We would also like to thank Ken Johnson, Juli Cook, and Susan Geiselman who were working behind the scenes to put the final manuscript between covers and on the shelf.

We Want to Hear from You!

As the reader of this book, *you* are our most important critic and commentator. We value your opinion and want to know what we're doing right, what we could do better, what areas you'd like to see us publish in, and any other words of wisdom you're willing to pass our way.

As an executive editor for Que Publishing, I welcome your comments. You can email or write me directly to let me know what you did or didn't like about this book—as well as what we can do to make our books better.

Please note that I cannot help you with technical problems related to the *topic* of this book. We do have a User Services group, however, where I will forward specific technical questions related to the book.

When you write, please be sure to include this book's title and author as well as your name, email address, and phone number. I will carefully review your comments and share them with the author and editors who worked on the book.

Email: feedback@quepublishing.com

Mail: Jeff Riley
           Executive Editor
           Que Publishing
           800 East 96th Street
           Indianapolis, IN 46240 USA

For more information about this book or another Que Publishing title, visit our Web site at www.quepublishing.com. Type the ISBN (excluding hyphens) or the title of a book in the Search field to find the page you're looking for.

How to Use This Book

Que Certification has made an effort in its Training Guide series to make the information as accessible as possible for the purposes of learning the certification material. Here, you have an opportunity to view the many instructional features that have been incorporated into the books to achieve that goal.

CHAPTER OPENER

Each chapter begins with a set of features designed to allow you to maximize study time for that material.

List of Objectives: Each chapter begins with a list of the objectives as stated by Microsoft.

Objective Explanations: Immediately following each objective is an explanation of it, providing context that defines it more meaningfully in relation to the exam. Because Microsoft can sometimes be vague in its objectives list, the objective explanations are designed to clarify any vagueness by relying on the authors' test-taking experience.

OBJECTIVES

This chapter covers the following Microsoft-specified objective for the "Creating and Managing Microsoft Windows Services, Serviced Components, .NET Remoting Objects, and XML Web Services" section of the "Developing XML Web Services and Server Components with Microsoft Visual C# .NET and the Microsoft .NET Framework" exam:

Create and consume a .NET Remoting object.

- **Implement server-activated components.**
- **Implement client-activated components.**
- **Select a channel protocol and a formatter. Channel protocols include TCP and HTTP. Formatters include SOAP and binary.**
- **Create client configuration files and server configuration files.**
- **Implement an asynchronous method.**
- **Create the listener service.**
- **Instantiate and invoke a .NET Remoting object.**

▶ This exam objective tests your skill on designing distributed applications with .NET remoting, which is a part of the .NET Framework SDK. You should know how to create a remote object, how to make it available to all the users via a remoting server, and how to write client applications that instantiate remote objects and invoke methods on them.

▶ Remoting provides a very flexible and configurable environment to design distributed applications. By the virtue of flexibility, the .NET remoting applications can be designed in several different ways. In this exam you are required to know how to make choices for various remoting configurations, such as activation mode, channel, and formatter, for a given scenario.

CHAPTER 3

.NET Remoting

Chapter Outline: Learning always gets a boost when you can see both the forest and the trees. To give you a visual image of how the topics in a chapter fit together, you will find a chapter outline at the beginning of each chapter. You will also be able to use this for easy reference when looking for a particular topic.

STUDY STRATEGIES

▶ Write programs to create remotable objects, remoting hosts, and remoting clients. Understand what role each of them plays in a distributed computing scenario.

▶ Understand the difference between server-activated objects and client-activated objects, HTTP channel and TCP channel, SOAP formatter and binary formatter. You should be ready to answer questions that ask you to choose between these remoting elements in a given scenario.

▶ Use both declarative as well as programmatic configuration for distributed applications. Appreciate the advantages and shortcomings of each approach.

▶ Understand how to use the asynchronous programming techniques to make a client program responsive in spite of slow method calls across the network.

Study Strategies: Each topic presents its own learning challenge. To support you through this, Que Certification has included strategies for how to best approach studying in order to retain the material in the chapter, particularly as it is addressed on the exam.

INSTRUCTIONAL FEATURES WITHIN THE CHAPTER

These books include a large amount and different kinds of information. The many different elements are designed to help you identify information by its purpose and importance to the exam and also to provide you with varied ways to learn the material. You will be able to determine how much attention to devote to certain elements, depending on what your goals are. By becoming familiar with the different presentations of information, you will know what information will be important to you as a test-taker and which information will be important to you as a practitioner.

EXAM TIP

SOAP over Other Protocols You often read that SOAP messages travel over HTTP Although this is the default for SOAP as implemented by Visual Studio .NET, it's not a part of the SOAP specification. SOAP messages could be sent by email or File Transfer Protocol (FTP) without losing their content. As a practical matter, SOAP today uses HTTP in almost all cases.

Exam Tip: Exam Tips appear in the margins to provide specific exam-related advice. Such tips may address what material is covered (or not covered) on the exam, how it is covered, mnemonic devices, or particular quirks of that exam.

Warning: In using sophisticated information technology, there is always potential for mistakes or even catastrophes that can occur through improper application of the technology. Warnings appear in the margins to alert you to such potential problems.

---

404   Part I EXAM PREPARATION

WARNING

The FileSystemWatcher Component May Lose Track of Changes The FileSystemWatcher component stores the file system changes in a property named InternalBufferSize before it acts upon those changes. If there are too many changes in a short time, this buffer can overflow and cause the FileSystemWatcher component to lose track of the file system changes. This buffer's default size is 8192 bytes. You should not arbitrarily increase this buffer's size because this buffer is maintained in non-paged memory and increasing its size would directly impact the performance of other applications. Instead, you should use the Path, NotifyFilter, and IncludeSubdirectories properties to narrow down the scope of notifications that the FileSystemWatcher component receives.

TABLE 6.2 *continued*

IMPORTANT MEMBERS OF THE FileSystemWatcher CLASS

Member	Type	Description
IncludeSubdirectories	Property	Specifies whether the subdirectories within the specified path should be monitored.
InternalBufferSize	Property	Specifies the size of the internal buffer.
NotifyFilter	Property	Specifies the type of file system changes to monitor. Its value is a combination of values from the NotifyFilters enumeration.
Path	Property	Specifies the path of the directory to watch.
Renamed	Event	Occurs when a file or directory in the specified Path is renamed.
SynchronizingObject	Property	Specifies the object that is used to marshal the event handler calls.
WaitForChanged()	Method	This method is a synchronous method that returns a structure that contains specific information on the file system change.

Compilation of the StepByStep6_1 project creates an executable file just like other Windows applications. However, you cannot run this executable directly. If you try doing so, you get a Windows service start failure error with the following message:

```
Cannot start service from the command line or a
debugger. A Windows Service must first be installed
(using installutil.exe) and then started with the
Server Explorer, Windows Services Administrative
tool or the NET START command
```

Apparently, you need to install a Windows service application before you can start it, and you'll learn how to do that in the following section.

NOTE

Windows Service Description Unfortunately, the Installer class does not have a property to set the description for a Windows Service. If you need to set a description for a service, you have two choices: Either use the Service Control utility (sc.exe) or modify the Registry key corresponding to the Windows service, add a string value named Description, and set the data for this value with the description text.

INSTALLING A WINDOWS SERVICE

The .NET Framework enables you to create custom installer components. The custom installer components are the classes that an

Note: Notes appear in the margins and contain various kinds of useful information, such as tips on the technology or administrative practices, historical background on terms and technologies, or side commentary on industry issues.

STEP BY STEP

7.1 Creating a Serviced Component

1. Launch Visual Studio .NET. Select File, New, Blank Solution, and name the new solution 320C07. Click OK.

2. Add a new Visual C# .NET class library named StepByStep7_1 to the solution.

3. In the Solution Explorer, right-click project StepByStep7_1 and select Add Reference from the context menu. In the .NET tab of the Add Reference dialog box, select the System.EnterpriseServices component from the list view and click the Select button. Click OK to add the reference.

4. In the Solution Explorer, rename the default Class1.cs to NorthwindSC.cs.

5. Open NorthwindSC.cs and replace the code with the following code:

```
using System;

using System.Data;
using System.Data.SqlClient;
using System.EnterpriseServices;

namespace StepByStep7_1
{
```

FIGURE 7.9
You can manage the properties of a COM+ application via its Properties dialog box.

Step by Step: Step by Steps are hands-on tutorial instructions that walk you through a particular task or function relevant to the exam objectives.

Figure: To improve readability, the figures have been placed in the margins wherever possible so they do not interrupt the main flow of text.

Chapter 7 COMPONENT SERVICES 453

A .NET type can be exported as a COM type library in any of the following ways:

▶ In Visual Studio .NET, open the project's property pages and change the Register for COM Interop option to true. The Register for COM Interop option is in the Configuration Properties, Build page of the project's Property Pages dialog box.

▶ Use the Assembly Registration tool (regasm.exe) with its /tlb option.

▶ Use the Type Library Exporter tool (tlbexp.exe) that ships as a part of .NET Framework SDK.

▶ In a program, use the ConvertAssemblyToTypeLib() method of the TypeLibConverter class in the System.Runtime.InteropServices namespace.

The default extension of a type library is .tlb. You can use this library to compile the COM clients.

REVIEW BREAK

▶ Instead of providing a new version of component services, Microsoft .NET Framework relies on the COM+ component services that ship as a part of Windows 2000, Windows XP, and the Windows Server 2003.

▶ COM+ component services provide several features for increasing the security, reliability, availability, efficiency, and scalability of an enterprise application as part of the operating system infrastructure.

▶ COM+ does not understand .NET and therefore cannot directly provide services to the .NET component. Instead, a .NET component must be exposed as a COM component through an assembly registration process.

▶ To enable the communication between COM and .NET components, the .NET Framework generates a COM Callable Wrapper (CCW). The CCW enables communication between the calling COM code and the managed code. It also handles conversion between the data types, as well as other messages between the COM types and the .NET types.

Review Break: Crucial information is summarized at various points in the book in lists or tables. At the end of a particularly long section, you might come across a Review Break that is there just to wrap up one long objective and reinforce the key points before you shift your focus to the next section.

EXTENSIVE REVIEW AND SELF-TEST OPTIONS

At the end of each chapter, along with some summary elements, you will find a section called "Apply Your Knowledge" that gives you several different methods with which to test your understanding of the material and review what you have learned.

CHAPTER SUMMARY

Enterprise applications have special needs for availability, reliability, scalability, and performance. COM+ provides an infrastructure that provides common services required for an enterprise application.

In this chapter, you learned how to use COM+ component services from your .NET programs. You created a serviced component and registered the component with the COM+ Catalog.

You also learned how to expose a .NET component to COM or COM+ programs. When a .NET component is visible to COM+, you can use the Component Services administrative tool to configure a component.

You also learned how to apply various attributes to your assemblies, classes, and methods to use the COM+ services. You used and appreciated the ease and power of attribute-based declarative programming for programming the component services.

KEY TERMS

- ACID
- activation type
- COM+ application
- COM+ Catalog
- COM interface
- context
- DTC (Distributed Transaction Coordinator)
- just-in-time (JIT) activation
- object pooling

Chapter Summary: Before the Apply Your Knowledge section, you will find a chapter summary that wraps up the chapter and reviews what you should have learned.

Key Terms: A list of key terms appears at the end of each chapter. These are terms that you should be sure you know and are comfortable defining and understanding when you go in to take the exam.

Exercises: These activities provide an opportunity for you to master specific hands-on tasks. Our goal is to increase your proficiency with the product or technology. You must be able to conduct these tasks in order to pass the exam.

---

550   Part I   EXAM PREPARATION

APPLY YOUR KNOWLEDGE

Exercises

7.1   Exposing Serviced Components via .NET Remoting

In an enterprise application, you may be required to expose business objects remotely. A general practice in that case is to add an extra tier that handles remote communication between the client and server. You can use your knowledge of .NET remoting and XML Web services for creating such a tier.

In this exercise, you learn how to expose a serviced component via a remoting server. You create three sets of programs: a serviced component that allows access to the Northwind database, a Singleton remoting server that exposes the serviced component, and a client program that connects to the remoting server to invoke methods on the serviced component.

Estimated Time: 30 minutes.

1. Launch Visual Studio .NET. Select File, New, Blank Solution, and name the new solution 320C07Exercises. Click OK.

2. Add a new Visual C# .NET Class library project named Exercise7_1SC to the solution.

3. In the Solution Explorer, right-click project Exercise7_1SC and select Add Reference from the context menu to add a reference to the System.EnterpriseServices component.

4. In the Solution Explorer, rename the default Class1.cs to NorthwindSC.cs. Open the NorthwindSC.cs and replace the code with the following code (change the Guid attribute):

```
using System;
using System.Data;
using System.Data.SqlClient;
using System.EnterpriseServices;
using System.Runtime.InteropServices;
using System.Diagnostics;
```

Review Questions

1. What is the COM+ catalog and what is it used for?

2. What is the significance of using the AutoComplete attribute in a method declaration?

3. What is the use of the CanBePooled() method for a pooled object?

4. How does a client instantiate a queued component?

5. How can you use COM+ services to increase an application's throughput?

6. How would you specify the type of transaction available to a serviced component?

7. What is the use of the ContextUtil class?

8. What are some of the scenarios where you might want to use the COM+ object pooling service?

9. State a few guidelines for designing a queued component.

10. What is a COM Callable Wrapper (CCW)?

Review Questions: These open-ended, short-answer questions allow you to quickly assess your comprehension of what you just read in the chapter. Instead of asking you to choose from a list of options, these questions require you to state the correct answers in your own words. Although you will not experience these kinds of questions on the exam, these questions will indeed test your level of comprehension of key concepts.

Chapter 7 COMPONENT SERVICES 555

APPLY YOUR KNOWLEDGE

Exam Questions

1. You create a COM+ application named "Inventory Application." This application contains a single serviced component named InventoryStatus that is present in an assembly named inventorystatus.dll. The InventoryStatus component is used by many client applications to monitor the status of the inventory. The client applications access the serviced component on a frequent basis. Which of the following options should you choose to ensure that the methods on InventoryStatus are processed as quickly as possible?

   A. Configure Inventory Application to be a server application.

   B. Configure Inventory Application to be a library application.

   C. Configure the InventoryStatus component to use object pooling.

   D. Configure the InventoryStatus component to use just-in-time Activation.

2. You are creating a serviced component that will be called from both managed and unmanaged client applications. You use a class library project to write the business logic and then compile the project into a strongly named assembly. As a next step, you want to register the assembly in the COM+ Catalog. You want to detect and correct any registration errors before any client applications use the component. Which of the following tools should you use to register the assembly?

Answers to Exam Questions

1. **B.** Method calls execute fastest when the application is configured as a library application. The library application executes in the client's process. For more information, see the section "COM+ Applications" in this chapter.

2. **D.** Among the given options, the only tool that actually registers a strongly named assembly with the COM+ Catalog is the .NET Services Installation tool (regsvcs.exe). For more information, see the section "Registering the Serviced Component into the COM+ Catalog" in this chapter.

3. **A.** If no object is available and no new object can be created because of the size restriction of the pool, the client requests are queued to receive the first available object from the pool. If an object cannot be made available within the time specified in the CreationTimeOut property, an exception is thrown. For more information, see the section "How Object Pooling Works" in this chapter.

4. **B.** When you use the AutoComplete attribute with a method, COM+ intercepts the method call to set the done bit and consistent bits after the method call returns. If there are no errors in the method call then the consistent bit is set to True; otherwise the consistent bit is set to False. This setting ensures that the changes to the database are committed or rolled backed reliably. For more information, see the section "How Automatic Transaction Works" in this chapter.

Exam Questions: These questions reflect the kinds of multiple-choice questions that appear on the Microsoft exams. Use them to become familiar with the exam question formats and to help you determine what you know and what you need to review or study more.

Answers and Explanations: For each of the Review and Exam questions, you will find thorough explanations located at the end of the section.

done bit to true. Using the EnableCommit() method sets the consistent bit to true but also sets the done bit to false, which does not deactivate the object after the method call returns. For more information, see the section "Elements of Transaction Processing" in this chapter.

13. **C, D.** You must at least sign the component with a strong name and then register the component in the COM+ Catalog. Just registering the

you should use the COM+ queued component service. For more information, see the section "Queued Components" in this chapter.

15. **C, D.** For achieving maximum performance, you can use COM+ object pooling and just-in-time activation services. For more information, see the section "Using Just-in-Time Activation with Object Pooling—A Recipe for High Throughput" in this chapter.

Suggested Readings and Resources

1. Visual Studio .NET Combined Help Collection
   - Writing Serviced Components
   - Serviced Components Programming Guidelines
   - COM+ Programming Overview

2. Building Distributed Applications with .NET, msdn.microsoft.com/nhp/default.asp?contentid=28001271.

3. The .NET Six-week series guide, msdn.microsoft.com/net/guide.

4. MSDN Index of How-To Articles, msdn.microsoft.com/howto/howto_index.asp.

5. .NET Architectural Sample Applications. msdn.microsoft.com/library/en-us/dnbda/html/bdadotnetsamp0.asp.

6. Enterprise Development Technology Map, msdn.microsoft.com/library/en-us/Dndotnet/html/Techmap_enterprise1.asp.

7. Derek Beyer. *C# COM+ Programming*. M&T Books, 2001.

8. Juval Lowy. *COM and .NET Component Services*. O'Reilly, 2001.

9. Roger Sessions. *COM+ and the Battle for the Middle Tier*. John Wiley & Sons, Inc. 2000.

Suggested Readings and Resources: The very last element in every chapter is a list of additional resources you can use if you want to go above and beyond certification-level material or if you need to spend more time on a particular subject that you are having trouble understanding.

Introduction

MCAD/MCSD .NET Training Guide: Developing XML Web Services and Server Components with Visual C# .NET and the Microsoft .NET Framework is designed for developers who are pursuing the Microsoft Certified Application Developer (MCAD) or Microsoft Certified Solution Developer (MCSD) for Microsoft .NET certifications. This book covers the Developing XML Web Services and Server Components with Visual C# .NET and the Microsoft .NET Framework exam (70-320), which is a core exam for both of those certifications. The exam is designed to measure your skill in developing and implementing middle-tier components, server components, and XML Web services by using Visual Studio .NET, Microsoft .NET Framework, and the Visual C# .NET programming language.

This book is designed to cover all the objectives that Microsoft has created for this exam. It doesn't offer end-to-end coverage of the Visual C# .NET language or the .NET Framework; rather, it helps you develop the specific core competencies that you need to design and develop distributed applications. You can pass the exam by learning the material in this book, without taking a class. Of course, depending on your own personal study habits and learning style, you might benefit from studying this book *and* taking a class.

Even if you are not planning to take the exam, you might find this book useful. Understanding the wide range of topics covered by the exam objectives will certainly help you to accomplish programming tasks.

How This Book Helps You

This book gives you a self-guided tour of all the areas that are covered by the "Developing XML Web Services and Server Components with Visual C# .NET and the Microsoft .NET Framework" exam. The goal is to teach you the specific skills you need to achieve your MCAD or MCSD certification. You'll also find helpful hints, tips, examples, exercises, and references to additional study materials.

Organization

This book is organized around the individual objectives from Microsoft's preparation guide for the "Developing XML Web Services and Server Components with Visual C# .NET and the Microsoft .NET Framework" exam. Every objective is covered in this book. The objectives are not covered in exactly the same order in which you'll find them in the official preparation guide (which you can download from `www.microsoft.com/traincert/exams/70-320.asp`), but they are reorganized for more logical teaching. I have also tried to make the information more accessible in several ways:

▶ This introduction includes the full list of exam topics and objectives.

▶ The Study and Exam Tips section helps you develop study strategies. It also provides you with valuable exam-day tips and information. You should read it early on.

▶ Each chapter starts with a list of objectives that are covered in that chapter.

▶ Each chapter also begins with an outline that provides an overview of the material for that chapter, as well as the page numbers where specific topics can be found.

▶ Each objective is repeated in the text where it is covered in detail.

▶ **Instructional Features.** This book is designed to provide you with multiple ways to learn and reinforce the exam material. Here are some of the instructional features you'll find inside:

  • *Objective explanations.* As mentioned previously, each chapter begins with a list of the objectives covered in the chapter. In addition, immediately following each objective is a detailed explanation that puts the objective in the context of the product.

  • *Study strategies.* Each chapter offers a selected list of study strategies—exercises to try or additional material to read that will help you learn and retain the material in the chapter.

  • *Exam tips.* Exam tips appear in the margins and provide specific exam-related advice. Exam tips address what material is likely to be covered (or not covered) on the exam, how to remember it, or particular exam quirks.

  • *Review breaks and chapter summaries.* Crucial information is summarized at various points in the book, in lists of key points you need to remember. Each chapter ends with an overall summary of the material covered in that chapter as well.

  • *Guided practice exercises.* Guided Practice Exercises offer additional opportunities to practice the material within a chapter and to learn additional facets of the topic at hand.

  • *Key terms.* A list of key terms appears at the end of each chapter.

  • *Notes.* Notes appear in the margins and contain various kinds of useful information, such as tips on technology, historical background, side commentary, or notes on where to go for more detailed coverage of a particular topic.

  • *Warnings.* When you use sophisticated computing technology, there is always a possibility of mistakes or even catastrophes. Warnings appear in the margins and alert you of such potential problems, whether they occur in following along with the text or in implementing Visual C# .NET in a production environment.

  • *Step-by-Steps.* These are hands-on, tutorial instructions that lead you through a particular task or function related to the exam objectives.

  • *Exercises.* Found at the end of each chapter in the "Apply Your Knowledge" section, the exercises include additional tutorial material and more chances to practice the skills that you learned in the chapter.

▶ **Extensive Practice Test Options.** The book provides numerous opportunities for you to assess your knowledge and practice for the exam. The practice options include the following:

  • *Review questions.* These open-ended questions appear in the "Apply Your Knowledge" section at the end of each chapter. They enable you to quickly assess your comprehension of what you just read in the chapter. The answers are provided later in the section.

- *Exam questions.* These questions appear in the "Apply Your Knowledge" section. They reflect the kinds of multiple-choice questions that appear on the Microsoft exams. You should use them to practice for the exam and to help determine what you know and what you might need to review or study further. Answers and explanations are provided later in the section.

- *Practice Exam.* The "Final Review" section includes a complete exam that you can use to practice for the real thing. The Final Review section and the Practice Exam are discussed in more detail later in this chapter.

- *PrepLogic.* The PrepLogic, Preview Edition software included on the CD-ROM provides more practice questions.

> NOTE
> **PrepLogic Software** For a complete description of the PrepLogic test engine, please see Appendix F, "*Using the PrepLogic, Preview Edition Software.*"

▶ **Final Review.** The "Final Review" section of the book provides two valuable tools for preparing for the exam:

- *Fast Facts.* This condensed version of the information contained in the book is extremely useful for last-minute review.

- *Practice Exam.* A full practice test for the exam is included in this book. Questions are written in the style and format used on the actual exams. You should use the Practice Exam to assess your readiness for the real thing.

This book includes several valuable appendixes, including overviews of ADO.NET (Appendix A) and XML (Appendix B), as well as a glossary (Appendix C) and an overview of the Microsoft certification program (Appendix D). Appendix E reviews the content of the CD-ROM, and Appendix F covers the use of the PrepLogic software. Finally, Appendix G provides you with a list of suggested readings and resources that contain useful information on Visual C# .NET and the .NET Framework.

These and all the other book features mentioned previously will provide you with thorough preparation for the exam.

For more information about the exam or the certification process, you should contact Microsoft directly:

By E-mail: mcphelp@microsoft.com

By regular mail, telephone, or fax, contact the Microsoft Regional Education Service Center (RESC) nearest you. You can find lists of RESCs at www.microsoft.com/traincert/support/northamerica.asp (for North America) and www.microsoft.com/traincert/support/worldsites.asp (worldwide).

On the Internet: www.microsoft.com/traincert

WHAT THE "DEVELOPING XML WEB SERVICES AND SERVER COMPONENTS WITH VISUAL C# .NET AND THE MICROSOFT .NET FRAMEWORK" EXAM (EXAM 70-320) COVERS

The "Developing XML Web Services and Server Components with Visual C# .NET and the Microsoft .NET Framework" exam covers four major topic areas: "Creating and Managing Microsoft Windows Services, Serviced Components, .NET Remoting Objects, and XML Web Services," "Consuming and Manipulating Data," "Testing and Debugging," and "Deploying Windows Services, Serviced Components, .NET Remoting Objects, and XML Web Services." The exam objectives are listed by topic area in the following sections.

Creating and Managing Microsoft Windows Services, Serviced Components, .NET Remoting Objects, and XML Web Services

Create and manipulate a Windows service.

▶ Write code that is executed when a Windows service is started or stopped.

Create and consume a serviced component.

▶ Implement a serviced component.

▶ Create interfaces that are visible to COM.

▶ Create a strongly named assembly.

▶ Register the component in the global assembly cache.

▶ Manage the component by using the Component Services tool.

Create and consume a .NET Remoting object.

▶ Implement server-activated components.

▶ Implement client-activated components.

▶ Select a channel protocol and a formatter. Channel protocols include TCP and HTTP. Formatters include SOAP and binary.

▶ Create client configuration files and server configuration files.

▶ Implement an asynchronous method.

▶ Create the listener service.

▶ Instantiate and invoke a .NET Remoting object.

Create and consume an XML Web service.

▶ Control characteristics of Web methods by using attributes.

▶ Create and use SOAP extensions.

▶ Create asynchronous Web methods.

▶ Control XML wire format for an XML Web service.

▶ Instantiate and invoke an XML Web service.

Implement security for a Windows service, a serviced component, a .NET Remoting object, and an XML Web service.

Access unmanaged code from a Windows service, a serviced component, a .NET Remoting object, and an XML Web service.

Consuming and Manipulating Data

Access and manipulate data from a Microsoft SQL Server database by creating and using ad hoc queries and stored procedures.

Create and manipulate DataSets.

- ▶ Manipulate a DataSet schema.
- ▶ Manipulate DataSet relationships.
- ▶ Create a strongly typed DataSet.

Access and manipulate XML data.

- ▶ Access an XML file by using the Document Object Model (DOM) and an XmlReader.
- ▶ Transform DataSet data into XML data.
- ▶ Use XPath to query XML data.
- ▶ Generate and use an XSD schema.
- ▶ Write a SQL statement that retrieves XML data from a SQL Server database.
- ▶ Update a SQL Server database by using XML.
- ▶ Validate an XML document.

Testing and Debugging

Create a unit test plan.

Implement tracing.

- ▶ Configure and use trace listeners and trace switches.
- ▶ Display trace output.

Instrument and debug a Windows service, a serviced component, a .NET Remoting object, and an XML Web service

- ▶ Configure the debugging environment.
- ▶ Create and apply debugging code to components and applications.
- ▶ Provide multicultural test data to components and applications.
- ▶ Execute tests.

Use interactive debugging.

Log test results.

- ▶ Resolve errors and rework code.
- ▶ Control debugging in the Web.config file.
- ▶ Use SOAP extensions for debugging.

Deploying Windows Services, Serviced Components, .NET Remoting Objects, and XML Web Services

Plan the deployment of and deploy a Windows service, a serviced component, a .NET Remoting object, and an XML Web service.

Create a setup program that installs a Windows service, a serviced component, a .NET Remoting object, and an XML Web service.

- ▶ Register components and assemblies.

Publish an XML Web service.

- ▶ Enable static discovery.
- ▶ Publish XML Web service definitions in the UDDI.

Configure client computers and servers to use a Windows service, a serviced component, a .NET Remoting object, and an XML Web service.

Implement versioning.

Plan, configure, and deploy side-by-side deployments and applications.

Configure security for a Windows service, a serviced component, a .NET Remoting object, and an XML Web service.

- ▶ Configure authentication type. Authentication types include Windows authentication, Microsoft .NET Passport, custom authentication, and none.

- ▶ Configure and control authorization. Authorization methods include file-based authorization and URL-based authorization.

- ▶ Configure and implement identity management.

WHAT YOU SHOULD KNOW BEFORE READING THIS BOOK

The Microsoft Visual C# .NET exams assume that you're familiar with the Visual C# language and the use of Visual Studio .NET to create applications, even though there are no objectives that pertain directly to this knowledge. This book shows you tasks that are directly related to exam objectives, but it does not include a tutorial in Visual C# .NET itself. If you're just getting started with the language, you should check out some of the references in Appendix G for the information that you'll need to get you started. For beginners, I particularly recommend these references:

- ▶ The samples and QuickStart Tutorials, which are installed as part of the .NET Framework SDK (which is a component of a full Visual Studio .NET installation) are an excellent starting point for information on ASP.NET, Windows Forms, and common tasks.

- ▶ *C# How to Program,* by Harvey M. Deitel, et al. (Prentice Hall, 2002).

- ▶ *Special Edition Using C#,* by NIIT (Que, 2001).

- ▶ *C# Primer: A Practical Approach,* by Stanley B. Lippman (Addison-Wesley Professional, 2002).

- ▶ *Understanding .NET: A Tutorial and Analysis,* by David Chappell (Addison-Wesley Professional, 2002).

HARDWARE AND SOFTWARE YOU NEED

Although you can build Visual C# .NET applications by using nothing more than the tools provided in the free .NET Framework SDK, to pass the exam you need to have access to a copy of Visual Studio .NET. Visual Studio .NET includes many tools and features that are not found in the free command-line tools. There are three editions of Visual Studio .NET:

- ▶ **Professional.** Visual Studio .NET Professional is the entry-level product in the product line. This edition allows you to build Windows, ASP.NET, and Web services applications. It includes visual design tools, Crystal Reports, and the Microsoft Data Engine (MSDE) version of SQL Server 2000.

▶ **Enterprise Developer.** Building on the Professional edition, the Enterprise Developer edition adds the full version of SQL Server 2000, Visual SourceSafe, Application Center Test, and Visual Studio Analyzer, as well as developer licenses for Exchange Server, Host Integration Server, and Commerce Server. It also contains additional samples and templates.

▶ **Enterprise Architect.** The high-end Enterprise Architect edition adds Visio Enterprise Architect, a development license for SQL Server, and high-end enterprise templates.

You should be able to complete all the exercises in this book with any of the three editions of Visual Studio .NET. Your computer should meet the minimum criteria required for a Visual Studio .NET installation:

▶ A Pentium II or better CPU, running at 450MHz or faster.

▶ Windows NT 4.0 or later.

▶ The following memory, depending on the operating system you have installed: 64MB for Windows NT 4.0 Workstation, 96MB for Windows 2000 Professional, 160MB for Windows NT 4.0 Server or Windows XP Professional, or 192MB for Windows 2000 Server.

▶ 3.5GB of disk space for a full installation.

▶ A CD-ROM or DVD drive.

▶ A video card running at 800¥600, with at least 256 colors.

▶ A Microsoft or compatible mouse.

Of course, those are *minimum* requirements. I recommend the following more realistic requirements:

▶ A Pentium III or better CPU running at 800MHz or faster.

▶ Windows 2000.

▶ At least 256MB of RAM, and as much more as you can afford.

▶ 5GB of disk space for a full installation.

▶ A CD-ROM or DVD drive.

▶ A video card running at 1280¥1024 or higher, with at least 65,000 colors.

▶ A Microsoft or compatible mouse.

You might find it easiest to obtain access to the necessary computer hardware and software in a corporate environment. It can be difficult, however, to allocate enough time within a busy workday to complete a self-study program. Most of your study time will probably need to occur outside normal working hours, away from the everyday interruptions and pressures of your job.

ADVICE ON TAKING THE EXAM

You will find more extensive tips in the section, "Study and Exam Prep Tips," but keep this advice in mind as you study:

▶ Read all the material in this book. Microsoft has been known to include material that is not expressly specified in the objectives for an exam. This book includes additional information that is not reflected in the objectives, in an effort to give you the best possible preparation for the examination—and for the real-world experiences to come.

▶ Complete the Step-by-Steps, Guided Practice Exercises, and exercises in each chapter. They will help you gain experience with Visual C# .NET. All Microsoft exams are task and experience based and require you to have experience using the Microsoft products, not just reading about them.

▶ Use the review and exam questions to assess your knowledge. Don't just read the chapter content; use the review and exam questions to find out what you know and what you don't. Study some more, review, and then assess your knowledge again.

▶ Review the exam objectives. Develop your own questions and examples for each topic listed. If you can develop and answer several questions for each topic, you should not find it difficult to pass the exam.

Remember, the primary objective is not to pass the exam: It is to understand the material. After you understand the material, passing the exam should be simple. To really work with Visual C# .NET, you need a solid foundation in practical skills. This book, and the Microsoft Certified Professional program, are designed to ensure that you have that solid foundation.

Good luck!

> **EXAM TIP**
>
> **There's No Substitute for Experience** The single best study tip that anyone can give you is to actually work with the product that you're learning! Even if you could become a "paper MCAD" simply by reading books, you wouldn't get the real-world skills that you need to be a Visual C# .NET success.

This section of the book provides you with some general guidelines for preparing for the exam "Developing XML Web Services and Server Components with Microsoft Visual C# .NET and the Microsoft .NET Framework" (exam 70-320). It is organized into three parts. The first part addresses your pre-exam preparation activities and covers general study tips. This is followed by an extended look at the Microsoft Certification exams, including a number of specific tips that apply to the Microsoft exam formats. Finally, changes in Microsoft's testing policies and how they might affect you are discussed.

To better understand the nature of preparation for the test, it is important to understand learning as a process. You are probably aware of how you best learn new material. You might find that outlining works best for you, or, as a visual learner, you might need to see things. Whatever your learning style, test preparation takes place over time. Obviously, you can't start studying for this exam the night before you take it. It is very important to understand that learning is a developmental process. Understanding it as a process helps you focus on what you know and what you have yet to learn.

Thinking about how you learn should help you recognize that learning takes place when you are able to match new information to old. You have some previous experience with computers and software development, and now you are preparing for this certification exam. Using this book, software, and supplementary materials will not just add incrementally to what you know; as you study, you actually change the organization of your knowledge and integrate this new information into your existing knowledge base. This leads you to a more comprehensive understanding of the tasks and concepts outlined in the objectives and of computing in general. Again, this happens as a repetitive process rather than as a single event. Keep this model of learning in mind as you prepare for the exam, and you will make good

Study and Exam Prep Tips

decisions concerning what to study and how much more studying you need to do.

STUDY TIPS

There are many ways to approach studying, just as there are many different types of material to study. However, the tips that follow should work well for the type of material covered on this certification exam.

Study Strategies

Although individuals vary in the ways they learn information, some basic principles of learning apply to everyone. You should adopt some study strategies that take advantage of these principles. One of these principles is that learning can be broken into various depths. *Recognition* (of terms, for example) exemplifies a surface level of learning in which you rely on a prompt of some sort to elicit recall. *Comprehension or understanding* (of the concepts behind the terms, for example), represents a deeper level of learning. The ability to analyze a concept and apply your understanding of it in a new way represents a further depth of learning.

Your learning strategy should enable you to know the material at a level or two deeper than mere recognition. This will help you do well on the exam. You will know the material so thoroughly that you can easily handle the recognition-level types of questions used in multiple-choice testing. You will also be able to apply your knowledge to solve new problems.

Macro and Micro Study Strategies

One strategy that can lead to deep learning involves preparing an outline that covers all the objectives and subobjectives for the particular exam you are working on. Then you should delve a bit further into the material and include a level or two of detail beyond the stated objectives and subobjectives for the exam. Then you should expand the outline by coming up with a statement of definition or a summary for each point in the outline.

An outline provides two approaches to studying. First, you can study the outline by focusing on the organization of the material. Work your way through the points and subpoints of your outline, with the goal of learning how they relate to one another. For example, be sure you understand how each of the main objective areas is similar to and different from the others. Then do the same thing with the subobjectives; be sure you know which subobjectives pertain to each objective area and how they relate to one another.

Next, you can work through the outline, focusing on learning the details. You should memorize and understand terms and their definitions, facts, rules and strategies, advantages and disadvantages, and so on. In this pass through the outline, you should attempt to learn detail rather than the big picture (the organizational information that you worked on in the first pass through the outline).

Research has shown that attempting to assimilate both types of information at the same time seems to interfere with the overall learning process. Split your study into these two approaches, using one after another, and you will perform better on the exam.

Active Study Strategies

The process of writing down and defining objectives, subobjectives, terms, facts, and definitions promotes a more active learning strategy than merely reading the material. In human information-processing terms, writing forces you to engage in more active encoding of the information. Simply reading over the information exemplifies more passive processing.

Next, you should determine whether you can apply the information you have learned by attempting to create examples and scenarios on your own. You should think about how or where you could apply the concepts you are learning. Again, you should write down this information so you can process the facts and concepts in a more active fashion.

Because of their hands-on nature, the Step-by-Step tutorials, the Guided Practice Exercises, and the exercises at the ends of the chapters provide further active learning opportunities that will reinforce concepts as well.

Common-Sense Strategies

Finally, you should also follow common-sense practices when studying. You should study when you are alert, reduce or eliminate distractions, take breaks when you become fatigued, and so on.

Pre-Testing Yourself

Pre-testing enables you to assess how well you are learning. One of the most important aspects of learning is what has been called meta-learning. *Meta-learning* has to do with realizing when you know something well or when you need to study some more. In other words, you recognize how well or how poorly you have learned the material you are studying.

For most people, this can be difficult to assess objectively. Practice tests are useful because they objectively reveal what you have learned and what you have not learned. You should use this information to guide your review and further study. Developmental learning takes place as you cycle through studying, assessing how well you have learned, reviewing, and assessing again until you feel you are ready to take the exam.

You might have noticed the practice exam included in this book, and the PrepLogic, Preview Edition, software on the CD-ROM. These tools are excellent for providing extra exam preparation opportunities. Use these extensively as part of the learning process.

You should set a goal for your pre-testing. A reasonable goal would be to score consistently in the 90% range.

See Appendix F, "Using the *PrepLogic, Preview Edition*, Software," for a more detailed explanation of the test engine.

EXAM PREP TIPS

Having mastered the subject matter, the final preparatory step is to understand how the exam will be presented. Make no mistake: A Microsoft Certified Professional (MCP) exam will challenge both your knowledge and test-taking skills. This section starts with the basics of exam design, reviews new question type formats, and concludes with hints targeted to each of the exam formats.

The MCP Exam

Every MCP exam is released in one of two basic formats. What is called *exam format* here is really little more than a combination of the overall exam structure and the presentation method for exam questions.

Each exam format uses the same types of questions. These types or styles of questions include multiple-rating (or scenario-based) questions, traditional multiple-choice questions, and simulation-based questions. You may also see visual question types, such as select-and-place questions (which require you to drag and drop elements on the screen) and hot area questions (which require you to click on an appropriate item on the screen). It is important that you understand the types of questions you will be asked and the actions required to answer them properly.

Understanding the exam formats is key to good preparation because the format determines the number of questions presented, the difficulty of those questions, and the time allowed to complete the exam.

Exam Forms

There are two basic formats for the MCP exams: the traditional fixed-form exam and the adaptive form. As its name implies, the fixed-form exam presents a fixed set of questions during the exam session. The adaptive form, however, uses only a subset of questions drawn from a larger pool during any given exam session.

> **NOTE**
> **Microsoft Exams and Testing Procedures** You can find the latest information about the testing procedure for Microsoft exams at
> `www.microsoft.com/traincert/mcpexams/faq/procedures.asp`.

Both forms of an exam use the same set of exam objectives and exam questions; the difference is only in the way the questions are presented. Microsoft changes the exam format and questions from time to time; therefore, they do not identify the format of any given exam at the time of registration. You should know the content well and be ready to answer questions in any way they are presented.

Fixed-Form Exams

A fixed-form computerized exam is based on a fixed set of exam questions. The individual questions are presented in random order during a test session. If you take the same exam more than once, you won't

necessarily see exactly the same questions because two or three final forms are typically assembled for every fixed-form exam Microsoft releases. These are usually labeled Forms A, B, and C.

The final forms of a fixed-form exam are identical in terms of content coverage, number of questions, and allotted time, but the questions are different. Microsoft replaces exam questions regularly to minimize their exposure and to ensure that exams remain current. As the questions are replaced, any changes in the difficulty level of the exam are counterbalanced by changes in the passing score. This ensures that consistent standards are used to certify candidates while preventing exam piracy at the same time.

Microsoft has stopped providing numerical scores for all the exams released after December 2001. This allows them to constantly change the contents of the exam and vary the passing score according to the difficulty level of the exam. At the end of the exam, you receive a result showing whether you passed or failed in the exam.

The typical format for the fixed-form exam is as follows:

▶ The exam contains 50–70 questions.

▶ You are allowed 60–300 minutes of testing time.

▶ Question review is allowed, and you have the opportunity to change your answers.

> **EXAM TIP**
> **Confirm the time duration** It is a good idea to confirm the exact time duration for an exam at the time you register for that exam.

The PrepLogic, Preview Edition software on the CD-ROM that accompanies this book contains fixed-form exams. However, PrepLogic, Preview Edition does provide your numerical results to help you in your preparation.

Adaptive Exams

An adaptive-form exam has the same appearance as a fixed-form exam, but its questions differ in quantity and process of selection. Although the statistics of adaptive testing are fairly complex, the process is concerned with determining your level of skill or ability with the exam subject matter. This ability assessment begins by presenting questions of varying levels of difficulty and ascertaining at what difficulty level you can reliably answer them. Finally, the ability assessment determines whether that ability level is above or below the level required to pass that exam.

Examinees at different levels of ability see quite different sets of questions. Examinees who demonstrate little expertise with the subject matter continue to be presented with relatively easy questions. Examinees who demonstrate a high level of expertise are presented progressively more difficult questions. Individuals with both levels of expertise might answer the same number of questions correctly, but because the higher-expertise examinee can correctly answer more difficult questions, he or she receives a higher score and is more likely to pass the exam.

The typical design for an adaptive form exam is as follows:

- ▶ The exam contains 20–25 questions.

- ▶ You are allowed 90 minutes of testing time, although this is likely to be reduced to 45–60 minutes in the near future.

- ▶ Question review is not allowed, providing no opportunity to change your answers.

The Adaptive Exam Process

Your first adaptive exam will be unlike any other testing experience you have had. In fact, many examinees have difficulty accepting the adaptive testing process because they feel that they are not provided the opportunity to adequately demonstrate their full expertise.

You can take consolation in the fact that adaptive exams are painstakingly put together after months of data gathering and analysis and are just as valid as fixed-form exams. The rigor introduced through the adaptive testing methodology means that there is nothing arbitrary about what you see. It is also a more efficient means of testing, requiring less time to conduct and complete than the traditional fixed-form methodology.

As you can see in Figure 1, a number of statistical measures drive the adaptive examination process. The measure that is most immediately relevant to you is the ability to estimate. Accompanying this test statistic are the standard error of measurement, the item characteristic curve, and the test information curve.

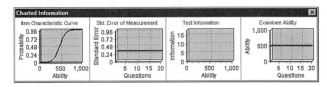

FIGURE 1
Microsoft's adaptive testing demonstration program.

The standard error, which is the key factor in determining when an adaptive exam will terminate, reflects the degree of error in the exam ability estimate. The item characteristic curve reflects the probability of a correct response relative to examinee ability. Finally, the test information statistic provides a measure of the information contained in the set of questions the examinee has answered, again relative to the ability level of the individual examinee.

When you begin an adaptive exam, the standard error has already been assigned a target value below which it must drop for the exam to conclude. This target value reflects a particular level of statistical confidence in the process. The examinee's ability is initially set to the mean possible exam score (which is 500 for MCP exams).

As the adaptive exam progresses, questions of varying difficulty are presented. Based on your pattern of responses to these questions, the ability estimate is recalculated. Simultaneously, the standard error estimate is refined from its first estimated value toward the target value. When the standard error reaches the target value, the exam terminates. Thus, the more consistently you answer questions of the same degree of difficulty, the more quickly the standard error estimate drops and the fewer questions you end up seeing during the exam session. This situation is depicted in Figure 2.

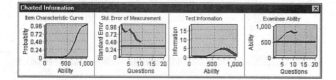

FIGURE 2
The changing statistics in an adaptive exam.

As you might suspect, one good piece of advice for taking an adaptive exam is to treat every exam question as if it is the most important. The adaptive scoring algorithm attempts to discover a pattern of responses that reflects a level of proficiency with the subject matter. Incorrect responses almost guarantee that additional questions must be answered (unless, of course, you get every question wrong) because the scoring algorithm must adjust to information that is not consistent with the emerging pattern.

New Question Types

A variety of question types can appear on MCP exams. Examples of multiple-choice questions and scenario-based questions appear throughout this book and the PrepLogic, Preview Edition software. Simulation-based questions are new to the MCP exam series.

Simulation Questions

Simulation-based questions reproduce the look and feel of key Microsoft product features for the purpose of testing. The simulation software used in MCP exams has been designed to look and act, as much as possible, just like the actual product. Consequently, answering simulation questions in an MCP exam entails completing one or more tasks just as if you were using the product itself.

The format of a typical Microsoft simulation question consists of a brief scenario or problem statement, along with one or more tasks that must be completed to solve the problem.

A Typical Simulation Question

It sounds obvious, but your first step when you encounter a simulation is to carefully read the question. Do not go straight to the simulation application! You must assess the problem being presented and identify the conditions that make up the problem scenario. You should note the tasks that must be performed or outcomes that must be achieved to answer the question and review any instructions on how to proceed.

The next step is to launch the simulator by using the button provided. After clicking the button, you see a product feature, presented in a dialog box. The simulation application is likely to partially cover the question text. You should feel free to reposition the simulation or move between the question text screen and the simulation by using hotkeys, by using point-and-click navigation, or by clicking the simulation launch button again.

It is important to understand that your answer to the simulation question will not be recorded until you move on to the next exam question. This gives you the added capability to close and reopen the simulation application on the same question without losing any partial answer you may have made.

The third step is to use the simulator as you would the actual product, to solve the problem or perform the defined tasks. Again, the simulation software is designed to function, within reason, just as the product does. But don't expect the simulation to reproduce product behavior perfectly. Most importantly, do not allow yourself to become flustered if the simulation does not look or act exactly like the product.

Two final points will help you tackle simulation questions. First, respond only to what is being asked in the question; do not solve problems that you are not asked to solve. Second, accept what is being asked of you. You may not entirely agree with the conditions in the problem statement, the quality of the desired solution, or the sufficiency of defined tasks to adequately solve the problem. Always remember that you are being tested on your ability to solve the problem as it is presented. If you make any changes beyond those required by the question, the item will be scored as wrong on an MCP exam.

Putting It All Together

Given all these different pieces of information, the task now is to assemble a set of tips that will help you successfully tackle the different types of MCP exams.

More Pre-Exam Preparation Tips

Generic exam-preparation advice is always useful. Tips include the following:

▶ Become familiar with the product. Hands-on experience is one of the keys to success on any MCP exam. Review the exercises, the Guided Practice Exercises, and the Step-by-Steps in the book.

▶ Review the current exam-preparation guide on the Microsoft MCP Web site. The documentation Microsoft makes available on the Web identifies the skills every exam is intended to test.

▶ Memorize foundational technical detail, but remember that MCP exams are generally heavy on questions that test problem solving and application of knowledge, rather than those that require only rote memorization.

▶ Take any of the available practice tests. I recommend the one included in this book and the ones you can complete using the PrepLogic, Preview Edition, software on the CD-ROM, and visiting the PrepLogic Web site for purchase of further practice exams if you feel the need for more examination practice. Although these are fixed-form exams, they provide preparation that is just as valuable for taking an adaptive exam. Because of the nature of adaptive testing, these practice exams cannot be done in the adaptive form. However, fixed-form exams use the same types of questions as adaptive exams and are the most effective way to prepare for either type.

▶ Look on the Microsoft MCP Exam Resources Web site (www.microsoft.com/traincert/ mcpexams) for samples and demonstration items. These tend to be particularly valuable for one significant reason: They help you become familiar with any new testing technologies before you encounter them on an MCP exam.

Tips for the Exam Session

The following pieces of generic exam-taking advice you've heard for years apply when you're taking an MCP exam:

- Take a deep breath and try to relax when you first sit down for your exam session. It is very important to control the pressure you might (naturally) feel when taking exams.

- You will be provided with scratch paper. Take a moment to write down any factual information and technical detail that you have committed to short-term memory.

- Carefully read all information and instruction screens. These displays have been put together to give you information relevant to the exam you are taking.

- Accept the nondisclosure agreement and preliminary survey as part of the examination process. Complete them accurately and quickly move on.

- Read the exam questions carefully. Reread each question to identify all relevant detail.

- On a standard exam, tackle the questions in the order in which they are presented. Skipping around won't build your confidence; the clock is always counting down. On an adaptive exam, of course, you don't have any choice.

- Don't rush, but also don't linger on difficult questions. The questions vary in degree of difficulty. Don't let yourself be flustered by a particularly difficult or verbose question.

Tips for Fixed-Form Exams

Besides considering this basic preparation and test-taking advice, you also need to consider the challenges presented by the different exam designs. Because a fixed-form exam is composed of a fixed, finite set of questions, you should add these tips to your strategy for taking a fixed-form exam:

- Note the time allotted and the number of questions on the exam you are taking. Make a rough calculation of how many minutes you can spend on each question and use this to pace yourself through the exam.

- Take advantage of the fact that you can mark a question that you want to review later before you finish your exam. When you have answered all other questions, you can easily locate marked questions and return to them. However, you should remember that if you answer a question but leave it marked, it is considered as unanswered. Be sure to unmark any marked question before you end the exam.

- Do not leave any questions unanswered. You do not get any negative marks for a wrong answer; therefore, at the end it is best to answer all questions. If you cannot determine the correct answer by reading the question, you may want to start by eliminating the choices that look incorrect and then try to guess the answer with remaining choices. Sometimes you may be able to deduce an answer by reading the information presented in other questions.

- If session time is remaining after you have completed all questions (and if you aren't too fatigued), review your answers. Pay particular attention to questions that seem to have a lot of detail or that require graphics.

- As for changing your answers, the general rule of thumb here is *don't!* If you read a question carefully and completely and you felt like you knew the right answer, you probably did. Don't second-guess yourself. If, as you check your answers, one clearly stands out as incorrectly marked, however, of course you should change it in that instance. If you are at all unsure, go with your first instinct.

Tips for Adaptive Exams

If you are planning to take an adaptive exam, keep these additional tips in mind:

▶ Read and answer every question with great care. When reading a question, identify every relevant detail, requirement, or task that must be performed and double-check your answer to be sure that you have addressed every one of them.

▶ If you cannot answer a question, use the process of elimination to reduce the set of potential answers, and then take your best guess. Careless mistakes invariably mean that additional questions will be presented.

▶ You cannot review questions and change your answers. When you leave a question, whether you've answered it or not, you cannot return to it. Do not skip any questions either; if you do, the item is counted as incorrect.

Tips for Simulation Questions

You might encounter simulation questions on either the fixed-form or adaptive-form exam. If you do, keep these tips in mind:

▶ Avoid changing any simulation settings that don't pertain directly to the problem solution. Solve the problem you are being asked to solve and nothing more.

▶ Assume default settings when related information has not been provided. If something has not been mentioned or defined, it is a noncritical detail that does not factor into the correct solution.

▶ Be sure your entries are syntactically correct and pay particular attention to your spelling. Enter relevant information just as the product would require it.

▶ Close all simulation application windows after you complete the simulation tasks. The testing system software is designed to trap errors that could result when using the simulation application, but you should trust yourself over the testing software.

▶ If simulations are part of a fixed-form exam, you can return to skipped or previously answered questions and change your answers. However, if you choose to change an answer to a simulation question or even attempt to review the settings you've made in the simulation application, your previous response to that simulation question is deleted. If simulations are part of an adaptive exam, you cannot return to previous questions.

Tips for Select-and-Place Questions

You might encounter select-and-place questions on either the fixed-form or adaptive-form exam. If you do, keep these tips in mind:

▶ You must always drag your answers from the answer objects section to the answer field section. If you drag an answer object from one answer field directly to another answer field, it will not count as a correct answer.

▶ Although you can review a select-and-place question, the answers will be cleared if you do so, and you'll need to answer the question all over again.

Tips for Hot Area Questions

You might encounter hot area questions on either the fixed-form or adaptive-form exam. If you do, keep these tips in mind:

▶ Remember, it's your final mouse click that counts on a hot area question. Be sure to click your answer area immediately before moving to the next question.

▶ Although you can review a hot area question, the answers will be cleared if you do so, and you'll need to answer the question all over again.

FINAL CONSIDERATIONS

Finally, a number of changes in the MCP program affect how frequently you can repeat an exam and what you see when you do:

▶ Microsoft's policy on retaking exams is simple. You can attempt any exam twice with no restrictions on the time between attempts; your second try can follow the first on the very next day if you like. But after the second attempt, you must wait two weeks before you can attempt that exam again. After that, you are required to wait two weeks between subsequent attempts. Plan to pass the exam in two attempts or plan to increase your time horizon for receiving an MCP credential.

▶ New questions are being seeded into the MCP exams. After performance data is gathered on new questions, the examiners replace older questions on all exam forms. This means that the questions that appear on exams regularly change.

▶ Many of the current MCP exams will be republished in adaptive form in the coming months. Prepare yourself for this significant change in testing as it is entirely likely that this will become the preferred MCP exam format.

These changes mean that the brute-force strategies for passing MCP exams are much less viable than they once were. So if you don't pass an exam on the first or second attempt, it is entirely possible that the exam's form will change significantly before the next time you take it. It could be updated to an adaptive form from a fixed form, or it could have a different set of questions or question types.

Microsoft's intention is clearly not to make the exams more difficult by introducing unwanted change, but to create and maintain valid measures of the technical skills and knowledge associated with the different MCP credentials. Preparing for an MCP exam has always involved not only studying the subject matter, but also planning for the testing experience itself. With the recent changes, this is now truer than ever.

EXAM PREPARATION

This chapter covers the following Microsoft-specified objective for the "Consuming and Manipulating Data" section of the "Developing XML Web Services and Server Components with Microsoft Visual C# .NET and the Microsoft .NET Framework" exam:

Create and Manipulate DataSets.

- **Manipulate a DataSet Schema.**

- **Manipulate DataSet Relationships.**

- **Create a strongly typed DataSet.**

▶ Databases are at the core of many applications. Visual C# .NET allows you to work with databases in many different ways. Many Web services and other applications manipulate DataSet objects rather than work directly with a database. The DataSet object provides you with an in-memory relational store that abstracts away many of the differences between database implementations. To pass the Web services and server components exam, you need a strong background in working with DataSet objects. In particular, you should know how to manipulate the schema of a DataSet. The schema of a DataSet describes the types of data that the DataSet contains; it is the *metadata* for the DataSet. You can use Visual Studio .NET to manage DataSet schemas. This includes designing schemas from scratch, editing existing schemas, and editing the relationships between multiple tables contained in the same schema. When your application contains a DataSet schema, you can use that schema to construct a strongly typed DataSet. A strongly typed DataSet allows you to use an early-binding syntax to refer to data contained in the DataSet. This enables you to write code that is clearer and less error prone.

CHAPTER 1

Creating and Manipulating DataSets

Access and manipulate data from a Microsoft SQL Server database by creating and using ad hoc queries and stored procedures.

▶ You also need to know how to manipulate the data at the database level. This objective tests your ability to work with data in a Microsoft SQL Server database. You'll learn how to use both SQL statements and stored procedures to work with this data.

S TUDY S TRATEGIES

▶ Create a DataSet schema by dragging and dropping a table from Server Explorer to a Visual C#
.NET application. Then use the schema designer to edit the schema.

▶ Add an additional table to your test DataSet
schema, and use the XML designer to create a
relationship between the two tables.

▶ Write code to work with data in a generic
DataSet object. Then create a strongly typed
DataSet object to hold the same data and
update the code to use early binding.

▶ You should understand how to construct and
interpret simple Transact SQL statements
including SELECT, INSERT, UPDATE, and DELETE, as
well as SQL Server stored procedures. Spend
some time practicing with the Visual Data Tools
inside of .NET or with another query front-end
such as SQL Server Query Analyzer. Make sure
you work with the raw T-SQL, not just the graphical tools.

INTRODUCTION

Just about any application you can think of will need to store data. Database integration is important to many of these applications, and Web services and server applications are no exception to the rule. Fortunately, the .NET Framework and Visual C# .NET offer a rich and productive set of tools for working with data stored in databases.

The Web services and server components exam presumes that you already have a working knowledge of ADO.NET. (If you need a refresher course, refer to Appendix A for the basics of ADO.NET.) The core object of ADO.NET is the DataSet, which provides a complete in-memory relational database. A DataSet object can contain multiple tables with keys and relationships, mimicking the structure of a relational database while abstracting away the implementation differences between various databases. You can use a DataSet object to hold data from Microsoft Jet, Microsoft SQL Server, Oracle, or many other databases, without changing any of your code.

In this chapter, you'll learn how to work with DataSet schemas. A DataSet schema is an XML representation of the metadata that defines a DataSet object's structure. Visual Studio .NET includes tools that enable you to work with this metadata directly, defining and altering the structure of DataSet objects.

When you've created a DataSet schema, you can use that schema to instantiate a strongly typed DataSet object. A strongly typed DataSet object behaves like any other DataSet object, but you can use an early-bound syntax to manipulate its contents. This makes it easier to write code, and makes the code less prone to errors.

After showing you how to work with DataSet schemas and strongly typed DataSet objects, I'll review the basics of the Structured Query Language (SQL) and show you how you can use SQL statements and stored procedures to interact with a Microsoft SQL Server database from within your .NET applications.

MANIPULATING A DataSet SCHEMA

Create and Manipulate DataSets: Manipulate a DataSet Schema.

A DataSet schema is an XML file that describes the structure of a DataSet object. You can work with such files as raw XML, but if you have Visual Studio .NET, there's a better way. Visual Studio .NET includes a specialized XML designer that provides a visual representation of DataSet schema files. In this section, you'll learn how to use this designer. You'll see that you can create a DataSet schema and edit it easily with the same sort of drag-and-drop operations that are used to create Windows forms or Web forms.

The XML Designer is also integrated with the database support in Server Explorer. You can add items to a DataSet schema file by dragging and dropping from Server Explorer.

To use the XML designer in Visual Studio .NET with a DataSet schema file, you need to create a new Visual Studio .NET project to host the file. After you've done that, you can perform many design tasks. In this section, you learn how to perform the following tasks on a DataSet schema:

▶ Create a new schema

▶ Add items such as elements, attributes, types, and facets to the schema

▶ Use items from Server Explorer in a schema

▶ Create element groups and attribute groups

Creating a DataSet Schema

Visual Studio .NET allows you to create a DataSet schema from scratch, without reference to an existing DataSet or to a table stored on a database server. Step-by-Step 1.1 demonstrates how you can do this.

STEP BY STEP

1.1 Creating a New DataSet Schema

1. Create a new Visual C# .NET Windows application. Name the application 320C01.

2. Right-click on the project node in Solution Explorer and select Add, Add New Item.

3. Select the Local Project Items node in the Categories tree view. Select the DataSet template. Name the new DataSet dsCustomers.xsd, as shown in Figure 1.1, and click OK.

FIGURE 1.1

The Add New Item dialog box enables you to create a new DataSet schema file.

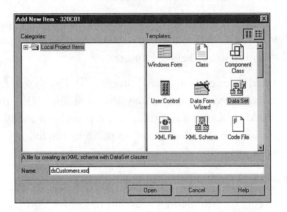

4. The new DataSet schema file is opened in the XML Designer, as shown in Figure 1.2. The Toolbox displays tools appropriate for creating new content in the schema file.

An empty DataSet schema is not very interesting or useful. In the next section of the chapter, you learn how to add information to the schema to help dictate the layout of the DataSet object that it defines.

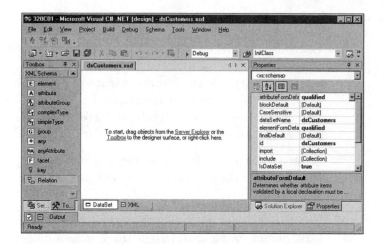

FIGURE 1.2
You can place objects from Server Explorer or the Toolbox to the create a `DataSet` schema file in the XML Designer.

Elements and Attributes

Like other XML files, `DataSet` schema files are made up of XML elements. You can think of an element as a unit of information. For example, if you're designing a `DataSet` to hold data from a database table named `Customers` with columns named `CustomerID` and `CompanyName`, then `Customers`, `CustomerID`, and `CompanyName` would all be represented by XML elements. Step-by-Step 1.2 shows you how to add elements to a `DataSet` schema file.

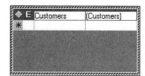

FIGURE 1.3
The top-level element—Customers—represents a table in a `DataSet` schema file.

STEP BY STEP

1.2 Adding Elements to a `DataSet` Schema

1. Ensure that the `DataSet` schema file that you created in Step-by-Step 1.1 is open in the XML Designer.

2. Select the Element tool in the Toolbox. Drag the element from the Toolbox and drop it on the design surface. This creates an element named `element1`. Rename the element `Customers` by typing over the name, as shown in Figure 1.3.

3. Drag another element and drop it on top of the first element. Name the new element `CustomerID`. This creates a nested element, as shown in Figure 1.4.

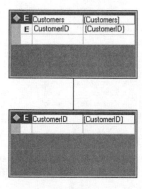

continues

FIGURE 1.4
You can create a nested element by dropping a child element on top of the parent element.

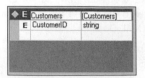

FIGURE 1.5
You can create a simple element by selecting an elementary data type.

continued

4. The XML Designer assumes that the new element will be a complex element—that is, one that contains other elements. To change the `CustomerID` element to a simple element, select a data type from the drop-down list to the right of the element. Figure 1.5 shows the result of defining the `CustomerID` element to be a string.

5. Create a `CompanyName` element by dragging another element from the Toolbox, renaming it, and changing its data type to `string`.

6. Switch to the XML view of the schema file (using the tab at the bottom of the XML Designer) and inspect the generated XML.

You can also use the XML designer to add attributes to a `DataSet` schema. Attributes provide an alternative way to represent columns within a `DataSet` object. Step-by-Step 1.3 shows how to add attributes to a `DataSet` schema.

STEP BY STEP

1.3 Adding Attributes to a `DataSet` Schema

1. Ensure that the `DataSet` schema file that you edited in Step-by-Step 1.2 is open in the XML Designer.

2. Select the Attribute tool in the Toolbox. Drag the attribute from the Toolbox and drop it on top of the complex element named `Customers`. This creates an attribute named `attribute1`. Rename the attribute `ContactName` by typing over the name. You'll see that the attribute is assigned the string data type by default. Attributes cannot be used for complex data types.

3. Drag a second attribute to the `Customers` element. Rename the attribute `ContactTitle`. Figure 1.6 shows the state of the `DataSet` schema after this change.

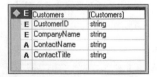

FIGURE 1.6
You can represent columns by either elements or attributes within a `DataSet` schema file.

Given that you can represent columns by either elements or attributes within a `DataSet` schema file, how do you decide which representation to use? Here are some points to consider:

▶ If you need to exchange the schema file with other applications, you must be sure that it is compatible with those applications. Microsoft Access, for example, can import a schema defined with elements but not one defined with attributes.

▶ If your `DataSet` requires that a custom data type be used to define columns, you must use elements for those columns. Attributes are restricted to the built-in data types defined by the World Wide Web Consortium (W3C).

▶ To represent a child table in a hierarchy, you must use an element.

Using Simple Types

When you define a column with an element or an attribute, there are no restrictions on that column beyond those imposed by the data type that you choose for the element or attribute. For example, you may want to require that the CustomerID column be a string consisting of somewhere between five and ten characters. To do this, you can define a simple type in the XML Designer, using the technique from Step-by-Step 1.4.

> **EXAM TIP**
>
> **Visual Studio .NET Default**   When you use Visual Studio .NET's built-in tools to create a DataSet schema from a database, Visual Studio .NET always uses elements to represent the database columns.

STEP BY STEP

1.4 Adding a Simple Type to a `DataSet` Schema

1. Ensure that the `DataSet` schema file that you edited in Step-by-Step 1.3 is open in the Designer.

2. Select the `SimpleType` tool in the Toolbox. Drag the simple type from the Toolbox and drop it in a blank area of the XML designer. This creates a simple type named `simpleType1`. Rename the simple type `CustomerIDType` by typing over the name. You'll see that the simple type is assigned the string data type by default.

continues

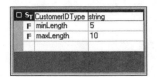

FIGURE 1.7
You can create a custom simple type in the
XML Schema designer as per the requirements.

◆ E	Customers	(Customers)
E	CustomerID	CustomerIDType
E	CompanyName	string
A	ContactName	string
A	ContactTitle	string

□ ST	CustomerIDType	string
F	minLength	5
F	maxLength	10

FIGURE 1.8
You can associate a custom-created simple
type to an XML element in the XML Schema
designer.

> **NOTE**
>
> **Facets in the XML Designer** At any
> time, the XML designer shows you
> only the facets that are applicable to
> the current data type. For example, if
> you're basing a simple data type on
> the string data type, you can set only
> the enumeration, length, minLength,
> maxLength, pattern, and whiteSpace
> facets.

continued

3. Click in the second row of the simple type, directly under the ST icon. This produces a drop-down arrow. Click the arrow and select Facet from the list (it is the only item in the list). In the next column select minLength. In the last column type the value **5**.

4. Add another facet to the simple type. Select the maxLength facet and set the maximum length to 10. Figure 1.7 shows the simple type at this point.

5. Click the data type drop-down for the CustomerID element. You'll find that this list now contains the CustomerIDType data type. Set the element to use this data type, as shown in Figure 1.8.

In this Step-by-Step, minLength and maxLength are data type facets. Facets help define the acceptable range of data for an element. Table 1.1 shows the data type facets that are available in the DataSet schema designer. This table gives you a sense of what restrictions you can place on DataSet elements.

TABLE 1.1

DATA TYPE FACETS

Facet Name	Description
enumeration	Set of allowable values.
fractionDigits	Maximum number of digits in the fractional part of a number.
length	Fixed length of the data.
maxExclusive	Maximum allowed value must be less than this number.
maxInclusive	Maximum allowed value must be less than or equal to this number.
maxLength	Maximum length of a variable length field.
minExcusive	Minimum allowed value must be greater than this number.
minInclusive	Minimum allowed value must be greater than or equal to this number.
minLength	Minimum length of a variable length field.

Facet Name	*Description*
pattern	Regular expression that specifies a pattern to which the data must conform.
totalDigits	Maximum number of total decimal digits in a number.
whiteSpace	Can be set to preserve (to leave whitespace unchanged), replace (to replace tabs, line feeds, and carriage returns with spaces) or collapse (to replace all contiguous whitespace characters with a single space character).

Using Server Explorer with the XML Designer

You can also create DataSet schemas quickly by using the Server Explorer, which enables you to interact directly with SQL Server or other databases. You may not have used Server Explorer in the past, so before I show you this particular use I'll give you a quick overview.

By default, the Server Explorer window in Visual Studio .NET is displayed as a small vertical tab to the left of the Toolbox. When you hover the mouse over this tab, the Server Explorer slides out to cover the Toolbox. Figure 1.9 shows the two states of the Server Explorer window.

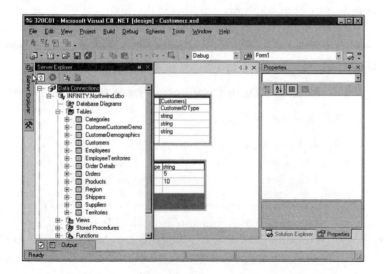

FIGURE 1.9
The Server Explorer is normally displayed as a small vertical tab; when you hover the mouse over this tab, the window slides out to cover the Toolbox.

Although we're going to use the Server Explorer to work with databases, it's really a general-purpose tool for managing server resources of many types. Table 1.2 lists the resources that you can manage with Server Explorer.

TABLE 1.2

RESOURCES THAT YOU CAN MANAGE WITH SERVER EXPLORER

Resource Type	Represents
Data Connection	A connection to a particular database
Crystal Services	Options for Crystal Reports
Event Logs	Windows event logs
Message Queues	Windows message queues
Performance Counters	Windows performance counters
Services	Windows services
SQL Servers	Microsoft SQL Servers

To work with `DataSet` schema files, you'll use the Data Connection node in Server Explorer and its children. To start working with those objects, you need to add a Data Connection to the Server Explorer tree. Step-by-Step 1.5 shows you how to do this.

STEP BY STEP

1.5 Adding a Data Connection from Server Explorer

1. Open Server Explorer.

2. Right-click the Data Connections node and then select Add Connection. This opens the Data Link Properties dialog box.

3. Fill in the connection information for your data source. The dialog box defaults to using the Microsoft OLE DB Provider for SQL Server, but you can change that on the Provider tab if you like.

4. Click OK to create the Data Connection. For ease in completing the other Step-by-Steps in this chapter, you should create at least one Data Connection based on an instance of the SQL Server Northwind sample database.

Visual Studio .NET remembers your Data Connections across sessions and projects. Any Data Connection that you've created appears in Server Explorer in all your projects, unless you right-click the Data Connection and choose Delete.

After you've created a Data Connection, you can use objects from that Data Connection in DataSet schema design. Step-by-Step 1.6 demonstrates this process.

STEP BY STEP

1.6 Using a Server Explorer Table in the DataSet Schema Designer

1. With the DataSet schema from Step-by-Step 1.4 open in the Designer, open Server Explorer.

2. Expand the Server Explorer tree view to show a Data Connection to the Northwind sample database. Drill into the Tables folder within this database.

3. Drag the Orders table from Server Explorer and drop it on the DataSet schema designer. This creates a new element with all the necessary included elements to represent the Orders table.

4. Repeat the process to bring the Order Details table into the DataSet schema designer. Figure 1.10 shows the DataSet schema designer with three tables and one simple type on the design surface.

FIGURE 1.10
You can create an element by dragging and dropping a table from the Server Explorer to the DataSet schema designer.

If you're an experienced database developer, you may have noticed that there's no sign of any relationship between the three tables in the DataSet schema. I'll show you how to create such a relationship in the next section of the chapter.

▶ `DataSet` schema files represent the metadata that describes a `DataSet` object's allowable content.

▶ You can create a `DataSet` schema file from scratch by dragging and dropping elements and attributes within the DataSet schema designer.

▶ Simple types enable you to apply constraints to the data that will be allowed in a `DataSet` object.

▶ You can quickly create a `DataSet` schema to represent an existing table by dragging and dropping the table from Server Explorer to the DataSet schema designer.

MANIPULATING DataSet RELATIONSHIPS

Create and Manipulate DataSets: Manipulate DataSet Relationships.

As an in-memory representation of a database, the `DataSet` object retains the notion of relations between tables. As you would expect, this means that a `DataSet` schema can also store information on keys and relationships in the `DataSet` object that it represents. In this section, you'll see how to add keys to a `DataSet` schema, and then how to create relationships betweeen multiple tables that are part of the same `DataSet` schema.

Adding Keys to a DataSet Schema

The DataSet schema designer allows you to create two types of keys. You can identify a field or a set of fields as the primary key for a table, or you can identify a field or a set of fields as making up a unique key. Step-by-Step 1.7 lets you practice these skills.

STEP BY STEP

1.7 Creating Keys in the DataSet Schema Designer

1. Ensure that the DataSet schema file that you edited in Step-by-Step 1.6 is open in the DataSet schema designer.

2. Select the key tool in the Toolbox. Drag the key from the Toolbox and drop it on the CustomerID element within the Customers table. This will open the Edit Key dialog box.

3. Name the key CustomersPrimaryKey. Select CustomerID in the Fields list, if it is not already selected. Check the DataSet Primary Key check box, as shown in Figure 1.11. Click OK to create the key. A key icon appears next to the CustomerID element.

4. Select the key tool in the Toolbox. Drag the key from the Toolbox and drop it on the CompanyName element within the Customers table. This will open the Edit Key dialog box.

5. Name the key CompanyNameUniqueKey. Select CompanyName in the Fields list, if it is not already selected. Click OK to create the key. A key icon appears next to the CompanyName element. Figure 1.12 shows the Customers table with both keys created.

FIGURE 1.11
The Edit Key dialog box allows you to define and edit keys in the DataSet schema designer.

FIGURE 1.12
You can create primary and unique keys for an element in the DataSet schema designer.

You can create one primary key, and as many unique keys as you like, for each table in the DataSet schema designer. The primary key identifies the field (or combination of fields) that uniquely specifies an individual row in the table. Unique keys identify other fields or combinations of fields that cannot be repeated in different records of the same table.

> **EXAM TIP**
>
> **Deleting a Key** To delete a primary key or a unique key in the DataSet schema designer, you must first click in the row containing the key to select the row. Then you can right-click on that row and select Delete Key.

One-to-Many Relationships

A one-to-many relationship is the most common type of relationship in a relational database. In a one-to-many relationship, a record in TableA can have more than one matching record in TableB, but a record in TableB has, at most, one matching record in TableA.

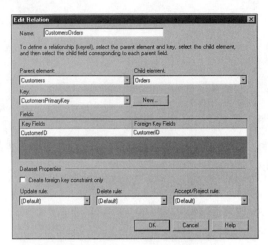

FIGURE 1.13
The Edit Relation dialog box enables you to create and edit relationships between tables in the DataSet schema designer.

FIGURE 1.14
You can associate one-to-many relationships between tables in the DataSet schema designer.

One way to relate two tables in a DataSet schema is to identify common key columns and then use those columns to create a relationship between the tables. This is similar to the way that relational database products handle relationships. Step-by-Step 1.8 demonstrates this technique.

STEP BY STEP

1.8 Creating One-to-Many Relationships in the DataSet Schema Designer

1. Ensure that the DataSet schema file that you edited in Step-by-Step 1.7 is open in the DataSet schema designer.

2. Select the Relation tool in the Toolbox. Drag the Relation from the Toolbox and drop it on the Orders table. This opens the Edit Relation dialog box.

3. Name the relation CustomersOrders. Select Customers as the parent element and Orders as the child element. Select CustomersPrimaryKey as the key to use. Select CustomerID as both the key field and the foreign key field. Leave all other options at their default values. Figure 1.13 shows this dialog box.

4. Click OK to create the relation. The DataSet schema designer draws a relation object and connecting lines between the two tables, as shown in Figure 1.14.

You can also specify a number of optional behaviors in the Edit Relation dialog box:

▶ To create a relationship that is used only as a constraint, but not for fetching child records, check the Create Foreign Key Constraint Only check box.

▶ To specify the behavior of child records when the key field in the parent record is updated, select a value from the Update Rule combo box. You can choose to automatically cascade changes to the child records, to set the key field in the child records to Null, or to set the key field in the child records to its default value.

▶ To specify the behavior of child records when a parent record is deleted, select a value from the Delete Rule combo box. You can choose to automatically cascade deletions to the child records, to set the key field in the child records to Null, or to set the key field in the child records to its default value.

▶ To specify the behavior of child records when a change to a parent record is accepted or rejected, select a value from the Accept/Reject Rule combo box. You can choose to automatically accept changes to the child records, or to leave those changes to be accepted separately.

Nested Relationships

Although one-to-many relationships are the only kind you'll find in a typical relational database, the DataSet schema designer also supports nested relationships. In a nested relationship, the child table is stored as a complex data type within the parent table. Step-by-Step 1.9 helps you set up a nested relationship.

STEP BY STEP

1.9 Creating Nested Relationships in the DataSet Schema Designer

1. Ensure that the DataSet schema file that you edited in Step-by-Step 1.8 is open in the DataSet schema designer.

2. Select the Order Details table. Drag the Order Details table and drop it on top of the Orders table. This creates a relationship between the Orders table and the Order Details table, as shown in Figure 1.15.

3. Note that in this case, there's no explicit relationship object; the line between the two tables does not have a diamond on it. Instead, the Order Details table has been added as a complex type to the Orders table.

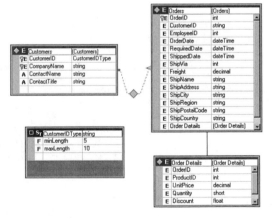

FIGURE 1.15
You can also create a nested relationship in the DataSet schema designer.

Because there are two different ways to relate tables in a DataSet schema, you have to choose between the two. Here are some points to help you decide whether to use one-to-many or nested relationships in your DataSet schemas:

▶ One-to-many relationships more directly represent the way that data is stored in a relational database. If your data is primarily stored in a database, this provides the most natural mapping.

▶ Nested relationships are more natural to represent in XML. If your data is not stored in a relational database, nested relationships provide a cleaner and more succinct XML representation of the connections between tables.

▶ If you require interoperability with other XML applications, nested relationships are more likely to be correctly interpreted.

REVIEW BREAK

▶ To create a primary key or a unique key in a DataSet schema, drag and drop the key tool from the Toolbox to an XML element.

▶ To create a one-to-many relationship, drag and drop the relation tool from the Toolbox to the relationship's child table.

▶ To create a nested relationship, drag and drop the child table to the parent table.

CREATING AND USING STRONGLY TYPED DataSet OBJECTS

Create and manipulate DataSets: Create a strongly typed DataSet.

The best way to understand strongly typed DataSet objects is to see what you can do with one syntactically. Suppose you have a normal DataSet object, and you've extracted a DataTable object named dt from this DataSet object. Then you can refer to a value in the DataTable object with any of these syntaxes:

```
dt.Rows[0][0]
dt.Rows[0]["ColumnName"]
```

All these syntaxes have one thing in common: They're all late-bound. That is, .NET doesn't know until runtime that `ColumnName` is a valid column name in the `DataTable`. By contrast, in a strongly typed `DataSet`, the columns actually become properties of the row. With a strongly typed `DataSet`, an early-bound version of the data-retrieval code becomes available:

```
dt.Rows[0].ColumnName
```

In addition to being faster than the late-bound syntax, this syntax also has the benefit that column and table names show up in the applicable IntelliSense lists.

In this section, you'll learn two different ways to create strongly typed `DataSet` objects. After that, I'll show you how to use a strongly typed `DataSet` in code.

Using the Component Designer to Create a Strongly Typed DataSet Object

One way to create a strongly typed `DataSet` object is to derive it directly from a table or other data-bearing object in a database. Step-by-Step 1.10 demonstrates this technique.

STEP BY STEP

1.10 Creating a Strongly Typed DataSet with the Component Designer

1. In Solution Explorer, right-click the project and select Add, Add Windows Form from the context menu. This opens the Add New Item dialog box. Name the form `StepByStep1_10.cs` and click Open.

2. Expand the Server Explorer tree view to show the Data Connection node. Drill into the Tables folder within the Northwind sample database.

continues

continued

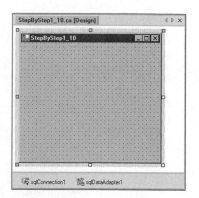

FIGURE 1.16
You can create ADO.NET objects by dragging and dropping tables and other data elements from the Server Explorer.

FIGURE 1.17▶
You can generate a DataSet object by clicking the Generate DataSet hyperlink in the Properties window for a SqlDataAdapter object.

3. Drag the Employees table from Server Explorer and drop it on the form. This adds a SqlConnection object named sqlConnection1 and a SqlDataAdapter object named sqlDataAdapter1 to the component tray of the form, as shown in Figure 1.16.

4. Select the SqlDataAdapter object. Click the Generate DataSet hyperlink at the bottom of the Properties window, as shown in Figure 1.17.

5. Clicking the hyperlink opens the Generate DataSet dialog box, as shown in Figure 1.18. Name the new DataSet object dsEmployees and select the check box to add the DataSet to the DataSet schema designer. Click OK.

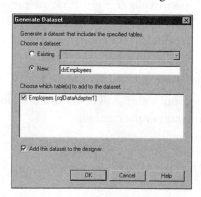

FIGURE 1.18▶
The Generate DataSet dialog box enables you to create new DataSet objects.

6. You'll see a new object, `dsEmployees.xsd`, appear in the Solution Explorer. This is a `DataSet` schema file that describes the new strongly typed `DataSet` object. Click the Show All Files button on the Solution Explorer toolbar. Expand the `dsEmployees.xsd` node to see the `dsEmployees.cs` file, as shown in Figure 1.19. This is a class file that can be instantiated to produce the strongly typed `DataSet` object.

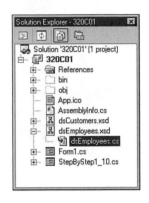

FIGURE 1.19
The `dsEmployees.cs` file contains the source code for the strongly typed `DataSet`.

In addition to the new objects in Solution Explorer, this example also adds a new component, `dsEmployees1`, to the component tray underneath the form. This is an instance of the class defined in `dsEmployees.cs`. If you inspect the code behind the form, you can find the declaration for the new component:

```
private _320C01.dsEmployees dsEmployees1;
```

Creating a Strongly Typed `DataSet` from a `DataSet` Schema

You can also create a strongly typed `DataSet` from a `DataSet` schema file. More precisely, if you've created a `DataSet` schema in your Visual C# .NET project, Visual C# .NET automatically creates a strongly typed `DataSet` class that matches the structure defined in the schema. As you edit the schema, Visual C# .NET keeps the `DataSet` class synchronized with your edits.

If you've been following along with the Step-by-Steps in this chapter, take a look at the files in Solution Explorer. If you click the Show All Files toolbar button, you'll find two files as children of the `dsCustomers.xsd` `DataSet` schema file:

▶ `dsCustomers.cs`—This file is the class definition for a strongly typed `DataSet` based on the `DataSet` schema that you've been working with.

▶ `dsCustomers.xsx`—This file contains information on the layout of objects within the DataSet schema designer window.

WARNING

Naming a Strongly Typed `DataSet` Object You should not name the `DataSet` schema file `dsCustomers.xsd` with the name of its enclosing tables—that is, `Customers.xsd` or `Orders.xsd`. The corresponding code file (that is, the `.cs` file) created for this `DataSet` object contains properties to provide access to their enclosing members—that is, `Customers` or `Orders`. If you named a class with the same name as its enclosing table, you would get the error `Member names cannot be the same as their enclosing type`.

Using a Strongly Typed DataSet Object

Now that you've built a strongly typed DataSet object, what can you do with it? Step-by-Step 1.11 demonstrates the syntax for using such a DataSet object.

STEP BY STEP

1.11 Using a Strongly Typed DataSet Object

1. Open the form StepByStep1_10.cs that you created in Step by Step 1.10 in the DataSet schema designer. Add a new ListBox control to the form, and name the control lbEmployees.

2. Double-click on the form to open the event handler for the form's Load event. Add this code to handle the Load event:

```
private void StepByStep1_10_Load(object sender,
    System.EventArgs e)
{
    sqlDataAdapter1.Fill(dsEmployees1, "Employees");
    foreach(dsEmployees.EmployeesRow EmpRow
            in dsEmployees1.Employees)
    {
        lbEmployees.Items.Add(
            EmpRow.FirstName + " " + EmpRow.LastName);
    }
}
```

Notice as you type this code that the IntelliSense feature fills in the names of tables and columns for you.

3. Insert the Main() method to launch the form as follows:

```
[STAThread]
static void Main()
{
    Application.Run(new StepByStep1_10());
}
```

4. Modify the properties of project 320C01 to set the form StepByStep1_10 as the startup object for the project. Run the project. You'll see a list of employees on the form, as shown in Figure 1.20.

FIGURE 1.20

You can perform early binding with data objects with the help of a strongly typed DataSet object.

A strongly typed `DataSet` class inherits from the base `DataSet` class, so it has all the methods and properties of the `DataSet`. The strong typing gives you the benefits of design-time IntelliSense and type checking. It also makes your code easier to read. Given the ease with which Visual Studio .NET can create strongly typed `DataSet` classes, you should plan to use them whenever possible.

REVIEW BREAK

► A strongly typed DataSet object brings the benefits of early binding to your data access code.

► You can create a strongly typed `DataSet` object by using the component designer with components dragged from Server Explorer, or by building a `DataSet` schema file.

► When you're working with a strongly typed `DataSet` object in code, IntelliSense will show you the names of the tables and columns contained within the `DataSet` object.

ACCESSING AND MANIPULATING SQL SERVER DATA

Access and manipulate data from a Microsoft SQL Server database by creating and using ad hoc queries and stored procedures.

You might be a bit surprised to find a Microsoft SQL Server objective on a Visual C# .NET certification exam, but it really makes perfect sense. Many Visual C# .NET applications require a database to enable them to store data on a permanent basis, and SQL Server is one of the best databases to use with the .NET framework. As you'll see later in this chapter, an entire namespace (`System.Data.SqlClient`) is devoted to efficient communication between .NET applications and SQL Server.

The objects in System.Data.SqlClient, though, won't do you any good unless you understand the language used to communicate with SQL Server, *Transact SQL (T-SQL)*. T-SQL is Microsoft's implementation of SQL (Structured Query Language), which is defined by a standard from the American National Standards Institute (ANSI).

SQL Statement Capitalization   You usually see SQL keywords (such as SELECT, INSERT, UPDATE, and DELETE) formatted entirely in upper-case. I follow that convention in this book, but uppercase formatting isn't required by SQL Server. You might see these same keywords in mixed case or lowercase on an exam. As far as SQL Server is concerned, there's no difference between SELECT, Select, and select.

SQL Dialects   Microsoft SQL Server isn't the only product that implements the SQL-92 standard. Other products, including Microsoft Access and Oracle, also use SQL-92–based query languages. However, databases differ in their treatment of SQL in many sub-tle ways. Most databases contain extensions to SQL-92 (that is, key-words that are understood only by that particular database), and most don't implement the entire SQL-92 standard. The SQL statements in this chapter are from the shared core of SQL-92 that's identical in nearly all database products, so they should work whether you're using SQL Server, Access, or Oracle (among others). But as you study the more advanced fea-tures of SQL Server, you should keep in mind that T-SQL statements do not necessarily run on other database servers without changes.

The core of T-SQL is based on the ANSI SQL-92 standard. SQL-92 defines a query-oriented language in which you submit queries to the database and get back a resultset consisting of rows and columns of data. Other queries cause changes to the database (for example, adding, deleting, or updating a row of data) without returning any resultset.

You can submit T-SQL to a SQL Server database for processing in two ways. First, you can write *ad hoc queries*, SQL statements that are executed directly. Second, you can write *stored procedures*, SQL statements that are stored on the server as named objects. Stored procedures can also include complex programming logic. The .NET Framework includes facilities for running both ad hoc queries and stored procedures.

Using Ad Hoc Queries

Ad hoc T-SQL queries provide an extremely flexible way to retrieve data from a SQL Server database or to make changes to that data-base. In this section, I'll show several ways to send an ad hoc query to SQL Server. Then you'll learn the basics of the four main T-SQL statements that help manipulate SQL Server data:

▶ SELECT statements enable you to retrieve data stored in the database.

▶ INSERT statements enable you to add new data to the database.

▶ UPDATE statements enable you to modify data already in the database.

▶ DELETE statements enable you to delete data from the database.

Running Queries

When learning T-SQL, it's useful to be able to send queries to a SQL Server database and to see the results (if any) that the server returns. You should be familiar with the many ways that are available to communicate with SQL Server. I'll show you four of them in this section:

▶ Using the Visual Studio .NET Integrated Development Environment (IDE)

▶ Using OSQL

▶ Using the SQL Query Analyzer

▶ Using a Visual C# .NET Application

Using the Visual Studio .NET IDE

When you just need to run a query in the course of working with a project, you can run it directly from the Visual Studio .NET IDE. Step-by-Step 1.12 shows you how.

STEP BY STEP

1.12 Running a Query from the Visual Studio .NET IDE

1. Open a Visual C# .NET Windows Application in the Visual Studio .NET IDE.

2. Open Server Explorer.

3. Expand the tree under Data Connections to show a SQL Server data connection that points to the Northwind sample database, and then expand the Views node of the selected SQL Server data connection.

4. Right-click the Views node and select New View.

5. Click Close in the Add Table dialog box.

6. In the SQL pane of the View Designer (which is the area that starts by displaying the text SELECT FROM), type this SQL statement (replacing the already existing text):

```
SELECT * FROM Employees
```

7. Select Query, Run from the Visual Studio menu, or click the Run Query button on the View toolbar. The SQL statement is sent to SQL Server and the results are displayed, as shown in Figure 1.21.

NOTE

The Northwind Sample Database
Whenever I've used data from a database in this book, I've used the `Northwind` sample database that comes as part of SQL Server 2000. If you don't have SQL Server, you can use Microsoft Data Engine (MSDE) that installs as a part of the Microsoft .NET Framework SDK QuickStarts, Tutorials, and Samples installation. Microsoft .NET SDK installs as a part of Visual Studio .NET. If you use MSDE, you'll need to change the name of the database server in this book's examples from `(local)` to `(local)\NetSDK`.

FIGURE 1.21
You can run an ad hoc query directly from the Visual Studio .NET IDE.

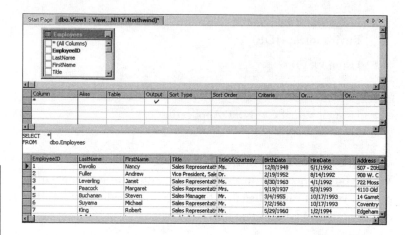

When you run the query, Visual Studio .NET sends the SQL statement to the SQL Server that is specified by the database connection you chose in step 3. The server then processes the query (this particular query tells it to return all columns in all rows of the Employees table) and sends the results back to the client (in this case, Visual Studio .NET). The IDE then displays the results, formatted as a grid.

The View Designer in Visual Studio .NET displays up to four panes. From top to bottom, the panes are as follows:

▶ The Diagram pane, which displays the tables involved in the query and the relationships between these tables, as well as all the columns that the tables contain.

▶ The Grid pane, which shows the columns that have been selected as part of the query, as well as additional sorting and filtering information.

▶ The SQL pane, which shows the actual SQL statement that will be executed.

▶ The Results pane, which shows the results (if any) after the query has been executed.

The View toolbar includes buttons that you can use to hide or show any of these four panes. For this chapter, you need only the SQL pane and the Results pane.

Using OSQL

A second option for executing ad hoc queries is to use one of the utilities that ships as a part of SQL Server, such as *OSQL*. OSQL is a command-line utility that can execute SQL Server queries (see Step-by-Step 1.13).

STEP BY STEP

1.13 Running a Query from OSQL

1. Open a Windows command prompt.

2. Type the following to launch OSQL, and log in using Windows integrated authentication:

```
osql -E
```

3. To execute a query in OSQL, you must first tell it which database to use. To do so, type this:

```
use Northwind
```

4. Enter the query to execute:

```
SELECT FirstName, LastName FROM Employees
```

5. Tell OSQL to execute the SQL statements that you just entered:

```
GO
```

6. When you're finished with OSQL, type this:

```
exit
```

Here's the entire OSQL session, including the prompts from OSQL:

```
C:\>osql -E
1> use Northwind
2> SELECT FirstName, LastName FROM Employees
3> GO
 FirstName  LastName
 ---------- --------------------
 Nancy      Davolio
 Max        Fuller
 Janet      Leverling
 Margaret   Peacock
```

continues

continued

```
Steven      Buchanan
Michael     Suyama
Robert      King
Laura       Callahan
Anne        Dodsworth

(9 rows affected)
1> exit

C:\>
```

EXAM TIP

Obtaining the SQL Query Analyzer
The SQL Query Analyzer is not
included in the MSDE version of
SQL Server. It's a part of all the
other editions of SQL Server, so if
you have another edition installed,
you should have the SQL Query
Analyzer available. Otherwise, you
can download the 120-day trial version of SQL Server 2000 from
www.microsoft.com/sql/
evaluation/trial/2000/
default.asp. This version also
contains the SQL Query Analyzer.

I chose a slightly different query for the OSQL session than I used
in Step-by-Step 1.12. The SELECT query in Step-by-Step 1.13 specifies two columns from the table (FirstName and LastName), telling
SQL Server to return only the contents of those two columns. If you
execute SELECT * FROM Employees in OSQL, you might get a bit of a
shock because the Employees table includes a bitmap image column,
and the contents of that column will fill a command session with
junk characters.

Using the SQL Query Analyzer

Although OSQL can be convenient for quick queries, it doesn't offer
much in the way of tools. SQL Server also offers a full-featured
query environment called *SQL Query Analyzer* (see Step-by-
Step 1.14).

STEP BY STEP

1.14 Running a Query from SQL Query Analyzer

1. Select Start, Programs, Microsoft SQL Server, Query
   Analyzer. The SQL Query Analyzer is launched, and the
   Connect to SQL Server dialog box appears.

2. To choose a SQL Server to work with, you can type the
   name of a SQL Server or the special name (local) to use a
   SQL Server on the same computer as SQL Query
   Analyzer. You can also use the Browse button to list all
   servers on the network. After you select a server and fill in
   your authentication information, click OK.

3. Select the Northwind database from the Databases combo box on the SQL Query Analyzer toolbar.

4. Type this query in the Query window:

```
SELECT * FROM Employees
```

5. Select Query, Execute, click the Execute button on the toolbar, or press F5 to run the query. The SQL statement is sent to SQL Server, and the results are displayed, as shown in Figure 1.22.

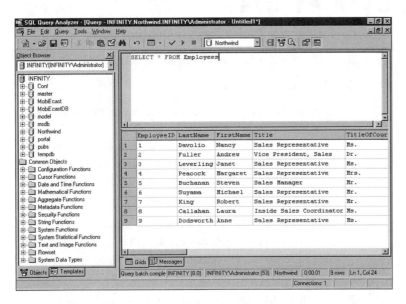

FIGURE 1.22
You can run an ad hoc query in the SQL Query Analyzer.

The SQL Query Analyzer offers an extremely flexible environment for running ad hoc queries. The features of the SQL Query Analyzer include the following:

▶ The ability to have multiple query windows open at the same time.

▶ An Object Browser in which you can see the structure of SQL Server objects

▶ Performance analysis tools

▶ Templates for common queries

For more information on using the SQL Query Analyzer, refer to SQL Server Books Online, the help file installed as part of SQL Server.

Using a Visual C# .NET Application

As a final alternative for executing ad hoc queries, you can build your own Visual C# .NET form to execute any query. Step-by-Step 1.15 shows you how.

STEP BY STEP

1.15 Running a Query from a Custom Form

1. Add a new form to your Visual C# .NET project.

2. Open Server Explorer.

3. Expand the tree under Data Connections to show a SQL Server data connection that points to the Northwind sample database. Drag and drop the data connection to the form. A `sqlConnection1` object is created on the form, and this object represents a connection to SQL Server.

4. Add a `TextBox` control named `txtQuery`, a `Button` control named `btnExecute`, and a `DataGrid` control named `dgResults` to the form. Set the `Multiline` property of the `TextBox` to `true`. Set the `CaptionVisible` property of the `DataGrid` to `false`.

5. Switch to the code view and add the following `using` directives to make the ADO.NET objects available:

```
using System.Data;
using System.Data.SqlClient;
```

6. Double-click the `Button` control and enter this code to execute the query when the Execute Query button is clicked:

```
private void btnExecute_Click(object sender,
    System.EventArgs e)
{
    // Create a SqlCommand object to represent the query
    SqlCommand cmd = sqlConnection1.CreateCommand();
    cmd.CommandType = CommandType.Text;
    cmd.CommandText = txtQuery.Text;
    // Create a SqlDataAdapter object
```

```
    // To talk to the database
    SqlDataAdapter da = new SqlDataAdapter();
    da.SelectCommand = cmd;
    // Create a DataSet to hold the results
    DataSet ds = new DataSet();
    // Fill the data set
    da.Fill(ds, "Results");
    // And bind it to the data grid
    dgResults.DataSource = ds;
    dgResults.DataMember = "Results";
}
```

7. Insert the `Main()` method to launch the form. Set the form as the startup object for the project.

8. Run the project. Enter this query in the Query text box:

```
SELECT * FROM Employees
```

9. Click the Execute Query button. The code runs, retrieving the results to the `DataGrid` control, as shown in Figure 1.23.

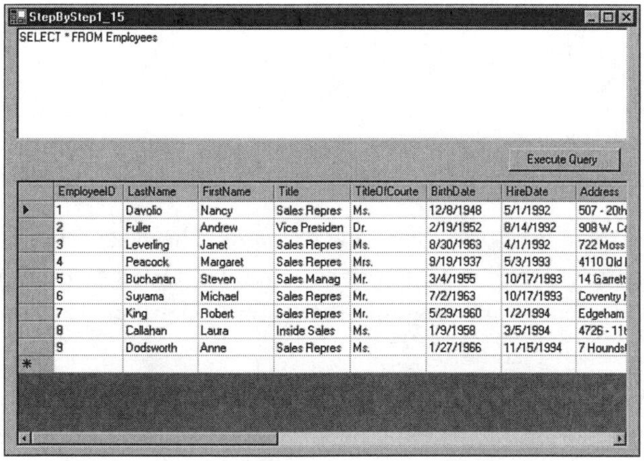

FIGURE 1.23
You can run an ad hoc query from a custom form.

You can learn about the ADO.NET objects that this example uses in Appendix A, "ADO.NET Basics." For now, I'll give a quick preview of the objects I just used:

▶ The `SqlConnection` object represents a connection to a database.

▶ The `SqlCommand` object represents a single query that you can send to the server.

▶ The `DataSet` object represents the results of one or more queries.

▶ The `SqlDataAdapter` object acts as a pipeline between the `SqlConnection` and `DataSet` objects.

The code in Step-by-Step 1.15 uses these objects to retrieve data from SQL Server to the data set, and it uses the SQL statement that you typed in to know which data to retrieve. It then uses complex data binding to display the results on the user interface in the `DataGrid` control.

The `SELECT` Statement

Now that you know a variety of ways to execute ad hoc queries, it's time to dig into the T-SQL language to see some of the possible queries, starting with the `SELECT` statement.

The most basic SQL statement is the `SELECT` statement, which is used to create a resultset. In skeleton form, a `SELECT` statement looks like this:

```
SELECT field_list
FROM table_list
WHERE where_clause
GROUP BY group_by_clause
HAVING having_clause
ORDER BY sort_clause
```

Each of these lines of code is called a *clause*. The `SELECT` and `FROM` clauses are required, and the rest are optional. Here's an example of a SQL statement containing only the required clauses:

```
SELECT OrderID, CustomerID
FROM Orders
```

The resultset for this statement contains the values of the `OrderID` and `CustomerID` fields from every record in the Orders table.

The `SELECT` clause can be used to obtain results other than just lists of fields. You've already seen the shortcut for all fields:

```
SELECT *
FROM Orders
```

You can also perform calculations in the `SELECT` clause:

```
SELECT OrderID,
CAST(ShippedDate - OrderDate AS integer) AS Delay
FROM Orders
```

The expression `ShippedDate - OrderDate` calculates the number of days between the two dates. The `CAST` function tells SQL Server to return the result as an integer. If you try this example, you'll see the `AS` clause supplies a name for the calculated column. If you omit `AS Delay`, the query still works, but SQL Server returns the calculation without assigning a name to the column.

You're not limited to fields from a single table. For instance, you might try retrieving information from both the Customers and Orders tables by using this query:

```
SELECT OrderID, Customers.CustomerID
FROM Orders, Customers
```

`Customers.CustomerID` is what's known as a *fully qualified name*, because it specifies both the table name and the field name. This is necessary because both the Customers and the Orders tables contain fields named `CustomerID`, and you need to tell SQL Server which one you want to display.

If you try the previous query, though, you get more than 75,000 records back—many more than the number of orders in the database! This happens because although the query includes all the proper tables, it doesn't tell SQL Server how to relate those tables.

This sort of query is called a *cross-product* query. SQL Server constructs the resultset by including one row in the output for each row in each combination of input table rows. That is, there's an output row for the first order and the first customer, for the first order and the second customer, and so on.

A more useful query, of course, would match each order with the corresponding customer.

That's the job of the `INNER JOIN` keyword. `INNER JOIN` tells SQL Server how to match two tables. Here's how the query looks for a fixed version of the original query:

```
SELECT OrderID, Customers.CustomerID
FROM Orders INNER JOIN Customers
ON Orders.CustomerID = Customers.CustomerID
```

This fixed query tells SQL Server to look at each row in the Orders table and match it with all rows in the Customers table where the `CustomerID` of the order equals the `CustomerID` of the customer. Because `CustomerID`s are unique in the Customers table, using the preceding code example is the same as including only a single row for each order in the resultset.

NOTE **One Keyword or Two?** Even though it's two words, INNER JOIN is referred to as a single SQL keyword because you can't have INNER in T-SQL unless you immediately follow it with JOIN.

The INNER JOIN keyword can appear more than once in a query if there are more than two tables to join. For example, the following query shows EmployeeIDs along with OrderIDs and CustomerIDs:

```
SELECT Orders.OrderID, Customers.CustomerID,
       Employees.EmployeeID
FROM Employees INNER JOIN
(Customers INNER JOIN Orders
ON Customers.CustomerID = Orders.CustomerID)
ON Employees.EmployeeID = Orders.EmployeeID
```

Note the use of parentheses to specify the order in which the joins should be performed.

The basic SELECT query allows you to see all the data in a table; for example:

```
SELECT * FROM Orders
```

That query returns every bit of data in the Orders table—every column, every row. You've already seen that you can use a field list to limit the number of columns returned:

```
SELECT OrderID, CustomerID, EmployeeID FROM Orders
```

But what if you want to see only some of the rows in a table? That's where the WHERE clause comes into the picture. You can think of a WHERE clause as making a simple, yes-or-no decision for each row of data in the original table, deciding whether to include that row in the resultset.

The simplest form of the WHERE clause checks for the exact contents of a field. Here's an example:

```
SELECT * FROM Orders
WHERE ShipCountry = 'Brazil'
```

This query looks at every row in the Orders table and determines whether the ShipCountry field contains the exact value Brazil. If it does, the row is included in the results. If it does not, the row is discarded.

However, WHERE clauses need not be exact. The following is also a valid SQL statement:

```
SELECT * FROM Orders
WHERE Freight > 50
```

In this case, you get all the rows where the amount in the Freight field is greater than 50.

Note, by the way, that in the first of these WHERE clause examples, Brazil appears in single quotation marks but 50 does not. This is simply a matter of syntax: Text and date data need quotation marks, but numeric columns do not.

You can combine multiple tests in a single WHERE clause. Here's an example:

```
SELECT * FROM Orders
WHERE ShipCountry = 'Brazil'
 AND Freight > 50
 AND OrderDate <= '12/31/97'
```

This retrieves all orders that went to Brazil, had more than $50 of freight charges, and were shipped before the end of 1997.

The entire WHERE clause must be a single logical predicate. That is, after all the pieces are evaluated, the result must be a true or false value. Rows for which the WHERE clause evaluates to true are included in the results; rows for which it evaluates to false are excluded.

You can also use wildcards in a WHERE clause. Consider this simple SELECT statement:

```
SELECT * FROM Customers
WHERE CustomerID = 'BLONP'
```

If you run that query, you find that it returns the record for Blondel pere et fils, the customer that is assigned the CustomerID BLONP. So far, that's easy. But what if you remember that the CustomerID starts with *B*, but not what it is exactly? That's when you'd use a wildcard:

```
SELECT * FROM Customers
WHERE CustomerID LIKE 'B%'
```

The % wildcard matches zero or more characters, so the result of this query is to retrieve all the customers whose CustomerIDs begin with *B*. Note the switch from = to LIKE when using a wildcard. (If you searched for CustomerID = 'B%', you'd only find a customer with that exact ID.) Now suppose you almost remember the CustomerID, but not quite: Is it BLOND or BLONP? Try this query:

```
SELECT * FROM Customers
WHERE CustomerID LIKE 'BLON_'
```

The _ wildcard matches precisely one character—so that would match BLONA, BLONB, and so on. If you're sure that it's either *D* or *P*, you can try the following:

```
SELECT * FROM Customers
WHERE CustomerID LIKE 'BLON[DP]'
```

The [DP] is a character set wildcard. The square brackets tell SQL Server to match any one of the characters listed in the set. You can also use a dash in a character set to indicate a range:

```
SELECT * FROM Customers
WHERE CustomerID LIKE 'BLON[D-P]'
```

This matches BLOND, BLONE, and so on, through BLONP. You can also invert a character set by using the ^ character; for example:

```
SELECT * FROM Customers
WHERE CustomerID LIKE 'BLON[^A-O]'
```

This matches BLONP, BLONQ, and so on, but not BLONA, BLONB, or anything else that would match the character set without the ^ character.

SQL is a set-oriented language; by default, the database engine is free to return the set of results in any order it likes. To guarantee a sort order, include an ORDER BY clause in your SQL statement. For example, to see the customers from Venezuela in postal code order, you could use this statement:

```
SELECT * FROM Customers
WHERE Country = 'Venezuela'
ORDER BY PostalCode
```

This example shows the basic ORDER BY clause: a field name to sort by. You can use two keywords to modify this: ASC, for ascending sort (the default), and DESC, for descending sort. Therefore, you could equally well write the previous SQL statement as follows:

```
SELECT * FROM Customers
WHERE Country = 'Venezuela'
ORDER BY PostalCode ASC
```

And you could get the customers sorted in reverse postal code order by using this statement:

```
SELECT * FROM Customers
WHERE Country = 'Venezuela'
ORDER BY PostalCode DESC
```

You're not limited to sorting by a single field. For example, you might want to see the entire customer list, sorted first by country and then by postal code within country:

```
SELECT * FROM Customers
ORDER BY Country, PostalCode
```

You can specify on a field-by-field basis the sort's order:

```
SELECT * FROM Customers
ORDER BY Country ASC, PostalCode DESC
```

This would sort by country in ascending order, and then by postal code in descending order within each country.

You can also calculate a sort. For example, you can sort the customers by the length of their company names:

```
SELECT * FROM Customers
ORDER BY Len([CompanyName])
```

Here the square brackets tell the Len() function that it's being passed a column name, and to retrieve that column value for each row as the input to the function.

A calculation need not have anything to do with the fields returned by the SELECT statement, as in this example:

```
SELECT * FROM Customers
ORDER BY 2+2
```

This is a perfectly valid SQL statement, although the effect is to put the records in whatever order the database engine decides it wants to use.

So far, all the SELECT statements you've seen in this chapter have returned results where each row corresponds to one row in the underlying tables. However, it's possible (and indeed common) to use SQL to return aggregate, summarized information.

For example, suppose you want to know how many customers you have in each country. Here's a query that gives you the answer:

```
SELECT Count(CustomerID) AS CustCount, Country
FROM Customers
GROUP BY Country
```

You can think of the GROUP BY clause as creating "buckets,"—in this case, one for each country. As the database engine examines each record, it tosses it in the appropriate bucket. After this process is done, the database engine counts the number of records that ended up in each bucket and outputs a row for each one. Figure 1.24 shows the start of the resultset from this query.

You can use ORDER BY in conjunction with GROUP BY. For example, you could sort by the number of customers in each country:

```
SELECT Count(CustomerID) AS CustCount, Country
FROM Customers
GROUP BY Country
ORDER BY Count(CustomerID) DESC
```

FIGURE 1.24
You can use GROUP BY clause in a query to retrieve a resultset with summarized information.

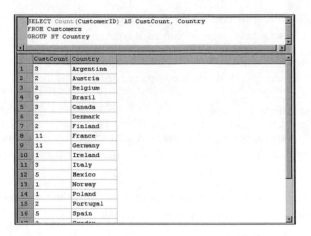

Or you could sort by the country name:

```
SELECT Count(CustomerID) AS CustCount, Country
FROM Customers
GROUP BY Country
ORDER BY Country
```

In these SQL statements, `Count()` is an *aggregate function*—that is, a function that returns a result based on a number of rows. T-SQL supports a number of aggregate functions. Here are some of the most common:

▶ `Count()`—Returns the number of records.

▶ `Sum()`—Returns the total value of records.

▶ `Avg()`—Returns the average value of records.

▶ **`Min()`**—Returns the smallest record.

▶ `Max()`—Returns the largest record.

You can also group on more than one field. Here's an example:

```
SELECT Count(CustomerID) AS CustCount, Region, Country
FROM Customers
GROUP BY Region, Country
```

This statement sets up one bucket for each combination of region and country, and it categorizes the customers by both fields simultaneously.

So far, the GROUP BY statements you've seen have included all the records in the table. For example, consider this query:

```
SELECT ProductID,
Sum(Quantity) AS TotalSales
FROM [Order Details]
GROUP BY ProductID
ORDER BY Sum(Quantity) DESC
```

This query returns a resultset that has one row for each product found in the Order Details table, with the product ID and the total quantity of the product that was ordered. This query uses all the rows in the Order Details table to come up with its totals. There are two ways you can limit this to use only part of the table.

First, you can use a WHERE clause to limit the rows from the original query that will be included in the totals:

```
SELECT ProductID,
Sum(Quantity) AS TotalSales
FROM [Order Details]
WHERE Quantity > 10
GROUP BY ProductID
ORDER BY Sum(Quantity) DESC
```

> **NOTE**
>
> **Quoting Names** This query uses square brackets to quote the name of the "Order Details" table. This is necessary because the table name has a space in it, and without the square brackets, SQL Server would try to interpret it as two names.

This has the same effect as the first query, except that it just ignores any row in the Order Details table that has a quantity of 10 or under.

The other way to limit the results is by filtering the totals with a HAVING clause:

```
SELECT ProductID, Sum(Quantity) AS TotalSales
FROM [Order Details]
GROUP BY ProductID
HAVING Sum(Quantity) > 1000
ORDER BY Sum(Quantity) DESC
```

A HAVING clause filters on the results, rather than on the input. That is, this query sums everything from the Order Details table, and then it shows you only rows where the total is greater than 1,000.

You can also combine the two types of filtering, as in this example:

```
SELECT ProductID, Sum(Quantity) AS TotalSales
FROM [Order Details]
WHERE Quantity > 10
GROUP BY ProductID
HAVING Sum(Quantity) > 1000
ORDER BY Sum(Quantity) DESC
```

This query goes through the source table, sums up all the rows where the quantity is greater than 10, and then keeps only the rows where the total is greater than 1,000.

Note that WHERE and HAVING go in two different places in the SQL statement. The order of clauses is fixed, not optional.

The INSERT Statement

The purpose of the INSERT statement is to add a row or multiple rows to a table by executing a SQL statement. In its simplest form, the INSERT statement lists a target table and a set of values to insert. For example, this query (with the optional INTO keyword) adds a new row to the Order Details table:

```
INSERT INTO [Order Details]
VALUES (10248, 1, 12.00, 5, 0)
```

This simple form of the statement has two drawbacks. There are two drawbacks to this simple form of the INSERT statement. First, it's very difficult to tell which field is getting which piece of data; the values are inserted into the table fields in the order in which the fields show up in design view, but you need to remember (in this example) that the quantity is the fourth field. Second, if you use this format, you need to supply a value for every field. This is a problem when you want the default value for a field or when a field can't have data inserted into it (for example, an identity field, whose values are automatically generated by SQL Server). To get around these problems, a second format explicitly lists the fields for the target table:

```
INSERT INTO [Order Details]
  (OrderID, ProductID, UnitPrice, Quantity, Discount)
VALUES (10248, 2, 12.00, 5, 0)
```

Here, the first set of parentheses holds a column list, and the second set holds the values to insert. If a field has a default value, or can be null, or is an identity field, you can leave it out of the field list, as in this example:

```
INSERT INTO Products
  (ProductName, SupplierID, CategoryID)
VALUES ('Turnips', 25, 7)
```

This works even though no value is specified for most of the fields in the Products table. Also, you can rearrange the field list as long as you rearrange the value list to match:

```
INSERT INTO Products
  (SupplierID, ProductName, CategoryID)
VALUES (20, 'Lettuce',  7)
```

The INSERT statement isn't limited to inserting a single record. A second format inserts the results of a SELECT statement into the target table. For example, this query inserts a product from every supplier into the Products table:

```
INSERT INTO Products
  (SupplierID, ProductName, CategoryID )
SELECT SupplierID, 'Trout', 8
FROM Suppliers
```

This works by building the results of the SELECT statement and then putting each row returned by the SELECT statement into the target table. Of course, the columns still need to match up properly.

The UPDATE Statement

Another very useful SQL statement is the UPDATE statement. As you can probably guess, the purpose of an UPDATE query is to update data. For example, you could update a field in a record in the Northwind database by using this query:

```
UPDATE Customers
 SET ContactName = 'Maria Anderson'
 WHERE CustomerID = 'ALFKI'
```

In this query, the UPDATE statement introduces an UPDATE query. The SET keyword tells SQL Server what to update. In this case, it's setting a field equal to a literal value. The WHERE clause tells SQL Server which row in the table to update.

You're not limited to updating a single record. If the WHERE clause selects multiple records, they are all updated, as in this example:

```
UPDATE Customers
 SET Country = 'United States'
 WHERE Country = 'USA'
```

You can even update every row in a table by leaving out the WHERE clause:

```
UPDATE Products
 SET Discontinued = 1
```

This updates every row in the Products table—even those where the Discontinued field already has the value 1.

You can also update more than one field at a time by using an UPDATE query:

```
UPDATE Customers
 SET ContactName = 'Maria Anders', City = 'Berlin'
 WHERE CustomerID = 'ALFKI'
```

And you can update by using the result of an expression:

```
UPDATE Products
 SET UnitPrice = UnitPrice * 1.1
```

If only it were so simple to raise prices in real life!

Finally, you can update based on joined tables:

```
UPDATE Suppliers INNER JOIN Products
 ON Suppliers.SupplierID = Products.SupplierID
 SET Discontinued = 1
 WHERE Suppliers.Country = 'Italy'
```

This has the effect of discontinuing all the products that are imported from Italy.

The DELETE Statement

The DELETE statement removes data from a table. The rule for constructing a DELETE query is simple: Construct a SELECT query to select the records you want to delete and then change the SELECT keyword to DELETE. Remove any * identifier from the SELECT clause as well. That's it!

To avoid destroying existing data, let's set the stage for the DELETE statement by using the SELECT INTO statement to create a new table. For example, this statement creates a table named BadCustomers, with all the data from the existing Customers table:

```
SELECT * INTO BadCustomers
FROM Customers
```

Here's a SELECT query for selecting a single row from the new table:

```
SELECT * FROM BadCustomers WHERE CustomerID = 'GODOS'
```

Now change the SELECT * clause to DELETE:

```
DELETE FROM BadCustomers WHERE CustomerID = 'GODOS'
```

If you run this query, the specified row is deleted. There's no need for a WHERE clause if you want to get really extreme:

```
DELETE FROM BadCustomers
```

This statement deletes all the rows from the BadCustomers table.

▶ T-SQL is the Microsoft SQL Server dialect of the ANSI SQL-92 standard query language.

▶ You can execute T-SQL statements from a variety of interfaces, including the Visual Studio .NET IDE, OSQL, the SQL Query Analyzer, and custom applications.

▶ SELECT statements retrieve data from tables in a database.

▶ INSERT statements add new data to tables in a database.

▶ UPDATE statements modify existing data in tables in a database.

▶ DELETE statements remove data from tables in a database.

Using Stored Procedures

When you use an ad hoc query to interact with SQL Server, the SQL statements in the query are completely transient—that is, they vanish as soon as you close whatever tool you've used to execute the query. In contrast, *stored procedures* are stored permanently on the SQL Server itself. Stored procedures have two main benefits. First, you can use them to save complex SQL statements for future execution so that you don't have to re-create them from scratch. Second, SQL Server compiles stored procedures so that they run faster than ad hoc queries.

In the following sections you'll learn how to create and run stored procedures. You'll also learn about parameters, which make stored procedures flexible, and the @@IDENTITY variable, which can supply useful information any time you use a stored procedure to insert data into a table that has an identity column.

Creating a Stored Procedure

T-SQL includes a CREATE PROCEDURE keyword to create stored procedures. You can run CREATE PROCEDURE statements from any interface that allows you to enter and execute T-SQL (see Step-by-Step 1.16).

> **EXAM TIP**
>
> **When to Use Stored Procedures**
> In almost every case, stored procedures are preferable to ad hoc queries in production applications. The only time you should consider using ad hoc queries is when you're writing an application that must allow completely free-form querying by the end user. Otherwise, the additional development time required to implement stored procedures will be worth it in the end.

STEP BY STEP

1.16 Creating a Stored Procedure from the Visual Studio .NET IDE

1. Open Server Explorer in the Visual Studio .NET IDE.

2. Expand the tree under Data Connections to show a SQL Server data connection that points to the Northwind sample database, and then expand the Stored Procedures node of the selected SQL Server data connection.

3. Right-click the Stored Procedures node and select New Stored Procedure. This step opens the Stored Procedure designer.

4. Replace the boilerplate code in the Stored Procedure designer with this code:

```
CREATE PROCEDURE procFranceCustomers
AS
    SELECT * FROM Customers
    WHERE Country = 'France'
```

5. Click the Save button to save the stored procedure to the database.

6. Select Database, Run Stored Procedure to run the CREATE PROCEDURE statement. This creates the stored procedure in the database.

7. Execute the new procFranceCustomers stored procedure from any tool that allows you to execute SQL statements. For example, Figure 1.25 shows the results of executing the stored procedure in the custom form you built in Step-by-Step 1.15.

You can see from Step-by-Step 1.16 that there are two separate executing steps in the process. Executing the CREATE PROCEDURE statement (which is itself an ad hoc query) is necessary to create the stored procedure. After that has been done, you can execute the stored procedure itself to return results.

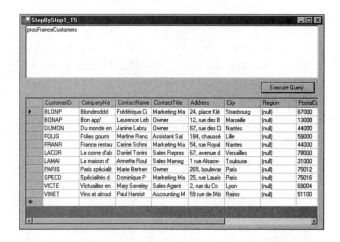

FIGURE 1.25
The results of running a stored procedure are the same as the results of running the T-SQL statements contained in the stored procedure.

Running Stored Procedures from the .NET Framework

Executing a stored procedure from the .NET Framework is very similar to executing an ad hoc query. The difference is that when you execute a stored procedure from the .NET Framework, you supply the name of the stored procedure instead of the actual SQL code as the CommandText property of a SqlCommand object and set the CommandType property to CommandType.StoredProcedure (see Step-by-Step 1.17).

STEP BY STEP

1.17 Running a Stored Procedure from Visual C# .NET

1. Add a new form to your Visual C# .NET project.

2. Open Server Explorer.

3. Expand the tree under Data Connections to show a SQL Server data connection that points to the Northwind sample database. Drag and drop the data connection to the form. A sqlConnection1 object is created on the form.

4. Add a DataGrid control named dgResults to the form.

continues

continued

5. Switch to the code view and add the following using directives to make the ADO.NET objects available:

```
using System.Data;
using System.Data.SqlClient;
```

6. Double-click the form control and enter this code to execute the stored procedure when you load the form:

```
private void StepByStep1_17_Load(object sender,
    System.EventArgs e)
{
    // Create a SqlCommand object to represent
    // the stored procedure
    SqlCommand cmd = sqlConnection1.CreateCommand();
    cmd.CommandType = CommandType.StoredProcedure;
    cmd.CommandText = "procFranceCustomers";
    // Create a SqlDataAdapter to talk to the database
    SqlDataAdapter da = new SqlDataAdapter();
    da.SelectCommand = cmd;
    // Create a DataSet to hold the results
    DataSet ds = new DataSet();
    // Fill the DataSet
    da.Fill(ds, "Customers");
    // And bind it to the DataGrid
    dgResults.DataSource = ds;
    dgResults.DataMember = "Customers";
}
```

7. Insert the Main() method to launch the form. Set the form as the startup object for the project.

8. Run the project. This will run the code, retrieving the results to the DataGrid, as shown in Figure 1.26.

FIGURE 1.26
You should set the CommandType property of SqlCommand to CommandType.StoredProcedure to run a stored procedure from the SqlCommand object.

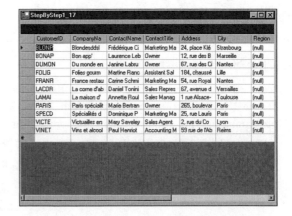

Stored procedures are not limited to containing SELECT statements. You can place any SQL statement inside a stored procedure. For example, you might use this SQL statement to create a stored procedure to update the Customers table:

```
CREATE PROCEDURE procExpandCountry
AS
UPDATE Customers
 SET Country = 'United States'
 WHERE Country = 'USA'
```

When a stored procedure doesn't return a resultset, you need to use a slightly different code structure to execute it (see Step-by-Step 1.18). Guided Practice Exercise 1.1 offers additional practice in this technique.

STEP BY STEP

1.18 Running a Stored Procedure That Does Not Return Results

1. Add a new form to your Visual C# .NET project.

2. Open Server Explorer.

3. Expand the tree under Data Connections to show a SQL Server data connection that points to the Northwind sample database. Drag and drop the data connection to the form. A sqlConnection1 object is created on the form.

4. Using a tool such as the SQL Query Analyzer or the Visual Studio .NET IDE, create this stored procedure:

```
CREATE PROCEDURE procExpandCountry
AS
UPDATE Customers
 SET Country = 'United States'
 WHERE Country = 'USA'
```

5. Place a Button control on the form and name it btnExecute.

6. Switch to the code view and add the following using directives to make the ADO.NET objects available:

```
using System.Data;
using System.Data.SqlClient;
```

continues

continued

7. Double-click the Button control and enter this code to execute the stored procedure when the Execute button is clicked:

```
private void btnExecute_Click(object sender,
    System.EventArgs e)
{
    // Create a SqlCommand object to represent
    // the stored procedure
    SqlCommand cmd = sqlConnection1.CreateCommand();
    cmd.CommandType = CommandType.StoredProcedure;
    cmd.CommandText = "procExpandCountry";
    // Open the connection and
    // execute the stored procedure
    sqlConnection1.Open();
    cmd.ExecuteNonQuery();
    // Close the connection
    sqlConnection1.Close();
    MessageBox.Show("SQL statement was executed.");
}
```

8. Insert the Main() method to launch the form. Set the form as the startup object for the project.

9. Run the project and click the Execute Stored Procedure button. The stored procedure executes, and you are informed of that fact via a message box.

EXAM TIP

Opening and Closing Connections
When you call the methods of the SqlDataAdapter object, the .NET Framework automatically opens and closes the associated SqlConnection object as necessary. For any other operation (such as using the SqlCommand.ExecuteNonQuery() method) you must explicitly call the SqlConnection.Open() and SqlConnection.Close() methods in your code.

You can use the ExecuteNonQuery() method of the SqlCommand object to execute any ad hoc query or stored procedure that doesn't return any results.

Using Parameters in Stored Procedures

The examples that you've seen so far in this chapter don't begin to tap the real power of stored procedures. SQL Server supports *parameterized stored procedures*, which enable you to pass information to the stored procedure at runtime (you can think of these as the T-SQL analogue of Visual C# .NET methods). For example, this SQL statement defines a stored procedure that returns the total sales for a particular customer, with the CustomerID specified at runtime:

```
CREATE PROC procCustomerSales
  @CustomerID char(5),
  @TotalSales money OUTPUT
AS
```

```
SELECT @TotalSales = SUM(Quantity * UnitPrice)
FROM ((Customers INNER JOIN Orders
ON Customers.CustomerID = Orders.CustomerID)
INNER JOIN [Order Details]
ON Orders.OrderID = [Order Details].OrderID)
WHERE Customers.CustomerID = @CustomerID
```

In this SQL statement, both `@CustomerID` and `@TotalSales` are variables (called *parameters* in T-SQL). To use the stored procedure, you must supply a value for the `@CustomerID` parameter. The `@TotalSales` parameter is marked as an `OUTPUT` parameter; it returns a value from the stored procedure to the calling code.

In the .NET Framework, the `SqlCommand` object has a collection of parameters that enable you to manage parameterized stored procedures (see Step-by-Step 1.19).

STEP BY STEP

1.19 Running a Parameterized Stored Procedure

1. Add a new form to your Visual C# .NET project.

2. Open Server Explorer.

3. Expand the tree under Data Connections to show a SQL Server data connection that points to the Northwind sample database. Drag and drop the data connection to the form to create a `sqlConnection1` object on the form.

4. Using a tool such as the SQL Query Analyzer or the Visual Studio .NET IDE, create a stored procedure with this code:

```
CREATE PROC procCustomerSales
  @CustomerID char(5),
  @TotalSales money OUTPUT
AS
  SELECT @TotalSales = SUM(Quantity * UnitPrice)
  FROM ((Customers INNER JOIN Orders
  ON Customers.CustomerID = Orders.CustomerID)
  INNER JOIN [Order Details]
  ON Orders.OrderID = [Order Details].OrderID)
  WHERE Customers.CustomerID = @CustomerID
```

5. Place two `Label` controls, two `TextBox` controls (`txtCustomerID` and `txtTotalSales`), and a `Button` control (`btnGetTotalSales`) on the form, as shown in Figure 1.27.

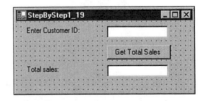

FIGURE 1.27
You can accept a parameter's value at the run-time and then execute a parameterized stored procedure.

continues

continued

6. Switch to the code view and add the following using directives to make the ADO.NET objects available:

```
using System.Data;
using System.Data.SqlClient;
using System.Data.SqlTypes;
```

7. Double-click the Button control and enter this code to execute the stored procedure when the button is clicked:

```
private void btnGetTotalSales_Click(object sender,
    System.EventArgs e)
{
    // Create a SqlCommand to represent
    // the stored procedure
    SqlCommand cmd = sqlConnection1.CreateCommand();
    cmd.CommandType = CommandType.StoredProcedure;
    cmd.CommandText = "procCustomerSales";
    // Add the input parameter and set its value
    cmd.Parameters.Add(new SqlParameter("@CustomerID",
        SqlDbType.Text, 5));
    cmd.Parameters["@CustomerID"].Value =
        txtCustomerID.Text;
    // Add the output parameter and set its direction
    cmd.Parameters.Add(new SqlParameter("@TotalSales",
        SqlDbType.Money));
    cmd.Parameters["@TotalSales"].Direction =
        ParameterDirection.Output;
    // Execute the stored procedure
    // Display the formatted results
    sqlConnection1.Open();
    cmd.ExecuteNonQuery();
    txtTotalSales.Text = String.Format("{0:c}",
        cmd.Parameters["@TotalSales"].Value);
    sqlConnection1.Close();
}
```

8. Insert the Main() method to launch this form and set the form as the startup object for the project.

9. Run the project and enter a CustomerID from the Customers table in the first text box. Click the button. The form executes the stored procedure and returns the total sales for this customer in the second text box.

In ADO.NET parameters are represented by `SqlParameter` objects. The code in Step-by-Step 1.19 uses two different forms of the constructor for `SqlParameters`. The first takes the parameter name, the parameter data type, and the size of the parameter; the second omits the parameter size (because the money type has a fixed size). The code works by setting the `Value` property of the `@CustomerID` parameter, executing the `SqlCommand` object, and then retrieving the `Value` property of the `@TotalSales` parameter.

Using the `@@IDENTITY` Variable

A SQL Server table can have a single *identity* column. An identity column is a column whose value is assigned by SQL Server itself whenever you add a new row to the table. The purpose of the identity column is to guarantee that each row in the table has a unique primary key.

If you're working with a table that contains an identity column, you are likely to add a new row to the table and then immediately retrieve the value of the identity column for the new row. SQL Server provides a variable named `@@IDENTITY` for just this purpose. The `@@IDENTITY` variable returns the most recently assigned identity column value.

Step-by-Step 1.20 shows how to use a stored procedure to insert a new row in a table and return the value of the identity column so that your code can continue to work with the new row.

STEP BY STEP

1.20 Retrieving a New Identity Value

1. Add a new form to your Visual C# .NET project.

2. Open Server Explorer.

3. Expand the tree under Data Connections to show a SQL Server data connection that points to the Northwind sample database. Drag and drop the data connection to the form to create a `sqlConnection1` object on the form.

continues

continued

4. Using a tool such as the SQL Query Analyzer or the Visual Studio .NET IDE, create this stored procedure:

```
CREATE PROC procInsertShipper
  @CompanyName nvarchar(40),
  @ShipperID int OUTPUT
AS
  INSERT INTO Shippers (CompanyName)
    VALUES (@CompanyName)
  SELECT @ShipperID = @@IDENTITY
```

This stored procedure contains two SQL statements. The first inserts a row into the Shippers table, and the second retrieves the value of the identity column for the new row.

5. Place two `Label` controls, two `TextBox` controls (`txtCompanyName` and `txtShipperID`) and a Button control (`btnAddShipper`) on the form.

6. Switch to the code view and add the following using directives to make the ADO.NET objects available:

```
using System.Data;
using System.Data.SqlClient;
using System.Data.SqlTypes;
```

7. Double-click the `Button` control and enter this code to execute the stored procedure when the button is clicked:

```
private void btnAddShipper_Click(object sender,
    System.EventArgs e)
{
    // Create a SqlCommand to represent
    // the stored procedure
    SqlCommand cmd = sqlConnection1.CreateCommand();
    cmd.CommandType = CommandType.StoredProcedure;
    cmd.CommandText = "procInsertShipper";
    // Add the input parameter and set its value
    cmd.Parameters.Add(new SqlParameter(
        "@CompanyName",
        SqlDbType.VarChar, 40));
    cmd.Parameters["@CompanyName"].Value =
        txtCompanyName.Text;
    // Add the output parameter and set its direction
    cmd.Parameters.Add(new SqlParameter("@ShipperID",
        SqlDbType.Int));
    cmd.Parameters["@ShipperID"].Direction =
        ParameterDirection.Output;
    // Execute the stored procedure and
```

```
    // display the result
    sqlConnection1.Open();
    cmd.ExecuteNonQuery();
    txtShipperID.Text =
        cmd.Parameters["@ShipperID"].Value.ToString();
    sqlConnection1.Close();
}
```

8. Insert the `Main()` method to launch the form. Set the form as the startup object for the project.

9. Run the project and enter a company name for the new shipper in the first text box. Click the button. The form executes the stored procedure and returns the identity value assigned to the new shipper in the second text box.

Step-by-Step 1.20 uses the same code pattern as Step-by-Step 1.19. The variable names and control names are different, but the two Step-by-Step examples show a common pattern for using stored procedures in code:

1. Create a `SqlCommand` object to represent the stored procedure.

2. Create `SqlParameter` objects to represent the parameters of the stored procedure.

3. Supply values for any input parameters.

4. Open the `SqlConnection` object for this stored procedure.

5. Execute the stored procedure by using the `ExecuteNonQuery()` method of the `SqlCommand` object.

6. Retrieve values of any output parameters.

7. Close the `SqlConnection` object.

GUIDED PRACTICE EXERCISE 1.1

In this exercise, you design a form to enter new products into the Northwind database. Table 1.3 shows the columns that the `Products` table contains.

continues

continued

TABLE 1.3

THE NORTHWIND PRODUCTS TABLE'S COLUMNS

Column Name	Data Type	Is the Column Nullable?	Is This an Identity Column?
ProductID	Int	No	Yes
ProductName	nvarchar(40)	No	No
SupplierID	Int	Yes	No
CategoryID	Int	Yes	No
QuantityPerUnit	nvarchar(20)	Yes	No
UnitPrice	money	Yes	No
UnitsInStock	smallint	Yes	No
UnitsOnOrder	smallint	Yes	No
ReorderLevel	smallint	Yes	No
Discontinued	Bit	No	No

Allow the user to enter at least the ProductName and CategoryID, to add the product to the table, and to see the ProductID that's assigned to the new row in the table. You might optionally allow the user to input any other data that you like.

Valid values for the CategoryID column can be determined by retrieving the CategoryID values from the Categories table, which also contains a CategoryName column. You should use a ComboBox control to display valid CategoryID values.

How would you design such a form?

You should try working through this problem on your own first. If you get stuck, or if you'd like to see one possible solution, follow these steps:

1. Add a new form to your Visual C# .NET project.

2. Open Server Explorer.

3. Expand the tree under Data Connections to show a SQL Server data connection that points to the Northwind sample database. Drag and drop the data connection to the form to create a sqlConnection1 object on the form.

4. Add Label controls, a `ComboBox` control (`cboCategoryID`), a Button control (`btnAddProduct`), and two `TextBox` controls (`txtProductName` and `txtProductID`) to the form. Figure 1.28 shows a possible design for the form.

5. Using a tool such as the SQL Query Analyzer or the Visual Studio .NET IDE, create this stored procedure:

```
CREATE PROC procInsertProduct
  @ProductName nvarchar(40),
  @CategoryID int,
  @ProductID int OUTPUT
AS
  INSERT INTO Products (ProductName, CategoryID)
    VALUES (@ProductName, @CategoryID)
  SELECT @ProductID = @@IDENTITY
```

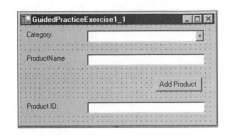

FIGURE 1.28
A possible design of a form that queries product information.

6. Switch to the code view and add the following using directives to make the ADO.NET objects available:

```
using System.Data;
using System.Data.SqlClient;
using System.Data.SqlTypes;
```

7. Double-click the form and enter the following code to fill the list in the `ComboBox` control in the form's `Load` event handler:

```
private void GuidedPracticeExercise1_1_Load
   (object sender, System.EventArgs e)
{
    // Retrieve data for the combo box
    SqlCommand cmdCategories =
                sqlConnection1.CreateCommand();
    cmdCategories.CommandType = CommandType.Text;
    cmdCategories.CommandText =
       "SELECT CategoryID, CategoryName FROM " +
       "Categories ORDER BY CategoryName";
    DataSet ds = new DataSet();
    SqlDataAdapter da = new SqlDataAdapter();
    da.SelectCommand = cmdCategories;
    da.Fill(ds, "Categories");
    cboCategoryID.DataSource =
       ds.Tables["Categories"];
    cboCategoryID.DisplayMember = "CategoryName";
    cboCategoryID.ValueMember = "CategoryID";
}
```

8. Attach a `Click` event handler to the Button control. Enter this code to execute the stored procedure when the button is clicked:

```
private void btnAddProduct_Click(object sender,
    System.EventArgs e)
```

continues

continued

```
{
    // Create a SqlCommand to represent
    // the stored procedure
    SqlCommand cmd = sqlConnection1.CreateCommand();
    cmd.CommandType = CommandType.StoredProcedure;
    cmd.CommandText = "procInsertProduct";
    // Add the input parameters and set their values
    cmd.Parameters.Add(new SqlParameter("@ProductName",
        SqlDbType.VarChar, 40));
    cmd.Parameters["@ProductName"].Value =
        txtProductName.Text;
    cmd.Parameters.Add(new SqlParameter("@CategoryID",
        SqlDbType.Int));
    cmd.Parameters["@CategoryID"].Value =
        cboCategoryID.SelectedValue;
    // Add the output parameter and set its direction
    cmd.Parameters.Add(new SqlParameter("@ProductID",
        SqlDbType.Int));
    cmd.Parameters["@ProductID"].Direction =
        ParameterDirection.Output;
    // Execute the stored procedure
    // and display the result
    sqlConnection1.Open();
    cmd.ExecuteNonQuery();
    txtProductID.Text =
        cmd.Parameters["@ProductID"].Value.ToString();
    sqlConnection1.Close();
}
```

9. Insert the `Main()` method to launch this form and set the form as the startup object for the project.

10. Run the project. Select a category for the new product from the combo box. Enter a name for the new product in the first text box. Click the button. The form executes the stored procedure and returns the identity value assigned to the new shipper in the second text box.

If you have difficulty following this exercise, review the sections "Running Queries," "The SELECT Statement," "The INSERT Statement," and "Using the Stored Procedures" from this chapter. The text and examples should help you relearn this material and help you understand what happens in this exercise. After doing that review, try this exercise again.

- ▶ Stored procedures provide a way to keep compiled SQL statements on the database server.

- ▶ The ADO.NET `SqlCommand` object lets you execute stored procedures.

- ▶ Stored procedures can have both input and output parameters. Input parameters are variables that are used by the stored procedure. Output parameters let the stored procedure return results to the caller.

- ▶ The `@@IDENTITY` variable returns the most recent identity value from the connection.

CHAPTER SUMMARY

The .NET Framework and Visual Studio .NET include pervasive XML integration. One place where this integration comes into play is with `DataSet` schema files. A `DataSet` schema provides an XML representation of the metadata that defines the structure of a `DataSet` object. Visual Studio .NET offers both text and graphical editing of these files.

In this chapter, you learned how to perform basic schema file operations. This includes creating schemas with elements and attributes, as well as using Server Explorer in conjunction with the XML Designer. You also saw how you could use the DataSet schema designer to add keys and relationships to a `DataSet` schema. Finally, you learned how to use schemas to create and use strongly typed `DataSet` objects.

KEY TERMS

- ad hoc query
- `DataSet`
- `DataSet` schema
- identity column
- key
- MetaData
- nested relationship
- one-to-many relationship
- OSQL
- parameter
- simple type
- SQL-92

CHAPTER SUMMARY

- SQL Query Analyzer

- stored procedure

- strongly typed `DataSet`

- Transact-SQL

- XML attribute

- XML element

SQL Server is an important data source for .NET applications. To deal effectively with SQL Server data, you must have an understanding of the T-SQL language. In this chapter, you learned the basics of T-SQL, including the SELECT, INSERT, UPDATE, and DELETE statements. You also saw how to execute SQL in ad hoc queries and in stored procedures.

APPLY YOUR KNOWLEDGE

Exercises

1.1 Preselecting Data with Parameterized Stored Procedures

One of the biggest issues in working with server-side data, such as SQL Server data, is to minimize the amount of data that you load into an application. Communication with such servers is typically comparatively slow, and the servers themselves have enough processing power to quickly locate the exact data that you want. In this exercise, you'll see how you can minimize the amount of data retrieved by using a series of stored procedures with parameters.

Estimated Time: 30 minutes.

1. Create a new Visual C# .NET project to use for the Exercises in this chapter. Name the project 320C01Exercises.

2. Add a new form to the project.

3. Place a ComboBox control (cboCustomers), a Button control (btnLoad), and a DataGrid control (dgMain) on the form.

4. Switch to the code view and add the following using directives to make the ADO.NET objects available:

   ```
   using System.Data;
   using System.Data.SqlClient;
   ```

5. Using a tool such as the SQL Query Analyzer or the Visual Studio .NET IDE, create this stored procedure:

   ```
   CREATE PROC procCustomerList
   AS
   SELECT CustomerID, CompanyName
   FROM Customers
   ORDER BY CompanyName
   ```

6. Using a tool such as the SQL Query Analyzer or the Visual Studio .NET IDE, create this stored procedure:

   ```
   CREATE PROC procCustomerDetails
     @CustomerID char(5)
   AS
   SELECT * FROM Customers
   WHERE CustomerID = @CustomerID
   ```

7. Using a tool such as the SQL Query Analyzer or the Visual Studio .NET IDE, create this stored procedure:

   ```
   CREATE PROC procOrdersForCustomer
     @CustomerID char(5)
   AS
   SELECT * FROM Orders
   WHERE CustomerID = @CustomerID
   ```

8. To minimize load time, the form starts by loading only the customer list into the ComboBox control. Enter this code to load the customer list in the form's Load event handler:

   ```
   SqlConnection cnn = new SqlConnection(
       "Data Source=(local); " +
       "Initial Catalog=Northwind;" +
       " Integrated Security=SSPI");

   private void Exercise1_1_Load(
       object sender, System.EventArgs e)
   {
       // Load the customer list
       SqlCommand cmdCustomers =
           cnn.CreateCommand();
       cmdCustomers.CommandType =
           CommandType.StoredProcedure;
       cmdCustomers.CommandText =
           "procCustomerList";
       DataSet ds = new DataSet();
       SqlDataAdapter da =
           new SqlDataAdapter();
       da.SelectCommand = cmdCustomers;
       da.Fill(ds, "Customers");
       cboCustomers.DataSource =
           ds.Tables["Customers"];
       cboCustomers.DisplayMember =
   ```

APPLY YOUR KNOWLEDGE

```
         "CompanyName";
    cboCustomers.ValueMember =
         "CustomerID";
}
```

9. When the user clicks the Load button, the other stored procedures should load only the data of interest. Enter this code to build the `DataSet` object and bind it to the `DataGrid` control in the `btnLoad Click` event handler:

```
private void btnLoad_Click(
    object sender, System.EventArgs e)
{
    // Create a new DataSet
    DataSet ds = new DataSet();
    // Load only the customer of interest
    SqlCommand cmdCustomer =
        cnn.CreateCommand();
    cmdCustomer.CommandType =
        CommandType.StoredProcedure;
    cmdCustomer.CommandText =
        "procCustomerDetails";
    cmdCustomer.Parameters.Add(
        new SqlParameter(
        "@CustomerID", SqlDbType.Text, 5));
    cmdCustomer.Parameters[
        "@CustomerID"].Value =
        cboCustomers.SelectedValue;
    SqlDataAdapter daCustomer =
        new SqlDataAdapter();
    daCustomer.SelectCommand = cmdCustomer;
    daCustomer.Fill(ds, "Customers");
    // Load the orders for this customer
    SqlCommand cmdOrders =
        cnn.CreateCommand();
    cmdOrders.CommandType =
        CommandType.StoredProcedure;
    cmdOrders.CommandText =
        "procOrdersForCustomer";
    cmdOrders.Parameters.Add(
        new SqlParameter(
        "@CustomerID", SqlDbType.Text, 5));
    cmdOrders.Parameters[
        "@CustomerID"].Value =
        cboCustomers.SelectedValue;
    SqlDataAdapter daOrders =
```

```
        new SqlDataAdapter();
    daOrders.SelectCommand = cmdOrders;
    daOrders.Fill(ds, "Orders");
    // Relate the two DataTables
    DataRelation relCustOrder =
        ds.Relations.Add(
        "CustOrder",
        ds.Tables["Customers"].
        Columns["CustomerID"],
        ds.Tables["Orders"].
        Columns["CustomerID"]);
    // Bind the data to the user interface
    dgMain.DataSource = ds;
    dgMain.DataMember = "Customers";
}
```

10. Insert the `Main()` method to launch the form. Set the form as the startup form for the project.

11. Run the project. Select a customer from the list in the combo box and then press the Load button. The form displays only the information for that customer. Click on the + sign next to the customer to see the order information, as shown in Figure 1.29.

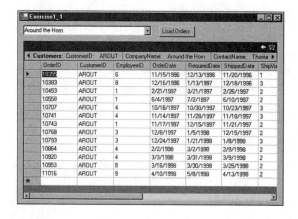

FIGURE 1.29
Use Parameterized Stored Procedures to minimize the amount of data that you need to load into an application.

APPLY YOUR KNOWLEDGE

1.2   Using a Schema with a Stored Procedure

You saw both schema files and stored procedures in this chapter, but you didn't see how to use the two of them together. In this exercise, you'll use a SQL Server stored procedure to create both a schema file and the corresponding Command object, and you'll see how to connect them to one another.

Estimated Time: 15 minutes.

1. Right-click on the 320C01Exercises project in Solution Explorer and select Add, Add New Item. Add a new DataSet object to the project and name it dsOrdersForCustomer.xsd.

2. Expand the Server Explorer tree view to show a data connection to the Northwind sample database. Drill into the Stored Procedures folder within this database.

3. Drag the procOrdersForCustomer stored procedure from Server Explorer and drop it on the DataSet schema designer. This creates a new element with all the necessary included elements to represent the stored procedure.

4. Add a new form to the project.

5. Place a ComboBox control named cboCustomers, a Button control named btnLoad, and a DataGrid control named dgMain on the form.

6. Switch to the code view and add the following using directives to make the ADO.NET objects available:

```
using System.Data;
using System.Data.SqlClient;
```

7. Drag the procOrdersForCustomer stored procedure from Server Explorer and drop it on the form. This creates a SqlConnection object and a SqlCommand object.

8. Select the SqlCommand object and change its name to cmdOrdersForCustomer.

9. Double-click the form and enter this code to load the customer list in the Load event handler:

```
private void Exercise1_2_Load(
    object sender, System.EventArgs e)
{
    // Load the customer list
    SqlCommand cmdCustomers =
        sqlConnection1.CreateCommand();
    cmdCustomers.CommandType =
        CommandType.StoredProcedure;
    cmdCustomers.CommandText =
        "procCustomerList";
    DataSet ds = new DataSet();
    SqlDataAdapter da =
        new SqlDataAdapter();
    da.SelectCommand = cmdCustomers;
    da.Fill(ds, "Customers");
    cboCustomers.DataSource =
        ds.Tables["Customers"];
    cboCustomers.DisplayMember =
        "CompanyName";
    cboCustomers.ValueMember =
        "CustomerID";
}
```

10. Double-click the button control and enter this code to build the DataSet and bind it to the DataGrid in the Click event handler:

```
private void btnLoad_Click(
    object sender, System.EventArgs e)
{
    // Create a new DataSet
    dsOrdersForCustomer ds =
        new dsOrdersForCustomer();
```

APPLY YOUR KNOWLEDGE

```
// Load only the data of interest
cmdOrdersForCustomer.Parameters[
    "@CustomerID"].Value =
        cboCustomers.SelectedValue;
SqlDataAdapter daCustomer =
    new SqlDataAdapter();
daCustomer.SelectCommand =
    cmdOrdersForCustomer;
daCustomer.Fill(ds, "Orders");
// Bind the data to the user interface
dgMain.DataSource = ds;
dgMain.DataMember = "Orders";
}
```

11. Insert the Main() method to launch the form. Set the form as the startup form for the project.

12. Run the project. Select a customer from the list in the combo box and then press the Load button. The form will display only the orders for that customer.

Review Questions

1. What is metadata?

2. What is the difference between an XML element and an XML attribute?

3. What is the use of a simple type in the XML schema designer?

4. What is a facet in an XML schema?

5. When should you use one-to-many relationships rather than nested relationships in an XML schema?

6. Describe the difference between an ad hoc query and a stored procedure.

7. List and describe the four basic T-SQL statements.

8. Name four ways to execute SQL statements.

9. In a T-SQL SELECT statement, what is the difference between the WHERE clause and the HAVING clause?

10. What is the purpose of the @@IDENTITY variable?

Exam Questions

1. You are creating a schema file to represent the Vehicles table in your database. You need to represent a field named SerialNo in this schema. Data entered in the SerialNo field must have precisely 14 digits. What should you use to represent this field in the XML schema?

   A. Complex type

   B. Simple type

   C. Element

   D. Attribute

2. Your application contains a DataSet schema file that represents students taking a laboratory course. Each student is assigned a unique student ID upon enrollment in the university. Each student is also assigned to a lab bench, and no two students can be assigned to the same lab bench. What XML settings should you use for the StudentID and LabBench rows in the schema file?

   A. Mark StudentID as a primary key and mark LabBench as a primary key.

   B. Mark StudentID as a unique key and mark LabBench as a primary key.

   C. Mark StudentID as a primary key and mark LabBench as a unique key.

   D. Mark StudentID as a unique key and mark LabBench as a unique key.

APPLY YOUR KNOWLEDGE

3. You are developing an XML schema file for an application that will retrieve data from an Oracle database. The database includes an `Orders` table and a `LineItems` table. Each order has one or more line items associated with it. You've already created the `Orders` table within the XML schema file. How should you represent the `LineItems` table within the XML schema file?

   A. Add `LineItems` as a separate table. Use a one-to-many relationship to relate the `LineItems` table to the `Orders` table.

   B. Add `LineItems` as a separate table. Use a nested relationship to relate the `LineItems` table to the `Orders` table.

   C. Add `LineItems` as a simple type. Add a row using this simple type to the `Orders` table.

   D. Add `LineItems` as an element. Add a row using this element to the `Orders` table.

4. Your application includes a strongly typed DataSet object named `dsWarehouse`. You have extracted a table named `Inventory` from the `DataSet` object to a `DataTable` object named `dtInventory`. The `Inventory` table contains a column named `StockOnHand`. Which syntax can you use to refer to a value in this column? (Select two.)

   A. `dtInventory.Rows[0].StockOnHand`

   B. `dtInventory.Rows[0]."StockOnHand"`

   C. `dtInventory.Rows[0]["StockOnHand"]`

   D. `dtInventory.Rows[0].Item.StockOnHand`

5. You are developing an XML schema file for an application that will retrieve data from web applications developed by your company's trading partners. These web applications use XML as their native format. The information you will retrieve includes a list of parts and a list of prices. Each part has one or more prices associated with it. You've already created the Parts table within the XML schema file. How should you represent the Prices table within the XML schema file?

   A. Add `Prices` as a separate table. Use a one-to-many relationship to relate the `Prices` table to the `Parts` table.

   B. Add `Prices` as a separate table. Use a nested relationship to relate the `Prices` table to the `Parts` table.

   C. Add `Prices` as a simple type. Add a row using this simple type to the `Parts` table.

   D. Add `Prices` as an element. Add a row using this element to the `Parts` table.

6. You have been assigned the task of developing an XML schema file to serve as part of the data layer of your company's new Web application. The application will deliver details on sporting events to subscribers. Each sporting event is characterized by several pieces of information, including the date, sport, and teams involved. What should you use to represent a sporting event in the XML schema?

   A. Complex type

   B. Simple type

   C. Element

   D. Attribute

APPLY YOUR KNOWLEDGE

7. You are developing an XML schema file that will hold information about your company's customers. Which of these data restrictions can you represent by a facet in the schema?

   A. The values of the `CustomerType` element are limited to `"Active"` and `"Inactive"`.

   B. The values of the `CustomerID` element must be four characters long for active customers and five characters long for inactive customers.

   C. Each customer may have one or more representatives.

   D. Each customer is associated with precisely one company.

8. You are writing a SQL query to retrieve information about all customers whose offices are in Germany. You have written the following SQL statement:

   ```
   SELECT * FROM Customers
   WHERE Country = Germany
   ```

   When you execute this query, you receive an error message:

   ```
   Server: Msg 207, Level 16, State 3, Line 1
   Invalid column name 'Germany'.
   ```

   How should you modify the SQL statement to fix this problem?

   A.
   ```
   SELECT * FROM Customers
   WHERE Country = [Germany]
   ```

   B.
   ```
   SELECT * FROM Customers
   WHERE Country = #Germany#
   ```

   C.
   ```
   SELECT * FROM Customers
   WHERE Country = "Germany"
   ```

   D.
   ```
   SELECT * FROM Customers
   WHERE Country = 'Germany'
   ```

9. You are using a SQL `INSERT` statement to insert records in a table named `Products`. The `Products` table has the following structure:

   ```
   ProductID integer, identity, no default value,
   cannot be null
   ProductName varchar(50), no default value, cannot be
   null
   UnitPrice money, default value 10.00, cannot be null
   Color varchar(10), no default value, can be null
   ```

   Which column must you explicitly specify in the `INSERT` statement?

   A. `ProductID`

   B. `ProductName`

   C. `UnitPrice`

   D. `Color`

10. You are designing an application that will manage customers and their orders. Which of the following situations is not a good candidate for implementation with stored procedures?

    A. Retrieving the list of all customers in the database.

    B. Retrieving the list of all orders for particular customers.

    C. Inserting a new order into the `Orders` table.

    D. Free-form querying by the database administrator.

11. Your application needs to return the total number of customers in the database. What is the fastest way to do this?

    A. Write ad hoc SQL to return the total number of customers. Use the `SqlCommand.ExecuteScalar()` method to execute the SQL statement.

    B. Write ad hoc SQL to return the total number of customers. Use the `SqlDataAdapter.Fill()` method to execute the SQL statement.

    C. Create a stored procedure to return the total number of customers. Use the `SqlCommand.ExecuteScalar()` method to execute the stored procedure.

    D. Create a stored procedure to return the total number of customers. Use the `SqlDataAdapter.Fill()` method to execute the stored procedure.

12. Your SQL Server database contains a table, Sales, with these columns:

```
SalesID (int, identity)
StoreNumber (int)
DailySales (int)
```

You want to see a list of the stores, together with their total daily sales. The list should be filtered to include only stores whose total daily sales are more than 10. Which SQL statement should you use?

    A.

```
SELECT StoreNumber, DailySales
FROM Sales
WHERE DailySales > 10
```

    B.

```
SELECT StoreNumber, SUM(DailySales)
FROM Sales
WHERE DailySales > 10
GROUP BY StoreNumber
```

    C.

```
SELECT StoreNumber, SUM(DailySales)
FROM Sales
GROUP BY StoreNumber
HAVING SUM(DailySales) > 10
```

    D.

```
SELECT StoreNumber, SUM(DailySales)
FROM Sales
WHERE DailySales > 10
GROUP BY StoreNumber
HAVING SUM(DailySales) > 10
```

13. Your SQL Server database contains a table, Sales, with these columns:

```
SalesID (int, identity)
StoreNumber (int)
DailySales (int)
```

You want to see a list of the stores, together with their total daily sales. The list should be filtered to include only rows from the table where the daily sales are more than 10. Which SQL statement should you use?

    A.

```
SELECT StoreNumber, DailySales
FROM Sales
WHERE DailySales > 10
```

    B.

```
SELECT StoreNumber, SUM(DailySales)
FROM Sales
WHERE DailySales > 10
GROUP BY StoreNumber
```

    C.

```
SELECT StoreNumber, SUM(DailySales)
FROM Sales
GROUP BY StoreNumber
HAVING SUM(DailySales) > 10
```

    D.

```
SELECT StoreNumber, SUM(DailySales)
FROM Sales
WHERE DailySales > 10
GROUP BY StoreNumber
HAVING SUM(DailySales) > 10
```

APPLY YOUR KNOWLEDGE

14. Your SQL Server database contains a table, Experiments, with the following columns:

```
ExperimentID (int, identity)
ExperimentType (char(1))
ExperimentDate (datetime)
```

You want to delete all rows from the table where the ExperimentType value is either A or C. You do not want to delete any other rows. Which SQL statement should you use?

A.

```
DELETE FROM Experiments
WHERE ExperimentType LIKE '[AC]'
```

B.

```
DELETE FROM Experiments
WHERE ExperimentType LIKE '[A-C]'
```

C.

```
DELETE FROM Experiments
WHERE ExperimentType LIKE 'A' OR 'C'
```

D.

```
DELETE * FROM Experiments
WHERE ExperimentType IN ('A', 'C')
```

15. Your SQL Server database contains a table, Sales, with these columns:

```
SalesID (int, identity)
StoreNumber (int)
DailySales (int)
```

You want to create a stored procedure that accepts as inputs the store number and daily sales, inserts a new row in the table with this information, and returns the new identity value. Which SQL statement should you use?

A.

```
CREATE PROCEDURE procInsertSales
  @StoreNumber int,
  @DailySales int,
  @SalesID int
AS
  INSERT INTO Sales (StoreNumber, DailySales)
  VALUES (@StoreNumber, @DailySales)
  SELECT @SalesID = @@IDENTITY
```

B.

```
CREATE PROCEDURE procInsertSales
  @StoreNumber int,
  @DailySales int,
  @SalesID int OUTPUT
AS
  INSERT INTO Sales (SalesID, StoreNumber,
DailySales)
  VALUES (@SalesID, @StoreNumber, @DailySales)
```

C.

```
CREATE PROCEDURE procInsertSales
  @StoreNumber int,
  @DailySales int,
  @SalesID int OUTPUT
AS
  INSERT INTO Sales (SalesID, StoreNumber,
DailySales)
  VALUES (0, @StoreNumber, @DailySales)
  SELECT @SalesID = @@IDENTITY
```

D.

```
CREATE PROCEDURE procInsertSales
  @StoreNumber int,
  @DailySales int,
  @SalesID int OUTPUT
AS
  INSERT INTO Sales (StoreNumber, DailySales)
  VALUES (@StoreNumber, @DailySales)
  SELECT @SalesID = @@IDENTITY
```

APPLY YOUR KNOWLEDGE

Answers to Review Questions

1. Metadata is information that describes data. For example, an XML schema file is data that describes the structure of other data.

2. An element is a standalone XML entity. An attribute is a value that further describes an element.

3. The simple type in the XML schema designer is useful for describing data with restrictions. For example, an integer that must be between 0 and 50 could be represented by a simple type.

4. A facet is a piece of information, such as minimum length, describing an XML simple type.

5. One-to-many relationships are most useful in an XML schema when the schema is being used in conjunction with a relational database.

6. An ad hoc query consists of SQL statements that are sent to the server. A stored procedure consists of SQL statements permanently stored on the server.

7. The SELECT statement retrieves data; the UPDATE statement updates existing data; the INSERT statement adds new data; and the DELETE statement deletes data.

8. You can execute T-SQL statements by using the Visual Studio IDE, through OSQL, through SQL Query Analyzer, or with your own home-grown solutions.

9. The WHERE clause restricts the output of the statement. The HAVING clause restricts the rows used as input to an aggregate.

10. The @@IDENTITY variable returns the last identity value to have been assigned to a table.

Answers to Exam Questions

1. **B.** A simple type can be modified by facets, which enable you to specify data restrictions such as minimum, maximum, or exact length. For more information, see the section "Using Simple Types" in this chapter.

2. **C.** A schema file can have only a single primary key. You should choose as the primary key the element that most distinctly identifies the entity that is represented by the schema file. Unique keys can then be used to enforce uniqueness on other elements. For more information, see the section "Manipulating DataSet Relationships" in this chapter.

3. **A.** For data stored in a relational database, one-to-many relationships provide the most natural mapping in an XML schema file. For more information, see the section "Manipulating DataSet Relationships" in this chapter.

4. **A, C.** The early-bound syntax of answer A is possible only with a strongly typed DataSet object. But you're not required to use early binding with strongly typed DataSet objects, so the late-bound syntax of answer C also works. For more information, see the section "Creating and Using Strongly Typed DataSet Objects" in this chapter.

5. **B.** For data coming from XML sources, nested relationships generally provide the most natural mapping in an XML schema file. For more information, see the section "Manipulating DataSet Relationships" in this chapter.

APPLY YOUR KNOWLEDGE

6. **A.** Because the sporting event will contain several pieces of information, it is best represented as a complex type. The constituent pieces of information within this type can be represented by elements, attributes, or simple types. For more information, see the section "Manipulating DataSet Relationships" in this chapter.

7. **A.** You can represent a fixed set of choices within a simple type by using the enumeration facet. Facets are not suited for representing relationships between elements within a table, or for representing relationships between different tables. For more information, see the section "Manipulating DataSet Relationships" in this chapter.

8. **D.** In T-SQL for SQL Server, you use single quotes to surround a literal value. For more information, see the section "Using Ad Hoc Queries" in this chapter.

9. **B.** An INSERT statement must specify explicit values for any columns that are not identity columns, are not nullable, and do not have a default value. For more information, see the section "The INSERT Statement" in this chapter.

10. **D.** Stored procedures can be used to carry out any SQL statement. These statements can have parameters, and they need not be SELECT statements. However, stored procedures are not useful for executing completely free-form SQL. For more information, see the section "The SELECT Statement" in this chapter.

11. **C.** Stored procedures execute faster than the corresponding ad hoc SQL statements because stored procedures are stored in the database in compiled form. The ExecuteScalar() method is faster than filling a DataSet object for returning a single value. For more information, see the section "Using Stored Procedures" in this chapter and Appendix A.

12. **C.** The GROUP BY clause is required to obtain aggregate numbers. The HAVING clause filters the results after the aggregation has been performed. The answers containing the WHERE clause are incorrect because WHERE filters the input to the aggregations. For more information, see the section "The SELECT Statement" in this chapter.

13. **B.** The GROUP BY clause is required to obtain aggregate numbers. The WHERE clause filters rows before aggregating them. The answers containing the HAVING clause are incorrect because HAVING filters the results after aggregation. For more information, see the section "The SELECT Statement" in this chapter.

14. **A.** Answer B would also delete rows with an ExperimentType of B. Answer C would take the OR of 'A' and 'C' before evaluating the LIKE clause. DELETE * is not valid T-SQL syntax. For more information, see the section "The DELETE Statement" in this chapter.

15. **D.** Answer A does not indicate that @SalesID is an output parameter. Answers B and C attempt to insert values into the identity column, rather than letting SQL Server assign the new value. For more information, see the section "Using Stored Procedures" in this chapter.

APPLY YOUR KNOWLEDGE

Suggested Readings and Resources

1. Visual Studio .NET Combined Help Collection

   - Accessing Data

   - Building and Editing XML Schema

2. Kalen Delaney. *Inside SQL Server 2000.* Microsoft Press, 2000.

3. Mike Gunderloy. *ADO and ADO.NET Programming.* Sybex, 2002.

4. SQL Server Books Online

   - Transact-SQL Reference

5. Dan Wahlin. *XML For ASP.NET Developers.* Sams, 2002.

This chapter covers the following Microsoft-specified objective for the "Consuming and Manipulating Data" section of the "Developing XML Web Services and Server Components with Microsoft Visual C# .NET and the Microsoft .NET Framework" exam:

Access and manipulate XML Data.

- **Access an XML file by using the Document Object Model (DOM) and an XmlReader.**

- **Transform DataSet data into XML data.**

- **Use XPath to query XML data.**

- **Generate and use an XSD schema.**

- **Write a SQL statement that retrieves XML data from a SQL Server database.**

- **Update a SQL Server database by using XML.**

- **Validate an XML document.**

▶ Extensible Markup Language (far better known as XML) is pervasive in .NET. It's used as the format for configuration files, as the transmission format for SOAP messages, and in many other places. It's also rapidly becoming the most widespread common language for many development platforms.

This objective tests your ability to perform many XML development tasks. To pass this section of the exam, you need to know how to read an XML file from disk, and how to create your own XML from a DataSet object in your application. You also need to be familiar with the XPath query language, and with the creation and use of XSD schema files.

You'll also need to understand the connections that Microsoft SQL Server has with the XML universe. You need to be able to extract SQL Server data in XML format, and to be able to update a SQL Server database by sending it properly formatted XML.

CHAPTER 2

Accessing and Manipulating XML Data

Finally, the exam tests your ability to validate XML to confirm that it conforms to a proper format. The .NET Framework includes several means of validating XML that you should be familiar with.

STUDY STRATEGIES

▶ Use the XmlDocument and XmlNode objects to navigate through some XML files. Inspect the node types that you find and understand how they relate to the original XML.

▶ Use the XmlDataDocument class to synchronize a DataSet object with an XML file. Save the XML file to disk and inspect its contents. Understand how the generated XML relates to the original DataSet object.

▶ Use an XPath processor to run XPath queries against an XML file. Make sure you know the XPath syntax to select portions of the XML.

▶ Use the methods of the DataSet object to create XSD files. Inspect the generated XSD and understand how it relates to the original objects.

▶ Use XML to read and write SQL Server data. You can install the MSDE version of SQL Server from your Visual Studio .NET CD-ROMs if you don't have a full SQL Server to work with.

▶ Use the XmlValidatingReader class to validate an XML file. Make a change to the file that makes it invalid and examine the results when you try to validate the file.

▶ Review the XML Data section of the Common Tasks QuickStart Tutorials that ship as part of the .NET Framework SDK.

INTRODUCTION

You can't use the .NET Framework effectively unless you're familiar with XML. That's true even if you're working only with desktop applications, but if you want to write XML Web Services and other distributed applications, XML knowledge is even more important. The .NET Framework uses XML for many purposes itself, but it also makes it very easy for you to use XML in your own applications.

The FCL's support for XML is mainly contained in the System.Xml namespace. This namespace contains objects to parse, validate, and manipulate XML. You can read and write XML, use XPath to navigate through an XML document, or check to see whether a particular document is valid XML by using the objects in this namespace.

As you're learning about XML, you'll become familiar with some other standards as well. These include the XPath query language and the XSD schema language. You'll see in this chapter how these other standards are integrated into the .NET Framework's XML support.

> **NOTE**
>
> **XML Basics**   In this chapter, I've assumed that you're already familiar with the basics of XML, such as elements and attributes. If you need a refresher course on XML Basics, refer to Appendix B, "XML Standards and Syntax."

ACCESSING AN XML FILE

Access and Manipulate XML Data: Access an XML file by using the Document Object Model (DOM) and an XmlReader.

The most basic thing you can do with an XML file is open it and read it to find out what the file contains. The .NET Framework offers both unstructured and structured ways to access the data within an XML file. That is, you can treat the XML file either as a simple stream of information or as a hierarchical structure composed of different entities, such as elements and attributes.

In this section of the chapter you'll learn how to extract information from an XML file. I'll start by showing you how you can use the XmlReader object to move through an XML file, extracting information as you go. Then you'll see how other objects, including the XmlNode and XmlDocument objects, provide a more structured view of an XML file.

I'll work with a very simple XML file named Books.xml that represents three books that a computer bookstore might stock. Here's the
raw XML file:

```xml
<?xml version="1.0" encoding="UTF-8"?>
<Books>
    <Book Pages="1088">
        <Author>Delaney, Kalen</Author>
        <Title>Inside Microsoft SQL Server 2000</Title>
        <Publisher>Microsoft Press</Publisher>
    </Book>
    <Book Pages="997">
        <Author>Burton, Kevin</Author>
        <Title>.NET Common Language Runtime</Title>
        <Publisher>Sams</Publisher>
    </Book>
    <Book Pages="392">
        <Author>Cooper, James W.</Author>
        <Title>C# Design Patterns</Title>
        <Publisher>Addison Wesley</Publisher>
    </Book>
</Books>
```

Understanding the DOM

The Document Object Model, or DOM, is an Internet standard for
representing the information contained in an HTML or XML document as a tree of nodes. Like many other Internet standards, the
DOM is an official standard of the World Wide Web Consortium,
better known as the W3C.

Even though there is a DOM standard, not all vendors implement
the DOM in exactly the same way. The major issue is that there are
actually several different standards grouped together under the general name of DOM. Also, vendors pick and choose which parts of
these standards to implement. The .NET Framework includes support for the DOM Level 1 Core and DOM Level 2 Core specifications, but it also extends the DOM by adding additional objects,
methods, and properties to the specification.

Structurally, an XML document is a series of nested items, including
elements and attributes. Any nested structure can be transformed to
an equivalent tree structure if the outermost nested item is made the
root of the tree, the next-in items the children of the root, and so
on. The DOM provides the standard for constructing this tree,
including a classification for individual nodes and rules for which

NOTE **DOM Background** You can find the
official DOM specifications at
www.w3.org/DOM. For details of
Microsoft's implementation in the
.NET Framework, see the "XML
Document Object Model (DOM)" topic
in the .NET Framework Developer's
Guide.

nodes can have children. Figure 2.1 shows how the Books.xml file might be represented as a tree.

FIGURE 2.1
You can represent an XML file as a tree of nodes.

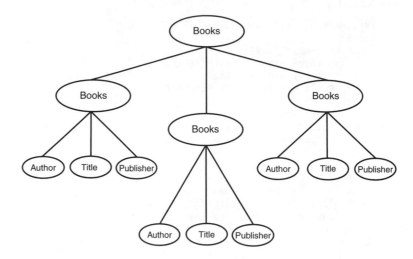

In its simplest form, the DOM defines an XML document as a tree of nodes. The root element in the XML file becomes the root node of the tree, and other elements become child nodes.

Using an XmlReader Object

The XmlReader class is designed to provide forward-only, read-only access to an XML file. This class treats an XML file similarly to the way that a cursor treats a resultset from a database. At any given time, there is one current node within the XML file, represented by a pointer that you can move around within the file. The class implements a Read() method that returns the next XML node to the calling application. There are also many other members in the XmlReader class; I've listed some of these in Table 2.1.

TABLE 2.1

IMPORTANT MEMBERS OF THE XmlReader CLASS

Member	Type	Description
Depth	Property	Specifies the depth of the current node in the XML document
EOF	Property	Represents a Boolean property that is true when the current node pointer is at the end of the XML file
GetAttribute()	Method	Gets the value of an attribute
HasAttributes	Property	Returns true when the current node contains attributes
HasValue	Property	Returns true when the current node can have a Value property
IsEmptyElement	Property	Returns true when the current node represents an empty XML element
IsStartElement()	Method	Determines whether the current node is a start tag
MoveToElement()	Method	Moves to the element containing the current attribute
MoveToFirstAttribute()	Method	Moves to the first attribute of the current element
MoveToNextAttribute()	Method	Moves to the next attribute
Name	Property	Specifies a qualified name of the current node
NodeType	Property	Specifies the type of the current node
Read()	Method	Reads the next node from the XML file
Skip()	Method	Skips the children of the current element
Value	Property	Specifies the value of the current node

The XmlReader class is a purely abstract class. You cannot create an instance of XmlReader in your own application. Generally, you'll use the XmlTextReader class instead. The XmlTextReader class implements

XmlReader for use with text streams. Step-by-Step 2.1 shows you how to use the XmlTextReader class.

STEP BY STEP

2.1 Using the XmlTextReader Class

1. Create a new Visual C# .NET Windows application. Name the application 320C02.

2. Right-click on the project node in Solution Explorer and select Add, Add New Item.

3. Select the Local Project Items node in the Categories tree view. Select the XML File template. Name the new file Books.xml and click OK.

4. Modify the code for the Books.xml file as follows:

```xml
<?xml version="1.0" encoding="UTF-8"?>
<Books>
    <Book Pages="1088">
        <Author>Delaney, Kalen</Author>
        <Title>Inside Microsoft SQL Server 2000</Title>
        <Publisher>Microsoft Press</Publisher>
    </Book>
    <Book Pages="997">
        <Author>Burton, Kevin</Author>
        <Title>.NET Common Language Runtime</Title>
        <Publisher>Sams</Publisher>
    </Book>
    <Book Pages="392">
        <Author>Cooper, James W.</Author>
        <Title>C# Design Patterns</Title>
        <Publisher>Addison Wesley</Publisher>
    </Book>
</Books>
```

5. Add a new form to the project. Name the new form StepByStep2_1.cs.

6. Add a Button control (btnReadXml) and a ListBox control (lbNodes) to the form.

7. Switch to the code view and add the following using directives:

```csharp
using System.Xml;
using System.Text;
```

8. Double-click the Button control and add the following code to handle the button's Click event:

```
private void btnReadXML_Click(
    object sender, System.EventArgs e)
{
    StringBuilder sbNode = new StringBuilder();

    // Create a new XmlTextReader on the file
    XmlTextReader xtr = new
        XmlTextReader(@"..\..\Books.xml");
    // Walk through the entire XML file
    while(xtr.Read())
    {
        sbNode.Length = 0;
        for(int intI=1; intI <= xtr.Depth ; intI++)
        {
            sbNode.Append(" ");
        }
        sbNode.Append(xtr.Name + " ");
        sbNode.Append(xtr.NodeType.ToString());

        if (xtr.HasValue)
        {
            sbNode.Append(": " + xtr.Value);
        }
        lbNodes.Items.Add(sbNode.ToString());
    }
    // Clean up
    xtr.Close();
}
```

9. Insert the Main() method to launch the form. Set the form as the startup object for the project.

10. Run the project. Click the button. You'll see a schematic representation of the XML file, as shown in Figure 2.2.

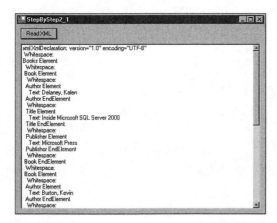

FIGURE 2.2

An XML file translated into schematic form by an XmlTextReader object.

As you can see in Step-by-Step 2.1, the output has everything in the XML file, including the XML declaration and any whitespace (such as the line feeds and carriage returns that separate lines of the files). On the other hand, the output doesn't include XML attributes. But the XmlTextReader is flexible enough that you can customize its behavior as you like.

Step-by-Step 2.2 shows an example where the code displays only elements, text, and attributes.

STEP BY STEP

2.2 Using the XmlTextReader Class to Read Selected XML Entities

1. Add a new form to the project. Name the new form StepByStep2_2.cs.

2. Add a Button control (btnReadXml) and a ListBox control (lbNodes) to the form.

3. Switch to the code view and add the following using directives:

```
using System.Xml;
using System.Text;
```

4. Double-click the button and add the following code to handle the button's Click event:

```
private void btnReadXML_Click(
    object sender, System.EventArgs e)
{
    StringBuilder sbNode = new StringBuilder();

    // Create a new XmlTextReader on the file
    XmlTextReader xtr = new
        XmlTextReader(@"..\..\Books.xml");
    // Walk through the entire XML file
    while(xtr.Read())
    {
        if((xtr.NodeType == XmlNodeType.Element) ||
            (xtr.NodeType == XmlNodeType.Text) )
        {
            sbNode.Length = 0;
            for(int intI=1;
```

```
        intI <= xtr.Depth ; intI++)
    {
        sbNode.Append(" ");
    }
    sbNode.Append(xtr.Name + " ");
    sbNode.Append(xtr.NodeType.ToString());

    if (xtr.HasValue)
    {
        sbNode.Append(": " + xtr.Value);
    }
    lbNodes.Items.Add(sbNode.ToString());
    // Now add the attributes, if any
    if (xtr.HasAttributes)
    {
        while(xtr.MoveToNextAttribute())
        {
            sbNode.Length=0;
            for(int intI=1;
                intI <= xtr.Depth;intI++)
            {
                sbNode.Append(" ");
            }
            sbNode.Append(xtr.Name + " ");
            sbNode.Append(
                xtr.NodeType.ToString());
            if (xtr.HasValue)
            {
                sbNode.Append(": " +
                    xtr.Value);
            }
            lbNodes.Items.Add(
                sbNode.ToString());
        }
    }
    }
    }
}
// Clean up
xtr.Close();
}
```

5. Insert the `Main()` method to launch the form. Set the form as the startup form for the project.

6. Run the project. Click the button. You'll see a schematic representation of the elements and attributes in the XML file, as shown in Figure 2.3.

continues

continued

FIGURE 2.3
Selected entities from an XML file translated into schematic form by an `XmlTextReader` object.

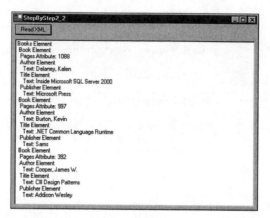

Note that `XmlTextReader` does not consider attributes to be nodes; however, `XmlTextReader` provides the `MoveToNextAtttibute()` method to treat them as nodes. Alternatively, you can retrieve attributes by using indexers on the `XmlTextReader` object. If the current node represents an element in the XML file, then this code retrieves the value of the first attribute of the element:

```
xtr[0]
```

This code retrieves the value of an attribute named `Pages`:

```
xtr["Pages"]
```

The `XmlNode` Class

The individual items in the tree representation of an XML file are called *nodes*. As you've seen in Step-by-Steps 2.1 and 2.2, many different entities within the XML file can be represented by nodes: elements, attributes, whitespace, end tags, and so on. The DOM distinguishes these different types of nodes by assigning a node type to each one. In the .NET Framework, the possible node types are listed by the `XmlNodeType` enumeration. Table 2.2 lists the members of this enumeration.

TABLE 2.2

MEMBERS OF THE XmlNodeType ENUMERATION

Member	Represents
Attribute	An XML attribute
CDATA	An XML CDATA section
Comment	An XML comment
Document	The outermost element of the XML document (that is, the root of the tree representation of the XML)
DocumentFragment	The outermost element of an XML document's subsection
DocumentType	A Document Type Description (DTD) reference
Element	An XML element
EndElement	The closing tag of an XML element
EndEntity	The end of an included entity
Entity	An XML entity declaration
EntityReference	A reference to an entity
None	An XmlReader object that has not been initialized
Notation	An XML notation
ProcessingInstruction	An XML processing instruction
SignificantWhitespace	Whitespace that must be preserved to re-create the original XML document
Text	The text content of an attribute, element, or other node
Whitespace	Space between actual XML markup items
XmlDeclaration	The XML declaration

The code you've seen so far in this chapter deals with nodes as part of a stream of information returned by the XmlTextReader object. But the .NET Framework also includes another class, XmlNode, which can be used to represent an individual node from the DOM representation of an XML document. If you instantiate an XmlNode object to represent a particular portion of an XML document, you can alter the properties of the object and then write the changes back to the original file. The DOM provides two-way access to the underlying XML in this case.

The XmlNode class has a rich interface of properties and methods. You can retrieve or set information about the entity represented by an XmlNode object, or you can use its methods to navigate the DOM. Table 2.3 shows the important members of the XmlNode class.

TABLE 2.3

IMPORTANT MEMBERS OF THE XmlNode CLASS

Member	Type	Description
AppendChild()	Method	Adds a new child node to the end of this node's list of children
Attributes	Property	Returns the attributes of the node as an XmlAttributeCollection object
ChildNodes	Property	Returns all child nodes of this node
CloneNode()	Method	Creates a duplicate of this node
FirstChild	Property	Returns the first child node of this node
HasChildNodes	Property	Returns true if this node has any children
InnerText	Property	Specifies the value of the node and all its children
InnerXml	Property	Specifies the markup representing only the children of this node
InsertAfter()	Method	Inserts a new node after this node
InsertBefore()	Method	Inserts a new node before this node
LastChild	Property	Returns the last child node of this node
Name	Property	Specifies the node's name
NextSibling	Property	Returns the next child of this node's parent node
NodeType	Property	Specifies this node's type
OuterXml	Property	Specifies the markup representing this node and its children
OwnerDocument	Property	Specifies the XmlDocument object that contains this node
ParentNode	Property	Returns this node's parent

Member	Type	Description
PrependChild()	Method	Adds a new child node to the beginning of this node's list of children
PreviousSibling	Property	Returns the previous child of this node's parent node
RemoveAll()	Method	Removes all children of this node
RemoveChild()	Method	Removes a specified child of this node
ReplaceChild()	Method	Replaces a child of this node with a new node
SelectNodes()	Method	Selects a group of nodes matching an XPath expression
SelectSingleNode()	Method	Selects the first node matching an XPath expression
WriteContentTo()	Method	Writes all children of this node to an XmlWriter object
WriteTo()	Method	Writes this node to an XmlWriter object

The XmlDocument Class

There's no direct way to create an XmlNode object that represents an entity from a particular XML document. Instead, you can retrieve XmlNode objects from an XmlDocument object. The XmlDocument object represents an entire XML document. Step-by-Step 2.3 shows how you can use the XmlNode and XmlDocument objects to navigate through the DOM representation of an XML document.

STEP BY STEP

2.3 Using the XmlDocument and XmlNode Classes

1. Add a new form to the project. Name the new form StepByStep2_3.cs.

2. Add a Button control (btnReadXml) and a ListBox control (lbNodes) to the form.

continues

continued

3. Switch to the code view and add the following using directives:

```
using System.Xml;
using System.Text;
```

4. Double-click the button and add the following code to handle the button's Click event:

```
private void btnReadXML_Click(
    object sender, System.EventArgs e)
{

    // Create a new XmlTextReader on the file
    XmlTextReader xtr = new
        XmlTextReader(@"..\..\Books.xml");
    // Load the XML file to an XmlDocument
    xtr.WhitespaceHandling = WhitespaceHandling.None;
    XmlDocument xd = new XmlDocument();
    xd.Load(xtr);
    // Get the document root
    XmlNode xnodRoot = xd.DocumentElement;
    // Walk the tree and display it
    XmlNode xnodWorking;
    if (xnodRoot.HasChildNodes)
    {
        xnodWorking = xnodRoot.FirstChild;
        while (xnodWorking != null)
        {
            AddChildren(xnodWorking, 0);
            xnodWorking = xnodWorking.NextSibling;
        }
    }
    // Clean up
    xtr.Close();
}

private void AddChildren(XmlNode xnod, Int32 intDepth)
{
    // Adds a node to the ListBox,
    // together with its children.
    // intDepth controls the depth of indenting

    StringBuilder sbNode = new StringBuilder();
    // Process only Text and Element nodes
    if((xnod.NodeType == XmlNodeType.Element) ||
       (xnod.NodeType == XmlNodeType.Text) )
    {
        sbNode.Length = 0;
        for(int intI=1;
            intI <= intDepth ; intI++)
        {
```

```
            sbNode.Append(" ");
    }
    sbNode.Append(xnod.Name + " ");
    sbNode.Append(xnod.NodeType.ToString());
    sbNode.Append(": " + xnod.Value);
    lbNodes.Items.Add(sbNode.ToString());

    // Now add the attributes, if any
    XmlAttributeCollection atts = xnod.Attributes;
    if(atts != null)
    {
        for(int intI = 0;
            intI < atts.Count; intI++)
        {
            sbNode.Length = 0;
            for (int intJ = 1;
                    intJ <= intDepth + 1; intJ++)
            {
                sbNode.Append(" ");
            }
            sbNode.Append(atts[intI].Name + " ");
            sbNode.Append(
                atts[intI].NodeType.ToString());
            sbNode.Append(": " +
                atts[intI].Value);
            lbNodes.Items.Add(sbNode);
        }
    }
    // And recursively walk
    // the children of this node
    XmlNode xnodworking;
    if (xnod.HasChildNodes)
    {
        xnodworking = xnod.FirstChild;
        while (xnodworking != null)
        {
            AddChildren(
                xnodworking, intDepth + 1);
            xnodworking = xnodworking.NextSibling;
        }
    }
}
}
```

5. Insert the `Main()` method to launch the form. Set the
form as the startup form for the project.

6. Run the project. Click the button. You'll see a schematic
representation of the elements and attributes in the XML
file.

Step-by-Step 2.3 uses recursion to visit all the nodes in the XML file. That is, it starts at the document's root node (returned by the DocumentElement property of the XmlDocument object) and visits each child of that node in turn. For each child, it displays the desired information, and then visits each child of that node in turn, and so on.

In addition to the properties used in Step-by-Step 2.3, the XmlDocument class includes a number of other useful members. Table 2.4 lists the most important of these.

TABLE 2.4

IMPORTANT MEMBERS OF THE XmlDocument CLASS

Member	Type	Description
CreateAttribute()	Method	Creates an attribute node
CreateElement()	Method	Creates an element node
CreateNode()	Method	Creates an XmlNode object
DocumentElement	Property	Returns the root XmlNode object for this document
DocumentType	Property	Returns the node containing the DTD declaration for this document, if it has one
ImportNode()	Method	Imports a node from another XML document
Load()	Method	Loads an XML document into the XmlDocument object
LoadXml()	Method	Loads the XmlDocument object from a string of XML data
NodeChanged	Event	Occurs after the value of a node has been changed
NodeChanging	Event	Occurs when the value of a node is about to be changed
NodeInserted	Event	Occurs when a new node has been inserted
NodeInserting	Event	Occurs when a new node is about to be inserted
NodeRemoved	Event	Occurs when a node has been removed
NodeRemoving	Event	Occurs when a node is about to be removed

Member	Type	Description
PreserveWhitespace	Property	Returns true if whitespace in the document should be preserved when loading or saving the XML
Save()	Method	Saves the XmlDocument object as a file or stream
WriteTo()	Method	Saves the XmlDocument object to an XmlWriter object

REVIEW BREAK

▶ The Document Object Model (DOM) is a W3C standard for representing the information contained in an HTML or XML document as a tree of nodes.

▶ The XmlReader class defines an interface for reading XML documents. The XmlTextReader class inherits from the XmlReader class to read XML documents from streams.

▶ The XmlNode object can be used to represent a single node in the DOM.

▶ The XmlDocument object represents an entire XML document.

SYNCHRONIZING DataSet OBJECTS WITH XML

Access and Manipulate XML Data: Transform DataSet data into XML data.

One area in which the .NET Framework's use of XML is especially innovative is in connecting databases with XML. You already know that ADO.NET provides a complete in-memory representation of the structure and data of a relational database through its DataSet object. What the System.Xml namespace adds to this picture is the capability to automatically synchronize a DataSet object with an equivalent XML file. In this section of the chapter, you'll learn about the classes and techniques that make this synchronization possible.

The `XmlDataDocument` Class

The `XmlDocument` class is useful for working with XML via the DOM, but it's not a data-enabled class. To bring the `DataSet` class into the picture, you need to use an `XmlDataDocument` class, which inherits from the `XmlDocument` class. Table 2.5 shows the additional members that the `XmlDataDocument` class adds to the `XmlDocument` class.

TABLE 2.5

ADDITIONAL MEMBERS OF THE `XmlDataDocument` CLASS

Member	Type	Description
DataSet	Property	Retrieves a `DataSet` object representing the data in the `XmlDataDocument` object
GetElementFromRow()	Method	Retrieves an `XmlElement` object representing a specified `DataRow` object
GetRowFromElement()	Method	Retrieves a `DataRow` object representing a specified `XmlElement` object
Load()	Method	Loads the `XmlDataDocument` object and synchronizes it with a `DataSet` object

Synchronizing a `DataSet` Object with an `XmlDataDocument` Object

The reason the `XmlDataDocument` class exists is to allow you to exploit the connections between XML documents and `DataSet` objects. You can do this by synchronizing the `XmlDataDocument` object (and hence the XML document that it represents) with a particular `DataSet` object. When you synchronize an `XmlDataDocument` object with `DataSet` object, any changes made in one are automatically reflected in the other. You can start the synchronization process with any of these objects:

▶ An `XmlDataDocument` object

▶ A full `DataSet` object

▶ A schema-only `DataSet` object

I'll demonstrate these three options in the remainder of this section.

Starting with an `XmlDataDocument` Object

One way to synchronize a `DataSet` object and an `XmlDataDocument` object is to start with the `XmlDataDocument` object and to retrieve the `DataSet` object from its `DataSet` property. Step-by-Step 2.4 demonstrates this technique.

STEP BY STEP

2.4 Retrieving a `DataSet` Object from an `XmlDataDocument` Object

1. Add a new form to the project. Name the new form `StepByStep2_4.cs`.

2. Add a `Button` control (`btnLoadXml`) and a `DataGrid` control (`dgXML`) to the form.

3. Switch to the code view and add the following `using` directives:

```
using System.Data;
using System.Xml;
```

4. Double-click the `Button` control and add the following code to handle the button's `Click` event:

```
private void btnLoadXml_Click(
    object sender, System.EventArgs e)
{
    // Create a new XmlTextReader on the file
    XmlTextReader xtr = new
        XmlTextReader(@"..\..\Books.xml");
    // Create an object to synchronize
    XmlDataDocument xdd = new XmlDataDocument();
    // Retrieve the associated DataSet
    DataSet ds = xdd.DataSet;
    // Initialize the DataSet by reading the schema
    // from the XML document
```

continues

continued

```
        ds.ReadXmlSchema(xtr);
        // Reset the XmlTextReader
        xtr.Close();
        xtr = new XmlTextReader(@"..\..\Books.xml");
        // Tell it to ignore whitespace
        xtr.WhitespaceHandling = WhitespaceHandling.None;
        // Load the synchronized object
        xdd.Load(xtr);
        // Display the resulting DataSet
        dgXML.DataSource = ds;
        dgXML.DataMember = "Book";
        // Clean up
        xtr.Close();
    }
```

5. Insert the `Main()` method to launch the form. Set the
   form as the startup object for the project.

6. Run the project. Click the button. The code will load the
   XML file and then display the corresponding `DataSet`
   object on the `DataGrid` control, as shown in Figure 2.4.

FIGURE 2.4
You can synchronize a `DataSet` object with an
`XmlDataDocument` object.

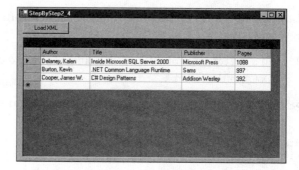

The code in Step-by-Step 2.4 performs some extra setup to make
sure that the `DataSet` object can hold the data from the
`XmlDataDocument` object. Even when you're creating the `DataSet`
object from the `XmlDataDocument` object, you must still explicitly
create the schema of the `DataSet` object before it will contain data.
That's necessary because in this technique you can also use a `DataSet`
object that represents only a portion of the `XmlDataDocument` object.
In this case, the code takes advantage of the `ReadXmlSchema()`

method of the `DataSet` object to automatically construct a schema that matches the XML document. Because the `XmlTextReader` object is designed for forward-only use, the code closes and reopens this object after reading the schema so that it can also be used to read the data.

Starting with a Full `DataSet` Object

A second way to end up with a `DataSet` object synchronized to an `XmlDataDocument` object is to start with a `DataSet` object. Step-by-Step 2.5 demonstrates this technique.

EXAM TIP

Automatic Schema Contents
When you use the `ReadXmlSchema()` method of the `DataSet` object to construct an XML schema for the `DataSet`, both elements and attributes within the XML document become `DataColumn` objects in the `DataSet` object.

STEP BY STEP

2.5 Creating an `XmlDataDocument` Object from a `DataSet` Object

1. Add a new form to the project. Name the new form `StepByStep2_5.cs`.

2. Add a `Button` control (`btnLoadDataSet`) and a `ListBox` control (`lbNodes`) to the form.

3. Open Server Explorer.

4. Expand the tree under Data Connections to show a SQL Server data connection that points to the Northwind sample database. Expand the Tables node of this database. Drag and drop the Employees table to the form to create a `SqlConnection` object and a `SqlDataAdapter` object on the form.

5. Select the `SqlDataAdapter` object. Click the Generate DataSet hyperlink beneath the Properties Window. Name the new `DataSet` `dsEmployees` and click OK.

6. Add a new class to the project. Name the new class `Utility.cs`. Alter the code in `Utility.cs` as follows:

```
using System;
using System.Windows.Forms;
using System.Xml;
using System.Text;
```

continues

continued

```
namespace _320C02
{
    public class Utility
    {
        public Utility()
        {
        }
        public void XmlToListBox(
            XmlDocument xd, ListBox lb)
        {
            // Get the document root
            XmlNode xnodRoot = xd.DocumentElement;
            // Walk the tree and display it
            XmlNode xnodWorking;
            if(xnodRoot.HasChildNodes)
            {
                xnodWorking = xnodRoot.FirstChild;
                while(xnodWorking != null)
                {
                    AddChildren(xnodWorking, lb, 0);
                    xnodWorking =
                        xnodWorking.NextSibling;
                }
            }
        }

        public void AddChildren(XmlNode xnod,
            ListBox lb, Int32 intDepth)
        {
            // Adds a node to the ListBox,
            // together with its children. intDepth
            // controls the depth of indenting

            StringBuilder sbNode =
                new StringBuilder();
            // Only process Text and Element nodes
            if((xnod.NodeType == XmlNodeType.Element)
                ||(xnod.NodeType == XmlNodeType.Text))
            {
                sbNode.Length = 0;
                for(int intI=1;
                    intI <= intDepth ; intI++)
                {
                    sbNode.Append("  ");
                }
                sbNode.Append(xnod.Name + " ");
                sbNode.Append(
                    xnod.NodeType.ToString());
                sbNode.Append(": " + xnod.Value);
                lb.Items.Add(sbNode.ToString());

                // Now add the attributes, if any
                XmlAttributeCollection atts =
                    xnod.Attributes;
```

```
            if(atts != null)
            {
                for(int intI = 0;
                    intI < atts.Count; intI++)
                {
                    sbNode.Length = 0;
                    for (int intJ = 1;
                        intJ <= intDepth + 1;
                        intJ++)
                    {
                        sbNode.Append(" ");
                    }
                    sbNode.Append(
                        atts[intI].Name + " ");
                    sbNode.Append(atts[
                        intI].NodeType.ToString());
                    sbNode.Append(": " +
                        atts[intI].Value);
                    lb.Items.Add(sbNode);
                }
            }
            // And recursively walk
            // the children of this node
            XmlNode xnodworking;
            if (xnod.HasChildNodes)
            {
                xnodworking = xnod.FirstChild;
                while (xnodworking != null)
                {
                    AddChildren(xnodworking, lb,
                        intDepth + 1);
                    xnodworking =
                        xnodworking.NextSibling;
                }
            }
        }
    }
}
```

7. Switch to the code view of the form `StepByStep2_5.cs`
and add the following using directives:

```
using System.Data;
using System.Xml;
```

8. Double-click the `Button` control and add the following
code to handle the button's `Click` event:

```
private void btnLoadDataSet_Click(
    object sender, System.EventArgs e)
{
    // Fill the DataSet
    sqlDataAdapter1.Fill(dsEmployees1, "Employees");
```

continues

continued

```
// Retrieve the associated document
XmlDataDocument xd =
     new XmlDataDocument(dsEmployees1);
// Display it in the ListBox
Utility util = new Utility();
util.XmlToListBox(xd, lbNodes);
}
```

9. Insert the Main() method to launch the form. Set the form as the startup object for the project.

10. Run the project. Click the button. The code loads the DataSet object from the Employees table in the SQL Server database. It then converts the DataSet object to XML and displays the results in the ListBox, as shown in Figure 2.5.

FIGURE 2.5
The XmlDataDocument object allows structured data to be retrieved and manipulated through a DataSet object.

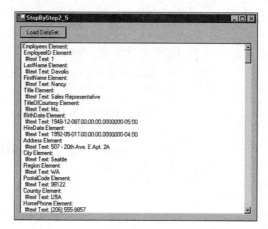

Starting with an XML Schema

The third method to synchronize the two objects is to follow a three-step process:

1. Create a new DataSet object with the proper schema to match an XML document, but no data.

2. Create the `XmlDataDocument` object from the `DataSet` object.

3. Load the XML document into the `XmlDataDocument` object.

Step-by-Step 2.6 demonstrates this technique.

STEP BY STEP

2.6 Synchronization Starting with an XML Schema

1. Add a new form to the project. Name the new form `StepByStep2_6.cs`.

2. Add a `Button` control (`btnLoadXml`), a `DataGrid` control (`dgXML`), and a `ListBox` control (`lbNodes`) to the form.

3. Add a new XML Schema file to the project from the Add New Item dialog box. Name the new file `Books.xsd`.

4. Switch to the XML view of the schema file and add this code:

```
<?xml version="1.0" encoding="utf-8" ?>
<xs:schema id="Books" xmlns=""
 xmlns:xs="http://www.w3.org/2001/XMLSchema">
    <xs:element name="Books">
        <xs:complexType>
            <xs:choice maxOccurs="unbounded">
                <xs:element name="Book">
                    <xs:complexType>
                        <xs:sequence>
                            <xs:element name="Author"
                             type="xs:string" />
                            <xs:element name="Title"
                             type="xs:string" />
                        </xs:sequence>
                        <xs:attribute name="Pages"
                         type="xs:string" />
                    </xs:complexType>
                </xs:element>
            </xs:choice>
        </xs:complexType>
    </xs:element>
</xs:schema>
```

5. Switch to the code view of the form `StepByStep2_6.cs` and add the following using directives:

```
using System.Data;
using System.Xml;
```

continues

continued

6. You need the `Utility.cs` class created in Step-by-Step 2.5, so create it now if you didn't already create it.

7. Double-click the `Button` control and add the following code to handle the button's `Click` event:

```
private void btnLoadXml_Click(
    object sender, System.EventArgs e)
{
    // Create a dataset with the desired schema
    DataSet ds = new DataSet();
    ds.ReadXmlSchema(@"..\..\Books.xsd");
    // Create a matching document
    XmlDataDocument xdd = new XmlDataDocument(ds);
    // Load the XML
    xdd.Load(@"..\..\Books.xml");
    // Display the XML via the DOM
    Utility util = new Utility();
    util.XmlToListBox(xdd, lbNodes);
    // Display the resulting DataSet
    dgXML.DataSource = ds;
    dgXML.DataMember = "Book";
}
```

8. Insert the `Main()` method to launch the form. Set the form as the startup object for the project.

9. Run the project. Click the button. The code loads the `DataSet` object and the `XmlDataDocument` object. It then displays the `DataSet` object in the `DataGrid` control and the XML document content in the `ListBox` control, as shown in Figure 2.6.

FIGURE 2.6

You can start synchronization with a schema file to hold only the desired data in the `DataSet` object.

The advantage to using this technique is that you don't have to represent the entire XML document in the `DataSet` schema; the schema needs to include only the XML elements that you want to work with. For example, in this case the `DataSet` object does not contain the `Publisher` column, even though the `XmlDataDocument` includes that column (as you can verify by inspecting the information in the `ListBox` control).

GUIDED PRACTICE
EXERCISE 2.1

As you might guess, the `XmlTextReader` is not the only class that provides a connection between the DOM and XML documents stored on disk. There's a corresponding `XmlTextWriter` class that is designed to take an `XmlDocument` object and write it back to a disk file.

For this exercise, you should write a form that enables the user to open an XML file and edit the contents of the XML file on a `DataGrid` control. Users who are finished editing should be able to click a button and save the edited file back to disk. You can use the `WriteTo()` method of an `XmlDocument` or `XmlDataDocument` object to write that object to disk through an `XmlTextWriter` object.

How would you design such a form?

You should try working through this problem on your own first. If you get stuck, or if you'd like to see one possible solution, follow these steps:

1. Add a new form `GuidedPracticeExercise2_1.cs` to your Visual C# .NET project.

2. Add two `Button` controls (btnLoadXml and btnSaveXml) and a `DataGrid` control (dgXML) to the form.

3. Switch to the code view and add the following using directives:

   ```
   using System.Data;
   using System.Xml;
   ```

4. Double-click the form and add the following code in the class definition:

   ```
   // Define XmlDataDocument object and DataSet
   // object at the class level
   XmlDataDocument xdd = new XmlDataDocument();
   DataSet ds;

   private void GuidedPracticeExercise2_1_Load(
       object sender, System.EventArgs e)
   {
       // Retrieve the associated DataSet and store it
       ds = xdd.DataSet;
   }
   ```

continues

continued

5. Double-click both the `Button` controls and add the following code in their `Click` event handlers:

```
private void btnLoadXml_Click(
    object sender, System.EventArgs e)
{
    // Create a new XmlTextReader on the file
    XmlTextReader xtr = new
        XmlTextReader(@"..\..\Books.xml");
    // Initialize the DataSet by reading the schema
    // from the XML document
    ds.ReadXmlSchema(xtr);
    // Reset the XmlTextReader
    xtr.Close();
    xtr = new XmlTextReader(@"..\..\Books.xml");
    // Tell it to ignore whitespace
    xtr.WhitespaceHandling = WhitespaceHandling.None;
    // Load the synchronized object
    xdd.Load(xtr);
    // Display the resulting DataSet
    dgXML.DataSource = ds;
    dgXML.DataMember = "Book";
    // Clean up
    xtr.Close();
}

private void btnSaveXml_Click(
    object sender, System.EventArgs e)
{
    // Create a new XmlTextWriter on the file
    XmlTextWriter xtw = new XmlTextWriter(
        @"..\..\Books.xml",
        System.Text.Encoding.UTF8);
    // And write the document to it
    xdd.WriteTo(xtw);
    xtw.Close();
}
```

6. Insert the `Main()` method to launch the form. Set the form as the startup object for the project.

7. Run the project. Click the Load XML button to load the `Books.xml` file to the `DataGrid` control. Change some data on the `DataGrid` control, and then click the Save XML button. Close the form. Open the `Books.xml` file to see the changed data.

The code in this exercise keeps the `XmlDataDocument` and `DataSet` objects at the class level so that they remain in scope while the user is editing data. To make the data available for editing, a `DataSet` object is synchronized to an XmlDataDocument object and then that DataSet object is bound to a DataGrid control. As the user makes changes on the DataGrid control, those changes are automatically saved back to the DataSet object, which in turn keeps the XmlDataDocument object synchronized to reflect the changes. When the user clicks the Save XML button, the contents of the XmlDataDocument object are written back to disk.

If you have difficulty following this exercise, review the section "Synchronizing DataSet Objects with XML." After doing that review, try this exercise again.

▶ The XmlDataDocument class is a subclass of the XmlDocument class that can be synchronized with a DataSet object.

▶ You can start the synchronization process with the XmlDataDocument object or with the DataSet object, or you can use a schema file to construct both objects.

▶ Changes to one synchronized object are automatically reflected in the other.

▶ You can use an XmlTextWriter object to persist an XmlDocument object back to disk.

UNDERSTANDING XPATH

Access and Manipulate XML Data: Use XPath to query XML data.

To pass the exam, you should also have basic knowledge of XPath. XPath is another W3C standard, formally known as the XML Path Language. XPath is described by the W3C as "a language for addressing parts of an XML document." The .NET implementation of XPath supports the Version 1.0 Recommendation standard for XPath, which you can find at www.w3.org/TR/xpath.

You can think of XPath as being a query language, conceptually similar to SQL. Just as SQL allows you to select a set of information from a table or group of tables, XPath allows you to select a set of nodes from the DOM representation of an XML document. In this section, I'll introduce you to the basic syntax of XPath, and then show you how you can use XPath in the .NET `System.Xml` namespace.

The XPath Language

XPath is not itself an XML standard. XPath expressions are not valid XML documents. Rather, XPath is a language for talking *about* XML. By writing an appropriate XPath expression, you can select particular elements or attributes within an XML document.

XPath starts with the notion of current context. The current context defines the set of nodes that an XPath query will inspect. In general, there are four choices for specifying the current context for an XPath query:

- ▶ `./` uses the current node as the current context.

- ▶ `/` uses the root of the XML document as the current context.

- ▶ `.//` uses the entire XML hierarchy starting with the current node as the current context.

- ▶ `//` uses the entire XML document as the current context.

To use XPath to identify a set of elements, you use the path down the tree structure to those elements, separating elements by forward slashes. For example, this XPath expression selects all the `Author` elements in the `Books.xml` file:

```
/Books/Book/Author
```

You can also select all the `Author` elements without worrying about the full path to get to them by using this expression:

```
//Author
```

You can use * as a wildcard at any level of the tree. So, for example, this expression selects all the `Author` nodes that are grandchildren of the `Books` node:

```
/Books/*/Author
```

XPath expressions select a set of elements, not a single element. Of course, the set might have only a single member, or no members at all. In the context of the XmlDocument object, an XPath expression can be used to select a set of XmlNode objects to operate on later.

To identify a set of attributes, you trace the path down the tree to the attributes, just as you do with elements. The only difference is that attribute names must be prefixed with an @ character. For example, this XPath expression selects all the Pages attributes from Book elements in the Books.xml file:

```
/Books/Book/@Pages
```

Of course, in the Books.xml file, only Book elements have a Pages attribute. So in this particular context, this XPath expression is equivalent to the previous one:

```
//@Pages
```

You can select multiple attributes with the @* operator. To select all attributes of Book elements anywhere in the XML, use this expression:

```
//Book/@*
```

XPath also offers a predicate language to enable you to specify smaller groups of nodes or even individual nodes in the XML tree. You might think of this as a filtering capability similar to a SQL WHERE clause. One thing you can do is specify the exact value of the node that you'd like to work with. To find all Publisher nodes with the value Addison Wesley you could use the XPath expression

```
/Books/Book/Publisher[.="Addison Wesley"]
```

Here the [] operator specifies a filter pattern and the dot operator stands for the current node. Filters are always evaluated with respect to the current context. Alternatively, you can find all Book elements published by Addison Wesley:

```
/Books/Book[./Publisher="Addison Wesley"]
```

Note that there is no forward slash between an element and a filtering expression in XPath.

Of course, you can filter on attributes as well as elements. You can also use operators and Boolean expressions within filtering specifications. For example, you might want to find Books that have a thousand or more pages:

```
/Books/Book[./@Pages>=1000]
```

Because the current node is the default context, you can simplify this expression a little bit:

```
/Books/Book[@Pages>=1000]
```

XPath also supports a selection of filtering functions. For example, to find books whose title starts with A you could use this XPath expression:

```
/Books/Book[starts-with(Title,"A")]
```

Table 2.6 lists some additional XPath functions.

TABLE 2.6

SELECTED XPATH FUNCTIONS

Function	Description
concat()	Concatenates strings
contains()	Determines whether one string contains another
count()	Returns the number of nodes in an expression
last()	Specifies the last element in a collection
normalize-space()	Removes whitespace from a string
not()	Negates its argument
number()	Converts its argument to a number
position()	Specifies the ordinal of a node within its parent
starts-with()	Determines whether one string starts with another
string-length()	Returns the number of characters in a string
substring()	Returns a substring from a string

Square brackets are also used to indicate indexing. Collections are indexed starting at one. To return the first Book node, you'd use this expression:

```
/Books/Book[1]
```

To return the first title of the second book:

```
/Books/Book[2]/Title[1]
```

To return the first author in the XML file, regardless of the book:

```
(/Books/Book/Author)[1]
```

The parentheses are necessary because the square brackets have a higher operator precedence than the path operators. Without the brackets, the expression would return the first author of every book in the file. There's also a `last()` function that you can use to return the last element in a collection, no matter how many elements are in the collection:

```
/Books/Book[last()]
```

Another useful operator is the vertical bar, which is used to form the union of two sets of nodes. This expression returns all the authors for books published by Addison Wesley or Microsoft Press:

```
/Books/Book[./Publisher="Addison Wesley"]/Author ¦
➥ /Books/Book[./Publisher="Microsoft Press"]/Author
```

One way to see XPath in action is to use the `SelectNodes()` method of the `XmlNode` object, as shown in Step-by-Step 2.7.

STEP BY STEP

2.7 Selecting Nodes with XPath

1. Add a new form to the project. Name the new form `StepByStep2_7.cs`.

2. Add a `Label` control, a `TextBox` control (`txtXPath`), a `Button` control (`btnEvaluate`), and a `ListBox` control (`lbNodes`) to the form.

3. Switch to the code view and add the following using directive:

```
using System.Xml;
```

4. Double-click the `Button` control and add the following code to handle the button's `Click` event:

```
private void btnEvaluate_Click(
    object sender, System.EventArgs e)
{
    // Load the Books.xml file
    XmlTextReader xtr = new
        XmlTextReader(@"..\..\Books.xml");
    xtr.WhitespaceHandling = WhitespaceHandling.None;
    XmlDocument xd = new XmlDocument();
    xd.Load(xtr);
    // Retrieve nodes to match the expression
```

continues

continued

```
XmlNodeList xnl = xd.DocumentElement.SelectNodes(
    txtXPath.Text);
// And dump the results
lbNodes.Items.Clear();
foreach (XmlNode xnod in xnl)
{
    // For elements, display the corresponding
    // Text entity
    if (xnod.NodeType == XmlNodeType.Element)
    {
        lbNodes.Items.Add(
            xnod.NodeType.ToString() + ": " +
            xnod.Name + " = " +
            xnod.FirstChild.Value);
    }
    else
    {
        lbNodes.Items.Add(
            xnod.NodeType.ToString()+ ": " +
            xnod.Name + " = " + xnod.Value);
    }
}
// Clean up
xtr.Close();
}
```

5. Insert the `Main()` method to launch the form. Set the form as the startup object for the project.

6. Run the project. Enter an XPath expression in the `TextBox` control. Click the button to see the nodes that the expression selects from the `Books.xml` file, as shown in Figure 2.7.

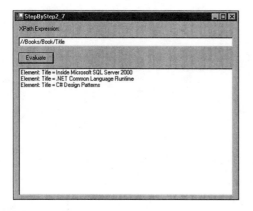

FIGURE 2.7
You can use XPath expressions to query an XML document.

The `SelectNodes()` method of the `XmlNode` object takes an XPath expression and evaluates that expression over the document. The resulting nodes are returned in an `XmlNodeList` object, which is just a collection of XML nodes.

Using the `XPathNavigator` Class

You've seen how you can use the `XmlReader` class to move through an XML document. But the `XmlReader` allows only forward-only, read-only access to the document. There is another set of navigation classes in the `System.Xml.XPath` namespace. In particular, the

`XPathNavigator` class provides you with read-only, random access to XML documents.

You can perform two distinct tasks with an `XPathNavigator` object:

▶ Selecting a set of nodes with an XPath expression

▶ Navigating the DOM representation of the XML document

In the remainder of this section, I'll show you how to use the `XPathNavigator` class for these tasks.

Selecting Nodes with XPath

To use the `XPathNavigator` class, you should start with an `XmlDocument`, `XmlDataDocument`, or `XPathDocument` object. In particular, if you're mainly interested in XPath operations, you should use the `XPathDocument` class. The `XPathDocument` class provides a representation of the structure of an XML document that is optimized for query operations. You can construct an `XPathDocument` object from a URI (including a local file name), a stream, or a reader containing XML.

The `XPathDocument` object has a single method of interest, `CreateNavigator()`. (You'll also find this method on the `XmlDocument` and `XmlDataDocument` objects.) As you've probably guessed, the `CreateNavigator()` method returns an `XPathNavigator` object that can perform operations with the XML document represented by the `XPathDocument` object. Table 2.7 lists the important members of the `XPathNavigator` object.

TABLE 2.7

IMPORTANT MEMBERS OF THE XPathNavigator CLASS

Member	Type	Description
`Clone()`	Method	Creates a duplicate of this object with the current state
`ComparePosition()`	Method	Compares two `XPathNavigator` objects to determine whether they have the same current node

continues

TABLE 2.7 *continued*

IMPORTANT MEMBERS OF THE XPathNavigator CLASS

Member	Type	Description
Compile()	Method	Compiles an XPath expression for faster execution
Evaluate()	Method	Evaluates an XPath expression
HasAttributes	Property	Indicates whether the current node has any attributes
HasChildren	Property	Indicates whether the current node has any children
IsEmptyElement	Property	Indicates whether the current node is an empty element
Matches()	Method	Determines whether the current node matches an XSLT pattern
MoveToFirst()	Method	Moves to the first sibling of the current node
MoveToFirstAttribute()	Method	Moves to the first attribute of the current node
MoveToFirstChild()	Method	Moves to the first child of the current node
MoveToNext()	Method	Moves to the next sibling of the current node
MoveToNextAttribute()	Method	Moves to the next attribute of the current node
MoveToParent()	Method	Moves to the parent of the current node
MoveToPrevious()	Method	Moves to the previous sibling of the current node
MoveToRoot()	Method	Moves to the root node of the DOM
Name	Property	Specifies the qualified name of the current node
Select()	Method	Uses an XPath expression to select a set of nodes
Value	Property	Specifies the value of the current node

Like the `XmlReader` class, the `XPathNavigator` class maintains a pointer to a current node in the DOM at all times. But the `XPathNavigator` brings additional capabilities to working with the DOM. For example, you can use this class to execute an XPath query, as shown in Step-by-Step 2.8.

> **EXAM TIP**
>
> **`XPathNavigator` Object Can Move Backward** Note that unlike the `XmlReader` class, the `XPathNavigator` class implements methods such as `MoveToPrevious()` and `MoveToParent()` that can move backward in the DOM. The `XPathNavigator` class provides random access to the entire XML document.

STEP BY STEP

2.8 Selecting Nodes with an `XPathNavigator` Object

1. Add a new form to the project. Name the new form `StepByStep2_8.cs`.

2. Add a `Label` control, a `TextBox` control (`txtXPath`), a `Button` control (`btnEvaluate`), and a `ListBox` control (`lbNodes`) to the form.

3. Switch to the code view and add the following using directive:

```
using System.Xml.XPath;
```

4. Double-click the `Button` control and add the following code to handle the button's `Click` event:

```
private void btnEvaluate_Click(
    object sender, System.EventArgs e)
{
    // Load the Books.xml file
    XPathDocument xpd = new
        XPathDocument(@"..\..\Books.xml");
    // Get the associated navigator
    XPathNavigator xpn = xpd.CreateNavigator();
    // Retrieve nodes to match the expression
    XPathNodeIterator xpni =
        xpn.Select(txtXPath.Text);
    // And dump the results
    lbNodes.Items.Clear();
    while (xpni.MoveNext())
    {
        lbNodes.Items.Add(
            xpni.Current.NodeType.ToString() + ": "
            + xpni.Current.Name + " = " +
            xpni.Current.Value);
    }
}
```

continues

continued

5. Insert the `Main()` method to launch the form. Set the form as the startup object for the project.

6. Run the project. Enter an XPath expression in the `TextBox` control. Click the button to see the nodes that the expression selects from the `Books.xml` file.

The `Select()` method of the `XPathNavigator` class returns an `XPathNodeIterator` object, which lets you visit each member of the selected set of nodes in turn. It has `Count` and `Current` properties, and (as you saw in the code for Step-by-Step 2.8) a `MoveNext()` method that advances it through the set of nodes.

Navigating Nodes with XPath

You can also use the `XPathNavigator` object to move around in the DOM. Step-by-Step 2.9 demonstrates the `MoveTo` methods of this class.

STEP BY STEP

2.9 Navigating with an `XPathNavigator` Object

1. Add a new form to the project. Name the new form `StepByStep2_9.cs`.

2. Add four `Button` controls (`btnParent`, `btnPrevious`, `btnNext`, and `btnChild`), and a `ListBox` control (`lbNodes`) to the form.

3. Switch to the code view and add the following `using` directive:

```
using System.Xml.XPath;
```

4. Double-click the form and add the following code to the class definition:

```
XPathDocument xpd;
XPathNavigator xpn;
```

```
private void StepByStep2_9_Load(
    object sender, System.EventArgs e)
{
    // Load the Books.xml file
    xpd = new XPathDocument(@"..\..\Books.xml");
    // Get the associated navigator
    xpn = xpd.CreateNavigator();
    xpn.MoveToRoot();
    ListNode();
}

private void ListNode()
{
    // Dump the current node to the listbox
    lbNodes.Items.Add(xpn.NodeType.ToString() +
        ": " + xpn.Name + " = " + xpn.Value);
}
```

5. Double-click the Button controls and add the following
   code to their Click event handlers:

```
private void btnParent_Click(
    object sender, System.EventArgs e)
{
    // Move to the parent of the current node
    if(xpn.MoveToParent())
        ListNode();
    else
        lbNodes.Items.Add("No parent node");
}

private void btnChild_Click(
    object sender, System.EventArgs e)
{
    // Move to the first child of the current node
    if(xpn.MoveToFirstChild())
        ListNode();
    else
        lbNodes.Items.Add("No child node");
}

private void btnPrevious_Click(
    object sender, System.EventArgs e)
{
    // Move to the previous sibling
    // of the current node
    if(xpn.MoveToPrevious())
        ListNode();
    else
        lbNodes.Items.Add("No previous node");
}

private void btnNext_Click(
    object sender, System.EventArgs e)
```

continues

continued

```
{
    // Move to the next sibling of the current node
    if(xpn.MoveToNext())
        ListNode();
    else
        lbNodes.Items.Add("No next node");
}
```

6. Insert the Main() method to launch the form. Set the form as the startup object for the project.

7. Run the project. Experiment with the buttons. You'll find that you can move around in the DOM, as shown in Figure 2.8.

FIGURE 2.8
You can navigate an XML Document by using an XpathNavigator object.

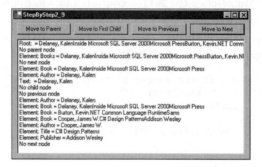

Step-by-Step 2.9 demonstrates two important things about the XPathNavigator class. First, the value of a node is the concatenated text of all the nodes beneath that node. Second, the MoveTo methods of the XPathNavigator will never throw an error, whether or not there is an appropriate node to move to. Instead, they simply return false when the requested navigation cannot be performed.

R E V I E W   B R E A K

▶ XPath is a language for specifying or selecting parts of an XML document. XPath is a query language for XML.

▶ An XPath expression returns a set of zero or more nodes from the DOM representation of an XML document.

▶ The SelectNodes() method of the XmlNode object returns a set of nodes selected by an XPath expression.

▶ The `XPathDocument` and `XPathNavigator` objects are optimized for fast execution of XPath queries.

▶ The `XPathNavigator` object allows random-access navigation of the structure of an XML document.

GENERATING AND USING XSD SCHEMAS

Access and Manipulate XML Data: Generate and use an XSD schema.

In Chapter 1, "Creating and Manipulating `DataSets`," you learned how to create an XSD schema in the Visual Studio .NET user interface by dragging and dropping XML elements from the toolbox. This method is useful when you need to create a schema from scratch. But there will be times when you want to create a schema to match an existing object. In this section, you'll learn about the methods that are available to programmatically generate XSD schemas.

Generating an XSD Schema

One obvious source for an XML Schema is an XML file. An XML file can contain explicit schema information (in the form of an embedded schema) or it can contain implicit schema information in its structure. If the file contains explicit schema information, you can use the `DataSet` object to read that information and create the corresponding schema as a separate file, as shown in Step-by-Step 2.10.

STEP BY STEP

2.10 Extracting an XML Schema

1. Add a new form to the project. Name the new form `StepByStep2_10.cs`.

continues

continued

2. Add a `Button` control (`btnGetSchema`) and a `TextBox` control (`txtSchema`) to the form. Set the `MultiLine` property of the `TextBox` to `true` and set its `ScrollBars` property to `Vertical`.

3. Switch to the code view and add the following using directives:

```
using System.Xml;
using System.Data;
using System.IO;
```

4. Double-click the `Button` controls and add code to process an XML document when you click the `Button` control:

```
private void btnGetSchema_Click(
    object sender, System.EventArgs e)
{
    // Load the XML file with inline schema info
    XmlTextReader xtr = new
        XmlTextReader(@"..\..\Products.xml");
    // Read the schema (only) into a DataSet
    DataSet ds = new DataSet();
    ds.ReadXmlSchema(xtr);
    // Write the schema out as a separate stream
    StringWriter sw = new StringWriter();
    ds.WriteXmlSchema(sw);
    txtSchema.Text = sw.ToString();
    // Clean up
    xtr.Close();
}
```

5. Add a new XML file to the project. Name the new file `Products.xml`. Add this XML to the new file:

```
<?xml version="1.0" encoding="UTF-8"?>
<root xmlns:xsd="http://www.w3.org/2001/XMLSchema"
  xmlns:od="urn:schemas-microsoft-com:officedata">
<xsd:schema>
 <xsd:element name="dataroot">
  <xsd:complexType>
   <xsd:choice maxOccurs="unbounded">
    <xsd:element ref="Products"/>
   </xsd:choice>
  </xsd:complexType>
 </xsd:element>
 <xsd:element name="Products">
  <xsd:annotation>
   <xsd:appinfo/>
  </xsd:annotation>
  <xsd:complexType>
   <xsd:sequence>
```

```
<xsd:element name="ProductID"
   od:jetType="autonumber"
   od:sqlSType="int" od:autoUnique="yes"
   od:nonNullable="yes">
 <xsd:simpleType>
  <xsd:restriction base="xsd:integer"/>
 </xsd:simpleType>
</xsd:element>
<xsd:element name="ProductName" minOccurs="0"
    od:jetType="text" od:sqlSType="nvarchar">
 <xsd:simpleType>
  <xsd:restriction base="xsd:string">
   <xsd:maxLength value="40"/>
  </xsd:restriction>
 </xsd:simpleType>
</xsd:element>
<xsd:element name="SupplierID" minOccurs="0"
    od:jetType="longinteger" od:sqlSType="int">
 <xsd:simpleType>
  <xsd:restriction base="xsd:integer"/>
 </xsd:simpleType>
</xsd:element>
<xsd:element name="CategoryID" minOccurs="0"
    od:jetType="longinteger" od:sqlSType="int">
 <xsd:simpleType>
  <xsd:restriction base="xsd:integer"/>
 </xsd:simpleType>
</xsd:element>
<xsd:element name="QuantityPerUnit" minOccurs="0"
    od:jetType="text" od:sqlSType="nvarchar">
 <xsd:simpleType>
  <xsd:restriction base="xsd:string">
   <xsd:maxLength value="20"/>
  </xsd:restriction>
 </xsd:simpleType>
</xsd:element>
<xsd:element name="UnitPrice" minOccurs="0"
    od:jetType="currency"
    od:sqlSType="money" type="xsd:double"/>
<xsd:element name="UnitsInStock" minOccurs="0"
    od:jetType="integer"
    od:sqlSType="smallint" type="xsd:short"/>
<xsd:element name="UnitsOnOrder" minOccurs="0"
    od:jetType="integer"
    od:sqlSType="smallint" type="xsd:short"/>
<xsd:element name="ReorderLevel" minOccurs="0"
    od:jetType="integer"
    od:sqlSType="smallint" type="xsd:short"/>
<xsd:element name="Discontinued"
    od:jetType="yesno"
    od:sqlSType="bit" od:nonNullable="yes"
    type="xsd:byte"/>
</xsd:sequence>
</xsd:complexType>
```

continues

continued

```
        </xsd:element>
      </xsd:schema>
      <dataroot xmlns:xsi=
        "http://www.w3.org/2000/10/XMLSchema-instance">
        <Products>
          <ProductID>1</ProductID>
          <ProductName>Chai</ProductName>
          <SupplierID>1</SupplierID>
          <CategoryID>1</CategoryID>
          <QuantityPerUnit>10 boxes x 20 bags
          </QuantityPerUnit>
          <UnitPrice>18</UnitPrice>
          <UnitsInStock>39</UnitsInStock>
          <UnitsOnOrder>0</UnitsOnOrder>
          <ReorderLevel>10</ReorderLevel>
          <Discontinued>0</Discontinued>
        </Products>
        <Products>
          <ProductID>2</ProductID>
          <ProductName>Chang</ProductName>
          <SupplierID>1</SupplierID>
          <CategoryID>1</CategoryID>
          <QuantityPerUnit>24 - 12 oz bottles
          </QuantityPerUnit>
          <UnitPrice>19</UnitPrice>
          <UnitsInStock>17</UnitsInStock>
          <UnitsOnOrder>40</UnitsOnOrder>
          <ReorderLevel>25</ReorderLevel>
          <Discontinued>0</Discontinued>
        </Products>
        <Products>
          <ProductID>3</ProductID>
          <ProductName>Aniseed Syrup</ProductName>
          <SupplierID>1</SupplierID>
          <CategoryID>2</CategoryID>
          <QuantityPerUnit>12 - 550 ml bottles
          </QuantityPerUnit>
          <UnitPrice>10</UnitPrice>
          <UnitsInStock>13</UnitsInStock>
          <UnitsOnOrder>70</UnitsOnOrder>
          <ReorderLevel>25</ReorderLevel>
        <Discontinued>0</Discontinued>
        </Products>
        <Products>
          <ProductID>4</ProductID>
          <ProductName>
           <![CDATA[Chef Anton's Cajun Seasoning]]>
          </ProductName>
          <SupplierID>2</SupplierID>
          <CategoryID>2</CategoryID>
          <QuantityPerUnit>48 - 6 oz jars</QuantityPerUnit>
          <UnitPrice>22</UnitPrice>
          <UnitsInStock>53</UnitsInStock>
          <UnitsOnOrder>0</UnitsOnOrder>
```

```
      <ReorderLevel>0</ReorderLevel>
      <Discontinued>0</Discontinued>
    </Products>
    <Products>
      <ProductID>5</ProductID>
      <ProductName><![CDATA[Chef Anton's Gumbo Mix]]>
      </ProductName>
      <SupplierID>2</SupplierID>
      <CategoryID>2</CategoryID>
      <QuantityPerUnit>36 boxes</QuantityPerUnit>
      <UnitPrice>21.35</UnitPrice>
      <UnitsInStock>0</UnitsInStock>
      <UnitsOnOrder>0</UnitsOnOrder>
      <ReorderLevel>0</ReorderLevel>
      <Discontinued>1</Discontinued>
    </Products>
    <Products>
      <ProductID>6</ProductID>
      <ProductName>
      <![CDATA[Grandma's Boysenberry Spread]]>
      </ProductName>
      <SupplierID>3</SupplierID>
      <CategoryID>2</CategoryID>
      <QuantityPerUnit>12 - 8 oz jars</QuantityPerUnit>
      <UnitPrice>25</UnitPrice>
      <UnitsInStock>120</UnitsInStock>
      <UnitsOnOrder>0</UnitsOnOrder>
      <ReorderLevel>25</ReorderLevel>
      <Discontinued>0</Discontinued>
    </Products>
  </dataroot>
</root>
```

6. Insert the `Main()` method to launch the form. Set the form as the startup object for the project.

7. Run the project. Click the button to load the XML file and extract the inline schema information to the text box, as shown in Figure 2.9.

NOTE

Generating an Inline Schema The `Products.xml` file is generated by exporting a portion of the `Products` table from the `Northwind` sample database in Microsoft Access 2002.

FIGURE 2.9
You can extract XSD schema information from an XML file by using the `DataSet.ReadXmlSchema()` method.

The `DataSet` object must have the capability to read an XML schema so that it can construct a matching data structure in memory. The .NET Framework designers thoughtfully exposed this capability to you through the `ReadXmlSchema()` and `WriteXmlSchema()` methods of the `DataSet` object. But what if the file does not contain explicit schema information? It turns out that you can still use the `DataSet` object, because this object also can infer an XML schema based on the data in an XML file. Step-by-Step 2.11 demonstrates this technique.

STEP BY STEP

2.11 Inferring an XML Schema

1. Add a new form to the project. Name the new form StepByStep2_11.cs.

2. Add a Button control (btnInferSchema) and a TextBox control (txtSchema) to the form. Set the MultiLine property of the TextBox to true and set its ScrollBars property to Vertical.

3. Switch to the code view and add the following using directives:

```
using System.Xml;
using System.Data;
using System.IO;
```

4. Double-click the Button controls and add code to process an XML document when you click the Button control:

```
private void btnInferSchema_Click(
    object sender, System.EventArgs e)
{
    // Load an XML file with no schema information
    XmlTextReader xtr = new
        XmlTextReader(@"..\..\Books.xml");
    // Read the schema (only) into a DataSet
    DataSet ds = new DataSet();
    String[] ns = {};
    ds.InferXmlSchema(xtr, ns);
    // Write the schema out as a separate stream
    StringWriter sw = new StringWriter();
    ds.WriteXmlSchema(sw);
    txtSchema.Text = sw.ToString();
    // Clean up
    xtr.Close();}
```

5. Insert the Main() method to launch the form. Set the form as the startup object for the project.

6. Run the project. Click the button to load the XML file and infer the schema information to the text box, as shown in Figure 2.10.

FIGURE 2.10

You can infer schema information from an XML file by using the DataSet.InferXmlSchema() method.

To summarize, there are at least four ways that you can obtain XSD files for your applications:

▶ You can use a file generated by an external application such as Microsoft SQL Server or Microsoft Access.

▶ You can create your own schema files from scratch, using the techniques that you learned in Chapter 1.

▶ You can extract inline schema information from an XML file by using the DataSet.ReadXmlSchema() method.

▶ You can infer schema information from an XML file by using the DataSet.InferXmlSchema() method.

Using an XSD Schema

Access and Manipulate XML Data: Validate an XML Document.

The prime use of a schema file is to validate the corresponding XML file. Although any XML file that conforms to the syntactical rules for XML is well-formed, this does not automatically make the file valid. A valid XML file is one whose structure conforms to a specification. This specification can be in the form of an XML schema or a Document Type Description (DTD), for example. Any valid XML file is well-formed, but not every well-formed XML file is valid.

In this section, you'll see the programmatic support that the .NET Framework provides for validating XML files.

Validating Against XSD

To validate an XML document, you can use the XmlValidatingReader class. This class implements the XmlReader class and provides support for validating XML documents. It can also validate the XML document as it is read in to the XmlDocument object. Step-by-Step 2.12 shows how you can use the XmlValidatingReader object to validate an XML document with an inline schema.

NOTE

XML Schema Definition Tool (xsd.exe) You can use the .NET Framework XML Schema Definition Tool (xsd.exe) to:

· Generate an XML schema document from a DLL or EXE.

· Generate a C# class file that conforms to the given XML schema file.

· Generate an XML schema from an XML Data Reduced (XDR) schema file.

· Generate an XML schema from an XML file.

· Generate DataSet classes from an XML schema file.

STEP BY STEP

2.12 Validating an XML Document Against an Inline Schema

1. Add a new form to the project. Name the new form StepByStep2_12.cs.

2. Add a Button control (btnValidate) and a TextBox control (txtErrors) to the form. Set the MultiLine property of the TextBox to true and set its ScrollBars property to Vertical.

3. Switch to the code view and add the following using directives:

```
using System.Xml;
using System.Xml.Schema;
```

4. Double-click the Button controls and add code to validate an XML document when you click the Button control:

```
private void btnValidate_Click(
    object sender, System.EventArgs e)
{
    // Load a document with an inline schema
    XmlTextReader xtr =
        new XmlTextReader(@"..\..\Products.xml");
    // Prepare to validate it
    XmlValidatingReader xvr =
        new XmlValidatingReader(xtr);
    xvr.ValidationType = ValidationType.Schema;
    // Tell the validator what to do with errors
    xvr.ValidationEventHandler +=
        new ValidationEventHandler(ValidationHandler);
    // Load the document, thus validating
    XmlDocument xd = new XmlDocument();
    xd.Load(xvr);
    // Clean up
    xvr.Close();
}

public void ValidationHandler(
    object sender, ValidationEventArgs e)
{
    // Dump any validation errors to the UI
    txtErrors.AppendText(e.Message + "\n");
}
```

5. Insert the Main() method to launch the form. Set the form as the startup object for the project.

6. Run the project. Click the button to load and simultaneously validate the XML file, as shown in Figure 2.11.

7. Stop the project. Open the `Products.xml` file and make a change. For example, change the name of a child element from `SupplierID` to `SupplierIdentifier`.

8. Run the project. Click the button to load and simultaneously validate the XML file. You'll see additional validation errors, as shown in Figure 2.12.

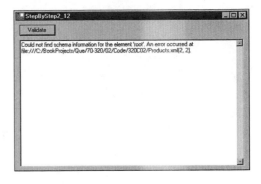

FIGURE 2.11
You can validate an XML document by using `XmlValidatingReader` class.

An inline schema cannot contain an entry for the root element of the document, so even when the document is otherwise valid, you'll get an error from that node. As you can see, the `XmlValidatingReader` object is constructed so that it does not stop on validation errors. Rather, it continues processing the file, but raises an event for each error. This lets your code decide how to handle errors while still filling the `XmlDocument` object.

When you change the name of an element in the XML, the XML remains well-formed. But because that name doesn't match the name in the schema file, that portion of the XML document becomes invalid. The `XmlValidatingReader` object responds by raising additional events.

You can also validate an XML file against an external schema. Step-by-Step 2.13 shows this technique in action.

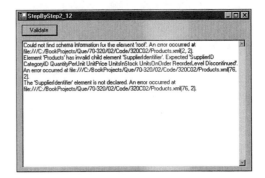

FIGURE 2.12
While the XML document is validated, the `XmlValidatingReader` object raises a `ValidationEventHandler` event for each error in the XML document.

STEP BY STEP

2.13 Validating an XML Document Against an External Schema

1. Add a new form to the project. Name the new form `StepByStep2_13.cs`.

2. Add a `Button` control (`btnValidate`) and a `TextBox` control (`txtErrors`) to the form. Set the `MultiLine` property of the `TextBox` to `true` and set its `ScrollBars` property to `Vertical`.

continues

continued

3. Switch to the code view and add the following using directives:

```
using System.Xml;
using System.Xml.Schema;
```

4. Double-click the Button controls and add code to validate an XML document when you click the Button control:

```
private void btnValidate_Click(
    object sender, System.EventArgs e)
{
    // Load a document with an external schema
    XmlTextReader xtr =
        new XmlTextReader(@"..\..\Books2.xml");
    // Prepare to validate it
    XmlValidatingReader xvr =
        new XmlValidatingReader(xtr);
    xvr.ValidationType = ValidationType.Schema;
    // Tell the validator what to do with errors
    xvr.ValidationEventHandler +=
        new ValidationEventHandler(ValidationHandler);
    // Load the schema
    XmlSchemaCollection xsc =
        new XmlSchemaCollection();
    xsc.Add("xsdBooks", @"..\..\Books2.xsd");
    // Tell the validator which schema to use
    xvr.Schemas.Add(xsc);
    // Load the document, thus validating
    XmlDocument xd = new XmlDocument();
    xd.Load(xvr);
    // Clean up
    xvr.Close();
}
public void ValidationHandler(
    object sender, ValidationEventArgs e)
{
    // Dump any validation errors to the UI
    txtErrors.AppendText(e.Message + "\n");
}
```

5. Add a new XML file to the project. Name the new file Books2.xml. Enter the following text for Books2.xml:

```
<?xml version="1.0" encoding="UTF-8"?>
<Books xmlns="xsdBooks">
    <Book Pages="1088">
        <Author>Delaney, Kalen</Author>
        <Title>Inside Microsoft SQL Server 2000</Title>
        <Publisher>Microsoft Press</Publisher>
    </Book>
    <Book Pages="997">
        <Author>Burton, Kevin</Author>
```

```
        <Title>.NET Common Language Runtime</Title>
        <Publisher>Sams</Publisher>
    </Book>
    <Book Pages="392">
        <Author>Cooper, James W.</Author>
        <Title>C# Design Patterns</Title>
        <Publisher>Addison Wesley</Publisher>
    </Book>
</Books>
```

6. Add a new schema file to the project. Name the new schema file `Books2.xsd`. Enter the following text for

   `Books2.xsd`:

```
<?xml version="1.0" encoding="utf-8" ?>
<xs:schema id="Books" xmlns="xsdBooks"
  elementFormDefault="qualified"
  targetNamespace="xsdBooks"
 xmlns:xs="http://www.w3.org/2001/XMLSchema">
    <xs:element name="Books">
        <xs:complexType>
            <xs:choice maxOccurs="unbounded">
                <xs:element name="Book">
                    <xs:complexType>
                        <xs:sequence>
                          <xs:element name="Author"
                            type="xs:string" />
                          <xs:element name="Title"
                            type="xs:string" />
                          <xs:element name="Publisher"
                            type="xs:string" />
                        </xs:sequence>
                        <xs:attribute name="Pages"
                          type="xs:string" />
                    </xs:complexType>
                </xs:element>
            </xs:choice>
        </xs:complexType>
    </xs:element>
</xs:schema>
```

7. Insert the `Main()` method to launch the form. Set the form as the startup object for the project.

8. Run the project. Click the button to load and simultaneously validate the XML file. Because the file exactly matches the schema, you won't see any errors.

9. Stop the project. Open the `Books2.xml` file and make a change. For example, change the name of a child element from `Author` to `Writer`.

continues

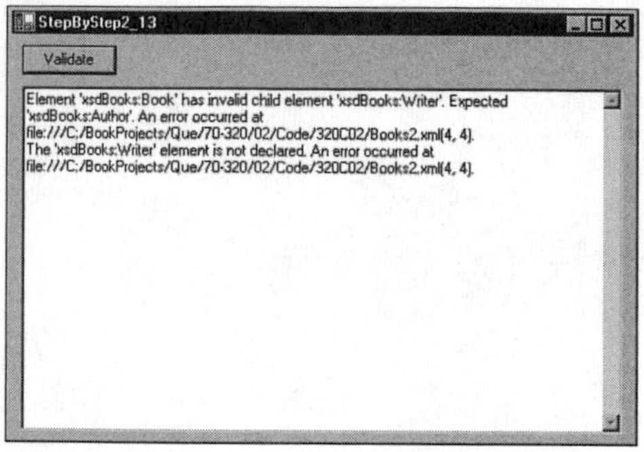

FIGURE 2.13
To validate against an external schema, you need to add the schema to the `XmlValidatingReader.Schemas` collection.

NOTE

DTD Tutorial   A good source for more information on DTDs is the XMLFiles.com DTD Tutorial, located at www.xmlfiles.com/dtd.

---

continued

10. Run the project. Click the button to load and simultaneously validate the XML file. You'll see validation errors, as shown in Figure 2.13.

Validating Against a DTD

Using schema files is not the only way to describe the structure of an XML file. An older standard for specifying structure is the Document Type Definition, or DTD. DTDs are part of the Standardized Generalized Markup Language (SGML) standard, from which both HTML and XML derive. The `XmlValidatingReader` class can also validate an XML document for conformance with a DTD, as you'll see in Step-by-Step 2.14.

STEP BY STEP

2.14 Validating an XML Document Against a DTD

1. Add a new form to the project. Name the new form `StepByStep2_14.cs`.

2. Add a `Button` control (`btnValidate`) and a `TextBox` control (`txtErrors`) to the form. Set the `MultiLine` property of the `TextBox` to `true` and set its `ScrollBars` property to `Vertical`.

3. Switch to the code view and add the following `using` directives:

```
using System.Xml;
using System.Xml.Schema;
```

4. Double-click the `Button` controls and add code to validate an XML document when you click the `Button` control:

```
private void btnValidate_Click(
    object sender, System.EventArgs e)
{
    // Load a document with a DTD
    XmlTextReader xtr =
        new XmlTextReader(@"..\..\Books3.xml");
```

```
    // Prepare to validate it
    XmlValidatingReader xvr =
        new XmlValidatingReader(xtr);
    xvr.ValidationType = ValidationType.DTD;
    // Tell the validator what to do with errors
    xvr.ValidationEventHandler +=
        new ValidationEventHandler(ValidationHandler);
    // Load the document, thus validating
    XmlDocument xd = new XmlDocument();
    xd.Load(xvr);
    // Clean up
    xvr.Close();
}

public void ValidationHandler(
    object sender, ValidationEventArgs e)
{
    // Dump any validation errors to the UI
    txtErrors.AppendText(e.Message + "\n");
}
```

5. Add a new XML file to the project. Name the new file `Books3.xml`. Enter the following text for `Books3.xml`:

```xml
<?xml version="1.0" encoding="UTF-8" ?>
<!DOCTYPE Books SYSTEM "books.dtd">
<Books>
    <Book Pages="1088">
        <Author>Delaney, Kalen</Author>
        <Title>Inside Microsoft SQL Server 2000</Title>
        <Publisher>Microsoft Press</Publisher>
    </Book>
    <Book Pages="997">
        <Author>Burton, Kevin</Author>
        <Title>.NET Common Language Runtime</Title>
        <Publisher>Sams</Publisher>
    </Book>
    <Book Pages="392">
        <Author>Cooper, James W.</Author>
        <Title>C# Design Patterns</Title>
        <Publisher>Addison Wesley</Publisher>
    </Book>
</Books>
```

6. Add a new text file to the project. Name the new schema file `Books.dtd`. Enter the following text for `Books.dtd`:

```
<!ELEMENT Books (Book)* >
<!ELEMENT Book (Author, Title, Publisher) >
<!ATTLIST Book Pages CDATA #REQUIRED>
<!ELEMENT Author (#PCDATA)>
<!ELEMENT Title (#PCDATA)>
<!ELEMENT Publisher (#PCDATA)>
```

NOTE

XDR Validation The `XmlValidatingReader` can also validate an XML file for conformance with an XML Data Reduced (XDR) specification. XDR is a standard that Microsoft briefly embraced for describing XML files before they settled on the more standard XSD. You're not likely to find many XDR files in common use.

continues

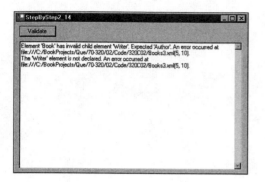

FIGURE 2.14
You can use the `XmlValidatingReader` class to validate an XML document against a DTD by setting its `ValidationType` property to `ValidationType.DTD`.

continued

7. Insert the `Main()` method to launch the form. Set the form as the startup object for the project.

8. Run the project. Click the button to load and simultaneously validate the XML file. Because the file exactly matches the schema, you won't see any errors.

9. Stop the project. Open the `Books3.xml` file and make a change. For example, change the name of a child element from `Author` to `Writer`.

10. Run the project. Click the button to load and simultaneously validate the XML file. You'll see validation errors, as shown in Figure 2.14.

If you inspect the code, you'll see that the only difference between validating against a schema file and validating against a DTD is in the constant chosen for the `ValidationType` property of the `XmlValidatingReader` object.

R E V I E W   B R E A K

▶ You can extract an inline schema from an XML file by using the `ReadXmlSchema()` method of the `DataSet` class.

▶ You can infer a schema from the structure of an XML file by using the `InferXmlSchema()` method of the `DataSet` class.

▶ You can validate an XML document for conformance with an inline schema, an external schema, a DTD, or an XDR file by using the `XmlValidatingReader` class.

USING XML WITH SQL SERVER

The .NET team is not the only group at Microsoft that's been working with XML. Over the past several releases, Microsoft SQL Server has become increasingly integrated with XML. In the current release, you can generate XML with SQL statements, using Microsoft T-SQL extensions to the SQL standard query language. You can also

update SQL Server tables by sending properly formed XML messages, called DiffGrams, to a SQL Server database. In this section,
you'll learn the basics of interacting with SQL Server via XML.

Generating XML with SQL Statements

**Access and Manipulate XML Data: Write a SQL statement
that retrieves XML data from a SQL Server database.**

Understanding the FOR XML Clause

SQL Server enables you to retrieve the results of any query as XML
rather than as a SQL resultset. To do this, you use the Microsoft-
specific FOR XML clause. You can use a variety of options in the FOR
XML clause to customize the XML that SQL Server generates.

The first option is FOR XML RAW. When you use raw mode with FOR
XML, SQL Server returns one element (always named row) for each
row of the resultset, with the individual columns represented as
attributes. For example, consider this query:

```
SELECT Customers.CustomerID, Customers.CompanyName,
  Orders.OrderID, Orders.OrderDate
  FROM Customers INNER JOIN Orders
  ON Customers.CustomerID = Orders.CustomerID
  WHERE Country = 'Brazil' AND
    OrderDate BETWEEN '1997-03-15' AND '1997-04-15'
  FOR XML RAW
```

If you execute this query (for example, using SQL Query Analyzer)
in the Northwind sample database, you'll get back these results:

```
<row CustomerID="RICAR"
  CompanyName="Ricardo Adocicados"
  OrderID="10481" OrderDate="1997-03-20T00:00:00"/>
<row CustomerID="QUEEN" CompanyName="Queen Cozinha"
  OrderID="10487" OrderDate="1997-03-26T00:00:00"/>
<row CustomerID="COMMI" CompanyName="Comércio Mineiro"
  OrderID="10494" OrderDate="1997-04-02T00:00:00"/>
<row CustomerID="TRADH"
  CompanyName="Tradiça[dd]o Hipermercados"
  OrderID="10496" OrderDate="1997-04-04T00:00:00"/>
```

NOTE

Result Formatting SQL Query
Analyzer returns XML results as one
long string. I've reformatted these
results for easier display on the printed page. If you have trouble seeing all
the results in SQL Query Analyzer,
select Tools, Options, Results, and
increase the Maximum Character
Width setting.

If the query output contains binary columns, you must include the
BINARY BASE64 option after the FOR XML clause to avoid a runtime
error:

```
SELECT EmployeeID, Photo
  FROM Employees
  FOR XML RAW, BINARY BASE64
```

With this option, standard Base64 coding is used to encode any binary columns in the output XML.

The second variant of the FOR XML clause is FOR XML AUTO. When you use auto mode with FOR XML, nested tables in the resultset are represented as nested elements in the XML. Columns are still represented as attributes. For example, here's a query that uses FOR XML AUTO:

```
SELECT Customers.CustomerID, Customers.CompanyName,
   Orders.OrderID, Orders.OrderDate
   FROM Customers INNER JOIN Orders
   ON Customers.CustomerID = Orders.CustomerID
   WHERE Country = 'Brazil' AND
      OrderDate BETWEEN '1997-03-15' AND '1997-04-15'
   FOR XML AUTO
```

Here's the corresponding resultset:

```
<Customers CustomerID="RICAR"
 CompanyName="Ricardo Adocicados">
 <Orders OrderID="10481"
    OrderDate="1997-03-20T00:00:00"/>
</Customers>
<Customers CustomerID="QUEEN"
    CompanyName="Queen Cozinha">
 <Orders OrderID="10487"
    OrderDate="1997-03-26T00:00:00"/>
</Customers>
<Customers CustomerID="COMMI"
 CompanyName="Comércio Mineiro">
 <Orders OrderID="10494"
    OrderDate="1997-04-02T00:00:00"/>
</Customers>
<Customers CustomerID="TRADH"
 CompanyName="Tradição Hipermercados">
 <Orders OrderID="10496"
     OrderDate="1997-04-04T00:00:00"/>
</Customers>
```

Note that in this resultset, the Orders element is nested within the Customers element for each order. If there were multiple orders for a single customer, the Orders element would repeat as many times as necessary.

There's a second variant of FOR XML AUTO. You can include the ELEMENTS option to represent columns as elements rather than as attributes. Here's a query that uses this option:

```
SELECT Customers.CustomerID, Customers.CompanyName,
   Orders.OrderID, Orders.OrderDate
   FROM Customers INNER JOIN Orders
   ON Customers.CustomerID = Orders.CustomerID
```

```
WHERE Country = 'Brazil' AND
  OrderDate BETWEEN '1997-03-15' AND '1997-04-15'
FOR XML AUTO, ELEMENTS
```

Here's the corresponding resultset:

```
<Customers>
  <CustomerID>RICAR</CustomerID>
  <CompanyName>Ricardo Adocicados</CompanyName>
  <Orders>
    <OrderID>10481</OrderID>
    <OrderDate>1997-03-20T00:00:00</OrderDate>
  </Orders>
</Customers>
<Customers>
  <CustomerID>QUEEN</CustomerID>
  <CompanyName>Queen Cozinha</CompanyName>
  <Orders>
    <OrderID>10487</OrderID>
    <OrderDate>1997-03-26T00:00:00</OrderDate>
  </Orders>
</Customers>
<Customers>
  <CustomerID>COMMI</CustomerID>
  <CompanyName>Comércio Mineiro</CompanyName>
  <Orders>
    <OrderID>10494</OrderID>
    <OrderDate>1997-04-02T00:00:00</OrderDate>
  </Orders>
</Customers>
<Customers>
  <CustomerID>TRADH</CustomerID>
  <CompanyName>Tradição Hipermercados</CompanyName>
  <Orders>
    <OrderID>10496</OrderID>
    <OrderDate>1997-04-04T00:00:00</OrderDate>
  </Orders>
</Customers>
```

The final variant of FOR XML is FOR XML EXPLICIT. In explicit mode, you must construct your query so as to create a resultset with the first column named Tag and the second column named Parent. These columns create a self-join in the resultset that is used to determine the hierarchy of the created XML file. Here's a relatively simple query in explicit mode:

```
SELECT 1 AS Tag, NULL AS Parent,
  Customers.CustomerID AS [Customer!1!CustomerID],
  Customers.CompanyName AS [Customer!1!CompanyName],
  NULL AS [Order!2!OrderID],
  NULL AS [Order!2!OrderDate]
  FROM Customers WHERE COUNTRY = 'Brazil'
UNION ALL
SELECT 2, 1,
  Customers.CustomerID, Customers.CompanyName,
```

```
Orders.OrderID, Orders.OrderDate
FROM Customers INNER JOIN Orders
ON Customers.CustomerID = Orders.CustomerID
WHERE Country = 'Brazil' AND
   OrderDate BETWEEN '1997-03-15' AND '1997-04-15'
ORDER BY [Customer!1!CustomerID], [Order!2!OrderID]
FOR XML EXPLICIT
```

The resulting XML from this query is as follows:

```
<Customer CustomerID="COMMI"
  CompanyName="Comércio Mineiro">
  <Order OrderID="10494"
     OrderDate="1997-04-02T00:00:00"/>
</Customer>
<Customer CustomerID="FAMIA"
  CompanyName="Familia Arquibaldo"/>
<Customer CustomerID="GOURL"
  CompanyName="Gourmet Lanchonetes"/>
<Customer CustomerID="HANAR"
   CompanyName="Hanari Carnes"/>
<Customer CustomerID="QUEDE"
   CompanyName="Que Delícia"/>
<Customer CustomerID="QUEEN"
   CompanyName="Queen Cozinha">
  <Order OrderID="10487"
      OrderDate="1997-03-26T00:00:00"/>
</Customer>
<Customer CustomerID="RICAR"
  CompanyName="Ricardo Adocicados">
  <Order OrderID="10481"
     OrderDate="1997-03-20T00:00:00"/>
</Customer>
<Customer CustomerID="TRADH"
  CompanyName="Tradição Hipermercados">
  <Order OrderID="10496"
      OrderDate="1997-04-04T00:00:00"/>
</Customer><Customer CustomerID="WELLI"
  CompanyName="Wellington Importadora"/>
```

Note that in this case even customers without orders in the specified time period are included, because the first half of the query retrieves all customers from Brazil. Explicit mode allows you the finest control over the generated XML, but it's also the most complex mode to use in practice. You should stick to raw or auto mode whenever possible.

Finally, you can generate schema information as part of a SQL Server query by including the XMLDATA option in the query. You can do this in any of the FOR XML modes. For example, here's a query you saw earlier in this section with the XMLDATA option added:

```
SELECT Customers.CustomerID, Customers.CompanyName,
  Orders.OrderID, Orders.OrderDate
```

```
FROM Customers INNER JOIN Orders
ON Customers.CustomerID = Orders.CustomerID
WHERE Country = 'Brazil' AND
  OrderDate BETWEEN '1997-03-15' AND '1997-04-15'
FOR XML AUTO, ELEMENTS, XMLDATA
```

The resulting XML is as follows:

```
<Schema name="Schema1"
  xmlns="urn:schemas-microsoft-com:xml-data"
  xmlns:dt="urn:schemas-microsoft-com:datatypes">
  <ElementType name="Customers" content="eltOnly"
    model="closed" order="many">
    <element type="Orders" maxOccurs="*"/>
    <element type="CustomerID"/>
    <element type="CompanyName"/>
  </ElementType>
  <ElementType name="CustomerID" content="textOnly"
    model="closed" dt:type="string"/>
  <ElementType name="CompanyName" content="textOnly"
    model="closed" dt:type="string"/>
  <ElementType name="Orders" content="eltOnly"
    model="closed" order="many">
    <element type="OrderID"/>
    <element type="OrderDate"/>
  </ElementType>
  <ElementType name="OrderID" content="textOnly"
    model="closed" dt:type="i4"/>
  <ElementType name="OrderDate" content="textOnly"
    model="closed" dt:type="dateTime"/>
</Schema>
<Customers xmlns="x-schema:#Schema1">
  <CustomerID>RICAR</CustomerID>
  <CompanyName>Ricardo Adocicados</CompanyName>
  <Orders>
    <OrderID>10481</OrderID>
    <OrderDate>1997-03-20T00:00:00</OrderDate>
  </Orders>
</Customers>
<Customers xmlns="x-schema:#Schema1">
  <CustomerID>QUEEN</CustomerID>
  <CompanyName>Queen Cozinha</CompanyName>
  <Orders>
    <OrderID>10487</OrderID>
    <OrderDate>1997-03-26T00:00:00</OrderDate>
  </Orders>
</Customers>
<Customers xmlns="x-schema:#Schema1">
  <CustomerID>COMMI</CustomerID>
  <CompanyName>Comércio Mineiro</CompanyName>
  <Orders>
    <OrderID>10494</OrderID>
    <OrderDate>1997-04-02T00:00:00</OrderDate>
  </Orders>
</Customers>
<Customers xmlns="x-schema:#Schema1">
```

```
      <CustomerID>TRADH</CustomerID>
      <CompanyName>Tradição Hipermercados</CompanyName>
      <Orders>
        <OrderID>10496</OrderID>
        <OrderDate>1997-04-04T00:00:00</OrderDate>
      </Orders>
    </Customers>
```

Using `ExecuteXmlReader()` Method

ADO.NET provides a means to integrate SQL Server's XML capabilities with the .NET Framework classes. The `ExecuteXmlReader()` method of the `SqlCommand` object enables you to retrieve an `XmlReader` directly from a SQL statement, provided that the SQL statement uses the `FOR XML` clause. Step-by-Step 2.15 shows you how.

STEP BY STEP

2.15 Using the `ExecuteXmlReader()` Method

1. Add a new form to the project. Name the new form `StepByStep2_15.cs`.

2. Add a `Button` control (`btnReadXml`) and a `ListBox` control (`lbNodes`) to the form.

3. Open Server explorer. Expand the Data Connections node and locate a node that represents the Northwind sample database from a SQL Server. Drag and drop the node to the form to create a `SqlConnection` object.

4. Switch to code view and add the following using directives:

```
using System.Text;
using System.Xml;
using System.Data;
using System.Data.SqlClient;
```

5. Double-click the `Button` control and add the following code to handle the button's `Click` event:

```
private void btnReadXML_Click(
    object sender, System.EventArgs e)
{
    SqlCommand cmd = sqlConnection1.CreateCommand();
    // Create a command to retrieve XML
```

```
cmd.CommandType = CommandType.Text;
cmd.CommandText = "SELECT Customers.CustomerID, "
+ "Customers.CompanyName," +
"Orders.OrderID, Orders.OrderDate " +
"FROM Customers INNER JOIN Orders " +
"ON Customers.CustomerID = Orders.CustomerID " +
"WHERE Country = 'Brazil' AND " +
"OrderDate BETWEEN '1997-03-15' AND '1997-04-15' "
+ "FOR XML AUTO, ELEMENTS";
sqlConnection1.Open();

// Read the XML into an XmlReader
XmlReader xr = cmd.ExecuteXmlReader();
StringBuilder sbNode = new StringBuilder();

// Dump the contents of the reader
while(xr.Read())
{
    if((xr.NodeType == XmlNodeType.Element) ||
        (xr.NodeType == XmlNodeType.Text) )
    {
        sbNode.Length = 0;
        for(int intI=1;
            intI <= xr.Depth ; intI++)
        {
            sbNode.Append(" ");
        }
        sbNode.Append(xr.Name + " ");
        sbNode.Append(xr.NodeType.ToString());

        if (xr.HasValue)
        {
            sbNode.Append(": " + xr.Value);
        }
        lbNodes.Items.Add(sbNode.ToString());

        // Now add the attributes, if any
        if (xr.HasAttributes)
        {
            while(xr.MoveToNextAttribute())
            {
                sbNode.Length=0;
                for(int intI=1;
                    intI <= xr.Depth;intI++)
                {
                    sbNode.Append(" ");
                }
                sbNode.Append(xr.Name + " ");
                sbNode.Append(
                    xr.NodeType.ToString());
                if (xr.HasValue)
                {
                    sbNode.Append(": " +
                        xr.Value);
```

WARNING

Close the XmlReader Object When you populate an XmlReader object with the ExecuteXmlReader() method, the XmlReader object gets exclusive use of the underlying SqlConnection object. You cannot perform any other operations through this SqlConnection object until you call the Close() method of the XmlReader object. Be sure to call the Close() method as soon as you are finished with the XmlReader object.

continues

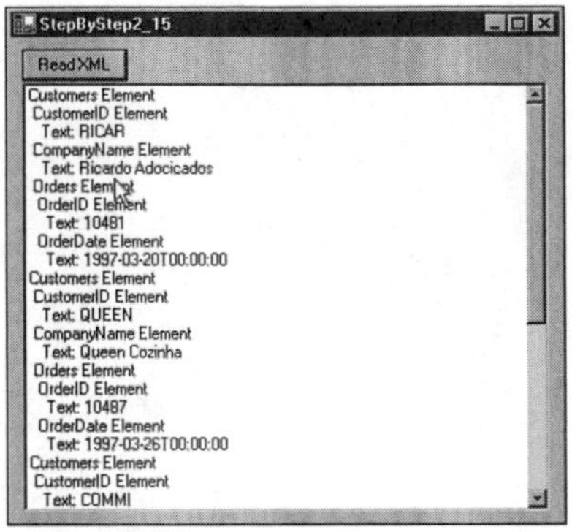

FIGURE 2.15
You can retrieve data as XML from a SQL Server database by using the `ExecuteXmlReader()` method.

continued

```
            }
            lbNodes.Items.Add(
                sbNode.ToString());
          }
        }
      }
    }
    // Clean up
    xr.Close();
    sqlConnection1.Close();
}
```

6. Insert the `Main()` method to launch the form. Set the form as the startup form for the project.

7. Run the project. Click the button to run the `FOR XML` query and display the results in the `ListBox` control, as shown in Figure 2.15.

> **WARNING**
>
> **Not a Valid Document** It's tempting to think that you can read an `XmlDocument` object directly from the `XmlReader` object returned by the `ExecuteXmlReader()` method. Unfortunately, if you try this you'll find that it generates an error. This is because the XML returned by `FOR XML` queries is well-formed, but it lacks an XML declaration and a root node, and is therefore an XML fragment and not a valid XML document.

Updating SQL Server Data by Using XML

Access and Manipulate XML Data: Update a SQL Server database by using XML.

You can also update SQL Server data by using special XML messages called DiffGrams. The .NET Framework uses DiffGrams internally as a means of serializing changes in a `DataSet` object. For example, if you pass the changes in a `DataSet` object from one tier to another, the .NET Framework uses a DiffGram to send the changes.

You can also use DiffGrams yourself to update data in SQL Server. However, before you can do so, you need to install some additional software. This software is the SQLXML Managed Classes, an interface between SQL Server and the .NET Framework. In this section, you learn how to install this software and then how to use DiffGrams to modify SQL Server data.

Installing SQLXML

Although SQL Server 2000 includes some XML support (for example, the FOR XML syntax is built into the product) there have been many advances in XML since that version of SQL Server was released. Microsoft has kept SQL Server in tune with these advances by issuing a series of free upgrade packages with the general name of SQLXML. As of this writing, the current release of SQLXML is SQLXML 3.0 SP1. This package includes the following features:

▶ A direct SOAP interface so that SQL Server can work with Web services without intervening components.

▶ XML views via XSD schemas.

▶ Client-side FOR XML support.

▶ An OLE DB provider for SQL XML data.

▶ Managed classes to expose SQLXML functionality in the .NET environment.

▶ Support for DiffGrams generated by .NET.

To install SQLXML, you need to download the current release directly from Microsoft's web site. You can always find the current release by starting at the SQLXML home page, msdn.microsoft.com/nhp/default.asp?contentid=28001300. Before you run the installation, be sure you have the following prerequisite software installed:

▶ Windows Installer 2.0

▶ Microsoft SOAP Toolkit 2.0 SP2

▶ SQL Server 2000 Client Tools

▶ MDAC 2.6 or later

▶ .NET Framework 1.0 or later.

SQLXML 3.0 also depends on release 4.0 of the MSXML parser. If this component is not present on your computer, it will be installed as part of the SQLXML installation.

To install SQLXML, download and run the executable. You can either choose to install all components, or select specific components to install.

Using DiffGrams

After you've installed SQLXML, you can use the `SqlXmlCommand`
object to execute a DiffGram, as shown in Step-by-Step 2.16.

STEP BY STEP

2.16 Executing a DiffGram

1. Add a new form to the project. Name the new form
`StepByStep2_16.cs`.

2. Add a `Button` control (`btnUpdate`) to the form.

3. In Solution Explorer, right-click on the References node
and select Add Reference. Select the .NET tab and click
the Browse button. Browse to the SQLXML .NET library.
By default this file is at `c:\Program Files\SQLXML`
`3.0\bin\Microsoft.Data.SqlXml.dll`. Click Open and
then OK to add the reference.

4. Switch to code view and add the following using directives:

```
using Microsoft.Data.SqlXml;
using System.IO;
```

5. Double-click the `Button` control and add code to execute a
DiffGram when you click the button. If your server
requires you to log in with a username and password,
modify the connection string accordingly:

```
private void btnUpdate_Click(
    object sender, System.EventArgs e)
{
    // Connect to the SQL Server database
    SqlXmlCommand sxc =
        new SqlXmlCommand("Provider=SQLOLEDB;" +
        "Server=(local);database=Northwind;" +
        "Integrated Security=SSPI");
    // Set up the DiffGram
    sxc.CommandType = SqlXmlCommandType.DiffGram;
    sxc.SchemaPath = @"..\..\diffgram.xsd";
    FileStream fs =
        new FileStream(@"..\..\diffgram.xml",
        FileMode.Open);
    sxc.CommandStream = fs;
```

```
    try
    {
        // And execute it
        sxc.ExecuteNonQuery();
        MessageBox.Show("Database was updated!");
    }
    catch (SqlXmlException ex)
    {
        ex.ErrorStream.Position = 0;
        string strErr = (new StreamReader(
            ex.ErrorStream).ReadToEnd());
        MessageBox.Show(strErr);
    }
    catch (Exception ex)
    {
        MessageBox.Show(ex.Message);
    }
    finally
    {
        fs.Close();
    }
}
```

6. Add a new XML file to the project. Name the new file `diffgram.xml`. Modify the XML for `diffgram.xml` as follows:

```xml
<?xml version="1.0" standalone="yes"?>
<diffgr:diffgram
  xmlns:msdata="urn:schemas-microsoft-com:xml-msdata"
  xmlns:diffgr=
  "urn:schemas-microsoft-com:xml-diffgram-v1">
  <NewDataSet>
    <Customers diffgr:id="Customers1"
     msdata:rowOrder="0"
     diffgr:hasChanges="modified">
      <CustomerID>ALFKI</CustomerID>
      <ContactName>Maria Anderson</ContactName>
    </Customers>
  </NewDataSet>
  <diffgr:before>
    <Customers diffgr:id="Customers1"
      msdata:rowOrder="0">
      <CustomerID>ALFKI</CustomerID>
      <ContactName>Maria Anders</ContactName>
    </Customers>
  </diffgr:before>
</diffgr:diffgram>
```

7. Add a new schema file to the project. Name the new file `diffgram.xsd`. Switch to XML view and modify the XML for this file as follows:

continues

continued

```xml
<xsd:schema xmlns:xsd=
 "http://www.w3.org/2001/XMLSchema"
 xmlns:sql="urn:schemas-microsoft-com:mapping-schema">
  <xsd:element name="Customers"
      sql:relation="Customers" >
   <xsd:complexType>
     <xsd:sequence>
        <xsd:element name="CustomerID"
            sql:field="CustomerID"
            type="xsd:string" />
        <xsd:element name="ContactName"
            sql:field="ContactName"
            type="xsd:string" />
     </xsd:sequence>
   </xsd:complexType>
  </xsd:element>
</xsd:schema>
```

8. Insert the `Main()` method to launch the form. Set the form as the startup form for the project.

9. Run the project. Click the button to update your SQL Server Northwind database. You can verify that the update worked by running a `SELECT` query in SQL Query Analyzer, as shown in Figure 2.16.

FIGURE 2.16
You can use the `SqlXmlCommand` object to apply DiffGrams to a SQL Server database.

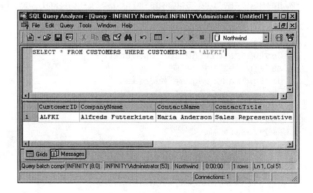

You can think of a DiffGram as a before-and-after snapshot of a part of a SQL Server table. In this case, the first part of the XML file lists a row in the `Customers` table and indicates that it has been modified.

The second part of the DiffGram contains the original data from the SQL Server table. SQL Server can use this data to find the row to be modified.

In addition to the DiffGram, this code requires a schema file that maps the element names in the DiffGram back to tables and columns in the SQL Server database. The `sql:relation` attribute in the schema file indicates the table mapping, whereas the `sql:field` attributes indicate the field mappings.

DiffGrams can insert or delete data as well as modify data. For an insertion, the DiffGram contains the data for the new row and no old data. For a deletion, the DiffGram contains the row to be deleted but no new row.

For more information on the DiffGram format, refer to the help files that are installed as a part of the SQLXML package.

REVIEW BREAK

▶ The `FOR XML` clause in the SQL Server `SELECT` statement lets you generate XML documents directly from SQL Server data.

▶ By choosing appropriate options in `FOR XML`, you can map SQL Server columns as either attributes or elements in the generated XML. You can also choose whether to use Base64 encoding in binary columns, and whether to embed schema information.

▶ You can use the `ExecuteXmlReader()` method of the `SqlCommand` object to retrieve XML from a SQL Server database and assign it to classes within the .NET Framework.

▶ The SQLXML package contains XML-related updates for SQL Server 2000.

▶ You can use DiffGrams to package updates to SQL Server tables as XML files. The `SqlXmlCommand` object can apply DiffGrams to a SQL Server database.

GUIDED PRACTICE EXERCISE 2.2

The SQLXML Managed Classes allow some additional flexibility in retrieving XML data from SQL Server to the .NET Framework classes. The key factor is that the `SqlXmlCommand` object includes a `RootTag` property. This property enables you to specify a root element to be included in the generated XML.

For this exercise, you'll use a `SqlXmlCommand` object to retrieve the results of a `FOR XML` query from a SQL Server database. You should load the results into an `XmlDocument` object and then display the contents of that object.

Try this on your own first. If you get stuck or would like to see one possible solution, follow the steps below.

1. Add a new form to the project. Name the new form `GuidedPracticeExercise2_2.cs`.

2. Add a `Button` control (`btnReadXml`) and a `ListBox` control (`lbNodes`) to the form.

3. Switch to code view and add the following using directives:
   ```
   using Microsoft.Data.SqlXml;
   using System.Xml;
   ```

4. You need the `Utility.cs` class created in Step-by-Step 2.5, so create it now if you didn't already create it.

5. Double-click the button control and add code to read XML from the SQL Server when you click the button:
   ```
   private void btnReadXML_Click(
       object sender, System.EventArgs e)
   {
       // Connect to the SQL Server database
       SqlXmlCommand sxc =
           new SqlXmlCommand("Provider=SQLOLEDB;" +
           "Server=(local);database=Northwind;" +
           "Integrated Security=SSPI");
       sxc.CommandType = SqlXmlCommandType.Sql;
       sxc.CommandText =
           "SELECT Customers.CustomerID, " +
           "Customers.CompanyName," +
           "Orders.OrderID, Orders.OrderDate " +
           "FROM Customers INNER JOIN Orders " +
           "ON Customers.CustomerID = Orders.CustomerID "
           + "WHERE Country = 'Brazil' AND " +
   ```

```
            "OrderDate BETWEEN '1997-03-15' " +
            "AND '1997-04-15' FOR XML AUTO, ELEMENTS";
    sxc.RootTag = "dataroot";
    // Read the XML into an XmlReader
    XmlReader xr = sxc.ExecuteXmlReader();
    XmlDocument xd = new XmlDocument();
    xd.Load(xr);
    Utility u = new Utility();
    u.XmlToListBox(xd, lbNodes);
    xr.Close();
}
```

6. Insert the `Main()` method to launch the form. Set the form as the startup object for the project.

7. Run the project. Click the button to run the `FOR XML` query and display the results in the `ListBox` control, as shown in Figure 2.17.

FIGURE 2.17
You can specify a root element for retrieved XML data from the SQL Server database by using the `RootTag` property of the `SqlXmlCommand` object.

CHAPTER SUMMARY

Extensible Markup Language (XML) is pervasive in the .NET Framework. It's used to pass messages between components, and as the serialization and configuration language for .NET, among other things. As you'd expect, the .NET Framework includes a rich set of classes for working with XML.

In this chapter you learned about some of the main classes in the `System.Xml` namespace and associated namespaces such as `System.Xml.Schema` and `System.Xml.XPath`. You learned how the Document Object Model (DOM) is used to represent an XML document as a tree of nodes. (Like many other parts of XML, the DOM is an official standard of the World Wide Web Consortium, better known as the W3C.) You saw how the `XmlReader` class gives you forward-only, read-only access to XML documents, and how the `XmlNode` and `XmlDocument` objects can be used to manipulate the DOM version of an XML document.

You learned about the `XmlDataDocument` class, which provides two-way synchronization between an XML document and the equivalent `DataSet` object. You saw how you could create such a synchronized hierarchical and relational view of your data by starting with either an XML document or an existing `DataSet` object.

KEY TERMS

- DiffGram
- DOM (Document Object Model)
- DTD
- valid XML document
- W3C (World Wide Web Consortium)
- well-formed XML document
- XPath

CHAPTER SUMMARY

This chapter also introduced the basic syntax of the XPath query language, which lets you address parts of an XML document. You learned how to use XPath in conjunction with the `XPathNavigator` class to select nodes of an XML document. You also learned how the `XPathNavigator` class provides random access to the nodes in the DOM representation of an XML document.

You explored XML schemas in a bit more depth, learning how to create a schema from an existing XML file. I also introduced the concept of XML validation, and showed you how to use the `XmlValidatingReader` class to validate an XML document.

Finally, you learned how to use XML to communicate with a Microsoft SQL Server database. You saw the syntax of the `FOR XML` clause of the T-SQL `SELECT` statement, which allows you to extract information from a SQL Server database directly as XML. You also learned about DiffGrams and saw how to use the SQLXML managed classes to execute a DiffGram on a SQL Server database.

APPLY YOUR KNOWLEDGE

Exercises

2.1 Compiling XPath Expressions

The .NET Framework developers invested a lot of
effort in finding ways to make code more efficient.
One performance enhancement in evaluating XPath
expressions is the capability to precompile an expression for reuse. This exercise shows you how to use the
`Compile()` method of the `XPathNavigator` class to create
a precompiled XPath expression, represented as an
`XPathExpression` object.

Estimated Time: 15 minutes.

1. Create a new Visual C# .NET project to use for
   the exercises in this chapter.

2. Add a new XML file to the project. Name the
   new file `Books1.xml`. Modify the XML for
   `Books1.xml` as follows:

```xml
<?xml version="1.0" encoding="UTF-8"?>
<Books>
    <Book Pages="1088">
        <Author>Delaney, Kalen</Author>
        <Title>
            Inside Microsoft SQL Server 2000
        </Title>
        <Publisher>Microsoft Press
        </Publisher>
    </Book>
    <Book Pages="997">
        <Author>Burton, Kevin</Author>
        <Title>.NET Common Language Runtime
        </Title>
        <Publisher>Sams</Publisher>
    </Book>
    <Book Pages="392">
        <Author>Cooper, James W.</Author>
        <Title>C# Design Patterns</Title>
        <Publisher>Addison Wesley
        </Publisher>
    </Book>
</Books>
```

3. Add a new XML file to the project. Name the
   new file `Books2.xml`. Modify the XML for
   `Books2.xml` as follows:

```xml
<?xml version="1.0" encoding="UTF-8" ?>
<Books>
    <Book Pages="792">
        <Author>LaMacchia, Brian A.
        </Author>
        <Title>.NET Framework Security
        </Title>
        <Publisher>Addison Wesley
        </Publisher>
    </Book>
    <Book Pages="383">
        <Author>Bischof Brian</Author>
        <Title>The .NET Languages:
          A Quick Translation Guide</Title>
        <Publisher>Apress</Publisher>
    </Book>
    <Book Pages="196">
        <Author>Simpson, John E.</Author>
        <Title>XPath and XPointer</Title>
        <Publisher>O'Reilly</Publisher>
    </Book>
</Books>
```

4. Add a new form to the project. Name the new
   form `Exercise2_1.cs`.

5. Add a `Label` control, a `TextBox` control
   (`txtXPath`), a `Button` control (`btnEvaluate`), and a
   `ListBox` control (`lbNodes`) to the form.

6. Switch to code view and add the following using
   directive:

```
using System.Xml.XPath;
```

7. Double-click the `Button` control and add code to
   handle the button's `Click` event:

```csharp
private void btnEvaluate_Click(
    object sender, System.EventArgs e)
{
    // Load the Books1.xml file
    XPathDocument xpd1 =
        new XPathDocument(
        @"..\..\Books1.xml");
```

APPLY YOUR KNOWLEDGE

```
// Get the associated navigator
XPathNavigator xpn1 =
    xpd1.CreateNavigator();
// Precompile an XPath expression
XPathExpression xpe =
    xpn1.Compile(txtXPath.Text);
// Retrieve nodes to match
// the expression
XPathNodeIterator xpni =
    xpn1.Select(xpe);
// And dump the results
lbNodes.Items.Clear();
lbNodes.Items.Add(
    "Results from Books1.xml:");
// Load the Books1.xml file

while(xpni.MoveNext())
{
    lbNodes.Items.Add("   " +
    xpni.Current.NodeType.ToString() +
    ": " + xpni.Current.Name + " = " +
    xpni.Current.Value);
}

// Now get the second document
XPathDocument xpd2 =
    new XPathDocument(
    @"..\..\Books2.xml");
// Get the associated navigator
XPathNavigator xpn2 =
    xpd2.CreateNavigator();
// Retrieve nodes to match
// the expression
// Reuse the precompiled expression
xpni = xpn2.Select(xpe);
// And dump the results
lbNodes.Items.Add(
    "Results from Books2.xml:");
while (xpni.MoveNext())
{
    lbNodes.Items.Add("   " +
    xpni.Current.NodeType.ToString() +
    ": " + xpni.Current.Name + " = " +
        xpni.Current.Value);
}
}
```

8. Insert the `Main()` method to launch the form. Set the form as the startup form for the project.

9. Run the project. Enter an XPath expression and click the button. The code precompiles the expression and then uses the precompiled version to select nodes from each of the two XML files, as shown in Figure 2.18.

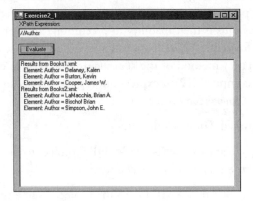

FIGURE 2.18
The `Compile()` method of the `XPathNavigator` class allows you to create a precompiled XPath expression.

2.2 Creating DiffGrams

If you'd like to experiment with the DiffGram format, you don't have to create DiffGrams by hand. You can use the `WriteXml()` method of the `DataSet` object to create a DiffGram containing all the changes made since the `DataSet` object was initialized. This exercise walks you through the process of creating a DiffGram.

Estimated Time: 15 minutes.

1. Add a new form to the project. Name the new form `Exercise2_2.cs`.

2. Add a `DataGrid` control (`dgProducts`) and a `Button` control (`btnWriteDiffGram`) to the form.

3. Expand the Server Explorer tree view to show a Data Connection to the Northwind sample database. Drag and drop the connection to the form.

4. Drag a `SaveFileDialog` component from the Toolbox and drop it on the form. Set the `FileName` property of the component to `diffgram.xml`.

5. Switch to code view and add the following `using` directive:

```
using System.Data;
using System.Data.SqlClient;
```

6. Add the following `DataSet` declaration to the class definition:

```
DataSet dsProducts = new DataSet();
```

7. Double-click the form and add the following code to handle the form's `Load` event:

```
private void Exercise2_2_Load(
    object sender, System.EventArgs e)
{
    // Create a command to retrieve data
    SqlCommand cmd =
        sqlConnection1.CreateCommand();
    cmd.CommandType = CommandType.Text;
    cmd.CommandText =
        "SELECT * FROM Products " +
        "WHERE CategoryID = 6";
    // Retrieve the data to the DataSet
    SqlDataAdapter da =
        new SqlDataAdapter();
    da.SelectCommand = cmd;
    da.Fill(dsProducts, "Products");
    // Bind it to the user interface
    dgProducts.DataSource = dsProducts;
    dgProducts.DataMember = "Products";
}
```

8. Double-click the button and add the following code to handle the button's `Click` event:

```
private void btnWriteDiffGram_Click(
    object sender, System.EventArgs e)
{
```

```
    // Prompt for a filename
    saveFileDialog1.ShowDialog();
    // Write out the DiffGram
    dsProducts.WriteXml(
        saveFileDialog1.FileName,
        XmlWriteMode.DiffGram);
}
```

9. Insert the `Main()` method to launch the form. Set the form as the startup form for the project.

10. Run the project. The form displays records from the Northwind Products table for the selected category ID. Make some changes to the data; you can use the DataGrid to add, edit, or delete records. Click the button and select a name for the DiffGram. Click the Write DiffGram button to create the DiffGram. Open the new DiffGram in a text editor and inspect it to see how your changes are represented.

2.3 Using XPath with Relational Data

By combining an XML-synchronized `DataSet` object with an XPath expression, you can use XPath to select information from a relational database. This exercise shows you how you can use a `DataSet` object, an `XmlDataDocument` object, and an `XPathNavigator` object together.

Estimated Time: 25 minutes.

1. Add a new form to the project. Name the new form `Exercise2_3.cs`.

2. Add two `Label` controls, two `TextBox` controls (`txtSQLStatement` and `txtXPath`), two `Button` controls (`btnCreateDataSet` and `btnSelectNodes`), and a `ListBox` control (`lbNodes`) to the form.

3. Expand the Server Explorer tree view to show a data connection to the Northwind sample database. Drag and drop the connection to the form.

APPLY YOUR KNOWLEDGE

4. Switch to code view and add the following using directives:

```
using System.Data;
using System.Data.SqlClient;
using System.Xml;
using System.Xml.XPath;
```

5. Add the following code to the class definition:

```
DataSet ds;
XmlDataDocument xdd;
```

6. Double-click the Create DataSet button and enter code to load a DataSet object and an XmlDataDocument object:

```
private void btnCreateDataSet_Click(
    object sender, System.EventArgs e)
{
    // Create a command to retrieve data
    SqlCommand cmd =
        sqlConnection1.CreateCommand();
    cmd.CommandType = CommandType.Text;
    cmd.CommandText = txtSQLStatement.Text;
    // Retrieve the data to the DataSet
    SqlDataAdapter da =
        new SqlDataAdapter();
    da.SelectCommand = cmd;
    ds = new DataSet();
    da.Fill(ds, "Table1");
    // Retrieve the XML form of the Dataset
    xdd = new XmlDataDocument(ds);
}
```

7. Double-click the Select Nodes button and enter code to evaluate the XPath expression:

```
private void btnSelectNodes_Click(
    object sender, System.EventArgs e)
{
    // Get the associated navigator
    XPathNavigator xpn =
        xdd.CreateNavigator();
    // Retrieve nodes to match
    // the expression
    XPathNodeIterator xpni =
        xpn.Select(txtXPath.Text);
    // And dump the results
    lbNodes.Items.Clear();
    while (xpni.MoveNext())
    {
```

```
        lbNodes.Items.Add(
            xpni.Current.NodeType.ToString()
            + ": " + xpni.Current.Name +
            " = " + xpni.Current.Value);
    }
}
```

8. Insert the Main() method to launch the form. Set the form as the startup form for the project.

9. Run the project. Enter a SQL Statement that retrieves rows and click the first button. Then enter an XPath expression and click the second button. You'll see the XPath query results as a set of XML nodes, as shown in Figure 2.19.

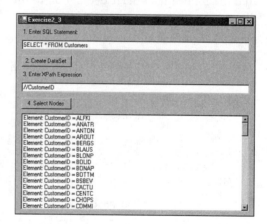

FIGURE 2.19
You can use XPath with an XmlDataDocument object.

Review Questions

1. How are XML elements and attributes represented in the DOM?

2. When should you use an XmlTextReader object by itself rather than with an XmlDocument object?

3. Explain three ways to synchronize an XmlDataDocument object with a DataSet object.

APPLY YOUR KNOWLEDGE

4. Why should you use an explicit path rather than a documentwide wildcard in an XPath expression?

5. What is the difference between the XPath expressions /Customers/Customer/Order[1] and (/Customers/Customer/Order)[1]?

6. How can you instantiate an XPathNavigator object?

7. What options are there for validating an XML file with the XmlValidatingReader object?

8. What are the three main variants of the FOR XML clause in T-SQL?

9. How can you generate schema information with the FOR XML clause in T-SQL?

10. What data operations can be represented in a DiffGram?

Exam Questions

1. Your application contains an XML file, Orders.xml, with the following content:

```
<?xml version="1.0" encoding="utf-8" ?>
<Orders>
  <Order OrderID="1">
    <OrderDate>1/1/2003</OrderDate>
  </Order>
  <Order OrderID="2">
    <OrderDate>1/2/2003</OrderDate>
  </Order>
  <Order OrderID="3">
    <OrderDate>1/3/2003</OrderDate>
  </Order>
</Orders>
```

Your application also contains a form with a Button control named btnProcess and a ListBox control named lbNodes. The Click event handler for the Button control has this code:

```
private void btnProcess_Click(
    object sender, System.EventArgs e)
{
    XmlTextReader xtr = new
        XmlTextReader(@"..\..\Orders.xml");
    while(xtr.Read())
    {
        if ((xtr.NodeType ==
                XmlNodeType.Attribute)
            || (xtr.NodeType ==
                XmlNodeType.Element)
            || (xtr.NodeType ==
                XmlNodeType.Text))
        {
            if(xtr.HasValue)
                lbNodes.Items.Add(xtr.Value);
        }
    }
    xtr.Close();
}
```

What will be the contents of the ListBox control after you click the button?

A.
```
1
1/1/2003
2
1/2/2003
3
1/3/2003
```

B.
```
1
2
3
```

C.
```
Orders
Order
1/1/2003
Order
1/2/2003
Order
1/3/2003
```

D.
```
1/1/2003
1/2/2003
1/3/2003
```

APPLY YOUR KNOWLEDGE

2. Your application contains the following XML file:

```
<?xml version="1.0" encoding="utf-8" ?>
<Orders>
  <Order OrderID="1">
    <OrderDate>1/1/2003</OrderDate>
  </Order>
  <Order OrderID="2">
    <OrderDate>1/2/2003</OrderDate>
  </Order>
  <Order OrderID="3">
    <OrderDate>1/3/2003</OrderDate>
  </Order>
</Orders>
```

Your application uses the ReadXmlSchema() method of the DataSet object to create a DataSet object with an appropriate schema for this XML file. Which of the following mappings between XML entities and DataSet object entities will this method create?

A. Orders and Order will become DataTable objects. OrderID will become a DataColumn object. OrderDate will not be mapped.

B. Orders and Order will become DataTable objects. OrderID and OrderDate will become DataColumn objects.

C. Orders and Order will become DataTable objects. OrderDate will become a DataColumn. OrderID will not be mapped.

D. Orders will become a DataTable. Order and OrderDate will become DataColumn objects.

3. Your application includes an XML file that represents inventory in a warehouse. Each inventory item is identified by 50 different elements. You need to work with 4 of these elements on a DataGrid control. You plan to create a DataSet object containing the appropriate data that can be bound to the DataGrid control. How should you proceed?

A. Load the XML file into an XmlDocument object. Create a DataSet object containing a single DataTable object with the desired column. Write code that loops through the nodes in the XmlDocument object and that transfers the data from the appropriate nodes to the DataSet object.

B. Load the XML file into an XmlDataDocument object. Retrieve the DataSet object from the XmlDataDocument object's DataSet property.

C. Load the XML file into a DataSet object by calling the DataSet object's ReadXml() method.

D. Create a schema that includes the four required elements. Create a DataSet object from this schema. Create an XmlDataDocument object from the DataSet object. Load the XML document into the XmlDataDocument object.

4. You use a SqlDataAdapter object to fill a DataSet object with the contents of the Customers table in your database. The CompanyName of the first customer is "Biggs Industries". You synchronize an XmlDataDocument object with the DataSet object. In the DataSet object, you change the CompanyName of the first customer to "Biggs Limited". After that, in the XmlDataDocument, you change the value of the corresponding node to "Biggs Co." When you call the Update() method of the SqlDataAdapter object, what is the effect?

A. The CompanyName in the database remains "Biggs Industries".

B. The CompanyName in the database is changed to "Biggs Limited".

C. The `CompanyName` in the database is changed to "Biggs Co."

D. A record locking error is thrown.

5. Your application contains the following XML file:

```
<?xml version="1.0" encoding="utf-8" ?>
<Customers>
  <Customer>
    <CustomerName>A Company</CustomerName>
    <Orders>
      <Order OrderID="1">
        <OrderDate>1/1/2003</OrderDate>
      </Order>
      <Order OrderID="2">
        <OrderDate>1/2/2003</OrderDate>
      </Order>
    </Orders>
  </Customer>
  <Customer>
    <CustomerName>B Company</CustomerName>
    <Orders>
      <Order OrderID="3">
        <OrderDate>1/2/2003</OrderDate>
      </Order>
      <Order OrderID="4">
        <OrderDate>1/3/2003</OrderDate>
      </Order>
    </Orders>
  </Customer>
  <Customer>
    <CustomerName>C Company</CustomerName>
    <Orders>
      <Order OrderID="5">
        <OrderDate>1/4/2003</OrderDate>
      </Order>
      <Order OrderID="6">
        <OrderDate>1/5/2003</OrderDate>
      </Order>
    </Orders>
  </Customer>
</Customers>
```

Which XPath expression will return the first `OrderID` for each customer?

A. `/Customers/Customer/Orders/Order/`
   `@OrderID[1]`

B. `(/Customers/Customer/Orders/`
   `Order)[1]/@OrderID`

C. `/Customers/Customer/Orders/Order[1]/`
   `@OrderID`

D. `(/Customers/Customer/Orders/Order/`
   `@OrderID)[1]`

6. Your application contains the following XML file:

```
<?xml version="1.0" encoding="utf-8" ?>
<Customers>
  <Customer>
    <CustomerName>A Company</CustomerName>
    <Orders>
      <Order OrderID="1">
        <OrderDate>1/1/2003</OrderDate>
      </Order>
      <Order OrderID="2">
        <OrderDate>1/2/2003</OrderDate>
      </Order>
    </Orders>
  </Customer>
  <Customer>
    <CustomerName>B Company</CustomerName>
    <Orders>
      <Order OrderID="3">
        <OrderDate>1/2/2003</OrderDate>
      </Order>
      <Order OrderID="4">
        <OrderDate>1/3/2003</OrderDate>
      </Order>
    </Orders>
  </Customer>
  <Customer>
    <CustomerName>C Company</CustomerName>
    <Orders>
      <Order OrderID="5">
        <OrderDate>1/4/2003</OrderDate>
      </Order>
      <Order OrderID="6">
        <OrderDate>1/5/2003</OrderDate>
      </Order>
    </Orders>
  </Customer>
</Customers>
```

Which XPath expression will return the `CustomerName` for all customers who placed an order on 1/3/2003?

APPLY YOUR KNOWLEDGE

A. `/Customers/Customer[./Orders/Order/ OrderDate="1/3/2003"]/CustomerName`

B. `/Customers/Customer[/Orders/Order/ OrderDate="1/3/2003"]/CustomerName`

C. `/Customers/Customer[//Orders/Order/ OrderDate="1/3/2003"]/CustomerName`

D. `/Customers[Orders/Order/ OrderDate="1/3/2003"]/CustomerName`

7. Your application allows the user to perform arbitrary XPath queries on an XML document. The user does not need to be able to alter the document. Which approach will give you the maximum performance for these requirements?

A. Read the document into an `XmlDocument` object. Use the `CreateNavigator()` method of the `XmlDocument` object to return an `XPathNavigator` object. Perform your queries by using the `XPathNavigator` object.

B. Read the document into an `XmlDataDocument` object. Use the `DataSet` property of the `XmlDataDocument` object to return a `DataSet` object. Perform your queries by using the `DataSet` object.

C. Read the document into an `XmlDataDocument` object. Use the `CreateNavigator()` method of the `XmlDataDocument` object to return an `XPathNavigator` object. Perform your queries by using the `XPathNavigator` object.

D. Read the document into an `XPathDocument` object. Use the `CreateNavigator()` method of the `XPathDocument` object to return an `XPathNavigator` object. Perform your queries by using the `XPathNavigator` object.

8. You are designing an application that will enable the user to explore the structure of an XML file. You need to allow the user to move to the parent node, next node, or first child node from the current node. Which object should you use to implement this requirement?

A. `XPathNavigator`

B. `XmlReader`

C. `XmlTextReader`

D. `XPathExpression`

9. Your XML document has an inline schema. What is the minimum number of errors that this document will generate if you validate it with the `XmlValidatingReader` class?

A. 0

B. 1

C. 2

D. 3

10. You are retrieving customer data from a SQL Server database into an XML document. You want the `CustomerName` and `ContactName` columns to be translated into XML elements. Which clause should you use in your SQL statement?

A. `FOR XML AUTO`

B. `FOR XML RAW`

C. `FOR XML EXPLICIT`

D. `FOR XML AUTO, XMLDATA`

11. Your application contains the following code:

```
private void btnReadXML_Click(
    object sender, System.EventArgs e)
{
```

APPLY YOUR KNOWLEDGE

```
// Create a command to retrieve XML
SqlCommand sc =
    SqlConnection1.CreateCommand();
sc.CommandType = SqlCommandType.Text;
sc.CommandText =
  "SELECT Customers.CustomerID, " +
  "Customers.CompanyName," +
  "Orders.OrderID, Orders.OrderDate " +
  "FROM Customers INNER JOIN Orders " +
  "ON Customers.CustomerID = " +
  "Orders.CustomerID "
  + "WHERE Country = 'Brazil' AND " +
  "OrderDate BETWEEN '1997-03-15' " +
  "AND '1997-04-15' " +
  "FOR XML AUTO, ELEMENTS";
// Read the XML into an XmlReader
XmlReader xr = sc.ExecuteXmlReader();
XmlDocument xd = new XmlDocument();
xd.Load(xr);
}
```

When you run this code, you receive an error on the line of code that attempts to load the XmlDocument. What can you do to fix the problem?

A. Use FOR XML RAW instead of FOR XML AUTO in the SQL statement.

B. Replace the XmlDocument object with an XmlDataDocument object.

C. Replace the SqlCommand object with a SqlXmlCommand object.

D. Replace the XmlReader object with an XmlTextReader object.

12. Your application contains the following code, which uses the SQLXML managed classes to apply a DiffGram to a SQL Server database:

```
private void btnUpdate_Click(
    object sender, System.EventArgs e)
{
    // Connect to the SQL Server database
    SqlXmlCommand sxc =
     new SqlXmlCommand(
```

```
      "Provider=SQLOLEDB;" +
      "Server=(local);database=Northwind;" +
      "Integrated Security=SSPI");

    // Set up the DiffGram
    sxc.CommandType =
        SqlXmlCommandType.DiffGram;
    FileStream fs =
     new FileStream(@"..\..\diffgram.xml",
        FileMode.Open);
    sxc.CommandStream = fs;
    // And execute it
    sxc.ExecuteNonQuery();
    MessageBox.Show(
        "Database was updated!");
}
```

When you run the code, it does not update the database. The DiffGram is properly formatted. What should you do to correct this problem?

A. Use a SqlCommand object in place of the SqlXmlCommand object.

B. Supply an appropriate schema mapping file for the DiffGram.

C. Store the text of the DiffGram in the CommandText property of the SqlXmlCommand object.

D. Use a SqlConnection object to make the initial connection to the database.

13. Which of these operations can be carried out in a SQL Server database by sending a properly-formatted DiffGram to the database? (Select two.)

A. Adding a row to a table

B. Adding a primary key to a table

C. Deleting a row from a table

D. Changing the data type of a column

APPLY YOUR KNOWLEDGE

14. You are developing code that uses the `XPathNavigator` object to navigate among the nodes in the DOM representation of an XML document. The current node of the `XPathNavigator` is an element in the XML document that does not have any attributes or any children. You call the `MoveToFirstChild()` method of the `XPathNavigator` object. What is the result?

    A. The current node remains unchanged and there is no error.

    B. The current node remains unchanged and a runtime error is thrown.

    C. The next sibling of the current node becomes the current node and there is no error.

    D. The next sibling of the current node becomes the current node and a runtime error is thrown.

15. Which of these operations requires you to have an XML schema file?

    A. Updating a SQL Server database with a DiffGram through the SQLXML Managed classes

    B. Validating an XML file with the `XmlValidatingReader` class

    C. Performing an XPath query with the `XPathNavigator` class

    D. Reading an XML file with the `XmlTextReader` class

Answers to Review Questions

1. XML elements are represented as nodes within the DOM. XML attributes are represented as properties of their parent nodes.

2. The `XmlTextReader` object provides forward-only, read-only access to XML data. For random access or for read-write access you should use the `XmlDocument` class or one of its derived classes.

3. You can synchronize an `XmlDataDocument` object and a `DataSet` object by creating a `DataSet` object from an `XmlDataDocument` object, by creating an `XmlDataDocument` object from a `DataSet` object, or by creating both a `DataSet` object and an `XmlDataDocument` object from a schema.

4. XPath expressions containing an explicit path, such as `/Customers/Customer/Order/OrderID`, are faster to evaluate than documentwide wildcard expressions such as `//OrderID`.

5. `/Customers/Customer/Order[1]` selects the first order for each customer, whereas `(/Customers/Customer/Order)[1]` selects the first order in the entire document.

6. You can instantiate an `XPathNavigator` object by calling the `CreateNavigator()` method of the `XmlDocument`, `XmlDataDocument`, or `XPathDocument` classes.

7. You can use an `XmlValidatingReader` object to validate an XML file for conformance with an embedded schema, an XSD file, a DTD file, or an XDR file.

8. The three main variants of `FOR XML` are `FOR XML RAW`, `FOR XML AUTO`, and `FOR XML EXPLICIT`.

9. To include schema information with a `FOR XML` query, specify the `XMLDATA` option.

10. DiffGrams can represent insertions, deletions, and modifications of the data in a `DataSet` object or SQL Server database.

Answers to Exam Questions

1. **D.** When you read XML data with the help of `XmlReader` or its derived classes, nodes are not included for XML attributes, but only for XML elements and the text that they contain. XML element nodes do not have a value. The only text that will be printed out is the value of the text nodes within the `OrderDate` elements. For more information, see the section "Accessing an XML File" in this chapter.

2. **B.** The `ReadXmlSchema()` method maps nested elements in the XML file to related `DataTable` objects in the `DataSet` object. At the leaf level of the DOM tree, both elements and attributes are mapped to `DataColumn` objects. For more information, see the section "Synchronizing `DataSet` Objects with XML" in this chapter.

3. **D.** Looping through all the nodes in an `XmlDocument` object is comparatively slow. If you start with the full XML document or by calling the `ReadXml()` method of the `DataSet` object, the `DataSet` object will contain all 50 elements. Using a schema file enables you to limit the `DataSet` object to holding only the desired data. For more information, see the section "Synchronizing `DataSet` Objects with XML" in this chapter.

4. **C.** The `DataSet` and the `XmlDataDocument` objects represent two different views of the same data structure. The last change made to either view is the change that is written back to the database.

For more information, see the section "Synchronizing `DataSet` Objects with XML" in this chapter.

5. **C.** `/Customers/Customer/Orders/Order/@OrderID[1]` selects the first OrderID for each order. `(/Customers/Customer/Orders/Order)[1]/@OrderID` selects the OrderID for the first order in the entire file. `(/Customers/Customer/Orders/Order/@OrderID)[1]` selects the first OrderID in the entire file. The remaining choice is the correct one. For more information, see the section "Understanding XPath" in this chapter.

6. **A.** The filtering expression needs to start with the `./` operator to indicate that it is filtering nodes under the current node at that point in the expression. For more information, see the section "Understanding XPath" in this chapter.

7. **D.** The `XPathDocument` class is optimized for read-only XPath queries. For more information, see the section "Understanding XPath" in this chapter.

8. **A.** The `XPathNavigator` object provides random access movement within the DOM. The `XmlReader` and `XmlTextReader` objects provide forward-only movement. The `XPathExpression` object is useful for retrieving a set of nodes, but not for navigating between nodes. For more information, see the section "Using the `XPathNavigator` Class" in this chapter.

9. **B.** An inline schema cannot contain validation information for the root node of the document, so XML documents with inline schemas will always have at least one validation error. For more information, see the section "Using an XSD Schema" in this chapter.

APPLY YOUR KNOWLEDGE

10. **C.** The raw and auto modes of the FOR XML statement always map columns to attributes, if the ELEMENTS option is not added in the FOR XML clause. Only explicit mode can map a column to an element. For more information, see the section "Understanding the FOR XML Clause" in this chapter.

11. **C.** The SqlCommand.ExecuteXmlReader() method returns an XML fragment rather than an XML document. To load a complete and valid XML document, you need to use the SqlXmlCommand object (from the SQLXML Managed Classes) instead. For more information, see the section "Updating SQL Data by Using XML" in this chapter.

12. **B.** When executing a DiffGram via the SQLXML managed classes, you must supply a mapping schema file. Otherwise, the code doesn't know which elements in the DiffGram map to which columns in the database. For more information, see the section "Using DiffGrams" in this chapter.

13. **A, C.** DiffGrams are useful for performing data manipulation operations, but not for data definition operations. For more information, see the section "Using DiffGrams" in this chapter.

14. **A.** The MoveTo methods of the XPathNavigator object always execute without error. If the requested move cannot be performed, the current node remains unchanged and the method returns false. For more information, see the section "Using the XPathNavigator Class" in this chapter.

15. **A.** You cannot perform a DiffGram update without a schema file that specifies the mapping between XML elements and database columns. Validation can be performed with a DTD or XDR file instead of a schema. XPath queries and reading XML files do not require a schema. For more information, see the section "Using DiffGrams" in this chapter.

Suggested Readings and Resources

1. Visual Studio .NET Combined Help Collection
   - Employing XML in the .NET Framework
   - XML and the DataSet
2. Microsoft SQL Server Books Online
   - Retrieving XML Documents Using FOR XML
   - SELECT Statement
3. .NET Framework QuickStart Tutorials, Common Tasks QuickStart, XML section.
4. Mike Gunderloy. *ADO and ADO.NET Programming.* Sybex, 2002.
5. John E. Simpson. *XPath and XPointer.* O'Reilly, 2002.
6. John Griffin. *XML and SQL Server.* New Riders, 2001.

This chapter covers the following Microsoft-specified objective for the "Creating and Managing Microsoft Windows Services, Serviced Components, .NET Remoting Objects, and XML Web Services" section of the "Developing XML Web Services and Server Components with Microsoft Visual C# .NET and the Microsoft .NET Framework" exam:

Create and consume a .NET Remoting object.

- **Implement server-activated components.**

- **Implement client-activated components.**

- **Select a channel protocol and a formatter. Channel protocols include TCP and HTTP. Formatters include SOAP and binary.**

- **Create client configuration files and server configuration files.**

- **Implement an asynchronous method.**

- **Create the listener service.**

- **Instantiate and invoke a .NET Remoting object.**

▶ This exam objective tests your skill on designing distributed applications with .NET remoting, which is a part of the .NET Framework SDK. You should know how to create a remote object, how to make it available to all the users via a remoting server, and how to write client applications that instantiate remote objects and invoke methods on them.

▶ Remoting provides a very flexible and configurable environment to design distributed applications. By the virtue of flexibility, the .NET remoting applications can be designed in several different ways. In this exam you are required to know how to make choices for various remoting configurations, such as activation mode, channel, and formatter, for a given scenario.

CHAPTER 3

.NET Remoting

▶ Remoting is configurable, too. All the remoting settings can be written in an XML-based configuration file. Writing the settings in separate configuration files allows easier modification and maintenance of remoting applications. This objective requires you to know about configuration files, such as the application configuration file, the `web.config` file, and the `machine.config` file.

▶ In distributed applications, methods are invoked across the network, and several factors such as network bandwidth and server availability may cause your application to respond slowly as compared to a desktop application. This exam objective also tests your skill with creating asynchronous or responsive distributed applications.

► Write programs to create remotable objects, remoting hosts, and remoting clients. Understand what role each of them plays in a distributed computing scenario.

► Understand the difference between server-activated objects and client-activated objects, HTTP channel and TCP channel, SOAP formatter and binary formatter. You should be ready to answer questions that ask you to choose between these remoting elements in a given scenario.

► Use both declarative as well as programmatic configuration for distributed applications. Appreciate the advantages and shortcomings of each approach.

► Understand how to use the asynchronous programming techniques to make a client program responsive in spite of slow method calls across the network.

INTRODUCTION

The .NET Framework provides a platform for building next-generation distributed applications. I start this chapter by introducing distributed application and how they are different from conventional applications. The .NET Framework allows you to create distributed applications in various ways. Two popular approaches are .NET remoting and ASP.NET Web services. I discuss .NET remoting in this chapter and cover ASP.NET Web services in the next two chapters.

In this chapter, you start learning about remoting by understanding its architecture first. You'll learn about various remoting elements such as the remotable class, remoting host, remoting client, channels, formatters, activation modes, and you'll also learn how these elements fit together to create a distributed application. I compare various choices available with each of the remoting elements and explain how to decide between those choices in a given scenario.

The next part of the chapter is code-intensive. You'll write code to practice creating small but fully functional distributed applications. While working with the Step-by-Step exercises you'll develop various skills instrumental for designing remoting applications and of course also for passing this exam.

I first show you how to create a class that can be remoted across the network and application boundaries. I then show how to create a remoting host that hosts the class so that the client program can take the services offered by the remotable class. I then show how to create a client program that can instantiate a remote object and invoke methods on it.

I discuss various types of applications that can work as remoting hosts, such as a console application, a Windows service, or IIS (Internet Information Services). I also discuss how you can use configuration files to conveniently modify the behavior of both the remoting host as well as the remoting client application.

Finally I show how to program the client application to invoke remote method calls asynchronously. Asynchronous method invocations, as you'll see, boost the responsiveness of the client application and keep users happy.

APPLICATION BOUNDARIES

An application boundary defines the scope of an application. It encompasses various resources critical to an application's execution, such as address space, executable code, and the data used by the application. A typical multiprogramming execution environment such as Windows uses application boundaries to protect one application from affecting the execution of another application.

In this section, you'll learn about application boundaries with respect to Windows and the .NET Framework. You'll understand how application boundaries protect applications from poorly designed or faulty code. You'll also learn how application boundaries make it difficult to design applications that want to communicate beyond the application boundaries.

Process Boundary

A process is an application under execution. Windows isolates processes from each other to ensure that code running in one process cannot adversely affect other processes. Windows achieves this isolation by creating a process boundary. A process boundary ensures that

- ▶ Each process has its own virtual address space, executable code, and data.

- ▶ A Windows process cannot directly access the code or data of another Windows process.

- ▶ A Windows process runs only one application, so if an application crashes, it does not affect other applications.

A process boundary allows processes to co-exist. However, it takes a lot of system resources to create, monitor, and terminate a process. In addition, when the processor switches between the processes, the processor must save and reset the execution context of the processes. Often an application involves several short-lived processes, which requires the system to spend a lot of resources just for process management.

Application Domain Boundary

The Common Language Runtime (CLR) provides a managed execution environment for .NET applications. The managed execution environment provides various services to the executing code, including cross-language integration, code access security, object lifetime management, and debugging and profiling support. The code executed by the CLR therefore is known also as managed code.

Unlike Windows, the CLR can verify type-safety of the programs to guarantee that a program does not request resources outside its own boundary. This characteristic of the CLR helps provide isolation between running programs at a lower cost than a process boundary incurs.

Instead of a process, the basic unit of isolation for running applications in the CLR is an application domain. An application domain (represented by System.AppDomain class) is the smallest execution unit for a .NET application. The CLR allows several application domains to run within a single Windows process and still provides the same level of isolation between applications as a Windows process does.

The application domains achieve isolation through application domain boundaries, which ensure that

- ▶ Each application domain contains its own set of code, data, and configuration settings.

- ▶ An application domain cannot directly access the code or data structures of another application domain.

- ▶ Code running in one application domain cannot affect other application domains. The CLR can terminate an application domain without stopping the entire process.

It is much cheaper to create, monitor, and maintain an application domain than a process. In addition, the capability of an application domain to run multiple applications within the same process consumes less overhead in process switching; therefore application domains increase application performance.

You can create an application domain in a program by using the AppDomain class of System namespace. However, in most cases the application domains created and managed by the runtime hosts execute your code. Runtime hosts provide the environment to run managed code on behalf of the user. When you install the .NET Framework, you get three runtime hosts already configured—the Windows shell, ASP.NET, and Internet Explorer.

DISTRIBUTED APPLICATIONS

As described in the previous sections, processes as well as application domains provide a close, protected environment. As a result, objects in a process or an application domain cannot talk directly to objects in another process or another application domain.

However, in the increasingly connected world, enterprises and users demand distributed applications. Distributed applications allow objects to talk across process boundaries. Often, distributed applications also meet the following objectives:

▶ Establish communication between objects that run in different application domains and processes, whether on the same computer or across the Internet.

▶ Enable enterprise application integration by establishing communication between objects that run on heterogeneous architectures.

▶ Enable application availability by making sure that portions of an application run even if some components are busy or have failed.

▶ Provide increased security and scalability by dividing the application into several layers (or tiers).

Evolution of Distributed Applications

A well-designed distributed application has the potential to be more connected, more available, more scalable, and more robust than an application where all components run on a single computer. This is a desirable model for an enterprise application.

Traditionally, there have been several efforts to design frameworks for developing distributed applications. A few well-known frameworks are Distributed Computing Environment/Remote Procedure Calls (DEC/RPC), Microsoft Distributed Component Object Model (DCOM), Common Object Request Broker Architecture (CORBA), and Java Remote Method Invocation (RMI). Some of these implementations are widely deployed in enterprises.

However, modern business requirements are different from those of earlier days. Today, businesses seek solutions that can be developed rapidly, that integrate well with their legacy applications, and that interoperate well with their business partners. Each of the technologies already mentioned failed to satisfy one or more of these requirements.

In 2000, Microsoft introduced the .NET Framework for designing next-generation distributed applications. As you'll explore more in this book, the .NET Framework is specifically targeted to meet the needs of modern business, whether the need is rapid development or integration or interoperability.

Using the .NET Framework to Develop Distributed Applications

The .NET Framework provides various mechanisms to support distributed application development. Most of this functionality is present in the following three namespaces of the Framework Class Library (FCL):

▶ The `System.Net` Namespace—This namespace includes classes to create standalone listeners and custom protocol handlers to start from scratch and create your own framework for developing a distributed application. Working with the `System.Net` namespace directly requires a good understanding of network programming.

▶ The `System.Runtime.Remoting` Namespace—This namespace includes the classes that constitute the .NET remoting framework. The .NET remoting framework allows communication between objects living in different application domains, whether or not they are on the same computer. Remoting provides an abstraction over the complex network programming and exposes a simple mechanism for inter-application domain communication. The key objectives of .NET remoting are flexibility and extensibility.

▶ The `System.Web.Services` Namespace—This namespace includes the classes that constitutes the ASP.NET Web services framework. ASP.NET Web services allow objects living in different application domains to exchange messages through standard protocols such as HTTP and SOAP. ASP.NET Web services, when compared to remoting, provide a much higher level of abstraction and simplicity. The key objectives of ASP.NET Web services are the ease of use and interoperability with other systems.

Both .NET remoting and ASP.NET Web services provide a complete framework for designing distributed applications. Most programmers will use either .NET remoting or ASP.NET Web services rather than build a distributed programming framework from scratch with the `System.Net` namespace classes.

The functionality offered by .NET remoting and ASP.NET Web services appears very similar. In fact, ASP.NET Web services are actually built on the .NET remoting infrastructure. It is also possible to use .NET remoting to design Web services. Given the amount of similarity, how do you choose one over the other in your project? Simply put, the decision depends on the type of application you want to create. You'll use

▶ .NET Remoting when both the end points (client and server) of a distributed application are in your control. This might be a case when an application has been designed for use within a corporate network.

▶ ASP.NET Web services when one end point of a distributed application is not in your control. This might be a case when your application is interoperating with your business partner's application.

You will learn more about architectural differences and specific features of both the technologies as you progress through this book. I will discuss .NET remoting in this chapter and will discuss ASP.NET Web services in Chapter 4, "Basic Web Services," and Chapter 5, "Advanced Web Services."

▶ An Application domain, `AppDomain`, is the smallest execution unit for a .NET application. The CLR allows several application domains to run within a single Windows process.

▶ Distributed Applications enable communication between objects that run in different application domains and processes.

▶ `System.Net`, `System.Runtime.Remoting`, and `System.Web.Services` namespaces enable the .NET Framework to support distributed application development.

.NET REMOTING ARCHITECTURE

.NET remoting enables objects in different application domains to talk to each other. The real strength of remoting is in enabling the communication between objects when their application domains are separated across the network. In this case, remoting transparently handles details related to network communication.

Before I get into details, I'll first answer a basic question: How come remoting is able to establish cross-application domain communication when the application domains do not allow direct calls across their boundaries?

Remoting takes an indirect approach to application domain communication by creating proxy objects as shown in Figure 3.1. Both application domains communicate with each other by following these steps:

FIGURE 3.1
In this simplified view of .NET remoting, you can see that client and server communicate indirectly through a proxy object.

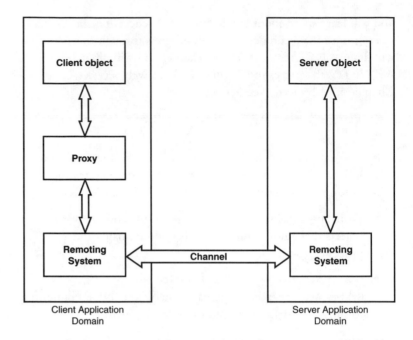

1. When a client object requests an instance of the server object, the remoting system at the client side instead creates a proxy of the server object. The proxy object lives at the client but behaves just like the remote object; this leaves the client with the impression that the server object is in the client's process.

2. When the client object calls a method on the server object, the proxy passes the call information to the remoting system on the client. This remoting system in turn sends the call over the channel to the remoting system on the server.

3. The remoting system on the server receives the call information and, on the basis of it, invokes the method on the actual object on the server (creating the object if necessary).

4. The remoting system on the server collects the result of the method invocation and passes it through the channel to the remoting system on the client.

5. The remoting system at the client receives the server's response and returns the results to the client object through the proxy.

The process of packaging and sending method calls among objects, across application boundaries, via serialization and deserialization, as shown in the preceding steps, is also known as *marshaling*.

Now that you have a basic idea of how .NET remoting works, it's time to get into the details. In the next few sections, I'll explain various key components and terminology of .NET remoting.

Object Marshaling

Remotable objects are the objects that can be marshaled across the application domains. In contrast, all other objects are known as non-remotable objects. There are two types of remotable objects:

▶ Marshal-by-value (MBV) Objects—These objects are copied and passed out of the server application domain to the client application domain.

▶ Marshal-by-reference (MBR) Objects—A proxy is used to access these objects on the client side. The clients hold just a reference to these objects.

Marshal-by-value Objects

MBV objects reside on the server. When a client invokes a method on the MBV object, the MBV object is serialized, transferred over the network, and restored on the client as an exact copy of the server-side object. Now, the MBV object is locally available and therefore any method calls to the object do not require any proxy object or marshaling.

The MBV objects can provide faster performance by reducing the network roundtrips, but in the case of large objects, the time taken to transfer the serialized object from server to the client can be very significant. Furthermore, the MBV objects do not provide the privilege of running the remote object in the server environment.

You can create an MBV object by declaring a class with the `Serializable` attribute. For example:

```
//define a MBV remoting object
[Serializable()]
public class MyMBVObject
{
    //...
}
```

If a class needs to control its own serialization, it can do so by implementing the `ISerializable` interface as follows:

```
//define a MBV remoting object
[Serializable()]
public class MyMBVObject : ISerializable
{
    //...
    //Implement custom serialization here
    public void GetObjectData(
        SerializationInfo info,
        StreamingContext context)
    {
        //...
    }
    //...
}
```

Marshal-by-reference Objects

The MBR objects are remote objects. They always reside on the server and all methods invoked on these objects are executed at the server side. The client communicates with the MBR object on the server by using a local proxy object that holds the reference to the MBR object.

Although the use of MBR objects increases the number of network roundtrips, they are a likely choice when the objects are prohibitively large or when the functionality of the object is available only in the server environment on which it is created.

You can create an MBR object by deriving the MBR class from the `System.MarshalByRefObject` class. For example:

```
//define a MBR remoting object
public class MyMBRObject : MarshalByRefObject
{
    //...
}
```

The `NonSerialized` Attribute   By default public and private fields of a class are serialized, if a `Serializable` attribute is applied to the class. If you do not want to serialize a specific field in a `serializable` class, apply the `NonSerialized` attribute on that field. For example, in the class Sample, although `field1` and `field2` are serialized, `field3` is not serialized because of the `NonSerialized` attribute.

```
[Serializable()]
public class Sample
{
    public int field1;
    public string field2;
    // A field that is not
serialized.
    [NonSerialized()]
    public string field3;
    .
    .
    .
}
```

Channels

Create and consume a .NET remoting object

- **Select a channel protocol and a formatter. Channel protocols include TCP and HTTP. Formatters include SOAP and binary.**

Channels are the objects that transport messages across remoting boundaries such as application domains, processes, and computers. When a client calls a method on the remote objects, the details of the method call—such as parameters and so on—are transported to the remote object through a channel. Any results returned from the remote object are communicated back to the client again through the same channel.

The .NET remoting framework ensures that before a remote object can be called, it has registered at least one channel with the remoting system on the server. Similarly, the client object should specify a channel before it can communicate with a remote object. If the remote object offers more than one channel, the client can connect by using the channel that best suits its requirements.

A channel has two end points. The channel object at the receiving end of a channel (the server) listens to a particular protocol through the specified port number, whereas the channel object at the sending end of the channel (the client) sends information to the receiving end by using the protocol and port number specified by the channel object on the receiving end.

To participate in the .NET remoting framework, the channel object at the receiving end must implement the IChannelReceiver interface, whereas the channel object at the sending end must implement the IChannelSender interface.

The .NET Framework provides implementations for HTTP (Hypertext Transmission Protocol) and TCP (Transmission Control Protocol) channels. If you want to use a different protocol, you can define your own channel by implementing the IChannelReceiver and IChannelSender interfaces.

> **EXAM TIP**
>
> **Port Numbers Should Be Unique on a Machine**   Each channel is uniquely associated with a TCP/IP port number. Ports are machine-wide resources; therefore, you cannot register a channel that listens on a port number that is already in use by some other channel on the same machine.

HTTP Channels

The HTTP channels use HTTP for establishing communication between the two ends. These channels are implemented through the classes of the `System.Runtime.Remoting.Channels.Http` namespace, as shown in Table 3.1.

TABLE 3.1

THE HTTP CHANNEL CLASSES

Class	*Implements*	*Purpose*
HttpServerChannel	IChannelReceiver	An implementation for a server channel that uses the HTTP to receive messages.
HttpClientChannel	IChannelSender	An implementation for a client channel that uses the HTTP to send messages.
HttpChannel	IChannelReceiver and IChannelSender	An implementation of a combined channel that provides the functionality of both the HttpServerChannel and the HttpClientChannel classes.

The following code example shows how to register a sender-receiver HTTP channel on port 1234:

```
using System;
using System.Runtime.Remoting.Channels;
using System.Runtime.Remoting.Channels.Http;
//...
 HttpChannel channel = new HttpChannel(1234);
 ChannelServices.RegisterChannel(channel);
 //...
```

The `ChannelServices` class used in the code provides various remoting-related services. One of its static methods is `RegisterChannel()`, which helps in registering a channel with the remoting framework.

TCP Channels

The TCP channel uses TCP for establishing communication between the two ends. The TCP channel is implemented through various classes of the `System.Runtime.Remoting.Channels.Tcp` namespace, as shown in Table 3.2.

TABLE 3.2

THE TCP CHANNEL CLASSES

Class	Implements	Purpose
TcpServerChannel	IChannelReceiver	An implementation for a server channel that uses the TCP to receive messages.
TcpClientChannel	IChannelSender	An implementation for a client channel that uses the TCP to send messages.
TcpChannel	IChannelReceiver and IChannelSender	An implementation of a combined channel that provides the functionality for both TcpServerChannel and TcpClientChannel classes.

The following code example shows how to register a sender-receiver TCP channel on port 1234:

```
using System;
using System.Runtime.Remoting.Channels;
using System.Runtime.Remoting.Channels.Tcp;
//...
 TcpChannel channel = new TcpChannel(1234);
 ChannelServices.RegisterChannel(channel);
//...
```

Choosing Between the HTTP and the TCP Channels

Table 3.3 helps you make a decision about which channel to use in a given scenario. In summary, you'll normally use the TCP channel within a low-risk intranet. For more wide-reach applications, using the HTTP channel makes more sense unless the application's efficiency requirements justify the cost of creating a customized security system.

EXAM TIP

Support for Security .NET remoting has no built-in support for security. It instead depends on the remoting hosts to provide security. The only built-in remoting host that provides security for remote objects is IIS. Therefore, any secured objects must be hosted in IIS.

TABLE 3.3

CHOOSING BETWEEN THE HTTP CHANNEL AND THE TCP CHANNEL

Channel	Scope	Efficiency	Security
HttpChannel	**Wide**, using the HTTP channel enables you to host the objects on a robust HTTP server such as IIS. HTTP channels can be used over the Internet, because firewalls do not generally block HTTP communication.	**Less**, because HTTP is a bulky protocol and has lots of extra overhead.	**More**, because when remote objects are hosted in IIS, the HttpChannel can immediately take advantage of Secure Sockets Layer (SSL), Integrated Windows Authentication or Kerberos.
TcpChannel	**Narrow**, using the TCP channel over the Internet would require opening certain ports in the firewall and could lead to security breaches.	**More**, because TCP uses raw sockets to transmit data across the network.	**Less**, until you implement a custom security system using the classes provided in the System.Security namespace.

Formatters

Create and consume a .NET Remoting object

- **Select a channel protocol and a formatter. Channel protocols include TCP and HTTP. Formatters include SOAP and binary.**

Formatters are the objects that are used to encode and serialize data into messages before they are transmitted over a channel. At the other end of the channel, when the messages are received, formatters decode and deserialize the messages.

To participate in the .NET remoting framework, the formatter classes must implement the `IFormatter` interface. The .NET Framework packages two formatter classes for common scenarios: the `BinaryFormatter` class and the `SoapFormatter` class. If you want to use a different formatter, you can define your own formatter class by implementing the `IFormatter` interface.

The SOAP Formatter

SOAP (Simple Object Access Protocol) is a simple, XML-based protocol for exchanging types and messages between applications. SOAP is an extensible and modular protocol; it is not bound to a particular transport mechanism such as HTTP or TCP.

The SOAP formatter is implemented in the `SoapFormatter` class of the `System.Runtime.Serialization.Formatters.Soap` namespace.

SOAP formatting is an ideal way of communicating between applications that use non-compatible architectures. However, SOAP is very verbose. SOAP messages require more bytes to represent the data as compared to the binary format.

The Binary Formatter

Unlike SOAP, the binary format used by the .NET Framework is proprietary and can be understood only within .NET applications. However, as compared to SOAP, the binary format of representing messages is very compact and efficient.

The binary formatter is implemented in the `BinaryFormatter` class of the `System.Runtime.Serialization.Formatters.Binary` namespace.

Channels and Formatters

The HTTP channel uses the SOAP formatter as its default formatter to transport messages to and from the remote objects. The HTTP channel uses `SoapClientFormatterSinkProvider` and `SoapServerFormatterSinkProvider` classes to serialize and deserialize messages through the `SoapFormatter` class. You can create industry-standard XML Web services when using SOAP formatter with the HTTP channel.

The TCP channel uses the binary format by default to transport messages to and from the remote object. The TCP channel uses `BinaryClientFormatterSinkProvider` and `BinaryServerFormatterSinkProvider` classes to serialize and deserialize messages through the `BinaryFormatter` class.

However, channels are configurable. You can configure the HTTP channel to use the binary formatter or a custom formatter rather than the SOAP formatter. Similarly, the TCP channel can be configured to use the SOAP formatter or a custom formatter rather than the binary formatter.

Figure 3.2 compares the various combinations of channels and formatters on the scale of efficiency and compatibility. You can use this information to decide which combination of channel and formatter you would chose in a given scenario.

Channel	Formatter	Efficiency	Interoperability
TCP	Binary		
TCP	SOAP		
HTTP	Binary		
HTTP	SOAP		

FIGURE 3.2
A TCP channel with a binary formatter provides maximum efficiency, whereas an HTTP channel with a SOAP formatter provides maximum interoperability.

REVIEW BREAK

▶ .NET remoting enables objects in different application domains to talk to each other even when they are separated by applications, computers, or the network.

▶ The process of packaging and sending method calls among the objects across the application boundaries via serialization and deserialization is called marshaling.

▶ Marshal-by-value (MBV) and Marshal-by-reference (MBR) are the two types of remotable objects. MBV objects are copied to the client application domain from the server application domain, whereas only a reference to the MBR objects is maintained in the client application domain. A proxy object is created at the client side to interact with the MBR objects.

▶ A channel is an object that transports messages across remoting boundaries such as application domains, processes, and computers. The .NET Framework provides implementations for HTTP and TCP channels to allow communication of messages over the HTTP and TCPs, respectively.

▶ A channel has two end points. A channel at the receiving end, the server, listens for messages at a specified port number from a specific protocol, and a channel object at the sending end, the client, sends messages through the specified protocol at the specified port number.

▶ Formatters are the objects that are used to serialize and deserialize data into messages before they are transmitted over a channel. You can format the messages in SOAP or the binary format with the help of `SoapFormatter` and `BinaryFormatter` classes in the FCL.

▶ The default formatter for transporting messages to and from the remote objects for the HTTP channel is the SOAP formatter and for the TCP channel is the binary formatter.

Remote Object Activation

Between the two types of objects you have studied—the MBV objects and the MBR objects—only MBR objects can be activated remotely. No remote activation is needed in the case of MBV objects because the MBV object itself is transferred to the client side.

Based on the activation mode, MBR objects are classified in the following two categories:

▶ Server-activated objects

▶ Client-activated objects

Server-Activated Objects

Server-activated objects (SAOs) are those remote objects whose lifetime is directly controlled by the server.

When a client requests an instance of a server-activated object, a proxy to the remote object is created in the client's application domain. The remote object is only instantiated (or activated) on the server when the client calls a method on the proxy object.

The server-activated objects provide limited flexibility because only their default (parameter-less) constructors can be used to instantiate them.

There are two possible activation modes for a server-activated object:

▶ SingleCall activation mode

▶ Singleton activation mode

SingleCall Activation Mode

In the SingleCall activation mode, an object is instantiated for the sole purpose of responding to just one client request. After the request is fulfilled, the .NET remoting framework deletes the object and reclaims its memory.

Objects activated in the SingleCall mode are also known as stateless because the objects are created and destroyed with each client request and therefore do not maintain state across the requests. This behavior of the SingleCall mode accounts for greater server scalability as an object consumes server resources for only a small period, therefore allowing the server to allocate resources to other objects.

The SingleCall activation mode is a desired solution when

▶ The overhead of creating an object is not significant.

▶ The object is not required to maintain its state.

▶ The server needs to support a large number of requests for the object.

▶ The object needs to be supported in a load-balanced environment.

NOTE

Well-Known Objects Remote objects activated in SingleCall or Singleton activation mode are also known as server-activated objects or well-known objects.

EXAM TIP

Load-Balancing and SingleCall Activation Sometimes to improve the overall efficiency of an application, the application may be hosted on multiple servers that share the incoming requests to it. In this case, a request can go to any of the available servers for processing. This scenario is called a load-balancing environment.

Because the SingleCall objects are stateless, it does not matter which server processes their requests. For this reason, SingleCall activation is ideally suited for load-balanced environments.

Scenarios that are often well suited for the SingleCall activation mode are those applications where the object is required by the client to do a small amount of work and then the object is no longer required. Some common examples include retrieving the inventory level for an item, displaying tracking information for a shipment, and so on.

Singleton Activation Mode

In the Singleton activation mode, there is at most one instance of the remote object, regardless of the number of clients accessing it.

A Singleton mode object can maintain state information across the method calls. Therefore, they are also sometimes known as stateful objects. The state maintained by the Singleton mode server-activated object is globally shared by all its clients.

A Singleton object does not exist on the server forever. Its lifetime is determined by the lifetime lease of the object. I'll discuss lifetime leases shortly in the section, "Lifetime Leases."

A Singleton object is a desired solution when

▶ The overhead of creating an object is substantial.

▶ The object is required to maintain its state over a prolonged period.

▶ Several clients need to work on the shared state.

Singleton activation mode is useful in scenarios such as in a chat server where multiple clients talk to the same remote object and share data between one another.

Client-Activated Objects

Client-activated objects (CAOs) are those remote objects whose lifetime is directly controlled by the client. This is in direct contrast with SAOs, where the server, not the client, has complete control over objects' lifetimes.

Client-activated objects are instantiated on the server as soon as the client requests the object to be created. Unlike SAOs, CAOs do not delay object creation until the first method is called on the object.

You can use any of the available constructors of the remotable class to create a CAO. A typical CAO activation involves the following steps:

1. When the client attempts to create an instance of the server object, an activation request message is sent to the remote server.

2. The server then creates an instance of the requested class by using the specified constructor and returns an `ObjRef` object to the client application that invoked it. The `ObjRef` object contains all the required information to generate a proxy object that is capable of communicating with a remote object.

3. The client uses the `ObjRef` object to create a proxy of the server object on the client side.

An instance of the CAO serves only the client that was responsible for its creation, and the CAO doesn't get discarded with each request. For this reason, a CAO can maintain state with each client that it is serving, but unlike Singleton SAOs, different CAOs cannot share a common state.

The lifetime of a CAO is determined by the lifetime leases. I'll talk more about this topic shortly in a section titled "Lifetime Leases."

A CAO is a desired solution when

▶ Clients want to maintain a private session with the remote object.

▶ Clients want to have more control over how the objects are created and how long they will live.

CAOs are useful in scenarios such as entering a complex purchase order where multiple roundtrips are involved and clients want to maintain their own private state with the remote object.

Comparing the Object Activation Techniques

Based on the discussions in the previous section, the various object activation techniques can be compared as shown in Figure 3.3.

SingleCall server activation mode offers maximum scalability because the remote object occupies server resources for the minimum length of the time. This enables the server to allocate its resources between many clients.

On the other hand, the client activation of remote objects offers maximum flexibility because you have complete control over the construction and lifetime of the remote object.

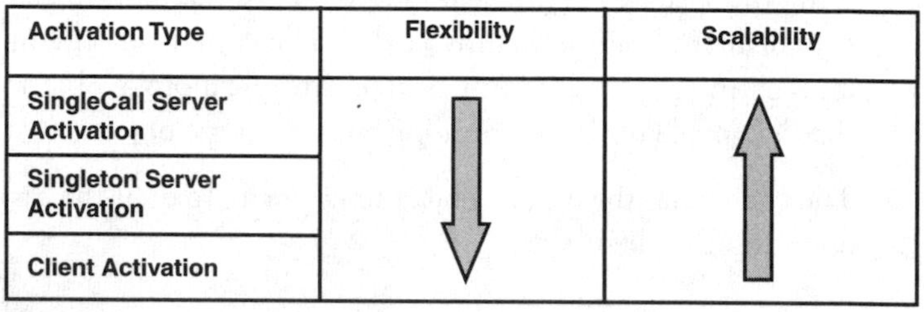

FIGURE 3.3
The SingleCall server activation offers maximum scalability, whereas the client activation offers maximum flexibility.

Activation Type	Flexibility	Scalability
SingleCall Server Activation		
Singleton Server Activation		
Client Activation		

Lifetime Leases

A lifetime lease is the period of time that a particular object shall be active in memory before the .NET framework deletes it and reclaims its memory. Both Singleton SAOs and CAOs use lifetime leases to determine how long they should continue to exist.

A lifetime lease is represented by an object that implements the ILease interface that is defined in the System.Runtime. Remoting.Lifetime namespace. Some of the important members of this interface are listed in Table 3.4.

TABLE 3.4

IMPORTANT MEMBERS OF THE ILease INTERFACE

Member Name	Type	Description
CurrentLeaseTime	Property	Gets the amount of time remaining on the lease before the object is marked for garbage collection.
InitialLeaseTime	Property	Gets or sets the initial time for the lease. If the object does not receive any method calls, it lives for only this period.
Register()	Method	Registers a sponsor for the lease.

EXAM TIP

Leases and Activation Mode Leases apply only to Singleton SAOs and CAOs. With SingleCall SAOs, objects are created and destroyed with each method call.

Custom and Infinite Lifetimes A remote object can choose to have a custom defined lifetime if the InitializeLifetimeService() method of the base class, MarshalByRefObject, is overridden. If the InitializeLifetimeService() method returns a null, the type tells the .NET remoting system that its instances are intended to have an infinite lifetime.

Member Name	*Type*	*Description*
`Renew()`	Method	Renews a lease for the specified time.
`RenewOnCallTime`	Property	Gets or sets the amount of time by which a call to the remote object will increase the `CurrentLeaseTime`.
`SponsorshipTimeout`	Property	Gets or sets the amount of time to wait for a sponsor to return with a lease renewal time.

Simply speaking, the lease works as follows:

▶ When an object is created, the value of the `InitialLeaseTime` property (which is by default 5 minutes) is used to set its lifetime lease (`CurrentLeaseTime`).

▶ Whenever the object receives a call, its `CurrentLeaseTime` is increased by the time specified by value of `RenewOnCallTime` property (which is by default 2 minutes).

▶ The client can also renew a lease for a remote object by directly calling the `ILease.Renew()` method:

```
ILease lease = (ILease)
        RemotingServices.GetLifetimeService(
        RemoteObject);
TimeSpan expireTime =
        lease.Renew(TimeSpan.FromSeconds(60));
```

▶ When the value of `CurrentLeaseTime` reaches 0, the .NET Framework contacts any sponsors registered with the lease to check whether they are ready to sponsor a renewal of the lease of the object.

▶ If the sponsor does not renew the object or the server cannot contact the sponsor within the duration specified by the `SponsorshipTimeout` property, then the object is marked for garbage collection.

Sponsors are the objects responsible for dynamically renewing an object's lease if its lease expires. Sponsors implement the `ISponsor` interface and are registered with the lease manager by calling the `ILease.Register()` method. When the lease for such an object expires, the lease manager calls the `ISponsor.Renewal()` method implemented by the sponsor objects to renew the lease time. For more information about sponsors, refer to the "Renewing Leases" topic in the .NET Framework Developer's Guide.

REVIEW BREAK

▶ The MBR remotable objects can be activated in two modes: server-activated mode and client-activated mode.

▶ Server-activated objects (SAOs) are those remote objects whose lifetime is directly controlled by the server.

▶ You can activate SAOs in two ways: SingleCall (object is created for each client request) and Singleton (object is created once on the server and is shared by all clients).

▶ The SingleCall activation mode provides the maximum scalability because it does not maintain any state and the object lives for the shortest duration possible.

▶ CAOs are created for each client when the client requests that a remote object be created. These objects maintain state for each client with which they are associated.

▶ The leased-based lifetime process determines how long Singleton SAOs and CAOs should exist.

APPLYING .NET REMOTING

So far, I have discussed the architecture and various concepts related to .NET remoting. In this section, you will learn how to apply these concepts to see remoting in action. In particular, you will learn to

▶ Create a remotable class.

▶ Create a server-activated object.

▶ Create a client-activated object.

▶ Use configuration files to configure the remoting framework.

▶ Use interface assemblies to compile remoting clients.

Creating a Remotable Class

Creating a remotable class is simple. All you need to do is to inherit a class from the `MarshalByRefObject` class or any of its derived classes. Step-by-Step 3.1 creates a remotable class named `DbConnect`. This class connects to a specified SQL Server database and enables you to execute a `SELECT` SQL statement by using its `ExecuteQuery()` method.

STEP BY STEP

3.1 Creating a Remotable Class

1. Launch Visual Studio .NET. Select File, New, Blank Solution, and name the new solution `320C03`. Click OK.

2. Add a new Visual C# .NET class library named `StepByStep3_1` to the solution.

3. In the Solution Explorer, rename the default `Class1.cs` to `DbConnect.cs`.

4. Open the `DbConnect.cs` and replace the code with the following code:

```csharp
using System;
using System.Data;
using System.Data.SqlClient;

namespace StepByStep3_1
{
    // Marshal-by-Reference Remotable Object
    public class DbConnect : MarshalByRefObject
    {
        private SqlConnection sqlconn;

        // Default constructor connects to the
        // Northwind database by calling
        // the overloaded constructor
        public DbConnect() : this("Northwind")
        {
        }

        // Parameterized constructor connects to the
        // specified database
        public DbConnect(string DbName)
        {
```

continues

continued

```
            // Open a connection to the specified
            // sample SQL Server database
            sqlconn = new SqlConnection(
                @"data source=(local);" +
                @"initial catalog=" + DbName +
                @";integrated security=SSPI");
            Console.WriteLine(
                "Created a new connection " +
                "to the {0} database.", DbName);
        }

        public DataSet ExecuteQuery(string strQuery)
        {
            Console.Write("Starting to execute " +
                "the query...");
            // Create a SqlCommand object
            // to represent the query
            SqlCommand sqlcmd =
                sqlconn.CreateCommand();
            sqlcmd.CommandType = CommandType.Text;
            sqlcmd.CommandText = strQuery;

            // Create a SqlDataAdapter object
            // to talk to the database
            SqlDataAdapter sqlda =
                new SqlDataAdapter();
            sqlda.SelectCommand = sqlcmd;
            // Create a DataSet to hold the results
            DataSet ds = new DataSet();
            try
            {
                // Fill the DataSet
                sqlda.Fill(ds, "Results");
            }
            catch (Exception ex)
            {
                Console.WriteLine(ex.Message,
                    "Error executing query");
            }
            Console.WriteLine("Done.");
            return ds;
        }
    }
}
```

5. Select Build, Build StepByStep3_1. This step packages the remotable class into the file StepByStep3_1.dll, which is located in the bin\Debug or bin\Release directory of your project. You can navigate to it through the Solution Explorer: Just select the project and click the Show All Files button in the Solution Explorer toolbar.

Although you now have a remotable class available to you, it cannot be called directly from the client application domains yet. For a remotable class to be activated, you need to connect the class to the remoting framework. You'll learn how to do that in the next section.

Creating a Server-Activated Object

Create and consume a .NET Remoting object.

- **Implement server-activated components.**

- **Instantiate and invoke a .NET Remoting object.**

A remotable class is usually connected with the remoting framework through a separate server program. The server program listens to the client request on a specified channel and instantiates the remote object or invokes calls on it as required.

It is a good idea to keep the remotable class and server program separate; this allows the design to be modular and the code to be reusable.

In this section, I'll show you how to create a remoting server. To achieve this, the remoting server must take the following steps:

1. Create a server channel that listens on a particular port to the incoming object activation requests from other application domains. The following code segment shows how to create a TCP server channel and an HTTP server channel:

   ```
   // Register a TCP server channel on port 1234
   TcpServerChannel channel = new TcpServerChannel(1234);

   // Register an HTTP server channel on port 1235
   HttpServerChannel channel = new HttpServerChannel(1235);
   ```

2. Register the channel with the remoting framework. This registration is performed through the RegisterChannel() method of the ChannelServices class:

   ```
   // Register the channel with the remoting framework
   ChannelServices.RegisterChannel(channel);
   ```

3. Register the remotable class with the remoting framework. For a server-activated object, the RegisterWellKnownServiceType() method of the RemotingConfiguration class is used to perform this registration, as follows:

```
//Register a remote object with the remoting framework
RemotingConfiguration.RegisterWellKnownServiceType(
    typeof(DbConnect),  // type of the remotable class
    "DbConnect",        // URI of the remotable class
    WellKnownObjectMode.SingleCall //Activation mode
);
```

Here, the first parameter is the type of the remotable class. The second parameter specifies the uniform resource identifier (URI) through which the server publishes the remote object's location. The last parameter specifies the activation mode. The activation mode should be one of the two possible values of the WellKnownObjectMode enumeration—SingleCall and Singleton.

As I discussed, earlier, an SAO can be activated in two different modes—SingleCall and Singleton. In the next few sections, I'll cover how to create a remoting server for activating objects in each of these modes. I'll also tell the story on the other side of the channel, that is, how to connect the client program to the remoting framework so that it can instantiate the SAO and call methods on it.

Using the SingleCall Activation Mode to Register a Remotable Class As a Server-Activated Object

In this section, I'll demonstrate how to create a server that exposes the remotable class through the remoting framework. The server process here is a long-running user interface-less process that continues to listen to incoming client requests on a channel.

Ideally, you should write this type of server program as a Windows service or use an existing Windows service such as Internet Information services (IIS) to work as the remoting server. But I have chosen to write the server program as a console application mainly because I'll use the console window to display various messages that will help you understand the workings of the remoting system.

However, later in this chapter, in the section "Using IIS As an Activation Agent," I cover how to use IIS as a remoting server. I talk about Windows services later in Chapter 6, "Windows Services."

> **EXAM TIP**
>
> **Accessing an Object Through Multiple Channels** From step 2 and step 3, note that the channel registration and the remote object registration are not related. In fact, a remote object can be accessed through all registered channels.

STEP BY STEP

3.2 Using the SingleCall Activation Mode to Register a Server-Activated Object

1. Add a new Visual C# .NET console application named StepByStep3_2 to the solution.

2. In the Solution Explorer, right-click project StepByStep3_2 and select Add Reference from the context menu. In the Add Reference dialog box, select the .NET tab, select the System.Runtime.Remoting component from the list view, and click the Select button. Now select the Projects tab, select the Project named StepByStep3_1 (contains the remotable object) from the list view, and click the Select button. Both the selected projects then appear in the Selected Components list, as shown in Figure 3.4. Click OK.

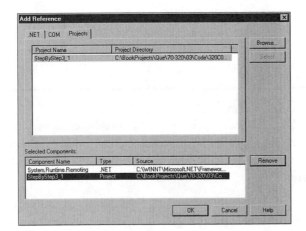

FIGURE 3.4
The Add Reference dialog box enables you to add references to components.

3. In the Solution Explorer, rename the default Class1.cs to DbConnectSingleCallServer.cs. Open the file and change the name of the class to DbConnectSingleCallServer in the class declaration.

4. Add the following using directives:

```
using System.Runtime.Remoting;
using System.Runtime.Remoting.Channels;
using System.Runtime.Remoting.Channels.Tcp;
```

continues

continued

5. Add the following code in the `Main()` method:

```
[STAThread]
static void Main(string[] args)
{
    // Create and register a TCP server channel
    // that listens on port 1234
    TcpServerChannel channel =
        new TcpServerChannel(1234);
    ChannelServices.RegisterChannel(channel);

    // Register the service that publishes
    // DbConnect for remote access in SingleCall mode
    RemotingConfiguration.RegisterWellKnownServiceType
        (typeof(StepByStep3_1.DbConnect), "DbConnect",
        WellKnownObjectMode.SingleCall);

    Console.WriteLine("Started server in the " +
        "SingleCall mode");
    Console.WriteLine("Press <ENTER> to terminate " +
        "server...");
    Console.ReadLine();
}
```

6. Build the project. This step creates a remoting server that is capable of registering the `StepByStep3_1.DbConnect` class for remote invocation by using the SingleCall activation mode.

Step-by-Step 3.2 uses a receiver TCP channel (`TcpServerChannel`) to register a remotable class with the remoting framework. However, converting this program to use the HTTP channel is not difficult—you just need to change all instances of `Tcp` to `Http`.

Step-by-Step 3.2 creates a remoting host that listens on port 1234. This is an arbitrary port number that may or may not work on your computer. A good idea is to check whether a port is already in use by some other application before running this program. You can do this from the command line by using the Windows `netstat` command.

This suggestion works only in a test scenario; it is not reasonable to instruct a customer to check whether the port is available before starting the application. If the application will run entirely on your company's network, you can safely use a port in the private port range of 49152 through 65535—provided, of course, that the port number you choose is not used by another internal application.

If you are distributing the application, you should get a port number registered from IANA (Internet Assigned Numbers Authority). You can see a list of already assigned port numbers at www.iana.org/assignments/port-numbers.

Instantiating and Invoking a Server-Activated Object

At this stage, you have a remotable object as well as a remoting server ready. In this section, I'll show you how to create a remoting client and use it to send messages to the remoting server to activate the remote object. To achieve this, the remoting client needs to take the following steps:

1. Create and register a client channel that is used by the remoting framework to send messages to the remoting server. The type of channel used by the client should be compatible with the channel used by the server. The following examples show how to create a TCP client channel and an HTTP client channel:

```
// Create and register a TCP client channel
TcpClientChannel channel = new TcpClientChannel();
ChannelServices.RegisterChannel(channel);

// Create and register an HTTP client channel
HttpClientChannel channel = new HttpClientChannel();
ChannelServices.RegisterChannel(channel);
```

2. Register the remotable class as a valid type in the client's application domain. The RegisterWellKnownClientType() method of the RemotingConfiguration class is used to perform this registration, as shown below:

```
// Register the remote class as a valid
// type in the client's application domain
RemotingConfiguration.RegisterWellKnownClientType(
    // Remote class
    typeof(DbConnect),
    // URL of the remote class
    "tcp://localhost:1234/DbConnect"
);
```

> **EXAM TIP**
>
> **Client Channel Registration** You do not specify a port number when you register the client channel. The port number is instead specified at the time of registering the remote class in the client's application domain.

Here, the first parameter is the type of the remotable class. The second parameter specifies the uniform resource identifier (URI) through which the server publishes the location of the remote object. *Localhost* maps to your local development machine. If the remote object is on some other computer, you'll replace *localhost* with the name of the computer.

3. Instantiate the SAO on the server. You can only use the default constructor.

```
// Instantiate the remote object
DbConnect dbc = new DbConnect();
```

I demonstrate the preceding steps in Step-by-Step 3.3, where I create the client program as a Windows application that accepts a SQL statement from the user and passes it to the remotable object. The rows returned by the remotable object are displayed in a DataGrid control.

STEP BY STEP

3.3 Instantiating and Invoking a Server-Activated Object

1. Add a new Visual C# .NET Windows application named StepByStep3_3 to the solution.

2. Add references to the .NET assembly System.Runtime.Remoting and the project StepByStep3_1 (the remotable class assembly).

3. In the Solution Explorer, rename the default Form1.cs to DbConnectClient.cs. Open the form in code view and change all occurrences of Form1 to refer to DbConnectClient instead.

4. Add the following using directives:

```
using System.Runtime.Remoting;
using System.Runtime.Remoting.Channels;
using System.Runtime.Remoting.Channels.Tcp;
using StepByStep3_1;
```

5. Place two GroupBox controls, a TextBox control (txtQuery, with its MultiLine property set to true), a Button control (btnExecute), and a DataGrid control (dgResults) on the form. Arrange the controls as shown in Figure 3.5.

6. Add the following code in the class definition:

```
// Declare a Remote object
DbConnect dbc;
```

7. Double-click the form and add the following code in the Load event handler:

```
private void DbConnectClient_Load(
    object sender, System.EventArgs e)
{
    // Register a TCP client channel
    TcpClientChannel channel = new TcpClientChannel();
    ChannelServices.RegisterChannel(channel);

    // Register the remote class as a valid
    // type in the client's application domain
    RemotingConfiguration.RegisterWellKnownClientType(
        // Remote class
        typeof(DbConnect),
        // URL of the remote class
        "tcp://localhost:1234/DbConnect"
        );

    // Instantiate the remote class
    dbc = new DbConnect();
}
```

8. Double-click the Button control and add the following code in the Click event handler:

```
private void btnExecute_Click
    (object sender, System.EventArgs e)
{
    try
    {   // Invoke a method on the remote object
        this.dgResults.DataSource =
            dbc.ExecuteQuery(this.txtQuery.Text);
        dgResults.DataMember = "Results";
    }
    catch(Exception ex)
    {
        MessageBox.Show(ex.Message,
            "Query Execution Error");
    }
}
```

continues

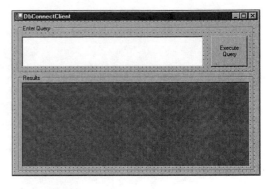

FIGURE 3.5
This form invokes a method of a remote object to execute the given query.

> **NOTE**
> **Starting Multiple Instances of a Program** When you run a project from the Visual Studio .NET IDE, the default behavior is to run the program in debug mode. However, debug mode does not allow you to start another program from the IDE until you finish the current execution. This can be inconvenient if you want to start multiple client programs from within Visual Studio. A solution is to set the project you want to run first as the startup object and select Debug, Run Without Debugging to run the project. This doesn't lock Visual Studio .NET in the debug mode and you can run more programs from within IDE by using the same technique.

continued

9. Right-click on the name of the solution in the Solution Explorer window and select Properties. This opens the Solution '320C03' Property Pages dialog box. In the dialog box, select the Multiple Startup Projects check box and then select the action Start for `StepByStep3_2` and `StepByStep3_3` and set the action to None for other projects, as shown in Figure 3.6. Make sure that `StepByStep3_2` is placed above `StepByStep3_3`, if it is not already in order, and then click on the Move Up and Move Down button to get the correct order.

FIGURE 3.6▶
Use the Solution Property Pages dialog box to control what projects are started and in what order.

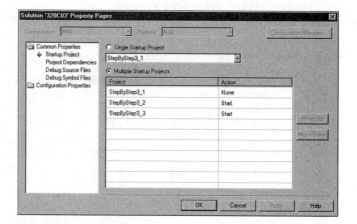

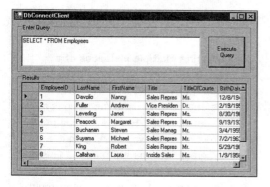

FIGURE 3.7▲
The remoting client populates the data grid with the result returned from the method invocation on a remote object.

10. Build the project. Select Debug, Start to run the project. You should see a command window displaying a message that the server is started in the SingleCall mode.

11. Shortly after, you'll see a Windows form for the client program. Enter a query in the text box and click the Execute Query button. The client invokes a method on the remote object and binds the results from the remote method to the `DataGrid` control, as shown in Figure 3.7.

In the preceding steps, I have chosen to start the client and server programs within the Visual Studio .NET IDE. You can also start these programs by clicking on `StepByStep3_2.exe` and `StepByStep3_3.exe`, respectively, from the Windows explorer. Note that the server program should be running before you click on the Execute Query button on the client program.

At the end of Step-by-Step 3.3, when you look at the console window of the server program, note the output as shown in Figure 3.8. The remote object is created every time you click on the Execute Query button. That's normal behavior based on what you have read so far in the chapter; however, what's peculiar is that for the first call, the constructor is called twice.

FIGURE 3.8
The SingleCall remoting server creates a new instance of the remote object with each request.

In fact, calling the constructor twice for the first request on a server is also a regular behavior of SingleCall object activation. The following two points explain why this happens:

▶ The first call to the constructor is made by the remoting framework at the server side to check whether it is okay to call this object remotely and to check the object's activation mode.

▶ The second constructor is called because of the client's call on the remote object. With SingleCall activation, the server does not preserve the state of the constructor that was called earlier and therefore the object has to be re-created with each client request.

Some of you might have a question about why I included a reference to StepByStep3_1.dll in this project. You may support your argument by saying that the DbConnect class contained in the StepByStep3_1.dll is a remotable class and its proper place is on the server—not on the client.

Well said, but I have included the reference to StepByStep3_1.dll for the following reasons:

▶ The client project StepByStep3_3 won't compile without it—I am referring to the DbConnect class in the project StepByStep3_3, and the project StepByStep3_3 by itself has no definition of DbConnect. When I include a reference to StepByStep3_1.dll, the project StepByStep3_3 can resolve the definition for DbConnect from there and enables me to compile the project.

▶ The client program `StepByStep3_3.exe` won't execute without it—I can't remove `StepByStep3_1.dll` from the project directory after the compilation is successfully completed. The `StepByStep3_1.dll` is required again at the time of running the client. To create the proxy object for the `DbConnect` class, the CLR must have the metadata that describes `DbConnect`. This metadata is read from the assembly stored in `StepByStep3_1.dll`.

However, you would say this won't work in real life, because the `StepByStep3_1.dll` may contain important business logic that you do not want your customers to decompile.

You're right! And I have a solution for that in the form of interface assemblies. With interface assemblies, you just share the interface of an assembly with your customers, not the actual business logic. I'll show you how to create interface assemblies later in this chapter in the section "Using Interface Assemblies to Compile Remoting Clients."

Using the Singleton Activation Mode to Register a Remotable Class As a Server-Activated Object

You can activate the same remotable object in different modes without making any changes to the remotable object itself. In the case of SAOs, the choice of activation mode is totally with the server. In this section, I'll show you how to create a remoting server that publishes the `DbConnect` class as an SAO by using the Singleton activation mode. I'll use the same client program that was created in Step-by-Step 3.3 to test this Singleton server.

STEP BY STEP

3.4 Using the Singleton Activation Mode to Register a Server-Activated Object

1. Add a new Visual C# .NET console application named `StepByStep3_4` to the solution.

2. Add references to the .NET assembly
System.Runtime.Remoting, and the project StepByStep3_1
(the remotable class assembly).

3. In the Solution Explorer, rename the default Class1.cs to
DbConnectSingletonServer.cs. Open the file and change
the name of the class to DbConnectSingletonServer in the
class declaration.

4. Add the following using directives:

```
using System.Runtime.Remoting;
using System.Runtime.Remoting.Channels;
using System.Runtime.Remoting.Channels.Tcp;
```

5. Add the following code in the Main() method:

```
[STAThread]
static void Main(string[] args)
{
    // Create and Register a TCP server channel
    // that listens on port 1234
    TcpServerChannel channel =
            new TcpServerChannel(1234);
    ChannelServices.RegisterChannel(channel);

    // Resgister the service that publishes
    // DbConnect for remote access in Singleton mode
    RemotingConfiguration.RegisterWellKnownServiceType
        (typeof(StepByStep3_1.DbConnect), "DbConnect",
         WellKnownObjectMode.Singleton);
    Console.WriteLine("Started server in the " +
        "Singleton mode");
    Console.WriteLine("Press <ENTER> to terminate " +
        "server...");
    Console.ReadLine();
}
```

6. Build the project. This step creates a remoting server that
is capable of registering the StepByStep3_1.DbConnect class
for remote invocation by using the Singleton activation
mode.

7. Set StepByStep3_4, the remoting server, as the startup project. Select Debug, Start Without Debugging to run the
project. You should see a command window displaying a
message that the server is started in the Singleton activation mode.

continues

continued

8. Now set StepByStep3_3, the remoting client, as the startup project. Select Debug, Start Without Debugging to run the project. Enter a query in the text box and click the button. The code invokes a method on the remote object, which is created when the form loads. The code binds the results from the remote method to the DataGrid control.

Although for the client there has been no changes in the output, if you note the messages generated by the server (see Figure 3.9), you can see that just one instance of the connection is created and is shared by all the clients that connect to this server.

FIGURE 3.9
The Singleton remoting server uses the same instance of the remote object with subsequent requests.

GUIDED PRACTICE EXERCISE 3.1

The objective of this exercise is to create a remoting server that exposes the DbConnect class of StepByStep3_1 as a Singleton SAO. However, the server and client should communicate via the HTTP channels and SOAP formatter. Other than this, the server and the client programs are similar to those created in Step-by-Step 3.4 and Step-by-Step 3.3, respectively.

How would you use the HTTP channel and SOAP formatter to establish communication between the remoting server and client?

This exercise helps you practice creating a remoting server and client that uses the HTTP channel and SOAP formatter for communication.

You should try working through this problem on your own first. If you get stuck, or if you'd like to see one possible solution, follow these steps:

1. Add a new Visual C# .NET console application named GuidedPracticeExercise3_1_Server to the solution.

2. Add references to the .NET assembly
   `System.Runtime.Remoting` and the project `StepByStep3_1` (the
   remotable class assembly).

3. In the Solution Explorer, rename the default `Class1.cs` to
   `DbConnectSingletonServer.cs`. Open the file and change the
   name of the class to `DbConnectSingletonServer` in the class
   declaration.

4. Add the following `using` directives:

```
using System.Runtime.Remoting;
using System.Runtime.Remoting.Channels;
using System.Runtime.Remoting.Channels.Http;
```

5. Add the following code in the `Main()` method:

```
[STAThread]
static void Main(string[] args)
{
    // Create and Register an HTTP server channel
    // that listens on port 1234
    HttpServerChannel channel =
        new HttpServerChannel(1234);
    ChannelServices.RegisterChannel(channel);

    // Register the service that publishes
    // DbConnect for remote access in Singleton mode
    RemotingConfiguration.RegisterWellKnownServiceType
        (typeof(StepByStep3_1.DbConnect), "DbConnect",
        WellKnownObjectMode.Singleton);
    Console.WriteLine("Started server in the " +
        "Singleton mode");
    Console.WriteLine("Press <ENTER> to terminate " +
        "server...");
    Console.ReadLine();
}
```

6. Build the project. This step creates a remoting server that is
   capable of registering the `StepByStep3_1.DbConnect` class (the
   remotable object) for remote invocation by using the Singleton
   activation mode via the HTTP channel.

7. Add a new Visual C# .NET Windows application named
   `GuidedPracticeExercise3_1_Client` to the solution.

8. Add references to the .NET assembly
   `System.Runtime.Remoting` and the project `StepByStep3_1` (the
   remotable class assembly).

continues

continued

9. In the Solution Explorer, rename the default `Form1.cs` to `DbConnectClient.cs`. Open the form in code view and change all occurrences of `Form1` to refer to `DbConnectClient` instead.

10. Add the following `using` directives:

```
using System.Runtime.Remoting;
using System.Runtime.Remoting.Channels;
using System.Runtime.Remoting.Channels.Http;
using StepByStep3_1;
```

11. Place two `GroupBox` controls, a `TextBox` control (`txtQuery`, with its `MultiLine` property set to `true`), a `Button` control (`btnExecute`) and a `DataGrid` control (`dgResults`) on the form. Refer to Figure 3.5 for the design of the form.

12. Add the following code in the class definition:

```
// Declare a Remote object
DbConnect dbc;
```

13. Double-click the form and add the following code in the `Load` event handler:

```
private void DbConnectClient_Load
    (object sender, System.EventArgs e)
{
    // Register an HTTP client channel
    HttpClientChannel channel =
        new HttpClientChannel();
    ChannelServices.RegisterChannel(channel);

    // Register the remote class as a valid
    // type in the client's application domain
    RemotingConfiguration.RegisterWellKnownClientType(
        // Remote class
        typeof(DbConnect),
        // URL of the remote class
        "http://localhost:1234/DbConnect"
        );

    // Instantiate the remote class
    dbc = new DbConnect();
}
```

14. Double-click the `Button` control and add the following code in the `Click` event handler:

```
private void btnExecute_Click
    (object sender, System.EventArgs e)
{
    try
    {   // Invoke a method on the remote object
```

continued

```
        this.dgResults.DataSource =
            dbc.ExecuteQuery(this.txtQuery.Text);
        dgResults.DataMember = "Results";
    }
    catch(Exception ex)
    {
        MessageBox.Show(ex.Message,
            "Query Execution Error");
    }
}
```

15. Build the project. Set the `GuidedPracticeExercise3_1_Server`, the remoting server, as the startup project. Select Debug, Start Without Debugging to run the project. You should see a command window displaying a message that the server is started in the Singleton activation mode. The remoting server is now ready to receive SOAP messages via HTTP.

16. Now set `GuidedPracticeExercise3_1_Client`, the remoting client, as the startup project. Select Debug, Start Without Debugging to run the project. Enter a query in the text box and click the button. The code invokes a method on the remote object and sends the messages in SOAP format via HTTP.

If you have difficulty following this exercise, review the sections "Channels," "Formatters," "Creating a Remotable Class," and "Creating a Server-Activated Object," earlier in this chapter. Make sure that you also perform Step-by-Step 3.1 to Step-by-Step 3.4. After doing that review, try this exercise again.

Creating a Client-Activated Object

Create and consume a .NET Remoting object.

- **Implement client-activated components.**

- **Instantiate and invoke a .NET Remoting object.**

When exposing a remotable class as a CAO, no changes are required on the remotable class. Instead, only the server and client differ on how the remotable class is registered with the remoting system.

In this section, I'll show you how to register a remotable class as a CAO and how to instantiate and invoke a CAO from a remoting client.

Registering a Remotable Class As a Client-Activated Object

You'll have to take the following steps to register a remotable class as a CAO on the server:

1. Create a server channel that listens on a particular port to the incoming object activation requests from other application domains. The following examples show how to create a TCP server channel and an HTTP server channel:

```
// Register a TCP server channel on port 1234
TcpServerChannel channel = new TcpServerChannel(1234);

// Register an HTTP server channel on port 1235
HttpServerChannel channel =
    new HttpServerChannel(1235);
```

2. Register the channel with the remoting framework. This registration is performed through the `RegisterChannel()` method of the `ChannelServices` class:

```
// Register the channel with the remoting framework
ChannelServices.RegisterChannel(channel);
```

3. Register the remotable class with the remoting framework. For a client-activated object, use the `RegisterActivatedServiceType()` method of the `RemotingConfiguration` class to perform the registration, as shown below:

```
// Register a remote object as a CAO
// with the remoting framework
RemotingConfiguration.RegisterActivatedServiceType(
    typeof(DbConnect)); // type of the remotable class
```

Here, the only parameter is the type of the remotable class.

Step-by-Step 3.5 shows how to expose the familiar `DbConnect` class from `StepByStep3_1` as a CAO.

STEP BY STEP

3.5 Registering a Remotable Class As a Client-Activated Object

1. Add a new Visual C# .NET console application named StepByStep3_5 to the solution.

2. Add references to the .NET assembly System.Runtime.Remoting and the project StepByStep3_1 (the remotable class assembly).

3. In the Solution Explorer, rename the default Class1.cs to DbConnectCAOServer.cs. Open the file and change the name of the class to DbConnectCAOServer in the class declaration.

4. Add the following using directives:

```
using System.Runtime.Remoting;
using System.Runtime.Remoting.Channels;
using System.Runtime.Remoting.Channels.Tcp;
using StepByStep3_1;
```

5. Add the following code in the Main() method:

```
[STAThread]
static void Main(string[] args)
{
    // Create and register a TCP channel on port 1234
    TcpServerChannel channel =
        new TcpServerChannel(1234);
    ChannelServices.RegisterChannel(channel);

    // Register the client-activated object
    RemotingConfiguration.RegisterActivatedServiceType
        (typeof(DbConnect));
    Console.WriteLine(
      "Started server in the Client Activation mode");
    Console.WriteLine(
        "Press <ENTER> to terminate server...");
    Console.ReadLine();
}
```

6. Build the project. This step creates a remoting server that is capable of registering the StepByStep3_1.DbConnect (the remotable object) class for remote invocation by using the client activation mode.

Instantiating and Invoking a Client-Activated Object

To instantiate and invoke a client-activated object, the remoting client needs to take the following steps:

1. Create and register a client channel that the remoting framework uses to send messages to the remoting server. The type of the channel the client uses should be compatible with the channel the server uses. The following examples show how to create a TCP client channel and an HTTP client channel:

    ```
    // Create and register a TCP client channel
    TcpClientChannel channel = new TcpClientChannel();
    ChannelServices.RegisterChannel(channel);

    // Create and register an HTTP client channel
    HttpClientChannel channel = new HttpClientChannel();
    ChannelServices.RegisterChannel(channel);
    ```

2. Register the remotable class as a valid type in the client's application domain. This registration is performed using the `RegisterActivatedClientType()` method of the `RemotingConfiguration` class as shown below:

    ```
    // Register DbConnect as a type on client,
    // which can be activated on the server
    RemotingConfiguration.RegisterActivatedClientType
            (typeof(DbConnect), "tcp://localhost:1234");
    ```

    Here, the first parameter is the type of the remotable class. The second parameter specifies the uniform resource identifier (URI) through which the server publishes the location of the remote object.

3. Instantiate the CAO on the server by using the desired constructor.

    ```
    // Instantiate the remote object
    DbConnect dbc = new DbConnect("Pubs");
    ```

I'll demonstrate the preceding steps in Step-by-Step 3.6. This step is similar to the client program created in Step-by-Step 3.3, but this time the client allows the user to choose between the databases on the server.

> **EXAM TIP**
>
> **Instantiating a Client-Activated Object**   You can instantiate a CAO at the client side by using any of its available constructors.

STEP BY STEP

3.6 Instantiating and Invoking a Client-Activated Object

1. Add a new Visual C# .NET Windows application named StepByStep3_6 to the solution.

2. Add references to the .NET assembly System.Runtime.Remoting, and the project StepByStep3_1 (the remotable class assembly).

3. In the Solution Explorer, rename the default Form1.cs to DbConnectClient.cs. Open the form in code view and change all occurrences of Form1 to refer to DbConnectClient instead.

4. Add the following using directives:

```
using System.Runtime.Remoting;
using System.Runtime.Remoting.Channels;
using System.Runtime.Remoting.Channels.Tcp;
using StepByStep3_1;
```

5. Place three GroupBox controls (grpDatabases, grpQuery and grpResults), a ComboBox control (cboDatabases), a TextBox control (txtQuery, with its MultiLine property set to true), two Button controls (btnSelect and btnExecute), and a DataGrid control (dgResults) on the form. Refer to Figure 3.10 for this form's design.

6. Select the Items property of the cboDatabases control in the Properties window and click on the (...) button. This opens the String Collection Editor dialog box. Enter the following database names in the editor:

```
Northwind
Pubs
GrocerToGo
```

Click OK to add the databases to the Items collection of the cboDatabases control.

7. Add the following code in the class definition:

```
// Declare a Remote object
DbConnect dbc;
```

continues

continued

8. Double-click the form and add the following code in the
Load event handler:

```
private void DbConnectClient_Load(
    object sender, System.EventArgs e)
{
    cboDatabases.SelectedIndex = 0;
    grpQuery.Enabled = false;
}
```

9. Double-click the btnSelect control and add the following
code in the Click event handler:

```
private void btnSelect_Click(
    object sender, System.EventArgs e)
{
    // Disable the Databases group box and
    // enable the Query group box
    grpDatabases.Enabled = false;
    grpQuery.Enabled = true;

    // Register a TCP client channel
    TcpClientChannel channel = new TcpClientChannel();
    ChannelServices.RegisterChannel(channel);

    // Register the remote class as a valid
    // type in the client's application domain
    // by passing the Remote class and its URL
    RemotingConfiguration.RegisterActivatedClientType
        (typeof(DbConnect), "tcp://localhost:1234");

    // Instantiate the remote class
    dbc = new DbConnect(
        cboDatabases.SelectedItem.ToString());
}
```

10. Double-click the btnExecute control and add the following code in the Click event handler:

```
private void btnExecute_Click
    (object sender, System.EventArgs e)
{
    try
    {   // Invoke a method on the remote object
        this.dgResults.DataSource =
            dbc.ExecuteQuery(this.txtQuery.Text);
        dgResults.DataMember = "Results";
    }
    catch(Exception ex)
    {
        MessageBox.Show(ex.Message,
            "Query Execution Error");
    }
}
```

11. Build the project. You now have a remoting client ready to use.

12. Set StepByStep3_5, the CAO remoting server, as the start-up project. Select Debug, Start Without Debugging to run the project. You should see a command window displaying a message that the server is started in the client activation mode.

13. Now set StepByStep3_6, the remoting client, as the startup project. Select Debug, Start Without Debugging to run the project. Select a database from the combo box and click the Select button. An instance of the remotable object, DbConnect, is created with the selected database. Now enter a query in the text box and click the button. The code invokes a method on the remote object. The code binds the results from the remote method to the DataGrid control as shown in Figure 3.10.

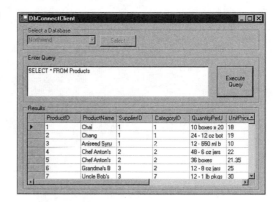

FIGURE 3.10
A CAO client allows database selection by taking advantage of the capability to call various constructors.

14. Again select Debug, Start Without Debugging to run one more instance of the remoting client. Select a different database from the combo box and click the Select button. An instance of the remotable object, DbConnect, is created with the selected database. Now enter a query in the text box and click the button. You should see that the second instance of the client fetches the data from the selected database. Switch to the server command window. You can see that the remote object is instantiated twice with different databases, as shown in Figure 3.11. This shows that the client activation creates an instance of a remotable object for each client.

FIGURE 3.11
The client-activated remoting server creates a new instance of a remote object for each client.

REVIEW BREAK

▶ To create a remotable class, inherit the remotable class from the `MarshalByRefObject` class.

▶ A remotable class is usually connected with the remoting framework through a separate server program. The server program listens to the client request on a specified channel and instantiates the remote object or invokes calls on it as required.

▶ You should create a server channel that listens on a given port number and register the channel with the remoting framework before you register the remotable class.

▶ The type of channel the client registers should be compatible with the type of channel the server uses for receiving messages.

▶ You do not specify a port number when you register the client channel. The port number is instead specified when the remote class is registered in the client's application domain.

▶ To register SAO objects, on the server side you call the `RemotingConfiguration.RegisterWellKnownServiceType()` method and on the client side you call the `RemotingConfiguration.RegisterWellKnownClientType()` method.

▶ To register CAO objects, on the server side you call the `RemotingConfiguration.RegisterActivatedServiceType()` method and on the client side you call the `RemotingConfiguration.RegisterActivatedClientType()` method.

▶ You can instantiate SAOs only at the client side by using their default constructor, whereas you can instantiate CAOs by using any of the constructors.

Using Configuration Files to Configure the Remoting Framework

Create and consume a .NET Remoting object: Create client configuration files and server configuration files.

In all the examples written so far, I have written code to register the channel and remote object with the remoting framework. This approach of specifying settings is also known as *programmatic configuration*. Although this approach works fine, there is a drawback: Every time you decide to make any changes in how the channel and the remote objects are registered, you have to recompile the code to see the effect of the changes.

Alternatively, you can store the remoting settings in an XML-based configuration file instead of the code file. The program can automatically pick up any changes made to the configuration file when it executes the next time. You need not recompile the sources. This approach of specifying configuration settings is also known as *declarative configuration.*

The declarative configuration can be specified at two levels:

▶ Machine-Level—The configuration settings at the machine level can be specified through the machine.config file. The machine.config file is present in the CONFIG subdirectory of the .NET Framework installation directory (typically, Microsoft.NET\Framework\v1.0.3705\CONFIG in the Windows directory of your computer, if you're running version 1.0 of the .NET Framework). Any settings specified in this file apply to all the .NET applications running on the machine.

▶ Application-Level—The configuration settings for a specific application can be specified through the application configuration file. In a Windows application, the name of the application-level configuration file includes the full application name and the extension, with .config appended to the extension. For example, the configuration file name for StepByStep3_7.exe is StepByStep3_7.exe.config. In an ASP.NET application, the name of the configuration file is web.config.

The general format of the configuration file is as follows:

```
<configuration>
<system.runtime.remoting>
 <application>
   <lifetime>
     <!-- Use this section to specify the -->
     <!-- lifetime information for all    -->
     <!-- the objects in the application. -->
   </lifetime>
```

NOTE

Visual Studio .NET Projects and Application Configuration File You should write the application configuration settings for Visual Studio .NET Windows application and Console application projects in a file named App.config in the project's folder. When you build the project, Visual Studio .NET copies the App.config file to the output folder and rename it to *OutputFileName.config*. For example, if the name of the output file for the project is StepByStep3_7.exe, then the name of the configuration file will be StepByStep3_7.exe.config. For a Web application project, the configuration settings are written directly to the Web.config file.

NOTE

Use Naming Conventions for the Application-Level Configuration Files Although it is not required, you should prefer using the .NET Framework naming convention for naming the application-level configuration file. This ensures that configuration settings for an application, whether remoting-related or security-related, are all in one place.

EXAM TIP

Application-Level Configuration File Takes Precedence over Machine-Level Configuration When you specify both application-level configuration as well as machine-level configuration for an application, the application-level configuration takes priority over the machine-level configuration.

```
<service>
  <!-- Use this section to specify how a remote-->
  <!-- object is exposed by the remoting server-->
  <!-- Use the <wellknown> tag to configure-->
  <!-- an SAO and use the <activated> tag     -->
  <!-- to configure a CAO                      -->
  <wellknown />
  <activated />
</service>
<client>
  <!-- Use this section to specify how a remote-->
  <!-- object is consumed by the client       -->
  <!-- Use the <wellknown> tag to configure a  -->
  <!-- call to the SAO and use the <activated> -->
  <!-- tag to configure a call to the CAO      -->
  <wellknown />
  <activated />
</client>
<channels>
  <!-- Use this section to configure the       -->
  <!-- channels that the application uses       -->
  <!-- to communicate with the remote objects  -->
</channels>
</application>
</system.runtime.remoting>
</configuration>
```

Server-Side Configuration

In Step-by-Step 3.7, I create a remoting server with Singleton activation mode, similar to one created in Step-by-Step 3.4. However, you'll note that the code itself is reduced, as most of the configuration-related code is now moved to a separate configuration file.

STEP BY STEP

3.7 Using Configuration Files to Register a Server-Activated Object in the Singleton Activation Mode

1. Add a new Visual C# .NET console application named StepByStep3_7 to the solution.

2. Add references to the .NET assembly System.Runtime.Remoting and the project StepByStep3_1 (the remotable class assembly).

3. In the Solution Explorer, right-click project `StepByStep3_7` and select Add, Add New Item from the context menu. Add an item named `App.config` based on the Application configuration file template.

4. Open the `StepByStep3_7.exe.config` file and modify it to contain the following code:

```
<configuration>
    <system.runtime.remoting>
        <application>
            <service>
                <!-- Set the activation mode,
                remotable object, and its URL -->
                <wellknown mode="Singleton"
                    type=
                "StepByStep3_1.DbConnect, StepByStep3_1"
                    objectUri="DbConnect" />
            </service>
            <channels>
                <!-- Set the channel and port -->
                <channel ref="tcp server"
                    port="1234" />
            </channels>
        </application>
    </system.runtime.remoting>
</configuration>
```

5. In the Solution Explorer, rename the default `Class1.cs` to `DbConnectSingletonServer.cs`. Open the file and change the name of the class to `DbConnectSingletonServer` in the class declaration.

6. Add the following `using` directive:

```
using System.Runtime.Remoting;
```

7. Add the following code in the `Main()` method:

```
[STAThread]
static void Main(string[] args)
{
```

continues

continued

```
// Load remoting configuration
RemotingConfiguration.Configure
    ("StepByStep3_7.exe.config");
Console.WriteLine("Started server in the " +
    "Singleton mode");
Console.WriteLine("Press <ENTER> to terminate " +
    "server...");
Console.ReadLine();
}
```

8. Build the project. This step creates a remoting server that is capable of registering the StepByStep3_1.DbConnect class for remote invocation by using the Singleton activation mode via its settings in the configuration file.

9. Set StepByStep3_7, the remoting server, as the startup project. Select Debug, Start Without Debugging to run the project. You should see a command window displaying a message that the server is started in the Singleton activation mode by retrieving the remoting configuration settings from the configuration file.

10. Now set StepByStep3_3, the remoting client, as the startup project. Select Debug, Start Without Debugging to run the project. Enter a query in the text box and click the button. The code invokes a method on the remote object, which is created when the form loads. The code binds the results from the remote method to the DataGrid control.

The most important thing to note in Step-by-Step 3.7 is the way I have written the <service> and <channels> elements in the configuration file.

The <service> element is written as follows:

```
<service>
    <!-- Set the activcation mode,
        remotable object, and its URL -->
    <wellknown mode="Singleton"
            type=
            "StepByStep3_1.DbConnect, StepByStep3_1"
            objectUri="DbConnect" />
</service>
```

For an SAO, you need to use the <wellknown> element, where you specify the activation mode, type, and the object URI. The type

attribute is specified as a pair made up of the qualified classname
(StepByStep3_1.DbConnect) and the name of the assembly
(StepByStep3_1). The objectUri attribute specifies the endpoint of
the URI where the client program will attempt to connect.

The <channels> element can be used to specify the channels the
server uses to expose the remotable class. The ref attribute specifies
the ID of the channel you want to use. The value ref="tcp server"
specifies that the channel is a TCP server channel. If I instead write
ref="tcp", the channel becomes a receiver-sender channel.

```
<channels>
    <!-- Set the channel and port -->
    <channel ref="tcp server" port="1234" />
</channels>
```

With the use of configuration files, the remoting code inside the
Main() method of the server is now just one statement:

```
// Load remoting configuration
RemotingConfiguration.Configure(
    "StepByStep3_7.exe.config");
```

The Configure() method of the RemotingConfiguration class loads
the configuration file into memory, parses its contents to locate the
<system.runtime.remoting> section, and based on the settings, calls
the relevant methods to register the channels and the remoting
objects.

Client-Side Configuration

The configuration of the remoting client is quite similar to that of
the remoting server. However, you configure the <client> element
of the configuration file instead of the <service> element.

Step-by-Step 3.8 demonstrates how to use the client-side configuration files.

STEP BY STEP

3.8 Instantiating and Invoking a Server-Activated Object

1. Add a new Visual C# .NET Windows application named
StepByStep3_8 to the solution.

continues

continued

2. Add references to the .NET assembly
`System.Runtime.Remoting`, and the project `StepByStep3_1`
(the remotable class assembly).

3. In the Solution Explorer, right-click project `StepByStep3_8`
and select Add, Add New Item from the context menu.
Add an Item named `App.config`, based on the Application
configuration file template.

4. Modify the `App.config` file to contain the following code:

```
<configuration>
    <system.runtime.remoting>
        <application>
            <client>
                <!-- Set the remotable object
                and its URL -->
                <wellknown
                  type=
                "StepByStep3_1.DbConnect, StepByStep3_1"
                  url="tcp://localhost:1234/DbConnect"
                  />
            </client>
        </application>
    </system.runtime.remoting>
</configuration>
```

5. In the Solution Explorer, rename the default `Form1.cs` to
`DbConnectClient.cs`. Open the form in code view and
change all occurrences of `Form1` to refer to
`DbConnectClient` instead.

6. Place two `GroupBox` controls (`grpQuery` and `grpResults`), a
`TextBox` control (`txtQuery`, with its `MultiLine` property set
to true), a `Button` control (`btnExecute`), and a `DataGrid`
control (`dgResults`) on the form. Refer to Figure 3.5 for
this form's design.

7. Add the following using directives:

```
using System.Runtime.Remoting;
using StepByStep3_1;
```

8. Add the following code in the class definition:

```
// Declare a Remote object
DbConnect dbc;
```

9. Double-click the form and add the following code in the Load event handler:

```
private void DbConnectClient_Load(
    object sender, System.EventArgs e)
{
    // Load remoting configuration
    RemotingConfiguration.Configure
        ("StepByStep3_8.exe.config");

    // Instantiate the remote class
    dbc = new DbConnect();
}
```

10. Double-click the Button control and add the following code in the Click event handler:

```
private void btnExecute_Click(
    object sender, System.EventArgs e)
{
    try
    {   // Invoke a method on the remote object
        this.dgResults.DataSource =
            dbc.ExecuteQuery(this.txtQuery.Text);
        dgResults.DataMember = "Results";
    }
    catch(Exception ex)
    {
        MessageBox.Show(ex.Message,
            "Query Execution Error");
    }
}
```

11. Build the project. Set StepByStep3_7, the remoting server, as the startup project. Select Debug, Start Without Debugging to run the project. You should see a command window displaying a message that the server is started in the Singleton activation mode by retrieving the remoting configuration settings from the configuration file.

12. Set StepByStep3_8, the remoting client, as the startup project. Select Debug, Start Without Debugging to run the project. Enter a query in the text box and click the

continues

continued

button. The code invokes a method on the remote object, which is created from the settings stored in the configuration file. The code binds the results from the remote method to the DataGrid control.

The most important thing to note in Step-by-Step 3.8 is the use of the <client> element in the configuration file. The mode attribute is not part of the <wellknown> element of the client and the objectUri attribute is replaced with the url attribute that specifies the address to connect to the remote object.

```
<client>
    <!-- Set the remotable object
         and its URL -->
    <wellknown
            type=
               "StepByStep3_1.DbConnect, StepByStep3_1"
            url="tcp://localhost:1234/DbConnect"
    />
</client>
```

Unlike the server configuration file, the <channel> element is not required for the client because the client uses the URL to determine protocol and the port number.

GUIDED PRACTICE EXERCISE 3.2

In this exercise, you are required to expose the DbConnect class from Step-by-Step 3.1 as a CAO through a remoting server through the HTTP channel. You also need to invoke methods on this client-activated object by creating a form similar to the one created in Step-by-Step 3.6.

However, you should be able to change various parameters such as the channel protocol, port number, URL, name, and type of the remote object without needing to recompile the server.

How would you design such a remoting client and server?

This exercise helps you practice creating configuration files for the remoting server and the client to remote a CAO. You should try working through this problem on your own first. If you get stuck, or if you'd like to see one possible solution, follow these steps:

1. Add a new Visual C# .NET console application named
   GuidedPracticeExercise3_2_Server to the solution.

2. Add references to the .NET assembly
   System.Runtime.Remoting and the project StepByStep3_1 (the
   remotable class assembly).

3. In the Solution Explorer, right-click the project
   GuidedPracticeExercise3_2_Server and select Add, Add New
   Item from the context menu. Add an Item named App.config
   based on the Application configuration file template.

4. Modify the App.config file to contain the following code:

```
<configuration>
    <system.runtime.remoting>
        <application>
            <service>
                <!-- Set the remotable object -->
                <activated
                    type=
                "StepByStep3_1.DbConnect, StepByStep3_1"
                    />
            </service>
            <channels>
                <channel ref="http" port="1234" />
            </channels>
        </application>
    </system.runtime.remoting>
</configuration>
```

5. In the Solution Explorer, rename the default Class1.cs to
   DbConnectCAOServer.cs. Open the file and change the name of
   the class to DbConnectCAOServer in the class declaration.

6. Add the following using directive:

```
using System.Runtime.Remoting;
```

continues

continued

7. Add the following code in the `Main()` method:

```
[STAThread]
static void Main(string[] args)
{
    // Load remoting configuration
    RemotingConfiguration.Configure
      ("GuidedPracticeExercise3_2_Server.exe.config");

    Console.WriteLine(
      "Started server in the Client Activation mode");
    Console.WriteLine(
      "Press <ENTER> to terminate server...");
    Console.ReadLine();
}
```

8. Build the project. This step creates a remoting server that is capable of registering the `StepByStep3_1.DbConnect` class for remote invocation by using the client activation mode via its settings in the configuration file.

9. Add a new Visual C# .NET Windows application named `GuidedPracticeExercise3_2_Client` to the solution.

10. Add references to the .NET assembly `System.Runtime.Remoting` and the project `StepByStep3_1` (the remotable class assembly).

11. In the Solution Explorer, right-click the project `GuidedPracticeExercise3_2_Client` and select Add, Add New Item from the context menu. Add an Item named `App.config` based on the Application configuration file template.

12. Modify the `App.config` file to contain the following code:

```
<configuration>
    <system.runtime.remoting>
        <application>
            <!-- Set the url for the
              client activation -->
            <client url="http://localhost:1234">
                <!-- Set the remote object
                type and its assembly -->
                <activated
                  type=
                "StepByStep3_1.DbConnect, StepByStep3_1"
                  />
            </client>
```

```
        </application>
      </system.runtime.remoting>
</configuration>
```

13. In the Solution Explorer, rename the default `Form1.cs` to `DbConnectClient.cs`. Open the form in code view and change all occurrences of `Form1` to refer to `DbConnectClient` instead.

14. Place three `GroupBox` controls (`grpDatabases`, `grpQuery` and `grpResults`), a `ComboBox` control (`cboDatabases`), a `TextBox` control (`txtQuery`, with its `MultiLine` property set to `true`), two `Button` controls (`btnSelect` and `btnExecute`), and a `DataGrid` control (`dgResults`) on the form. Refer to Figure 3.10 for the design of this form.

15. Select the `Items` property of the `cboDatabases` control in the Properties window and click on the (…) button. This opens the String Collection Editor dialog box. Enter the following database names in the editor:

```
Northwind
Pubs
GrocerToGo
```

Click OK to add the databases to the `Items` collection of the `cboDatabases` control.

16. Add the following `using` directives:

```
using System.Runtime.Remoting;
using StepByStep3_1;
```

17. Add the following code in the class definition:

```
// Declare a Remote object
DbConnect dbc;
```

18. Double-click the form and add the following code in the `Load` event handler:

```
private void DbConnectClient_Load(
    object sender, System.EventArgs e)
```

continues

continued

```
{
    cboDatabases.SelectedIndex = 0;
    grpQuery.Enabled = false;
}
```

19. Double-click the `btnSelect` control and add the following code in the `Click` event handler:

```
private void btnSelect_Click(
    object sender, System.EventArgs e)
{
    grpDatabases.Enabled = false;
    grpQuery.Enabled = true;

    // Load remoting configuration
    RemotingConfiguration.Configure
      ("GuidedPracticeExercise3_2_Client.exe.config");

    // Instantiate the remote class
    dbc = new DbConnect(
        cboDatabases.SelectedItem.ToString());
}
```

20. Double-click the `btnExecute` control and add the following code in the `Click` event handler:

```
private void btnExecute_Click(
    object sender, System.EventArgs e)
{
    try
    {   // Invoke a method on the remote object
        this.dgResults.DataSource =
            dbc.ExecuteQuery(this.txtQuery.Text);
        dgResults.DataMember = "Results";
    }
    catch(Exception ex)
    {
        MessageBox.Show(ex.Message,
            "Query Execution Error");
    }
}
```

21. Build the project. Set `GuidedPracticeExercise3_2_Server`, the remoting server, as the startup project. Select Debug, Start Without Debugging to run the project. You should see a command window displaying a message that the server is started in the client activation mode by retrieving the remoting configuration settings from the configuration file.

22. Set `GuidedPracticeExercise3_2_Client`, the remoting client, as the startup project. Select Debug, Start Without Debugging to

run the project. Enter a query in the text box and click the button. The code invokes a method on the remote object, which is created from the settings stored in the configuration file. The code binds the results from the remote method to the `DataGrid` control.

If you have difficulty following this exercise, review the sections "Creating a Client-Activated Object" and "Using Configuration Files to Configure the Remoting Framework" earlier in this chapter. After doing that review, try this exercise again.

Using Interface Assemblies to Compile Remoting Clients

So far, in all the examples, I had to copy the assembly containing the remotable class to the client project for the client to work. However, this is not a desirable solution in most cases because you may not want to share the implementation of the remotable object with your customers or business partners who are writing the client application.

An advisable solution in that case is to share only the interface of the remotable class with the client application. An interface does not contain any implementation; instead, it just contains the members that are supplied by the class.

In the following sections I demonstrate how you can create interfaces that will enable you to create remote SAOs and CAOs without sharing the implementation. I also introduce the Soapsuds tool, which can help you in automatically creating the interfaces for a remotable class.

Creating an Interface Assembly

In this section, I create an assembly that contains an interface named `IDbConnect`. The interface defines a contract (as shown in

Step-by-Step 3.9). All the classes or structs that implement the interface must adhere to this contract.

STEP BY STEP

3.9 Creating an Interface Assembly

1. Add a new Visual C# .NET class library named StepByStep3_9 to the solution.

2. In the Solution Explorer, rename the default Class1.cs to IDbConnect.cs.

3. Open the IDbConnect.cs and replace the code with the following code:

```
using System;
using System.Data;

namespace StepByStep3_9
{
    public interface IDbConnect
    {
        DataSet ExecuteQuery(string strQuery);
    }
}
```

4. Build the project. This step creates an assembly that contains the definition of the IDbConnect interface.

Creating a Remotable Object That Implements an Interface

Now that you have created the interface IDbConnect, you can implement this interface in a class named DbConnect. You must ensure that the class DbConnect adheres to the contract defined by the IDbConnect interface. This means you must implement the method ExecuteQuery() and the data types of parameters, and the return value must match with that defined in the interface.

Step-by-Step 3.10 creates the class DbConnect, which adheres to the IDbConnect interface.

STEP BY STEP

3.10 Creating a Remotable Object That Implements an Interface Assembly

1. Add a new Visual C# .NET class library named `StepByStep3_10` to the solution.

2. Add references to the .NET assembly `System.Runtime.Remoting` and the project `StepByStep3_9` (the interface assembly).

3. In the Solution Explorer, rename the default `Class1.cs` to `DbConnect.cs`.

4. Open the `DbConnect.cs` and replace the code with the following code:

```
using System;
using System.Data;
using System.Data.SqlClient;
using StepByStep3_9;

namespace StepByStep3_10
{
    // Marshal-by-Reference Remotable Object
    // Inheriting from MarshalByRefObject and
    // Implementing IDbConnect interface
    public class DbConnect :
        MarshalByRefObject, IDbConnect
    {
        private SqlConnection sqlconn;

        // Default constructor connects to the
        // Northwind database
        public DbConnect() : this("Northwind")
        {
        }

        // Parameterized constructor connects to the
        // specified database
        public DbConnect(string DbName)
        {
            // Open a connection to the specified
            // sample SQL Server database
            sqlconn = new SqlConnection(
                "data source=(local);" +
                "initial catalog=" + DbName +
                ";integrated security=SSPI");
            Console.WriteLine(
                "Created a new connection to " +
                "the {0} database.", DbName);
        }
```

continues

continued

```
public DataSet ExecuteQuery(string strQuery)
{
    Console.Write("Starting to execute " +
        "the query...");
    // Create a SqlCommand object
    // to represent the query
    SqlCommand sqlcmd =
        sqlconn.CreateCommand();
    sqlcmd.CommandType = CommandType.Text;
    sqlcmd.CommandText = strQuery;

    // Create a SqlDataAdapter object
    // to talk to the database
    SqlDataAdapter sqlda =
        new SqlDataAdapter();
    sqlda.SelectCommand = sqlcmd;
    // Create a DataSet to hold the results
    DataSet ds = new DataSet();
    try
    {
        // Fill the DataSet
        sqlda.Fill(ds, "Results");
    }
    catch (Exception ex)
    {
        Console.WriteLine(ex.Message,
            "Error executing query");
    }
    Console.WriteLine("Done.");
    return ds;
    }
  }
}
```

5. Build the project. This step creates
`StepByStep3_10.DbConnect`, a remotable class that implements the `IDbConnect` interface.

This program is similar to the one created in Step-by-Step 3.1, except that the `DbConnect` class is now implementing the `IDbConnect` interface in addition to deriving from the `MarshalByRefObject` class:

```
public class DbConnect :
    MarshalByRefObject, IDbConnect
{...}
```

You can expose this remotable object to the clients via the remoting framework by using the techniques that you already know. Step-by-Step 3.11 creates a remoting server that registers the `DbConnect` class created in Step-by-Step 3.10 as an SAO in Singleton mode.

STEP BY STEP

3.11 Creating a Remoting Server to Register the Remotable Object That Implements an Interface Assembly

1. Add a new Visual C# .NET console application named StepByStep3_11 to the solution.

2. Add references to the .NET assembly System.Runtime.Remoting, the project StepByStep3_9 (the interface assembly), and StepByStep3_10 (the remotable class assembly).

3. In the Solution Explorer, rename the default Class1.cs to DbConnectSingletonServer.cs. Open the file and change the name of the class to DbConnectSingletonServer in the class declaration.

4. Add the following using directives:

```
using System.Runtime.Remoting;
using System.Runtime.Remoting.Channels;
using System.Runtime.Remoting.Channels.Tcp;
```

5. Add the following code in the Main() method:

```
[STAThread]
static void Main(string[] args)
{
    // Register a TCP server channel that
    // listens on port 1234
    TcpServerChannel channel =
        new TcpServerChannel(1234);
    ChannelServices.RegisterChannel(channel);

    // Register the service that publishes
    // DbConnect for remote access in Singleton mode
    RemotingConfiguration.RegisterWellKnownServiceType
        (typeof(StepByStep3_10.DbConnect), "DbConnect",
        WellKnownObjectMode.Singleton);
    Console.WriteLine("Started server in the " +
        "Singleton mode");
    Console.WriteLine("Press <ENTER> to terminate " +
        "server...");
    Console.ReadLine();
}
```

6. Build the project. This step creates a remoting server that is capable of registering StepByStep3_10.DbConnect, the remotable object that implements StepByStep3_9.

continues

continued

IDbConnect interface, for remote invocation by using the Singleton activation mode.

Creating a Remoting Client That Uses an Interface Instead of the Implementation

When the remotable class is implementing an interface, you can include just the reference to the interface assembly rather than the implementation assembly itself at the client side. The client then extracts the necessary type information and metadata for compiling and running the program from the interface. Step-by-Step 3.12 shows you how to create such a client.

STEP BY STEP

3.12 Creating a Remoting Client to Invoke the Remotable Object That Implements an Interface Assembly

1. Add a new Visual C# .NET Windows application named StepByStep3_12 to the solution.

2. Add references to the .NET assembly System.Runtime.Remoting and the project StepByStep3_9 (the interface assembly).

3. In the Solution Explorer, rename the default Form1.cs to DbConnectClient.cs. Open the form in code view and change all occurrences of Form1 to refer to DbConnectClient instead.

4. Add the following using directives:

```
using System.Runtime.Remoting;
using System.Runtime.Remoting.Channels;
using System.Runtime.Remoting.Channels.Tcp;
using StepByStep3_9;
```

5. Place two GroupBox controls (grpQuery and grpResults), a TextBox control (txtQuery, with its MultiLine property set to true), a Button control (btnExecute), and a DataGrid

control (dgResults) on the form. Refer to Figure 3.5 for the design of this form.

6. Add the following code in the class definition:

```
// Declare a Remote object
IDbConnect dbc;
```

7. Double-click the form and add the following code in the Load event handler:

```
private void DbConnectClient_Load(
    object sender, System.EventArgs e)
{
    // Register a TCP client channel
    TcpClientChannel channel = new TcpClientChannel();
    ChannelServices.RegisterChannel(channel);

    // Instantiate the remote class
    dbc = (IDbConnect)
        Activator.GetObject(typeof(IDbConnect),
        @"tcp://localhost:1234/DbConnect");
}
```

8. Double-click the Button control and add the following code in the Click event handler:

```
private void btnExecute_Click
    (object sender, System.EventArgs e)
{
    try
    {   // Invoke a method on the remote object
        this.dgResults.DataSource =
            dbc.ExecuteQuery(this.txtQuery.Text);
        dgResults.DataMember = "Results";
    }
    catch(Exception ex)
    {
        MessageBox.Show(ex.Message,
            "Query Execution Error");
    }
}
```

9. Build the project. Set StepByStep3_11, the remoting server, as the startup project. Select Debug, Start Without Debugging to run the project. You should see a command window displaying a message that the server is started in the Singleton activation mode.

10. Now, set StepByStep3_12, the remoting client, as the start-up project. Select Debug, Start Without Debugging to

continues

continued

> run the project. Enter a query in the text box and click the button. The code invokes a method on the remote object, which is created when the form loads. The code binds the results from the remote method to the DataGrid control.

In the preceding program, you add the reference to StepByStep3_9.dll. This assembly contains the interface IDbConnect. However, an interface variable cannot be instantiated, and therefore you cannot create the instance of the remote object by using the new operator.

But there is an alternative way of creating instances of remote objects, which is especially helpful in the case of interfaces: You can use the methods of the Activator class of the System namespace as follows:

▶ The Activator.GetObject() Method—Calls the proxy to send messages to the remote object. No messages are sent over the network until a method is called on the proxy. This method is useful for activating the server-activated objects.

▶ The Activator.CreateInstance() Method—Uses the constructor that best matches the specified parameters to create an instance of the specified type. This method is useful for activating the client-activated objects.

In Step-by-Step 3.12, I am using the Activator.GetObject() method to create a proxy for the server-activated object indicated by the type IDbConnect and the server URL.

Using the Soapsuds Tool to Automatically Generate an Interface Assembly

In the previous section, you learned how you can distribute the interface assemblies, rather than the implementation assembly, to the client, and still enable clients to instantiate the remote objects.

However, when you have large numbers of clients, distribution of interface files to each of them is another big issue. However, the .NET Framework SDK provides you the Soapsuds tool (soapsuds.exe) to overcome this issue.

Given the URL for a remotable object, the Soapsuds tool can auto-matically generate an interface assembly for the remote object. All the clients need to know is the URL of the remotable object. They can then generate interface assemblies on their own by using the Soapsuds tool. A typical usage of the `soapsuds.exe` is:

```
soapsuds -nowrappedproxy
➥ -urltoschema:http://MyServer.com/DbConnect?wsdl
➥ -outputassemblyfile:DbConnectInterface.dll
```

where the `urltoschema` (or `url`) switch specifies the remote object's URL, you normally have to append the URL with `?wsdl` to enable the Soapsuds tool to generate the metadata from the URL. The `outputassemblyfile` (or `oa`) switch specifies the name of the file in which you want the output assembly to be created. The `nowrappedproxy` (or `nowp`) switch instructs the Soapsuds tool to generate an unwrapped proxy.

By default the Soapsuds tool generates wrapped proxies. Wrapped proxies are the proxies that store various connection details such as the channel formatting and the URL within the proxy itself. Although this means that you need not write the code for these things, this is not recommended because it reduces the flexibility to change the configuration. If you want to avoid specifying these details in the code, a better way is to use the configuration files.

In Step-by-Step 3.13 you create a client that uses the soapsuds-generated unwrapped proxy to connect with the HTTP server created in Guided Practice Exercise 3.1.

> **NOTE**
>
> **Wrapped Proxies** Wrapped proxies are useful when you need to quickly test a Web service because with the use of wrapped proxies you don't have to write code for channel config-uration and remote object registration. However, for better flexibility, you should use unwrapped proxies.

> **EXAM TIP**
>
> **Soapsuds Tool** The Soapsuds tool can be used only with the HTTP channel. If you are using the TCP channel, you still need to depend on manually creating and distribut-ing the interfaces for remotable classes.

STEP BY STEP

3.13 Using the Soapsuds Tool (soapsuds.exe) to Automatically Generate an Interface Assembly

1. Add a new Visual C# .NET Windows Application project named `StepByStep3_13` to the solution.

2. Set the `GuidedPracticeExercise3_1_Server` as the startup project. Select Debug, Start Without Debugging to run the project.

3. Select Start, Programs, Microsoft Visual Studio .NET, Visual Studio .NET Tools, Visual Studio .NET Command Prompt to launch a .NET command prompt.

continues

continued

4. Make sure that `GuidedPracticeExercise3_1_Server` is running. Navigate to the `StepByStep3_13` project and run the following command to automatically generate an interface assembly for the remotable object `DbConnect`, registered by the remoting server, `GuidedPracticeExercise3_1_Server`:

```
soapsuds -url:http://localhost:1234/DbConnect?wsdl
➥ -oa:DbConnectInterface.dll -nowp
```

5. Add references to the .NET assembly `System.Runtime.Remoting` and `DbConnectInterface.dll` (the interface assembly auto-generated by `soapsuds.exe` in step 3).

6. In the Solution Explorer, rename the default `Form1.cs` to `DbConnectClient.cs`. Open the form in code view and change all occurrences of `Form1` to refer to `DbConnectClient` instead.

7. Add the following using directives:

```
using System.Runtime.Remoting;
using System.Runtime.Remoting.Channels;
using System.Runtime.Remoting.Channels.Http;
using StepByStep3_1;
```

8. Place two `GroupBox` controls (`grpQuery` and `grpResults`), a `TextBox` control (`txtQuery`, with its `MultiLine` property set to `true`), a `Button` control (`btnExecute`), and a `DataGrid` control (`dgResults`) on the form. Refer to Figure 3.5 for the design of this form.

9. Add the following code in the class definition:

```
// Declare a Remote object
DbConnect dbc;
```

10. Double-click the form and add the following code in the Load event handler:

```
private void DbConnectClient_Load(
    object sender, System.EventArgs e)
{
    // This step is not required if you use
    // a wrapped proxy
    // Register an HTTP client channel
    HttpClientChannel channel =
        new HttpClientChannel();
    ChannelServices.RegisterChannel(channel);
```

```
            // This step is not required if you use
            // a wrapped proxy.
            // Register the remote class as a valid
            // type in the client's application domain
            RemotingConfiguration.RegisterWellKnownClientType(
                // Remote class
                typeof(DbConnect),
                // URL of the remote class
                "http://localhost:1234/DbConnect");

            // Instantiate the remote class
            dbc = new DbConnect();
        }
```

11. Double-click the Button control and add the following
code in the Click event handler:

```
private void btnExecute_Click
    (object sender, System.EventArgs e)
{
    try
    {   // Invoke a method on the remote object
        this.dgResults.DataSource =
            dbc.ExecuteQuery(this.txtQuery.Text);
        dgResults.DataMember = "Results";
    }
    catch(Exception ex)
    {
        MessageBox.Show(ex.Message,
            "Query Execution Error");
    }
}
```

12. Build the project. If the
GuidedPracticeExercise3_1_Server project is not running,
set the GuidedPracticeExercise3_1_Server as the startup
project and select Debug, Start Without Debugging to
run the project. You should see a command window displaying a message that the server is started in the
Singleton activation mode.

13. Set StepByStep3_13, the remoting client, as the startup
project. Select Debug, Start Without Debugging to run
the project. Enter a query in the text box and click the
button. The code invokes a method on the remote object,
which is created when the form loads. The code binds the
results from the remote method to the DataGrid control.

> **Soapsuds Tool and Client-Activated Objects**   You cannot use the Soapsuds tool with the client-activated object because the metadata generated by the Soapsuds tool can use only the default constructor to create the remote objects.

In Step-by-Step 3.13, you learned how to use the Soapsuds tool to automatically generate the interface for the remotable object.

Also, the interface generated by the Soapsuds tool enables you to directly use the name of the remotable class, which means you can access the remotable class directly in the client as if you had a direct reference to the remotable class at the client side. Therefore you can use the `RegisterWellKnownClientType()` method of the `RemotingConfiguration` class, rather than the `Activator.GetObject()` method, to register the remote object on the client side.

Creating an Interface Assembly That Works with the Client-Activated Objects

Both the techniques for generating interface assemblies discussed so far, in the sections, "Creating an Interface Assembly" and "Using the Soapsuds Tool to Automatically Generate an Interface Assembly" are not useful for CAO.

The problem lies with the constructors. The CAOs have capabilities of invoking even the non-default constructors of the remotable class. However, interfaces cannot contain the declaration for a constructor because they contain only method and property declarations.

This common problem is generally solved by following these steps:

1. Create an interface and the remotable class as shown in the previous examples. For easy reference, I'll call them `IDbConnect` and `DbConnect`, respectively. `IDbConnect` contains definitions of all the methods that the `DbConnect` class wants exposed to the clients.

2. Create an interface that declares as many different methods as there are constructors in the remotable class. Each method is responsible for creating an object in a way defined by its corresponding constructor. This technique is also called as an *abstract factory pattern*. The name contains the word "factory" because it enables you to create objects in different ways. Let's call this interface `IDbConnectFactory`.

3. Create a class that derives from the `MarshalByRefObject` class and implements the interface created in step 2 (`IDbConnectFactory`). Implement all methods to actually create

the remotable object (DbConnect) based on the given parameters and return the created instance (DbConnect). Let's call this class DbConnectFactory.

4. Create a remoting server that registers the class created in step 3 (DbConnectFactory) as the remotable class.

5. Create a client that connects to the server and create an instance of the remotable class created in step 3 (DbConnectFactory).

6. Invoke the methods corresponding to a constructor on the remotable object created in step 5. The return value of the constructor is a remotable object of the type defined in step 1 (DbConnect).

7. You now have an object of a type that you originally wanted to remote (DbConnect). You can use this object to invoke methods.

In this section I show you how to implement the preceding technique to create a client-activated object that allows you to use any of its available constructors to create objects.

I use the same remotable class that I defined in Step-by-Step 3.10 (DbConnect), and its interface (IDbConnect), which I defined in Step-by-Step 3.9. I'll start directly with Step 2 of preceding list by creating an IDbConnectFactory interface in Step-by-Step 3.14.

STEP BY STEP

3.14 Creating an Assembly That Works As an Abstract Factory for the IDbConnect Objects.

1. Add a new Visual C# .NET class library named StepByStep3_14 to the solution.

2. Add references to the project StepByStep3_9 (the interface assembly).

3. In the Solution Explorer, rename the default Class1.cs to IDbConnectFactory.cs.

4. Open the IDbConnectFactory.cs and replace the code with the following code:

continues

continued

```
using System;
using System.Data;
using StepByStep3_9;

namespace StepByStep3_14
{
    public interface IDbConnectFactory
    {
        IDbConnect CreateDbConnectInstance();
        IDbConnect CreateDbConnectInstance(
            string dbName);
    }
}
```

5. Build the project. The class library now contains an interface to a class that can act as a factory of objects implementing the IDbConnect interface.

The next step is to create a class that implements the IDbConnectFactory interface and then expose that class as a remotable class through the remoting framework. Step-by-Step 3.15 shows the steps for doing so.

STEP BY STEP

3.15 Creating a Remoting Server That Exposes the DbConnectFactory As a Remotable Class

1. Add a new Visual C# .NET console application named StepByStep3_15 to the solution.

2. Add references to the .NET assembly System.Runtime.Remoting, the project StepByStep3_9 (the interface assembly containing IDbConnect) StepByStep3_14 (the new interface assembly containing the IDbConnectFactory) and StepByStep3_10 (the remotable class assembly).

3. Add a new class to the project that will create another remotable object that inherits from MarshalByRefObject class and implements the IDbConnectFactory interface, created in Step-by-Step 3.14. Name it DbConnectFactory.cs. Open the DbConnectFactory.cs and replace the code with the following code:

```csharp
using System;
using StepByStep3_9;
using StepByStep3_10;
using StepByStep3_14;

namespace StepByStep3_15
{
    class DbConnectFactory :
       MarshalByRefObject, IDbConnectFactory
    {
        public IDbConnect CreateDbConnectInstance()
        {
            return new DbConnect();
        }
        public IDbConnect CreateDbConnectInstance(
            string dbName)
        {
            return new DbConnect(dbName);
        }
    }
}
```

4. In the Solution Explorer, rename the default `Class1.cs` to `DbConnectFactoryServer.cs`. Open the file and change the name of the class to `DbConnectFactoryServer` in the class declaration.

5. Add the following using directives:

```csharp
using System.Runtime.Remoting;
using System.Runtime.Remoting.Channels;
using System.Runtime.Remoting.Channels.Tcp;
```

6. Add the following code in the `Main()` method:

```csharp
[STAThread]
static void Main(string[] args)
{
    // Register a TCP server channel that
    // listens on port 1234
    TcpServerChannel channel =
        new TcpServerChannel(1234);
    ChannelServices.RegisterChannel(channel);

    RemotingConfiguration.RegisterWellKnownServiceType
        (typeof(DbConnectFactory),
         "DbConnectFactory",
         WellKnownObjectMode.Singleton);
    Console.WriteLine("Started server in " +
        "client-activated mode");
    Console.WriteLine("Press <ENTER> to terminate " +
        "server...");
    Console.ReadLine();
}
```

continues

continued

7. Build the project. This step uses the Singleton activation mode to create a remoting server that is capable of registering `StepByStep3_15.DbConnectFactory`, the remotable object that implements the `StepByStep3_14.IDbConnectFactory` interface, for remote invocation.

Step-by-Step 3.15 exposes the `DbConnectFactory` as an SAO in Singleton mode. Although the `DbConnectFactory` object is registered as an SAO, the objects returned by various methods of `DbConnectFactory` (`DbConnect`) are CAOs because they are created only on an explicit request from the client.

Step-by-Step 3.16 is the final step for creating a CAO using the abstract factory pattern.

STEP BY STEP

3.16 Using the Abstract Factory Pattern to Instantiate and Invoke a Client-Activated Object

1. Add a new Visual C# .NET Windows application named `StepByStep3_16` to the solution.

2. Add references to the .NET assembly `System.Runtime.Remoting` and the projects `StepByStep3_9` (the `IDbConnect` interface assembly) and `StepByStep3_14` (the `IDbConnectFactory` interface assembly).

3. In the Solution Explorer, rename the default `Form1.cs` to `DbConnectClient.cs`. Open the form in code view and change all occurrences of `Form1` to refer to `DbConnectClient` instead.

4. Add the following using directives:

```
using System.Runtime.Remoting;
using System.Runtime.Remoting.Channels;
using System.Runtime.Remoting.Channels.Tcp;
using StepByStep3_9; // contains IDbConnect
using StepByStep3_14; // contains IDbConnectFactory
```

5. Place three `GroupBox` controls (`grpDatabases`, `grpQuery`, and `grpResults`), a `ComboBox` control (`cboDatabases`), a `TextBox` control (`txtQuery`, with its `MultiLine` property set to true), two `Button` controls (`btnSelect` and `btnExecute`), and a `DataGrid` control (`dgResults`) on the form. Refer to Figure 3.10 for this form's design.

6. Select the `Items` property of the `cboDatabases` control in the Properties window and click on the (...) button. This opens the String Collection Editor dialog box. Enter the following database names in the editor:

```
Northwind
Pubs
GrocerToGo
```

Click OK to add the databases to the `Items` collection of the `cboDatabases` control.

7. Add the following code in the class definition:

```
// Declare a Remote object
IDbConnect dbc;
```

8. Double-click the form and add the following code in the `Load` event handler:

```
private void DbConnectClient_Load(
    object sender, System.EventArgs e)
{
    cboDatabases.SelectedIndex = 0;
    grpQuery.Enabled = false;
}
```

9. Double-click the `btnSelect` control and add the following code in the `Click` event handler:

```
private void btnSelect_Click(
    object sender, System.EventArgs e)
{
    // Disable the Databases group box and
    // enable the Query group box
    grpDatabases.Enabled = false;
    grpQuery.Enabled = true;

    // Register a TCP client channel
    TcpClientChannel channel = new TcpClientChannel();
    ChannelServices.RegisterChannel(channel);
```

continues

continued

```
// Register the remote class as a valid
// type in the client's application domain
// by passing the Remote class and its URL
IDbConnectFactory dbcf = (IDbConnectFactory)
    Activator.GetObject(typeof(IDbConnectFactory),
        "tcp://localhost:1234/DbConnectFactory");

dbc = dbcf.CreateDbConnectInstance
    (cboDatabases.SelectedItem.ToString());
}
```

10. Double-click the `btnExecute` control and add the following code in the `Click` event handler:

```
private void btnExecute_Click
    (object sender, System.EventArgs e)
{
    try
    {   // Invoke a method on the remote object
        this.dgResults.DataSource =
            dbc.ExecuteQuery(this.txtQuery.Text);
        dgResults.DataMember = "Results";
    }
    catch(Exception ex)
    {
        MessageBox.Show(ex.Message,
            "Query Execution Error");
    }
}
```

11. Build the project. This step creates a remoting client that is capable of activating `DbConnect` as a CAO.

12. Set `StepByStep3_15`, the remoting server, as the startup project. Select Debug, Start Without Debugging to run the project. You should see a command window displaying a message that the server is started in client-activation mode.

13. Set `StepByStep3_16`, the remoting client, as the startup project. Select Debug, Start Without Debugging to run the project. Select a database from the combo box and click the Select button. An instance of the remotable object, `DbConnect` is created with the selected database. Now enter a query in the text box and click the button. The code invokes a method on the remote object. The code binds the results from the remote method to the `DataGrid` control.

14. Again select Debug, Start Without Debugging to run the remoting client. Select a different database from the combo box and click the Select button. An instance of the remotable object, DbConnect, is created with the selected database. Now enter a query in the text box and click the button. You should see that the second instance of the client fetches the data from the selected database. Now switch to the Server command window. You see that two times the remote object is instantiated with different databases, as shown earlier in Figure 3.10. This shows that client activation creates an instance of the remotable object per client.

In Step-by-Step 3.16, it is important to note that although the object for DbConnectFactory is created as a server-activated object, the DbConnect object is always created as the client-activated object. For the DbConnectFactory object, there is only one instance for all the clients; however, there is one DbConnect object for each client.

REVIEW BREAK

▶ The .NET Framework allows you to store remoting configuration details in an XML-based configuration file rather than the code file. This causes any changes in the configuration file to be automatically picked up and eliminates the need to recompile the code files.

▶ To configure remoting configuration details from configuration files, you should call the RemotingConfiguration.Configure() method and pass the configuration file's name.

▶ You can distribute the interface assemblies to the client rather than the implementation assembly by creating an interface that defines the contract and exposes the member definitions to the client. The remotable class should implement this interface.

▶ You can use the Soapsuds tool to automatically generate the interface for the remotable object rather than manually define

continues

continued

the interface. However, the Soapsuds tool works only when the HTTP channel is used for communication.

▶ To create an interface that allows client-activated remote objects to be created, you should create an additional interface that declares as many different methods as there are constructors in the remotable class. Each of these methods should be able to create the object in a way that its corresponding constructor defines.

Using IIS As an Activation Agent

Create and consume a .NET Remoting object: Create the listener service.

So far in this chapter, you are hosting the remotable class by creating your own server that is a console application. The major disadvantage with this approach is that you have to manually start the server if it is not already running.

As discussed before, remoting provides two alternatives to overcome this disadvantage: You can either run the server process as a Windows service instead of a console application, or use IIS as an activation agent (which is a built-in Windows service) for the server process. I'll talk about the former in Chapter 6, and the latter in this section.

Using IIS as an activation agent offers the following advantages:

▶ You need not write a separate server program to register the remotable classes.

▶ You need not worry about finding an available port for your server application. You can just host the remotable object and IIS automatically uses port 80.

▶ IIS can provide other functionality, such as authentication and secure socket layers (SSL).

The following list specifies what you need to do to host a remotable class in IIS:

▶ Place the assembly containing the remotable objects into the \bin directory of an IIS Web application or place the assembly in the GAC (Global Assembly Cache).

▶ Configure the remoting settings by placing the `<system.runtime.remoting>` configuration section into the `web.config` file for the Web application. Alternatively, you can write the configuration code in the `Application_Start()` event handler of the `global.asax` file in the same way you would register a remote object in an `.exe` host.

▶ You should not specify a channel. IIS already listens on port 80. Specifying a port for a channel causes exceptions to be thrown when new IIS worker processes are started.

▶ The well-known object URIs must end with `.rem` or `.soap` because these are the two extensions that are registered with both IIS (via the `aspnet_isapi.dll`) as well as the remoting system (in `machine.config`).

Step-by-Step 3.17 demonstrates how to use IIS for activating the `DbConnect` remotable class from Step-by-Step 3.10.

EXAM TIP

IIS Does Not Support CAO   When creating IIS-hosted remote objects, you cannot specify constructor parameters; therefore it is not possible to use IIS to activate CAO.

NOTE

Channels and IIS Activation   IIS Activation supports only HTTP channels. The default formatting is SOAP, but IIS also supports binary and other custom formatting.

NOTE

Database Access Permission   In order for the Step By Step 3.17 to work, the ASP.NET user account must have permission to access the SQL Server database.

STEP BY STEP

3.17 Using IIS As an Activation Agent

1. Add a new empty Web project named `StepByStep3_17` to the solution.

2. Add references to the project `StepByStep3_9` (the interface assembly) and `StepByStep3_10` (the remotable object) by selecting Add Reference from the context menu.

3. Add a Web configuration file to the project. Open the `web.config` file and add the following `<system.runtime.remoting>` element inside the `<configuration>` element:

```
<configuration>
    <system.runtime.remoting>
        <application>
            <service>
            <!-- Set the activation mode,
                 remotable object, and its URL -->
                <wellknown mode="Singleton"
```

continues

continued

```
                                type="StepByStep3_10.DbConnect,
   ➥ StepByStep3_10"
                                objectUri="DbConnect.rem"
                        />
                    </service>
                </application>
            </system.runtime.remoting>
    ...
    </configuration>
```

4. IIS is now hosting the `StepByStep3_10.DbConnect` remotable class as a server-activated object by using the Singleton activation mode.

Note that the `objectUri` of the SAO in the preceding example ends with the extension `.rem`.

Step-by-Step 3.18 demonstrates how to invoke a remote object hosted in the IIS.

STEP BY STEP

3.18 Instantiating and Invoking an IIS-Hosted Remote Object

1. Add a new Visual C# .NET Windows application named `StepByStep3_18` to the solution.

2. Add references to the .NET assembly `System.Runtime.Remoting` and the project `StepByStep3_9` (the interface assembly).

3. In the Solution Explorer, rename the default `Form1.cs` to `DbConnectClient.cs`. Open the form in code view and change all occurrences of `Form1` to refer to `DbConnectClient` instead.

4. Add the following using directives:

```
using System.Runtime.Remoting;
using System.Runtime.Remoting.Channels;
using System.Runtime.Remoting.Channels.Http;
using StepByStep3_9; // contains IDbConnect
```

5. Place two GroupBox controls, a TextBox control (txtQuery, with its MultiLine property set to true), a Button control (btnExecute), and a DataGrid control (dgResults) on the form. Refer to Figure 3.5 for the design of this form.

6. Add the following code in the class definition:

```
// Declare a Remote object
IDbConnect dbc;
```

7. Double-click the form and add the following code in the Load event handler:

```
{
    // Register a Http client channel
    HttpClientChannel channel = new HttpClientChannel();
    ChannelServices.RegisterChannel(channel);

    // Instantiate the remote class
    dbc = (IDbConnect)
        Activator.GetObject(typeof(IDbConnect),

@"http://localhost/StepByStep3_17/DbConnect.rem");

    //  pass default credentials
    // (user name, password, and domain) to the server
    IDictionary props =
        ChannelServices.GetChannelSinkProperties(dbc);
    props["credentials"] =
        System.Net.CredentialCache.DefaultCredentials;
}
```

8. Double-click the Button control and add the following code in the Click event handler:

```
private void btnExecute_Click
    (object sender, System.EventArgs e)
{
    try
    {   // Invoke a method on the remote object
        this.dgResults.DataSource =
            dbc.ExecuteQuery(this.txtQuery.Text);
        dgResults.DataMember = "Results";
    }
    catch(Exception ex)
    {
        MessageBox.Show(ex.Message,
            "Query Execution Error");
    }
}
```

9. Build the project. This step creates the remoting client that can invoke an IIS-hosted remote object.

continues

continued

> **10.** Set StepByStep3_18, the remoting client, as the startup project. Select Debug, Start Without Debugging to run the project. Enter a query in the text box and click the button. The code invokes a method on the remote object, which is created when the form loads. The code binds the results from the remote method to the DataGrid control.

This client was similar to the client created in Step-by-Step 3.12; however, there are a few things to note. The client is using the HTTP channel to communicate with the server, there is no port number specified in the URL, and the URL ends with .rem.

Asynchronous Remoting

Create and consume a .NET Remoting object: Implement an asynchronous method.

So far, all the method invocations that you've studied in this chapter have been synchronous. In a synchronous method call, the thread that executes the method call waits until the called method finishes execution.

Such types of synchronous calls can make the user interface very non-responsive if the client program is waiting for a long process to finish executing on the server. This is especially true for remote method calls where additional time is involved because the calls are made across the network.

The .NET framework has a solution for this in the form of asynchronous methods. An asynchronous method calls the method and returns immediately, leaving the invoked method to complete its execution.

Understanding the Model of Asynchronous Programming in the .NET Framework

In the .NET Framework, asynchronous programming is implemented with the help of delegate types. Delegates are types that are capable of storing references to methods of a specific signature. A delegate declared as follows is capable of invoking methods that take a string parameter and return a string type:

```
delegate string LongProcessDelegate(string param);
```

So if there is a method definition, such as the following:

```
string LongProcess(string param)
{
...
}
```

then the `LongProcessDelegate` can hold references to this method like this:

```
LongProcessDelegate delLongProcess;
delLongProcess = new LongProcessDelegate(LongProcess);
```

After you have the delegate object available, you can call its `BeginInvoke()` method to call the `LongProcess()` method asynchronously, such as in the following:

```
IAsyncResult ar =
   delLongProcess.BeginInvoke("Test", null, null);
```

Here the `IAsyncResult` interface is used to monitor an asynchronous call and relate the beginning and the end of an asynchronous method call. When you use the `BeginInvoke()` method, the control immediately comes back to the next statement while the `LongProcess()` method may still be executing.

To return the value of an asynchronous method call, you can call the `EndInvoke()` method on the same delegate, such as in the following:

```
String result = delLongProcess.EndInvoke(ar);
```

However, it is important to know where to place this method call, because when you call the `EndInvoke()` method, if the `LongProcess()` method has not yet completed execution, the `EndInvoke()` method causes the current thread to wait for the completion of the `LongProcess()` method. A poor use of the `EndInvoke()` method, such as placing it in just the next statement after the `BeginInvoke()` method, can cause an asynchronous method call to result in a synchronous method call.

One of the alternatives to this problem is to use the `IsCompleted` property of the `IAsyncResult` object to check whether the method has completed the execution, and then call the `EndInvoke()` method only in such a case.

```
string result;
if(ar.IsCompleted)
{
    result = delLongProcess.EndInvoke(ar);
}
```

But regular polling of the `IAsyncResult.IsCompleted` property requires additional work at the client side.

You can also use a `WaitHandle` object to manage asynchronous remote method calls. When you are ready to wait for the results of the remote method call, you can retrieve a `WaitHandle` object from the `IAsyncResult` object's `AsyncWaitHandle` property:

```
ar.AsyncWaitHandle.WaitOne();
String result = delLongProcess.EndInvoke(ar);
```

The `WaitOne()` method of the `WaitHandle` object causes the thread to pause until the results are ready. The `WaitHandle` object has other methods that are useful if you have multiple outstanding asynchronous remote method calls. You can wait for all the method calls to come back by using the static `WaitHandle.WaitAll()` method, or for the first one to return by using the static `WaitHandle.WaitAny()` method. Therefore, the `WaitHandle` object essentially lets you turn the asynchronous process back into a synchronous process.

There is, in fact, a better technique for managing asynchronous method invocation—callback methods. In this technique, you can register a method that is automatically invoked as soon as the remote method finishes execution. You can then place a call to the `EndInvoke()` method inside the callback method to collect the result of remote method execution.

To implement the callback technique with an asynchronous method invocation, you need to take the following steps in the client program:

1. Define a callback method that you want to execute when the remote method has finished execution.

2. Create an object of delegate type `AsyncCallback` to store the reference to the method created in step 1.

3. Create an instance of the remote object on which you wish to invoke remote method calls.

4. Declare a delegate type capable of storing references to the remote method.

5. Using the object in step 3, create a new instance of delegate declared in step 4 to refer to the remote method.

6. Call the `BeginInvoke()` method on the delegate created in step 5, passing any arguments and the `AsyncCallback` object.

7. Wait for the server object to call your callback method when the method has completed.

Applying Asynchronous Programming

In the following sections I create a set of three projects to demonstrate the use of the callback method for an asynchronous method call:

▶ The Remotable Class—The remotable class exposes the remote methods that are called from the client program.

▶ The Remote Server—I use IIS to host the remotable object.

▶ The Client Program—The client program calls the remote method asynchronously. I use the Soapsuds tool to automatically generate the metadata required to invoke the remote object.

I create a remotable class that is different from other remotable classes used in this chapter to help you properly understand synchronous and asynchronous method calls.

The remotable class used in Step-by-Step 3.19 is named `RemotableClass` and it has a single method named `LongProcess()`. The `LongProcess()` method waits for about 5 seconds to simulate a long process call.

STEP BY STEP

3.19 Creating a Remotable Class

1. Add a new Visual C# .NET class library named `StepByStep3_19` to the solution.

2. In the Solution Explorer, rename the default `Class1.cs` to `RemotableClass.cs`.

3. Open the `RemotableClass.cs` and replace the code with the following code:

continues

continued

```
using System;
using System.Threading;

namespace StepByStep3_19
{
    public class RemotableClass : MarshalByRefObject
    {
        public string LongProcess(string param)
        {
            Thread.Sleep(5000);
            return param;
        }
    }
}
```

4. Select Build, Build StepByStep3_19. This step generates the code for your class library and packages it into the file StepByStep3_19.dll, which is located in the bin\Debug or bin\Release directory of your project.

RemotableClass is now ready to be hosted in a remoting host. In Step-by-Step 3.20, I decided to use IIS to host the remotable class because it requires only a minimum amount of code. I control the remoting configuration by modifying the web.config file.

STEP BY STEP

3.20 Using IIS to Host a Remotable Class

1. Add a new Visual C# ASP.NET application named StepByStep3_20 to the solution.

2. Add references the project StepByStep3_19 (the remotable class assembly).

3. Open the web.config file and add the following <system.runtime.remoting> element inside the <configuration> element:

```
<configuration>
  <system.runtime.remoting>
    <application>
      <service>
        <!-- Set the activation mode,
             remotable object, and its URL -->
        <wellknown mode="Singleton"
```

```
                type="StepByStep3_19.RemotableClass,
➡ StepByStep3_19"
                objectUri="RemotableClass.rem" />
        </service>
    </application>
  </system.runtime.remoting>
...
</configuration>
```

4. The remoting server is now hosting the `RemotableClass`
contained in the assembly `StepByStep3_19` for remote
invocation by using the Singleton activation mode.

Both `RemotableClass`, the remote object and the remoting host contain no additional information that supports an asynchronous
method call. The asynchronous call is completely dependent on the
client code. So in the final step, I create a client application that calls
a remote method synchronously as well as asynchronously. Seeing
both ways of calling a method will help you note the difference.

STEP BY STEP

3.21 Instantiating and Invoking a Client That Calls Remote Object Methods Synchronously and Asynchronously

1. Add a new Visual C# .NET Windows application named
`StepByStep3_21` to the solution.

2. Add references to the .NET assembly
`System.Runtime.Remoting`.

3. Select Start, Programs, Microsoft Visual Studio .NET,
Visual Studio .NET Tools, Visual Studio .NET
Command Prompt to launch a .NET command prompt.

4. Navigate to the `StepByStep3_9` project and run the following command to automatically generate the source code
for the interface of the remotable class `RemotableClass`,
registered by the IIS Web server:

```
soapsuds -nowp -gc
➡ -url:http://localhost/StepByStep3_20/RemotableClass.
rem?wsdl
```

continues

continued

This step generates a file named StepByStep3_19.cs, which contains the interface code for the RemotableClass class.

5. In the Solution Explorer, right-click project StepByStep3_21 and select Add, Add Existing Item to add the StepByStep3_19.cs file (generated by the soapsuds.exe in step 4).

6. Open the file StepByStep3_19.cs. You will notice that the RemotableClass class definition is applied with two attributes—Serializable and SoapType. Remove the SoapType attribute definition so that the class definition looks like this:

```
[Serializable]
public class RemotableClass :
    System.MarshalByRefObject
{
    ...
}
```

7. In the Solution Explorer, rename the default Form1.cs to SyncAsync.cs. Open the form in code view and change all occurrences of Form1 to refer to SyncAsync instead.

8. Add the following using directives:

```
using System.Runtime.Remoting;
using System.Runtime.Remoting.Channels;
using System.Runtime.Remoting.Channels.Http;
// Contains RemotableClass interface
using StepByStep3_19;
```

9. Place a Label control, a TextBox control (txtResults), and two Button controls (btnSync and btnAsync) on the form. Refer to Figure 3.12 for the design of this form.

10. Add the following code to the class definition:

```
// Remotable object
RemotableClass remObject;

// Create a delegate for the LongProcess method
// of the Remotable object
delegate string LongProcessDelegate(string param);

// Declare a LongProcessDelegate object,
// an AsyncCallback delegate object,
// and an IAsyncResult object
LongProcessDelegate delLongProcess;
```

```
AsyncCallback ab;
IAsyncResult ar;

// Declare a static integer variable to hold
// the number of times the method is called
static int counter;
```

11. Double-click the form and add the following code in the
Load event handler:

```
private void SyncAsync_Load(
    object sender, System.EventArgs e)
{
    // Register an HTTP client channel
    HttpClientChannel channel =
        new HttpClientChannel();
    ChannelServices.RegisterChannel(channel);

    // Instantiate the remote class
    remObject = (RemotableClass) Activator.GetObject(
        typeof(RemotableClass),
        @"http://localhost/StepByStep3_20/
➥RemotableClass.rem");

    // Create an AsyncCallback delegate object to hold
    // the reference of the LongProcessCompleted
    // callback method, which is called when
    // the asynchronous call is completed
    ab = new AsyncCallback(LongProcessCompleted);

    // Create a LongProcessDelegate delegate object to
    // hold the reference of the LongProcess method
    delLongProcess = new LongProcessDelegate(
        remObject.LongProcess);
}
```

12. Double-click the btnSync control and add the following
code in the Click event handler:

```
private void btnSync_Click(
    object sender, System.EventArgs e)
{
    // Increment the method call counter
    counter++;
    string param = String.Format(
        "Call: {0}, Type=Synchronous", counter);

    // Append the start message to the text box
    txtResults.AppendText(String.Format(
        "{0}, Started at: {1}\n",
        param, DateTime.Now.ToLongTimeString()));
```

continues

continued

```
// Call the LongProcess method of the
// remotable object
remObject.LongProcess(param);

// Append the completed message to the text box
txtResults.AppendText(
    String.Format("{0},  Completed at: {1}\n",
    param, DateTime.Now.ToLongTimeString()));
}
```

13. Double-click the btnAsync control and add the following code in the Click event handler:

```
private void btnAsync_Click(
    object sender, System.EventArgs e)
{
    // Increment the method call counter
    counter++;
    string param = String.Format(
        "Call: {0}, Type=Asynchronous",
        counter);
    // Append the start message to the text box
    txtResults.AppendText(
        String.Format("{0}, Started at: {1}\n",
        param, DateTime.Now.ToLongTimeString()));

    // Call the BeginInvoke method to start
    // the asynchronous method call
    ar = delLongProcess.BeginInvoke(param, ab, null);
}
```

14. Add the following callback method definition for LongProcessCompleted() to the class:

```
void LongProcessCompleted(IAsyncResult ar)
{
    // Call the EndInvoke method to retrieve the
    // return value of the asynchronous method call
    string result = delLongProcess.EndInvoke(ar);

    // Append the completed message to the text box
    txtResults.AppendText(
        String.Format("{0}, Completed at: {1}\n",
        result, DateTime.Now.ToLongTimeString()));
}
```

15. Build the project. This step creates a remoting client for the RemotableClass remotable object.

16. Set StepByStep3_21, the remoting client, as the startup project. Select Debug, Start Without Debugging to run the project. Click the Call Long Process Synchronously button to call the LongProcess() method synchronously.

You should see the start message appended to the text box, and the application freezes for the next five seconds. After the method call is completed you notice a completed message and you are now able to work with the application. Now click the Call Long Process Asynchronously button to call the `LongProcess()` method asynchronously. As soon as the method starts, the start message is appended to the text box. While the method is executing, you can still work with the application (such as by moving the form, clicking buttons, and so on, although clicking the synchronous call button freezes the application). When the method is completed, you notice a completed message in the text box, as shown in Figure 3.12.

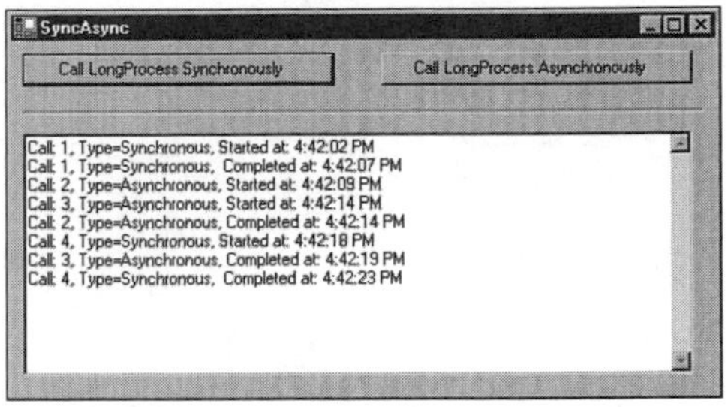

FIGURE 3.12
The asynchronous method call invokes the method and transfers the control back to the form. The asynchronous call can use a callback method to get a notification when the remote method finishes execution.

In this program I am following the same steps for an asynchronous method call that were discussed earlier in the previous section, "Understanding the Model of Asynchronous Programming in the .NET Framework."

The only surprise in Step-by-Step 3.21 is the special use of the Soapsuds tool. Step 4 uses the Soapsuds tool to generate the source code of the interface assembly instead of the assembly itself. The soapsuds-generated assembly uses a `SoapType` attribute that doesn't work with delegates. The advantage of soapsuds-generated source code is that I can manually remove the problematic `SoapType` attribute and compile the program to generate the interface assembly.

REVIEW BREAK

▶ You can choose to run the remoting host as a console application, as a Windows service, or as an IIS application.

▶ You can use IIS as an activation agent only when the underlying communication is in the HTTP channel. Using IIS as an activation agent eliminates the need to write a separate server program that listens on a unique port number (IIS uses the port 80).

▶ When creating IIS-hosted remote objects, you cannot specify constructor parameters; therefore using IIS to activate CAO is not possible.

continues

continued

▶ You can invoke a method asynchronously by calling the
`BeginInvoke()` method on that method's delegate.

▶ You can automatically get a notification when an asynchronous method ends. However, you must first create another
delegate object (of `AsyncCallback` type) that refers to the callback method that you need to execute when the remote
method ends. And then you should pass the delegate to the
callback method as an argument to the `BeginInvoke()`
method.

CHAPTER SUMMARY

KEY TERMS

• application domain

• asynchronous call

• channel

• marshaling

• proxy

• synchronous call

• remoting

• runtime host

The .NET Framework is a modern platform for building distributed
applications. In this chapter you learned how to create distributed
applications by using the remoting library of the .NET Framework.

You learned that the remoting framework is made up of several elements, such as remotable classes, remoting hosts, remoting clients,
channels, formatters, and so on. Each of these elements is configurable and extensible. You practiced creating a remotable class and
hosting that class in several modes such as server-activated
SingleCall, server-activated Singleton, and client-activated. You also
used different channels, such as HTTP and TCP, and different formatters, such as SOAP and binary.

I also demonstrated the use of a configuration file to configure the
remoting configuration for a remoting host and the remoting client.
You noted that depending on your requirements, you can write
remoting configurations at two level: one at the application level
(`.exe.config`, or `web.config` for IIS) and the other at the machine
level (`machine.config`).

Finally, I discussed the technique of invoking remote methods asynchronously. An asynchronous method call makes a user
interface–based application, such as a Windows forms application,
quite responsive to user input despite the delays caused in a remote
method call.

APPLY YOUR KNOWLEDGE

Exercises

3.1   Using HTTP Channels with Binary Formatters

As I discussed in the chapter, the default formatter for the HTTP channel is SOAP, and for the TCP channel is Binary. The formatters are used for serializing and deserializing messages in the specified encoding.

The chapter has made use of these default formatters in the examples. In this exercise, you'll learn how to configure a channel to use a formatter different from the default one.

In particular I'll demonstrate how to use the binary formatter with the HTTP channel. This combination is especially useful when you want to optimize the performance of a remote object that is hosted on IIS. However, you should note that binary format is proprietary to the .NET Framework.

Estimated Time: 30 minutes.

1. Launch Visual Studio .NET. Select File, New, Blank Solution, and name the new solution `320C03Exercises`. Click OK.

2. Add a new empty Web project named `Exercise3_1_Server` to the solution.

3. Add references to `StepByStep3_9.dll` (the interface assembly containing `IDbConnect`) and `StepByStep3_10.dll` (the remotable object, `DbConnect`).

4. Add a new Web configuration file to the project. Open the `web.config` file and add the following `<system.runtime.remoting>` element inside the `<configuration>` element:

```
<configuration>
    <system.runtime.remoting>
        <application>
            <service>
```

```
            <!--Set the activation mode,
               remotable object,
               and its URL -->
            <wellknown mode="Singleton"
                type=
                "StepByStep3_10.DbConnect,
➥ StepByStep3_10"
                    objectUri=
                        "DbConnect.rem" />
            </service>
        </application>
    </system.runtime.remoting>
...
</configuration>
```

IIS is now hosting the `StepByStep3_10.DbConnect` remotable class as a server-activated object by using the Singleton activation mode.

5. Add a new Visual C# .NET Windows application named `Exercise3_1_Client` to the solution.

6. Add references to `StepByStep3_9.dll` (the interface assembly containing `IDbConnect`).

7. Add an Application configuration file (`App.config`) to the project and modify it to contain the following code:

```
<configuration>
    <system.runtime.remoting>
        <application>
            <channels>
                <channel ref="http">
                    <serverProviders>
                        <formatter ref =
                            "binary" />
                    </serverProviders>
                </channel>
            </channels>
        </application>
    </system.runtime.remoting>
</configuration>
```

8. In the Solution Explorer, rename the default `Form1.cs` to `DbConnectClient.cs`. Open the form in code view and change all occurrences of `Form1` to refer to `DbConnectClient` instead.

9. Place two `GroupBox` controls (`grpQuery` and `grpResults`), a `TextBox` control (`txtQuery`, with its `MultiLine` property set to `true`), a `Button` control (`btnExecute`), and a `DataGrid` control (`dgResults`) on the form. Refer to Figure 3.5 for the design of this form.

10. Add the following `using` directives:

```
using System.Runtime.Remoting;
using StepByStep3_9;
```

11. Add the following code in the class definition:

```
// Declare a Remote object
IDbConnect dbc;
```

12. Double-click the form and add the following code in the `Load` event handler:

```
private void DbConnectClient_Load(
    object sender, System.EventArgs e)
{
    // Load remoting configuration
    RemotingConfiguration.Configure
        ("Exercise3_1_Client.exe.config");

    // Instantiate the remote class
    dbc = (IDbConnect)
    Activator.GetObject(typeof(IDbConnect),
    @"http://localhost/Exercise3_1_Server/
➥DbConnect.rem");
}
```

13. Double-click the `Button` control and add the following code in the `Click` event handler:

```
private void btnExecute_Click(
    object sender, System.EventArgs e)
{
```

```
    try
    {
        // Invoke a method on
        // the remote object
        this.dgResults.DataSource =
            dbc.ExecuteQuery(
                this.txtQuery.Text);
        dgResults.DataMember = "Results";
    }
    catch(Exception ex)
    {
        MessageBox.Show(ex.Message,
            "Query Execution Error");
    }
}
```

14. Build the project. Set `Exercise3_1_Client`, the remoting client, as the startup project. Select Debug, Start Without Debugging to run the project. Enter a query in the text box and click the button. The code invokes a method on the remote object. The remote object is serialized and deserialized in binary format and is transported over the HTTP. The code binds the results from the remote method to the `DataGrid` control.

Note that you can specify the desired formatter for the client and need not specify the formatter for the server. The formatter requested by the client will be used to format data by the server for that client.

3.2 Dynamically Publishing a Well-Known Object

Well-known objects cannot be invoked from a client with a non-default constructor. However, you can create an object using any constructor you wish, initialize it any way you wish, and then make it available to clients.

You should use the `RemotingServices.Marshal()` method to publish an existing object instance.

Estimated Time: 30 minutes.

1. Add a new Visual C# console application named `Exercise3_2_Server` to the solution.

2. Add references to the .NET assembly `System.Runtime.Remoting`, the `StepByStep3_9.dll` (the interface assembly containing `IDbConnect`), and `StepByStep3_10.dll` (the remotable object, `DbConnect`).

3. In the Solution Explorer, rename the default `Class1.cs` to `DbConnectServer.cs`. Open the file and change the name of the class to `DbConnectServer` in the class declaration.

4. Add the following using directives:

```
using System.Runtime.Remoting;
using System.Runtime.Remoting.Channels;
using System.Runtime.Remoting.Channels.Tcp;
using StepByStep3_10;
```

5. Add the following code in the `Main()` method:

```
[STAThread]
static void Main(string[] args)
{
    // Create and register a TCP server
    // channel that listens on port 1234
    TcpServerChannel channel =
        new TcpServerChannel(1234);
    ChannelServices.RegisterChannel(
        channel);

    // Create the remotable object here
    // itself. Call the
    // RemotingServices.Marshal() method
    // to marshal (serialize) the created
    // remotable object to transfer the
    // object beyond application boundaries
    // with the specified uri
    DbConnect dbcPubs =
        new DbConnect("Pubs");
    RemotingServices.Marshal(
        dbcPubs, "Pubs.uri");
```

```
    DbConnect dbcNorthwind =
        new DbConnect("Northwind");
    RemotingServices.Marshal(
        dbcNorthwind, "Northwind.uri");

    Console.WriteLine(
        "Started server in the " +
        "Singleton mode");
    Console.WriteLine(
        "Press <ENTER> to terminate " +
        "server...");
    Console.ReadLine();
}
```

6. Build the project. This step creates a remoting server that creates the remotable object `StepByStep3_1.DbConnect` and is capable of marshaling the remote object across application boundaries.

7. Add a new Visual C# .NET Windows application named `Exercise3_2_Client` to the solution.

8. Add references to the .NET assembly `System.Runtime.Remoting` and the project `StepByStep3_9` (the interface assembly).

9. In the Solution Explorer, rename the default `Form1.cs` to `DbConnectClient.cs`. Open the form in code view and change all occurrences of `Form1` to refer to `DbConnectClient` instead.

10. Add the following using directives:

```
using System.Runtime.Remoting;
using System.Runtime.Remoting.Channels;
using System.Runtime.Remoting.Channels.Tcp;
using StepByStep3_9;
```

11. Place three `GroupBox` controls (`grpDatabases`, `grpQuery`, and `grpResults`), a `ComboBox` control (`cboDatabases`), a `TextBox` control (`txtQuery`), a `Button` control (`btnExecute`), and a `DataGrid` control (`dgResults`) on the form. Set the `DropDownStyle` to `DropDownList`.

APPLY YOUR KNOWLEDGE

12. Select the `Items` property of the `cboDatabases` control in the Properties window and click on the (...) button. This opens the String Collection Editor dialog box. Enter the following database names in the editor:

    ```
    Northwind
    Pubs
    ```

13. Click OK to add the databases to the `Items` collection of the `cboDatabases` control.

14. Add the following code in the class definition:

    ```
    // Declare a remote object
    IDbConnect dbc;
    ```

15. Double-click the form and add the following code in the `Load` event handler:

    ```
    private void DbConnectClient_Load(
        object sender, System.EventArgs e)
    {
        // Register a TCP client channel
        TcpClientChannel channel =
            new TcpClientChannel();
        ChannelServices.RegisterChannel(
            channel);

        cboDatabases.SelectedIndex = 0;
    }
    ```

16. Double-click the `cboDatabases` control and add the following code in the `SelectedIndexChanged` event handler:

    ```
    private void
        cboDatabases_SelectedIndexChanged(
        object sender, System.EventArgs e)
    {
        switch (
          cboDatabases.SelectedItem.ToString())
        {
          case "Pubs":
          {
              // Instantiate the remote class
              dbc = (IDbConnect)
                  Activator.GetObject(
                  typeof(IDbConnect),
                  @"tcp://localhost:1234/
    ➥Pubs.uri");
    ```

    ```
              break;
          }
          case "Northwind":
          {
              // Instantiate the remote class
              dbc = (IDbConnect)
                  Activator.GetObject(
                  typeof(IDbConnect),
                  @"tcp://localhost:1234/
    ➥Northwind.uri");
              break;
          }
        }
    }
    ```

17. Double-click the `btnExecute` control and add the following code in the `Click` event handler:

    ```
    private void btnExecute_Click
        (object sender, System.EventArgs e)
    {
        try
        {
            // Invoke a method on
            // the remote object
            this.dgResults.DataSource =
                dbc.ExecuteQuery(
                this.txtQuery.Text);
            dgResults.DataMember = "Results";
        }
        catch(Exception ex)
        {
            MessageBox.Show(ex.Message,
                "Query Execution Error");
        }
    }
    ```

18. Build the project. You now have a remoting client ready to use.

19. Set the `Exercise3_2_Server`, the remoting server, as the startup project. Select Debug, Start Without Debugging to run the project. You should see a command window displaying a message that the server is started in the singleton activation mode. You should also see messages that the remote object is already created.

APPLY YOUR KNOWLEDGE

20. Set `Exercise3_2_Client`, the remoting client, as the startup project. Select Debug, Start Without Debugging to run the project. Select a desired database from the combo box, enter a query in the text box, and click the button. The code invokes a method on the remote object that is already created on the server. The code binds the results from the remote method to the `DataGrid` control.

21. Again select Debug, Start Without Debugging to run one more instance of the remoting client. Select a different database from the combo box, enter a query in the text box, and click the button. You should see that the second instance of the client fetches the data from the selected database.

Review Questions

1. What is an application domain? How does the CLR manage an application domain?

2. What are MBR objects? What are their advantages and disadvantages?

3. What do you mean by a channel? What are the different types of channels the .NET Framework provides?

4. What are the advantages and disadvantanges of the binary and SOAP formatters?

5. What are the two modes for creating Server-Activated objects?

6. When should you choose to create a client-activated object?

7. What is the benefit of using declarative configuration over programmatic configuration?

8. What are the two methods of the `Activator` class that enable you to create instances of remote objects?

9. What are the advantages of using an IIS server as an activation agent?

10. What should you do while creating a remotable class so that its methods can be called asynchronously?

Exam Questions

1. You are designing a distributed application that hosts a remote object. You want only the authorized client applications to activate the remote object. You want to write the application with the minimum amount of code. Which of the following channels enables you to achieve this objective? (Select two.)

   A. `HttpChannel`

   B. `HttpServerChannel`

   C. `TcpChannel`

   D. `TcpServerChannel`

2. You are designing a company-wide order processing system. This application is hosted on a server in the company's headquarters in Redmond, Washington, and is accessed by 1500 franchise locations throughout the world. The application specification mentions that the franchisees should be able to access the order-processing system even through firewalls. A large number of franchisees access the application over a slow connection and your objective is to maximize the performance of the application. Which of the following combinations of channel and formatter would you choose in this scenario?

APPLY YOUR KNOWLEDGE

A. Use a TCP channel with a binary formatter.

B. Use a TCP channel with a SOAP formatter.

C. Use an HTTP channel with a binary formatter.

D. Use an HTTP channel with a SOAP formatter.

3. You are designing a distributed application for a large automotive company. The application allows the part suppliers across the globe to collect the latest design specifications for a part. The application is heavily accessed by the suppliers. For greater scalability, you are required to design the application so that it can be deployed in a load-balanced environment. How should you host the remotable object in this scenario?

A. As a server-activated object in SingleCall activation mode.

B. As a server-activated object in Singleton activation mode.

C. As a client-activated object using the HTTP channel.

D. As a client-activated object using the SOAP formatter.

4. You have been hired by Great Widgets Inc., to create an application that enables their suppliers to access the purchase order information in real time. You create the required classes that the suppliers can activate remotely and package them into a file named gwpoinfo.dll. You plan to use IIS as the remoting host for this file. After the application has been deployed, minimal steps should be involved in changing the remoting configuration for this application. Any configuration changes made to the purchase order

information system should not affect any other applications running on that server. Which of the following files would you choose to configure remoting for the purchase order information system?

A. gwpoinfo.dll

B. web.config

C. global.asax

D. machine.config

5. You have designed a remotable class named ProductDesign. You now want to register this class with the remoting system in such a way that client programs should be able to remotely instantiate objects of this class and invoke methods on it. You want to have only one instance of this class on the server, no matter how many clients connect to it. Which of the following code segments fulfills your requirement?

A.
```
RemotingConfiguration.
    RegisterWellKnownServiceType(
    typeof(ProductDesign),
    "ProductDesign",
    WellKnownObjectMode.SingleCall
);
```

B.
```
RemotingConfiguration.
    RegisterWellKnownServiceType(
    typeof(ProductDesign),
    "ProductDesign",
    WellKnownObjectMode.Singleton
);
```

C.
```
RemotingConfiguration.
    RegisterActivatedServiceType(
    typeof(ProductDesign),
    "ProductDesign"
);
```

APPLY YOUR KNOWLEDGE

D.

```
RemotingConfiguration.
    RegisterWellKnownClientType(
    typeof(ProductDesign),
    "ProductDesign"
);
```

6. You have designed a remotable class that allows the user to retrieve the latest weather information for their region. You do not want to write a lot of code to create a custom remoting host, so you decide to use IIS to host the application. The name of the remotable class is `RemotingWeather.WeatherInfo` and it is stored in an assembly named `WeatherInfo.dll`. You want the users to access this remotable class by using the URL `http://RemoteWeather.com/users/WeatherInfo.rem`. Which of the following remoting configurations would you place in the `web.config` file so that client applications can correctly retrieve weather information?

   A.

```
<system.runtime.remoting>
   <application>
      <service>
         <activated type=
            "RemotingWeather.WeatherInfo,
➥ WeatherInfo"
            />
      </service>
      <channels>
         <channel ref="http" port="80" />
      </channels>
   </application>
</system.runtime.remoting>
```

   B.

```
<system.runtime.remoting>
   <application>
      <service>
         <wellknown mode="Singleton"
            type=
            "RemotingWeather.WeatherInfo,
➥ WeatherInfo"
```

```
            objectUri="WeatherInfo.rem"
            />
      </service>
   </application>
</system.runtime.remoting>
```

   C.

```
<system.runtime.remoting>
   <application>
      <service>
         <activated type=
            "RemotingWeather.WeatherInfo,
➥ WeatherInfo"
            />
      </service>
      <channels>
         <channel ref="http server"
            port="80" />
      </channels>
   </application>
</system.runtime.remoting>
```

   D.

```
<system.runtime.remoting>
   <application>
      <client>
         <wellknown mode="Singleton"
            type=
            "RemotingWeather.WeatherInfo,
➥ WeatherInfo"
            objectUri="WeatherInfo.rem"
            />
      </client>
   </application>
</system.runtime.remoting>
```

7. You are a software developer for LubriSol, Inc., which manufactures chemicals for automobile industries. Your company does a lot of business with ReverseGear, Inc., which is the largest manufacturer of heavy vehicles in the country. ReverseGear, Inc., uses a .NET remoting application that allows its suppliers to check its daily parts requirements. Your objective is to create a client application to the ReverseGear's application that retrieves the information for parts produced

by your company. All you know about the server application is its URL, which is `http://ReverseGearInc.com/Suppliers/Req.rem`. You want the quickest solution. What should you do to write a client application successfully?

A. Contact ReverseGear, Inc., to ask for the interface and include reference to the interface in the client project.

B. Open the URL in the Web browser and select View, Source to find how the remote class is structured.

C. Use the Visual Studio .NET Add Web Reference feature to add a reference to the remote class in the client project.

D. Use the Soapsuds tool to automatically generate the metadata and include the reference to this metadata in the client project.

8. You want to host a remotable class via the .NET remoting framework so that remote clients can instantiate the class and invoke methods on it. The remotable class does not have any user interface but it must use Integrated Windows authentication to authenticate the users. Which of the following techniques you should use to host the remotable class? You want a solution that requires you to write minimal code.

A. Use a console application as a remoting host.

B. Create a Windows service and use that to host the remotable class.

C. Use a Windows forms application to host the remotable class.

D. Use Internet Information Services (IIS) as a remoting host.

9. You are developing a remoting client to access a server-activated remotable object hosted at the URL `tcp://finance:1234/Budget`. You have obtained an interface assembly of this remote object. This assembly contains an interface named `IBudget` that is implemented by the remote class. You want to instantiate the remote object to invoke a method name `GetDepartmentBudget()`, which accepts a string value and returns a double value containing the department budget. Given the following code, what should you write in line 06 to successfully invoke the `GetDepartmentBudget()` method?

```
01: // Register a TCP client channel
02: TcpClientChannel channel =
        new TcpClientChannel();
03: ChannelServices.RegisterChannel(
        channel);
04: IBudget budget;
05: // Instantiate the remote class
06:
07: // Invoke the remote method
08: double budgetValue =
        budget.GetDepartmentBudget("HR");
```

A.

```
budget = (IBudget)
    Activator.GetObject(typeof(IBudget),
    @"tcp://finance:1234/Budget");
```

B.

```
budget = (IBudget)
     Activator.CreateInstance(
       typeof(IBudget),
       @"tcp://finance:1234/Budget");
```

C.

```
budget = new IBudget();
```

D.

```
RemotingConfiguration.
RegisterWellKnownClientType(
      typeof(IBudget),
      @"tcp://finance:1234/Budget");
Budget = new IBudget();
```

APPLY YOUR KNOWLEDGE

10. You are developing an application that allows the client programs to instantiate a class named `Inventory`. You want the remote object to be created on the server so that it can access the inventory database. However, you want client programs to control the creation and the lifetime of the remote objects. Which of the following methods of the `RemotingConfiguration` class would you choose to register the remotable class with the remoting system on the server?

    A. `RegisterWellKnownServiceType()`

    B. `RegisterWellKnownClientType()`

    C. `RegisterActivatedServiceType()`

    D. `RegisterActivatedClientType()`

11. You work for a large chemical manufacturing company that has four production units across the country. Your team has the responsibility of designing a distributed application that allows different production units to share and update material safety information for various products. One of your co-workers is using the following code to create a remoting host to host a server-activated object. She is getting an error. What should she do to resolve this error?

```
01: using System.Runtime.Remoting;
02: using System.Runtime.Remoting.Channels;
03: using
System.Runtime.Remoting.Channels.Tcp;
04: using
        System.Runtime.Remoting.Channels.Http;
05: [STAThread]
06: static void Main(string[] args)
07: {
08:     TcpServerChannel tcpChannel =
            new TcpServerChannel(7777);
09:     HttpServerChannel httpChannel =
            new HttpServerChannel(8888);
10:     RemotingConfiguration.
        RegisterWellKnownServiceType
```

```
        (typeof(MsdsInfo), "MsdsInfo",
        WellKnownObjectMode.Singleton);
11: }
```

    A. Remove the statement at line 09.

    B. Add the following statements just before line 10:

```
ChannelServices.RegisterChannel(tcpChannel);
ChannelServices.RegisterChannel(httpChannel);
```

    C. In the statement at line 08, replace `TcpServerChannel` with `TcpChannel`, and similarly in the statement in line 09, replace `HttpServerChannel` with `HttpChannel`.

    D. Use the same port numbers in the statements in line 08 and line 09.

12. One of your coworkers has written the following code as part of a client application that activates a remote object. She is complaining that her program is not compiling. What should she modify in the program to remove this error? (Select all that apply.)

```
01: DbConnect CreateObject()
02: {
03:     TcpClientChannel channel =
            new TcpClientChannel(1234);
04:     ChannelServices.RegisterChannel(
            channel);
05:     RemotingConfiguration.
        RegisterWellKnownClientType(
06:         typeof(DbConnect),
07:         "tcp://localhost/DbConnect"
08:         );
09:     dbc = new DbConnect();
10:     return dbc;
11: }
```

    A. Change line 05 to use the `RegisterWellKnownServiceType()` method instead of the `RegisterWellKnownClientType()` method.

APPLY YOUR KNOWLEDGE

B. Change the URL in line 07 to `"tcp://localhost:1234/DbConnect"`

C. Remove the port number from the constructor of `TcpClientChannel()` in line 03

D. Change the code in line 07 to `objectUri="DbConnect"`

13. The Soapsuds tool (`soapsuds.exe`) can be used to automatically generate the interface assembly for the remotable object. Which of the following statements are FALSE related to the Soapsuds tool? (Select two options.)

   A. The Soapsuds tool can be used to generate metadata for server-activated objects.

   B. The Soapsuds tool can be used to generate metadata for client-activated objects.

   C. The Soapsuds tool can be used to generate metadata for remotable objects registered through the HTTP channel.

   D. The Soapsuds tool can be used to generate metadata for remotable objects registered through the TCP channel.

14. You have designed a Windows application that is used by the shipping department of a large distribution house. The Windows application instantiates a remotable class hosted on Internet Information Services (IIS). The remotable class provides various services to the Windows application, such as address validation and calculation of shipping rates. When you deploy the application, users complain that when they click the Validate Address button, the Windows application freezes and they can't take further action till the address has been verified. What should you do to improve the application's responsiveness?

A. Use the binary formatter instead of the SOAP formatter.

B. Use the TCP channel to communicate instead of the HTTP channel.

C. Modify the remotable class to support asynchronous method calls.

D. Modify the Windows application to call the methods asynchronously on the remote object.

15. When you derive a class from the `MarshalByRefObject` to make the class remotable, which of the following members of the class are not remoted? (Select all that apply.)

A. non-static public methods

B. static methods

C. non-static private methods

D. non-static public properties

Answers to Review Questions

1. The application domain, represented by the `AppDomain` class, is the basic unit of isolation for running applications in the CLR. The CLR allows several application domains to run within a single Windows process. The CLR ensures that code running in one application domain cannot affect other application domains. The CLR can terminate an application domain without stopping the entire process.

2. MBR objects are remotable objects that derive from the `System.MarshalByRefObject` class. The MBR objects always reside on the server; the client application domain holds only a reference

to the MBR objects and uses a proxy object to interact with the MBR objects. They are best suited when the remotable objects are large or when the functionality of the remotable objects is available only in the server environment on which it is created. However, they increase the number of network roundtrips between the server application domain and the client application domain.

3. A channel is an object that transports messages across remoting boundaries such as application domains, processes, and computers. The .NET Framework provides implementations for HTTP and TCP channels.

4. The binary formatter represents messages in a compact and efficient way, whereas the SOAP formatters are very verbose. The SOAP formatters can be used to communicate in heterogeneous environments, whereas the binary formatters can be understood only by .NET applications.

5. The two modes for creating SAOs are SingleCall and Singleton. SingleCall activation mode creates a remote object for each client request. The object is discarded as soon as the request completes. Singleton activation mode creates a remote object only once and all the clients share the same copy. Hence SingleCall SAOs are stateless and Singleton SAOs maintain state global to all clients.

6. CAOs are created for each client whenever the client requests. Hence CAOs are best suited when clients want to maintain private sessions with remote objects, when the clients want to control the lifetimes of the objects, or when they want to create customized remote objects with non-default properties.

7. The main benefit of using declarative configuration over programmatic configuration is that you need not recompile the application after changing the remoting settings in the configuration file. The changes are picked up automatically.

8. The `GetObject()` method (for server-activated objects) and `CreateInstance()` method (for client-activated objects) are the two methods of the `Activator` class that enable you to create instances of remote objects.

9. Using IIS as an activation agent offers the following advantages:

   • You need not write a separate server program to register the remotable classes.

   • You need not worry about finding an available port for your server application. You can just host the remotable object and IIS automatically uses port 80.

   • IIS can provide other functionality, such as authentication and Secure Sockets Layer (SSL).

10. A remotable object by default is capable of being called asynchronously; therefore no extra efforts are required to create remote objects that can be called asynchronously.

Answers to Exam Questions

1. **A, B.** Your objective is to provide access to only authorized clients. Authorization is a function of the remoting host. IIS is the only available remoting host that provides you with this capability. IIS supports only HTTP communication. Therefore, you can use either the `HttpChannel` or

APPLY YOUR KNOWLEDGE

`HttpServerChannel` channel because both allow you to listen to incoming messages from clients. IIS does not support `TcpChannel` and `TcpServerChannel`, so if you use these channels you have to write additional code to implement security and this is not desired in the given scenario. For more information, see the section "Choosing Between the HTTP and the TCP Channels" in this chapter.

2. **C.** Firewalls generally allow HTTP messages to pass through, and the binary formatter provides a size-optimized format for encoding data. Using TCP may require administrators to open additional ports in the firewall, and the SOAP format is verbose when compared to binary and would take additional bandwidth, which is not a desirable solution for clients using slow connections. For more information, see the section "Choosing Between the HTTP and the TCP Channels" and "Channels and Formatters" in this chapter.

3. **A.** Only server-activated objects in SingleCall activation mode support load-balancing because they do not maintain state across the method calls. For more information, see the section "Server-Activated Objects" in this chapter.

4. **B.** You should store the remoting configuration in the `web.config` file. This file is an XML-based configuration file that is easy to modify and does not require a separate compilation step. Storing configuration settings in `gwpoinfo.dll` or `global.asax` requires the additional step of compilation before the settings come into effect. The `machine.config` file is not suggested because any changes made to it affect all the applications running on the server. For more information, see the section "Using Configuration Files to Configure the Remoting Framework" in this chapter.

5. **B.** When you want to create just one instance of a remote object, without regard to the number of clients, you must create a server-activated object in the Singleton activation mode. For more information, see the section "Server-Activated Objects" in this chapter.

6. **B.** IIS supports only `well-known` or server-activated objects. Therefore, you must use the `<wellknown>` element rather than the `<activated>` element. Also, you are specifying the configuration for the server, so you must use the `<server>` element rather than the `<client>` element inside the `<application>` element to configure the `WellKnown` object. For more information, see the section "Using Configuration Files to Configure the Remoting Framework" and "Using IIS As an Activation Agent" in this chapter.

7. **D.** Because you know that the server's .NET remoting application is using HTTP, you can use the Soapsuds tool to automatically generate the metadata for the server. For more information, see the section "Using the Soapsuds Tool to Automatically Generate an Interface Assembly" in this chapter.

8. **D.** You should use IIS as the remoting host because IIS has built-in support for Integrated Windows authentication. You'll have to write additional code to achieve this with other techniques. For more information, see the section "Using IIS As an Activation Agent" in this chapter.

9. **A.** When you have an interface to a class and not the original class, you cannot use the `new` operator to instantiate the remote object. You should instead use the static methods of the `Activator` class. The `Activator.GetObject()` method is used

to instantiate a server-activated object. For more information, see the section "Using Interface Assemblies to Compile Remoting Clients" in this chapter.

10. **C.** Your requirement is to register a client-activated remote object on the server, so you'll use the `RegisterActivatedServiceType()` method. The `RegisterActivatedClientType()` method is used to register the CAO with the remoting system in the client's application domain. The other two options are for creating the server-activated objects. For more information, see the section "Creating a Client-Activated Object" in this chapter.

11. **B.** In this program, although you have created an instance of `TcpServerChannel` and `HttpServerChannel` objects, you haven't yet registered them with the remoting framework. You'll register the channels by using the `RegisterChannel()` method of the `ChannelServices` class. For more information, see the sections "Using the SingleCall Activation Mode to Register a Remotable Class As a Server-Activated Object," "Using the Singleton Activation Mode to Register a Remotable Class As a Server-Activated Object," and "Registering a Remotable Class As a Client-Activated Object" in this chapter.

12. **B, C.** When creating a client channel you should not specify a port number when calling the channel constructor. Instead, the port number should be used with the URL of the remote object. After the channels are created they should be registered with the remoting system. For more information, see the section "Channels" in this chapter.

13. **B, D.** The Soapsuds tool is capable of generating metadata for server-activated objects on the HTTP channel. For more information, see the section "Using the Soapsuds Tool to Automatically Generate an Interface Assembly" in this chapter.

14. **D.** The issue in the question is not of speed but of responsiveness. This behavior occurs because the Windows application is calling the methods on the remote object synchronously. You can make the user interface more responsive by simply calling the remote method asynchronously. No modifications are needed on the remotable object to achieve this behavior. For more information, see the section "Asynchronous Remoting" in this chapter.

15. **B, C.** Only non-static public methods, properties, and fields participate in remoting. For more information, see the section "Remote Object Activation" in this chapter.

APPLY YOUR KNOWLEDGE

Suggested Readings and Resources

1. Visual Studio .NET Combined Help Collection

   - .NET Remoting Overview

   - Remoting Examples

2. Ingo Rammer. *Advanced .NET Remoting.* Apress, 2002.

3. www.iana.org/assignments/port-numbers— List of assigned port numbers.

This chapter covers the following Microsoft-specified objective for the "Creating and Managing Microsoft Windows Services, Serviced Components, .NET Remoting Objects, and XML Web Services" of the "Developing XML Web Services and Server Components with Microsoft Visual C# .NET and the Microsoft .NET Framework" exam:

Create and consume an XML Web service.

- **Control characteristics of Web methods by using attributes.**

- **Instantiate and invoke an XML Web service.**

▶ One of the major advances of Visual Studio .NET over previous versions of Visual Studio is its support for XML Web services. As you'll learn in this chapter, XML Web services enable the use of remote objects over common Internet protocols. This objective tests your ability to use Visual Studio .NET to create a Web service, and to use objects that are made available by a Web service created by another developer.

This chapter also covers the following Microsoft-specified objectives for the "Deploying Windows Services, Serviced Components, .NET Remoting Objects, and XML Web Services" section of the "Developing XML Web Services and Server Components with Microsoft Visual C# .NET and the Microsoft .NET Framework" exam:

Publish an XML Web Service.

- **Enable static discovery.**

- **Publish XML Web service definitions in the UDDI.**

CHAPTER 4

Basic Web Services

OBJECTIVES

▶ The exam also tests your familiarity with the publishing side of Web services. Publishing a Web service makes its objects and methods publicly available. By using Web services protocols such as WSDL and UDDI, you can make your Web service available to other developers for use in their own applications.

OUTLINE

STUDY STRATEGIES

▶ Use ASP.NET to create a simple Web service. Then use the `wsdl.exe` tool to create a proxy class for that Web service, and instantiate the Web service within another ASP.NET application. Make sure you understand how to make all of the pieces of the process work together.

▶ Use the registry at `www.uddi.org` to explore some available Web services.

▶ If you're reviewing references on Web services to study for the exam, make sure that they're specifically about Microsoft's approach to Web services. Although Web services are broadly interoperable between manufacturers, there are implementation differences.

▶ Use a tool such as the .NET WebService Studio to inspect SOAP messages and WSDL files to see what's happening as you interact with a Web service.

INTRODUCTION

You have probably heard quite a bit of hype about *Web services* in conjunction with the .NET Framework. In fact, Microsoft has gone so far as to sometimes describe the .NET Framework as "an XML Web services platform that will enable developers to create programs that transcend device boundaries and fully harness the connectivity of the Internet" (`msdn.microsoft.com/net`). You may also run across a lot of complex and confusing explanations of the architecture of these Web services. But at their most basic level, Web services are simple: They are a means for interacting with objects over the Internet.

Seen in that light, Web services are part of a natural progression:

1. Object-oriented languages such as C++ and C# enable two objects within the same application to interact.

2. Protocols such as the Component Object Model (COM) enable two objects on the same computer, but in different applications, to interact.

3. Protocols such as the Distributed Component Object Model (DCOM) enable two objects on different computers, but in the same local network, to interact.

4. Web services enable two objects on different computers—even if they're only connected by the Internet—to interact.

In this chapter I'll introduce you to Web services as they exist in the .NET Framework. You'll see how to build and use Web services in your .NET applications, and you'll learn about the major protocols that are used when you communicate with a Web service.

UNDERSTANDING WEB SERVICES

Create and consume an XML Web service.

- **Instantiate and invoke an XML Web service.**

Before I get into the nuts and bolts of actually working with Web services, I'll give you an overview of the way they work. The key to understanding Web services is to know something about the protocols that make them possible:

▶ Simple Object Access Protocol (SOAP)

▶ Disco and Universal Description, Discovery, and Integration (UDDI)

▶ Web Services Description Language (WSDL)

One important thing to realize is that, by default, all communication between Web services servers and their clients is through Extensible Markup Language (XML) messages transmitted over the Hypertext Transfer Protocol (HTTP) protocol. This has two benefits. First, because Web services messages are formatted as XML, they're reasonably easy for human beings to read and understand. Second, because those messages are transmitted over the pervasive HTTP, they can normally reach any machine on the Internet without being blocked by firewalls.

NOTE

Naming Web Services As with many rapidly-developing technologies, different companies use different names for Web services. Some prefer the capitalized form "Web Services," and others use the explicit "XML Web Services." In this book, I've gone along with the MCAD exam objectives guide, which calls them "Web services."

SOAP

For Web services to manipulate objects through XML messages, there has to be a way to translate objects (as well as their methods and properties) into XML. SOAP is a way to encapsulate object calls as XML sent via HTTP.

There are two major advantages to using SOAP to communicate with Web services. First, because HTTP is so pervasive, it can travel to any point on the Internet, regardless of intervening hardware or firewalls. Second, because SOAP is XML based, it can be interpreted by a wide variety of software on many operating systems. Although you'll only work with the Microsoft implementation of Web services in this chapter, numerous Web services tools from other vendors can interoperate with Microsoft-based Web services.

EXAM TIP

SOAP over Other Protocols You often read that SOAP messages travel over HTTP. Although this is the default for SOAP as implemented by Visual Studio .NET, it's not a part of the SOAP specification. SOAP messages could be sent by email or File Transfer Protocol (FTP) without losing their content. As a practical matter, SOAP today uses HTTP in almost all cases.

Here's a typical SOAP message sent from a Web services client to a Web services server:

```
<?xml version="1.0" encoding="utf-8"?>
<soap:Envelope
  xmlns:soap=
    "http://schemas.xmlsoap.org/soap/envelope/"
  xmlns:soapenc=
    "http://schemas.xmlsoap.org/soap/encoding/"
```

```
xmlns:tns=
  "http://www.capeclear.com/AirportWeather.wsdl"
xmlns:types="http://www.capeclear.com/
  AirportWeather.wsdl/encodedTypes"
xmlns:xsi=
  "http://www.w3.org/2001/XMLSchema-instance"
xmlns:xsd="http://www.w3.org/2001/XMLSchema">
<soap:Body soap:encodingStyle=
  "http://schemas.xmlsoap.org/soap/encoding/">
  <q1:getLocation
    xmlns:q1="capeconnect:AirportWeather:Station">
    <arg0 xsi:type="xsd:string">KSEA</arg0>
  </q1:getLocation>
</soap:Body>
</soap:Envelope>
```

Even without digging into this file in detail, you can see some obvious points:

▶ The SOAP message consists of an envelope and a body, each marked with a specific XML tag.

▶ This particular message invokes a method named `getLocation()` from a specified uniform resource locator (URL).

▶ The method takes a single parameter, `arg0`, which is transmitted as an XML element.

Here's the SOAP message that comes back from the server:

```
<?xml version="1.0" encoding="utf-8"?>
<SOAP-ENV:Envelope
  xmlns:SOAP-ENV=
    "http://schemas.xmlsoap.org/soap/envelope/"
  xmlns:xsd="http://www.w3.org/2001/XMLSchema"
  xmlns:cc1=
    "http://www.capeclear.com/AirportWeather.xsd"
  xmlns:xsi=
    "http://www.w3.org/2001/XMLSchema-instance"
  xmlns:SOAP-ENC=
    "http://schemas.xmlsoap.org/soap/encoding/">
  <SOAP-ENV:Body SOAP-ENV:encodingStyle=
    "http://schemas.xmlsoap.org/soap/encoding/">
    <cc2:getLocationResponse
      xmlns:cc2="capeconnect:AirportWeather:Station"
      SOAP-ENC:root="1">
      <return xsi:type="xsd:string">
        Seattle, Seattle-Tacoma International Airport,
        WA, United States</return>
    </cc2:getLocationResponse>
  </SOAP-ENV:Body>
</SOAP-ENV:Envelope>
```

In the response message, the getLocationResponse element is the result of the call to the object on the server. It includes a string wrapped up as an XML element.

Disco and UDDI

Before you can use a Web service, you need to know where to find the service. Handling such requests is the job of several protocols, including Disco and UDDI. These protocols enable you to communicate with a Web server to discover the details of the Web services that are available at that server. You'll learn more about these protocols later in the chapter.

WSDL

Another prerequisite for using a Web service is knowledge of the SOAP message types that it can receive and send. You can obtain this knowledge by parsing WSDL files. WSDL is a standard by which a Web service can tell clients what messages it accepts and which results it will return.

Here's a portion of a WSDL file:

```
<?xml version="1.0" encoding="utf-16"?>
<definitions
  xmlns:http="http://schemas.xmlsoap.org/wsdl/http/"
  xmlns:soap="http://schemas.xmlsoap.org/wsdl/soap/"
  xmlns:s="http://www.w3.org/2001/XMLSchema"
  xmlns:s0=
    "http://www.capeclear.com/AirportWeather.xsd"
  xmlns:soapenc=
    "http://schemas.xmlsoap.org/soap/encoding/"
  xmlns:tns=
    "http://www.capeclear.com/AirportWeather.wsdl"
  xmlns:tm=
    "http://microsoft.com/wsdl/mime/textMatching/"
  xmlns:mime="http://schemas.xmlsoap.org/wsdl/mime/"
  targetNamespace=
    "http://www.capeclear.com/AirportWeather.wsdl"
  name="AirportWeather"
  xmlns="http://schemas.xmlsoap.org/wsdl/">
  <types>
    <s:schema targetNamespace=
      "http://www.capeclear.com/AirportWeather.xsd">
      <s:complexType name="WeatherSummary">
        <s:sequence>
          <s:element minOccurs="1" maxOccurs="1"
```

```
              name="location" nillable="true"
              type="s:string" />
            <s:element minOccurs="1" maxOccurs="1"
              name="wind" nillable="true"
              type="s:string" />
            <s:element minOccurs="1" maxOccurs="1"
              name="sky" nillable="true"
              type="s:string" />
            <s:element minOccurs="1" maxOccurs="1"
              name="temp" nillable="true"
              type="s:string" />
            <s:element minOccurs="1" maxOccurs="1"
              name="humidity" nillable="true"
              type="s:string" />
            <s:element minOccurs="1" maxOccurs="1"
              name="pressure" nillable="true"
              type="s:string" />
            <s:element minOccurs="1" maxOccurs="1"
              name="visibility" nillable="true"
              type="s:string" />
          </s:sequence>
        </s:complexType>
      </s:schema>
    </types>
    <message name="getHumidity">
      <part name="arg0" type="s:string" />
    </message>
    <message name="getHumidityResponse">
      <part name="return" type="s:string" />
    </message>
    <message name="getLocation">
      <part name="arg0" type="s:string" />
    </message>
    <message name="getLocationResponse">
      <part name="return" type="s:string" />
    </message>
    <message name="getOb">
      <part name="arg0" type="s:string" />
    </message>
...
</definitions>
```

WSDL files define everything about the public interface of a Web service, including the following:

▶ The data types that it can process

▶ The methods that it exposes

▶ The URLs through which those methods can be accessed

> **EXAM TIP**
>
> **Exposure Is Optional** Although UDDI and WSDL files make it possible to interact with Web services without any prior knowledge, these files are not required for a Web service to function. You can make a Web service available on the Internet without any UDDI or WSDL file. In that case, only clients who know the expected message formats and the Web service's location are able to use it.

Invoking Your First Web Service

At this point, I'd like to show you a Web service in action. Step-by-Step 4.1 shows how you can use a Web service, in this case one that supplies the weather at any airport worldwide.

STEP BY STEP

4.1 Invoking a Web Service

1. Create a new Visual C# .NET Windows application in the Visual Studio .NET Integrated Development Environment (IDE). Name the project 320C04.

2. Right-click the References folder in Solution Explorer and select Add Web Reference. This opens the Add Web Reference dialog box.

3. Type **http://live.capescience.com/wsdl/ AirportWeather.wsdl** in the Address bar of the Add Web Reference dialog box and press Enter. This connects you to the Airport Weather Web service and downloads the information shown in Figure 4.1.

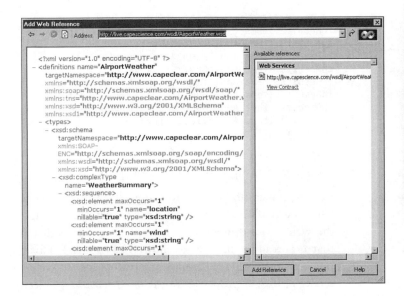

continues

WARNING **Working with the Internet** Most of the examples in this chapter assume that you're working on a computer that is connected to the Internet. It's okay if there's a proxy server between you and the Internet, as long as you can connect to Web sites.

NOTE **Airport Codes** You can find a list of four-letter ICAO airport codes to use with this Web service at www. house747.freeserve.co.uk/ aptcodes.htm. Codes for airports in the United States all start with K; codes for Canadian airports all start with C.

WARNING **Web Service Stability** Web services come and go, and there's no guarantee that the one I'm using in this chapter will still be available when you go to test it. If the Airport Weather Web service doesn't seem to be available, one good way to find others is to use your favorite search engine to look for the term "Web service examples." You can also search for Web services through public UDDI directories such as, uddi.microsoft.com and uddi.ibm.com.

FIGURE 4.1
The Add Web Reference dialog box enables you to connect to a Web service over the Internet.

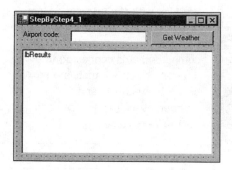

FIGURE 4.2
Design of a form that invokes an Airport
Weather Web service.

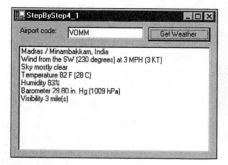

FIGURE 4.3
You can invoke a remote Web service and
access the objects returned by the Web
service.

continued

4. Click the Add Reference button.

5. In the Solution Explorer, rename the default `Form1.cs` to
   `StepByStep4_1.cs`. Open the form in code view and
   change all occurrences of `Form1` to refer to `StepByStep4_1`
   instead.

6. Place a `Label` control, a `TextBox` control (`txtCode`), a
   `Button` control (`btnGetSummary`), and a `ListBox` control
   (`lbResults`) on the form. Figure 4.2 shows the design of
   the form.

7. Double-click the `Button` control and enter the following
   code to invoke the Web service when the user clicks the
   Get Weather button:

```
private void btnGetWeather_Click(object sender,
    System.EventArgs e)
{
    // Declare the Web service main object
    com.capescience.live.AirportWeather aw =
        new com.capescience.live.AirportWeather();

    // Invoke the service to get a summary object
    com.capescience.live.WeatherSummary ws =
        aw.getSummary(txtCode.Text);

    // And display the results
    lbResults.Items.Clear();
    lbResults.Items.Add(ws.location);
    lbResults.Items.Add("Wind " + ws.wind);
    lbResults.Items.Add("Sky " + ws.sky);
    lbResults.Items.Add("Temperature " + ws.temp);
    lbResults.Items.Add("Humidity " + ws.humidity);
    lbResults.Items.Add("Barometer " + ws.pressure);
    lbResults.Items.Add("Visibility " +
        ws.visibility);
}
```

8. Set the form as the startup object for the project.

9. Run the project and enter a four-digit ICAO airport code.
   Click the Get Weather button. After a brief pause while
   the Web service is invoked, you see the current weather at
   that airport in the list box, as shown in Figure 4.3. This
   information is delivered from the server where the Web
   service resides, as properties of the `WeatherSummary` object.

You'll learn more about the techniques in Step by Step 4.1 in the rest of the chapter, but you should be able to see the broad outlines of Web services already. In one sense, there's not much new here, compared to invoking any other object. After you've set a reference to the server, you can create objects from that server, invoke their methods, and examine the results. You could do the same with objects from a .NET library on your own computer.

But in another sense, there's a lot of revolutionary work going on here, even though you don't see most of it happening. When you create the Web reference, for example, Visual Studio .NET reads the appropriate WSDL file to determine which classes and methods are available from the remote server. When you call a method on an object from that server, the .NET infrastructure translates your call and the results into SOAP messages and transmits them without any intervention on your part.

Depending on the speed of your Internet connection, you may notice that the Web service client that you created in Step-by-Step 4.1 "freezes" when you invoke the Web service. This program uses a synchronous method to communicate with the Web service, waiting for the SOAP response before allowing any other code to execute. You will learn later in this chapter, in Exercise 4.1 and in Chapter 5, "Advanced Web Services," how to call a Web service asynchronously to increase the responsiveness of the client program.

REVIEW BREAK

▶ Web services provide you with the means to create objects and invoke their methods even though your only connection to the server is via the Internet.

▶ Communication with Web services is via XML messages transported by the HTTP.

▶ Because they communicate over HTTP, Web services are typically not blocked by firewalls.

▶ The Simple Object Access Protocol (SOAP) encapsulates object-oriented messages between Web service clients and servers.

continues

continued

▶ The Universal Description, Discovery, and Integration (UDDI) protocol enables you to find Web services by connecting to a directory.

▶ The Web Services Description Language (WSDL) lets you retrieve information on the classes and methods that are supported by a particular Web service.

CREATING WEB SERVICES

To better understand Web services, you should be familiar with both sides of the conversation. In this section, you'll learn how to create a Web service by using the tools built into ASP.NET.

Creating a Web Service Project

To create a Web service, you can build an ASP.NET project in Visual Studio .NET.

NOTE

Web Server Required   You need to have an IIS Web server available to you to complete the examples and exercises in this chapter that create Web services and Web applications. You get IIS as a part of the Windows 2000 Professional, Windows XP Professional, and Windows Server operating systems.

STEP BY STEP

4.2 Creating a Web Service

1. Create a new project in Visual Studio .NET. Select the ASP.NET Web Service template and name the new project StringProc, as shown in Figure 4.4. (substituting your own Web server name for *localhost*, if the Web server is not on your local machine).

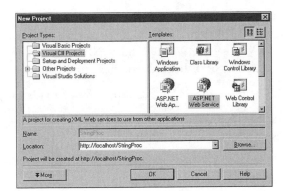

FIGURE 4.4
The New Project dialog box enables you to create a new Web service project in the Visual Studio .NET IDE.

2. Right-click the `Service1.asmx` file in Solution Explorer and rename it `Strings.asmx`. Open the form in code view and change all occurrences of `Service1` to refer to `Strings` instead.

3. Click the hyperlink on the `Strings.asmx` design surface to switch to the code view. Add the following attribute before the `Strings` class definition:

```
[WebService(
  Namespace="http://NetExam.org/StringProc")]
public class Strings : System.Web.Services.WebService
```

4. Enter the following methods in the class definition:

```
[WebMethod()]
public String ToUpper(String inputString)
{
    return inputString.ToUpper();
}

[WebMethod()]
public String ToLower(String inputString)
{
    return inputString.ToLower();
}
```

5. Save the project.

6. Select Build, Build Solution to create the Web service on the server.

EXAM TIP

The Web Service Namespace   The `WebService` attribute requires you to supply a value for the `Namespace` property. This value (`http://NetExam.org/StringProc` in Step-by-Step 4.2) is purely arbitrary. It doesn't have to resolve to an actual Web site. This string is just a unique identifier for your Web service. If you leave the default value instead of changing it, you get a warning from Visual Studio .NET.

You now have a functioning Web service on your Web server. Congratulations! Although lots of plumbing is involved in properly hooking up a Web service, Visual Studio .NET protects you from having to set up any of it. Instead, you have to do only three things:

▶ Build the project from the ASP.NET Web Service template.

▶ Mark the classes that should be available via the Web service by using the `WebService` attribute.

▶ Mark the methods that should be available via the Web service by using the `WebMethod` attribute.

The methods marked with the `WebMethod` attribute are also known as Web methods.

Testing the Web Service Project

Visual Studio .NET includes built-in tools, hosted on an HTML test page, for testing a Web service project without building any client applications for the Web service. Step-by-Step 4.3 shows you how to use these tools, which can save you time when you're debugging a Web service.

STEP BY STEP

4.3 Testing a Web Service

1. Run the Web Service project from Step-by-Step 4.2. Run the project. A browser is launched that shows the test page shown in Figure 4.5.

FIGURE 4.5
When you view a Web service in a browser, a Web service test page with hyperlinks to Web methods is displayed.

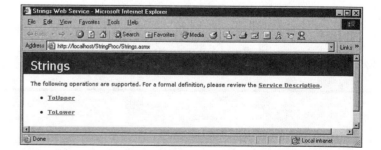

2. Click the Service Description link on the test page. This lets you view the WSDL for this Web service. Click the Back button in the browser to return to the test page.

3. Click the ToUpper link on the test page. This opens a page for testing the ToUpper() method, as shown in Figure 4.6.

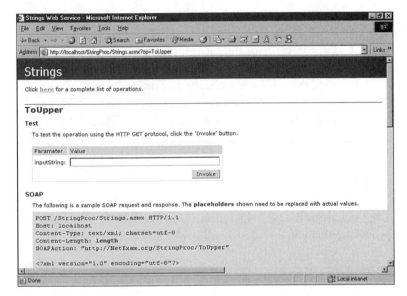

FIGURE 4.6
The Web method test page allows you to test the Web method by using the HTTP GET protocol.

4. The Web method test page shows the SOAP messages and other messages that the Web service understands. It also contains a form that allows you to test the Web method.

5. Enter a string with mixed uppercase and lowercase characters at the inputString prompt.

6. Click the Invoke button. A second browser window opens, as shown in Figure 4.7, with the XML message that the Web service sends back when you call the ToUpper() method on the test string.

continues

continued

FIGURE 4.7
The Web service returns the results in the XML format.

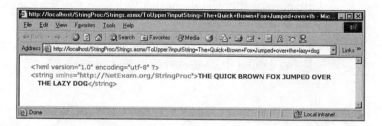

7. Experiment with the ToLower() method in the same way you experimented with the ToUpper() method. When you click the Invoke button, the test page constructs the appropriate XML message and passes it to the Web service, which returns the results.

REVIEW BREAK

▶ Visual Studio .NET includes an ASP.NET Web Service template that you can use to build your own Web services.

▶ To make a class available via a Web service, you mark the class with the WebService attribute.

▶ To make a method available via a Web service, you mark the method with the WebMethod attribute.

▶ To test a Web service, run the project in the Visual Studio .NET IDE.

GUIDED PRACTICE EXERCISE 4.1

In this exercise, you are required to create a Web service to allow the client applications to perform database lookup for a SQL Server database.

Specifically, you need to perform these tasks:

1. Build a Web service that exposes a single class named Customer. The Customer class should expose a Web method named GetCustomers(). The GetCustomers() Web method

should accept a country name and return a DataSet object that contains all the customers from that country. You should use the data from the Customers table of the Northwind sample database.

2. Build a client application that uses the Web service from step 1. The user should be able to enter a country name and see all the customers from that country.

How would you accomplish these tasks?

You should try working through this problem on your own first. If you are stuck, or if you'd like to see one possible solution, follow these steps:

1. Create a new project in Visual Studio .NET. Select the ASP.NET Web Service template and name the new project Northwind.

2. Right-click the Service1.asmx file in Solution Explorer and rename it Customer.asmx. Open the form in code view and change all occurrences of Service1 to refer to Customer instead.

3. Add the following using directive:

```
using System.Data.SqlClient;
```

4. Enter this code to create the GetCustomers() Web method:

```
[WebMethod()]
public DataSet GetCustomers(String Country)
{
    // Create a SqlConnection
    SqlConnection cnn = new SqlConnection(
    "Data Source=(local);" +
    "Initial Catalog=Northwind;" +
    "Integrated Security=SSPI");
    // Create a SqlCommand
    SqlCommand cmd = cnn.CreateCommand();
    cmd.CommandType = CommandType.Text;
    cmd.CommandText = "SELECT * FROM Customers " +
        " WHERE Country = '" + Country + "'";
    // Set up the DataAdapter and
    // fill the Dataset object
    SqlDataAdapter da = new SqlDataAdapter();
    da.SelectCommand = cmd;
    DataSet ds = new DataSet();
    da.Fill(ds, "Customers");
```

continues

FIGURE 4.8
You can test the Web methods that return complex objects through a Windows form.

continued

```
        // And return it to the client
        return ds;
    }
```

5. Select Build, Build Solution to create the Web service on the server.

6. Build the client application. Open your Windows application for this chapter and add a new form to the project.

7. Place a `Label` control, a `TextBox` control (`txtCountry`), a `Button` control (`btnGetCustomers`), and a `DataGrid` control (`dgCustomers`) on the form. Figure 4.8 shows a possible design of the form.

8. Right-click the References folder in Solution Explorer and select Add Web Reference. The Add Web reference dialog box appears.

9. Type `http://localhost/Northwind/Customer.asmx` (substituting your own Web server name for *localhost*, if the Web server is not on your local machine) in the Address bar of the Add Web Reference dialog box, and press Enter. You are then connected to the server, where you can and download the information about the `Northwind` Web service.

10. Click the Add Reference button.

11. Switch to the code view of the form. Add the following `using` directives:

```
using System.Data;
using System.Data.SqlClient;
```

12. Double-click the `Button` control on the form. Enter the following code to handle the button's `Click` event (replace *localhost* with the name of your own Web server, if *localhost* is not applicable):

```
private void btnGetCustomers_Click
    (object sender, System.EventArgs e)
{
    // Create a DataSet object
    // to hold the customers of interest
    DataSet dsCustomers;
    // Connect to the Web service
    // and retrieve customers
    localhost.Customer cust =
```

```
        new localhost.Customer();
    dsCustomers = cust.GetCustomers(txtCountry.Text);
    // Bind the results to the user interface
    dgCustomers.DataSource = dsCustomers;
    dgCustomers.DataMember = "Customers";
}
```

13. Insert the `Main()` method to launch the form. Set the form as the startup object for the project.

14. Run the project and enter a country name (such as France). Click the Get Customers button. After a brief delay while the project contacts the Web service, the `DataGrid` control fills with data, as shown in Figure 4.9.

As this exercise shows, you can return complex objects from a Web service as easily as you can return simple types. The Web service takes care of all the details of converting the `DataSet` object to an XML representation, wrapping it in a SOAP message, sending it to the client, and reconstituting the `DataSet` object there.

If you have difficulty following this exercise, review the sections "Invoking Your First Web Service" and "Creating a Web Service Project" earlier in this chapter. Also, review the section "Running Queries" in Chapter 1, "Creating and Manipulating DataSets." After doing that review, try this exercise again.

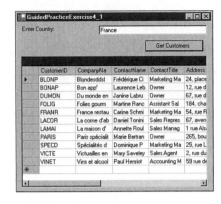

FIGURE 4.9
The Web form displaying the contents of the `DataSet` object returned by the `GetCustomers()` Web method.

CUSTOMIZING THE WebMethod ATTRIBUTE

Create and consume an XML Web service.

- **Control characteristics of Web methods by using attributes.**

You've seen how easy it is to generate a Web service by using Visual Studio .NET, simply by marking published methods with the `WebMethod` attribute. But there are also a number of ways to customize your Web service by adding properties to that attribute. Table 4.1 shows the properties that you can use to customize the `WebMethod` attribute.

TABLE 4.1

PROPERTIES OF THE WebMethod ATTRIBUTE

Property	Meaning
BufferResponse	Indicates whether the response should be buffered. If set to true (the default) the entire response is buffered until the message is completely serialized and is then sent to the client. If set to false, the response is sent to the client as it is serialized.
CacheDuration	Specifies the number of seconds that ASP.NET should cache results on the server. The default is 0, which disables caching.
Description	Supplies a description for the Web method.
EnableSession	Indicates whether the session state should be enabled. The default is false.
MessageName	Specifies the name by which the method will be called in SOAP messages. The default is the method name.
TransactionOption	If set to TransactionOption.Required or TransactionsOption.RequiredNew, enables the Web method to participate as the root object of a transaction. The default is TransactionOption.Disabled.

In the Step-by-Step 4.4, you'll see how you can use several of these properties to customize a Web method.

STEP BY STEP

4.4 Customizing a Web Service

1. Open the StringProc Web Service project that you created in Step-by-Step 4.2.

2. Add this Web methods definition to the existing Strings class definition:

```
[WebMethod(CacheDuration = 60,
     Description = "Method to demonstrate caching")]
public String CachedString(int intInput)
{
    return "The time is " +
        DateTime.Now.ToLongTimeString();
}

[WebMethod(Description = "Method without caching")]
public String UncachedString(int intInput)
```

```
{
    return "The time is " +
        DateTime.Now.ToLongTimeString();
}

[WebMethod(EnableSession = true,
    Description = "Store a value in session state")]
public String SetSession(int intInput)
{
    Session["StoredInt"] = intInput;
    return "Value " +  intInput +
        " stored in session state";
}

[WebMethod(EnableSession = true,
    MessageName = "Get Session",
    Description=
      "Retrieve a value from session state")]
public String GetSession()
{
    if (Session["StoredInt"] != null)
    {
        int intOutput = (int) Session["StoredInt"];
        return "Value " +  intOutput +
            " retreived from session state";
    }
    return "";
}
```

3. Run the project. This opens the test page shown in Figure
   4.10. Notice that the test page displays the description
   property of each Web method.

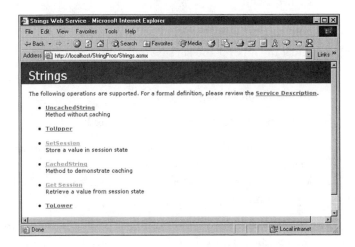

FIGURE 4.10
The test page for a Web service displays the
Web method with its description, if the Web
method attribute has the `Description` property
defined.

continues

continued

4. Click on the `UncachedString` link to open a test page for the `UncachedString()` method.

5. Enter a value for the input parameter and click Invoke. You should see a return message with the current time.

6. Click Invoke again. You should now see the updated current time.

7. Click the link to return to the complete list of operations.

8. Click on the `CachedString` link to open a test page for the `CachedString()` method.

9. Enter a value for the input parameter and click Invoke. You should see a return message with the current time.

10. Click Invoke again. You should now see the same current time. That's because the result from the `CachedString()` method is cached for sixty seconds. ASP.NET returns the cached value during that time without calling the original method.

11. Change the input parameter and click Invoke again. You should see a return message with the current time. When an input parameter changes, ASP.NET does not use the cached result.

12. Click the link to return to the complete list of operations.

13. Click the link for the `SetSession()` method.

14. Enter an input value and click Invoke. You should see a confirmation message.

15. Click the link to return to the complete list of operations.

16. Click on the link for the `GetSession()` method. Notice that this link uses the `MessageName` property of the `WebMethod` attribute rather than the name of the underlying method.

17. Click Invoke. You should now see the value retrieved from the session state.

Step-by-Step 4.4 demonstrates all the WebMethod attribute properties except for BufferResponse and TransactionOption. The only time that you'll want to set BufferResponse to true is when you're returning more than 16KB of data, and that data is being constructed on the fly—for example, when you are retrieving and formatting records from a database.

If you're interested in performing transactions within a Web service, you should look at the WS-Transaction portion of the new Global XML Architecture (GXA) specification, rather than use the TransactionOption property. See msdn.microsoft.com/ library/default.asp?url=/library/en-us/dngxa/html/ gloxmlws500.asp for more information on this advanced topic, which you will not find on the exam.

> **WARNING**
>
> **Be Wary of Session State** You should be cautious about using session state in a Web service. Session state can tie up server resources for an extended period of time. If you use session state with a popular Web service, you will apply heavy demands to Random Access Memory (RAM) on your Web server.

DISCOVERING WEB SERVICES

Publish an XML Web Service

- **Enable static discovery.**
- **Publish XML Web Service definitions in the UDDI.**

One of the problems with Web services is simply finding them. Because Web services aren't installed on your computer, you need some way to determine what messages they accept and what services they provide. The usual term for this process is *discovery*, which encompasses both finding Web services and determining their interfaces. You should know about three protocols in this area:

▶ Disco

▶ UDDI

▶ WSDL

Disco and UDDI

Disco is a Microsoft standard for the creation of discovery documents. A Disco document is kept at a standard location on a Web services server and it contains paths and other information for retrieving useful information, such as the WSDL file that describes a service. This document is used for static discovery. That is, a potential user of your Web service must know the location of the Disco document to use it.

For Visual Studio .NET projects, you ordinarily won't want to build a Disco document. Such projects are designed to generate discovery information from their base URL. For example, if your Web service is named `StringProc` and is stored on a server with the name `INFINITY`, and a base class name of `Strings.asmx`, you can retrieve static discovery information by navigating to `http://INFINITY/StringProc/Strings.asmx?wsdl`.

Sometimes, though, you'll want to generate a completely static discovery document that does not require processing to create. Step-by-Step 4.5 shows you how.

STEP BY STEP

4.5 Creating a Discovery Document

1. Open the `StringProc` Web Service project that you created in Step-by-Step 4.2.

2. Right-click the `StringProc` Web service project and select Add, Add New Item from the context menu. In the Add New Item dialog box select the Web Project Items Categories and the Static Discovery File template. Name the new document `StringProc.disco` and click Open.

3. Enter this code in the new file:

```
<?xml version="1.0" encoding="utf-8" ?>
<discovery xmlns="http://schemas.xmlsoap.org/disco/">
<contractRef ref="Strings.asmx?WSDL"
 xmlns="http://schemas.xmlsoap.org/disco/scl/" />
</discovery>
```

4. In another Visual Studio .NET project, right-click the References node in Solution Explorer and select Add Web Reference. Enter `http://localhost/StringProc/StringProc.disco` (substituting your own Web server name for `localhost`, if the Web server is not on your local machine) to view the discovery file, as shown in Figure 4.11.

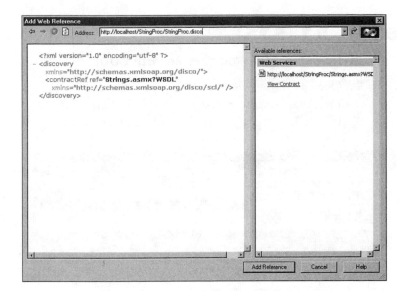

FIGURE 4.11
You can also set a Web reference through a static discovery file.

5. Click on the View Contract link to see the WSDL for the Web service.

UDDI (Universal Description, Discovery, and Integration) is a method for finding services by referring to a central directory. These can be Web services, URLs for information, or any other online resources. UDDI registries are sites that contain information that is available via UDDI; you can search such a registry to find information about Web services. UDDI thus provides dynamic discovery, allowing you to find Web services even when you do not know their location in advance.

UDDI registries come in two forms: *public* and *private*. A public UDDI registry is available to all comers via the Internet and serves as a central repository of information about Web and other services for businesses. A private UDDI registry follows the same specifications as a public UDDI registry but is located on an intranet for the use of workers at one particular enterprise.

To add your own services to a UDDI registry, you must use the tools provided by that particular registry. Step-by-Step 4.6 shows you how to add your Web service to the Microsoft Test UDDI Registry.

> **NOTE**
>
> **The UDDI Project**   The UDDI specification is developed jointly by several industry partners, including Microsoft and IBM. For more information and a public directory, visit `www.uddi.org`.

FIGURE 4.12
You can add your own Web services to a UDDI Registry.

STEP BY STEP

4.6 Registering a Web service with UDDI

1. Open a browser window and navigate to `http://test.uddi.microsoft.com/default.aspx`. This opens the UDDI Test Registry, as shown in Figure 4.12.

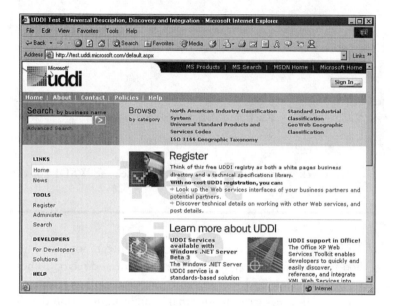

2. Click the Register link.

3. Sign in using your Microsoft Passport. If you do not already have a Microsoft Passport, follow the instructions to create one.

4. Fill in the registration form to create a UDDI publisher account. Follow the directions to respond to the validation email if you do not share your Passport email address.

5. Click the Administer link.

6. Click the Add a New Business link.

7. Fill in your business details and click Publish to add your business to the UDDI registry.

8. Return to the Administer page.

9. Click the Add a New tModel link.

10. Fill in the details of your Web service. You can provide the URL of a static discovery document, or an ASP.NET WSDL URL such as `http://infinity/StringProc/Strings.asmx?WSDL` (substituting your own Web server name for *infinity*), as the document location.

11. After you have published your business and service details, you can use the Search link to locate your information in the UDDI Test Registry.

> **N O T E**
>
> **Use a Test UDDI Registry For Testing** To test your Web service without impacting other UDDI users you should use a test UDDI Registry such as `test.uddi.microsoft.com` instead of a production UDDI Registry such as `uddi.microsoft.com`.

Using the Web Services Discovery Tool (`disco.exe`)

When you set a Web reference inside Visual Studio .NET, the software handles the details of discovery automatically for you. But you can also get into the details of the process yourself. One of the tools included in the .NET Framework Software Development Kit (SDK) (and also in Visual Studio .NET) is the Web Services Discovery tool, `disco.exe`. This command-line tool assists you in the discovery process, as seen in Step-by-Step 4.7.

STEP BY STEP

4.7 Using the Web Services Discovery Tool

1. Select Start, Programs, Microsoft Visual Studio .NET, Visual Studio .NET Tools, Visual Studio .NET Command Prompt. This opens a command prompt window and sets the environment up so that you can use any of the command-line tools from the .NET Framework SDK.

2. Enter the following command to discover the details of the Airport Weather Web Service:

```
disco http://live.capescience.com/wsdl/
➥AirportWeather.wsdl
```

As you can see, you need to know the Web service's base address to use this tool.

continues

continued

NOTE

Discovery File (`.disco`)—The `disco.exe` also retrieves a discovery document, if the Web service includes a static discovery document (`.disco` file). The discovery file is an XML file containing useful URLs. These include the URL for the WSDL file describing the service, the URL for the documentation of the service, and the URL to which SOAP messages should be sent.

Dynamic Discovery   Visual Studio .NET also creates a dynamic discovery document (`.vsdisco` file) for ASP.NET Web service applications. The dynamic discovery document is an XML-based file that contains links to resources that provide discovery information for a Web service.

3. The tool contacts the Web service and (in this case) creates two files of results: `AirportWeather.wsdl` and `results.discomap`. If the Web service includes a static discovery document (`.disco` file), the tool also retrieves that document.

4. Open these files in Visual Studio .NET to see the results of the discovery process.

   The `results.discomap` file is an XML file that shows you the name of the other file (`AirportWeather.wsdl`) and the URL from which its contents were retrieved.

   The `AirportWeather.wsdl` file is an XML file that contains information about the Web service's interface. This includes details of the messages, parameters, and objects with which you can interact. It's this file that gives Visual Studio .NET the details that it needs to let you use a Web service from your code.

REVIEW BREAK

▶ Disco is Microsoft's standard format for discovery documents, which contain information on Web services.

▶ UDDI, the Universal Description, Discovery, and Integration protocol, is a multi-vendor standard for discovering online resources, including Web services.

▶ The Web Services Discovery tool, `disco.exe`, can retrieve discovery information from a server that exposes a Web service.

INSTANTIATING AND INVOKING WEB SERVICES

After you have discovered a Web service and retrieved information about its interface, you can instantiate an object that represents that

Web service and then invoke its methods. In this section you'll learn about two methods to integrate Web services in your applications, and you'll learn about testing a Web service as a consumer.

Creating Proxy Classes with the Web Services Description Language Tool (`wsdl.exe`)

The .NET Framework SDK includes the Web Services Description Language tool, `wsdl.exe`. This tool can take a WSDL file and generate a corresponding proxy class that you can use to invoke the Web service, as shown in Step-by-Step 4.8.

STEP BY STEP

4.8 Using the Web Services Description Language Tool

1. Select Start, Programs, Microsoft Visual Studio .NET, Visual Studio .NET Tools, Visual Studio .NET Command Prompt. This opens a command prompt window and sets the environment up so that you can use any of the command-line tools from the .NET Framework SDK.

2. Navigate to the folder that contains the WSDL file that you created in Step-by-Step 4.7.

3. Enter the following command to create a proxy class to call the Airport Weather Web service:

```
wsdl /language:CS /out:AirportWeatherProxy.cs
➡ AirportWeather.wsdl
```

   The tool reads the WSDL file and creates a new file named `AirportWeatherProxy.cs`.

4. Add the `AirportWeatherProxy.cs` file to your Visual Studio .NET Windows application project by selecting File, Add Existing Item.

continues

continued

5. Add a new Windows form to your Visual C# .NET project.

6. Place a `Label` control, a `TextBox` control (`txtCode`), a `Button` control (`btnGetWeather`), and a `Listbox` control (`lbResults`) on the form. Refer to Figure 4.2 for the design of this form.

7. Double-click the `Button` control and enter the following code to invoke the Web service when the user clicks the Get Weather button:

```
private void btnGetWeather_Click(object sender,
    System.EventArgs e)
{
    // Connect to the Web service by declaring
    // a variable of the appropriate type
    // available in the proxy
    AirportWeather aw = new AirportWeather();

    // Invoke the service to get a summary object
    WeatherSummary ws = aw.getSummary(txtCode.Text);

    // And display the results
    lbResults.Items.Clear();
    lbResults.Items.Add(ws.location);
    lbResults.Items.Add("Wind " + ws.wind);
    lbResults.Items.Add("Sky " + ws.sky);
    lbResults.Items.Add("Temperature " + ws.temp);
    lbResults.Items.Add("Humidity " + ws.humidity);
    lbResults.Items.Add("Barometer " + ws.pressure);
    lbResults.Items.Add("Visibility " +
        ws.visibility);
}
```

8. Insert the `Main()` method to launch the form. Set the form as the startup object for the project.

9. Run the project and fill in a value for the airport code. Click the Get Weather button. After a brief pause while the Web service is invoked, you'll see some information in the `ListBox` control, as shown in Figure 4.3. This information is delivered from the server where the Web service resides, as properties of the `WeatherSummary` object. The difference between this and the version in Step-by-Step 4.1 is that this code explicitly defines the objects that it

uses rather than discovering them at runtime. The
AirportWeather and WeatherSummary objects are proxy
objects that pass calls to the Web service and return results
from the Web service. This information is delivered from
the server where the Web service resides, as properties of
the WeatherSummary object.

Table 4.2 shows some of the command-line options that you can use
with wsdl.exe. You don't need to memorize this material, but you
should be familiar with the tool's overall capabilities. You can use
either the path to a local WSDL or Disco file or the URL of a
remote WSDL or Disco file with this tool.

TABLE 4.2

COMMAND-LINE OPTIONS FOR wsdl.exe

Option	Meaning
/domain:*DomainName* /d:*DomainName*	Specifies the domain name to use when connecting to a server that requires authentication.
/language:*LanguageCode* /l:*LanguageCode*	Specifies the language for the generated class. The LanguageCode parameter can be CS (for C#), VB (for Visual Basic .NET) or JS (for JScript).
/namespace:*Namespace* /n:*Namespace*	Specifies a namespace for the generated class.
/out:*Filename* /o:*FileName*	Specifies the filename for the generated output. If this option is not specified, the filename is derived from the Web service name.
/password:*Password* /p:*Password*	Specifies the password to use when connecting to a server that requires authentication.
/server	Generates a class to create a server based on the input file. By default, the tool generates a client proxy object.
/username:*Username* /u:*Username*	Specifies the username to use when connecting to a server that requires authentication.
/?	Displays full help for the tool.

Using Web References

FIGURE 4.13
When you add a Web reference, the proxy class is automatically generated.

As an alternative to using the Web Services Discovery tool and the Web Services Description Language tool to create explicit proxy classes, you can simply add a Web reference to your project to enable the project to use the Web service. You've seen Web references several times in this chapter, starting in Step-by-Step 4.1.

In fact, there's no difference in the end result between using the tools to create a proxy class and adding a Web reference. Behind the scenes, the Web reference creates its own proxy class. To see this, click the Show All Files toolbar button in Solution Explorer, and then expand the Solution Explorer node for a Web reference. You'll see a set of files similar to that shown in Figure 4.13.

The `.disco` and `.wsdl` files are the same files that would be generated by running the Web Services Discovery tool on the URL of the Web reference. The `.map` file is same as the `.discomap` file generated by the Web Services Discovery tool. The `.cs` file defines the proxy objects to be used with the Web service represented by this Web reference, as you can see by opening this file. The major difference between this file and the proxy that you generate with the Web Services Description Language tool is that the auto-generated file uses a namespace that is based on the name of the Web reference.

Testing a Web Service

If you'd like to test a Web service without building an entire client application, you can use a testing tool. Several such tools are easily available:

▶ NetTool is a free Web services proxy tool from CapeClear. You can get a copy from `capescience.capeclear.com/articles/using_nettool`.

▶ The .NET WebService Studio tool comes from Microsoft. You can download a free copy from `www.gotdotnet.com/team/tools/web_svc/default.aspx`.

▶ XML Spy includes a SOAP debugger that can be used to test Web services. You can download a trial copy of this XML editor and toolkit from `www.xmlspy.com/default.asp`.

All three of these tools work in the same basic way: They intercept SOAP messages between Web services clients and servers so that you can inspect, and if you like, alter the results. In Step-by-Step 4.9 you use one of these tools to see a Web service in action.

STEP BY STEP

4.9 Testing a Web Service without a Client Project

1. Download the .NET WebService Studio tool from `www.gotdotnet.com/team/tools/web_svc/default.aspx` and install it on your computer.

2. Launch the WebServiceStudio.exe application.

3. Enter `http://live.capescience.com/wsdl/` `AirportWeather.wsdl` as the WSDL endpoint and click the Get button.

4. The tool reads the WSDL file from the Web service and constructs the necessary proxy classes to invoke it. Click the getSummary entry on the Invoke tab to use the `getSummary` Web method.

5. In the Input section, select the arg0 item. You can now enter a value for this item in the Value section. Enter an airport code such as **KSEA** for the value.

6. Click the Invoke button. The tool sends a SOAP message to the Web service, using your chosen parameters, and then displays the results, as shown in Figure 4.14.

7. Click the Request/Response tab to view the outgoing and incoming SOAP messages.

8. Click the WSDLs & Proxy tab to see the WSDL file and the generated proxy class for this Web service.

continues

continued

FIGURE 4.14
The .NET WebService Studio tool allows you to test a Web service without creating any client application.

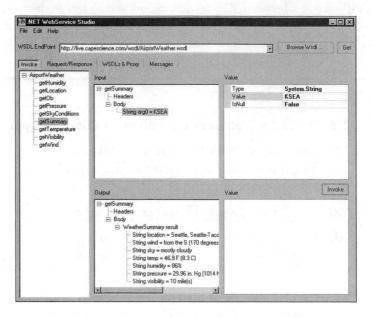

R E V I E W   B R E A K

▶ You can manually generate proxy classes for a Web service by using the Web Services Description Language tool.

▶ You can automatically generate proxy classes for a Web service by setting a Web reference to point to the Web service.

▶ You can test and debug a Web service without a client application by using one of several SOAP proxy tools.

CHAPTER SUMMARY

Web service support is one of the most significant advances in the .NET architecture. The .NET Framework supports both creating and consuming Web services through command-line tools as well as the Visual Studio .NET IDE.

Web services provide a way to invoke objects over the Internet. A Web service can expose one or more Web methods, each of which can accept parameters and return objects.

Web services use protocols and standards, including SOAP, Disco, UDDI, and WSDL to communicate. These protocols and standards are designed to use HTTP as their transmission mechanism so that they are generally not blocked by firewalls.

The .NET Framework includes command-line tools to aid in the discovery and use of Web services. Visual Studio .NET enables you to easily use these tools in the simple act of setting a Web reference. Either of these methods produces local proxy classes that you can use to send messages to a Web service and that will return the results from the Web service to the rest of the application.

KEY TERMS

- Web service
- Web service proxy
- SOAP
- Disco
- UDDI
- WSDL
- Web method
- Web reference

APPLY YOUR KNOWLEDGE

Exercises

4.1   Calling a Web Service Asynchronously

Depending on the speed of your Internet connection, you may have noticed that the Web service client applications you constructed earlier in this chapter "freeze" when you invoke the Web service. By default these applications use synchronous methods to communicate with the Web service, waiting for the SOAP response before allowing any other code to execute. But the proxy classes constructed by .NET include asynchronous methods as well. In this exercise, you'll learn how to call a Web service asynchronously.

Estimated Time: 30 minutes.

1. Create a Visual C# .NET Windows Application in the Visual Studio .NET IDE.

2. Right-click the References folder in Solution Explorer and select Add Web Reference. The Add Web Reference dialog box appears.

3. Type `http://live.capescience.com/wsdl/` `AirportWeather.wsdl` in the Address bar of the Add Web Reference dialog box and press Enter. This connects you to the `StringProc` Web service and creates the appropriate proxy classes.

4. Click the Add Reference button.

5. Add a new Windows form to your Visual C# .NET project.

6. Place a `Label` control, a `TextBox` control (txtCode), a `Button` control (btnGetWeather), and a `Listbox` control (lbResults) on the form. Refer to Figure 4.2 for the design of this form.

7. Double-click the `Button` control and enter the following code to invoke the Web service when the user clicks the Get Weather button:

```
private void btnGetWeather_Click(
    object sender, System.EventArgs e)
{
    // Declare the Web service main object
    com.capescience.live.AirportWeather aw=
 new com.capescience.live.AirportWeather();

    // Invoke the Web service.
    // This may take some time, so
    // call it asynchronously.
    // First, create a callback method
    AsyncCallback wcb = new AsyncCallback(
        WebServiceCallback);
    // Initiate the asynchronous call
    aw.BegingetSummary(
        txtCode.Text, wcb, aw);
}
// This method will get called
// when the Web service call is done
public void WebServiceCallback(
    IAsyncResult ar)
{
    // Retrieve the state of
    // the proxy object
    com.capescience.live.AirportWeather aw=
      (com.capescience.live.AirportWeather)
      ar.AsyncState;

    // Call the End method
    // to finish processing
    com.capescience.live.WeatherSummary ws=
        aw.EndgetSummary(ar);

    // And display the results
    lbResults.Items.Clear();
    lbResults.Items.Add(ws.location);
    lbResults.Items.Add(
        "Wind " + ws.wind);
    lbResults.Items.Add(
        "Sky " + ws.sky);
    lbResults.Items.Add(
        "Temperature " + ws.temp);
    lbResults.Items.Add(
        "Humidity " + ws.humidity);
    lbResults.Items.Add(
        "Barometer " + ws.pressure);
    lbResults.Items.Add(
        "Visibility " + ws.visibility);
}
```

APPLY YOUR KNOWLEDGE

8. Insert the `Main()` method to launch the form. Set the form as the startup object for the project.

9. Run the project and enter a four-digit ICAO airport code. Click the Get Weather button. Wait a few moments; you will see the current weather at that airport in the list box. Note that while you're waiting, you can still drag the form around the screen, which shows that it is not blocked by the Web service call.

If you compare the code for this exercise with the code that you saw in Step-by-Step 4.1, you'll find some significant changes. In the .NET Framework, asynchronous Web service calls are managed by call-back methods. When you add a Web reference, the proxy class includes Begin and End methods for each Web method. In this case, those are the `BegingetSummary()` and `EndgetSummary()` methods.

The Begin method takes all the same parameters as the underlying Web method, plus two others. The first is the address of a callback method, and the second is an object whose properties should be available in the call-back method. When you call the Begin method, the .NET Framework launches the call to the Web service in the background. When the Web method call completes, the callback method is invoked. The code in this exercise shows how you can then retrieve the original object and use its End method to finish the work of using the Web service.

4.2 Using a Web Service from ASP.NET

Although the examples in this chapter were written as Windows applications, Web services work equally well when called from ASP.NET Web applications. In this exercise, you use ASP.NET to retrieve information from the Airport Weather Web service.

Estimated Time: 25 minutes.

1. Create a new Visual C# .NET Web Application project.

2. Right-click the References folder in Solution Explorer and select Add Web Reference. This opens the Add Web Reference dialog box.

3. Type **http://live.capescience.com/wsdl/ AirportWeather.wsdl** into the Address bar of the Add Web Reference dialog box and press Enter. This connects you to the Airport Weather Web service and creates the appropriate proxy classes.

4. Click the Add Reference button.

5. Add a new Web form to the project.

6. Place a `Label` control, a `TextBox` control (txtCode), a `Button` control (btnGetSummary), and a `ListBox` control (lbResults) on the Web form in the project.

7. Double-click the `Button` control and enter the following code to invoke the Web service when the user clicks the Get Weather button:

```
private void btnGetWeather_Click(
    object sender, System.EventArgs e)
{
    // Declare the Web service main object
    com.capescience.live.AirportWeather aw=
new com.capescience.live.AirportWeather();

    // Invoke the service
    // to get a summary object
    com.capescience.live.WeatherSummary ws=
        aw.getSummary(txtCode.Text);

    // And display the results
    lbResults.Items.Clear();
    lbResults.Items.Add(ws.location);
    lbResults.Items.Add("Wind " + ws.wind);
    lbResults.Items.Add("Sky " + ws.sky);
    lbResults.Items.Add(
        "Temperature " + ws.temp);
```

APPLY YOUR KNOWLEDGE

```
lbResults.Items.Add(
    "Humidity " + ws.humidity);
lbResults.Items.Add(
    "Barometer " + ws.pressure);
lbResults.Items.Add(
    "Visibility " + ws.visibility);
}
```

8. Set the Web form as the start page for the project.

9. Run the project and fill in an airport code. Click the button. Wait a few moments, and the list box will show the details of the weather for that airport, as shown in Figure 4.15.

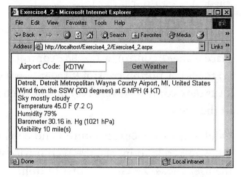

FIGURE 4.15
You can also invoke a Web service from an ASP.NET application.

Review Questions

1. What is the purpose of a Web service proxy class?

2. Describe the general purpose of SOAP.

3. Describe the general purpose of Disco and UDDI.

4. Describe the general purpose of WSDL.

5. Can a Web service exist without a WSDL file?

6. Explain two ways in which you can create proxy classes for a Web service.

7. List three steps involved in using Visual Studio .NET to build a Web service.

8. What tools can you use to make local copies of the configuration files for a Web service?

9. How can you test a Web service without building a client application?

10. What is the advantage of sending SOAP messages over the HTTP?

Exam Questions

1. You want to use a Web service that supplies inventory level information in your application. You know the URL of the .asmx file published by the Web service. What step should you take first?

   A. Open the .asmx file in a Web browser.

   B. Run the XML Schema Definition tool.

   C. Run the Web Services Discovery tool.

   D. Copy the .asmx file to your client project.

2. Your application includes a Web reference to a Web service that delivers customer information as an object with multiple properties. The developer of the Web service has added a new property named CreditRating to the object. What should you do to be able to use the CreditRating property in your code?

   A. Create an entirely new client application, and add a Web reference for the Web service to the new application.

   B. Delete and re-create the Web reference in the existing application.

C. Update the Web reference in the existing application.

D. Use a generic `Object` variable to hold customer information, so you can call any property you like.

3. You have used ASP.NET to create a Web service that returns financial information. One of the methods in your Web service is defined with this code:

```
public Double Cash()
{
    // Calculations omitted
}
```

Potential consumers of your Web service report that although they can set a reference to the Web service, the `Cash()` method is not available. What could be the problem?

A. The `.asmx` file for the Web service is not available on your Web server.

B. The Web service class is not marked with the `[WebService]` attribute.

C. The `Cash()` method is not marked with the `[WebMethod]` attribute.

D. Web services can return only string values.

4. You have created a new Web service to perform financial calculations. You're working in an ASP.NET project within Visual Studio .NET. What's the easiest way to test your new Web service to make sure that it's returning the proper results?

A. Cut and paste the code into a Windows application project and test it in the new project.

B. Run the Web service project and use the test page that it opens in the browser.

C. Use a tool such as .NET WebService Studio to send SOAP requests directly to the server.

D. Have a large number of beta testers use the application, and monitor the server for odd behavior.

5. Your application uses a Web service named `Northwind`. The `Northwind` Web service includes a Web method named `Suppliers()` that returns a `DataSet` containing all the company's suppliers. What data type should you use to declare an object to hold the result of the `Suppliers()` method?

A. `Suppliers.DataSet`

B. `DataSet`

C. `Northwind.DataSet`

D. `DataRow[]`

6. You're using the Web Services Discovery tool to determine information about a Web service on a particular server. You receive the error message `The HTML document does not contain Web service discovery information`. What could be the problem?

A. The server address that you typed does not exist.

B. The server requires authentication and you have entered improper credentials.

C. The Web Services Discovery tool works only on your local computer.

D. There is no WSDL or Disco file available at the address that you typed.

APPLY YOUR KNOWLEDGE

7. You are using the Web Services Description Language tool to create a proxy class for a Web service. The Web service exposes a class named `Customer`. You already have a `Customer` class in your application. What should you do to allow both classes to coexist in the same application?

   A. Use the `/namespace` option of the Web Services Description Language tool to specify a unique namespace for the new class.

   B. Rename the existing class.

   C. Use the `/out` option of the Web Services Description Language tool to specify a unique output file name for the new class.

   D. Manually edit the generated proxy class to change the classname that it contains.

8. You have used a UDDI registry to locate a Web service that might be able to supply information for your business. You want to test the interface of the Web service to make sure that it meets your requirements before you invest the effort to build a client application. How should you proceed?

   A. Use the Web Services Discovery tool to download the WSDL file for the Web service and inspect it in an XML editor.

   B. Use the Web Services Description Language tool to create a proxy class for the Web service and to use a text editor to inspect the class.

   C. Craft SOAP messages in an XML editor and use them to test the Web service.

   D. Use a tool such as the .NET WebService Studio to test the Web service's interface.

9. Your application calls a Web service that performs complex, time-consuming calculations. Users complain that the user interface of the application freezes while it's recalculating. Which of the following approaches is guaranteed to solve this problem?

   A. Move the application to a faster computer.

   B. Install a faster link to the Internet.

   C. Install more memory in the computer.

   D. Use asynchronous calls to invoke the Web service.

10. One of your partner businesses has informed you that it is making its inventory information available via a Web service. You do not know the Web service's URL. How can you discover the URL?

   A. Use the Web Services Discovery tool to download the information.

   B. Use the Web Services Description Language tool to create a proxy class.

   C. Use a UDDI registry to locate the Web service.

   D. Use a search engine to explore your partner's Web site.

11. What must a developer do to make a Web service built with Visual Studio .NET available asynchronously?

   A. Nothing. The client can always call a Web service asynchronously.

   B. Use a separate `Thread` object for each invocation of the Web service.

   C. Provide callback methods to invoke the Web service.

   D. Host the Web service on an Internet Information Server 6.0 server.

12. You are invoking a Web service that returns a `DataSet` object. Your client application is written in Visual C# .NET, whereas the Web service itself is written in Visual Basic .NET. The Web service is outside of your corporate firewall. You receive an `object not found` error when you call the method that returns the `DataSet`. What could be the problem?

    A. The client project and the Web service project must use the same language.

    B. Objects supplied by a Web service cannot cross a firewall.

    C. The client project does not contain a reference to the `System.Data` namespace.

    D. Web services cannot properly serialize a complex object such as the `DataSet` object.

13. Your application invokes a Web service named Northwind that includes a Web method named `GetOrders()`. `GetOrders()` returns a `DataSet` object containing order information. What must you do to use this `DataSet` object in your client application?

    A. Create a new `DataSet` object and use the `ReadXml()` method of the `DataSet` object to initialize it from the returning SOAP message.

    B. Obtain an XSD file that specifies the schema of the `DataSet` object. Use this XSD file to instantiate a `DataSet` object from the returned data from the `GetOrders()` method.

    C. Assign the return value from the `GetOrders()` method to an array of `DataRow` variables. Loop through the array to build the `DataSet`.

    D. Assign the return value from the `GetOrders()` method to a `DataSet` variable.

14. You have used the Web Services Discovery tool to retrieve information about a Web service named `ZipcodeService`. Which file will contain the URL for any documentation of the `ZipcodeService` Web service?

    A. `disco.exe`

    B. `results.discomap`

    C. `ZipcodeService.wsdl`

    D. `ZipcodeService.disco`

15. You have used the Web Services Description Language tool to create a proxy class for a Web service. When you add the proxy class to your project, you discover that it is coded in the Visual Basic .NET language. What must you do to get the proxy class in Visual C# .NET instead of Visual Basic .NET?

    A. Manually convert the Visual Basic .NET code to C# code.

    B. Rerun the tool, using the `/language:CS` option.

    C. Rerun the tool, using the `/namespace:CS` option.

    D. Select File, Save As and save the file with the `.cs` extension.

Answers to Review Questions

1. A Web service proxy class is an object that you can create on the client to communicate with a Web service. The proxy accepts messages, forwards them to the Web service, and returns the results of those messages.

APPLY YOUR KNOWLEDGE

2. SOAP is an XML-based protocol designed to exchange structured information on the Web. The purpose of SOAP is to enable Web services based on the Web infrastructure such as HTTP, SMTP, and so on.

3. Disco and UDDI are designed to help discover the interface details of a Web service.

4. WSDL exists to supply information on the interface of a Web service.

5. A Web service can exist without a WSDL file, but you must then know the exact incoming SOAP message that the Web service expects before you can use it.

6. You can create proxy classes for a Web service by using the `disco.exe` and `wsdl.exe` tools or by creating a Web reference within Visual Studio .NET.

7. To build a Web service you must create a new Web service application, mark the classes to be exposed with the `[WebService]` attribute, and mark the methods to be exposed with the `[WebMethod]` attribute.

8. The `disco.exe` tool makes local copies of the configuration files for a Web service. Creating a new Web reference also creates these files.

9. You can use a tool such as .NET WebService Studio to test a Web service without building a client application. You can also use Microsoft Internet Explorer to test Web services using the HTTP GET protocol.

10. Using HTTP as the transport protocol for SOAP messages means that the messages can take advantage of pervasive Internet connectivity to reach their destination; they are not blocked by firewalls.

Answers to Exam Questions

1. **C.** The Web Services Discovery tool retrieves copies of the files that you need to proceed with this project. For more information, see the section "Discovering Web Services" in this chapter.

2. **C.** The Update Web Reference menu item for a Web reference refreshes local configuration information from the server that hosts the Web service. For more information, see the section "Using Web References" in this chapter.

3. **C.** All exposed methods of a Web service must be marked with the `[WebMethod]` attribute. For more information, see the section "Creating Web Services" in this chapter.

4. **B.** When you're creating a Web service in ASP.NET, running the project opens a testing form in a browser window. For more information, see the section "Testing a Web Service" in this chapter.

5. **B.** The client needs to declare the same data type that the server is returning, in this case the `DataSet` object. For more information, see the section "Testing the Web Service Project" and Guided Practice Exercise 4.1 in this chapter.

6. **D.** The Web Services Discovery tool requires the URL to a Disco or WSDL file in order to function. For more information, see the section "Using the Web Services Discovery Tool (`disco.exe`)" in this chapter.

7. **A.** Specifying a unique namespace for the new object removes the chance that it can clash with a pre-existing object name. For more information, see the section "Creating Proxy Classes with the Web Services Description Language Tool (`wsdl.exe`)" in this chapter.

8. **D.** By using an automated tool you can avoid tedious and error-prone inspection of XML files. For more information, see the section "Testing a Web Service" in this chapter.

9. **D.** Speeding up the client computer will do nothing to speed up the Web service, which runs on the server computer. For more information, see the section "Invoking Your First Web Service" and Exercise 4.1 in this chapter.

10. **C.** UDDI registries exist so that you can find business services by browsing or searching. For more information, see the section "Disco and UDDI" in this chapter.

11. **A.** Building the proxy class, either with wsdl.exe or by setting a Web reference, automatically creates methods to invoke the Web service asynchronously. For more information, see the section "Instantiating and Invoking Web Services" and Exercise 4.1 in this chapter.

12. **C.** Web services client and server applications must agree on the definition of the data to be exchanged. For more information, see the section "Instantiating and Invoking Web Services" in this chapter.

13. **D.** The only thing you need to do to use a complex variable returned by the Web service is to declare an instance of the same data type in the client application. For more information, see the section "Instantiating and Invoking Web Services" in this chapter.

14. **D.** The Disco (.disco) file is the only one that contains pointers to non-XML resources. For more information, see the section "Discovering Web Services" in this chapter.

15. **B.** The /language option controls the output language of the wsdl.exe tool. For more information, see the section "Creating Proxy Classes with the Web Services Description Language Tool (wsdl.exe)" in this chapter.

Suggested Readings and Resources

1. Visual Studio .NET Combined Help Collection.

2. .NET Framework SDK Documentation, including "XML Web Services Created Using ASP.NET and XML Web Service Clients."

3. Kenn Scribner & Mark C. Stiver. *Applied SOAP: Implementing .NET XML Web Services.* Sams, 2001.

4. Scott Short. *Building XML Web Services for the Microsoft .NET Platform.* Microsoft Press, 2002.

5. Eric Newcomer. *Understanding Web Services: XML, WSDL, SOAP, and UDDI.* Addison-Wesley, 2002.

This chapter covers the following Microsoft-specified objective for the "Creating and Managing Microsoft Windows Services, Serviced Components, .NET Remoting Objects, and XML Web Services" of the "Developing XML Web Services and Server Components with Microsoft Visual C# .NET and the Microsoft .NET Framework" exam:

Create and Consume an XML Web service.

▶ **Create and use SOAP extensions.**

▶ **Create asynchronous Web methods.**

▶ **Control XML wire format for an XML Web service.**

In most cases, you can treat using the .NET Framework to create Web services as something that "just works." But there will be times when the simple approach of letting Visual Studio .NET and the .NET Framework do everything for you won't quite work. To pass this section of the exam, you need to understand several ways in which you can customize your Web services. Specifically, you'll learn about SOAP extensions, which let you apply your own processing to SOAP messages; asynchronous Web methods, which allow you to issue non-blocking calls to Web services; and wire format attributes, which let you control the low-level formatting of your SOAP messages.

CHAPTER 5

Advanced Web Services

STUDY STRATEGIES

▶ Understand the order of events in a SOAP extension. Be sure you know what actions your extension should perform in each event.

▶ Write code to call a Web service asynchronously, and compare it with code to call the same Web service synchronously.

▶ Experiment with the options for customizing SOAP messages. Use a tool such as the .NET WebService Studio to inspect the actual messages sent and received by a customized Web service.

INTRODUCTION

As you saw in Chapter 4, "Basic Web Services," Visual Studio .NET makes it very easy to create and consume Web services. Whether you use the `wsdl.exe` tool explicitly, or use a Web reference to call it implicitly, your client applications can use WSDL to create fully-functional proxy classes that tie them seamlessly to Web services servers. But you may find situations in which this automatic connection isn't quite flexible enough to do everything that you want. In this chapter, you'll learn about three advanced Web service techniques:

▶ SOAP extensions

▶ Asynchronous calls

▶ Custom wire formatting

Each of these techniques has its own set of applications. SOAP extensions enable you to modify the SOAP messages between client and server by inserting your own custom code into the message creation process. Usually SOAP extensions are deployed in pairs, with matching extensions on client and server.

Asynchronous calls are a client-side technique for making more efficient use of Web services. When your code calls a Web method asynchronously, it is not blocked while waiting for the results of the call. Although the proxy classes created by `wsdl.exe` automatically enable asynchronous calls, you need to understand the various techniques for using these calls.

Finally, custom wire formatting lets you dictate the formatting of the SOAP messages a Web service uses (the messages that are sent "over the wire"). This is most useful when you're developing a Web service that must interoperate with client software that expects messages in a particular format. By using attributes within your code, you can control the formatting of these messages precisely.

CREATING AND USING SOAP EXTENSIONS

Create and Consume an XML Web service: Create and use SOAP extensions.

SOAP extensions enable you to perform your own processing on SOAP messages that pass between a Web service client and a Web service server. A SOAP extension can perform tasks such as encryption, signature verification, translation, or any other modification of the SOAP messages that are being passed. In this section of the chapter, you'll learn the mechanics of writing and using a SOAP extension.

The Extensible Web Services Architecture

To understand how SOAP extensions fit into Web services, it's helpful to have an understanding of the general Web services architecture. Figure 5.1 shows schematically how Web services clients and servers communicate with one another.

FIGURE 5.1
How the Web service communication works.

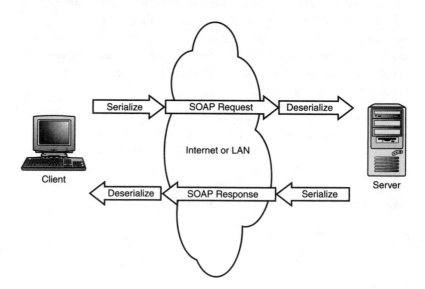

When a Web service client invokes a Web method that is on a Web service server, the client takes the objects and parameters involved and turns them into an XML message: the SOAP request. This process of converting objects to XML is called *serialization*. On the server end, the reverse process (called *deserialization*) is used to turn the XML back into objects. The server then sends back the SOAP response, which goes through a similar process of serialization and deserialization.

SOAP extensions allow you to run your own code as part of the serialization or deserialization process. Figure 5.2 shows schematically how SOAP extensions fit into the Web services architecture.

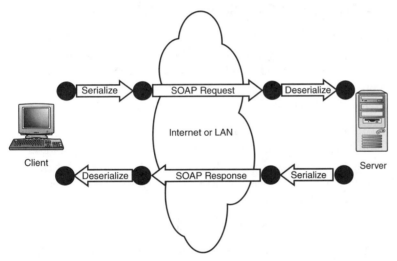

FIGURE 5.2
How the Web service communication works with SOAP extensions.

In Figure 5.2, the circles show the points at which you can insert a SOAP extension into the Web services architecture. As you can see, SOAP extensions are quite flexible: you can run code in a SOAP extension before or after a serialization or deserialization operation.

Soap extensions can be deployed on the client or on the server, and singly or in pairs. Here are some examples to suggest how particular types of SOAP extensions might fit into the overall Web services picture:

▶ A SOAP extension designed to measure overall server traffic for a Web service would be deployed only on the server. Clients would never know anything about this SOAP extension.

EXAM TIP

Multiple SOAP Extensions   It's entirely possible to have more than one SOAP extension working with a single SOAP message. You'll see later on that you can configure SOAP extensions with a priority. The SOAP extension with the lowest priority modifies the message first; the SOAP extension with the highest priority modifies the message last.

▶ A SOAP extension designed to translate requests from English measurements to metric measurements, and responses from metric measurements to English measurements, could be deployed only on the client. As far as the server knows, it's still dealing with a client making requests in metric measurements.

▶ A SOAP extension designed to digitally sign messages, and to verify the digital signature on delivery, would need to be deployed on both the client and the server. Each side would sign outgoing messages and verify incoming signatures.

Writing a Server-side SOAP Extension

Writing a SOAP extension is one of the more difficult Web service tasks that you're likely to tackle for this exam. There is quite a bit of intricate code involved, in addition to the code that you'll need to implement the Web service itself. But if you examine each piece of code carefully, you'll see how it all fits together.

In Step-by-Step 5.1, you'll put together a Web service that includes a SOAP extension. This SOAP extension will log incoming and outgoing messages to a disk file. Before getting started, it may help to have a high-level overview of the process that the SOAP extension code must follow:

1. Derive a new class from the `SoapExtension` class.

2. Implement the `GetInitializer()` and `Initialize()` methods to handle startup chores.

3. Implement the `ChainStream()` method to intercept the SOAP messages being serialized and deserialized.

4. Implement the `ProcessMessage()` method to work with the SOAP messages.

5. Derive a new class from the `SoapExtensionAttribute` class to mark methods that will use the new extension.

You'll see each of these tasks in Step-by-Step 5.1.

STEP BY STEP

5.1 Creating a Server-side SOAP Extension

1. Launch Visual Studio .NET. Select File, New, Blank Solution and name the new solution `320C05`.

2. Add a new Visual C# ASP.NET Web Service application in the Visual Studio .NET IDE. Name the new Web service `BugTracker`.

3. In the Solution Explorer, rename the default `Service1.asmx` to `Bugs.asmx`. Open the form in code view and change all occurrences of `Service1` to refer to `Bugs` instead.

4. Add the following attribute before the `Bugs` class definition:

```
[WebService(Namespace="http://BugTracker.que.com/")]
public class Bugs : System.Web.Services.WebService
```

5. Add a new class file to the project. Name the new class `Bug.cs`. Modify the `Bug.cs` class to contain this code:

```
using System;
namespace BugTracker
{
    public class Bug
    {
        private int bugID;
        private string description;

        public Bug()
        {
            Description = "";
        }


        public Bug(int bugID)
        {
            this.bugID = bugID;
            // Test data
            // A real implementation would retrieve
            // details from a database
            // or other store here
            this.description = "Initializing the " +
                "thingamabob causes the " +
                "whatsit to crash.";
        }
```

continues

continued

```
                    public int BugID
                    {
                        get
                        {
                            return bugID;
                        }
                        set
                        {
                            bugID = value;
                        }
                    }

                    public string Description
                    {
                        get
                        {
                            return description;
                        }
                        set
                        {
                            description = value;
                        }
                    }
                }
            }
        }
```

6. Add a Web method to the `Bugs.asmx.cs` file to return a Bug object when it is passed a Bug ID from the client:

```
[WebMethod]
public Bug GetBug(int bugID)
{
    Bug b = new Bug(bugID);
    return b;
}
```

7. Add a new class to the project. Name the new class `SoapDisplayExtension.cs`. This class implements a SOAP extension that writes incoming and outgoing messages to a file.

8. Add these using directives at the top of the `SoapDisplayExtension` class:

```
using System.IO;
using System.Text;
using System.Web.Services;
using System.Web.Services.Protocols;
```

9. Modify the class declaration to make the `SoapDisplayExtension` class derive from the `SoapExtension` class:

```
public class SoapDisplayExtension : SoapExtension
```

10. Add two variables to the `SoapExtension` class. These variables store the original SOAP message (passed to your SOAP extension as a stream object) and the possibly-modified SOAP message from your extension to the next stage of processing:

```
// Variables to hold the original stream
// and the stream that is returned
private Stream originalStream;
private Stream internalStream;
```

11. Invoke the Class View. Navigate to the SoapDisplayExtension node and select Bases and Interface. Select the SoapExtension node and then expand the node. You should see nodes showing `GetInitializer()` and `Initialize()` methods. Right-click each method and select Add, Override from the context menu to add overridden versions for these methods. Although these methods are not used in this particular example, you still need to implement them, because they are defined as abstract methods in the base class.

```
// Version called if configured with a config file
public override object GetInitializer(
    System.Type serviceType)
{
    // Not used in this example, but it's
    // declared abstract in the base class
    return null;
}

// Called the first time the Web service is used
// Version called if configured with an attribute
public override object GetInitializer(
    LogicalMethodInfo methodInfo,
    SoapExtensionAttribute attribute)
{
    // Not used in this example, but it's
    // declared abstract in the base class
    return null;
}

// Called each time the Web service is used
// And gets passed the data from
```

continues

continued

```
// GetInitializer() method
public override void Initialize(
    object initializer)
{
    // Not used in this example, but it's
    // declared abstract in the base class
}
```

12. Add code to override the `ChainStream()` method of the `SoapExtension` class. This method enables you to intercept the stream that the Web service is working with and substitute your own stream in its place:

```
// The ChainStream() method gives a chance
// to grab the SOAP messages as they go by
public override System.IO.Stream ChainStream(
    System.IO.Stream stream)
{
    // Save the original stream
    originalStream = stream;
    // Create and return your own in its place
    internalStream = new MemoryStream();
    return internalStream;
}
```

13. Add code to handle SOAP messages in the `ProcessMessage()` method. Note that this method is called in four different situations (before and after serialization and deserialization), and that you can use the passed parameter to determine in which stage you are:

```
// The ProcessMessage() method is where
// soap messages are handled
public override void ProcessMessage(
    System.Web.Services.Protocols.SoapMessage message)
{
    // Determine the stage and take appropriate action
    switch(message.Stage)
    {
        case SoapMessageStage.BeforeSerialize:
            // About to prepare a SOAP Response
            break;

        case SoapMessageStage.AfterSerialize:
            // SOAP response is all prepared
            // Open a log file and write a status line
            FileStream fs = new FileStream(
                @"c:\temp\BugTracker.log",
                FileMode.Append, FileAccess.Write);
            StreamWriter sw = new StreamWriter(fs);
            sw.WriteLine("AfterSerialize");
            sw.Flush();
```

EXAM TIP

GetInitializer() and Initialize() Methods The `GetInitializer()` method is called once when your SOAP extension is first initialized. There are two forms of this method, depending on whether the SOAP extension was configured with an attribute or with a configuration file. You can pass any object you like as the return value from the `GetInitializer()` method. The `Initialize()` method is called once for every SOAP message serialized or deserialized by the Web service. The object passed to the `Initialize()` method is the same object that you return from the `GetInitializer()` method. So, for example, you might open a file in the `GetInitializer()` method, and pass a `FileStream` object as the return value from that method to become the input parameter to the `Initialize()` method.

NOTE

override The override keyword indicates that a method in a derived class has the same signature as a method in the base class, and that the derived class method should be called by the runtime rather than the base class method.

```
                    // Copy the passed message to the file
                    internalStream.Position = 0;
                    CopyStream(internalStream, fs);
                    fs.Close();
                    // Copy the passed message
                    // to the other stream
                    internalStream.Position = 0;
                    CopyStream(
                        internalStream, originalStream);
                    internalStream.Position = 0;
                    break;

                case SoapMessageStage.BeforeDeserialize:
                    // About to handle a SOAP request
                    // Copy the passed message
                    // to the other stream
                    CopyStream(
                        originalStream, internalStream);
                    internalStream.Position = 0;
                    // Open a log file and write a status line
                    FileStream fs1 = new FileStream(
                        @"c:\temp\BugTracker.log",
                        FileMode.Append, FileAccess.Write);
                    StreamWriter sw1 = new StreamWriter(fs1);
                    sw1.WriteLine("BeforeDeserialize");
                    sw1.Flush();
                    // Copy the passed message to the file
                    CopyStream(internalStream, fs1);
                    fs1.Close();
                    internalStream.Position = 0;
                    break;

                case SoapMessageStage.AfterDeserialize:
                    // SOAP request has been deserialized
                    break;
            }
        }
        // Helper function to copy one stream to another
        private void CopyStream(Stream fromStream,
            Stream toStream)
        {
            try
            {
                StreamReader sr  =
                    new StreamReader(fromStream);
                StreamWriter sw =
                    new StreamWriter(toStream);
                sw.WriteLine(sr.ReadToEnd());
                sw.Flush();
            }
            catch (Exception ex)
            {
                // Log the exception
            }
        }
```

> **EXAM TIP**
>
> **Streams, Serialization, and Deserialization** If your SOAP extension is called during serialization, then the internal variable that you returned contains the SOAP message, and you should copy it to the original variable before you finish processing. If your SOAP extension is called during deserialization, then the original variable will contain the SOAP message, and you should copy it to the internal variable before you finish processing. And remember, the client serializes requests and deserializes responses, whereas the server deserializes requests and serializes responses.

continues

continued

14. Add a new class file to the project. Name the new class SoapDisplayExtensionAttribute.cs. Modify the SoapDisplayExtensionAttribute.cs class to contain this code:

```
using System;
using System.Web.Services;
using System.Web.Services.Protocols;
namespace BugTracker
{
    [AttributeUsage(AttributeTargets.Method)]
    public class SoapDisplayExtensionAttribute
        : SoapExtensionAttribute
    {
        private int priority =1;

        // Member to store the extension's priority
        public override int Priority
        {
            get
            {
                return priority;
            }
            set
            {
                priority = value;
            }
        }
        // Specifies the class of the SOAP
        // Extension to use with this method
        public override System.Type ExtensionType
        {
            get
            {
                return typeof(
                    BugTracker.SoapDisplayExtension);
            }
        }
    }
}
```

15. Modify the Web method's declaration in the Bugs.asmx.cs class to include the SoapDisplayExtensionAttribute. This is what tells the CLR that it should apply your SOAP extension to this Web method:

```
[WebMethod, SoapDisplayExtension]
public Bug GetBug(int bugID)
{
    Bug b = new Bug(bugID);
    return b;
}
```

When a request comes in for the GetBug() method, the Web service notices the SoapDisplayExtension attribute and routes the request and response through the SoapDisplayExtension class. Within that class, the SOAP messages are logged to a disk file and then passed on. In Step-by-Step 5.2, you'll build a client project to confirm that this works.

STEP BY STEP

5.2 Testing a Server-side SOAP Extension

1. Add a new Visual C# .NET Windows application named BugTrackerClient to the solution.

2. Right-click the References folder in Solution Explorer and select Add Web Reference. This opens the Add Web reference dialog box.

3. Type **http://*localhost*/BugTracker/Bugs.asmx** (substituting *localhost* with your own Web server name) into the Address bar of the Add Web Reference dialog box and press Enter. This connects to the server and downloads the information about the BugTracker Web service.

4. In the Solution Explorer, rename the default Form1.cs to StepByStep5_2.cs. Open the form in code view and change all occurrences of Form1 to refer to StepByStep5_2 instead.

5. Place a Button control (btnGetBug) and a TextBox control (txtDescription) on the form. Set the MultiLine property of the txtDescription control to true.

6. Double-click the Button control and add the following code to handle the Button control's Click event:

```
private void btnGetBug_Click(
    object sender, System.EventArgs e)
{
    localhost.Bugs bugs = new localhost.Bugs();
    localhost.Bug bug = bugs.GetBug(1);
    txtDescription.Text = bug.Description;
}
```

7. Set the project as the startup project.

continues

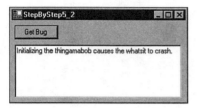

FIGURE 5.3
A client program that tests server-side SOAP extensions.

continued

8. Run the solution and click the Get Bug button on the form. You should see the bug description, as shown in Figure 5.3.

9. On the Web server where the Web service is located, open the file `C:\Temp\BugTracker.log`. This file contains both the incoming SOAP request and the outgoing SOAP response, as saved by the SOAP extension. I've reformatted the file contents here for easier reading:

```
BeforeDeserialize
<?xml version="1.0" encoding="utf-8"?>
<soap:Envelope
  xmlns:soap=
    "http://schemas.xmlsoap.org/soap/envelope/"
  xmlns:xsi=
    "http://www.w3.org/2001/XMLSchema-instance"
  xmlns:xsd="http://www.w3.org/2001/XMLSchema">
  <soap:Body>
    <GetBug xmlns="http://BugTracker.que.com/">
      <bugID>1</bugID>
    </GetBug>
  </soap:Body>
</soap:Envelope>

AfterSerialize
<?xml version="1.0" encoding="utf-8"?>
<soap:Envelope
  xmlns:soap=
    "http://schemas.xmlsoap.org/soap/envelope/"
  xmlns:xsi=
    "http://www.w3.org/2001/XMLSchema-instance"
  xmlns:xsd="http://www.w3.org/2001/XMLSchema">
  <soap:Body>
    <GetBugResponse
      xmlns="http://BugTracker.que.com/">
      <GetBugResult>
        <BugID>1</BugID>
        <Description>Initializing the thingamabob
        causes the whatsit to crash.</Description>
      </GetBugResult>
    </GetBugResponse>
  </soap:Body>
</soap:Envelope>
```

Writing a Client-side SOAP Extension

SOAP Extensions can also, as I said, run on the client. In Step-by-Step 5.3, you'll develop a version of the `SoapDisplayExtension` class to run on the client. You'll see that the client SOAP extension is very similar to the server SOAP extension. However, you can take advantage of Windows forms to display the information as it's received, rather than dump it to a log file.

STEP BY STEP

5.3 Creating a Client-side SOAP Extension

1. Add a new form to the `BugTrackerClient` project that you created in Step-by-Step 5.2. Name the new form `DisplayMessage.cs`. Set the form's `Text` property to `SOAP Message`.

2. Place a `TextBox` control (`txtMessage`) on the form. Set the `Multiline` property to `true` and the `Modifiers` property to `Internal` for the `txtMessage` control.

3. Add a new XSLT file to the project. Name the new XSLT file `Identity.xslt` and edit its contents as follows:

```
<?xml version = "1.0"?>
<xsl:stylesheet xmlns:xsl=
    "http://www.w3.org/1999/XSL/Transform"
version="1.0">
  <xsl:output method="xml" indent="yes"/>
  <xsl:template match="node()|@*">
    <xsl:copy>
      <xsl:apply-templates select="node()|@*"/>
    </xsl:copy>
  </xsl:template>
</xsl:stylesheet>
```

4. Add a new class to the project. Name the new class `SoapDisplayExtension.cs`. This class will implement a SOAP extension that writes incoming and outgoing messages to a file.

continues

continued

5. Add these using directives at the top of the
`SoapDisplayExtension` class:

```
using System.IO;
using System.Xml;
using System.Xml.Xsl;
using System.Web.Services;
using System.Web.Services.Protocols;
```

6. Modify the class declaration to make the
`SoapDisplayExtension` class derive from the `SoapExtension`
class:

```
public class SoapDisplayExtension : SoapExtension
```

7. Add two variables to the `SoapExtension` class. These variables will store the original SOAP message (passed to your
SOAP extension as a stream object) and the possibly-
modified SOAP message from your extension to the next
stage of processing:

```
// Variables to hold the original stream
// and the stream that is returned
private Stream originalStream;
private Stream internalStream;
```

8. Add code to override the `GetInitializer()` and
`Initialize()` methods. Although these methods are not
used in this particular example, you still need to implement them, because they are defined as abstract methods
in the base class.

```
// Version called if configured with a config file
public override object GetInitializer(
    System.Type serviceType)
{
    // Not used in this example, but it's
    // declared abstract in the base class
    return null;
}

// Called the first time the Web service is used
// Version called if configured with an attribute
public override object GetInitializer(
    LogicalMethodInfo methodInfo,
    SoapExtensionAttribute attribute)
{
    // Not used in this example, but it's
    // declared abstract in the base class
    return null;
}
```

```
// Called each time the Web service is used
// And gets passed the data from
// GetInitializer() method
public override void Initialize(
    object initializer)
{
    // Not used in this example, but it's
    // declared abstract in the base class
}
```

9. Add code to override the `ChainStream()` method of the
   `SoapExtension` class. This method allows you to intercept
   the stream that the Web service is working with and substitute your own stream in its place:

```
// The ChainStream() method gives a chance
// to grab the SOAP messages as they go by
public override System.IO.Stream ChainStream(
    System.IO.Stream stream)
{
    // Save the original stream
    originalStream = stream;
    // Create and return your own in its place
    internalStream = new MemoryStream();
    return internalStream;
}
```

10. Add code to handle SOAP messages in the
    `ProcessMessage()` method:

```
// The ProcessMessage() method is where
// the soap messages are handled
public override void ProcessMessage(
    System.Web.Services.Protocols.SoapMessage message)
{
    // Determine the stage and take appropriate action
    switch(message.Stage)
    {
        case SoapMessageStage.BeforeSerialize:
            // About to prepare a SOAP Response
            break;

        case SoapMessageStage.AfterSerialize:
            // SOAP response is all prepared
            internalStream.Position = 0;
            // Get a Transform ready
            XslTransform xslt = new XslTransform();
            xslt.Load(@"..\..\Identity.xslt");
            // Load the raw XML into an XML document
            XmlDocument xd = new XmlDocument();
            xd.Load(internalStream);
            // Use the transform to pretty print it
            MemoryStream ms = new MemoryStream();
```

continues

continued

```
                    xslt.Transform(xd, null, ms);
                    // And drop the results
                    // to a TextBox control
                    ms.Position = 0;
                    StreamReader sr = new StreamReader(ms);
                    DisplayMessage f = new DisplayMessage();
                    f.txtMessage.Text = sr.ReadToEnd();
                    f.Show();
                    // Copy the passed message
                    // to the other stream
                    internalStream.Position = 0;
                    CopyStream(
                        internalStream, originalStream);
                    internalStream.Position = 0;
                    break;

            case SoapMessageStage.BeforeDeserialize:
                    // About to handle a SOAP request
                    // Copy the passed message
                    // to the other stream
                    CopyStream(
                        originalStream, internalStream);
                    internalStream.Position = 0;
                    // Get a Transform ready
                    XslTransform xslt1 = new XslTransform();
                    xslt1.Load(@"..\..\Identity.xslt");
                    // Load the raw XML into an XML document
                    XmlDocument xd1 = new XmlDocument();
                    xd1.Load(internalStream);
                    // Use the transform to pretty print it
                    MemoryStream ms1 = new MemoryStream();
                    xslt1.Transform(xd1, null, ms1);
                    // And drop the results
                    // to a TextBox control
                    ms1.Position = 0;
                    StreamReader sr1 = new StreamReader(ms1);
                    DisplayMessage f1 = new DisplayMessage();
                    f1.txtMessage.Text = sr1.ReadToEnd();
                    f1.Show();
                    internalStream.Position = 0;
                    break;

            case SoapMessageStage.AfterDeserialize:
                    // SOAP request has been deserialized
                    break;
        }
    }

    // Helper function to copy one stream to another
    private void CopyStream(Stream fromStream,
        Stream toStream)
    {
        try
        {
```

```
        StreamReader sr  =
            new StreamReader(fromStream);
        StreamWriter sw =
            new StreamWriter(toStream);
        sw.WriteLine(sr.ReadToEnd());
        sw.Flush();
    }
    catch (Exception ex)
    {
        // Log the exception
    }
}
```

> **XSL Transforms** This code uses an XSL transform to "pretty print" the SOAP messages with indenting to make them easier to read. For more information on XSL transforms in .NET, see the documentation for the System.Xml.Xsl namespace.

11. Add a new class file to the project. Name the new class SoapDisplayExtensionAttribute.cs. Modify the SoapDisplayExtensionAttribute.cs class to contain this code:

```
using System;
using System.Web.Services;
using System.Web.Services.Protocols;
namespace BugTrackerClient
{
    [AttributeUsage(AttributeTargets.Method)]
    public class SoapDisplayExtensionAttribute
        : SoapExtensionAttribute
    {
        private int priority =1;

        // Member to store the extension's priority
        public override int Priority
        {
            get
            {
                return priority;
            }
            set
            {
                priority = value;
            }
        }
        // Specifies the class of the SOAP
        // Extension to use with this method
        public override System.Type ExtensionType
        {
            get
            {
                return typeof(
                BugTrackerClient.SoapDisplayExtension);
            }
        }
    }
}
```

continues

FIGURE 5.4
The SOAP extension attribute is applied to the Web method declaration in the proxy class to implement a client-side soap extension.

continued

12. Click the Show All Files button on the Solution Explorer toolbar. Expand the Web References folder to find the `Reference.cs` file, as shown in Figure 5.4. This is the proxy class that was created when you set the Web reference in the project. Double-click the `Reference.cs` file to open it in the editor.

13. Locate the `GetBug()` method in the proxy class and modify it by adding the `SoapDisplayExtension` attribute to the class declaration, as follows:

```
[SoapDisplayExtension,
  System.Web.Services.Protocols.
    SoapDocumentMethodAttribute(
    "http://BugTracker.que.com/GetBug",
    RequestNamespace="http://BugTracker.que.com/",
    ResponseNamespace="http://BugTracker.que.com/",
    Use=System.Web.Services.Description.
      SoapBindingUse.Literal,
    ParameterStyle=System.Web.Services.Protocols.
      SoapParameterStyle.Wrapped)]
public Bug GetBug(int bugID) {
    object[] results = this.Invoke(
        "GetBug", new object[] {bugID});
    return ((Bug)(results[0]));
}
```

14. Run the solution. Click the Get Bug button on the default form. The project retrieves information from the Web service, and displays both the SOAP request and the SOAP response on separate instances of the `DisplayMessage` form, as shown in Figure 5.5.

FIGURE 5.5
SOAP messages displayed by a client-side SOAP extension.

▶ A SOAP extension allows you to intercept SOAP messages at all stages of processing: before and after serialization and before and after deserialization.

▶ SOAP extensions are classes that are derived from the base `SoapExtension` class.

▶ SOAP extensions can run on a Web services client, server, or both.

▶ The `GetInitializer()` method is called once when the SOAP extension is first loaded.

▶ The `Initialize()` method is called once for each call to a Web method being monitored by the SOAP extension.

▶ The `ChainStream()` method enables you to intercept the actual SOAP message stream.

▶ The `ProcessMessage()` method is called with the actual SOAP requests and responses.

CREATING ASYNCHRONOUS WEB METHODS

Create and Consume an XML Web service: Create asynchronous Web methods.

If you simply call a Web service method from a client program (via a Web service proxy), the call is synchronous. That is, your client application will not process any other commands until the SOAP response comes back from the server. For example, if you click the Get Bug button in Step-by-Step 5.2 and then try to move the form, you'll discover that the form is unresponsive until the response from the server has been processed and displayed.

The proxy classes generated by Visual Studio .NET (or by `wsdl.exe`) also enable you to make asynchronous calls to a Web service. When you make an asynchronous call, the client sends the SOAP request, but it is not blocked while waiting for the SOAP response. The Web service server does not require any special configuration to support asynchronous calls. In fact, as far as the server knows, the call is synchronous. All the additional processing is done at the client. The CLR sends the SOAP request and then monitors a system I/O completion port to wait for the SOAP response.

In this section, you'll see several ways to make an asynchronous call to a Web service. I'll also show you the code that the proxy class uses to enable asynchronous calls.

Using a Callback Delegate

The first way to handle an asynchronous Web method call is to provide a delegate that the runtime can invoke when the results are returned. Step-by-Step 5.4 illustrates this technique.

STEP BY STEP

5.4 Using a Callback Delegate for Asynchronous Web Method Calls

1. Add a new form to the BugTrackerClient project that you created in Step-by-Step 5.2. Name the new form StepByStep5_4.cs.

2. Place a Button control (btnGetBug) and a TextBox control (txtDescription) on the form. Set the MultiLine property of the txtDescription control to true. Set the control's ScrollBars property to Vertical.

3. Double-click the button and add the following code to handle the button's Click event:

```
private void btnGetBug_Click(
    object sender, System.EventArgs e)
{
    // Connect to the Web service
    localhost.Bugs b = new localhost.Bugs();
    // Create a delegate to handle the callback
    AsyncCallback cb = new
        AsyncCallback(WebServiceCallback);
    // Launch the asynchronous call
    b.BeginGetBug(1, cb, b);
    // Do some work while waiting for it to return
    for (int intI=1; intI <= 100; intI++)
    {
```

```
        txtDescription.AppendText(intI + "\n");
    }
}
```

4. Add code to implement the callback function:

```
// Callback to handle the asynchronous return
private void WebServiceCallback(IAsyncResult ar)
{
    // Get the returned Web service instance
    localhost.Bugs b = (localhost.Bugs) ar.AsyncState;
    // Finish the work
    localhost.Bug b1 = b.EndGetBug(ar);
    // And display the result
    txtDescription.AppendText(b1.Description + "\n");
}
```

5. Open the `Reference.cs` proxy class and remove the `SoapDisplayExtension` attribute from the `GetBug()` method:

```
[System.Web.Services.Protocols.
    SoapDocumentMethodAttribute(
    "http://BugTracker.que.com/GetBug",
    RequestNamespace="http://BugTracker.que.com/",
    ResponseNamespace="http://BugTracker.que.com/",
    Use=System.Web.Services.Description.
        SoapBindingUse.Literal,
    ParameterStyle=System.Web.Services.Protocols.
        SoapParameterStyle.Wrapped)]
public Bug GetBug(int bugID) {
    object[] results = this.Invoke(
        "GetBug", new object[] {bugID});
    return ((Bug)(results[0]));
}
```

6. Insert the `Main()` method to launch the form. Set the form as the startup object for the project.

7. Run the solution. Click the Get Bug button on the form. This invokes the Web method asynchronously. You should see the output of the other work before the Web service returns value, as shown in Figure 5.6.

NOTE

Asynchronous Is Unpredictable
There's no guarantee that the project will print all 100 numbers to the TextBox control before the Web method returns; it depends on how fast your network is, how heavily loaded your client computer is, and so on.

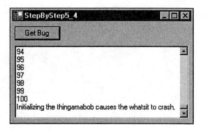

FIGURE 5.6
A callback delegate is invoked when an asynchronous call to a Web method completes its execution.

The callback method for an asynchronous Web method call must have the signature shown in Step-by-Step 5.4, taking a single argument of type `IAsyncResult`. For each Web method, the proxy class will contain corresponding Begin and End methods. The Begin method takes all the arguments of the original method, plus a reference to the Web service object itself (necessary because you can have multiple asynchronous calls outstanding at any given time), and the address of the callback method (contained in an `AsyncCallback` object). When the results of the call are available, the callback method will be invoked. Within the callback method, you can retrieve the original Web service object and then call its End method to get the result of the method call.

Using the `WaitHandle` Object

You can also use a `WaitHandle` object to manage asynchronous Web method calls. The `WaitHandle` object essentially lets you turn the asynchronous process back into a synchronous process, as shown in Step-by-Step 5.5.

STEP BY STEP

5.5 Using a `WaitHandle` Object with Asynchronous Web Method Calls

1. Add a new form to the `BugTrackerClient` project. Name the new form `StepByStep5_5.cs`.

2. Place a Button control (`btnGetBug`) and a TextBox control (`txtDescription`) on the form. Set the `MultiLine` property of the `txtDescription` control to `true`. Set the `ScrollBars` property of the control to `Vertical`.

3. Switch to the code view and add the following using directive:

```
using System.Threading;
```

4. Double-click the button control and add this code to handle the button's `Click` event:

```
private void btnGetBug_Click(
    object sender, System.EventArgs e)
{
    // Connect to the Web service
    localhost.Bugs b = new localhost.Bugs();
    // Create a result object to hold
    // the status of the asynchronous call
    IAsyncResult ar;
    // Launch the asynchronous call
    ar = b.BeginGetBug(1, null, null);
    // Do some work while waiting for it to return
```

```
    for (int intI=1; intI <= 90; intI++)
        txtDescription.AppendText(intI + "\n");
    // Now wait for the method to come back
    WaitHandle wh = ar.AsyncWaitHandle;
    wh.WaitOne();
    localhost.Bug b1 = b.EndGetBug(ar);
    // And display the result
    txtDescription.AppendText(b1.Description + "\n");
    // Do some final work
    for (int intI=91; intI <= 100; intI++)
        txtDescription.AppendText(intI + "\n");
}
```

5. Insert the Main() method to launch the form. Set the form as the startup object for the project.

6. Run the solution. Click the Get Bug button on the form. This invokes the Web method asynchronously. You should see the output of the other work before and after the Web service return value, as shown in Figure 5.7.

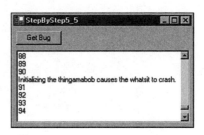

FIGURE 5.7
You can also use a WaitHandle object to manage asynchronous Web method calls.

In Step-by-Step 5.5, I didn't use a callback method at all. Rather, I used the BeginGetBug() method to start the asynchronous method call, and saved the result from this call as an IAsyncResult object. When I was ready to wait for the results of the call, I retrieved a WaitHandle object from this object's AsyncWaitHandle property. The WaitOne() method of this object causes the thread to pause until the results are ready.

There are two other ways that you can manage asynchronous Web method calls if you like:

▶ You can use a loop to poll the value of the IAsyncResult.IsCompleted property. This property returns false while the method is still doing work, and true when the End method is ready to call.

▶ You can simply call the End method in your code when you're ready to wait synchronously for the result. This is equivalent to using the WaitHandle.WaitOne() method that you saw in Step-by-Step 5.5.

EXAM TIP

Waiting for Multiple Results If you have multiple outstanding asynchronous Web method calls, you can wait for them all to come back by using the static WaitHandle.WaitAll() method, or for the first one to return by using the static WaitHandle.WaitAny() method.

Inside the Asynchronous Proxy Methods

Although you probably won't need to write your own asynchronous methods, it's worth having a look at the code that Visual Studio .NET or `wsdl.exe` builds for you to create these methods. Here are the `BeginGetBug()` and `EndGetBug()` methods from the sample project that I've been working with:

```
public System.IAsyncResult BeginGetBug(
    int bugID,
    System.AsyncCallback callback,
    object asyncState)
{
    return this.BeginInvoke("GetBug",
        new object[] {bugID},
        callback, asyncState);
}

public Bug EndGetBug(System.IAsyncResult asyncResult)
{
    object[] results = this.EndInvoke(asyncResult);
    return ((Bug)(results[0]));
}
```

The proxy class is derived from the `SoapHttpClientProtocol` class. The Begin and End methods are simply lightweight wrappers around the generic `BeginInvoke()` and `EndInvoke()` methods provided by the base class. The work performed in the specific methods consists of converting parameters to and from the parameter types used by the generic classes. The `BeginInvoke()` method takes the name of the Web method being called, an array of objects that represent the parameters of the method, a callback delegate, and an arbitrary object passed from the caller. The `EndInvoke()` method returns the results of the call as an array of objects. The return wrapper extracts items from this array (here the single item stored in `results[0]`) and casts them back to the data types that the caller is expecting.

GUIDED PRACTICE EXERCISE 5.1

The .NET Framework also makes provisions for aborting an asynchronous Web method call. To abort an asynchronous Web method call, you can cast the applicable `IAsyncResult` to a `WebClientAsyncResult` object and call the `Abort()` method of the latter object.

In this exercise, you should create a form that calls the `GetBug()` method. The form should call the method asynchronously and perform some processing after the method call. You should also add a button to the form that will abort the asynchronous call, if the button is pressed before the result of the call is available.

How would you accomplish this task?

You should try working through this problem on your own first. If you are stuck, or if you'd like to see one possible solution, follow these steps:

1. Add a new form to the project. Name the new form
   `GuidedPracticeExercise5_1.cs`.

2. Place two `Button` controls (`btnGetBug` and `btnAbort`) and one
   `TextBox` control (`txtDescription`) on the form. Set the
   `MultiLine` property to `true` and the `ScrollBars` property to
   `Vertical` for the `txtDescription` control. Set the `Enabled`
   property of the `btnAbort` control to `false`.

3. Switch to code view and add the following using directive:

   ```
   using System.Web.Services.Protocols;
   ```

4. Double-click the `Button` controls and add this code to handle
   their `Click` events:

   ```
   IAsyncResult ar;
   Boolean fAborted=true;

   private void btnGetBug_Click(
       object sender, System.EventArgs e)
   {
       // Connect to the Web service
       localhost.Bugs b = new localhost.Bugs();
       // Create a delegate to handle the callback
       AsyncCallback cb = new
           AsyncCallback(WebServiceCallback);
   ```

continues

continued

```
            // Launch the asynchronous call
            ar = b.BeginGetBug(1, cb, b);
            btnAbort.Enabled = true;
            fAborted = false;
            // Do some work while waiting for it to return
            for (int intI=1; intI <= 100; intI++)
            {
                txtDescription.AppendText(intI + "\n");
            }
        }

        // Define callback method to
        // handle the asynchronous return
        private void WebServiceCallback(IAsyncResult ar)
        {
            if(!fAborted)
            {
                // Get the returned Web service instance
                localhost.Bugs b =
                    (localhost.Bugs) ar.AsyncState;
                // Finish the work
                localhost.Bug b1 = b.EndGetBug(ar);
                // And display the result
                txtDescription.AppendText(
                    b1.Description + "\n");
            }
        }

        private void btnAbort_Click(
            object sender, System.EventArgs e)
        {
            // Retrieve an appropriate object
            WebClientAsyncResult w =
                (WebClientAsyncResult) ar;
            // and call its Abort method
            w.Abort();
            fAborted = true;
            btnAbort.Enabled = false;
        }
```

5. Insert the Main() method to launch the form. Set the form as the startup object for the project.

6. Run the solution. Click the Get Bug button. When the code enables the Abort button, click the Abort button. The loop displays its results, but the Web service does not return any results.

If you have difficulty following this exercise, review the section "Creating Asynchronous Web Methods." After doing that review, try this exercise again.

▶ By default, calls to a Web method are synchronous, and block the client program until the SOAP response is returned.

▶ Proxies generated by `wsdl.exe` also allow you to make asynchronous calls to a Web service.

▶ One way to make an asynchronous Web method call is to supply a delegate method that the .NET Framework will call back when the SOAP response is ready.

▶ Another way to make an asynchronous Web method call is to use a `WaitHandle` object to wait for one or more calls to complete.

▶ Asynchronous Web method calls can be aborted by calling the `Abort()` method of an appropriate `WebClientAsyncResult` object.

CONTROLLING XML WIRE FORMAT

Create and Consume an XML Web service: Control XML wire format for an XML Web service.

So far in this book I've been treating the SOAP format as if it were completely specified by the SOAP standard. But in fact the standard allows a good deal of flexibility in converting objects to XML messages. There are variations in formatting for both the parameters within the body of a SOAP message and for the format of the body itself:

▶ Literal parameter formatting formats parameters according to an XSD schema. This is the default parameter formatting for .NET Web services.

▶ Encoded parameter formatting formats parameters according to what are called the SOAP Section 5 encoding rules. These rules encode data type information directly into the SOAP message.

▶ Document-based body formatting is the default .NET body formatting. In this method of body formatting, parameters may be broken up into multiple elements inside the message body. Elements may be wrapped within an overall element, or placed in the body as bare elements.

▶ RPC-based body formatting is sometimes known as SOAP Section 7 formatting. In this style of body formatting, all parameters are contained within a single element in the body of the SOAP message.

Given these choices, there are three different legal combinations:

▶ Document-based body formatting with literal parameter formatting (the .NET default).

▶ Document-based body formatting with encoded parameter formatting.

▶ RPC-based body formatting with encoded parameter formatting.

These formatting choices control the *XML wire format* of the messages, so-called because the resulting messages travel "over the wire" between client and server.

You can apply attributes indicating these choices to both Web methods and to proxy classes that call those methods. It should be obvious that you must match such choices: If the Web method is using encoded parameter formatting, then any proxy class that calls that method must also use encoded parameter formatting.

Finally, you can also use attributes to change details about the SOAP message, such as the names used for XML elements representing parameters.

Why would you make these changes? If you're working in a purely .NET world, you probably wouldn't. But there may come a time when you need to write code that interoperates with Web services developed under other environments, or with clients that can't use the .NET defaults. In those cases, it's helpful to be able to fine-tune the XML that your code can accept to match the XML sent and received by less flexible components.

In this section of the chapter, I'll demonstrate all these choices and their effects on the SOAP messages produced by .NET code. Rather than write entire applications for each option, I'll show you how to modify the Web service code, and then use .NET WebService Studio (`http://www.gotdotnet.com/team/tools/web_svc/default.aspx`) to display the request and response messages. For more information on .NET WebService Studio, see Chapter 4.

Using Literal Parameter Formatting

Literal parameter formatting is the default for Web services created with Visual Studio .NET. But if you like, you can use attributes to specify this default explicitly. Step-by-Step 5.6 shows how you can do this.

STEP BY STEP

5.6 Using Literal Parameter Formatting in a Web Service

1. Add a new Visual C# ASP.NET Web service application to the solution. Name the new Web service `WeatherService`.

2. In the Solution Explorer, rename the default `Service1.asmx` to `Weather.asmx`. Open the form in code view and change all occurrences of `Service1` to refer to `Weather` instead.

3. Add the `WebService` attribute before the `Weather` class definition:

```
[WebService(Namespace="http://weather.que.com/")]
public class Weather : System.Web.Services.WebService
```

4. Add a new class file to the project. Name the new class `WindObservation.cs`. Modify the `WindObservation.cs` class to contain this code:

```
using System;
namespace WeatherService
{
    public class WindObservation
    {
```

continues

continued

```
        public string Direction;
        public int Speed;
    }
}
```

5. Switch to the code view of the `Weather.asmx` Web service and add the following using directive:

```
using System.Web.Services.Description;
using System.Web.Services.Protocols;
```

6. Add two Web methods to the `Weather.asmx.cs` file:

```
[WebMethod()]
public bool Store(
    string Station, WindObservation Wind)
{
    // Here a full implementation would store
    // the data in the database
    // Return true to indicate success
    return true;
}

[WebMethod()]
public WindObservation GetLatest(string Station)
{
    // Simulate retrieving the most
    // recent observation from the database
    WindObservation w = new WindObservation();
    w.Direction = "NNW";
    w.Speed = 14;
    return w;
}
```

7. Modify the declaration of the `Weather` Web service class to specify that it should use document-based body formatting with literal parameters:

```
[SoapDocumentService(Use=SoapBindingUse.Literal),
WebService(Namespace="http://weather.que.com/")]
public class Weather : System.Web.Services.WebService
```

8. Build the Web service.

9. Launch .NET WebService Studio. Enter **http://localhost/WeatherService/Weather.asmx** as the WSDL EndPoint and click the Get button.

10. Select the Invoke tab and click on the `Store()` Web method. In the Input treeview, click on the `Station` parameter. Enter **AAA** as the value for this parameter. Similarly,

---

EXAM TIP

Applying Web Service Attributes
In this case, you used the `SoapDocumentService` attribute to apply formatting to an entire Web service where the service is defined. You can also use the `SoapDocumentMethod` attribute to a specific Web method. You can also use either one of these attributes in a proxy class to specify the corresponding format on the client side.

enter values of N for the Direction parameter and 5 for the Speed parameter. Click the Invoke button to call the Store() Web method.

11. Select the Request/Response tab to view the SOAP request and the SOAP response. You'll find this SOAP request:

```
<?xml version="1.0" encoding="utf-8"?>
<soap:Envelope
xmlns:soap="http://schemas.xmlsoap.org/soap/envelope/"
 xmlns:xsi="http://www.w3.org/2001/XMLSchema-instance"
 xmlns:xsd="http://www.w3.org/2001/XMLSchema">
  <soap:Body>
    <Store xmlns="http://weather.que.com/">
      <Station>AAA</Station>
      <Wind>
        <Direction>N</Direction>
        <Speed>5</Speed>
      </Wind>
    </Store>
  </soap:Body>
</soap:Envelope>
```

You'll also find the corresponding SOAP response:

```
<?xml version="1.0" encoding="utf-8"?>
<soap:Envelope
xmlns:soap="http://schemas.xmlsoap.org/soap/envelope/"
 xmlns:xsi="http://www.w3.org/2001/XMLSchema-instance"
 xmlns:xsd="http://www.w3.org/2001/XMLSchema">
  <soap:Body>
    <StoreResponse xmlns="http://weather.que.com/">
      <StoreResult>true</StoreResult>
    </StoreResponse>
  </soap:Body>
</soap:Envelope>
```

As you can see, literal parameter formatting keeps things very simple. Starting from the outside in, here's what you'll find in these messages:

▶ The <soap:Envelope> element, which includes the namespace declarations that identify this as a SOAP message.

▶ The <soap:Body> element, which identifies the application-specific body of the SOAP message.

▶ The top-level application-specific element (`<Store>` or `<StoreResponse>`). These elements specify the namespace of the Web service itself (`http://weather.que.com/`), indicating that all the contained elements will be from this namespace.

▶ Elements representing the actual parameters of the messages. Note that the complex parameter `<Wind>` is handled by creating nested XML elements for each of its properties.

Literal parameter formatting does not insert any information about data types into the SOAP messages. It assumes that your code will know how to handle the data that it sends and receives.

Using Encoded Parameter Formatting

Encoded parameter formatting inserts additional information into the SOAP messages to conform with section 5 of the SOAP specification. Step-by-Step 5.7 shows how you can specify encoded parameter formatting and displays the results.

STEP BY STEP

5.7 Using Encoded Parameter Formatting in a Web Service

1. Start with the `WeatherService` Web service application that you created in Step-by-Step 5.6. Modify the declaration of the `Weather` class to specify that it should use document-based body formatting with encoded parameters:

```
[SoapDocumentService(Use=SoapBindingUse.Encoded),
WebService(Namespace="http://weather.que.com/")]
public class Weather : System.Web.Services.WebService
```

2. Build the Web service.

3. Launch .NET WebService Studio. Enter **http:// localhost/WeatherService/Weather.asmx** as the WSDL EndPoint and click the Get button.

4. Select the Invoke tab and click on the `Store()` Web method. In the Input treeview, click on the `Station` parameter. Enter **AAA** as the value for this parameter. Similarly,

enter values of **N** for the Direction parameter and **5** for the Speed parameter. Click the Invoke button to call the Store() Web method.

5. Select the Request/Response tab to view the SOAP request and the SOAP response. You'll find this SOAP request:

```xml
<?xml version="1.0" encoding="utf-8"?>
<soap:Envelope
 xmlns:soap=
  "http://schemas.xmlsoap.org/soap/envelope/"
 xmlns:soapenc=
  "http://schemas.xmlsoap.org/soap/encoding/"
 xmlns:tns="http://weather.que.com/"
 xmlns:types="http://weather.que.com/encodedTypes"
 xmlns:xsi="http://www.w3.org/2001/XMLSchema-instance"
 xmlns:xsd="http://www.w3.org/2001/XMLSchema">
  <soap:Body soap:encodingStyle=
    "http://schemas.xmlsoap.org/soap/encoding/">
    <tns:Store>
      <Station xsi:type="xsd:string">AAA</Station>
      <Wind href="#id1" />
    </tns:Store>
    <tns:WindObservation id="id1"
      xsi:type="tns:WindObservation">
      <Direction xsi:type="xsd:string">N</Direction>
      <Speed xsi:type="xsd:int">5</Speed>
    </tns:WindObservation>
  </soap:Body>
</soap:Envelope>
```

You'll also find the corresponding SOAP response:

```xml
<?xml version="1.0" encoding="utf-8"?>
<soap:Envelope
 xmlns:soap=
    "http://schemas.xmlsoap.org/soap/envelope/"
 xmlns:soapenc=
    "http://schemas.xmlsoap.org/soap/encoding/"
 xmlns:tns="http://weather.que.com/"
 xmlns:types="http://weather.que.com/"
 xmlns:xsi="http://www.w3.org/2001/XMLSchema-instance"
 xmlns:xsd="http://www.w3.org/2001/XMLSchema">
  <soap:Body soap:encodingStyle=
    "http://schemas.xmlsoap.org/soap/encoding/">
    <types:StoreResponse>
      <StoreResult xsi:type="xsd:boolean">
          true</StoreResult>
    </types:StoreResponse>
  </soap:Body>
</soap:Envelope>
```

Note that encoded parameter formatting is somewhat more complex than literal parameter formatting. The `<soap:Envelope>` element includes additional namespaces to allow each parameter to be explicitly marked with its data type. Elements that are specific to this Web service (such as the method name or the parameter names) are each explicitly marked with the `tns` namespace indicator. The complex data element `<Wind>` is handled by a reference to a separate XML element outside the `<tns:Store>` element.

Encoded parameter formatting conforms more closely to the SOAP standard than literal parameter formatting, and thus may be helpful when interoperability with Web service components defined outside the .NET Framework is a consideration. However, this standards compliance comes at the cost of additional message size. Table 5.1 shows how the request and response sizes compare between literal and encoded parameter formatting in this simple example.

TABLE 5.1

COMPARISON OF LITERAL AND ENCODED PARAMETER FORMATTING

SOAP Message	Literal Size	Encoded Size	Increase
Request	368 bytes	705 bytes	92%
Response	341 bytes	538 bytes	58%

Using RPC-Style Body Formatting

Another major decision to make about SOAP message formatting is whether to use document-style or RPC-style (SOAP Section 7) body formatting. So far all the SOAP messages you've seen have used document-style body formatting. Step-by-Step 5.8 demonstrates the use of RPC-style body formatting.

STEP BY STEP

5.8 Using RPC-style Body Formatting in a Web Service

1. Start with the Web service that you created in Step-by-Step 5.6. Modify the declaration of the Weather class to specify that it should use RPC-style body formatting:

```
[SoapRpcService(),
WebService(Namespace="http://weather.que.com/")]
public class Weather : System.Web.Services.WebService
```

2. Build the Web service application.

3. Launch .NET WebService Studio. Enter **http://localhost/WeatherService/Weather.asmx** as the WSDL EndPoint and click the Get button.

4. Select the Invoke tab and click on the `Store()` Web method. In the Input tree view, click on the `Station` parameter. Enter **AAA** as the value for this parameter. Similarly, enter values of **N** for the `Direction` parameter and **5** for the `Speed` parameter. Click the Invoke button to call the `Store()` Web method.

5. Select the Request/Response tab to view the SOAP request and the SOAP response. You'll find this SOAP request:

```
<?xml version="1.0" encoding="utf-8"?>
<soap:Envelope
  xmlns:soap=
    "http://schemas.xmlsoap.org/soap/envelope/"
  xmlns:soapenc=
    "http://schemas.xmlsoap.org/soap/encoding/"
  xmlns:tns="http://weather.que.com/"
  xmlns:types="http://weather.que.com/encodedTypes"
  xmlns:xsi=
    "http://www.w3.org/2001/XMLSchema-instance"
  xmlns:xsd="http://www.w3.org/2001/XMLSchema">
  <soap:Body soap:encodingStyle=
    "http://schemas.xmlsoap.org/soap/encoding/">
    <tns:Store>
      <Station xsi:type="xsd:string">AAA</Station>
      <Wind href="#id1" />
    </tns:Store>
    <tns:WindObservation id="id1"
      xsi:type="tns:WindObservation">
```

continues

> **NOTE**
>
> **Method-by-Method Encoding** There is also a `SoapRpcMethod` attribute that you can apply to format an individual Web method with the RPC style.

continued

```
            <Direction xsi:type="xsd:string">N</Direction>
            <Speed xsi:type="xsd:int">5</Speed>
         </tns:WindObservation>
      </soap:Body>
   </soap:Envelope>
```

You'll also find the corresponding SOAP response:

```
<?xml version="1.0" encoding="utf-8"?>
<soap:Envelope
  xmlns:soap=
   "http://schemas.xmlsoap.org/soap/envelope/"
  xmlns:soapenc=
   "http://schemas.xmlsoap.org/soap/encoding/"
  xmlns:tns="http://weather.que.com/"
  xmlns:types="http://weather.que.com/"
  xmlns:xsi=
    "http://www.w3.org/2001/XMLSchema-instance"
  xmlns:xsd="http://www.w3.org/2001/XMLSchema">
  <soap:Body soap:encodingStyle=
   "http://schemas.xmlsoap.org/soap/encoding/">
    <types:StoreResponse>
      <StoreResult xsi:type="xsd:boolean">
            true</StoreResult>
    </types:StoreResponse>
  </soap:Body>
</soap:Envelope>
```

EXAM TIP

RPC Body Forces Encoded Parameters   If you select an RPC-style message body, the parameters within that body will automatically be encoded according to the SOAP section 5 rules.

If you compare the results of Step-by-Step 5.8 to those of Step-by-Step 5.7, you'll discover that they're identical! What's going on here? The answer is that the Document style of body formatting is more flexible than the RPC style. When you use RPC style, you can't make any further choices about how to encode the parameters within the body. With Document style, though, there are additional options that you can supply to the SoapDocumentService attribute. I'll cover those in the next section.

Wrapped and Bare Parameters

In both RPC-style body formatting and the default document body formatting, all the parameters within the SOAP message are contained within a single XML element identified with the name of the Web method. This is referred to as the wrapped parameter style. If you're using document body formatting, you can specify the bare parameter style as an alternative. Step-by-Step 5.9 shows how this works.

STEP BY STEP

5.9 Using Bare Parameters in a Web Service

1. Start with the Web service that you created in Step-by-Step 5.6. Modify the declaration of the Weather class to specify that it should use document body formatting and bare literal parameters:

```
[SoapDocumentService(Use=SoapBindingUse.Literal,
ParameterStyle=SoapParameterStyle.Bare),
WebService(Namespace="http://weather.que.com/")]
public class Weather : System.Web.Services.WebService
```

2. Build the Web service.

3. Launch .NET WebService Studio. Enter **http://localhost/WeatherService/Weather.asmx** as the WSDL EndPoint and click the Get button.

4. Select the Invoke tab and click on the Store() Web method. In the Input tree view, click on the Station parameter. Enter **AAA** as the value for this parameter. Similarly, enter values of **N** for the Direction parameter and **5** for the Speed parameter. Click the Invoke button to call the Store() Web method.

5. Select the Request/Response tab to view the SOAP request and the SOAP response. You'll find this SOAP request:

```
<?xml version="1.0" encoding="utf-8"?>
<soap:Envelope
  xmlns:soap=
    "http://schemas.xmlsoap.org/soap/envelope/"
  xmlns:xsi=
    "http://www.w3.org/2001/XMLSchema-instance"
  xmlns:xsd="http://www.w3.org/2001/XMLSchema">
  <soap:Body>
    <Station xmlns="http://weather.que.com/">
        AAA</Station>
    <Wind xmlns="http://weather.que.com/">
```

continues

continued

```
        <Direction>N</Direction>
        <Speed>5</Speed>
      </Wind>
    </soap:Body>
</soap:Envelope>
```

You'll also find the corresponding SOAP response:

```
<?xml version="1.0" encoding="utf-8"?>
<soap:Envelope
  xmlns:soap=
    "http://schemas.xmlsoap.org/soap/envelope/"
  xmlns:xsi=
    "http://www.w3.org/2001/XMLSchema-instance"
  xmlns:xsd="http://www.w3.org/2001/XMLSchema">
  <soap:Body>
    <StoreResult xmlns="http://weather.que.com/">
      true</StoreResult>
  </soap:Body>
</soap:Envelope>
```

If you compare the results of Step-by-Step 5.9 with those of Step-by-Step 5.6, you'll see that the bare parameter formatting makes the parameter elements direct children of the `<soap:Body>` element, instead of wrapping them in a single element that represents the entire Web method. You can also apply bare parameter formatting to encoded parameters, with similar results.

Using the `XmlElement` Attribute

The last level of customization of which you should be aware involves the `XmlElement` attribute. This attribute allows you to specify the low-level XML formatting details for messages, as shown in Step by-Step 5.10.

STEP BY STEP

5.10 Using the `XmlElement` Attribute

1. Start with the `WeatherService` Web service application that you created in Step-by-Step 5.6. Modify the declaration of the `Weather` class to specify that it should use document body formatting and literal parameters:

```
[SoapDocumentService(Use=SoapBindingUse.Literal),
WebService(Namespace="http://weather.que.com/")]
public class Weather : System.Web.Services.WebService
```

2. Add the following using directive:

```
using System.Xml.Serialization;
```

3. Modify the declaration of the `Store()` Web method as follows:

```
[WebMethod()]
public bool Store(
    [XmlElement("ReportingStation")]string Station,
    [XmlElement("WindReading")]WindObservation Wind)
```

As you can see, the `XmlElement` attribute can be applied to individual parameters.

4. Build the Web service.

5. Launch .NET WebService Studio. Enter **http://localhost/WeatherService/Weather.asmx** as the WSDL EndPoint and click the Get button.

6. Select the Invoke tab and click on the `Store()` Web method. In the Input tree view, click on the `ReportingStation` parameter. Enter **AAA** as the value for this parameter. Similarly, enter values of **N** for the `Direction` parameter and **5** for the `Speed` parameter. Click the Invoke button to call the `Store()` Web method.

7. Select the Request/Response tab to view the SOAP request and the SOAP response. You'll find this SOAP request:

```
<?xml version="1.0" encoding="utf-8"?>
<soap:Envelope
  xmlns:soap=
    "http://schemas.xmlsoap.org/soap/envelope/"
```

continues

continued

```
xmlns:xsi=
  "http://www.w3.org/2001/XMLSchema-instance"
xmlns:xsd="http://www.w3.org/2001/XMLSchema">
<soap:Body>
  <Store xmlns="http://weather.que.com/">
    <ReportingStation>AAA</ReportingStation>
    <WindReading>
      <Direction>N</Direction>
      <Speed>5</Speed>
    </WindReading>
  </Store>
</soap:Body>
</soap:Envelope>
```

You'll also find the corresponding SOAP response:

```
<?xml version="1.0" encoding="utf-8"?>
<soap:Envelope
  xmlns:soap=
    "http://schemas.xmlsoap.org/soap/envelope/"
  xmlns:xsi=
    "http://www.w3.org/2001/XMLSchema-instance"
  xmlns:xsd="http://www.w3.org/2001/XMLSchema">
  <soap:Body>
    <StoreResponse xmlns="http://weather.que.com/">
      <StoreResult>true</StoreResult>
    </StoreResponse>
  </soap:Body>
</soap:Envelope>
```

Ordinarily, the parameter names within a SOAP message exactly match the parameter names in the Visual C# .NET code for the corresponding Web method. In Step-by-Step 5.10, though, I've used the XmlElement attribute to override the default naming in several cases. As you can see in the SOAP messages, the names in the XmlElement attribute are used, instead of the default names.

In addition to the element names, you can control other aspects of the generated XML with properties of the XmlElement attribute. For example, you can force the element to include a namespace qualifier with the Form property:

```
[XmlElement(ElementName="Name",  Form=XmlSchemaForm.Qualified)]
```

Table 5.2 shows the properties of the XmlElement attribute that you can set.

TABLE 5.2

PROPERTIES OF THE XMLELEMENT ATTRIBUTE

Property	Description
DataType	XSD data type to use for the element.
ElementName	Name of the element. This is the default property.
Form	Indicates whether to use a namespace qualifier with the element name.
IsNullable	Indicates whether to include an element in the XML for null values.
Namespace	Namespace of the element.
Type	Native data type of the element.

REVIEW BREAK

▶ SOAP messages can be formatted in a variety of ways. You can use literal or encoded parameter formatting, document or RPC-style body formatting, and wrapped or bare parameters.

▶ The .NET Framework enables you to dictate the format of SOAP messages through applying attributes to the Web service or Web method at both the server and the proxy class.

▶ The XmlElement attribute enables you to specify the name and other details of a parameter in a SOAP message.

CHAPTER SUMMARY

In this chapter you learned about some of the more advanced aspects of Web services, including SOAP extensions, asynchronous Web method calls, and control of XML wire formatting.

SOAP extensions enable you to insert your own code into the SOAP request and SOAP response processing loop. SOAP extensions can be executed before or after either serialization or deserialization operations on either the client or the server. To develop a SOAP extension, you derive a class from the SoapExtension class, and then implement custom GetInitializer(), Initialize(), ChainStream(), and ProcessMessage() methods.

KEY TERMS

- SOAP Request
- SOAP Response
- serialization
- deserialization
- SOAP Extension

CHAPTER SUMMARY

KEY TERMS

- asynchronous call
- XML wire format

The .NET Framework automatically enables asynchronous calls to Web methods whenever you create a proxy class on the client. The Web services server neither knows nor cares that a call is asynchronous; the changes are entirely on the client. You can use a callback delegate to run code when an asynchronous call is ready to complete, or you can use a WaitHandle object to wait for such calls either singly or in groups.

Although SOAP is a standard, it is implemented differently in different products. The .NET Framework enables you to tailor the XML wire format of SOAP messages with the help of attributes. This facility lets you create SOAP messages that will interoperate with other Web services components that were not created with the .NET Framework or languages.

APPLY YOUR KNOWLEDGE

Exercises

5.1 Configuring a SOAP Extension with a Config File

In the chapter you saw how to configure a SOAP extension to run with a particular Web method by applying a custom attribute to that method. However, there's a second way to configure a SOAP extension. Instead of applying attributes one method at a time, you can use a configuration file to cause a SOAP extension to run with every Web method in the scope of the configuration file.

Estimated Time: 35 minutes.

1. Add a new Visual C# .NET Class library project to the 320C05 solution. Name the new library SoapExt.

2. Rename the default Class1.cs file to SoapDisplayExtension.cs.

3. Right-click the References node in Solution Explorer and select Add Reference. Add a reference to System.Web.Services.dll.

4. Modify the code in the SoapDisplayExtension.cs with the following code:

```csharp
using System;
using System.IO;
using System.Text;
using System.Web.Services;
using System.Web.Services.Protocols;

namespace SoapExt
{
    public class SoapDisplayExtension
        : SoapExtension
    {
        // Variables to hold the original
        // stream and the stream
        // that is returned
        private Stream originalStream;
        private Stream internalStream;
```

```csharp
        // Version called if configured
        // with a config file
        public override object
            GetInitializer(
            System.Type serviceType)
        {
            // Not used in this example,
            // but it's declared abstract
            // in the base class
            return null;
        }

        // Called the first time the Web
        // service is used. Version called
        // if configured with an attribute
        public override object
            GetInitializer(
            LogicalMethodInfo methodInfo,
            SoapExtensionAttribute attribute)
        {
            // Not used in this example,
            // but it's declared abstract
            // in the base class
            return null;
        }

        // Called each time the Web service
        // is used and gets passed the data
        // from GetInitializer() method
        public override void Initialize(
            object initializer)
        {
            // Not used in this example,
            // but it's declared abstract
            // in the base class
        }

        // The ChainStream() method gives
        // a chance to grab the
        // SOAP messages as they go by
        public override System.IO.Stream
            ChainStream(
            System.IO.Stream stream)
        {
            // Save the original stream
            originalStream = stream;
            // Create and return your
            // own in its place
            internalStream =
                new MemoryStream();
            return internalStream;
        }
```

APPLY YOUR KNOWLEDGE

```
// The ProcessMessage() method
// is where the soap messages
// are handled
public override void
    ProcessMessage(
    System.Web.Services.Protocols.
    SoapMessage message)
{
    // Determine the stage
    // and take appropriate action
    switch(message.Stage)
    {
        case SoapMessageStage.
              BeforeSerialize:
            // About to prepare
            // a SOAP Response
            break;

        case SoapMessageStage.
              AfterSerialize:
            // SOAP response is all
            // prepared. Open a log
            // file and write status
            FileStream fs =
            new FileStream(
            @"c:\temp\SoapExt.log",
            FileMode.Append,
            FileAccess.Write);
            StreamWriter sw =
              new StreamWriter(fs);
            sw.WriteLine(
                "AfterSerialize");
            sw.Flush();
            // Copy the passed
            // message to the file
            internalStream.Position
                = 0;
            CopyStream(
                internalStream, fs);
            fs.Close();
            // Copy the passed
            // message to the
            // other stream
            internalStream.Position
                = 0;
            CopyStream(
                internalStream,
                originalStream);
            internalStream.Position
                = 0;
            break;
```

```
        case SoapMessageStage.
              BeforeDeserialize:
            // About to handle a
            // SOAP request. Copy
            // the passed message
            // to the other stream
            CopyStream(
                originalStream,
                internalStream);
            internalStream.Position
                = 0;
            // Open a log file and
            // write a status line
            FileStream fs1 =
            new FileStream(
            @"c:\temp\SoapExt.log",
            FileMode.Append,
            FileAccess.Write);
            StreamWriter sw1 =
             new StreamWriter(fs1);
            sw1.WriteLine(
              "BeforeDeserialize");
            sw1.Flush();
            // Copy the passed
            // message to the file
            CopyStream(
                internalStream, fs1);
            fs1.Close();
            internalStream.Position
                = 0;
            break;

        case SoapMessageStage.
              AfterDeserialize:
            // SOAP request has
            // been deserialized
            break;
    }
}

// Helper function to copy
// one stream to another
private void CopyStream(
    Stream fromStream,
    Stream toStream)
{
    try
    {
        StreamReader sr  =
            new StreamReader(
            fromStream);
        StreamWriter sw =
```

APPLY YOUR KNOWLEDGE

```
            new StreamWriter(
            toStream);
        sw.WriteLine(
            sr.ReadToEnd());
        sw.Flush();
    }
    catch (Exception ex)
    {
        // Log the exception
    }
  }
 }
}
```

5. Build the class library project.

6. Locate the bin folder of the `WeatherService` project that you developed in Step-by-Step 5.6. Copy the compiled `SoapExt.dll` file to this folder.

7. In the `WeatherService` project, right-click the References folder and select Add Reference. Add a reference to the `SoapExt.dll` file that you just copied.

8. Open the `web.config` file from the `WeatherService` application. Add the `<webServices>` element at the bottom of the file:

```
<configuration>
  <system.web>
...

    <webServices>
      <soapExtensionTypes>
        <add
          type=
            "SoapExt.SoapDisplayExtension,
➥SoapExt"
          priority="1" group="0" />
      </soapExtensionTypes>
    </webServices>

  </system.web>
</configuration>
```

9. Build the `WeatherService` project.

10. Launch .NET WebService Studio. Enter **http://localhost/WeatherService/Weather.asmx** as the WSDL EndPoint and click the Get button.

11. Select the Invoke tab and click on the `Store()` Web method. In the Input tree view, click on the `ReportingStation` parameter. Enter **AAA** as the value for this parameter. Similarly, enter values of **N** for the `Direction` parameter and **5** for the `Speed` parameter. Click the Invoke button to call the `Store()` Web method.

12. Open the `C:\Temp\SoapExt.log` file in the server to view the SOAP request and response.

When you configure a SOAP extension in a config file, the extension applies to all Web methods within the scope of the file. If you add a SOAP extension to the `machine.config` file, then the extension will be used with all Web methods served from that computer.

The `type` attribute of the add element specifies the SOAP extension to use. There are two parameters within this attribute. The first is the fully-qualified classname of the extension class. The second is the name of the DLL file containing the class, without the `.dll` extension.

The `priority` attribute of the add element specifies the relative priority of the SOAP extension as compared to other SOAP extensions. The lower the priority value, the higher the relative priority.

The `group` attribute of the add element specifies whether the SOAP extension is in group `0` or group `1`. SOAP extensions in group `0` are all executed first, in order of their relative priority. After that, SOAP extensions configured via attributes are executed. Finally, SOAP extensions in group `1` are executed, in order of their relative priority.

APPLY YOUR KNOWLEDGE

Review Questions

1. Describe the round-trip process of a Web method invocation.

2. At what points in the Web method lifecycle can SOAP extensions modify messages?

3. What is the difference between the `GetInitializer()` method and the `Initialize()` method in a SOAP extension?

4. Name two ways to run code when an asynchronous Web method call completes its work.

5. What are two ways in which parameters can be formatted in a SOAP message?

6. What are two ways that the body of a SOAP message can be formatted?

7. How can you control the name of a parameter within a SOAP message?

8. How can you configure a SOAP extension to apply to all Web methods on a computer?

Exam Questions

1. You are installing two SOAP extensions to a particular Web service. The first extension, named `SoapEncrypt`, is designed to use symmetric cryptography to encrypt SOAP messages. The second extension, named `SoapTranslate`, is designed to translate key words in the SOAP message from English to French.

   You want the `SoapTranslate` extension to be invoked before the `SoapEncrypt` extension. Which priorities should you set for the two extensions?

A. Set the priority of the `SoapTranslate` extension to -1, and the priority of the `SoapEncrypt` extension to 0.

B. Set the priority of the `SoapTranslate` extension to 0, and the priority of the `SoapEncrypt` extension to 1.

C. Set the priority of the `SoapTranslate` extension to 1, and the priority of the `SoapEncrypt` extension to 0.

D. Set the priority of the `SoapTranslate` extension to 0, and the priority of the `SoapEncrypt` extension to -1.

2. You are developing a SOAP extension that will record the average number of requests for a particular Web method each minute. These results will be written to a file for later analysis. The filename is specified in a configuration file, and will not change while the Web service is running. In which method should you read the name of this file?

A. `GetInitializer()`

B. `Initialize()`

C. `ChainStream()`

D. `ProcessMessage()`

3. You are creating a SOAP extension to log incoming SOAP request messages. In the `ChainStream()` method of the SOAP extension, you have the following code:

```
private Stream originalStream;
private Stream internalStream;

public override System.IO.Stream
    ChainStream(
    System.IO.Stream stream)
{
```

```
    originalStream = stream;
    internalStream =
        new MemoryStream();
    return internalStream;
}
```

In the `ProcessMessage()` method of the SOAP extension you have the following code:

```
public override void
    ProcessMessage(
    System.Web.Services.Protocols.
    SoapMessage message)
{
    // Determine the stage
    // and take appropriate action
    switch(message.Stage)
    {
        case SoapMessageStage.
                BeforeDeserialize:
            StreamReader sr =
                new StreamReader(
                internalStream);
            StreamWriter sw =
                new StreamWriter(
                originalStream);
            sw.WriteLine(
              sr.ReadToEnd());
            sw.Flush();
            LogMessage(
              internalStream);
            internalStream.Position
                = 0;
            break;
    }
}
```

You have tested the `LogMessage()` method and have verified that it works as desired. When you deploy this SOAP extension, users of your Web service report that they are receiving an error indicating that the root element is missing whenever they attempt to invoke a Web method from the service.

How should you fix this problem?

A. Open the `StreamReader` object on the `originalStream` and open the `StreamWriter` object on the `internalStream`.

B. Declare the `originalStream` and `internalStream` variables as being of type `MemoryStream` rather than type `Stream`.

C. Move your processing code from the `BeforeDeserialize` case to the `AfterDeserialize` case.

D. Move the call to the `LogMessage()` method ahead of the call to the `WriteLine()` method.

4. You are designing a SOAP extension to modify incoming Web method calls. The extension will run on the server, and when it discovers an obsolete parameter name in the SOAP request, it will replace this with the new parameter name. In which message stage should you invoke this SOAP extension?

A. `BeforeSerialize`

B. `AfterSerialize`

C. `BeforeDeserialize`

D. `AfterDeserialize`

5. You are designing a SOAP extension to modify outgoing Web method calls. The extension will run on the client, and when it discovers an obsolete parameter name in the SOAP request, it will replace this with the new parameter name. In which message stage should you invoke this SOAP extension?

APPLY YOUR KNOWLEDGE

A. `BeforeSerialize`

B. `AfterSerialize`

C. `BeforeDeserialize`

D. `AfterDeserialize`

6. You are developing a client-side SOAP extension named `TraceExt`. Your project includes the `TraceExt` class and an attribute class named `TraceExtAttribute`. It also includes a form with a button that uses the following code to invoke a Web method:

```
private void btnRunMethod_Click(
    object sender, System.EventArgs e)
{
  // Call a Web method on the Sales object
  SalesWebService.Sales S = _
    new SalesWebService.Sales();
    txtSales.Text = S.GetSales();
}
```

Where should you apply the `TraceExtAttribute` attribute to activate the SOAP extension?

A. To the `GetInitializer()` method in the `TraceExt` class.

B. To the `Initialize()` method in the `TraceExt` class.

C. To the `btnRunMethod_Click()` event handler in the form.

D. To the `GetSales()` method in the Web service proxy class.

7. Your code is making asynchronous calls to two different Web methods. You want other processing in your code to continue while these methods execute. When either asynchronous call is finished, you want to process its results. How should your code wait for the results of the asynchronous calls?

A. Use a separate `WaitHandle.WaitOne()` method call for each Web method.

B. Use a separate callback delegate method for each Web method.

C. Use a `WaitHandle.WaitAny()` method call, specifying both Web methods.

D. Use a `WaitHandle.WaitAll()` method call, specifying both Web methods.

8. Your code is making asynchronous calls to two different Web methods. You then execute other code until you arrive at a point where you require results from one or the other of the asynchronous calls. You can proceed with further processing as soon as either result is available. How should your code wait for the results of the asynchronous calls?

A. Use a separate `WaitHandle.WaitOne()` method call for each Web method.

B. Use a separate callback delegate method for each Web method.

C. Use a `WaitHandle.WaitAny()` method call, specifying both Web methods.

D. Use a `WaitHandle.WaitAll()` method call, specifying both Web methods.

9. You are writing a Web service named `Sales` in Visual C# .NET. The Web service will be consumed by a client that expects to use SOAP Section 7 formatting for all messages and SOAP Section 5 formatting for all parameters. How should you declare the `Sales` Web service?

APPLY YOUR KNOWLEDGE

A.

```
[SoapDocumentService(
  Use=SoapBindingUse.Encoded),
WebService(
  Namespace="http://sales.myco.com/")]
public class Sales
```

B.

```
[SoapRpcService(
  Use=SoapBindingUse.Encoded),
WebService(
  Namespace="http://sales.myco.com/")]
public class Sales
```

C.

```
[SoapDocumentService(
  Use=SoapBindingUse.Encoded,
  ParameterStyle=
    SoapParameterStyle.Wrapped), _
WebService(
  Namespace="http://sales.myco.com/")]
public class Sales
```

D.

```
[SoapRpcService(),
WebService(
  Namespace="http://sales.myco.com/")]
public class Sales
```

10. You are developing a Web service to work with an existing client application. The client application generates SOAP requests in this form:

```
<?xml version="1.0" encoding="utf-8"?>
<soap:Envelope
  xmlns:soap=
"http://schemas.xmlsoap.org/soap/envelope/"
  xmlns:xsi=
"http://www.w3.org/2001/XMLSchema-instance"
  xmlns:xsd=
"http://www.w3.org/2001/XMLSchema">
  <soap:Body>
    <CustomerID
      xmlns="http://sales.myco.com/">427
    </CustomerID>
    <OrderID
      xmlns="http://sales.myco.com/">18918
    </OrderID>
  </soap:Body>
</soap:Envelope>
```

Which Web service declaration can you use to process these messages?

A.

```
[SoapDocumentService(
  Use=SoapBindingUse.Encoded,
  ParameterStyle=
    SoapParameterStyle.Bare),
WebService(
  Namespace="http://sales.myco.com/")]
public class SalesClass
```

B.

```
[SoapDocumentService(
  Use=SoapBindingUse.Literal,
  ParameterStyle=
    SoapParameterStyle.Wrapped),
WebService(
  Namespace="http://sales.myco.com/")]
public class SalesClass
```

C.

```
[SoapDocumentService(
  Use=SoapBindingUse.Literal,
  ParameterStyle=SoapParameterStyle.Bare),
WebService(
  Namespace="http://sales.myco.com/")]
public class SalesClass
```

D.

```
[SoapRpcService(
  ParameterStyle=SoapParameterStyle.Bare),
WebService(
  Namespace="http://sales.myco.com/")]
public class SalesClass
```

11. You have created a Web method named `GetSales()` with the following declaration:

```
[WebMethod()]
public int GetSales(string strCompanyName)
```

Your corporate standards call for using Hungarian naming (with the `str` prefix) for variables. However, the developer of the client application that will call this Web method used the name `CompanyName` (without a prefix) for the parameter. How should you fix this problem?

APPLY YOUR KNOWLEDGE

A. Rewrite your code to use `CompanyName` as the parameter name.

B. Use the `SoapDocumentMethod` attribute to specify the `SoapParameterStyle.Bare` parameter style for this method.

C. Use the `XmlElement` attribute to rename the parameter in the SOAP messages.

D. Use the `SoapDocumentMethod` attribute with `Use=SoapBindingUse.Literal` to specify literal encoding for this method.

12. Your Web service includes a SOAP extension named `Ext1`, which is activated with an attribute. The priority of this extension is set to `3`. Now you are modifying the configuration file for the Web service to activate another SOAP extension named `Ext2`. The `Ext2` extension should run after the `Ext1` extension. What section should you add to the `web.config` file?

    A.

```
<webServices>
  <soapExtensionTypes>
    <add type="Ext2Namespace.Ext2, ext2"
     priority="0" group="0" />
  </soapExtensionTypes>
</webServices>
```

    B.

```
<webServices>
  <soapExtensionTypes>
    <add type="Ext2Namespace.Ext2, ext2"
     priority="1" group="0" />
  </soapExtensionTypes>
</webServices>
```

    C.

```
<webServices>
  <soapExtensionTypes>
    <add type="Ext2Namespace.Ext2, ext2"
     priority="5" group="1" />
  </soapExtensionTypes>
</webServices>
```

    D.

```
<webServices>
  <soapExtensionTypes>
    <add type="Ext2Namespace.Ext2, ext2"
     priority="1" group="2" />
  </soapExtensionTypes>
</webServices>
```

13. You have deployed a Web service and a set of client applications. Now you are ready to deploy version 2 of the Web service, which changes the name of a parameter in one of the Web methods. How can you deploy version 2 of the Web service without breaking the version 1 clients?

    A. Use the `XmlElement` attribute to rename the parameter in the Web method.

    B. Use the `SoapDocumentMethod` attribute to rename the parameter in the Web method.

    C. Use a try-catch block in the Web service to catch the error when the old parameter is invoked, and rename it to the new parameter.

    D. Use a SOAP extension on the server to detect the old parameter name and change it to the new parameter name before the message is processed.

14. You have developed a SOAP extension that will compress messages on the server and then decompress them on the client. You plan to use this extension for both requests and responses. Which of these processing stages would be an appropriate place to call this extension? (Select two.)

    A. `BeforeSerialize` on the server

    B. `AfterSerialize` on the client

    C. `BeforeDeserialize` on the client

    D. `AfterDeserialize` on the server

APPLY YOUR KNOWLEDGE

15. Your code has made an asynchronous call to a Web method and is now continuing with processing. You've reached a point where you could handle the return value from the asynchronous call, if it's available, or continue with other processing. How can you check to see whether the asynchronous call is finished without blocking?

    A. Test the value of the `IAsyncResult.IsCompleted` property.

    B. Call the `WaitHandle.WaitOne()` method.

    C. Call the `End` method for the asynchronous Web method.

    D. Call the `WaitHandle.WaitAny()` method.

Answers to Review Questions

1. When the client calls a Web method, the call is serialized into a SOAP request and sent to the server. On the server, the SOAP request is deserialized into objects and processed by the Web method code. The results of the call are then serialized into a SOAP response and sent to the client. On the client, the SOAP response is deserialized into the results of the call.

2. SOAP extensions can modify messages before or after serialization or deserialization on either the client or the server.

3. The `GetInitializer()` method is called once when a SOAP extension is first loaded, and it can return an arbitrary object. The `Initialize()` method is called each time that the SOAP extension is invoked, and it is passed the object that the `GetInitializer()` method returned.

4. You can run code when an asynchronous Web method call is finished by supplying a delegate callback, or by using a `WaitHandle` object to notify you when the results are ready.

5. Either literal formatting or SOAP section 5 encoding can be used to format parameters in a SOAP message.

6. The body of a SOAP message can be formatted in document style or in SOAP section 7 RPC style.

7. You can use the `XmlElement` attribute to control the name of a parameter within a SOAP message.

8. If you specify a SOAP extension within the `machine.config` file, it will be called for all Web methods invoked on that server.

Answers to Exam Questions

1. **B.** SOAP extensions with a lower priority value are invoked first. The lowest possible priority value is zero. For more information, see the section "Creating and Using SOAP Extensions" in this chapter.

2. **A.** The filename can be read once at the time when the SOAP extension is first loaded. The `GetInitializer()` method is called at this time. The `Initialize()` method is called every time the SOAP extension is invoked; setting up the file in this method would result in duplication of effort. For more information, see the section "Creating and Using SOAP Extensions" in this chapter.

APPLY YOUR KNOWLEDGE

3. **A.** If your SOAP extension is called during deserialization, then the original variable will contain the SOAP message, and you should copy it to the internal variable before you finish processing. As the code is currently structured, it copies the empty internal variable over the incoming request, causing the Web service to return an empty string. For more information, see the section "Creating and Using SOAP Extensions" in this chapter.

4. **C.** On the server side, incoming SOAP requests are deserialized into objects. The raw XML is available to be altered in the `BeforeDeserialize` message stage. For more information, see the section "Writing a Server-side SOAP Extension" in this chapter.

5. **B.** On the client side, outgoing SOAP requests are serialized from objects into XML. The XML is available in the `AfterSerialize` message stage, after which it is sent to the server. For more information, see the section "Creating and Using SOAP Extensions" in this chapter.

6. **D.** To invoke a SOAP extension, you can add an attribute for the extension to the Web method declaration. On the client side, you'll find this declaration in the proxy class. For more information, see the section "Writing a Client-side SOAP Extension" in this chapter.

7. **B.** Using any of the `WaitHandle` methods will block your code at the point where the method of the `WaitHandle` object is called until the method that you are waiting for returns. To continue processing until the results of the Web methods are available, you should use callback delegates. For more information, see the section "Creating Asynchronous Web Methods" in this chapter.

8. **C.** The `WaitHandle.WaitAny()` method blocks your code until any of the objects that it's waiting for are available. You can't use callback delegates in this situation because they won't block the code. You can't use separate `WaitHandle.WaitOne()` methods because the first one will block until its object is ready, and you can't use `WaitHandle.WaitAll()` because it requires all the objects that it's waiting for to be ready before it proceeds. For more information, see the section "Creating Asynchronous Web Methods" in this chapter.

9. **D.** For SOAP section 7 messages, you need to use the `SoapRpcService` attribute. This attribute automatically uses SOAP section 5 encoding for parameters; it does not include a `Use` property because this can't be configured. For more information, see the section "Controlling XML Wire Format" in this chapter.

10. **C.** The SOAP message does not have a top-level element wrapping all the parameters, so you must use the `Bare` parameter style. It also does not include any SOAP section 7 encoding, so you must use document-style body formatting. Finally, the parameters do not include SOAP section 5 encoding, so you must use literal parameters. For more information, see the section "Controlling XML Wire Format" in this chapter.

11. **C.** The `XmlElement` attribute allows you to specify a different name for a parameter in a SOAP message than the name that you use in your actual code. Although rewriting the code would solve the problem, there's no reason to ignore corporate standards when you don't have to do so. For more information, see the section "Controlling XML Wire Format" in this chapter.

APPLY YOUR KNOWLEDGE

12. **C.** Extensions configured with `group="1"` run after extensions configured with an attribute. It's not legal to specify `group="2"`. Extensions configured with `group="0"` run before extensions configured with an attribute, regardless of their relative priority values. For more information, see Exercise 5.1 in the Apply Your Knowledge section of this chapter.

13. **D.** The SOAP extension can rewrite incoming SOAP requests before they are deserialized into objects. The `XmlElement` attribute won't work, because it specifies the only name to use, not an alternate name. Exception handling won't work, because the code will fail during deserialization before the Web method is actually called. For more information, see the section "Controlling XML Wire Format" in this chapter.

14. **B, C.** This extension needs to be called during the `AfterSerialize` and `BeforeDeserialize` stages on both client and server. These are the stages during which you can work with the raw messages as they are passed over the wire. For more information, see the section "Creating and Using SOAP Extensions" in this chapter.

15. **A.** The `IsCompleted` property returns `true` if the results of the asynchronous Web method call are available, without blocking the code where you check the property. For more information, see the section "Creating Asynchronous Web Methods" in this chapter.

Suggested Readings and Resources

1. Visual Studio .NET Combined Help Collection

   - Altering the SOAP message using SOAP Extensions

   - Accessing an XML Web Service Asynchronously in Managed Code

   - Customizing SOAP messages

2. Kenn Scribner and Mark C Stiver. *Applied SOAP: Implementing .NET XML Web Services.* Sams, 2001.

3. Roger Jennings. *Visual C# .NET XML Web Services Developer's Guide.* McGraw-Hill/ Osborne, 2002.

4. William Oellerman. *Architecting Web Services.* Apress, 2002.

This chapter covers the following Microsoft-specified objective for the "Creating and Managing Microsoft Windows Services, Serviced Components, .NET Remoting Objects, and XML Web Services" section of the "Developing XML Web Services and Server Components with Microsoft Visual C# .NET and the Microsoft .NET Framework" exam:

Create and manipulate a Windows service.

- **Write code that is executed when a Windows service is started or stopped.**

▶ Many enterprise applications need components that run in the background and provide important services to other application components and users on an ongoing basis.

A standard way to create these types of components on the Windows operating system is in the form of Windows services. The programming model provided by the Microsoft .NET Framework makes it easy to design and implement Windows services like never before.

This exam objective requires you to know how to use the Microsoft .NET Framework to create and manipulate Windows services.

CHAPTER 6

Windows Services

▶ Understand the reasons why you would implement some applications as Windows services.

▶ Write programs to create a Windows Service. Make sure that you complete Guided Practice Exercise 6.1.

▶ Use `installutil.exe` to install a Windows service. Study Chapter 10, "Deployment," to learn more about the installation process and to learn how to create a setup package based on Windows installer technology to deploy a Windows service application.

▶ Know how to programmatically control a Windows service by passing control messages to it such as start, pause, continue and stop messages.

INTRODUCTION

You often need programs that run continuously in the background. For example, an email server is expected to listen continuously on a network port for incoming email messages, a print spooler is expected to listen continuously to print requests, and so on.

Most operating systems provide a way to create such long-running background tasks. In fact, operating systems themselves run a variety of background processes critical for their functionality. In Unix, the background tasks are called daemons; in Windows NT, the background tasks are called NT services; whereas in Window 2000, Windows XP, and Windows Server 2003 operating systems, the background tasks are called Windows services.

Although Windows services are created as normal executable files, they have at least two distinct characteristics:

1. Windows services must conform to the interface of the Service Control Manager (SCM). The SCM is a part of the Windows operating system responsible for managing Windows services.

2. Windows services must be installed in the Windows service database before they can be used.

In this chapter, you'll use the .NET Framework class libraries to develop the following skills that will help you to create your own Windows services:

▶ Creating a Windows service that conforms to the interface of the Windows Service Control Manager (SCM).

▶ Creating an installer class that is capable of installing a Windows service to the Windows service database.

▶ Using the Installer tool (`installutil.exe`) to install and uninstall a Windows service in the Windows service database.

▶ Connecting to a Windows service and issuing messages such as start, stop, pause, and continue.

▶ Querying a Windows service to retrieve its status.

UNDERSTANDING WINDOWS SERVICES

The Windows operating system provides a set of services that allow device manufacturers and software vendors to integrate their products with the operating system. These services include:

▶ **Kernel Services**—The kernel is the core part of the operating system responsible for process, thread, and memory management. Kernel services enable devices and applications to interact with the kernel and use its functionality.

▶ **Device Driver Services**—A device driver controls and manages the hardware devices. Device driver services enable applications to work with devices.

▶ **Windows Services**—Windows services enable operating system components and application programs to expose their functionality to other applications.

Kernel services and device driver services are used mostly by system programmers. As an application programmer, you'll be more interested in Windows services, and therefore Windows services are the focus of this chapter and Exam 70-320.

So what, exactly, is a Windows service? Precisely defined, a Windows service is a process that conforms to the interface rules of the Windows Service Control Manager (SCM). The SCM is a part of the Windows operating system that provides a unified way to control, configure, and access Windows services.

In general, a Windows service is a process that provides background services to other processes. Some typical examples of Windows services are World Wide Web Publishing, Print Spooler, Task Scheduler, Event Log, Plug and Play, and so on. Some common characteristics of Windows services are:

▶ **Conformance to SCM**—Each Windows service must implement a set of well-known methods, which enable the service to communicate with the SCM. These well-known methods define how a Windows service should handle the SCM messages. Some common messages sent by SCM to a service are Start, Pause, Continue, and Stop. How these messages are handled depends totally on the service, because not all Windows services accept all messages. For example, the Event Log and

NOTE

Windows Service Application A Windows service application is a normal executable file (with an .exe extension) that contains the code for one or more Windows services.

Support for Windows Services Windows services are available on Windows NT (where they are known as NT services), Windows 2000, Windows XP, and Windows Server 2003 operating systems. There is no support of Windows services on the Windows 95, Windows 98, or Windows ME operating systems.

NOTE

Communication via the Event Log
Windows services run in the background and generally do not provide a user interface. However, a Windows service may need to inform the user about an application state or an event in the environment. Most Windows services do so by writing informative messages in the event log.

EXAM TIP

Currently Logged On User   Most Windows services are started before a user logs on and they keep on running across multiple user sessions. Therefore, the functionality of a Windows service cannot depend on the permissions available to the currently logged on user. A Windows service always executes by using an assigned user identity that may be the same or different from the currently logged on user.

Plug and Play Windows services do not accept Pause and Stop messages and therefore cannot be paused or stopped. In contrast, the Print Spooler Windows service can be started or stopped but cannot be paused.

▶ **Lack of User Interface**—Although Windows services can interact with the desktop and provide a user interface, most services don't. Windows services perform system tasks that usually do not require any user interface. As an example, the job of IIS (Internet Information Services) is to serve the requested Web pages, and IIS does not require any user interface or desktop interaction to accomplish this job. IIS is launched when a computer is started and its process remains unseen by a Windows desktop user.

▶ **Long-lived Process**—Typically, a Windows service is started automatically when the computer is started and continues to live. Services can execute even when no user is logged on to the system. Most Windows services provide the functionality that enables them to be paused, resumed, started, or stopped.

▶ **Specific User Identity**—Most Windows services run with System privileges. System is a special account that Windows uses to perform privileged operations. However, each Windows service can be launched with a specific user identity. This feature can restrict services to the permissions defined for an individual user. Consider a scenario where an administrator requires that a Windows service have access to only a limited set of directories on a file system. The administrator can easily accomplish this by following these two steps:

1. Set up a user account with the set of permissions that the administrator wants the service to have.

2. Configure the Windows service to run with the user identity that was created in step 1.

▶ **Separate Windows Process**—A Windows service does not run in the process of the program that communicates with it. Instead, a Windows service runs in its own process. Sometimes, a Windows service can also share a process with another Windows service.

▶ **Special Installation Procedure**—Unlike a Windows application, a Windows service cannot be started by just executing its .exe file. Instead, a Windows service requires a special installation procedure. This installation procedure registers the Windows service with the Windows Service Control Manager (SCM). The SCM provides varied functionality to control (such as to start, pause, and stop a service) and configure (such as setting up a service user account) the Windows services.

ARCHITECTURE OF WINDOWS SERVICES

As shown in Figure 6.1, the Windows services architecture has five main components:

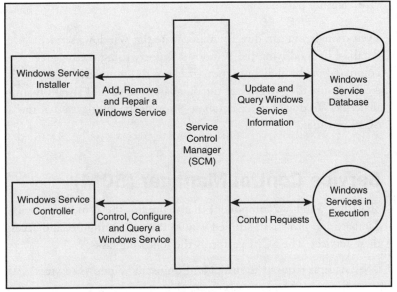

FIGURE 6.1
The Service Control Manager provides a unified way to control, configure, and access Windows services.

▶ Windows Service Database
▶ Service Control Manager
▶ Windows Service Installer

▶ Windows Services in Execution

▶ Windows Service Controller

The following sections discuss each of these components.

Windows Service Database

The Windows service database stores information about all the installed services. This database is a part of the Windows Registry and is stored in the HKEY_LOCAL_MACHINE\SYSTEM\ CurrentControlSet\Services key. The Windows service database typically contains the following information for each Windows service:

▶ Path to the executable file.

▶ Security settings.

▶ Startup parameters.

Even though you can directly manipulate the Windows service database by modifying the Windows Registry using the regedit command or through a program, it is not recommended that you do so. To ensure the integrity of the database, you should always manipulate the Windows service database through the interfaces that the SCM provides.

Service Control Manager (SCM)

SCM is a Windows component that maintains the Windows service database and provides a unified way to control, configure, and access these services. The SCM performs the following tasks:

▶ Accepts requests to install and uninstall Windows services from the Windows service database.

▶ Starts Windows services either on system startup or on demand.

▶ Enumerates installed Windows services.

▶ Maintains status information for running Windows services.

▶ Transmits control messages (such as Start, Stop, Pause, and Continue) to running Windows services.

▶ Locks and unlocks the Windows service database.

Windows provides a generic interface to work with the SCM through the Services and Computer Management MMC (Microsoft Management Console) snap-ins. These MMC snap-ins can be accessed through the Administrative tool section of the Windows Control Panel. Some applications, such as IIS and SQL Server, provide their own MMC snap-ins to control and configure their services.

Windows Service Installer

A Windows service installer uses the SCM to install, uninstall, and repair a Windows service. The install, uninstall, and repair actions respectively create, delete, and update a Windows service record in the Windows service database.

While installing a service, the Windows service installer also stores information about how the service will be started. This information includes

▶ A name that uniquely identifies the service in the Windows service database.

▶ The account name and password under whose identity the service runs.

▶ How the Windows service process is created (an independent process or a shared process).

▶ How the service is started (automatically when Windows starts, manual start, disabled).

Windows Services in Execution

Just installing a service in the Windows service database is not sufficient to enable you to use the service's functionality. By default, a Windows service must be explicitly started. However, it is also possible to set up a service in such a way that the service is started automatically with Windows.

NOTE

Microsoft Management Console (MMC)   MMC is an integrated administration environment for administrating Windows components and installed applications. By itself, MMC can't do much; however applications and Windows components provide snap-ins that integrate with the MMC and extend its Explorer-like user interface with menus, toolbars, property sheets, and wizards to perform specific administration tasks. All MMC snap-ins have a similar look and feel. This helps administrators to leverage their existing knowledge and quickly learn how to administer new applications.

Windows Services on Remote Machines   The SCM is started as a remote procedure call (RPC) server. This enables the Windows service control programs to manipulate services on remote machines.

When the SCM starts a service, it attempts to create a Windows process for that service based on the information stored in the Windows service database. The SCM also sends a Start message to the service; this message invokes an associated handler in the service (if any) that specifies the processing to be done.

After a Windows service is started, it continues to run until it receives a pause message or a stop message. When a Windows service is paused, the process for the Windows service continues to exist, but the service does not listen to the requests from the client programs. On the other hand, when a Windows service is stopped, its process is terminated and the memory is reclaimed.

Windows Service Controller Program

The Windows service controller program uses the SCM to perform the following tasks:

▶ Start a Windows service.

▶ Stop a Windows service.

▶ Pause a Windows service.

▶ Resume the execution of a paused Windows service.

▶ Query the Windows service database to retrieve the status for a Windows service.

▶ Install a new Windows service in the Windows service database.

▶ Uninstall an installed Windows service from the Windows service database.

▶ Modify the configuration information for a Windows service.

You may question the need for the Windows service controller program when the Services MMC snap-in is already available to perform various control and administrative tasks for a Windows service. Although the Services MMC snap-in provides generic control and configuration options for Windows services, it cannot take care of the individual configuration requirements and customized user interface for each Windows service. For example, IIS provides an Internet Information Services snap-in in the MMC to provide a customized interface to administer the World Wide Web Publishing, the File Transfer Protocol (FTP) Publishing, Network News Transfer Protocol (NNTP), and the Simple Mail Transfer Protocol (SMTP) services.

▶ Windows services are the applications that conform to the interface of the Windows Service Control Manager (SCM). SCM is the part of Windows that is responsible for managing Windows services.

▶ Windows services are quite distinct from regular Windows applications. One of most apparent distinctions is that Windows services usually lack a GUI. In addition, a Windows service typically runs in the background and runs in its own process with a specific user identity.

▶ Windows services must be installed in the Windows services database before they can be used. The Windows services database is a part of the Windows Registry. It is recommended that you not directly modify the database but rather modify the database through the SCM.

THE FCL SUPPORT FOR WINDOWS SERVICES

In the .NET Framework SDK, the `System.ServiceProcess` namespace provides the classes that enable you to implement, install, and control Windows services. The main classes involved in working with Windows service applications are

▶ **The `ServiceBase` Class**   A class that provides the base-level functionality for a Windows services application.

▶ **The `ServiceProcessInstaller` and `ServiceInstaller` Classes**   Classes that enable you to use an installation utility such as `installutil.exe` to install a Windows services application.

▶ **The `ServiceController` Class**   A class that enables a program to connect to a Windows service and perform various operations such as starting, stopping, querying etc.

CREATING A WINDOWS SERVICE APPLICATION

Create and manipulate a Windows service: Write code that is executed when a Windows service is started or stopped.

In this section, you use the `ServiceBase` class to create a Windows service application. You'll learn

- ▶ About the `ServiceBase` class and its functionality.

- ▶ How the SCM interacts with a Windows service derived from the `ServiceBase` class.

- ▶ How to create a Windows service by deriving a class from the `ServiceBase` class.

The `System.ServiceProcess.ServiceBase` Class

Programmatically, a Windows service is a class that derives its basic functionality from the `ServiceBase` class of the `System.ServiceProcess` namespace. The `ServiceBase` class provides its derived classes with some well-known methods and properties. The SCM knows these methods and properties and uses them to communicate with the Windows services. Table 6.1 lists the important members of the `ServiceBase` class.

TABLE 6.1

IMPORTANT MEMBERS OF THE ServiceBase CLASS

Member Name	Type	Description
AutoLog	Property	When set to `true`, automatically logs the call to `OnStart()`, `OnStop()`, `OnPause()`, and `OnContinue()` methods in the Application event log.
CanPauseAndContinue	Property	When set to `true`, indicates that the service can be paused and resumed.

Member Name	Type	Description
CanShutdown	Property	When set to true, indicates that the service should be notified when the system is shutting down.
CanStop	Property	When set to true, indicates that the service can be stopped after it has started.
EventLog	Property	Specifies an event log that can be used to write customized messages to the Application event log on method calls such as OnStart() and OnStop().
OnContinue()	Method	Specifies the actions to take when a service resumes normal functioning after being paused. This method is executed when the SCM sends a continue message to the Windows service.
OnPause()	Method	Specifies the actions to take when a service pauses. This method is executed when the SCM sends a pause message to the Windows service.
OnStart()	Method	Specifies the actions to take when a service starts running. This method is executed when the SCM sends a start message to the Windows service.
OnStop()	Method	Specifies the actions to take when a service stops running. This method is executed when the SCM sends a stop message to the Windows service.
Run()	Method	Provides the main entry point for a service executable.
ServiceName	Property	Specifies a name that identifies the service.

> **EXAM TIP**
>
> **Writing to a Custom Event Log**
> With the help of the AutoLog and the EventLog properties of the ServiceBase class, you can write messages to the Application event log only. If you want to write entries to a different event log, you should set AutoLog to false and create a new EventLog component and override the OnStart(), OnStop(), and other related methods to explicitly post entries to the custom log.

Understanding How the SCM Interacts with a Windows Service

A Windows service application contains one or more classes that inherit from the ServiceBase class to define a Windows service.

Only one of these classes can define a `Main()` method, which is the main entry point for the application. The `Main()` method specifies which Windows services should run by passing the instances of the Windows service to the static `ServiceBase.Run()` method.

The `Run()` method does not actually start the Windows service; instead, the `Run()` method just passes references to the Windows service objects to the SCM. The SCM uses these objects to send messages to the Windows service.

Figure 6.2 illustrates how the SCM interacts with a Windows service derived from the `ServiceBase` class.

FIGURE 6.2

The `ServiceBase` class provides the functionality that enables a Windows service application to interact with the SCM.

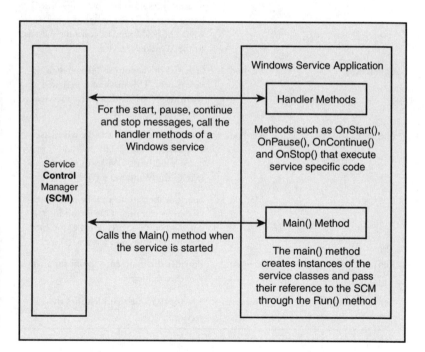

When the SCM sends a start message to the Windows service, the following things happen:

1. The SCM finds the path of the Windows service application's executable file from the Windows service database.

2. The SCM creates a Windows service process by executing the `Main()` method defined in the Windows service executable.

3. The `Main()` method of the Windows service executable creates one or more instances of the Windows service class and passes

their references to the SCM through the static `Run()` method of the `ServiceBase` class. The SCM uses these references to send messages to the Windows service.

4. The handler associated with the start message—the `OnStart()` method—is executed. The `OnStart()` method executes the code that is required for a Windows service to run, such as listening to a port for incoming requests, logging events to the event log, spooling print jobs, and so on.

After the Windows service is started, the SCM can use its reference to send various messages such as pause, continue, and stop to the Windows service. These messages respectively invoke the `OnPause()`, `OnContinue()`, and `OnStop()` methods of the Windows service.

Not all services implement the `OnPause()`, `OnContinue()`, and `OnStop()` methods. Whether a service needs to implement these methods depends on the `CanPauseAndContinue` and `CanStop` properties of the Windows service. If these properties are `true`, then the SCM can invoke the `OnPause()`, `OnContinue()`, and `OnStop()` methods. Some common examples of Windows services that can neither be paused nor be stopped include the Event Log, the Plug and Play, and the Security Accounts Manager services. Examples of Windows services that can be stopped but cannot be paused include the Print Spooler and the System Event Notification services.

There is no `CanStart` property in the `ServiceBase` class. This means that not starting is not an option for a Windows service. A Windows service class must provide a `OnStart()` method; otherwise the base class version of the method is called.

When the SCM sends a stop message to the Windows service, the associated handler `OnStop()` method is executed. After this, the Windows service process is unloaded from memory.

> **NOTE**
>
> **Controlling a Windows Service** If you set any of the `CanStop`, `CanShutdown`, or `CanPauseAndContinue` properties for a Windows service to `true`, then you also must implement a corresponding handler method (such as `OnStop()`, `OnPause()`, `OnContinue()`, and so on). Otherwise, when the SCM sends any of these messages, the Windows service throws an exception and ignores the message.

Creating the `OrderService` Application

To demonstrate how Windows services are created, I'll create an `OrderService` that listens for XML files containing order information in a particular disk directory (`c:\orders`). As soon an XML file is created in the directory, the service reads the files and based on its data, creates a new record in the Orders table of the Northwind database. This type of application is typically used for updating orders received from the Internet, from business partners, and from the legacy applications.

Step-by-Step 6.1 shows how to create the OrderService application.

STEP BY STEP

6.1 Creating a Windows Service Application

1. Launch Visual Studio .NET. Select File, New, Blank Solution, and name the new solution 320C06. Click OK.

2. Add a new project to the solution. In the Add New Project dialog box, select Visual C# .NET as the project type and Windows Service as the template. Name the project StepByStep6_1, as shown in Figure 6.3.

FIGURE 6.3
The Windows Service template allows you to easily create a Windows service application.

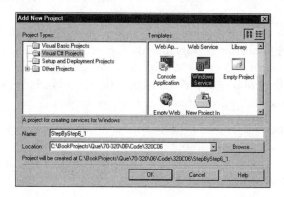

3. The Windows service project contains a file named Service1.cs. Rename this file to OrderService.cs. Click on the designer surface and then in the Properties window, set the Name and ServiceName properties to OrderService, and set the CanPauseAndContinue property to true. Note that the AutoLog and the CanStop properties are already true, as shown in Figure 6.4.

4. Switch to the code view and change all occurrences of
Service1 to OrderService. Add the following using directives to the code:

```
using System.Data.SqlClient;
using System.IO;
```

5. Switch to the design view. Open the Visual Studio .NET
toolbox. From its Components tab (see Figure 6.5), drag
and drop the FileSystemWatcher component onto the
OrderService component's surface.

6. Access the Properties window for the FileSystemWatcher
component and change its Name property to fswOrders, its
Filter property to *.xml, and its Path property to
c:\orders.

7. Click on the Events icon on the Properties window for the
FileSystemWatcher component and double-click on the
Created event to attach an event handler. Add the follow-
ing code to the event handler:

```
// Executes when an XML file is created in or
// copied to the c:\orders directory
private void fswOrders_Created(object sender,
        System.IO.FileSystemEventArgs e)
{
    DataSet dsOrders = new DataSet("Orders");
    // Read the contents of the XML file
    // into the Orders DataSet
    dsOrders.ReadXml(e.FullPath);

    // set up the database connection string
    string strConn = "data source=(local);" +
        "initial catalog=Northwind;" +
        "integrated security=SSPI";
    string strOrderQuery = "SELECT * FROM Orders";
    // Create a DataAdapter for the Orders
    // table of the Northwind database
    SqlDataAdapter daOrders =
        new SqlDataAdapter(strOrderQuery, strConn);
    // Automatically generate the update
    // command to reconcile the changes
    // made to the DataSet
    SqlCommandBuilder cbOrders =
        new SqlCommandBuilder(daOrders);
    //Update the DataSet
    daOrders.Update(dsOrders, "Orders");
    daOrders.Dispose();
```

continues

FIGURE 6.4
You can set the properties of a Windows service through the Properties window.

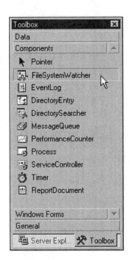

FIGURE 6.5
The FileSystemWatcher component listens to
the file system and raises events when there
are any changes.

continued

```
        FileInfo fi = new FileInfo(e.FullPath);
        // Create a subdirectory named "Updated"
        // if it does not already exist
        fi.Directory.CreateSubdirectory("Updated");
        // Copy the processed XML file to updated
        // directory, overwriting if needed
        File.Copy(e.FullPath, fi.DirectoryName +
            @"\Updated\" + fi.Name, true);
        // Delete the XML file from its
        // original location
        fi.Delete();
}
```

8. In the code, search for the skeletons of the OnStart() and OnStop() methods and modify them as follows:

```
protected override void OnStart(string[] args)
{
    fswOrders.EnableRaisingEvents = true;
}

protected override void OnStop()
{
    fswOrders.EnableRaisingEvents = false;
}
```

9. Add the following code to the OrderService class to override the OnPause() and the OnContinue() methods of the base class:

```
protected override void OnPause()
{
    fswOrders.EnableRaisingEvents = false;
}

protected override void OnContinue()
{
    fswOrders.EnableRaisingEvents = true;
}
```

10. Set the startup object for the project to OrderService.

11. Build the project. This step creates the OrderService Windows service application.

When you create a new project based on the Windows Service template, Visual Studio .NET automatically inserts a class that derives from the System.ServiceProcess.ServiceBase class in the project. To respond to various events raised by the SCM messages, I have overridden the base class version of the OnStart(), OnStop(), OnPause(), and OnContinue() methods.

In Step-by-Step 6.1, I'm using the FileSystemWatcher component. This component watches for any changes in the file system and raises events when a file or directory changes. In this example, I have set up the FileSystemWatcher component in such a way that it just watches for the creation of XML files in a directory named c:\orders. I have also instructed the FileSystemWatcher component to exclude any subdirectories of c:\orders to narrow down the scope of notifications.

When an XML file is created in the c:\orders directory, the FileSystemWatcher component raises the Created event. I am using the fswOrders_Created() event handler to retrieve the order information from the newly created XML file and insert this information as a new order to the Orders table of the Northwind database.

Table 6.2 lists some important members of the FileSystemWatcher component.

TABLE 6.2

IMPORTANT MEMBERS OF THE FileSystemWatcher CLASS

Member	Type	Description
Changed	Event	Occurs when a file or directory in the specified Path is changed.
Created	Event	Occurs when a file or directory in the specified Path is created.
Deleted	Event	Occurs when a file or directory in the specified Path is deleted.
EnableRaisingEvents	Property	Specifies whether the component is enabled. If its value is false, the component does not receive any events.
Error	Event	Occurs when the component's internal buffer overflows.
Filter	Property	Specifies which files are monitored in a directory. Its default value is *.*, which monitors for all types of files.

continues

W A R N I N G

The FileSystemWatcher Component May Lose Track of Changes   The FileSystemWatcher component stores the file system changes in a property named InternalBufferSize before it acts upon those changes. If there are too many changes in a short time, this buffer can overflow and cause the FileSystemWatcher component to lose track of the file system changes. This buffer's default size is 8192 bytes. You should not arbitrarily increase this buffer's size because this buffer is maintained in non-paged memory and increasing its size would directly impact the performance of other applications. Instead, you should use the Path, NotifyFilter, and IncludeSubdirectories properties to narrow down the scope of notifications that the FileSystemWatcher component receives.

TABLE 6.2   *continued*

IMPORTANT MEMBERS OF THE FileSystemWatcher CLASS

Member	Type	Description
IncludeSubdirectories	Property	Specifies whether the subdirectories within the specified path should be monitored.
InternalBufferSize	Property	Specifies the size of the internal buffer.
NotifyFilter	Property	Specifies the type of file system changes to monitor. Its value is a combination of values from the NotifyFilters enumeration.
Path	Property	Specifies the path of the directory to watch.
Renamed	Event	Occurs when a file or directory in the specified Path is renamed.
SynchronizingObject	Property	Specifies the object that is used to marshal the event handler calls.
WaitForChanged()	Method	This method is a synchronous method that returns a structure that contains specific information on the file system change.

Compilation of the StepByStep6_1 project creates an executable file just like other Windows applications. However, you cannot run this executable directly. If you try doing so, you get a Windows service start failure error with the following message:

```
Cannot start service from the command line or a
debugger. A Windows Service must first be installed
(using installutil.exe) and then started with the
Server Explorer, Windows Services Administrative
tool or the NET START command
```

Apparently, you need to install a Windows service application before you can start it, and you'll learn how to do that in the following section.

INSTALLING A WINDOWS SERVICE

The .NET Framework enables you to create custom installer components. The custom installer components are the classes that an installation tool, such as `installutil.exe`, can use to properly install an application.

The following three installation components are used when creating an installer for the Windows service applications:

▶ **The `System.ServiceProcess.ServiceProcessInstaller` Class**—This class creates the records for all the Windows services contained with the application in the Windows service database. You need to have just one instance of the `ServiceProcessInstaller` class in a Windows service application.

▶ **The `System.ServiceProcess.ServiceInstaller` Class**—This class writes specific information about a Windows service to the Windows service database. You'll have as many instances of the `ServiceInstaller` class as the number of services in a Windows service application.

▶ **The `System.Configuration.Install.Installer` Class**—This class works as the entry point for the installation process. The `Installer` class maintains a collection of custom installer objects, which can be accessed through the `Installers` property. You should add the instance of the `ServiceProcessInstaller` class and instances of the `ServiceInstaller` class of the Windows service application to this collection. You should also apply the `RunInstaller` attribute to this class and set its value to true.

When you use an installation tool such as `installutil.exe` to install a Windows service application, the installation tool takes the following steps:

1. It looks for an installer class in the Windows service application that has its `RunInstaller` attribute set to true and creates an instance of this class.

2. It gets a collection of custom installer objects from the `Installers` property and invokes the `Install()` method on each of these objects to perform the custom installation.

3. It rolls back the installation of all custom installers if any one of them failed.

The ServiceProcessInstaller and the ServiceInstaller Classes

I'll talk more about the installation process and the Installer class later in Chapter 10. This section focuses on some important properties of the ServiceProcessInstaller class and the ServiceInstaller class because these properties specify the values that are written to the Windows service database.

The ServiceProcessInstaller class specifies the security settings for the Windows services in the Windows service application. Table 6.3 lists some important properties of the ServiceProcessInstaller class.

TABLE 6.3

IMPORTANT PROPERTIES OF THE ServiceProcessInstaller CLASS

Property	Description
Account	Specifies the type of account under which the services run. This property takes one of the values from the ServiceAccount enumeration. These values are LocalService, LocalSystem, NetworkService, and User. If you set the Account property to User and do not specify a value for either the Username or Password property, then you are prompted to enter both username and password at the time of installation.
Password	This property is useful only when the Account property is set to User. In that case, this property specifies the password of the account under which the service application runs.
Username	This property is useful only when the Account property is set to User. In that case, this property specifies the username of the account under which the service application runs.

EXAM TIP

Some Accounts Are XP-only The LocalService and NetworkService accounts are only available on Windows XP and Windows Server 2003. These accounts do not exist on Windows 2000 or older operating systems.

The ServiceInstaller specifies the individual settings for each service in the Windows service database. Table 6.4 lists some important properties of the ServiceInstaller class.

TABLE 6.4

IMPORTANT MEMBERS OF THE ServiceInstaller CLASS

Property	Description
DisplayName	Specifies a descriptive friendly name that identifies the service to the user. This name is often used by interactive tools to display the service to the user.
ServiceName	Specifies a unique name by which the system identifies this service. The ServiceName must be between 1 to 256 characters. And it cannot contain '/', '\', or any character from the ASCII character set with a value less than decimal value 32.
ServicesDependedOn	Specifies an array of strings that represents the services that must be running for this service to run. If any service in the array is not running, the SCM tries to start that service before starting this service.
StartType	Indicates how and when this service is started. The value of this property is one of the ServiceStartMode enumeration value—Automatic, Disabled or Manual. The value Automatic specifies that the service is started automatically when Windows starts. The default value of this property is Manual, which means that the service will not start automatically with Windows.

> **EXAM TIP**
>
> **The ServiceName Property** The ServiceName property of a ServiceInstaller object must exactly match the ServiceName property of the corresponding Windows service class.

> **NOTE**
>
> **Windows Service Description** Unfortunately, the Installer class does not have a property to set the description for a Windows Service. If you need to set a description for a service, you have two choices: Either use the Service Control utility (sc.exe) or modify the Registry key corresponding to the Windows service, add a string value named Description, and set the data for this value with the description text.

Adding Installer Classes to a Windows Service Project

When you use Visual Studio .NET to create a Windows service application, it is easy to create the required installer classes. The Properties window of the Windows service, as shown earlier in Figure 6.4, displays a link called Add Installer. When you click on that link, Visual Studio .NET automatically adds a class named ProjectInstaller in your project. This class derives from the Installer class and contains an instance of the ServiceProcessInstaller class and one or more instances of the ProcessInstaller class (depending on the number of Windows services you have in the application).

Step-by-Step 6.2 demonstrates how to add installer classes to a Windows service project.

STEP BY STEP

6.2 Creating an Installer for the Windows Service

1. Open the project StepByStep6_1. Access the design view for the OrderService component. Click anywhere on the background of the designer to select the service itself, rather than any of its components. Access the Properties window for the service. In the gray area below the list of properties, you see a hyperlink named Add Installer (refer to Figure 6.4). Click on the hyperlink.

2. The preceding step adds a component named ProjectInstaller.cs to the StepByStep6_1 project. Access the design view for ProjectInstaller.cs to see that it has two components: serviceProcessInstaller1 and serviceInstaller1.

3. Access the properties for the serviceProcessInstaller1 component. You'll note that this component is an instance of the ServiceProcessInstaller class. Change its Account property from User to LocalSystem.

4. Access the properties for the serviceInstaller1 component. You'll note that this component is an instance of the ServiceInstaller class. Change its DisplayName and ServiceName properties to OrderService and the StartType property to Automatic.

5. Build the project StepByStep6_1. The Windows service is now ready to be installed.

At this stage, the OrderService application has both a Windows service and an installer.

Using Installer tool (installutil.exe) to Install a Windows Service Application

You can easily install an executable file that has the code for the installer class by using the command line Installer tool (installutil.exe) that comes as a part of the .NET Framework SDK.

Step-by-Step 6.3 demonstrates how to use installutil.exe to install a Windows service application in the Windows service database.

STEP BY STEP

6.3 Using installutil.exe to Install a Windows Service Application

1. Open the Visual Studio .NET command prompt by selecting Start, Programs, Microsoft Visual Studio .NET, Visual Studio .NET Tools, Visual Studio .NET Command Prompt. This opens a command window with necessary environment variables set to run the .NET Framework SDK tools. Change the directory to the bin\debug directory of the StepByStep6_1 project where the .exe file for the Windows service application is stored.

2. Issue the following command; you see the results as shown in Figure 6.6:

```
installutil StepByStep6_1.exe
```

continues

continued

FIGURE 6.6
You can use `installutil.exe` to install a Windows service application.

The Windows service application is now stored in the Windows service database. Not only this, but based on the information in the executable file, `installutil.exe` has also installed an event source named `OrderService` for writing to the Application event log.

Because the `StartType` of the `OrderService` Windows service is set as `Automatic`, it will start automatically when Windows starts next time.

Starting and Testing a Windows Service

To see the `OrderService` Windows service in action, you need to first create the directory `c:\orders` because `OrderService` depends on it. In most cases, it is helpful to create any such required files or directories at the time of installation itself. However, for that you have to install the Windows service using a setup package based on the Windows Installer. You'll learn how to do that later in Chapter 10.

Step-by-Step 6.4 shows how to use the `OrderService` service to automatically add new records in the `Orders` table of the `Northwind` database, whenever an XML file is created in the `c:\orders` directory.

STEP BY STEP

6.4 Starting a Windows Service

1. Create a directory c:\orders. This is the directory where the incoming orders will be created as an XML file.

2. Restart the computer; the OrderService is started automatically when Windows is started.

3. Right-click on the My Computer icon and select Manage from its shortcut menu. In the Computer Management window, navigate to System Tools, Event Viewer, Application. You'll see that OrderService has written an informational message to the Application event log. Double-click to open the message; you'll see that the message is about the successful start of OrderService, as shown in Figure 6.7.

4. Create an XML file named Orders.xml and store the following information in this file:

```xml
<?xml version="1.0" standalone="yes"?>
<dsOrders xmlns="http://www.tempuri.org/dsOrders.xsd">
  <Orders>
    <CustomerID>VINET</CustomerID>
    <EmployeeID>5</EmployeeID>
    <OrderDate>2002-10-11</OrderDate>
    <RequiredDate>2002-10-21</RequiredDate>
    <ShippedDate>2002-10-18</ShippedDate>
    <ShipVia>3</ShipVia>
    <Freight>22.38</Freight>
    <ShipName>Vins et alcools Chevalier</ShipName>
    <ShipAddress>59 rue de l'Abbaye</ShipAddress>
    <ShipCity>Reims</ShipCity>
    <ShipRegion>MI</ShipRegion>
    <ShipPostalCode>51100</ShipPostalCode>
    <ShipCountry>France</ShipCountry>
  </Orders>
</dsOrders>
```

5. Copy this file to the c:\orders directory. You'll note that in a few moments the Orders.xml file is moved from c:\orders to a new subdirectory, c:\orders\updated.

6. Query the Orders table in the Northwind database. You'll find that a record has been added to the Orders table with the information in the Orders.xml file.

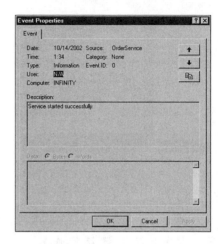

FIGURE 6.7

When the StartType for a Windows service is set to Automatic, the service is started automatically when Windows is started.

continues

continued

7. Create another orders file in the c:\orders directory.
You'll note that the file is moved again to the updated subdirectory and the Orders table is updated with the information in the XML file.

In Step-by-Step 6.4, you saw that as the new XML files are created,
they are inserted into the Northwind database's Orders table. After the
order record is inserted, the program also moves the XML file to the
c:\orders\updated subdirectory. The FileSystemWatcher is configured not to listen to any of the subdirectories inside c:\orders;
therefore XML files created in c:\orders\updated do not raise any
events of interest to the FileSystemWatcher component.

R E V I E W   B R E A K

▶ You can easily create Windows services by using the functionality provided by the System.ServiceProcess.ServiceBase
class.

▶ The System.ServiceProcess.ServiceProcessInstaller and the
System.ServiceProcess.ServiceInstaller classes provide the
functionality for custom installation of Windows service applications.

▶ For installation tools such as installutil.exe to install an
assembly, the assembly must have a class derived from
System.Configuration.Install.Installer. If any custom
installers (such as Windows service installers) need to be
installed, they are added to the Installers collection of the
Installer class.

▶ When the SCM sends a start message to a Windows service,
first the Main() method of the Windows service application is
executed. This method creates one or more instances of the
Windows services and passes them to the Run() method of the
ServiceBase class. This method provides the references of
Windows service objects to the SCM. SCM uses these references to communicate with the Windows service.

GUIDED PRACTICE EXERCISE 6.1

Recall from Chapter 3, ".NET Remoting," that when you want to remote an object by some method other than using IIS, you have to create a remoting server and manually start the service whenever the computer is restarted. When you implement a remoting server as a Windows service, it is easy to ensure that the remoting server is automatically started with Windows.

The objective of this exercise is to create a Windows service that exposes the DbConnect class of the StepByStep3_10 project as a Singleton server-activated object. You'll use a client program such as the one created in StepByStep3_12 project to connect to this service.

The server and client should communicate via the TCP channels and the binary formatter. The service should start automatically when Windows is started. The service should allow itself to be stopped but should not support pause and continue operations.

How would you create such a Windows service?

You should try working through this problem on your own first. If you get stuck, or if you'd like to see one possible solution, follow these steps:

1. Add a new Visual C# .NET Windows Service application named GuidedPracticeExercise3_1 to the solution.

2. Add references to the .NET assembly System.Runtime.Remoting, and to the project StepByStep3_9 and StepByStep3_10 that you created in Chapter 3 (the interface to the remotable class and the remotable class itself).

3. In the Solution Explorer, rename the default Service1.cs to DbConnectSingletonServer.cs. Click on the designer surface, and then in the Properties window. Set the Name and ServiceName properties to DbConnectSingletonServer. Note the CanPauseAndContinue property is already set to false.

4. Switch to the code view and change all occurrences of Service1 to DbConnectSingletonServer. Add the following using directives to the code:

continues

continued

```
using StepByStep3_9;
using StepByStep3_10;
using System.Runtime.Remoting;
using System.Runtime.Remoting.Channels;
using System.Runtime.Remoting.Channels.Tcp;
```

5. In the code, search for the skeleton of the OnStart() method and modify it as follows:

```
protected override void OnStart(string[] args)
{
    // Register a TCP server channel that
    // listens on port 1234
    TcpServerChannel channel =
        new TcpServerChannel(1234);
    ChannelServices.RegisterChannel(channel);

    // Resgister the service that publishes
    // DbConnect for remote access in Singleton mode
    RemotingConfiguration.RegisterWellKnownServiceType
        (typeof(StepByStep3_10.DbConnect), "DbConnect",
        WellKnownObjectMode.Singleton);
}
```

6. Access the Properties window for the DbConnectSingletonServer component. Click on the Add Installer hyperlink. This adds a component named ProjectInstaller.cs to the project. Access the design view for ProjectInstaller.cs to see that it has two components: serviceProcessInstaller1 and serviceInstaller1.

7. Access the properties for the serviceProcessInstaller1 component. You'll note that this component is an instance of the ServiceProcessInstaller class. Change its Account property from User to LocalSystem.

8. Access the properties for the serviceInstaller1 component. You'll note that this component is an instance of the ServiceInstaller class. Change its ServiceName and DisplayName properties to DbConnectSingletonServer and the StartType property to Automatic.

9. Set DbConnectSingletonServer.cs as the startup object for the project.

10. Build the project. This step creates a remoting server that is capable of using the Singleton activation mode via the TCP channel to register the StepByStep3_10.DbConnect class for remote invocation.

11. To install the Windows service, open the Visual Studio .NET command prompt and change the directory to the `bin\debug` directory in the project folder. Execute the following command:

    ```
    installutil GuidedPracticeExercise6_1.exe
    ```

12. Use the command prompt to execute the following command to start the Windows service:

    ```
    NET START DbConnectSingletonServer
    ```

13. Run the executable file `StepByStep3_12.exe` for the project created in Step-by-Step 3.12 in Chapter 3. In the window that appears type queries for retrieving data from the `Northwind` database.

If you have difficulty following this exercise, review the sections "Creating a Windows Service Application" and "Installing a Windows Service" earlier in this chapter. Also review the sections, "Creating a Remotable Class" and "Creating a Server-Activated Object" in Chapter 3. Make sure that you also perform Step-by-Step 6.1 through Step-by-Step 6.3 and Step-by-Step 3.9 to Step-by-Step 3.12. After doing that review, try this exercise again.

USING TOOLS TO MONITOR AND CONTROL A WINDOWS SERVICE

The .NET Framework SDK and Visual Studio .NET provide various tools that help you monitor and control a Windows service application. In this section, you'll learn how to work with each of these tools.

Using the Services MMC Snap-in

One of the easiest ways to manipulate a Windows service is through the Service MMC Snap-in. You can access this snap-in through either of the following:

▶ By using the Administrative Tools section of the Windows Control Panel.

▶ By navigating to the Services and Application, Services node of the Computer Management tool. You can open the Computer Management tool by right-clicking on My Computer and selecting Manage from the shortcut menu.

The Services snap-in lists all the Windows services installed on the computer, along with the Name, Description, Status, Startup Type and Logon Account for each one, as shown in Figure 6.8.

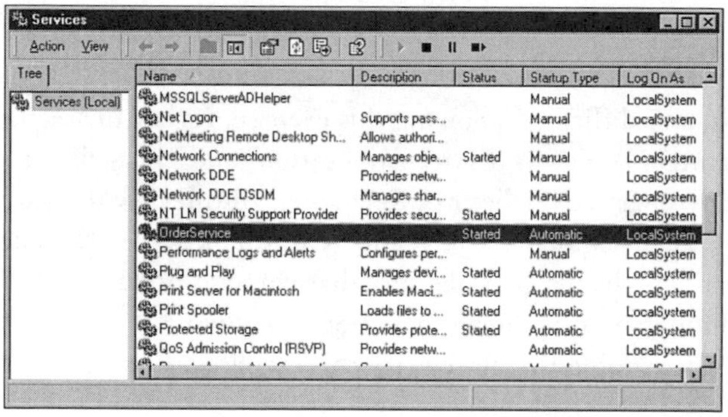

FIGURE 6.8
The Services snap-in enumerates the installed Windows services on a computer.

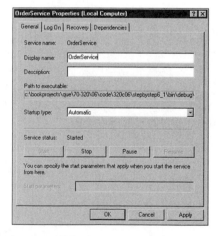

FIGURE 6.9
You can access the control options of a Windows service by using its Properties window in the Services snap-in.

You can select a service in this list, and use the Action menu or the toolbar buttons to start, pause, continue, or stop a Windows service.

For more control options, you can display the Properties window for a service (see Figure 6.9) by double-clicking on the service record in the Services snap-in.

From the service's Properties window, you can start, pause, continue, and stop the service. In addition to this, you have extra options to manipulate the startup type, start parameters, and service login account. The Recovery tab enables you to specify actions that need to be taken if the service fails to start.

Using Visual Studio .NET Server Explorer

When using Visual Studio .NET, you need not leave the development environment to manipulate the Windows services. Visual

Studio .NET enables you to manipulate services on both local and remote computers through the Server Explorer Window.

To access the services, open the Server Explorer Window and in the Server node select the computer where you want to access the service. Inside the selected computer, you will find the node containing all the services on that computer, as shown in Figure 6.10. You can right-click a service and select options to start, pause, continue, and stop the Windows service from the shortcut menu.

Using the NET Utility (`net.exe`)

The NET command-line utility comes installed with Windows. This utility enables you to perform various networking commands, including control of Windows services. Typical usage of the `net.exe` with Windows services is as follows:

- ▶ To enumerate a list of installed services

  NET START

- ▶ To start a Windows service

  NET START *WindowsServiceName*

- ▶ To pause a Windows service

  NET PAUSE *WindowsServiceName*

- ▶ To resume a paused Windows service

  NET CONTINUE *WindowsServiceName*

- ▶ To stop a Windows service

  NET STOP *WindowsServiceName*

Using the Service Control Utility (`sc.exe`)

The Service Control command line utility is the most powerful of all the service control tools that I discussed in this section. This utility comes installed with Windows XP and Windows Server 2003. This utility also comes as a part of the Win32 SDK and the .NET Framework SDK.

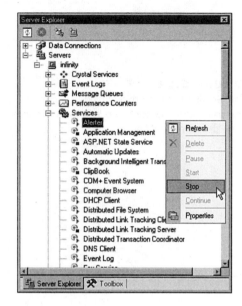

FIGURE 6.10
Visual Studio .NET Server Explorer enables you to control Windows services without leaving the development environment.

The Service Control utility provides various options to start, pause, continue, stop, configure, and query a Windows service as shown in Figure 6.11.

FIGURE 6.11

The Service Control utility provides a powerful way to control and configure Windows services from the command line.

As an example, you can use sc.exe to set the description for a Windows service. To change the description of OrderService, you can use the following form of the sc.exe command:

```
sc.exe description OrderService "This service listens
to creation of order files (*.XML) in c:\orders
directory. When a XML file is created in this
directory, the XML data in the file is added as a new
record to the Orders table of the NorthWind database"
```

You can query the description by using the following command:

```
sc.exe qdescription OrderService
```

The Service Control utility provides a large number of options to work with Windows services. I'd recommend you try several of these options to get familiar with the utility's usage.

CONTROLLING A WINDOWS SERVICE

Create and manipulate a Windows service.

In the previous section, I discussed several utilities for manipulating Windows services. You may also need to manipulate a Windows service programmatically from your program. You may use this in the scenario where you want to take some action based on the status of a service or you may want to take some actions in a program that require you to start, pause, continue, or stop a Windows service. You may also want to programmatically manipulate a Windows service when you want to provide your own custom user interface for configuring and controlling a Windows service.

You can use the `ServiceController` class of the `System.ServiceProcess` namespace to programmatically control Windows services from your programs. In the next two sections, you'll learn what the `ServiceController` class is and how you can use this class in your programs.

> **NOTE**
>
> **Creating MMC Snap-ins**   If you wish to provide an MMC-integrated administration module for your Windows service application, you can use classes from the `System.Management.Instrumentation` namespace. These classes make up a whole subject known as Windows Management Instrumentation (WMI), which is not a part of the Exam 70-320 objectives. However, if you are curious you can find more information in the "Managing Applications Using WMI" topic in the .NET Framework SDK documentation.

The `ServiceController` Class

The `ServiceController` class provides functionality to connect to a Windows service and control its behavior. Table 6.5 lists some important methods and properties of this class that you'll typically use in a Windows service control program.

TABLE 6.5

IMPORTANT MEMBERS OF THE `ServiceController` CLASS

Member	Type	Description
CanPauseAndContinue	Property	A value of `true` indicates that the service can be paused and resumed.
CanShutdown	Property	A value of `true` indicates that the service should be notified when the system is shutting down.
CanStop	Property	A value of `true` indicates that the service can be stopped after it has started.

continues

TABLE 6.5 *continued*

IMPORTANT MEMBERS OF THE ServiceController CLASS

Member	Type	Description
Close()	Method	Disconnects the ServiceController object from the Windows service.
Continue()	Method	Continues a Windows service after it has been paused.
DisplayName	Property	Specifies a friendly name for the service.
ExecuteCommand()	Method	Executes a custom command on the service.
GetServices()	Method	Retrieves the Windows services installed on a computer.
MachineName	Property	Specifies the name of the computer on which this service resides. Its default value is set to the local computer. You need to change the MachineName property only if you want to control the Windows services on a remote machine.
Pause()	Method	Suspends a Windows service's operation.
Refresh()	Method	Refreshes the values of all the properties with their latest values.
ServiceName	Property	Specifies the name of the Windows service.
ServicesDependedOn	Property	Specifies the set of services on which this Windows service depends.
ServiceType	Property	One of the ServiceType enumeration values that specifies how the Windows service is used. A Windows service can be of type—InteractiveProcess (can communicate with the desktop), Win32OwnProcess (runs in its own process), or Win32ShareProcess (shares the process with other Windows services).
Start()	Method	Starts the Windows service.
Status	Property	Retrieves the status of the Windows service.
Stop()	Method	Stops the Windows service and other services that are dependent on this service.

Member	*Type*	*Description*
WaitForStatus()	Method	Waits for the service to reach the specified status, which is a value of the ServiceControllerStatus enumeration. Its possible values are: ContinuePending, Paused, PausePending, Running, StartPending, Stopped, and StopPending

Creating a Windows Service Controller Application

In this section, I'll show you how to use various methods and properties of the ServiceController class to create a simple service controller application.

The application enumerates the list of installed services on the local machine and enables users to start, stop, pause, continue, and refresh the list of services. Step-by-Step 6.5 shows you how to accomplish this.

STEP BY STEP

6.5 Creating a Windows Service Controller Application

1. Add a new Windows Application project to the solution. Name the project StepByStep6_5.

2. Rename the default Form1.cs file to WindowsServiceController.cs. Access the properties window for this form and change the Name property to WindowsServiceController and the Text property to Windows Service Controller. Switch to the code view and change all instances of Form1 to WindowsServiceController.

continues

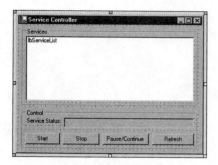

FIGURE 6.12
Arrange controls to create a user interface for the service controller program.

continued

3. Add a ListBox control (lbServiceList), a TextBox control (txtStatus), and 4 Button controls (btnStart, btnStop, btnPauseContinue, and btnRefresh) on the form. Arrange the controls as shown in Figure 6.12.

4. Add a reference to the System.ServiceProcess.dll to the project. Add the following using directive to the code:

```
using System.ServiceProcess;
```

5. Double-click on an empty area on the form to attach an event handler with its Load event. Add the following code to its event handler:

```
private void WindowsServiceController_Load
            (object sender, System.EventArgs e)
{
    PopulateServiceList();
}

// Get the list of installed services
protected void PopulateServiceList()
{
    // Populate services in the list box
    lbServiceList.DataSource =
        ServiceController.GetServices();
    // Display friendly name
    lbServiceList.DisplayMember = "DisplayName";
}
```

6. Double-click on the ListBox to attach an event handler with its SelectedIndexChanged event. Add the following code to its event handler:

```
private void lbServiceList_SelectedIndexChanged
            (object sender, System.EventArgs e)
{
    // Retrieve the selected service
    ServiceController service =
        (ServiceController) lbServiceList.SelectedItem;
    // and get status for it
    GetServiceStatus(service);
}

// Find the latest service status
protected void GetServiceStatus(ServiceController sc)
{
    // Get the service status
    ServiceControllerStatus status = sc.Status;
    // Enable all buttons
```

```
    btnStart.Enabled = btnStop.Enabled =
        btnPauseContinue.Enabled = true;
// Disable the pause button if it does
// not support pause and continue messages
if (!sc.CanPauseAndContinue)
    btnPauseContinue.Enabled = false;
// Disable the stop button if it does
// not support stop message
if (!sc.CanStop)
    btnStop.Enabled = false;
// Enable and disable buttons based on
// service status, also display the text
// for the status
switch (status)
{
    case ServiceControllerStatus.ContinuePending:
        txtStatus.Text = "Continue Pending";
        btnPauseContinue.Enabled = false;
        break;
    case ServiceControllerStatus.Paused:
        txtStatus.Text = "Paused";
        btnPauseContinue.Text = "Continue";
        btnStart.Enabled = false;
        break;
    case ServiceControllerStatus.PausePending:
        txtStatus.Text = "Pause Pending";
        btnPauseContinue.Enabled = false;
        btnStart.Enabled = false;
        break;
    case ServiceControllerStatus.Running:
        txtStatus.Text = "Running";
        btnPauseContinue.Text = "Pause";
        btnStart.Enabled = false;
        break;
    case ServiceControllerStatus.StartPending:
        txtStatus.Text = "Start Pending";
        btnStart.Enabled = false;
        break;
    case ServiceControllerStatus.Stopped:
        txtStatus.Text = "Stopped";
        btnStop.Enabled = false;
        break;
    case ServiceControllerStatus.StopPending:
        txtStatus.Text = "Stop Pending";
        btnStop.Enabled = false;
        break;
    default:
        txtStatus.Text = "Unknown Status";
        break;
}
}
```

continues

continued

7. Add the following event handler and attach it to the
Click event of btnStart, btnStop, and btnPauseContinue
buttons.

```
// Common event handler for the Click event on
// start, stop, and pause/continue buttons
private void btnControl_Click
    (object sender, System.EventArgs e)
{
    // It might take time, so change the
    // cursor to a wait cursor
    Cursor.Current = Cursors.WaitCursor;
    // Retrieve the selected service
    ServiceController service =
        (ServiceController)
        lbServiceList.SelectedItem;
    if (sender == this.btnStart)
    {
        // Start the service and wait till
        // the status is Running
        service.Start();
        service.WaitForStatus
            (ServiceControllerStatus.Running);
    }
    else if (sender == this.btnStop)
    {
        // Stop the service and wait till
        // the status is Stopped
        service.Stop();
        service.WaitForStatus
            (ServiceControllerStatus.Stopped);
    }
    else if (sender == this.btnPauseContinue)
    {
        if (btnPauseContinue.Text == "Pause")
        {
            // Pause the service and wait till
            // the status is Paused
            service.Pause();
            service.WaitForStatus
                (ServiceControllerStatus.Paused);
        }
        else
        {
            // Resume the service and wait till
            // the status is Running
            service.Continue();
            service.WaitForStatus
                (ServiceControllerStatus.Running);
        }
    }
    // Refresh the list
    int intIndex = lbServiceList.SelectedIndex;
```

```
        PopulateServiceList();
        lbServiceList.SelectedIndex = intIndex;
        // Change the cursor back to normal
        Cursor.Current = Cursors.Default;
}
```

8. Add the following event handler to the `Click` event of the `btnRefresh` control:

```
private void btnRefresh_Click
        (object sender, System.EventArgs e)
{
    // Refresh the list
    int intIndex = lbServiceList.SelectedIndex;
    PopulateServiceList();
    lbServiceList.SelectedIndex = intIndex;
}
```

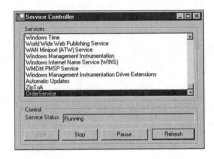

FIGURE 6.13

The Windows Service Controller form controls the Windows services programmatically.

9. Build the `StepByStep6_5` project. Set the project as the startup object. Run the project. You will see a window displaying a list of installed services, as shown in Figure 6.13.

10. Scroll through the list of services. Select `OrderService`. Pause the service and then continue. Stop the service and then start. As you do this, also create new XML files in the `c:\orders` directory. You should find that the files are not processed when the `OrderService` is paused or stopped.

11. Open the Application EventLog. You'll see that each time you start, pause, continue, or stop the `OrderService` service, an entry in the Application event log is written because you set the `AutoLog` property for the Windows service to `true`.

12. Click on the Refresh button to update the list of installed services with any newly installed or uninstalled services.

In Step-by-Step 6.5, most of the code is written to make the user interface work logically. For Windows service control, I am using the `ServiceController.GetServices()` static method to get a list of installed services that I populate in the `lbServiceList` control.

When the user clicks on the `btnStart` button, I am calling the `Start()` method to start the selected Windows service. The Windows service might take some time to start, and meanwhile I should restrict the user from pressing any other buttons; therefore I am calling the synchronous `WaitForStatus()` method that waits till the Windows service returns a Running status. I followed a similar logic for other control messages.

REVIEW BREAK

▶ Several tools are available for monitoring and controlling Windows services. Some notable tools are the Services MMC snap-in, Visual Studio .NET Server Explorer, the `net.exe` command-line utility, and the Service Control command-line utility (`sc.exe`).

▶ Service Control utility (`sc.exe`) is distributed as a part of Windows XP and later operating systems and as a part of Win32 SDK and the .NET Framework SDK. This utility is the most powerful tool for controlling and configuring Windows services.

▶ Some programs may also need to monitor Windows services programmatically. The FCL provides the `System.ServiceProcess.ServiceController` class to programmatically control the Windows services.

▶ The `ServiceController.GetServices()` method is used to enumerate installed services on a computer. You can use the `Start()`, `Stop()`, `Pause()`, and `Continue()` methods to change the status of a Windows service. The `WaitforStatus()` synchronous method is useful when you would like the current thread to pause execution and wait for the Windows service to enter in the specified state.

CHAPTER SUMMARY

Windows services are the programs that generally run in the background and follow the interface of the Windows Service Control Manager (SCM). In this chapter, I discussed the architecture of Windows services and how the SCM manages the Windows services and the Windows service database (which is stored in the Windows registry).

Traditionally it was considered difficult to create Windows services, but with .NET Framework, creating a Windows service is just like creating any other application. Credit for this simplicity goes to the improved programming model and the functionality of the `ServiceBase` class. This class acts as the base class for all the Windows services.

I also discussed how to add installation classes (the `ServiceProcessInstaller` and the `ServiceInstaller` classes) to a Windows service project so that the installation tools such as `installutil.exe` can be used to install the Windows service.

You also learned about various tools for controlling and managing Windows services, such as the Services MMC snap-in, Visual Studio .NET Server Explorer, the NET utility (`net.exe`) and the Service Control utility (`sc.exe`).

Finally, in this chapter I discussed how you could programmatically control a Windows service. I explained and used various members of the `ServiceController` class to accomplish this.

KEY TERMS

- SCM (Service Control Manager)
- Windows service

APPLY YOUR KNOWLEDGE

Exercises

6.1   Passing Startup Parameters to a Windows Service

When you start a Windows service, you can also pass startup parameters to the service.

In this exercise, I'll create a new Windows service named OrderServiceEx. This Windows service is almost same as OrderService, which was created in Step-by-Step 6.1. The only difference is that OrderServiceEx accepts the value of the NotifyFilter property and the Path property of the FileSystemWatcher component at the time of starting the Windows service.

The startup parameters to a Windows service are given the same way as command-line arguments are provided to a console application. However, the only difference is that rather than accepting the arguments in the Main() method, the Windows services accepts arguments in the OnStart() method. The Main() method here is common to several Windows services in an application. However, each of these services has its own individual OnStart() method.

Estimated Time: 30 minutes.

1. Launch Visual Studio .NET. Select File, New, Blank Solution, and name the new solution 320C06Exercises. Click OK.

2. Add a new C# Windows Service project named Exercise6_1 to the solution.

3. The Windows service project contains a file named Service1.cs. Rename this file to OrderServiceEx.cs. Click on the designer surface; then in the Properties windows, set the Name and ServiceName properties to OrderServiceEx, and set the CanPauseAndContinue property to true.

4. Switch to the code view and change all occurrences of Service1 to OrderServiceEx. Add the following using directives to the code:

```
using System.Data.SqlClient;
using System.IO;
```

5. Add a FileSystemWatcher component onto the surface of the OrderServiceEx component. Access the Properties window for the FileSystemWatcher component and change its Name property to fswOrders and its EnableRaisingEvent property to false.

6. Click on the Events icon on the Properties window and double-click on the Created event to attach an event handler. Add the following code to the event handler:

```
private void fswOrders_Created(
    object sender,
    System.IO.FileSystemEventArgs e)
{
    DataSet dsOrders =
        new DataSet("Orders");
    // Read the contents of the XML file
    // into the Orders DataSet
    dsOrders.ReadXml(e.FullPath);

    // Set up the database connection string
    string strConn =
        "data source=(local);" +
        "initial catalog=Northwind;" +
        "integrated security=SSPI";
    string strOrderQuery =
        "Select * from orders";
    // Create a DataAdapter for the Orders
    // table of the Northwind database
    SqlDataAdapter daOrders =
        new SqlDataAdapter(
        strOrderQuery, strConn);
    // Automatically generate the update
    // command to reconcile the changes
    // made to the DataSet
    SqlCommandBuilder cbOrders =
        new SqlCommandBuilder(daOrders);
    //Update the DataSet
    daOrders.Update(dsOrders, "Orders");
    daOrders.Dispose();
```

APPLY YOUR KNOWLEDGE

```
    FileInfo fi = new FileInfo(e.FullPath);
    // Create a subdirectory named "Updated"
    // if it does not already exist
    fi.Directory.CreateSubdirectory(
        "Updated");
    // Copy the processed XML file
    // to the updated directory,
    // overwriting if needed
    File.Copy(
        e.FullPath, fi.DirectoryName +
        @"\Updated\" + fi.Name, true);
    // Delete the XML file from its
    // original location
    fi.Delete();
}
```

7. In the code, search for the skeletons of the
   `OnStart()` and `OnStop()` methods and modify
   them as follows:

```
protected override void OnStart(
    string[] args)
{
    fswOrders.Filter = args[0];
    fswOrders.Path = args[1];
    fswOrders.EnableRaisingEvents = true;
}

protected override void OnStop()
{
    fswOrders.EnableRaisingEvents = false;
}
```

8. Add the following code to the `OrderService` class
   to override the `OnPause()` and the `OnContinue()`
   methods of the base class:

```
protected override void OnPause()
{
    fswOrders.EnableRaisingEvents = false;
}

protected override void OnContinue()
{
    fswOrders.EnableRaisingEvents = true;
}
```

9. Access the Properties window for the
   `OrderServiceEx` component and click on the Add
   Installer hyperlink.

10. Access the properties for the
    `serviceProcessInstaller1` component and
    change its `Account` property from `User` to
    `LocalSystem`.

11. Access the properties for the `serviceInstaller1`
    component, and change its `ServiceName` proper-
    ties to `OrderServiceEx` and its `StartType` property
    to `Automatic`.

12. Build the project `StepByStep6_1`. Open the Visual
    Studio .NET command prompt, switch to the
    `bin\debug` directory of the project and type the
    following command:

    `installutil.exe Exercise6_1.exe`

13. Open the Services MMC snap-in. Open the
    property window for `OrderServiceEx`. In the Start
    parameters text box type the following as shown
    in Figure 6.14 and click on the Start button:

    `*.xml c:\ordersEx`

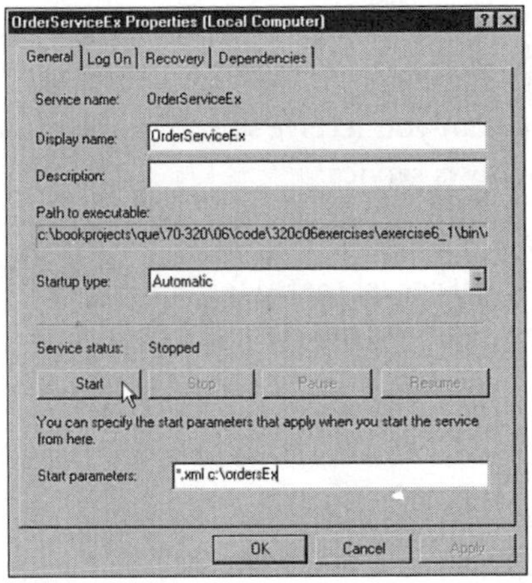

FIGURE 6.14
You can specify start parameters for a Windows service.

APPLY YOUR KNOWLEDGE

14. Create an XML file in the c:\OrdersEx folder. You may use the same XML file used in Step-by-Step 6.4. You'll note that the record has been updated to the Orders table in the Northwind database.

Review Questions

1. What is a Windows service?

2. What is the Service Control Manager (SCM) and what does it do?

3. How can you control and monitor a Windows service?

4. What is the significance of the Run() method of the ServiceBase class?

5. How can you programmatically enumerate the Windows services installed on a computer?

6. How do you write to an event log from a Windows service application?

7. How can you receive startup parameters in a Windows service?

8. What is the difference between the ServiceProcessInstaller and the ServiceInstaller classes?

Exam Questions

1. You are required to design an application that monitors incoming emails and analyzes them to filter out junk emails. The emails arrive at a well-known port and you use conditions stored in an XML file to determine whether an email is possibly a junk email. Your application bounces back all junk email while forwarding the other emails to a groupware application. You want this application to run continuously with minimal interaction with the desktop user. How should you design this application?

   A. Design the application as a Windows forms application

   B. Design the application as a Windows service application

   C. Design the application as a Web forms application

   D. Design the application as a Web service application

2. You are designing a Windows service application that will be used by other applications over the Internet. You want the users of the application to have access to only certain directories on your system. Which of the following techniques should you use?

   A. When installing the Windows service, set the Account property to User. Also, specify the username and password for an account that has access to only the required directories.

   B. When starting the Windows service, set the Account property to User. Also, specify the username and password for an account that has access to only the required directories.

APPLY YOUR KNOWLEDGE

C. When installing the Windows service, set the `Account` property to `NetworkService`. Also specify the username and password for an account that has access to only the required directories.

D. When starting the Windows service, set the `Account` property to `NetworkService`. Also, specify the username and password for an account that has access to only the required directories.

3. You are working on a team that is designing a Windows service that monitors Web server performance on an ongoing basis. You are given a task to make sure that an entry is written to the Application event log when the Windows service is started, paused, resumed, or stopped. You want to write a minimum amount of code to achieve this. Which of the following options would you choose?

A. Use the `EventLog` property of the Windows service class to write entries to the application log.

B. Set the `AutoLog` property of the Windows service class to `true`.

C. Create an `EventLog` component in the project and use this component to write entries in the event log.

D. Create a method that writes entries in the event log and call this method from `OnStart()`, `OnStop()`, `OnPause()`, and `OnContinue()` methods of the Windows service class.

4. You are developing a Windows service application that accepts startup parameters. Which of the following methods would you program to retrieve and process these parameters?

A. The `Main()` method

B. The `Run()` method

C. The `OnStart()` method

D. The constructor of the Windows service class

5. You are part of a team that is developing a Windows service application to monitor a legacy application for new data. Occasionally your application may encounter errors. You want to develop an error reporting mechanism that is easy to use for administrators who will monitor and maintain the application on day-to-day basis. You also want a scheme that is robust and requires a minimum amount of code. Which of the following techniques should you choose?

A. Event Log.

B. SQL Server tables.

C. XML-based log files.

D. Plain-text log files.

APPLY YOUR KNOWLEDGE

6. You have designed a Windows service application that contains two Windows services. You now want to add installer classes to this application so that the application can be installed with tools such as `installutil.exe`. You have added a new class inherited from the `Installer` class in your application. To the `Installers` collection of this class, you would like to add the custom installation components for properly installing the Windows services in your application. Which of the following combinations of custom components would you like to add to the `Installers` collection of the `Installer` class?

   A. Add two instances of the `ServiceProcessInstaller` class and one instance of the `ServiceInstaller` class.

   B. Add two instances of the `ServiceInstaller` class and one instance of the `ServiceProcessInstaller` class.

   C. Add two instances each of the `ServiceInstaller` class and the `ServiceProcessInstaller` classes.

   D. Add one instance each of the `ServiceInstaller` class and the `ServiceProcessInstaller` classes.

7. You are required to design a Windows service that cannot be paused. Which of the following options will help you to accomplish this requirement?

   A. Set the `CanStart` property of the Windows service to `true`, but set the `CanStop` property to `false`.

   B. Set the `CanPauseAndContinue` property of the Windows service to `false`.

   C. Do not include definitions for the `OnPause()` and `OnContinue()` methods in the class definition of the Windows service.

   D. Do not include a definition for the `OnStop()` method in the class definition for Windows service.

8. Your application is required to monitor changes to files in the `c:\Documents` directory. You are especially interested in taking actions when there are any changes to the PDF files in this directory. You are using a `FileSystemWatcher` component to accomplish this task. How should you set the `Filter` and `NotifyFilter` properties of this component? (Select two.)

   A. Set the `Filter` property to `"*.pdf"`.

   B. Set the `NotifyFilter` property to `LastWrite`.

   C. Set the `NotifyFilter` property to `"*.pdf"`.

   D. Set the `Filter` property to `LastWrite`.

9. You have recently designed a Windows service application. You now want to install the application to test its functionality. Which of the following options should you choose to install this application?

   A. Use the Visual Studio .NET Server Explorer.

   B. Use the Services MMC snap-in.

   C. Use `net.exe`.

   D. Use `installutil.exe`.

APPLY YOUR KNOWLEDGE

10. You are designing an application that needs to know the Windows services that are installed on a computer. Which of the following classes would allow you retrieve this information?

    A. `ServiceBase`

    B. `ServiceInstaller`

    C. `ServiceController`

    D. `ServiceProcessInstaller`

11. Your group is designing a Windows service application that constantly monitors the computer to keep it tuned. This service performs tasks such as disk defragmentation, Registry cleanup, and virus detection. The service needs to have high privilege to perform its task. In what security context should you set up this service to run?

    A. `LocalService`

    B. `LocalSystem`

    C. `NetworkService`

    D. `User`

12. Which of the following options correctly identifies the security context in which a Windows service is executed?

    A. In the context of the built-in SYSTEM account

    B. In the context of the currently logged-on user

    C. In the context of the `Administrator` account

    D. In the context of the account information specified at the time of installation of service

13. You are designing a Windows service application and you want to set the service to start automatically when the computer is restarted. Which of the following classes would allow you retrieve this information?

    A. `ServiceBase`

    B. `ServiceInstaller`

    C. `ServiceController`

    D. `ServiceProcessInstaller`

14. Your colleague has designed a Windows service application by inheriting a class from the `ServiceBase` class. She is complaining that she is able to compile the program successfully, but when she tries to run the program, she is getting an error. What should you suggest to resolve this problem? (Select two.)

    A. Ask your colleague to start the Windows service by using the Service MMC snap-in.

    B. Ask your colleague to restart the computer.

    C. Ask your colleague to add custom installation components in the Windows service application and install the application by using `installutil.exe`.

    D. Ask your colleague to modify the Windows Registry by using `regedit.exe` and write the Windows service details there.

APPLY YOUR KNOWLEDGE

15. Your colleagues are testing a Windows service application. They are arguing over the order in which the following constructs are called when a Windows service is started:

    • The Main() method of the Windows service application.

    • The Run() method of the ServiceBase class.

    • The OnStart() method of the Windows service.

    Which of the following order should you suggest to them?

    A. Main(), Run(), OnStart()

    B. Main(), OnStart(), Run()

    C. OnStart(), Main(), Run()

    D. Run(), Main(), OnStart()

Answers to Review Questions

1. A Windows service is a long-running process that usually runs in the background without any user interaction. A Windows service must conform to the interface provided by the Windows Service Control Manager.

2. The Service Control Manager (SCM) is a part of the operating system that manages Windows services. SCM also manages the Windows service database (which is stored in the Windows Registry) and provides a mechanism through which other programs can interact with the Windows service database and the Windows services in execution.

3. You can control and monitor a Windows service in several ways. The easiest is to use the tools that come installed with Windows, such as the NET utility (net.exe), Service Control utility (sc.exe), and the Services MMC snap-in. You can also control Windows services through the Server Explorer of Visual Studio .NET. Sometimes you may need to control the Windows service programmatically; in that case, you can use the methods and properties of the ServiceController class.

4. The Run() method is usually called from the Main() method of a Windows service executable file. The Run() method loads an application's Windows services in memory and passes references to the Windows service objects to the SCM. This enables the SCM to pass control messages to a Windows service.

5. You can get a list of the Windows services installed on a computer by calling the static ServiceController.GetServices() method. This method returns an array of ServiceController objects, each associated with a Windows service.

6. To write entries in the Application event log from a Windows service application, you just need to use the EventLog.WriteEntry() method. However, if you need to write entries to any other event log, you should create a new EventLog object in your application.

7. Any startup parameters provided to a Windows service are passed to the OnStart() method call as an array of strings. You can process this array to retrieve the startup parameters in the OnStart() method.

8. The `ServiceProcessInstaller` class performs the installation tasks that are common to all Windows services in an application. These include setting the logon account for the Windows service. The `ServiceInstaller` class, on the other hand, performs the installation tasks that are specific to a Windows service, such as setting the `ServiceName` and `StartType`.

Answers to Exam Questions

1. **B.** The application in question runs continuously and requires minimal user interaction. The application also just listens to email and is not required to listen to Web-based requests. Given these characteristics, you should design this application as a Windows service rather than any of the application types specified in the other options. For more information, see the section "Understanding Windows Services" in this chapter.

2. **A.** You can specify the security settings for a Windows service only at the time of installation. When you want to run the Windows service with a specific username and password, the `Account` property must be set to `User`. For more information, see the sections "Architecture of Windows Services" and "Installing a Windows Service" in this chapter.

3. **B.** When you set the `AutoLog` property to `true`, the Windows service class automatically writes events to the Application event log. All other options require more code to be written to achieve the same results. For more information, see the section "The `System.ServiceProcess.ServiceBase` Class" in this chapter.

4. **C.** When a Windows service is started, any start-up parameters are passed to the `OnStart()` method. For more information, see the section "The `System.ServiceProcess.ServiceBase` Class" in this chapter.

5. **A.** You should use the event log for error reporting from a Windows service. Event logs are easy to use for administrators because they already use event logs for monitoring notifications from other applications. The service base class provides an `EventLog` property that allows you to use a single line of code to write messages to the Application event log. For more information, see the section "The `System.ServiceProcess.ServiceBase` Class" in this chapter.

6. **B.** For installing a Windows service application, you need to have one instance of the `ServiceProcessInstaller` class and as many instances of the `ServiceInstaller` class as the number of services you want to install. For more information, see the section "The `ServiceProcessInstaller` and the `ServiceInstaller` Classes" in this chapter.

7. **B.** If you do not want a Windows service to be paused, you need to set the `CanPauseAndContinue` property of the Web service to `false`. If this property is `true`, the SCM may send pause and continue messages to your service. The `CanStop` property and the `OnStop()` method won't help because stopping a Windows service is different from pausing a Windows service. In case of stopping, the Windows service is unloaded from memory and all its resources are reclaimed. For more information, see the section "Creating a Windows Service Application" in this chapter.

8. **A** and **B.** For a `FileSystemWatcher` component, the `Filter` property specifies what files are to be monitored, whereas the `NotifyFilter` specifies the type of changes the application is to watch for. For more information, see the section "Creating the `OrderService` Application" in this chapter.

9. **D.** Although the Server Explorer, Services MMC snap-in, and the .NET utility enable you to control and monitor a Windows service, they do not enable you to install one. To install a Windows service, either you should use `installutil.exe` or you should create a Windows installer-based setup project. For more information, see the section "Installing a Windows Service" in this chapter.

10. **C.** The `ServiceController` class interacts with SCM to enumerate the list of services installed on a computer. You get this information by using the static `GetServices()` method of this class. For more information, see the section "The `ServiceController` Class" in this chapter.

11. **B.** The `LocalSystem` value defines a highly privileged account. As compared to this, the `LocalService` and `NetworkService` values provide a lower privilege level for the security context. Privileges for a `User` account depend on the specified username and password. For more information, see the section "The `ServiceProcessInstaller` and the `ServiceInstaller` Classes" in this chapter.

12. **D.** Most Windows services are started before a user logs on and they keep on running across multiple user sessions. Therefore, the functionality of a Windows service cannot depend on the permissions available to the currently logged on user. A Windows service always executes by using an assigned user identity that is specified at the time the Windows service is installed. For more information, see the sections "Understanding Windows Services" and "Installing a Windows Service" in this chapter.

13. **B.** The `StartType` property of the `ServiceInstaller` class is used to specify whether a service will be started manually, or will be started automatically when the computer starts, or will not start at all. For more information, see the section "The `ServiceProcessInstaller` and the `ServiceInstaller` Classes" in this chapter.

14. **A** and **C.** The Windows service must be installed in the Windows Registry before it can be started. Although the service is installed in the Windows Registry, it is not a good idea to manipulate the Registry directly. You should instead use installation tools such as `installutil.exe` that interact with SCM to install a Windows service in the Windows Registry. After the service is installed successfully, you should instruct your colleague to start the Windows service by using the Service MMC snap-in because if the start type of the service is not set up as automatic, the service will not start automatically when the computer restarts. For more information, see the section "Installing a Windows Service" in this chapter.

15. **A.** The `Main()` method of the application is always the first to execute. The `Main()` method executes the `Run()` method of the `ServiceBase` class, which passes the reference of the Windows service to the SCM. The SCM then invokes the `OnStart()` method of the Windows service. For more information, see the section "Understanding How the SCM Interacts with a Windows Service" in this chapter.

APPLY YOUR KNOWLEDGE

Suggested Readings and Resources

1. Visual Studio .NET Combined Help
   Collection

   - Windows Service Applications

   - Service Application Programming
     Architecture

   - Monitoring Windows Services

   - Walkthrough: Creating a Windows Service
     Application in the Component Designer

This chapter covers the following Microsoft-specified objective for the "Creating and Managing Microsoft Windows Services, Serviced Components, .NET Remoting Objects, and XML Web Services" section of the "Developing XML Web Services and Server Components with Microsoft Visual C# .NET and the Microsoft .NET Framework" exam:

Create and consume a serviced component.

- **Implement a serviced component.**

- **Create interfaces that are visible to COM.**

- **Create a strongly named assembly.**

- **Register the component in the global assembly cache.**

- **Manage the component by using the Component Services tool.**

▶ COM+ is a part of the Windows operating system that provides various infrastructure-level services to interested applications. These services include automatic transaction management, object pooling, just-in-time activation, queued components, and so on.

.NET components that make use of COM+ component services are called *serviced components*. This exam objective tests your skills on creating and consuming serviced components. Although not explicitly mentioned in the objective list, you should be ready to answer questions on specific COM+ services because the reason for the existence of a serviced component is mainly to use these services.

To use COM+ services, a serviced component must be registered with COM+. One of the requirements for the registration is that the assembly that contains the serviced component must be signed with a strong name. A strong name uniquely identifies the components in an assembly and avoids any identity clash with other components.

CHAPTER 7

Component Services

One of the preferred places to deploy a component that uses COM+ services is the global assembly cache (GAC). The exam objective also requires you to know the process of deploying a component to the GAC.

Windows provides a Component Services administrative tool. System administrators can use this tool to configure the serviced components at runtime. However, a serviced component's methods are not visible to this tool unless the component exposes the required interfaces. The exam objectives require you to know how to expose these interfaces and how to configure a component with the Component Services administrative tool.

▶ Understand the need for component services. Understand the reasons why you would implement some components as serviced components.

▶ Know how to create a serviced component and then register the component in the COM+ Catalog.

▶ Know how to use the Component Services administrative tool to configure the behavior of a serviced component.

▶ Use various COM+ services such as automatic transactions, just-in-time activation, and object pooling in your programs.

▶ Know how to create interfaces in a way that a serviced component's methods are visible to COM.

INTRODUCTION

Large-scale enterprise applications have special requirements: They need to be secure, reliable, available, efficient, and scalable. Of course, programmers can write tons of code and implement these features, but the problem is that they need to do the same for every enterprise application they develop. Reinventing the wheel is undesirable. Nevertheless, that's how the programmers traditionally used to develop enterprise applications on the Windows platform.

This paradigm changed when Microsoft introduced technologies such as Microsoft Transaction Server (MTS), and its improvement, COM+. COM+ incorporates functionality for security, reliability, availability, efficiency, and scalability as part of the operating system infrastructure. As a result, programmers need not write these features repeatedly in each application that they develop. Instead, they can just request the operating system to provide these services to the applications.

This chapter focuses on how to use various COM+ services from your .NET Framework applications. The chapter opens by discussing the evolution of the component services so that you can appreciate where they originated from.

COM+ understands the Component Object Model (COM) but does not understand .NET. However, the .NET Framework provides features by which you can expose a .NET component as a COM component. That's what I discuss next—how to expose a .NET component to COM or COM+.

The next part of the chapter discusses the architecture of component services. I discuss the declarative programming model and discuss how COM+ intercepts the cross-context calls to provide the component services.

I also discuss how to create a .NET component and to deploy, register, and configure a .NET component to use COM+ services.

Finally, I discuss a set of COM+ services such as object construction, object pooling, just-in-time activation, automatic transaction management, and queued components. I offer an insight on how each of these services works and provide systematic tutorials to illustrate how to use these services in your own applications.

EVOLUTION OF COMPONENT SERVICES

Historically, enterprise applications were written as large monolithic programs that ran on powerful but expensive mainframe computers. Over time, with experience developing monolithic applications and with the modern advancements in the personal computer technology, system architects were able to make some observations:

▶ It would be much better to write code as reusable components instead of monolithic tomes. Assembling an application from reusable components would be faster and cheaper because of the time saved in coding and testing.

▶ It would be much better if applications could talk to each other. It would be much more useful to have integrated applications working together than closed applications that could not understand each other.

▶ With the increasing power of personal computers, it would be a good idea to break down the application in multiple layers, each running on one or more personal computers. This way, the complete application could run on a set of inexpensive computers networked with each other, rather than expensive mainframes.

These observations were the foundation of the component-based distributed application development systems that would evolve over the next several years on the Windows platforms. I'll briefly summarize this evolution in the next few sections.

Component Object Model (COM)

COM was one of the first technologies to address component-based development on the Windows platform. COM allows applications to be built from components supplied by different software vendors. In addition to this, COM also defines a binary standard for component interoperability. This ensures that the components written by one developer can interoperate with components written by other developers without requiring users to have any knowledge of the inner workings of a component.

COM became immensely popular for developing enterprise applications. There was soon a large collection of libraries available from third-party software vendors to perform various common tasks. Programmers could now quickly design a large program by assembling various COM components that were readily available.

Many enterprise application developers started developing software that is divided in discrete logical parts called *tiers*. Tiers enable an application to be developed and deployed in modular fashion. Applications that have multiple tiers are commonly known as *n-tier* applications. One of the common approaches to tiered development is the three-tier approach, in which the application is divided into three parts, as shown in Table 7.1.

TABLE 7.1

A TYPICAL 3-TIER APPROACH TO DEVELOPING APPLICATIONS

Tier Name	Implementation Choice
Presentation	Active Server Pages (ASP)
Business Logic	COM components
Data	Database Management Systems (DBMS), such as SQL Server

Programmers prefer to write business logic in COM components instead of ASP and SQL Server stored procedures because the COM components provide better performance and are easy to develop and debug.

COM components that encapsulate business rules and logic to perform a specific task are also called *business objects*. In an enterprise application, several business objects interoperate with each other to perform a business transaction. In an online bookstore, for example, when a customer orders a book, a transaction needs to be performed. This transaction may involve several tasks, such as verifying and charging the customer's credit card, updating the inventory, and shipping the book to the customer. A business object may perform each of these tasks. Sometimes business objects may interoperate with each other while residing on different computers.

However, there is more to enterprise development than just components. As an example, for a successful transaction, all its tasks should succeed. If even one of these tasks fails then it is important to undo all the changes made to the system in its attempt to perform this transaction (also referred to as *rollback* of the transaction). Rollback is important to maintain the integrity of a system. Maintaining the system's integrity becomes increasingly difficult when you have a distributed application where each of these tasks is performed on a different computer.

With lack of any special support from the operating system, many efforts of enterprise developers were spent in writing code to coordinate transactions in each application that they developed. Microsoft realized the need to provide this infrastructure as part of Windows to position Windows as a platform for enterprise applications. The result came in the form of Microsoft Transaction Server (MTS).

Microsoft Transaction Server (MTS)

MTS represented a complete paradigm shift in how programmers looked at the application server. With MTS, the application server does not merely host the components but also provides useful services to them. One of the most important services provided by MTS is automatic transaction management.

To provide the automatic transaction service, MTS coordinates a set of business objects to perform an operation. Each of these objects then votes for the success or failure of the transaction based on the task that it individually performs. If all the business objects vote for the success of the transaction then the system changes are finalized or committed. On the other hand, if any of the business objects votes for a failure, any changes made to the system during the transaction are undone or rolled back and the system is restored to its original state as if nothing had happened.

In addition to transactions, MTS also provides other services such as concurrency management and component-based security.

With MTS providingall these services, the work of an enterprise application developer is simplified. The developer can now focus on writing the business logic instead of developing an application development framework on her own.

> **N O T E**
>
> **ACID Properties**   A well-designed transaction has ACID properties. ACID is an acronym that stands for the following:
>
> - **Atomicity**—Ensures that the entire transaction is either committed or rolled back.
>
> - **Consistency**—Ensures that the system is always left at the correct state in case of the failure or success of a transaction.
>
> - **Isolation**—Ensures data integrity by protecting concurrent transactions from seeing or being adversely affected by each other's partial and uncommitted results.
>
> - **Durability**—Ensures that the system can return to its original state in case of a failure.

The success of MTS encouraged Microsoft to consolidate other common services that an enterprise application developer may need and make them a part of the platform. The result of this initiative came with the launch of Windows 2000 in the form of COM+.

COM+ 1.0 and COM+ 1.5

Microsoft has positioned COM+ as a unified platform for developing component-oriented distributed applications. Although from its name the technology looks more like a new version of COM, COM+ is instead a new version of MTS. It is important to understand this distinction because COM+ is not a new standard for developing components but instead COM+ is a platform that provides application services to the COM components.

The initial release of COM+ (that is, COM+ 1.0), which comes with Windows 2000, upgrades MTS and provides a new set of services in addition to automatic transaction processing. These services include the following:

▶ **Object Pooling**—With object pooling, COM+ creates objects and keeps them in a pool, where they are ready to be used when the next client makes a request. This improves the performance of a server application that hosts the objects that are frequently used but are expensive to create.

▶ **Just-in-Time (JIT) Activation**—The objective of JIT activation is to minimize the amount of time for which an object lives and consumes resources on the server. With JIT activation, the client can hold a reference to an object on the server for a long time, but the server creates the object only when the client calls a method on the object. After the method call is completed, the object is freed and its memory is reclaimed. JIT activation enables applications to scale up as the number of users increases.

▶ **Role-Based Security**—In the role-based security model, access to parts of an application are granted or denied based on the role to which the callers belong. A role defines which members of a Windows domain are allowed to work with what components, methods, or interfaces.

▶ **Queued Components**—The queued components service enables you to create components that can execute asynchronously or in disconnected mode. Queued components ensure availability of a system even when one or more sub-systems are temporarily unavailable. Consider a scenario where salespeople take their laptop computers to the field and enter orders on the go. Because they are in disconnected mode, these orders can be queued up in a message queue. When salespeople connect back to the network, the orders can be retrieved from the message queue and processed by the order processing components on the server.

▶ **Loosely Coupled Events**—Loosely coupled events enable an object (publisher) to publish an event. Other objects (subscribers) can subscribe to an event. COM+ does not require publishers or subscribers to know about each other. Therefore, loosely coupled events greatly simplify the programming model for distributed applications.

Microsoft introduced an update of COM+—COM+ 1.5—with the release of Windows XP. COM+ 1.5 has several enhancements over the COM+ 1.0 features, including the following:

▶ Ability to Run a COM+ Application As a Windows Service— COM+ 1.5 allows you to configure a COM+ application to run as a Windows service. This enables an application to start as soon as Windows starts, rather than wait for an explicit request from the client. Starting an application as a Windows service enables the application to run under the system identity account. This is especially useful if an application needs to have high privilege on a given machine.

▶ Ability to Run a COM+ Application As a Web Service— COM+ 1.5 can expose any COM+ component as an XML Web service as long as the component complies with Web services design guidelines. COM+ installs the Web service with IIS and generates the proper Web service configuration and information files. Doing this involves no extra coding, but you must have IIS running on the Windows XP machine.

NOTE

Key Requirements for an Enterprise Application   The following list describes some of the key requirements that any enterprise application must include:

· **Scalability**—To ensure that an application meets its requirement for efficiency even if the number of users increases.

· **Reliability**—To ensure that the application generates correct and consistent information all the time.

· **Availability**—To ensure that users can depend on using the application when needed.

· **Security**—To ensure that the application's functioning is never disrupted or compromised by the efforts of malicious or ignorant users.

· **Manageability**—To ensure that the deployment and maintenance of the application is as efficient and painless as possible.

COM+ 2.0 (The .NET Framework)

In fact, the .NET Framework, in the initial phase of its development, was known as COM+ 2.0. However, later Microsoft renamed it because the first release of the .NET Framework is actually more of an upgrade of COM than of COM+.

The .NET Framework provides a new approach to creating components that replaces the need for COM. These components execute in a managed execution environment known as the Common Language Runtime (CLR), which provides low-level services such as memory management, versioning, and security to the components. In addition, the .NET Framework also provides a new set of object-oriented libraries that enables programmers to develop applications in a better and faster way.

The task of developing the .NET Framework was so huge in itself that instead of developing a new platform for component services for the .NET Framework, Microsoft relies on COM+. The .NET Framework uses COM+ 1.0 for component services on Windows 2000 and uses COM+ 1.5 for Windows XP and Windows Server 2003.

In the .NET Framework, the `System.EnterpriseServices` namespace contains the types that allow you to use COM+ services in the .NET Framework. These types are collectively known as enterprise services.

EXPOSING .NET COMPONENTS TO COM/COM+

When COM+ was developed, COM was the prevalent component development technology. Therefore COM+ was developed with COM in mind. COM+ recognizes only COM components; any .NET component that is exposed to COM+ must be exposed as a COM component. In this section, you learn how to expose a .NET component as a COM component. After you do that, the .NET components can be used from the COM clients as well as they can make use of the COM+ services.

Calling a .NET Component from COM/COM+

For COM+ (or any COM client) to find a .NET component, you need to register the .NET component as a COM server in the Windows Registry. This process is known as the assembly registration process and it can be performed by any of the following methods:

▶ When using Visual Studio .NET, open the project's property pages and change the Register for COM Interop option to `true`. The Register for COM Interop option is in the Configuration Properties, Build page of the project's Property Pages dialog box.

▶ Use the Assembly Registration tool (`regasm.exe`) that ships as a part of the .NET Framework.

▶ In a program, use the `RegistrationServices` class of the `System.Runtime.InteropServices` namespace.

However, before you use any of these options, you must sign a .NET assembly using the Strong Name tool (`sn.exe`). A strong name provides a unique identification to the assembly and avoids any possible conflicts with other programs. A strong name consists of the assembly's identity (its simple text name, version number, and culture information), a public key, and an optional digital signature.

Additionally you can also assign an assembly and each of its classes with distinct GUID values by using the `Guid` attribute. If you don't assign a GUID, the registration methods mentioned previously will assign one automatically for each element of the assembly (such as the assembly itself and its interfaces and classes). The GUID value is used to create a unique Registry key for the component, as shown in Figure 7.1.

Within each component's registry entry is a key named `InprocServer32`. The value of `InprocServer32` key specifies the path of the DLL that COM uses to create the component by invoking the `CoCreateInstance()` COM method. However, if the DLL is managed code, COM does not know how to load the DLL and create objects. To resolve this problem, the assembly registration process takes a different approach. Rather than store a path to managed code

DLL in the `InprocServer32` key, the assembly registration process stores a path to the `mscoree.dll` file. The `mscoree.dll` is a special file in the .NET Framework that knows how to launch the CLR process and execute a managed DLL.

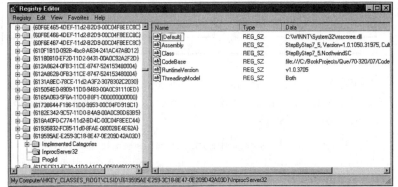

FIGURE 7.1
The assembly registration process creates registry entries that COM uses to instantiate a component.

How does `mscoree.dll` know which managed code DLL to execute? The assembly registration process stores this information for `mscoree.dll` in another registry key named `Assembly` (refer to Figure 7.1). The `Assembly` key store the identity of the managed code DLL but does not store its path. The `mscoree.dll` has the assembly name, but does `mscoree.dll` know where to find the code for this assembly for execution? The `mscoree.dll` instructs the CLR to locate the assembly. One of the first places where the CLR searches for a strongly named assembly is the Global Assembly Cache (GAC). If the CLR cannot find the assembly in the GAC, it tries to locate the assembly in several other places. I have covered the complete process of how the CLR locates an assembly in Chapter 10, "Deployment."

When `mscoree.dll` locates the assembly containing the requested type, it invokes a global method named `DllGetClassObject()` to create an instance of the type. This method also creates a COM Callable Wrapper (CCW) on the fly, based on the type. You can think of the CCW as a proxy to the COM object. CCW enables communication between the calling COM code and the managed code. It also handles any conversion between the data types, as well as other messages between the COM types and the .NET types. Figure 7.2 shows how a .NET component is invoked from COM.

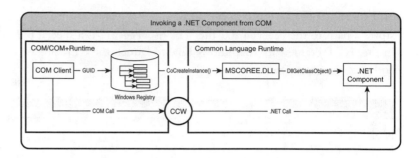

The CCW exposes an `IDispatch` interface that can be used by a
COM client to access methods or properties of a managed object in
the following two steps:

1. The COM client calls the `IDispatch.GetIdsOfName()` COM
   method on the CCW, passing it the name of the member you
   want to access. The method returns a unique dispatch id
   (`DispId`) for the member.

2. The COM client calls the `IDispatch.Invoke()` COM method
   and passes it the `DispId` as an argument. This method provides
   access to the members exposed by an object.

Exporting .NET Components As COM Type Libraries

In the previous section, you saw that the CCW is created on the fly
at runtime. The COM clients use a technique called *late binding* to
access the object. In late binding, resolution of the type references is
delayed until runtime. Although late binding is suitable for interpreted environments such as scripting languages, late binding is slow
and does not support compile-time type checking.

The .NET Framework also enables .NET programmers to export
their components as COM type libraries. A type library is a persistent CCW that makes the .NET types available to the COM
programs at compile time. COM programmers can use the type
information stored inside CCW to compile their programs and take
advantage of early binding to the .NET types. Early binding significantly reduces the time required to access an object and additionally
enables compilers to enforce type checking at compile time.

A .NET type can be exported as a COM type library in any of the following ways:

▶ In Visual Studio .NET, open the project's property pages and change the Register for COM Interop option to `true`. The Register for COM Interop option is in the Configuration Properties, Build page of the project's Property Pages dialog box.

▶ Use the Assembly Registration tool (`regasm.exe`) with its `/tlb` option.

▶ Use the Type Library Exporter tool (`tlbexp.exe`) that ships as a part of .NET Framework SDK.

▶ In a program, use the `ConvertAssemblyToTypeLib()` method of the `TypeLibConverter` class in the `System.Runtime.InteropServices` namespace.

The default extension of a type library is `.tlb`. You can use this library to compile the COM clients.

R E V I E W   B R E A K

▶ Instead of providing a new version of component services, Microsoft .NET Framework relies on the COM+ component services that ship as a part of Windows 2000, Windows XP, and the Windows Server 2003.

▶ COM+ component services provide several features for increasing the security, reliability, availability, efficiency, and scalability of an enterprise application as part of the operating system infrastructure.

▶ COM+ does not understand .NET and therefore cannot directly provide services to the .NET component. Instead, a .NET component must be exposed as a COM component through an assembly registration process.

▶ To enable the communication between COM and .NET components, the .NET Framework generates a COM Callable Wrapper (CCW). The CCW enables communication between the calling COM code and the managed code. It also handles conversion between the data types, as well as other messages between the COM types and the .NET types.

ARCHITECTURE OF COMPONENT SERVICES

In this section, you'll learn about the basic components of the COM+ architecture. You'll learn how a COM+ application is organized, how COM+ provides the component services, and how the .NET Framework interacts with COM+.

Serviced Components

One of the most important classes in the System.EnterpriseServices namespace is the ServicedComponent class. Any class that uses enterprise services must derive from the System.EnterpriseServices.ServicedComponent class. Such a class is also called a *serviced component*. Classes that derive from ServicedComponent must be public and concrete, and must provide a public default constructor. A basic serviced component declaration is as follows:

```
using System.EnterpriseServices;
namespace Exam70320
{
  public class MySampleSC : ServicedComponent
  {
    public MySampleSC() {…}
    ...
  }
}
```

The ServicedComponent class has methods but no properties or events. I have listed the important methods of this class in Table 7.2. All these methods are protected except the DisposeObject() method that is a public static method. You can override the protected methods in a class inherited from the ServicedComponent class.

NOTE

Non-Default Constructors COM can instantiate the .NET classes only with public default constructors via the CoCreateInstance() COM method. There is no way that COM can create an object and pass parameters for object creation at the same time. If you wish to create a .NET object in different ways from a COM client, you need to use the factory pattern (that is, by creating a separate .NET object that has methods to create the required object in different ways). Refer to the section "Creating an Interface Assembly That Works with the Client-Activated Objects" in Chapter 3, ".NET Remoting," for an example on using the factory pattern.

Configured Components You can apply declarative attributes on the serviced components that are configurable at runtime. For this reason, serviced components also can be called configured components.

TABLE 7.2

IMPORTANT METHODS OF THE ServicedComponent CLASS

Method	Description
Activate()	Can be used to perform startup operations. It is called when an object is created or allocated from a pool.
CanBePooled()	Indicates whether the object should be pooled. It is called when an object is to be moved to the pool.
Construct()	Provides access to the construction string of the serviced component. It is called after the serviced component object is created—that is, after the constructor is executed.
Deactivate()	Can be used to perform cleanup operations. It is called when an object is about to be deactivated—that is, destroyed or moved to a pool.
DisposeObject()	Finalizes the resources used by the serviced component and removes the associated COM+ reference.

NOTE

Component Versus Class You'll often find the terms "component" and "class" used apparently interchangeably in this chapter. They refer to the same thing but there is a slight distinction. A class is a unit of development, whereas a component is a unit of deployment. A component may provide features such as versioning and security, which are not of interest to a class.

Declarative Programming Model

Unlike the conventional procedural model, the programming model for enterprise services is mostly declarative. In the procedural model, you write code to accomplish a task, whereas in the declarative model you use declarative tags that instruct the underlying platform to accomplish a task. With a serviced component, the declarative tags specify the services that the component receives, such as transactions, just-in-time activation, object pooling, and so on.

In Visual C# .NET, the declarative tags are specified by attributes. You can place attributes on certain program elements such as an assembly, a class, and methods to specify runtime information. At runtime, the attribute values can be manipulated through a mechanism called *reflection*. After the application is deployed, administrators can use tools such as the Component Services administrative tool to manipulate the attribute values and change the application's behavior without any need to recompile the application.

For example, consider an application that needs to support transactions. In the procedural model, a programmer has to write code to commit or abort a transaction. As opposed to this, in the declarative programming model, programmers can just mark the code with attributes that tell the runtime environment that the code requires transaction support. A simple serviced component that requires transaction support may be defined as shown here:

```
[Transaction(TransactionOption.Required)]
public class MySampleSC : ServicedComponent
{
    ...
}
```

When this code executes, all the necessary details for enabling transactions are done behind the scenes by the runtime environment.

What's really the advantage of declarative programming over the procedural programming? There are many. The three most important advantages are

▶ **Reduced Development Cost**—Development cost is reduced because there is now less code to write and maintain.

▶ **Increased Reliability**—Applications' reliability is increased because it is very likely that the underlying platform would have gone through more testing than an average piece of application code.

▶ **Increased Flexibility**—Declarative code can be read and modified at runtime without any need to recompile the application. Therefore, it is easy to write programs that allow administrators to reconfigure the way an application behaves after it has been deployed.

As you progress through this chapter, you'll use several attributes that specify the runtime requirements for serviced components. I have listed important attributes of the System.EnterpriseServices namespace and their descriptions in Table 7.3.

TABLE 7.3

IMPORTANT ATTRIBUTES OF THE
System.EnterpriseServices NAMESPACE

Attribute	Scope	Description
ApplicationAccessControl	Assembly	Allows you to configure the security of an application hosting the serviced component.
ApplicationActivation	Assembly	Specifies whether the serviced components are activated in the creator's process (ActivationOption. Library, the default value) or in the system's process (ActivationOption. Server).
ApplicationID	Assembly	Specifies the GUID of the COM+ application.
ApplicationName	Assembly	Specifies the name of the COM+ application.
ApplicationQueuing	Assembly	Enables queuing support for the COM+ application.
AutoComplete	Method	Indicates whether the method should automatically notify the COM+ context about its success or failure when it completes.
ComponentAccessControl	Class	Enables security checking when the serviced component is accessed.
COMTIIntrinsics	Class	Allows passing of the context properties from the COM transaction integrator (COMTI) to the COM+ context.
ConstructionEnabled	Class	Allows the component to pass a construction string to enable object construction.
Description	Assembly Class Method Interface	Specifies the description of he assembly, class, method, or interface.

continues

TABLE 7.3   *continued*

IMPORTANT ATTRIBUTES OF THE
System.EnterpriseServices NAMESPACE

Attribute	*Scope*	*Description*
EventClass	Class	Indicates that a class can participate in loosely coupled events.
EventTrackingEnabled	Class	Enables event tracking on the component.
ExceptionClass	Class	Specifies the queuing exception class.
InterfaceQueuing	Class Interface	Enables queuing support on the specified interface or class.
JustInTimeActivation	Class	Indicates whether the serviced component supports just-in-time activation.
LoadBalancingSupported	Class	Indicates whether the serviced component supports load balancing.
MustRunInClientContext	Class	Indicates whether the serviced component must be created in the creator's context.
ObjectPooling	Class	Indicates whether the serviced component will be created in an object pool and configures the size of the pool.
PrivateComponent	Class	Specifies that a serviced component should not be visible and should not be activated outside its containing COM+ application.
SecureMethod	Assembly Class Method	Indicates that the methods of the serviced component should be called through an interface so that the security is applied.
SecurityRole	Assembly Class Interface	Indicates the security role that will have access to the serviced component.

Attribute	Scope	Description
Synchronization	Class	Specifies the synchronization support offered to the serviced component. It controls how multiple threads can execute the methods of the serviced component simultaneously.
Transaction	Class	Specifies the transaction support required by the serviced component.

COM+ Applications

A COM+ application is a group of serviced components that perform related functions. Each of these components further consists of interfaces and methods. A COM+ application is the primary unit of administration and deployment for the serviced components.

A COM+ application is always stored in a DLL file. A DLL file cannot run on its own, so a COM+ application is always configured to run in one of the following two ways:

- ▶ **Server Application**—In a server application, a COM+ application runs in its own process. To enable this, COM+ provides a surrogate process (`dllhost.exe`) that hosts the DLL file for the COM+ application.

- ▶ **Library Application**—In a library application, the COM+ application runs in the process of the client that creates it. To enable this, the components in a library application are always loaded into the process of the creator.

Now that you have two types of applications, you'll have to choose between them. Table 7.4 helps you make this decision based on various parameters.

TABLE 7.4

CHOOSING BETWEEN A SERVER AND LIBRARY APPLICATION

Parameter	*Server Application*	*Library Application*
Performance	Low, because communication between the objects involves marshaling across the processes or computer.	High, because the objects are locally available to the client programs and no marshaling is required.
Fault-tolerance	High, because any unhandled exception in the application affects only the `dllhost.exe` process that is hosting the application. A server application is therefore especially useful when you have any components that use unmanaged or unsafe code.	Low, because any unhandled exception in the application affects the client program that hosts the serviced component.
Security	High, because server applications can be more tightly secured, and you therefore can explicitly configure the process-wide security settings.	Low, because the components rely on security settings of the client process that hosts the serviced component.
Support for component services	High, because all COM+ component services are supported when a COM+ application runs as a server application.	Low, because services such as object pooling and queued components are not supported.

EXAM TIP

Server Application Versus Library Application   You should know the merits and drawbacks of configuring a COM+ application to run as a server application or as a library application. Use the information in Table 7.4 to make the decision.

COM+ Catalog

The COM+ Catalog stores the information about the COM+ applications. Each COM+ application and serviced component is uniquely identified in the COM+ Catalog by a globally unique identifier (GUID).

The other important information stored in the COM+ Catalog for a serviced component is its runtime requirements. For example, if a component requires a transaction, this information is stored in the COM+ Catalog. Later, when the component is activated, COM+ services use the catalog to determine the runtime requirements of components.

The COM+ Catalog itself is physically split between the following locations:

▶ COM+ Registration Database (`RegDB`), which is stored in the `Registration` directory of the Windows installation (such as `c:\windows\registration`).

▶ Windows Registry within a key named `HKEY_CLASSES_ROOT`.

However, you can access and update the catalog in an integrated way by using the Component Services administrative tool. This tool is available in the Administrative Tools section of the Windows Control Panel. This tool allows administrators to make changes to the installed COM+ application via a user interface as shown in Figure 7.3. Any changes made through the Component Services administrative tool are stored in the COM+ Catalog. You can also read or update the catalog through programs as described in the section "Registering the Serviced Component into the COM+ Catalog," later in this chapter.

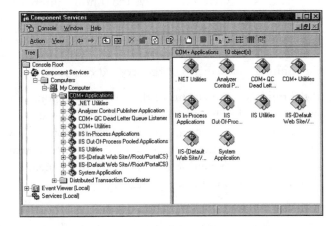

FIGURE 7.3
The Component Services administrative tool enables you to manage and configure COM+ applications.

Serviced Component Activation

At this point, you have a reasonably clear idea about how a serviced component is configured for development and deployment. What remains to be seen is how the .NET Framework and COM+ work together to activate a serviced component and enforce the configured semantics at runtime.

Activation of a serviced component can be summarized in the following steps:

1. When a client component (such as ComponentA as shown in Figure 7.4) creates a new instance of a serviced component (such as, ComponentB), the .NET enterprise services use the COM-based `CoCreateInstance()` COM method to request COM+ to instantiate the serviced component. The .NET enterprise services pass a GUID of the serviced component to the `CoCreateInstance()` COM method.

FIGURE 7.4

Components with similar runtime requirements may exist in a similar context.

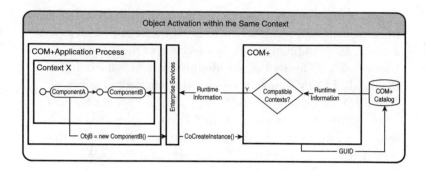

2. COM+ uses the GUID to retrieve the runtime information of a serviced component from the COM+ Catalog. COM+ then checks to see whether the client component is running in the same context (that is, an environment that is compatible with the runtime requirements of the serviced component).

3. If the runtime requirements of the serviced component match with those of the client component, then the new object is created in the same context as the client component, as shown in Figure 7.4. A reference to the newly created object is returned to the client component so that the client component can make direct calls on the newly created object.

4. If the runtime requirements of the serviced component are not compatible with that of the client component, COM+ creates a new context that matches the client's runtime requirements and creates the serviced component in that environment as shown in Figure 7.5. The COM+ component services then create a proxy and return the proxy to the client component.

FIGURE 7.5

Components with different runtime requirements exist in different contexts and communicate through a proxy.

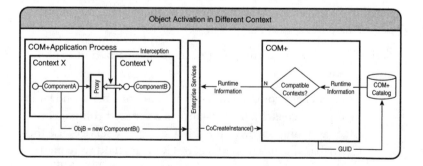

5. When the objects are in different context, they communicate with each other by using a proxy. In case of cross-context calls, the proxy uses a mechanism known as interception that enables the proxy to do some pre-processing and post-processing for each object and method invocation to ensure that the correct runtime policies are applied when a method call proceeds from one context to another.

The concept of context and interception is the key to understanding the activation process.

Context

A *context* is a set of runtime properties that defines the execution environment for a serviced component. A context is created during the activation process for a serviced component based on how the serviced component is configured.

COM+ uses context to group the like-minded objects while separating the incompatible objects. Objects having the same runtime requirements share a context (refer to Figure 7.4), whereas those having incompatible runtime requirements must reside in different contexts, as shown earlier in Figure 7.5.

An object can access its context-specific properties by using the `ContextUtil` class of the `System.EnterpriseServices` namespace. The `ContextUtil` class provides static methods and properties as listed in Table 7.5. You will use several of these properties throughout this chapter.

TABLE 7.5

IMPORTANT MEMBERS OF THE ContextUtil CLASS

Member	Type	Description
DeactivateOnReturn	Property	Indicates whether the object should be deactivated when the object's method returns.
DisableCommit()	Method	Indicates the COM+ context to vote for aborting the current transaction. This method does not deactivate the object when the object's method returns.

continues

TABLE 7.5 *continued*

IMPORTANT MEMBERS OF THE ContextUtil CLASS

Member	Type	Description
EnableCommit()	Method	Indicates the COM+ context to vote for committing the current transaction. This method does not deactivate the object when the object's method returns.
IsCallerInRole()	Method	Determines whether the caller is in a specified role.
IsInTransactional	Property	Indicates whether the current COM+ context is transactional.
IsSecurityEnabled	Property	Indicates whether the current COM+ context has role-based security enabled.
MyTransactionVote	Property	Specifies the COM+ context transaction vote—abort or commit.
Transaction	Property	Represents the current COM+ transaction object.
SetAbort()	Method	Indicates the COM+ context to vote for aborting the current transaction. This method also deactivates the object when the object's method returns.
SetComplete()	Method	Indicates the COM+ context to vote for committing the current transaction. This method also deactivates the object when the object's method returns.

Interception

Interception is a mechanism that allows COM+ to capture calls to any object and execute its own code before passing the call to the object. For example, a component in the COM+ Catalog may specify that only users authenticated with the Supervisors security role are allowed to call a method named ApproveOrder(). In this case, COM+ intercepts the call to the ApproveOrder() method and forwards or rejects the call to the object based on the identity of the user.

When two objects are in the same context, no interception is required because the objects have the same runtime requirements.

However, when the objects reside in different contexts, it is important to ensure that appropriate runtime requirements for individual contexts are satisfied. Therefore, the objects in a different context use a proxy to communicate rather than make direct calls to each other. The proxy uses interception to ensure that the runtime requirements are met. Interception is available at two levels:

▶ Object level—This level of interception allows the proxy to perform pre-processing and post-processing operations when an object is created and destroyed. This level of interception is helpful in providing object-level services such as object construction and object pooling.

▶ Method level—This level of interception allows the proxy to perform pre-processing and post-processing operations when a method is invoked on an object. This level of interception is useful in providing method-level services such as just-in-time activation and transactions.

REVIEW BREAK

▶ Classes that should use COM+ component services must derive from the `System.EnterpriseServices.ServicedComponent` class.

▶ To use the COM+ services in your program, you need not write a lot of code. Instead, you use declarative attributes to specify whether a class should receive particular services.

▶ The declarative attributes applied to a class are stored in the COM+ Catalog as part of the assembly registration process. At runtime, COM+ can read the COM+ Catalog to determine what services a component should receive and to provide those services.

▶ COM+ uses interception to provide various runtime services. Interception is a mechanism that allows COM+ to capture calls to any object and execute its own code before passing the call to the object.

▶ COM+ creates different contexts for the objects that have different runtime requirements. A proxy is used to provide interception services between the objects in different contexts.

CREATING AND CONSUMING A SERVICED COMPONENT

From the discussion in the previous sections, you know that it is easy to create a serviced component—all you need to do is to inherit from the ServicedComponent class and apply attributes to use various COM+ component services. However, to use the COM+ component services, the component must be registered into the COM+ Catalog. The following list summarizes the typical steps involved in creating and registering a serviced component.

1. Create a class that inherits from the ServicedComponent class.

2. Compile the class by assigning a strong name to create a strongly named assembly.

3. Run the .NET Services Installation tool (regsvcs.exe) to install the assembly into the COM+ Catalog.

After you have installed the serviced component in the COM+ Catalog, the component can be used by

▶ Application Programs—To create instances of the serviced components and execute methods on them.

▶ System Administrators—To use the Component Services administrative tool to configure various attributes of the serviced component.

In the following sub-sections, you will walk through the complete process of creating and consuming serviced components.

Creating a Serviced Component

In this section, you will learn how to create a simple serviced component. You will also learn how to set various assembly-level attributes to specify the COM+ application name, description, and activation type, as shown in Step-by-Step 7.1.

STEP BY STEP

7.1 Creating a Serviced Component

1. Launch Visual Studio .NET. Select File, New, Blank Solution, and name the new solution `320C07`. Click OK.

2. Add a new Visual C# .NET class library named `StepByStep7_1` to the solution.

3. In the Solution Explorer, right-click project `StepByStep7_1` and select Add Reference from the context menu. In the .NET tab of the Add Reference dialog box, select the `System.EnterpriseServices` component from the list view and click the Select button. Click OK to add the reference.

4. In the Solution Explorer, rename the default `Class1.cs` to `NorthwindSC.cs`.

5. Open `NorthwindSC.cs` and replace the code with the following code:

```
using System;

using System.Data;
using System.Data.SqlClient;
using System.EnterpriseServices;

namespace StepByStep7_1
{
    public class NorthwindSC : ServicedComponent
    {
        private SqlConnection sqlcnn;
        private SqlDataAdapter sqlda;
        private DataSet ds;

        public NorthwindSC()
        {
            // Create a connection to the
            // Northwind SQL Server database
            sqlcnn = new SqlConnection(
                "data source=(local);" +
                "initial catalog=Northwind;" +
                "integrated security=SSPI");
        }

        // This method executes a SELECT query and
        // returns the results in a DataSet object
```

continues

continued

```
public DataSet ExecuteQuery(string strQuery)
{
    // Create a SqlDataAdapter object to
    // talk to the database
    sqlda =
        new SqlDataAdapter(strQuery, sqlcnn);

    // Create a DataSet object
    // to hold the results
    ds = new DataSet();

    // Fill the DataSet object
    sqlda.Fill(ds, "Results");

    return ds;
}

// This method updates the database with
// the changes in a DataSet object
public int UpdateData(DataSet ds)
{
    // Update the database
    // and return the result
    SqlCommandBuilder sqlcb =
        new SqlCommandBuilder(sqlda);
    return sqlda.Update(ds.Tables["Results"]);
}
    }
}
```

6. Open the `AssemblyInfo.cs` file in the project and add the following using directive:

```
using System.EnterpriseServices;
```

7. Add assembly-level attributes `ApplicationName`, `Description`, and `ApplicationActivation` to `AssemblyInfo.cs` as follows:

```
[assembly: ApplicationName(
    "Northwind Data Application")]
[assembly: Description("Retrieve and Update data " +
    "from the Northwind database")]
[assembly: ApplicationActivation(
    ActivationOption.Library)]
```

8. Select Build, Build `StepByStep7_1`. This step packages the serviced component into the file `StepByStep7_1.dll`, which is located in the `bin\Debug` or `bin\Release` directory of your project. You can navigate to it through the Solution Explorer: Just select the project and click the Show All Files button in the Solution Explorer toolbar.

Step-by-Step 7.1 defines a class NorthwindSC that is a serviced component because the class derives from the ServicedComponent class. Using an assembly level attribute, I have also specified that the NorthwindSC serviced component should be activated in Library mode. The Library activation mode is the default; I have used it anyway to be explicit.

Recall from the previous sections that a serviced component must reside in a class library (DLL file). Therefore, I chose to create a class library project in Step-by-Step 7.1. A class library project can contain multiple class files, so Visual Studio .NET uses a separate file named AssemblyInfo.cs to store assembly-level attributes. You can, though, if you wish, write the assembly-level attributes directly in the class file.

Creating a Strongly Named Assembly

Every serviced component must be signed with a strong name before it can be registered into the COM+ Catalog. A strong name guarantees a unique identity for an assembly by relying on a pair of keys: a public key and a private key.

The Strong Name tool (sn.exe) that comes as a part of the .NET Framework SDK can be used to create a strong name. In Step-by-Step 7.2, you first create a strong name and then modify the program in Step-by-Step 7.1 to associate the strong name with the assembly StepByStep7_1.dll. StepByStep7_1.dll needs to be regenerated because an already created assembly cannot be signed with a strong name. Signing with the strong name must be a part of the assembly creation process.

STEP BY STEP

7.2 Creating a Strongly Named Assembly

1. From the Visual Studio .NET program group in the Windows Start menu, launch the Visual Studio .NET command prompt.

continues

continued

2. Change the directory to the folder where the `320C07` solution resides and issue the following command to create a pair of public/private keys (see Figure 7.6):

```
sn -k 70320.snk
```

FIGURE 7.6
You can create a public/private key pair by using the Strong Name tool.

Both the public and private keys are created and stored in a file named `70320.snk`.

3. Open the `AssemblyInfo.cs` file of the `StepByStep7_1` project. Scroll down in the file and change the `AssemblyKeyFile` attribute as follows:

```
[assembly: AssemblyKeyFile(@"..\..\..\70320.snk")]
```

4. Build the project. A `StepByStep7_1.dll` is generated, and a strong name is assigned to the file based on the specified key file.

> **WARNING**
>
> **Protecting Your Identity**   When you start using a strong name key file to sign your components, the key pair stored in the strong name key files uniquely identifies your components from the components written by other vendors. Anyone who has access to the key pair can potentially sign malicious code on your behalf. To protect their identities, most software development teams use a slightly different process for signing an assembly. This process is called *delay signing*, a technique that I discuss in detail, along with strong names, in Chapter 10.

This key file created in Step-by-Step 7.2 is also called a strong name key file. You will be reusing the key pair generated in Step-by-Step 7.2 to sign assemblies in many of the examples in this book.

Registering the Serviced Component into the COM+ Catalog

A serviced component must be registered into the COM+ Catalog to use any of the COM+ component services. A serviced component must be signed with a strong name before it may be registered. The registration process involves retrieving all the necessary runtime information from the class library and copying it to the COM+ Catalog. The runtime information is mostly specified in the form of attributes that are applied at the assembly level, class level, and on the method level in the class library.

Remember that the COM+ Catalog came before managed code; therefore any managed component must appear as a COM component before it can be registered in the COM+ Catalog. The .NET Framework Class Libraries (FCL) provide the `System.EnterpriseServices.RegistrationHelper` class to simplify the registration process. The `RegistrationHelper.InstallAssembly()` method performs the following steps to register a serviced component in the COM+ Catalog:

1. Use the `RegistrationServices.RegisterAssembly()` method to register the assembly in the Registry. All classes in the assembly therefore appear as COM components in the Registry.

2. Generate a COM type library (a TLB file) from the assembly using the `TypeLibConverter.ConvertAssemblyToTypeLib()` method.

3. Register the type library by using the COM `LoadTypeLibrary()` method.

4. Use the COM+ admin API to configure a COM+ Catalog based on the information stored in the type library.

Using the `RegistrationHelper` class requires you to write a program for registering the serviced components. Alternatively, the .NET Framework provides two other methods for registering a component that do not require writing any registration code. Both of these methods, however, use the `RegistrationHelper` class internally:

▶ Dynamic or Lazy Registration—In dynamic registration, the registration of a serviced component is delayed until the component is first used. When a client application attempts to create an instance of a serviced component for the first time, the CLR registers the assembly and the type library and configures the COM+ Catalog. Dynamic registration occurs only once for a particular version of an assembly.

▶ Manual Registration—The .NET Framework provides the .NET Services Installation tool (`regsvcs.exe`) to manually install a serviced component from the command line.

Table 7.6 compares the advantages and disadvantages of the dynamic and manual registration process.

<table>
<tr><td>N O T E</td><td>**Administrative Access Is Required for Registration** Installing a component to the COM+ Catalog requires a user or an application to have administrative privileges.</td></tr>
</table>

TABLE 7.6

ADVANTAGES AND DISADVANTAGES OF DYNAMIC AND MANUAL REGISTRATION

	Dynamic Registration	*Manual Registration*
Advantages	1. Dynamic registration allows applications to register components on the go. This may be especially helpful in the case of Web applications.	1. Manual registration is the only way for registering the Assemblies, which are placed in the GAC. 2. Manual registration enables the serviced components to be called by COM clients, in addition to the .NET clients.
Disadvantages	1. The registration process requires administrative privileges and sometimes the first user of the component or the Web application may not have those privileges. 2. Assemblies placed in the GAC cannot be dynamically registered. 3. If there is any error during the registration process, it is revealed only when the first client attempts to access the component.	1. Requires an additional registration step.

Step-by-Step 7.3 shows how to register a serviced component manually by using the .NET Services Installation tool (regsvcs.exe).

STEP BY STEP

7.3 Installing a Serviced Component in the COM+ Catalog

1. From the Visual Studio .NET program group in the Windows Start menu, launch the Visual Studio .NET command prompt.

2. Change the directory to the folder where the StepByStep7_1.dll file resides in the StepByStep7_1 project—in this case, the project's bin\Debug directory.

3. Issue the following command to install the service component assembly to the COM+ Catalog (see Figure 7.7):

```
regsvcs StepByStep7_1.dll
```

FIGURE 7.7
You can add a serviced component to the COM+ Catalog by using regsvcs.exe.

At this stage, the serviced component created in Step-by-Step 7.1 is installed in the COM+ Catalog and can be instantiated by the client programs or can be administered through the Component Services administrative tool.

Using the Component Services Administrative Tool to Manage Components

After an application is registered into the COM+ Catalog, the application can be configured easily by the system administrators using the Component Services administrative tool. In Step-by-Step 7.4, you will learn how to use this tool to configure COM+ applications.

STEP BY STEP

7.4 Managing the Serviced Component by Using the Component Services Administrative Tool

1. Open the Component Services administrative tool from the Administrative Tools section of Windows Control Panel. Using the tree on the left side, navigate to Computers, My Computer, COM+ Applications. You should be able to view the Northwind Data Application, which was added to the COM+ Catalog in Step-by-Step 7.3, as shown in Figure 7.8.

2. Right-click on the Northwind Data Application and select Properties from the context menu. This opens the Northwind Data Application Properties dialog box, as shown in Figure 7.9. Notice the Application ID that is automatically assigned to the Northwind Data Application. Browse through all the tabs to get an idea of the properties that can be managed with the Components Services administrative tool.

continues

continued

FIGURE 7.8
You can manage a serviced component application by using the Component Services administrative tool.

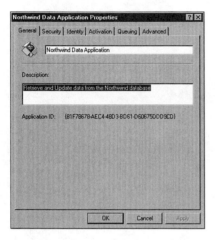

FIGURE 7.9
You can manage the properties of a COM+ application via its Properties dialog box.

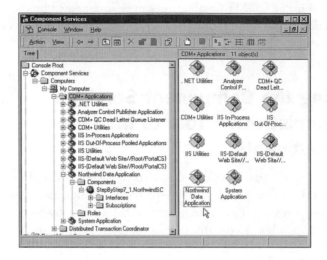

3. Click the Activation tab to view the activation option. Notice that the Library option is selected. This activation option, the name, and the description of the application were assigned by the attributes added to the AssemblyInfo.cs file in the StepByStep7_1 project.

4. Expand the Northwind Data Application node in the left pane and select the Components node to view the serviced components in the Northwind Data Application. In this case, you should find the StepByStep7_1.NorthwindSC serviced component.

5. Right-click the StepByStep7_1.NorthwindSC serviced component and select Properties from the context menu. This opens the serviced component's Properties dialog box, as shown in Figure 7.10. Notice the CLSID (Class Identifier) that is automatically assigned to the StepByStep7_1.NorthwindSC serviced component. Browse through all the tabs to get an idea of the properties that can be managed with the Components Services administrative tool.

6. Expand the StepByStep7_1.NorthwindSC node in the left pane to drill down into the list of interfaces as shown in Figure 7.11. Note that although you have not defined any interface in the C# program, there is an interface added to

FIGURE 7.10
You can manage the properties of a serviced component via its Properties dialog box.

the component. The name of the interface is the name of
the component preceded with an underscore. Expand the
methods node under this interface. You won't find any
methods listed there. Even if you explore all the interfaces,
you will not find any of the two methods that you defined
in the C# program for this component (refer to Step-by-
Step 7.1).

In Step-by-Step 7.4, you see various options for configuring a
COM+ application and the serviced components. At this time, you
may not have a good idea about what each of these options means
and how to configure them. Later in this chapter, when I discuss
individual COM+ services, I will return to the relevant property
pages and explain them in detail.

Configuration also can be performed at the level of methods.
However, the methods of a serviced component are not directly
accessible to the Component Services administrative tool. I discuss
in the next section what you need to do to make the methods of a
serviced component visible to the Component Services administrative tool as well as other COM applications.

Creating Interfaces That Are Visible to COM/COM+

COM clients and COM+ services communicate with the .NET
components by using the interfaces provided by the .NET component. The COM Callable Wrapper (CCW) automatically generates
these interfaces for a .NET class based on the setting of the
`ClassInterface` and the `InterfaceType` attributes of the
`System.Runtime.InteropServices` namespace. Additionally, you can
write an interface explicitly and inherit the .NET class from that
interface. These interfaces do not affect how a managed client calls
another managed component (or a serviced component), but they
surely affect how the COM programs (or COM+) interact with the
managed components. I discuss both of these attributes in this section.

FIGURE 7.11
A default interface is created for the serviced
component, but no methods of the serviced
components have been exposed.

The `ClassInterface` Attribute

The `ClassInterface` attribute specifies how the interfaces will be generated for a class (if they will be generated at all). This attribute can be applied either to a class or to an assembly. If you apply this attribute to an assembly, the attribute applies to all the classes in that assembly.

The `ClassInterface` attribute can be set with any of the three values specified by the `ClassInterfaceType` enumeration as shown in Table 7.7.

TABLE 7.7

MEMBERS OF THE `ClassInterfaceType` ENUMERATION

Member name	Description
AutoDispatch	This is the default setting for the `ClassInterface` attribute. This setting automatically generates a dispatch-only interface for the class, which means that the class supports only late binding for COM clients. When using this setting, no type information is published to the COM type libraries.
AutoDual	This setting is called AutoDual for two reasons. First, it automatically creates an interface that exposes all the public members of a class (such as methods, properties, fields, and events) and the public methods, properties, and fields of the base classes. Second, this setting generates dual interfaces. This means the COM client can use these interfaces for both late binding as well as early binding. When using this setting, all the type information is produced for the class interface and published in the type library. This is not a recommended setting and creates versioning problems.
None	This setting does not generate any automatic interfaces. In this case, you need to explicitly write the interface for your class. This is the recommended setting for the `ClassInterface` attribute.

Step-by-Step 7.5 shows how to use these attributes to generate different types of interfaces for a serviced component.

STEP BY STEP

7.5 Creating Interfaces That Are Visible to COM

1. Add a new C# class library project to solution 320C07. Name the project StepByStep7_5.

2. In the Solution Explorer, right-click project StepByStep7_5 and select Add Reference from the context menu to add a reference to the System.EnterpriseServices library.

3. In the Solution Explorer, copy the NorthwindSC.cs file from the StepByStep7_1 project to the current project. Open the file and change the namespace name to StepByStep7_5. Delete the default Class1.cs.

4. Add the following using directive to NorthwindSC.cs:

```
using System.Runtime.InteropServices;
```

5. Apply the following attribute to the NorthwindSC class:

```
[ClassInterface(ClassInterfaceType.AutoDual)]
public class NorthwindSC : ServicedComponent
{
    ...
}
```

6. Open the AssemblyInfo.cs file in the project and add the following using directive:

```
using System.EnterpriseServices;
```

7. Add assembly-level attributes ApplicationName, Description, and ApplicationActivation to AssemblyInfo.cs as follows:

```
[assembly: ApplicationName(
    "Northwind Data Application with Interfaces")]
[assembly: Description("Retrieve and Update data " +
    "from the Northwind database")]
[assembly: AssemblyKeyFile(@"..\..\..\70320.snk")]
```

Note that you are using the key file, 70320.snk, already created in Step-by-Step 7.2. If you haven't created one before, create it now by following step 2 of Step-by-Step 7.2.

continues

continued

8. Select Build, Build `StepByStep7_5`. This step packages the serviced component into the file `StepByStep7_5.dll`, which is located in the `bin\Debug` or `bin\Release` directory of your project.

9. Register `StepByStep7_5.dll` into the COM+ Catalog by using the .NET Services Installation tool:

```
regsvcs StepByStep7_5.dll
```

10. Open the Component Services administrative tool (or click on the Refresh toolbar icon if the tool is already open). You see an icon labeled Northwind Data Application with Interfaces. Double-click on the icon and use the tree view on the left to drill down to the interfaces of the NorthwindSC component of this application. Expand the _NorthwindSC interface to see its methods. Select the Methods node in the left pane and then select View, Detail from the menu. You see a list of methods as shown in Figure 7.12.

FIGURE 7.12

The `ClassInterfaceType.AutoDual` setting automatically generates the class interface for a class.

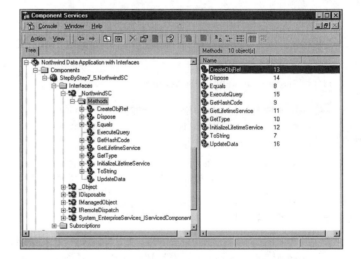

11. Right-click on the `ExecuteQuery()` method and select properties from the shortcut menu. The property sheet enables you to configure a method by means such as changing its description, as shown in Figure 7.13.

12. Switch back to Visual Studio .NET and open the `NorthwindSC.cs` file. Insert the following interface just before the class definition:

```
public interface INorthwind
{
    DataSet ExecuteQuery(string strQuery);
    int UpdateData(DataSet ds);
}
```

13. Modify the definition of `NorthwindSC` class and the `ClassInterface` attribute as follows:

```
[ClassInterface(ClassInterfaceType.None)]
public class NorthwindSC :
    ServicedComponent, INorthwind
{
    ...
}
```

14. Select Build, Build `StepByStep7_5`. Use the .NET Services Installation tool to register `StepByStep7_5.dll` into the COM+ Catalog:

```
regsvcs StepByStep7_5.dll
```

15. Open the Component Services administrative tool. Navigate to the Components node of the Northwind Data Application with Interfaces application. You now see a second instance of the `NorthwindSC` component. Expand the second instance of the component to see its interfaces and methods. You see that instead of the default interface `NorthwindSC`, the component now has the `INorthwind` interface with only the method that the serviced component implements and does not contain methods of its base classes (see Figure 7.14).

continues

FIGURE 7.13
You can configure a method by using its Properties dialog box.

continued

FIGURE 7.14
When ClassInterfaceType is set to None, you get only the interfaces, which you explicitly implement.

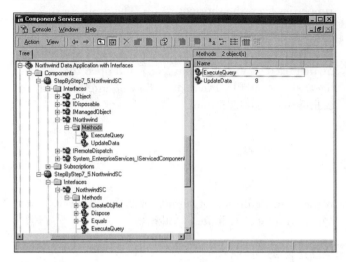

In Step-by-Step 7.5, I demonstrated how to use the ClassInterface attribute with ClassInterfaceType set to AutoDual or None. You already know how the AutoDispatch option works because that's the default one. If you don't apply the ClassInterface attribute at all, then in fact the ClassInterface attribute is implicitly applied with ClassInterfaceType set to AutoDispatch.

From Step-by-Step 7.4 and Step-by-Step 7.5, you also note that with both the AutoDispatch and AutoDual settings, an interface is automatically generated. The name of the automatic interface is the name of the class preceded by an underscore. For example, the class NorthwindSC has the interface _NorthwindSC. However, when you set the ClassInterfaceType to None no automatic interfaces are generated. Therefore, information about interfaces and methods are written to the COM+ Catalog only if you explicitly define and then implement an interface.

Versioning Problems and the ClassInterface Attribute

You can see from Step-by-Step 7.5 that the AutoDual setting of the ClassInterface exports the type information and DispId of the class and base class members to the COM type library. This enables COM clients to bind their programs with the `DispId` of the members at compile time.

The `DispIds` are generated based on the position of the member in the class. This causes a versioning problem because if in the next version of your component you change the order of the members and export the class to a COM type library, the `DispId` of the members will be changed. This will cause already compiled COM programs to fail. Because of this versioning issue, even if the `AutoDual` setting of the class interface looks flexible, it is not a recommended option.

The `AutoDispatch` setting, on the other hand, does not export the type information and `DispId`. Therefore, clients cannot bind to a particular `DispId` at compile time and no problems occur when the order of methods is changed in next version. Because of its late binding support, however, use of `AutoDispatch` is limited to only scripted or interpreted execution environments.

The last option, the `None` setting, prevents any automatic interface generation in the COM type library. If you want any interfaces to be written to the COM type library, you must explicitly define them. In this case, you get the benefit of both early binding and late binding. However, writing your own interface separates the view of a class from its implementation. Even if you decide to change the order of the methods in your implementation in the future, you are fine unless you modify the interface definition.

To summarize, the best practice is to mark the class with the `ClassInterface` attribute set to the `ClassInterfaceType.None` value and create your own interface explicitly. I will use this technique in the rest of the examples in this chapter.

The `InterfaceType` Attribute

The `InterfaceType` attribute can be applied to the interfaces that you declare. You can use this attribute to configure how the interfaces are exposed to the COM clients. The `InterfaceType` attribute can be set with any of the three values specified by the `ComInterfaceType` enumeration, as shown in Table 7.8.

NOTE

Configuring COM Visibility By default, all public members in your programs are visible to COM. You may sometimes want to hide certain elements from COM. You can mark those elements by setting the `Value` property of the `ComVisible` attribute to `false`. The hidden members are not included in the COM type library and the CCW rejects all requests to hidden elements from a COM client.

The `ComVisible` attribute can be set up in a hierarchy. That is, if you apply this attribute to an assembly and set its value to `false`, all the classes and members in the assembly are hidden from COM. However, if any of the classes in the assembly overrides the `ComVisible` attribute by setting its value to `true`, then that class will be visible to COM clients.

COM+ Partitions A COM+ partition is a logical container that allows multiple versions of COM+ applications to exist on a single computer. By default, all applications are installed in a partition named the Global Partition. However, administrators can define additional partitions to install the same or different versions of the application. Applications installed in different partitions can be configured and managed independent of each other. For more information on COM+ partitions, refer to the COM+ Platform SDK documentation in the MSDN Library (`msdn.microsoft.com/library`).

TABLE 7.8

MEMBERS OF THE `ComInterfaceType` ENUMERATION

Enumerators	Description
`InterfaceIsDual`	This is the default setting for an interface. This value specifies that the interface should be exposed to COM as a dual interface. This allows the COM client to get both a late-binding as well as an early-binding facility.
`InterfaceIsIDispatch`	This value specifies that the interface should be exposed to COM as a dispatch-only interface—that is, one supporting just the late binding.
`InterfaceIsIUnknown`	This value specifies that the interface should be exposed to COM as an `IUnknown`-derived interface.

In most cases, you should leave the value of the `InterfaceType` attribute unchanged.

Component Identification

COM+ uses GUIDs to uniquely identify each COM+ application and its components. If you don't use GUIDs to identify the COM+ application and components, the assembly registration process assigns them automatically.

Each assembly is registered as a separate COM+ application; you can use the assembly-level `ApplicationID` attribute to specify a GUID for the COM+ application. However, in most cases you may not want to specify a fixed `ApplicationID` because doing so prevents COM+ partitioning.

Each component in an assembly can be uniquely identified by applying the `Guid` attribute, as in the following code:

```
[Guid("0F1FD944-ADDC-4d34-A4D0-90F9AA707930")]
public class NorthwindSC : ServicedComponent,
                           INorthwind
{
  . . .
}
```

You pass a GUID to the constructor of the `Guid` attribute. You can generate a GUID by using the command-line GUID generation tool (`guidgen.exe`) or through the Tools, Create GUID menu option in Visual Studio .NET.

In Step-by-Step 7.5, you did not hardcode any GUID for the components; as a result, a GUID was automatically generated for the component by the registration process each time a different version of the component was registered into the COM+ Catalog.

When you are developing, you may need to register the component several times in the COM+ Catalog. In that case, unless you hardcode a GUID for the component, you end up registering multiple versions of the same component, each with a different GUID, in the COM+ Catalog.

Now when you use the Component Services administrative tool, you see multiple instances of a component in the COM+ application. It's hard to determine which component you need to configure. A good idea in this case is to hardcode each component with a GUID rather than depend on the automatically generated GUID.

Installing the Component in the Global Assembly Cache

Before the client programs can invoke methods on a serviced component, the serviced component must be installed at a location where the client programs can reliably locate it. Serviced components are usually shared by several applications on a computer; therefore, a common practice is to install a serviced component in the Global Assembly Cache (GAC). The GAC is a machine-wide central repository for storing shared components.

Installing the assembly in the GAC is not a requirement for using a serviced component. In fact, an application that uses the serviced component will work correctly as long as the CLR can load the corresponding assembly.

Installing the serviced component assembly in the GAC is the most recommended option when you deploy an application because it ensures that the CLR can always locate an assembly. To learn more about the GAC and how the CLR locates assemblies, refer to Chapter 10.

NOTE

Benefits of Installing a Component in the GAC   Apart from acting as a central repository for storing shared components, the GAC provides several other benefits, such as side-by-side versioning and file security. You will learn more about the GAC and its features in Chapter 10.

EXAM TIP

Strong Name Required for Installing a Component to the GAC   An assembly must be signed with a strong name before the assembly can be installed in the GAC.

> **NOTE**
>
> **Installing a Serviced Component for Use by Web Forms**   ASP.NET uses a technique called *shadow copy* to eliminate the need to stop a running Web application whenever any components of that application need to be updated or replaced. To participate in the shadow copy process, a component must be deployed in the bin directory of the virtual root of a Web application, instead of the GAC.

In Step-by-Step 7.6, you learn how to use the Global Assembly Cache tool (gacutil.exe) to install an assembly to the GAC and how to view the contents of the GAC.

STEP BY STEP

7.6 Installing a Serviced Component in the GAC by Using the Global Assembly Cache Tool (gacutil.exe)

1. From the Visual Studio .NET program group in the Windows Start menu, launch the Visual Studio .NET command prompt.

2. Change the directory to the folder where the StepByStep7_5.dll file resides in the StepByStep7_5 project—in this case, the project's bin\Debug directory.

3. Issue the following command to install the assembly to the GAC (see Figure 7.15):

```
gacutil /i StepByStep7_5.dll
```

4. Open Windows Explorer. Navigate to the assembly cache folder, which is the assembly folder in your windows installation folder, such as c:\WINNT\assembly or C:\Windows\assembly. Verify that the serviced component is added to the GAC, as shown in Figure 7.16.

FIGURE 7.15
You can add an assembly to the GAC by using the gacutil.exe.

Step-by-Step 7.6 uses the Global Assembly Cache tool to deploy an assembly to the GAC. This tool comes as a part of the .NET Framework SDK.

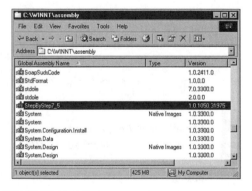

FIGURE 7.16
You can view the assemblies in the GAC by using Windows Explorer.

Internally, GAC is maintained as a bunch of directories nested within each other. To be able to view the contents of the GAC in an easily readable way, the .NET Framework installs an Assembly Cache Viewer (`shfusion.dll`) shell extension that integrates with the Windows shell and enables you to view the contents of the GAC just as you view files in a folder.

Component Versioning

All components in an assembly share the same version. You can specify the version of an assembly by using the assembly-level `AssemblyVersion` attribute. When working with Visual Studio .NET, each time when you modify and recompile a program, the version of the assembly is increased because the `AssemblyVersion` attribute is set to `1.0.*`, which means that the major and minor versions of the assembly are fixed to `1` and `0` respectively, but the `*` in the latter part specifies a build number and a revision number that changes automatically when the assembly is rebuilt.

A common destination for installing the serviced component is the GAC. The GAC is capable of installing different versions of an assembly side by side. During development, if you install several builds of an assembly in the GAC, you can easily clutter up the GAC with several versions of the assembly, even though you are interested in only the most recent one.

To keep the matter simple, you may fix the version number specified in the `AssemblyVersion` attribute so that the old copy of an assembly in the GAC is overwritten when a new copy of the assembly with the same version is installed in the GAC.

Consuming a Serviced Component

Instantiating and using a serviced component is no different from doing so with any other managed component. In Step-by-Step 7.7, I create a Windows form application that instantiates the serviced component and calls methods on it. This application enables users to retrieve and update data from the SQL Server sample `Northwind` database.

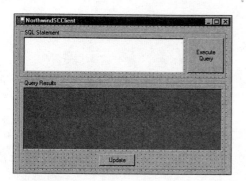

FIGURE 7.17
The design of a form that uses the
NorthwindSC serviced component.

STEP BY STEP

7.7 Using a Serviced Component

1. Add a new Visual C# .NET Windows application named StepByStep7_7 to the solution.

2. In the Solution Explorer, right-click project StepByStep7_7 and select Add Reference from the context menu to add references to the System.EnterpriseServices and StepByStep7_5 components.

3. In the Solution Explorer, rename the default Form1.cs to NorthwindSCClient.cs. Open the form in code view and change all occurrences of Form1 to refer to NorthwindSCClient instead.

4. Add the following using directives:

```
using System.Data.SqlClient;
using StepByStep7_5;
```

5. Place two GroupBox controls, a TextBox control (txtQuery), two Button controls (btnExecute and btnUpdate), and a DataGrid control (dgResults) on the form. Arrange the controls as shown in Figure 7.17.

6. Add the following code in the class definition:

```
// Declare the serviced component
private NorthwindSC nsc;
```

7. Double-click the form and add the following code in the Load event handler:

```
private void NorthwindSCClient_Load(
    object sender, System.EventArgs e)
{
    // Instantiate the serviced component
    nsc = new NorthwindSC();
}
```

8. Double-click the Button controls and add the following code to their Click event handlers:

```
private void btnExecute_Click(
    object sender, System.EventArgs e)
{
    try
    {
```

```
            // Call the ExecuteQuery() method of the
            // NorthwindSC serviced component to execute the
            // query and bind the results to the data grid
              dgResults.DataSource =
                    nsc.ExecuteQuery(txtQuery.Text);
              dgResults.DataMember = "Results";
        }
    catch(Exception ex)
    {
        MessageBox.Show(ex.Message, "Invalid Query",
          MessageBoxButtons.OK, MessageBoxIcon.Error);
    }
}

private void btnUpdate_Click(
    object sender, System.EventArgs e)
{
    try
    {
        // Call the UpdateData() method of the
        // NorthwindSC serviced component to update
        // the database and display the number
        // of updated rows in the database
        int intRows = nsc.UpdateData(
            (DataSet) dgResults.DataSource);
        MessageBox.Show(String.Format(
          "{0} row(s) updated successfully", intRows),
          "Row(s) Updated", MessageBoxButtons.OK,
          MessageBoxIcon.Information);

        // Load the updates and bind the grid
        // with the updates
        dgResults.DataSource =
            nsc.ExecuteQuery(txtQuery.Text);
        dgResults.DataMember = "Results";
    }
    catch(Exception ex)
    {
        MessageBox.Show(ex.Message, "Update Failed",
          MessageBoxButtons.OK, MessageBoxIcon.Error);
    }
}
```

9. Build the project. Set project StepByStep7_7 as the startup project.

10. Run the solution. Enter a query in the text box and click the button. The code invokes a method on the serviced component. The code binds the results from the method to the DataGrid control. Make some changes to the data in the DataGrid control and click the Update button to

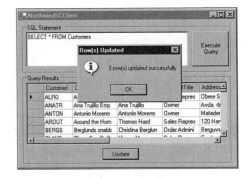

FIGURE 7.18
NorthwindSCClient uses the NorthwindSC serviced component to retrieve and update data from the Northwind database.

continues

continued

> save the changes to the database. If there is no error in the updates, a message box with the number of rows updated is displayed as shown in Figure 7.18.

Although Step-by-Step 7.7 uses a Windows application to use a serviced component, you have other options, too. For example, a distributed application can use a remoting server or a Web service to consume a serviced component.

REVIEW BREAK

▶ Administrators can use the Component Services administrative tool to configure COM+ applications at runtime. Using this tool, they can change certain behaviors of a COM+ application without needing to recompile the application.

▶ If configuration at the method level is required, a class must implement an interface with those methods.

▶ Depending on the ClassInterface attribute to automatically generate class interfaces is not advised because it leads to versioning problems. You should set the ClassInterface attribute for a class to the ClassInterfaceType.None and create your own interface explicitly.

▶ An assembly must be signed with a strong name before the assembly can be registered into the COM+ Catalog.

▶ A serviced component is generally shared by several client applications. Therefore, the most recommended place to install a serviced component assembly is the Global Assembly Cache (GAC) because it ensures that the CLR is always able to locate an assembly.

▶ A distributed application may use different types of applications, such as a Windows application, Windows service, Web application, Web service, Remoting server, and so on, to consume a serviced component.

GUIDED PRACTICE EXERCISE 7.1

You have just learned the basics of developing serviced components. You want to create a sample application that you will use to experiment with various COM+ services. You want to start with a serviced component similar to the one created in Step-by-Step 7.5.

You want to develop the application in a gradual manner. Each time you add a new feature, you should test whether the feature is working and then proceed with adding the new feature. You are interested in using only the most recent version of a component. You do not want multiple copies of a component registered with the COM+ Catalog and installed in the GAC.

How would you create such a serviced component?

This exercise helps you practice creating serviced components and controlling their versioning and identification.

You should try working through this problem on your own first. If you are stuck, or if you'd like to see one possible solution, follow these steps:

1. Add a new Visual C# .NET Class library named `GuidedPracticeExercise7_1` to the solution.

2. In the Solution Explorer, right-click project `GuidedPracticeExercise7_1` and select Add Reference from the context menu to add a reference to the `System.EnterpriseServices` component.

3. In the Solution Explorer, copy the `NorthwindSC.cs` file from the `StepByStep7_5` project to the current project. Open the file and change the namespace to `GuidedPracticeExercise7_1`. Delete the default `Class1.cs`.

4. Select Tools, Create GUID. In the create GUID dialog box, select the Registry format as the GUID format, as shown in Figure 7.19, and then click on the Copy button.

continues

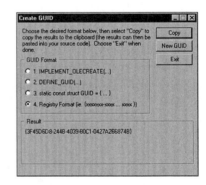

FIGURE 7.19
The Create GUID dialog box enables you to create a GUID.

continued

5. Open `NorthwindConstructSC.cs` and apply the `Guid` attribute to the `NorthwindSC` class as shown in the following code segment. Instead of the GUID shown in the following code segment, paste the value that you copied in Step 4. Remove any curly braces from the GUID value:

```
[ClassInterface(ClassInterfaceType.None)]
[Guid("3F45D6D8-244B-4039-80C1-0427A266874B")]
public class NorthwindSC :
    ServicedComponent, INorthwind
{
    ...
}
```

6. Open the `AssemblyInfo.cs` file in the project and add the following using directive:

```
using System.EnterpriseServices;
```

7. Add the following assembly-level attributes to the `AssemblyInfo.cs` file:

```
[assembly: ApplicationName(
    "Northwind Data Application with Fixed Version" +
    " and component identification")]
[assembly: Description("Retrieve and Update data" +
    " from the Northwind database")]
```

8. Change the `AssemblyVersion` and `AssemblyKeyFile` attribute in the `AssemblyInfo.cs` file as shown here:

```
[assembly: AssemblyVersion("1.0.0")]
[assembly: AssemblyKeyFile(@"..\..\..\70320.snk")]
```

Note that you are using the key file, `70320.snk`, already created in Step-by-Step 7.2. If you haven't created one before, create it now by following step 2 of Step-by-Step 7.2.

9. Build the project. A `GuidedPracticeExercise7_1.dll` is generated, and a strong name is assigned to the file based on the specified key file.

10. Launch the Visual Studio .NET command prompt and change the directory to the folder where the DLL file generated in step 9 resides. Issue the following command to install the assembly to the GAC:

```
gacutil /i GuidedPracticeExercise7_1.dll
```

11. At the command prompt, issue the following command to install the service component assembly to the COM+ Catalog:

```
regsvcs GuidedPracticeExercise7_1.dll
```

The serviced component with a fixed version and component identification information is now ready. When you rebuild and reregister this assembly in the COM+ Catalog, you will still have just one entry for the component. Similarly, when you install multiple builds of this assembly to the GAC, only the most recent copy is present in the GAC at all times.

If you have difficulty following this exercise, review the sections "Creating a Serviced Component," "Component Identification," and "Component Versioning," earlier in this chapter. After doing that review, try this exercise again.

UNDERSTANDING AND USING ENTERPRISE SERVICES

Although you know how to create and consume a serviced component, it's of little use unless you use one of the automatic services provided by COM+. In this section, you will learn how some of the key COM+ component services work and how to use them in an application. In particular, I discuss the following COM+ services:

▶ Object Pooling

▶ Just-in-Time Activation

▶ Object Construction

▶ Automatic Transaction Management

▶ Queued Components

Object Pooling

When you request that an object be created on the server, the server creates a process space, instantiates the object, and performs necessary initialization. For some large and complex objects, the number of resources consumed in creating them may be significantly high. An application may perform poorly if expensive-to-create objects are frequently created.

Wouldn't it be nice if you could maintain a pool of already created objects and then efficiently reuse them repeatedly without creating them from scratch? That's what the object pooling service of COM+ does. The object pooling service enables you to increase an application's scalability and performance by minimizing the time and resources required in creating objects repeatedly.

Configuring a Serviced Component to Use the Object Pooling Service

You can configure a class to use the object pooling service by applying the ObjectPooling attribute on the class. Table 7.9 lists various properties of the ObjectPooling attribute that you can use to configure the way object pooling works for the class.

TABLE 7.9

PROPERTIES OF THE ObjectPooling ATTRIBUTE

Property	Description
CreationTimeout	Specifies a length of time (in milliseconds) to wait for an object to become available in the pool before throwing an exception.
Enabled	Specifies whether object pooling is enabled for a component; the default value for this property is true.
MaxPoolSize	Specifies the maximum number of pooled objects that should be created for a component.
MinPoolSize	Specifies the minimum number of objects that should be available to a component at all times.

In addition to using the `ObjectPooling` attribute, a object-pooled class also overrides the `CanBePooled()` method of the `ServicedComponent` class. The overridden version of this method should return either `true` or `false`. You'll see in the following section that an object is pooled only if the `CanBePooled()` method returns `true`.

How Object Pooling Works

At a higher level, you can think of COM+ as placing a pooling manager between the client and the server, as shown in Figure 7.20.

The pooling manager is responsible for maintaining and controlling the object pool. All client requests to the server for an object are intercepted and instead processed by the pooling manager. The pooling manager follows an internal logic as shown in Figure 7.21.

The functionality of the pooling manager can be summarized by the following list:

▶ When the COM+ application is started, a `MinPoolSize` number of objects are created and thereafter maintained in the pool at all times when the application is running.

▶ Each time the pooling manager receives a request to create an object, the pooling manager checks whether the object is available in the pool. If the object is available, the pooling manager provides an already created object from the pool.

▶ If no objects are currently available in the pool, the pooling manager checks to see whether the number of objects currently in the pool has reached the `MaxPoolSize`. If it has not, then the pooling manager creates new objects to fulfill the request. The pooling manager tends to create as many objects as needed to keep the number of available objects at the level of `MinPoolSize` while not exceeding the `MaxPoolSize`.

▶ If no object is available and no new object can be created because of the size restriction of the pool, then the client requests are queued to receive the first available object from the pool. If an object cannot be made available within the time specified in the `CreationTimeOut` property, an exception is thrown.

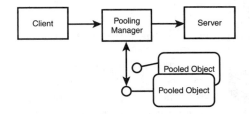

FIGURE 7.20
The pooling manager intercepts any requests for object creation and provides the object pooling service.

continued

FIGURE 7.21
The pooling manager maintains the object pool
based on the specified attributes.

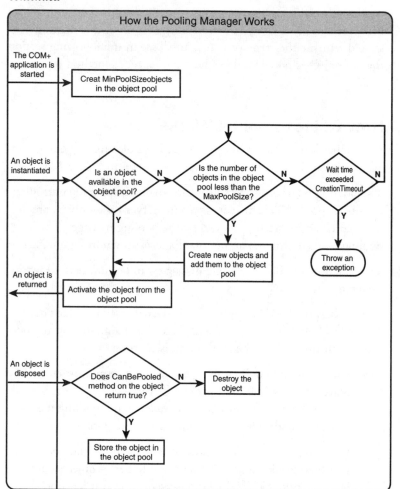

To Pool or Not to Pool?   Using the
object pooling service with every
application might not be a good
idea. Although object pooling has
benefits, it also has its own share
of overheads. You should use
object pooling in those applications
where the benefits of object pooling
exceed the overheads. Some of the
scenarios suitable for object pooling are

- When the costs of creating an
  object are relatively high.

- When usage costs are relatively
  low.

- When an object will be reused
  often.

- When you want to limit the
  number of object instances.

Some scenarios where object pooling may not be useful are

- When an object is inexpensive
  to create.

- When the object does not maintain any server-specific state.

- When the object must be activated in the caller's context.

- When you do not want to
  restrict the number of object
  instances.

▶ When the client finishes with an object, it invokes a `Dispose()`
method on the object. The pooling manager intercepts this
request and calls the `CanBePooled()` method on the object to
check whether the object is interested in being pooled. If the
method returns `true`, the object is stored in the object pool.
On the other hand, if the `CanBePooled()` method returns
`false`, then the object is destroyed.

▶ The pooling manager ensures that an optimum number of
objects are always available in the object pool. If the number

of available objects in the pool drops below the specified minimum, new objects are created to meet any outstanding object requests and refill the pool. If the number of available objects in the pool is greater than the minimum number, those surplus objects are destroyed during a clean-up cycle.

Creating an Object-Pooled Serviced Component

Step-by-Step 7.8 shows how to create an object-pooled serviced component by applying the ObjectPooling attribute and overriding the CanBePooled() method. In addition, the serviced component in Step-by-Step 7.8 also overrides the Activate() and Deactivate() methods of the ServicedComponent class. Recall from Table 7.2 that the Activate() method is invoked by enterprise services either when an object is created afresh or when an object is activated from the pool. The Deactivate() method is called just before an object is deactivated and returned to the pool or destroyed.

In Step-by-Step 7.8, I use the constructor, Activate(), and Deactivate() methods to write messages to the Windows event log. This helps you monitor how object activation and deactivation is being performed by the system.

> **WARNING**
>
> **Don't Pool Objects with Client-Specific States** When a client program repeatedly requests an instance of an object-pooled serviced component, there is no guarantee that the client will receive exactly the same instance of the object that it received in the earlier requests. Any object that needs to maintain client-specific state should not be pooled. Otherwise, you'll get undesirable results.

STEP BY STEP

7.8 Creating an Object-Pooled Serviced Component

1. Add a new Visual C# .NET Class library named StepByStep7_8 to the solution.

2. In the Solution Explorer, right-click project StepByStep7_8 and select Add Reference from the context menu to add a reference to the System.EnterpriseServices component.

3. In the Solution Explorer, rename the default Class1.cs to NorthwindSC.cs.

4. Open the NorthwindSC.cs and replace the code with the following code:

continues

continued

```
using System;
using System.Data;
using System.Data.SqlClient;
using System.EnterpriseServices;
using System.Runtime.InteropServices;
using System.Diagnostics;

namespace StepByStep7_8
{
    public interface INorthwind
    {
        DataSet ExecuteQuery(string strQuery);
        int UpdateData(string strQuery, DataSet ds);
    }

    [ObjectPooling(true, 2, 4)]
    [ClassInterface(ClassInterfaceType.None)]
    public class NorthwindSC : ServicedComponent,
                               INorthwind
    {
        private SqlConnection sqlcnn;
        private SqlDataAdapter sqlda;
        private DataSet ds;
        private EventLog eventLog;

        public NorthwindSC()
        {
            // Perform expensive start up operations

            // Create a Sqlconnection object
            sqlcnn = new SqlConnection(
                "data source=(local);" +
                "initial catalog=Northwind;" +
                "integrated security=SSPI");

            // Create an EventLog object
            // and assign its source
            eventLog = new EventLog();
            eventLog.Source = "NorthwindPool";

            // Write an entry to the event log
            eventLog.WriteEntry(
                "NorthwindSC object is created" +
                " and added to the object pool");
        }

        protected override bool CanBePooled()
        {
            return true;
        }

        protected override void Activate()
        {
```

```
        eventLog.WriteEntry(
            "A NorthwindSC object is activated" +
            " from the object pool");
    }

    protected override void Deactivate()
    {
        eventLog.WriteEntry(
            "A NorthwindSC object is deactivated"+
            " and is returned to the object pool");
    }

    // This method executes a SELECT query and
    // returns the results in a DataSet object
    public DataSet ExecuteQuery(string strQuery)
    {
        // Create a SqlDataAdapter object to
        // talk to the database
        sqlda =
            new SqlDataAdapter(strQuery, sqlcnn);

        // Create a DataSet object
        // to hold the results
        ds = new DataSet();

        // Fill the DataSet object
        sqlda.Fill(ds, "Results");

        return ds;
    }

    // This method updates the database with
    // the changes in a DataSet object
    public int UpdateData(string strQuery,
                          DataSet ds)
    {
        sqlda =
            new SqlDataAdapter(strQuery, sqlcnn);
        // Update the database
        // and return the result
        SqlCommandBuilder sqlcb =
            new SqlCommandBuilder(sqlda);
        return sqlda.Update(ds.Tables["Results"]);
    }
  }
}
```

5. Select Tools, Create GUID to open the Create GUID dialog box. Select the Registry Format option in the dialog box and click the Copy button. Paste the copied GUID to the Guid attribute of the NorthwindSC class (after removing the curly brackets) as shown here:

continues

continued

```
[Guid("2166AC45-7E24-407a-967A-DD614FE8727B")]
public class NorthwindSC : ServicedComponent
```

> Note that you will get a different GUID than the one mentioned earlier.

6. Open the `AssemblyInfo.cs` file in the project and add the following using directive:

```
using System.EnterpriseServices;
```

7. Add the following assembly-level attributes to the `AssemblyInfo.cs` file:

```
[assembly: ApplicationName("Northwind Data " +
    "Application with Object Pooling")]
[assembly: Description("Retrieve and Update data " +
    "from the Northwind database")]
[assembly: ApplicationActivation(
    ActivationOption.Server)]
```

8. Change the `AssemblyVersion` and `AssemblyKeyFile` attribute in the `AssemblyInfo.cs` file, as shown here:

```
[assembly: AssemblyVersion("1.0.0")]
[assembly: AssemblyKeyFile(@"..\..\..\70320.snk")]
```

9. Build the project. A `StepByStep7_8.dll` file is generated, and a strong name is assigned to the file based on the specified key file.

10. Launch the Visual Studio .NET command prompt and change the directory to the folder where the DLL file generated in step 9 resides. Issue the following command to install the assembly to the GAC:

```
gacutil /i StepByStep7_8.dll
```

11. At the command prompt, issue the following command to install the service component assembly to the COM+ Catalog:

```
regsvcs StepByStep7_8.dll
```

In Step-by-Step 7.8, I selected the `ActivationOption` to be `Server` instead of `Library` because I want to create the object in context of the server and not that of the client.

I also registered the assembly as a COM+ application. Now when you use the Component Services administrative tool to access the properties of the `NorthwindSC` component in this application, you get the options to configure the object pooling parameters as shown in Figure 7.22.

Using an Object-Pooled Serviced Component

In this section, I'll demonstrate how to use an object-pooled serviced component from a client program. I'll show you two different ways to use a serviced component—the greedy approach and a non-greedy approach. You'll understand what each of these approaches is and why you should use one over the other as you proceed. I'll first start with an example of the greedy approach to call a serviced component in Step-by-Step 7.9.

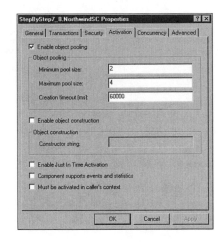

FIGURE 7.22
You can configure the object pooling parameters for a component at runtime by using the Component Services administrative tool.

STEP BY STEP

7.9 Using an Object-Pooled Serviced Component: Greedy Approach

1. Add a new Visual C# .NET Windows application named `StepByStep7_9` to the solution.

2. In the Solution Explorer, right-click project `StepByStep7_9` and select Add Reference from the context menu to add references to the `System.EnterpriseServices` and `StepByStep7_8` components.

3. In the Solution Explorer, copy the `NorthwindSCClient.cs` file from the `StepByStep7_7` project to the current project. Open the form in code view and change all occurrences of `NorthwindSCClient` to refer to `NorthwindSCGreedyClient` instead. Also, change the namespace name to `StepByStep7_9` and the using directive to refer to `StepByStep7_8` instead of `StepByStep7_5`. Delete the default `Form1.cs`.

4. Modify the `btnUpdate_Click()` method as follows:

continues

continued

```
private void btnUpdate_Click(
    object sender, System.EventArgs e)
{
    try
    {
        // Call the UpdateData() method of the
        // NorthwindSC serviced component to update
        // the database and display the number
        // of updated rows in the database
        int intRows = nsc.UpdateData(
            txtQuery.Text,
            (DataSet) dgResults.DataSource);
        MessageBox.Show(String.Format(
            "{0} row(s) updated", intRows),
            "Row(s) Updated", MessageBoxButtons.OK,
            MessageBoxIcon.Information);

        // Load the updates and bind the grid
        // with the updates
        dgResults.DataSource =
            nsc.ExecuteQuery(txtQuery.Text);
        dgResults.DataMember = "Results";
    }
    catch(Exception ex)
    {
        MessageBox.Show(ex.Message, "Update Failed",
        MessageBoxButtons.OK, MessageBoxIcon.Error);
    }
}
```

5. Build the project. Set project StepByStep7_9 as the startup project.

6. Select Debug, Start Without Debugging to launch the client form. Open the Component Services administrative tool and use the tree view on the left to navigate to the Event Viewer node. View the Application Log; you should notice that three messages from the NorthwindSC source are logged. When the application starts, the number of objects created equals the minimum size specified for the object pool. In this case, two objects are created and each of them logs a message to the event log when executing the constructor. The third message is generated from the Activate() method because the client program activates an object from the pool.

7. Select Debug, Start Without Debugging to launch another client form. View the messages in the event log and

you'll see that one new message is added to the event log. This message is generated from the `Activate()` method because the second serviced component object is already created and is just activated from the object pool. Now launch the third form and view the messages in the event log. You should notice this adds two more messages to the event log; one is added because the third serviced component object is created, and the other added is because the client also activates the object. Repeat the same process and launch the fourth form; you can see that two more messages are added to the event log because the fourth object is created and then activated from the pool. Now try launching the fifth form. The fifth form will not be created because the maximum size of the pool is 4, and the four objects are already created. If you wait for long (that is, the default timeout value of 60,000 milliseconds), you will get a connection timed out error. If instead you close one of the four open forms, the fifth form is launched immediately. View the event log and you will notice two messages, one from the `Deactivate()` method because you closed a form and another from the `Activate()` method because the fifth form does not create an object from scratch but instead fetches one from the object pool.

When the form in Step-by-Step 7.9 is loaded, it creates an object on the server and then holds the reference to this object until the form is closed. The client is holding the resource for longer than it actually needs to; therefore, I call this program a greedy client. You can also note from Step-by-Step 7.9 that the solution involving greedy clients does not scale well with an increasing number of clients.

An alternative to the greedy client is to create clients that are not greedy. That means the client occupies server resources as late as possible and releases them as early as possible. This scheme ensures that the server's resources are occupied for only the period during which they are actually used. As soon as a client frees a resource, the resource can be used by another client that may be waiting for it. Step-by-Step 7.10 shows one such solution.

STEP BY STEP

7.10 Using an Object-Pooled Serviced Component: Non-greedy Approach

1. Add a new Visual C# .NET Windows Application project named StepByStep7_10 to the solution.

2. In the Solution Explorer, right-click project StepByStep7_10 and select Add Reference from the context menu to add references to the System.EnterpriseServices and StepByStep7_8 components.

3. In the Solution Explorer, rename the default Form1.cs to NorthwindSCNonGreedyClient.cs. Open the form in code view and change all occurrences of Form1 to refer to NorthwindSCNonGreedyClient instead.

4. Add the following using directives:

```
using System.Data.SqlClient;
using StepByStep7_8;
```

5. Place two GroupBox controls, a TextBox control (txtQuery), two Button controls (btnExecute and btnUpdate), and a DataGrid control (dgResults) on the form (refer to Figure 7.17).

6. Double-click the Button controls and add the following code to their Click event handlers:

```
private void btnExecute_Click(
    object sender, System.EventArgs e)
{
    // Declare and Instantiate the serviced component
    NorthwindSC nsc= new NorthwindSC();

    try
    {
      // Call the ExecuteQuery() method of the
      // NorthwindSC serviced component to execute the
      // query and bind the results to the data grid
        dgResults.DataSource =
            nsc.ExecuteQuery(txtQuery.Text);
        dgResults.DataMember = "Results";
    }
    catch(Exception ex)
    {
        MessageBox.Show(ex.Message, "Invalid Query",
          MessageBoxButtons.OK, MessageBoxIcon.Error);
    }
```

```
    finally
    {
        nsc.Dispose();
    }
}

private void btnUpdate_Click(
    object sender, System.EventArgs e)
{
    // Declare and instantiate the serviced component
    NorthwindSC nsc= new NorthwindSC();
    try
    {
        // Call the UpdateData() method of the
        // NorthwindSC serviced component to update
        // the database and display the number
        // of updated rows in the database
        int intRows = nsc.UpdateData(
            txtQuery.Text,
            (DataSet) dgResults.DataSource);
        MessageBox.Show(String.Format(
            "{0} row(s) updated", intRows),
            "Row(s) Updated", MessageBoxButtons.OK,
            MessageBoxIcon.Information);

        // Load the updates and bind the grid
        // with the updates
        dgResults.DataSource =
            nsc.ExecuteQuery(txtQuery.Text);
        dgResults.DataMember = "Results";
    }
    catch(Exception ex)
    {
        MessageBox.Show(ex.Message, "Update Failed",
          MessageBoxButtons.OK, MessageBoxIcon.Error);
    }
    finally
    {
        nsc.Dispose();
    }
}
```

7. Build the project. Set project StepByStep7_10 as the start-up project.

8. Open the Component Services administrative tool. If "Northwind Data Application with Object Pooling" is still running, shut down the application. This purges any existing object pool. Select Debug, Start Without Debugging to launch the client form. Open the Event Viewer and view the Application Log; you should not see any messages added to the event log because in this

continues

continued

version of the client the object is created only when a method is invoked.

9. Enter a query in the text box and click the Execute Query button. View the Application Event log; you should notice four messages from the NorthwindSC source. Two of these messages are generated by the constructor because 2 is the minimum size of the pool and when the application starts, that many new objects are created. The third message comes from the Activate() method when the client program activates an object from the pool. Just before the ExecuteQuery() method finishes, the method calls a Dispose() method on the serviced component object. This causes the Deactivate() method to generate the fourth message when the object is being sent back to the pool.

10. Launch four more client forms. You will notice the fifth form is also launched, even though the maximum size of the pool is 4. This is because the object is not created when the form loads; instead the objects are created when you fire the method and are then destroyed. Execute queries in the forms; you notice that only messages from the Activate() and Deactivate() methods are added to the event log, which means that no new objects are created. The existing two objects (minimum size of the pool) in the pool can process all calls because they are tied with a client for only a small duration when a method is invoked. The object is returned to the pool as soon as the method returns. However, if you call more than two methods on the object simultaneously, then the third object is created. However, the maximum size of the pool is still not achieved and the clients don't have to wait for a server resource.

In Step-by-Step 7.10, I am creating the object each time within a method call and destroying it as soon as the method is completed. This ensures that the client holds a reference to the server object for only the period for which it is actually using the object.

From the perspective of conventional programming, this approach may look outright inefficient because if the client is repeatedly creating objects it will be slower compared to a client that creates an object only once and then holds onto it. However, in Step-by-Step 7.10, you can see that the benefits of scalability surpass the difference in speed. That is very important for enterprise applications, which must scale with increasing numbers of users.

In Step-by-Step 7.10, it is important for the client to call the Dispose() method on server objects as soon as the objects are not needed. If the client program doesn't do so, it will keep on holding the server resources for its lifetime. C# provides a using statement especially designed to help programmers with requirements like this. The btnExecute_Click() method can be programmed with the help of a using statement, like this:

```
private void btnExecute_Click(
    object sender, System.EventArgs e)
{
    // Declare and instantiate the serviced component
    using (NorthwindSC nsc= new NorthwindSC())
    {
        try
        {
            // Call the ExecuteQuery() method of the
            // NorthwindSC serviced component to
            // execute the query and bind the
            // results to the data grid
            dgResults.DataSource =
            nsc.ExecuteQuery(txtQuery.Text);
            dgResults.DataMember = "Results";
        }
        catch(Exception ex)
        {
            MessageBox.Show(ex.Message, "Invalid Query",
            MessageBoxButtons.OK, MessageBoxIcon.Error);
        }
    }
}
```

In this example, the NorthwindSC object is created in the scope of the using statement. C# automatically calls Dispose() on such objects when the using statement is exited.

Although the using statement provides a good option for dealing with the Dispose() problem, it is still not a good idea for an enterprise application to make scalability a factor for determining how well a client program is designed. Ideally, in these scenarios, a server application should automatically dispose of server objects as soon as

> **Using Object Pooling to Control Licensing**   Using object pooling, you can set the upper limit for the consumption of a server resource. This feature of object pooling can help you scale your application as the number of licensed users increases. Moreover, because of the declarative nature of COM+ services, it is easy to configure this setting at runtime with minimal administrative efforts.

the client finishes using them. So what is the solution? I'll tell you about a server-side solution to deal with the dispose problem in a forthcoming section, "Just-in-Time Activation."

Monitoring Statistics of a Serviced Component

When an object writes messages to the event log, that's a way to monitor how an object is functioning. However, you may also want to aggregate information about all objects that are currently instantiated and monitor how a component as a whole is working. In this section, you'll learn how to use the Component Services administrative tool to monitor the usage statistics for a serviced component.

STEP BY STEP

7.11 Monitoring Object Statistics of a Serviced Component

1. Open the Component Services administrative tool. Using the left pane, navigate to the `StepByStep7_8.NorthwindSC` component within the Northwind Data Application with Object Pooling COM+ application.

2. Right-click on the component to see the Properties dialog box for the `StepByStep7_8.NorthwindSC` component. Select the Activation tab and check the Component supports Event and Statistics option, as shown in Figure 7.23.

3. Shut down the Northwind Data Application with Object Pooling COM+ application. Then start the application.

4. Using the left pane, navigate to the Components node within the Northwind Data Application with Object Pooling COM+ application. Select Status View from the View menu.

5. Launch several instances of the resource hog program `StepByStep7_9.exe`. As you instantiate and work with the program, you will see the statistics of the component in the right pane of the Component Services administrative tool as shown in Figure 7.24.

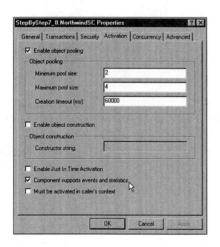

FIGURE 7.23
Select the Component Supports Events and Statistics option to monitor usage statistics for a component.

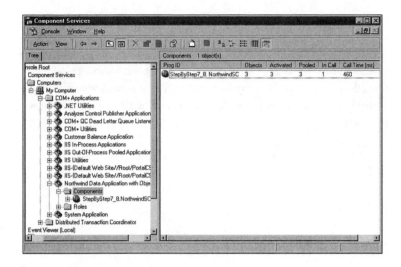

FIGURE 7.24
The status view of the component allows you to view the component's statistics.

Table 7.10 shows what each of the status view columns for a serviced component in the right pane of the Component Services administrative tool mean:

TABLE 7.10

WHAT EACH STATUS VIEW COLUMN REPRESENTS FOR A SERVICED COMPONENT

Column	Description
ProgID	Identifies a specific component.
Objects	Shows the number of objects that are currently held by the client programs.
Activated	Shows the number of objects that are currently activated.
Pooled	Shows the total number of objects created by the pooling manager. This number is the sum of objects that are in use and the objects that are deactivated.
In Call	Shows the number of objects that are currently executing some client request.
Call Time (ms)	Shows the average call duration (in milliseconds) of method calls made in the last 20 seconds (up to 20 calls).

NOTE

Fine Tuning an Application The initial estimated settings of the `MinPoolSize`, `MaxPoolSize`, and `CreationTimeOut` properties may not be optimal for your specific application and its environment. Usually administrators monitor an application's behavior and then fine-tune its configuration settings to suit to the environment. An administrator may have to experiment with several different values to reach the desired performance level. The fine-tuning of an application can be easily performed with the Component Services administrative tool.

In Step-by-Step 7.11, you checked the Component Supports Events and Statistics check box to specify that you are interested in recording the statistics for a serviced component. If you want your components to always install in the COM+ Catalog with this option turned on, you should apply the EventTrackingEnabled attribute to your class and set its Value property to true as shown in the following code snippet:

```
[EventTrackingEnabled(true)]
public class NorthwindPoolSC : ServicedComponent
{
    ...
}
```

Just-in-Time Activation

In the "Object Pooling" section, I used two different approaches for designing the client program:

▶ In the first approach, a client creates an object and holds onto it until the client no longer needs it. The advantage of this approach is that it's faster because the client need not create objects repeatedly. The disadvantage is that this approach can be expensive in terms of server resources in a large-scale application.

▶ In the second approach, a client can create, use, and release an object. The next time it needs the object, it creates it again. The advantage to this technique is that it conserves server resources. The disadvantage is that as your application scales up, your performance slows down. If the object is on a remote computer, each time an object is created, there must be a network round-trip, which negatively affects performance.

Although either of these approaches might be fine for a small-scale application, as your application scales up, they're both inefficient. Moreover, in an enterprise application, the server scalability should not be a factor of how the clients are designed. The just-in-time activation service of COM+ provides a server-side solution that includes advantages of both of the previous approaches while avoiding the disadvantages of each.

How Just-in-Time Activation Works

Just-in-time activation is an automatic service provided by COM+.
To use this service in a class, all you need to do is to mark the class
with the JustInTimeActivation attribute set to true.

Figure 7.25 shows how the just-in-time activation service works. I
have also summarized the process in the following list:

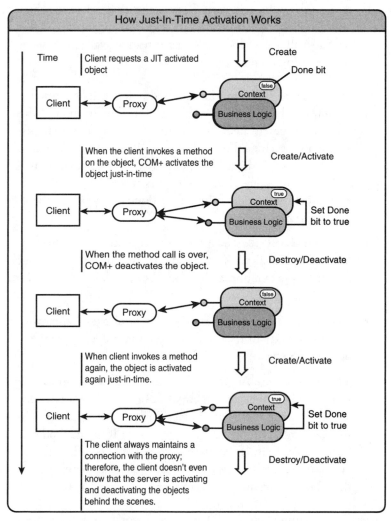

FIGURE 7.25
The just-in-time activation service saves server
resources by creating objects just in time—
when they are required.

▶ When the client requests an object from the server, COM+
  intercepts that request, creates a proxy, and returns the proxy

to the client. The client maintains a long-lived reference to the proxy, thinking that it is a reference to the actual object. This way the client does not spend time repeatedly creating the object. The server also saves resources because it can delay creating the object until the client invokes a method on it.

▶ When the client invokes a method on the object (using the proxy), COM+ actually creates the object, calls the method, return the results, and then destroys the object. Because the objects are short-lived, the server resources are consumed for only a small period and the server is readily available to serve other waiting clients.

As shown in Figure 7.25, any JIT-activated object will be created in its own context. The context maintains a "done bit" to specify when the object will be deactivated. The interception mechanism checks the done bit after each method call finishes. If the value of the done bit is true, the object is deactivated; otherwise the object continues to exist. The default value of the done bit is false. Nevertheless, you can programmatically set the value of the done bit by using any of the following techniques:

▶ The `ContextUtil.SetComplete()` or `ContextUtil.SetAbort()` Methods—Usually these methods are used to vote for the success or failure of a transaction, but they also set the done bit to `true`.

▶ The `ContextUtil.DeactivateOnReturn` Property—When you set this property to `true` in a method, the property sets the done bit to `true`.

▶ The `AutoComplete` Attribute—When you always want to deactivate an object when the method call returns, you can apply this attribute to the method definition. This attribute automatically calls `ContextUtil.SetComplete()` if the method completes successfully. If the method throws an exception, the `ContextUtil.SetAbort()` method is invoked. In both cases the done bit is automatically set to `true`.

After understanding how the JIT activation works, you can appreciate how JIT activation enables scalable programming. However, the server still has lots of work to do. If the client is frequently calling methods, the server frequently creates and destroys objects. The benefits of JIT activation are beaten when the cost of object creation is significantly high. However, you already know a COM+ service that saves the cost of object creation—object pooling. What will happen if you combine JIT activation and object pooling services together for a serviced component? You will create a recipe for high throughput.

Using Just-in-Time Activation with Object Pooling—A Recipe for High Throughput

Throughput is a measure of the processing done by an application during a given time. Often, as the number of users increases, so does the competition for a server's resources. This normally results in an overall decrease in throughput.

The JIT activation and object pooling services complement each other's features. When these services are used in combination, they can maximize the throughput for an application by providing the following benefits:

- ▶ JIT activation enables clients to hold long-lived references on the server object (through a proxy) without consuming server resources.

- ▶ JIT activation enables the server objects to be destroyed as soon as their work is over to minimize the resource consumption on the server.

- ▶ Object pooling caches the already created objects and saves time by activating and deactivating the objects from the pool rather than re-creating them from scratch.

> **NOTE**
>
> **TPC-C Benchmarks** Microsoft Windows 2000 and COM+ hold the top six places in the Transaction Processing Performance Council's TPC-C benchmark for performance. Additionally, Microsoft Windows 2000 and COM+ also hold all ten of the top ten positions in the TPC-C benchmark for price/performance ratio. One of the important parameters of the TPC-C benchmark is application throughput. Microsoft heavily relied on object pooling and just-in-time activation services to maximize application throughput and achieve world-record performance. TPC-C benchmark results can be found at the Transaction Processing Performance Council's web site at www.tpc.org.

Design Considerations for Using Just-in-Time Activation and Object Pooling

When using JIT activation in your programs, you need to consider the following points:

- ▶ An object's lifetime is controlled by the server instead of the client. Therefore, you need not call the Dispose() method on the server object from the client. Actually, if you do so, the object will be re-created on the server, just to be disposed of.

▶ The server does not automatically deactivate an object. You need to set the done bit to true for COM+ to destroy an object after the current method call has completed. You can use any of the techniques mentioned in the previous section to set the done bit to true. You can also configure a method administratively to control this behavior.

▶ The objects are created and destroyed after each method call. Therefore, you should consider the server object as stateless. JIT activation is not suitable for the objects that need to maintain state across method calls.

Creating a JIT-Activated Object-Pooled Serviced Component

In this section, you'll learn how to use just-in-time activation and object pooling to create an application that is more scalable and that has improved performance. In Step-by-Step 7.12, you will see how a few simple changes to a serviced component allow it to scale efficiently and support a large number of clients, without depending on the client to call the `Dispose()` method on the server objects.

STEP BY STEP

7.12 Creating a JIT-Activated Serviced Component

1. Add a new Visual C# .NET Class library project named `StepByStep7_12` to the solution.

2. In the Solution Explorer, right-click project `StepByStep7_12` and select Add Reference from the context menu to add a reference to the `System.EnterpriseServices` component.

3. In the Solution Explorer, copy the `NorthwindSC.cs` file from the `StepByStep7_8` project to the current project. Open the form in code view and change the namespace name to `StepByStep7_12`. Delete the default `Class1.cs`.

4. Apply the `JustInTimeActivation` and `EventTrackingEnabled` attributes on the `NorthWindSC` class and change the GUID in the `Guid` attribute:

```
[EventTrackingEnabled(true)]
[JustInTimeActivation(true)]
[ObjectPooling(true, 2,4)]
[Guid("EBC55B5E-090A-4515-9B91-A812E74A40E7")]
[ClassInterface(ClassInterfaceType.None)]
public class NorthwindSC : ServicedComponent,
                                INorthwind
{
  ...
}
```

5. Modify the ExecuteQuery() and UpdateData() methods as follows:

```
// This method executes a SELECT query and
// returns the results in a DataSet object
public DataSet ExecuteQuery(string strQuery)
{
    // Create a SqlDataAdapter object to
    // talk to the database
    sqlda =
        new SqlDataAdapter(strQuery, sqlcnn);

    // Create a DataSet object
    // to hold the results
    ds = new DataSet();

    // Fill the DataSet object
    sqlda.Fill(ds, "Results");
    // Deactivate the object
    // when the method returns
    ContextUtil.DeactivateOnReturn = true;
    return ds;
}

// This method updates the database with
// the changes in a DataSet object
[AutoComplete]
public int UpdateData(string strQuery, DataSet ds)
{
    // Update the database
    sqlda =
        new SqlDataAdapter(strQuery, sqlcnn);
    SqlCommandBuilder sqlcb =
        new SqlCommandBuilder(sqlda);
    return sqlda.Update(ds.Tables["Results"]);
}
```

6. Open the AssemblyInfo.cs file in the project and add the following using directive:

```
using System.EnterpriseServices;
```

7. Add the following assembly level attributes in the AssemblyInfo.cs file:

continues

continued

```
[assembly: ApplicationName("Northwind Data " +
    "Application with JIT activation")]
[assembly: Description("Retrieve and Update data " +
    "from the Northwind database")]
[assembly: ApplicationActivation(
    ActivationOption.Server)]
```

8. Change the `AssemblyVersion` and `AssemblyKeyFile` attribute in the `AssemblyInfo.cs` file as shown here:

```
[assembly: AssemblyVersion("1.0")]
[assembly: AssemblyKeyFile(@"..\..\..\70320.snk")]
```

9. Build the project. A `StepByStep7_12.dll` file is generated, and a strong name is assigned to the file based on the specified key file.

10. Launch the Visual Studio .NET command prompt and change the directory to the folder where the DLL file generated in step 9 resides. Issue the following command to install the assembly to the GAC:

```
gacutil /i StepByStep7_12.dll
```

11. At the command prompt, issue the following command to install the service component assembly to the COM+ Catalog:

```
regsvcs StepByStep7_12.dll
```

In Step-by-Step 7.12, I have applied the `JustInTimeActivation` attribute on the `NorthwindSC` class. This attribute instructs the runtime to check the value of the done bit after each method call. The object is deactivated if the done bit evaluated to true after a method call.

I use two different ways to set the done bit in this program. In the `ExecuteQuery()` method, I set the `DeactivateOnReturn` property of the `ContextUtil` class to true, whereas in the `UpdateData()` method, I apply the `AutoComplete` attribute. The `AutoComplete` attribute always deactivates the object after the method call is completed, whereas the `ContextUtil.DeactivateOnReturn` property is more flexible because it can be set to true or false, depending on a condition.

You can also configure the Just-in-Time Activation service using the Component Services administrative tool. To enable JIT activation for a component you need to check the Enable Just In Time Activation check box in the component's Properties dialog box, as shown in Figure 7.26.

To set the done bit after a method completes, you need to check the Automatically Deactivate This Object When This Method Returns check box in the method's Properties dialog box as shown in Figure 7.27.

Using a JIT-Activated Object-Pooled Serviced Component

Step-by-Step 7.13 demonstrates how to use a JIT-activated object-pooled serviced component. This program is similar to that of Step-by-Step 7.10, but is simpler because this time the server automatically takes care of disposing of the server objects and thus the client is not required to call `Dispose()` on the server objects.

STEP BY STEP

7.13 Using a JIT-Activated Serviced Component

1. Add a new Visual C# .NET Windows Application project named `StepByStep7_13` to the solution.

2. In the Solution Explorer, right-click project `StepByStep7_13` and select Add Reference from the context menu to add references to the `System.EnterpriseServices` and `StepByStep7_12` components.

3. In the Solution Explorer, copy the form `NorthwindSCNonGreedyClient.cs` from the `StepByStep7_10` project to the current project. Delete the default `Form1.cs`. Open the form in code view and change `using StepByStep7_8` to `using StepByStep7_12` instead. Change the namespace to `StepByStep7_13`.

4. Remove the `finally` block from the `btnExecute_Click()` and `btnUpdate_Click()` methods.

continues

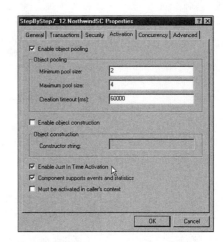

FIGURE 7.26
You can easily configure just-in-time activation for a serviced component by using the Component Services administrative tool.

FIGURE 7.27
Using the Component Services administrative tool, you can easily configure a method to deactivate the object when the method call returns.

continued

5. Build the project. Set the project StepByStep7_13 as the startup project.

Run the project as you did in Step-by-Step 7.10. Note that the results are the same despite the fact that the client program is not calling Dispose() on the server objects.

Object Construction

The object construction service of COM+ allows you to specify initialization information for a serviced component. The advantage of using the construction service is that it enables you to configure the string externally, using tools such as the Component Services administrative tool.

To use the object construction service in a serviced component you need to do the following:

▶ Apply the ConstructionEnabled Attribute—You need to apply the ConstructionEnabled attribute on a class that uses the object construction service. This attribute has two properties: Enabled and Default. The default values of these properties are true and empty string, respectively. The Default property specifies the constructor string.

▶ Override the Construct() Method—To receive the currently configured constructor string from the COM+ Catalog, an object must override the Construct() method of the ServicedComponent class. When the ConstructionEnabled attribute is true, enterprise services calls this method automatically after the constructor of the component has been executed. The Construct() method receives the currently configured construction string as its only parameter.

After the ConstructionEnabled attribute is applied, you can configure the constructor string by using the component's property sheet in the Component Services administrative tool.

NOTE

Using Object Construction with Object Pooling You can pair object construction with object pooling to have more control over how the clients reuse resources. For example, you can design a generic serviced component that exposes resources to the clients based on the constructor string. You can install this component several times in a COM+ application (ensuring that each component has a different CLSID) and then assign each of these components a distinct constructor string. The COM+ application now has distinct pools of objects, each usable by distinct groups of clients.

▶ The COM+ object pooling service enables you to maintain already created instances of a component that are ready to be used by any client that requests the component.

▶ To use the object pooling service, a class must override the `CanBePooled()` method of the `ServicedComponent` class. In addition, you need to apply the `ObjectPooling` attribute on the class or configure the component via the Component Services administrative tool to use object pooling.

▶ The COM+ Just-in-Time activation service allows you to minimize the period of time an object lives and consumes resources on the server.

▶ You can enable the just-in-time activation service declaratively in your programs by using the `JustInTimeActivation` attribute or administratively via the Component Services administrative tool. You must, however, indicate to COM+ whether an object should be deactivated after a method call by setting the done bit to `true`.

▶ The COM+ object construction service allows you to specify initialization information for a serviced component. It is possible to use the Component Services administrative tool and configure the initialization information for a component to change the way a component behaves.

GUIDED PRACTICE EXERCISE 7.2

You need to modify the serviced component created in Step-by-Step 7.10 in such a way that system administrators should be able to configure the database connection string for the component. To do this, there should not be a need to recompile the application. You do not want to log events to the event log from the serviced component.

How would you create such a serviced component and then configure the component with the help of Component Services administrative tool?

continues

continued

This exercise helps you practice creating serviced components that use COM+ services. You should try working through this problem on your own first. If you are stuck, or if you would like to see one possible solution, follow these steps:

1. Add a new Visual C# .NET Class library named GuidedPracticeExercise7_2 to the solution.

2. In the Solution Explorer, right-click the project GuidedPracticeExercise7_2 and select Add Reference from the context menu to add reference to the System.EnterpriseServices component.

3. In the Solution Explorer, rename the default Class1.cs to NorthwindSC.cs.

4. Open the NorthwindSC.cs and replace the code with the following code:

```csharp
using System;
using System.Data;
using System.Data.SqlClient;
using System.EnterpriseServices;
using System.Runtime.InteropServices;

namespace GuidedPracticeExercise7_2
{
    public interface INorthwind
    {
        DataSet ExecuteQuery(string strQuery);
        int UpdateData(string strQuery, DataSet ds);
    }

    // Default value for the Construction
    // string specified here
    [ConstructionEnabled(
        Default="data source=(local);" +
        "initial catalog=Northwind;" +
        "integrated security=SSPI")]
    [Guid("18C7C90F-FD2C-4a1a-88D4-E8FDEC530CDA")]
    [EventTrackingEnabled(true)]
    [JustInTimeActivation(true)]
    [ObjectPooling(true, 2,4)]
    [ClassInterface(ClassInterfaceType.None)]
    public class NorthwindSC : ServicedComponent,
                                    INorthwind
    {
        private SqlConnection sqlcnn;
        private SqlDataAdapter sqlda;
        private DataSet ds;
```

```csharp
public NorthwindSC()
{
}

protected override void Construct(string s)
{
    // Open a connection to the specified
    // sample SQL Server database
    sqlcnn = new SqlConnection(s);
}

protected override bool CanBePooled()
{
    return true;
}

// This method executes a SELECT query and
// returns the results in a DataSet object
public DataSet ExecuteQuery(string strQuery)
{
    // Create a SqlDataAdapter object to
    // talk to the database
    sqlda =
        new SqlDataAdapter(strQuery, sqlcnn);

    // Create a DataSet object
    // to hold the results
    ds = new DataSet();

    // Fill the DataSet object
    sqlda.Fill(ds, "Results");

    // Deactivate the object
    // when the method returns
    ContextUtil.DeactivateOnReturn = true;
    return ds;
}

// This method updates the database with
// the changes in a DataSet object
[AutoComplete]
public int UpdateData(string strQuery,
                      DataSet ds)
{
    // Update the database
    sqlda =
        new SqlDataAdapter(strQuery, sqlcnn);

    // Update the database
    // and return the result
    SqlCommandBuilder sqlcb =
        new SqlCommandBuilder(sqlda);
    return sqlda.Update(ds.Tables["Results"]);
}
```

continues

continued

```
        }
    }
```

5. Open the `AssemblyInfo.cs` file in the project and add the following using directive:

   ```
   using System.EnterpriseServices;
   ```

6. Add the following attributes to the `AssemblyInfo.cs` file:

   ```
   [assembly: ApplicationName("Northwind Data " +
       "Application with Object Construction")]
   [assembly: Description("Retrieve and Update data " +
       "from the Northwind database")]
   [assembly: ApplicationActivation(
       ActivationOption.Server)]
   ```

7. Change the `AssemblyVersion` and `AssemblyKeyFile` attribute in the `AssemblyInfo.cs` file as shown here:

   ```
   [assembly: AssemblyVersion("1.0.0")]
   [assembly: AssemblyKeyFile(@"..\..\..\70320.snk")]
   ```

8. Build the project. A `GuidedPracticeExercise7_2.dll` file is generated, and a strong name is assigned to the file based on the specified key file.

9. Launch the Visual Studio .NET command prompt and change the directory to `GuidedPracticeExercise7_2.dll` file, and issue the following command to install the assembly to the GAC:

   ```
   gacutil /i GuidedPracticeExercise7_2.dll
   ```

10. At the command prompt, issue the following command to install the service component assembly to the COM+ Catalog:

    ```
    regsvcs GuidedPracticeExercise7_2.dll
    ```

11. Open the Component Services Administrative tool by selecting Administrative Tools, Component Services, Computers, My Computer, COM+ Applications from the Windows Control Panel. You should be able to see that Northwind Data Application with Object Construction has been added to the COM+ Catalog.

12. Right-click the `NorthwindConstructSC` serviced component and select Properties from the context menu. Click the Activation tab; notice that the Enable Object Construction check box is selected and the Constructor string text box contains the connection string supplied to the `ConstructionEnabled` attribute in the `NorthwindSC.cs` file, as shown in Figure 7.28.

Guided Practice Exercise 7.2 registers the serviced component in the COM+ Catalog. Before you can use the component from a client application, you should deploy the component to the GAC. The design of the client application is unaffected by the application of the ConstructionEnabled attribute. You can easily modify the client program in Step-by-Step 7.13 to work with this serviced component.

If you have difficulty following this exercise, review the sections "Object Pooling," "Just-in-Time Activation," and "Object Construction," earlier in this chapter. After doing that review, try this exercise again.

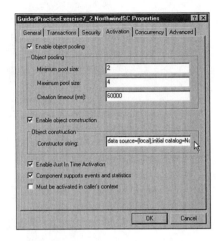

FIGURE 7.28
You can easily configure the object construction for a serviced component by using the Component Services administrative tool.

Automatic Transaction Processing

As discussed earlier, in the section "Microsoft Transaction Server (MTS)," a transaction is a series of operations performed as a single unit. A transaction is successful only when all the operations in that transaction succeed.

For example, consider a banking application that needs to perform a balance transfer from account A to account B for amount X. In this transaction, two atomic operations are involved. First, the balance in account A should be decreased by amount X, and second, the balance in account B should increased by amount X. For the balance transfer action to succeed, both of these atomic operations should succeed. If one of the actions fails, the system is in an inconsistent state (with wrong account balances) and the complete operation should be undone (rolled back). However, if both the atomic operations succeed, the balance transfer action also succeeds and the changes can be made permanent (committed).

Using transactions to ensure the reliability of applications is not a new concept. Transaction processing has been a part of database management systems long before the concept of transactions came to business objects. The COM+ transaction processing mechanism provides two significant advantages over traditional transaction processing techniques:

▶ Distributed Transactions—A local transaction is one whose scope is limited to a single transactional resource, such as a SQL Server database. On the other hand, a distributed transaction can span over several transaction-aware resources. The transaction-aware resources in a distributed transaction may be heterogeneous (such as a SQL Server database, Oracle database, or a Microsoft Messaging Queue) and may involve multiple computers over a network.

▶ Automatic Transactions—A typical database transaction, such as the one implemented with Transact SQL code or ADO.NET code, is manual in nature. With manual transactions, you explicitly begin and end the transaction and implement all the necessary logic to take care of the commit and rollback process. However, COM+ allows automatic transaction services that you can use in your program without writing any additional code. COM+ implements this with the help of a Windows service called Microsoft Distributed Transaction Coordinator (MSDTC).

In this section, I discuss how the COM+ automatic transaction processing service works and how to use this service to implement transactions across single-transaction–aware resources, as well as multiple-transaction–aware resources residing on separate processes.

Using Automatic Transaction Service for Local Transactions

Before I get any further, let me give you first-hand exposure to using automatic transaction processing for a local transaction in Step-by-Step 7.14.

In this example, I use the serviced component created in Step-by-Step 7.12 and demonstrate how you can use COM+ automatic transaction services without writing even a single line of additional code.

STEP BY STEP

7.14 Using a Local Automatic Transaction Processing Service

1. Start the Windows Application `StepByStep7_13.exe`. This is the client application that uses an object-pooled and just-in-time–enabled serviced component (`StepByStep7_12.NorthwindSC`). Together they enable you to query and update data from the `Northwind` sample database.

2. In the Windows form, type the following query and click on the Execute Query button.

`SELECT * FROM CUSTOMERS`

3. You see that a list of customers is displayed. Change the `ContactName` for a customer (for example, change "Maria Anders" to "Maria Anderson"). In the next record, change the `CustomerID` to any string of your choice (for example, change "ANATR" to "ANAT"). Click on the Update button. You get an error message because the `CustomerID` field has a check for referential integrity and the database doesn't allow you to change that.

4. Click on the Execute Query button. The fresh result shows that although you got an error in the previous execution, the database saved the record where you modified the `ContactName` but did not save the erroneous record where you modified the `CustomerID`. You now decide that both the database update operations performed in the previous step should be part of a transaction. If both of them succeed, the database should be updated with the changes; otherwise, the record should be rolled back to its old values.

5. Open the Component Services administrative tool. Open the property sheet for the `StepByStep7_12.NorthwindSC` serviced component. Select the Transactions tab and select the Required option in the Transaction Support group box, as shown in Figure 7.29.

FIGURE 7.29
You can configure a serviced component by using the Component Services administrative tool to use the COM+ automatic transaction processing service.

continues

continued

6. Switch to the Windows form and click on the Execute Query button for the same query. Now try updating the `ContactName` in one row and `CustomerID` in another row and click on the Update button. You get the same error message that you got in step 3. To verify the changes to the database, click on the Execute Query button and observe the results. Notice that both ContactName and CustomerID are unchanged. When you got an error while updating data, COM+ rolled back the complete operation, leaving the database in its original shape.

In Step-by-Step 7.14, you use the Component Services administrative tool to configure the automatic transaction service for a component. Like the other COM+ services, you can also accomplish this by writing declarative attributes in your programs. You'll learn about various attributes related to transaction processing in the next few sections.

Elements of Transaction Processing

The `System.EnterpriseServices` namespace provides various classes to work with transactions in your programs. These classes hide the complexity of automatic transaction processing and provide most of the functionality with declarative attributes. Under the covers, these classes negotiate with COM+ and MSDTC services to implement the transaction.

In this section, you'll learn how these classes work together to provide automatic transaction services.

The `Transaction` Attribute

Applying the `Transaction` attribute to a class is equivalent to enabling transactions through the Component Services administrative tool. The benefit of applying an attribute in the program is that the component can execute in a pre-configured state straight out of the box. The `Transaction` attribute takes a value from the `TransactionOption` enumeration to specify how a component participates in a transaction. The values of the `TransactionOption` enumeration are listed in Table 7.11.

TABLE 7.11

MEMBERS OF THE TransactionOption ENUMERATION

Member	Description
Disabled	Specifies that the component's capability to participate with COM+ in managing transactions has been disabled. This setting is used for compatibility reasons only.
NotSupported	Specifies that the component will never participate in transactions.
Required	Specifies that the component uses transactional resources such as databases and will participate in a transaction if one already exists; otherwise a new transaction must be created.
RequiresNew	Specifies that the component requires a new transaction to be created even if a transaction already exists.
Supported	Specifies that the component will participate in a transaction if one already exists. This setting is mostly used by components that do not themselves use any transactional resources.

For example, ComponentA may use the following code to request that a new transaction be created:

```
[Transaction(TransactionOption.RequiresNew)]
class ComponentA : ServicedComponent
{
    ...
}
```

When a transaction is created, it is uniquely identified by a transaction id. Several components can share a transaction, as in the following, when ComponentA calls a method on ComponentB, which has been defined as

```
[Transaction(TransactionOption.Supported)]
class ComponentB : ServicedComponent
{
    ...
}
```

Then ComponentB shares the transaction started by ComponentA. In this case, the tasks accomplish by ComponentA and ComponentB belong to the same unit of transaction. As a result, these tasks fail and succeed together.

> **EXAM TIP**
>
> **JIT Activation Is Required with Automatic Transaction Processing**
> To preserve the consistency of a transaction, a component must not carry state from one transaction to another. To enforce statelessness for all transactional components, COM+ uses JIT activation. JIT activation forces an object to deactivate and lose state before the object can be activated in another transaction.
>
> For a component, if you apply the Transaction attribute and set its value to TransactionOption. Supported, TransactionOption. Required, or TransactionOption. RequiresNew, then COM+ automatically sets the JustInTimeActivation attribute to true.

Context and Transaction

Each component that participates in a transaction has its own context. The context stores various flags that specify an object's state. Two such flags are the done bit and the consistent bit. In addition to objects, the transaction itself also has a context. The context of a transaction maintains an abort bit. The purpose of the abort bit is to determine whether the transaction as a whole failed or succeeded. I have summarized these bits and their influence on the outcome of a transaction in Table 7.12.

TABLE 7.12

THE ABORT, DONE, AND CONSISTENT BIT AND THEIR EFFECT ON THE TRANSACTION OUTCOME

Bit	Scope	Description	Affect on the Transaction Outcome
abort	Entire transaction	This bit is also called the doomed bit. COM+ sets this bit to `false` when creating a new transaction. In a transaction lifetime, if this bit is set to `true`, it cannot be changed back.	If the abort bit is set to `true`, then the transaction is aborted.
consistent	Each context	This bit is also called the happy bit. COM+ sets this bit to `true` when creating an object. A programmer can choose to set this bit to `true` or `false`, depending on the program logic to indicate that the object is either consistent or inconsistent.	If the consistent bit in any context is set to `false`, then the transaction is aborted. If the consistent bit in all the contexts is set to `true`, then the transaction is committed.
done	Each context	Each COM+ object that participates in a transaction must also support just-in-time activation and therefore must maintain a done bit. When a method call begins, the done bit is set to `false`. When a method call finishes, COM+ checks the status of the done bit. If the bit is `true` then the active object is deactivated.	When exiting a method, if the done bit is set to `true` and the consistent bit is set to `false` then the abort bit is set to `true`.

The .NET enterprise services library provides the `ContextUtil` class to work with an object's context. Table 7.13 shows those methods of the `ContextUtil` class that influence an object's done bit and its consistent bit.

TABLE 7.13

**HOW THE METHODS OF THE ContextUtil CLASS AFFECT
THE CONSISTENT BIT AND THE DONE BIT**

Method	Effect on Consistent Bit	Effect on Done Bit
DisableCommit()	false	false
EnableCommit()	true	false
SetAbort()	false	true
SetComplete()	true	true

How Automatic Transaction Works

In this section, you learn how the COM+ automatic transaction service works in a distributed scenario. Consider a scenario as shown in Figure 7.30. It shows an Ordering application that is divided into four layers:

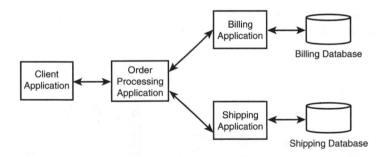

FIGURE 7.30
Distributed processing environments like the one shown in this figure are common in enterprises.

▶ Sales representatives use a Windows application to enter the order that they receive over the telephone.

▶ The client Windows application interacts with the Ordering application for order fulfillment. The Ordering application works as a service provider and interacts with other applications to fulfill an order. The main objective of this application is to keep the client from knowing how an order is processed. This scheme gives you flexibility in changing processes at the server side without making any changes to the client program.

▶ The Shipping application knows how to ship an order and the Billing application knows how to bill customers. These applications can reside on the same computer as the Ordering application, or may reside on different computers. If the applications are on different computers, they can use technologies such as remoting or XML Web services to communicate with the Ordering application.

▶ The Shipping application and the Billing application maintain their own sets of data that are independent of each other. The databases themselves may reside on different servers.

In this scenario, the need for transactions is clear. When a customer places an order, the order should be both billed and shipped as an integrated unit of work. Just billing the customer without shipping anything or vice-versa is not what most organizations want to do.

Let us now see how the automatic transaction service works in this scenario. For the sake of simplicity, I assume that each of the Ordering, Billing, and Shipping applications have just one component. The name of the component is the same as the name of application. Figure 7.31 shows how these components interact with each other to create a transaction.

FIGURE 7.31

Distributed processing environments like the one shown in this figure are common in enterprises.

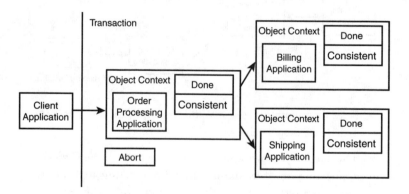

The process in Figure 7.31 is explained in the following steps:

1. When the client instantiates the Ordering component, an object context is created. The done bit is set to false, whereas the consistent bit is set to true. COM+ intercepts object invocation to check whether transaction services are needed. The Ordering component has a Transaction attribute set to the

`TransactionOption.RequiresNew` value. COM+ creates a new transaction and sets the abort bit to `false`. The `Ordering` component is designated as the root object of the transaction. A root object coordinates with all other objects in a transaction. The client fires a method on the `Ordering` component.

2. When the `Ordering` component instantiates the `Billing` component, COM+ intercepts to check whether transaction services are needed. The `Billing` component has a `Transaction` attribute set to the `TransactionOption.Supported` value. COM+ determines that the `Billing` component can support the transaction started by the `Ordering` component and extends the scope of the transaction to cover the `Billing` component. The context of the `Billing` object is initialized with the consistent bit set to true and the done bit set to `false`.

3. The `Ordering` component calls a method on the `Billing` component. The `Billing` object interacts with a SQL Server database to update a table of confirmed shipments. COM+ takes the help of MSDTC to record any new and old changes done to the database so that the changes can be rolled back at a later stage. If the update is successful, the consistent bit is set to `true`, but if there were any errors then the consistent bit is set to `false`. If the `Billing` object wishes to deactivate itself after the method call, it sets the done bit to `true`; otherwise the done bit remains set to `false`. If the done bit is `true` and the consistent bit is `false` then the abort bit of the transaction is set to `true` and the control transfers to Step 6.

4. When the method returns from the `Billing` object, COM+ intercepts the call and records the status of the consistent bit. If the done bit is `true`, the `Billing` object is deactivated.

5. The control comes back to the `Ordering` object and the `Ordering` component now repeats steps 2 to 4 to instantiate the `Shipping` component and invoke a method on the resulting object.

6. The control comes to the `Ordering` object. COM+ checks the status of the abort bit. If the abort bit is `true` then the entire transaction is aborted and COM+ requests DTC to roll back any changes that were made to the database. If the abort bit is `false` then the status of all the consistent bits is checked. If

NOTE

MSDTC and Two-phase Commit In a transaction, MSDTC works in two phases. The first phase is the prepare phase in which MSDTC interacts with resources managers for resources such as databases, message queues, and so on, and asks them to record new and old values in a durable place. Based on the resource manager's feedback, MSDTC determines the success or failure of an operation.

The second phase is the commit phase. In this phase, MSDTC asks all the individual resource managers to perform a commit operation on their resources. MSDTC collects the votes, and if all the commit operations are successful, then MSDTC instructs all resource managers to make the changes permanent. Otherwise, if any of the commits failed, MSDTC instructs all the resource managers to roll back their operations based on the information that they collected in the prepare phase.

any of these bits is false then the transaction is aborted and a rollback is performed. If all the consistent bits are true, then COM+ requests DTC to finally commit all the changes to the database.

7. Finally, the root object sets its done bit to true and returns from the method that was invoked by the client. COM+ intercepts to deactivate the root object and destroys the transaction. The control is transferred to the client.

In the preceding steps, if you wish to programmatically control the success or failure of an operation, you can do so by calling the methods of the ContextUtil class (see Table 7.5). However, a common choice is to apply the AutoComplete attribute on the method call. This attribute automatically calls ContextUtil.SetComplete() if the method completes successfully. Otherwise if the method throws an exception, ContextUtil.SetAbort() is called to abort the transaction.

Using Automatic Transaction Service for Distributed Transactions

Now that you are familiar with how transactions work, it's time to write a program that makes use of automatic transaction services in a distributed application. In this section, I use the distributed Ordering application already discussed and write a Shipping component, a Billing component, an Ordering component and a client application.

Step-by-Step 7.15 shows how to create a Shipping component that supports transactions and updates a database table with shipping records.

STEP BY STEP

7.15 Using Distributed Transactions: Creating a Shipping Component

1. Create a new table named Shipping in the Northwind database with the structure shown in Table 7.14.

TABLE 7.14

DESIGN OF THE Shipping TABLE

Column Name	Data Type	Length	Allow Nulls	Identity
ShippingID	int	4	No	Yes
CustomerID	nchar	5	No	No
ProductID	int	4	No	No
DateTime	datetime	8	No	No

2. Add a new Visual C# .NET Class library named StepByStep7_15 to the solution.

3. In the Solution Explorer, right-click project StepByStep7_15 and select Add Reference from the context menu to add a reference to the System.EnterpriseServices component.

4. In the Solution Explorer, rename the default Class1.cs to Shipping.cs.

5. Open Shipping.cs and replace the code with the following code:

```
using System;
using System.Data;
using System.Data.SqlClient;
using System.Data.SqlTypes;
using System.EnterpriseServices;
using System.Runtime.InteropServices;

namespace StepByStep7_15
{
    public interface IShipping
    {
        void ShipItem(
            string customerID, int productID);
    }

    [Transaction(TransactionOption.Supported)]
    [ClassInterface(ClassInterfaceType.None)]
    [Guid("660E0672-54E8-443f-9946-23C22E248034")]
    public class Shipping : ServicedComponent,
                            IShipping
    {
        SqlConnection sqlConn;
        public Shipping()
        {
```

continues

continued

```
                        sqlConn = new SqlConnection(
                            "data source=(local);" +
                            "initial catalog=Northwind;" +
                            "integrated security=SSPI");
                    }

                    [AutoComplete(true)]
                    public void ShipItem(string customerID,
                                         int productID)
                    {
                        SqlCommand sqlCmd = new SqlCommand();
                        SqlDateTime dt =
                            new SqlDateTime(DateTime.Now);
                        sqlCmd.CommandText = String.Format(
                            "insert into Shipping (CustomerID, " +
                            "ProductID, DateTime) values " +
                            "('{0}', {1}, '{2}')",
                            customerID, productID, dt);
                        sqlCmd.Connection = sqlConn;
                        sqlConn.Open();
                        sqlCmd.ExecuteNonQuery();
                    }
                }
            }
```

6. Open the `AssemblyInfo.cs` file in the project and add the following using directive:

```
using System.EnterpriseServices;
```

7. Add the following assembly-level attributes to the `AssemblyInfo.cs` file:

```
[assembly: ApplicationName("Shipping Application")]
[assembly: Description("Ship Orders")]
[assembly: ApplicationActivation(
    ActivationOption.Server)]
```

8. Change the `AssemblyVersion` and `AssemblyKeyFile` attribute in the `AssemblyInfo.cs` file as shown here:

```
[assembly: AssemblyVersion("1.0.0")]
[assembly: AssemblyKeyFile(@"..\..\..\70320.snk")]
```

9. Build the project. A `StepByStep7_15.dll` file is generated, and a strong name is assigned to the file based on the specified key file.

10. Launch the Visual Studio .NET command prompt and change the directory to the folder where the DLL file generated in step 9 resides. Issue the following command to install the assembly to the GAC:

```
gacutil /i StepByStep7_15.dll
```

11. At the command prompt, issue the following command to install the service component assembly to the COM+ Catalog:

```
regsvcs StepByStep7_15.dll
```

Note that in Step-by-Step 7.15 I used the `TransactionOption.Supported` option because the `Shipping` component is not invoked on its own. Instead, this component is invoked by the `Ordering` application as part of the order fulfillment process.

Step-by-Step 7.16 shows how to create a `Billing` component that supports transactions and updates a database table with billing records.

STEP BY STEP

7.16 Using Distributed Transactions: Creating a Billing Component

1. Create a new table named `Billing` in the `Northwind` database with the structure shown in Table 7.15.

TABLE 7.15

DESIGN OF THE Billing TABLE

Column Name	Data Type	Length	Allow Nulls	Identity
BillingID	int	4	No	Yes
CustomerID	nchar	5	No	No
ProductID	int	4	No	No
DateTime	datetime	8	No	No

2. Add a new Visual C# .NET Class library named `StepByStep7_16` to the solution.

continues

continued

3. In the Solution Explorer, right-click project
StepByStep7_16 and select Add Reference from the context
menu to add a reference to the
System.EnterpriseServices component.

4. In the Solution Explorer, rename the default Class1.cs to
Billing.cs.

5. Open Billing.cs and replace the code with the following
code:

```
using System;
using System.Data;
using System.Data.SqlClient;
using System.Data.SqlTypes;
using System.EnterpriseServices;
using System.Runtime.InteropServices;

namespace StepByStep7_16
{
    public interface IBilling
    {
        void BillCustomer(
            string customerID, int productID);
    }

    [Transaction(TransactionOption.Supported)]
    [ClassInterface(ClassInterfaceType.None)]
    [Guid("2F4B34B2-6140-41ce-9B57-AC7491F31203")]
    public class Billing : ServicedComponent,
                           IBilling
    {
        SqlConnection sqlConn;
        public Billing()
        {
            sqlConn = new SqlConnection(
                "data source=(local);" +
                "initial catalog=Northwind;" +
                "integrated security=SSPI");
        }

        [AutoComplete(true)]
        public void BillCustomer(string customerID,
                                 int productID)
        {
            SqlCommand sqlCmd = new SqlCommand();
            SqlDateTime dt =
                new SqlDateTime(DateTime.Now);

            sqlCmd.CommandText = String.Format(
                "insert into Billing (CustomerID, " +
```

```
                     "ProductID, DateTime) values " +
                     "('{0}', {1}, '{2}')",
                     customerID, productID, dt);

             sqlCmd.Connection = sqlConn;
             sqlConn.Open();
             sqlCmd.ExecuteNonQuery();
         }
     }
 }
```

6. Open the `AssemblyInfo.cs` file in the project and add the following using directive:

```
using System.EnterpriseServices;
```

7. Add the following assembly-level attributes to the `AssemblyInfo.cs` file:

```
[assembly: ApplicationName("Billing Application")]
[assembly: Description("Bill Customers")]
[assembly: ApplicationActivation(
    ActivationOption.Server)]
```

8. Change the `AssemblyVersion` and `AssemblyKeyFile` attributes in the `AssemblyInfo.cs` file as shown here:

```
[assembly: AssemblyVersion("1.0.0")]
[assembly: AssemblyKeyFile(@"..\..\..\70320.snk")]
```

9. Build the project. A `StepByStep7_16.dll` file is generated, and a strong name is assigned to the file based on the specified key file.

10. Launch the Visual Studio .NET command prompt and change the directory to the folder where the DLL file generated in step 9 resides. Issue the following command to install the assembly to the GAC:

```
gacutil /i StepByStep7_16.dll
```

11. At the command prompt, issue the following command to install the service component assembly to the COM+ Catalog:

```
regsvcs StepByStep7_16.dll
```

Note that in Step-by-Step 7.16, I used the `TransactionOption`. `Supported` option because the Billing component is not invoked on

its own. Instead, this component is invoked by the Ordering component as part of the order fulfillment process. Step-by-Step 7.17
shows how to create such an Ordering component.

STEP BY STEP

7.17 Using Distributed Transactions: Creating an Ordering Component

1. Add a new Visual C# .NET Class library named
   StepByStep7_17 to the solution.

2. In the Solution Explorer, right-click project
   StepByStep7_17 and select Add Reference from the context
   menu to add references to the System.EnterpriseServices
   component and to the projects StepByStep7_15 and
   StepByStep7_16.

3. In the Solution Explorer, rename the default Class1.cs to
   Ordering.cs.

4. Open Ordering.cs and replace the code with the following code:

```
using System;
using System.EnterpriseServices;
using System.Runtime.InteropServices;
using StepByStep7_15;
using StepByStep7_16;

namespace StepByStep7_17
{
    public interface IOrdering
    {
        void PlaceOrder(
            string customerID, int productID);
    }

    [Transaction(TransactionOption.RequiresNew)]
    [ClassInterface(ClassInterfaceType.None)]
    [Guid("C261BA4C-0B3E-49a7-87B5-7F6F909726A1")]
    public class Ordering : ServicedComponent,
                            IOrdering
    {
        public Ordering()
        {
        }
```

```
        [AutoComplete(true)]
        public void PlaceOrder(string customerID,
                                  int productID)
        {
            Billing billing = new Billing();
            billing.BillCustomer(
                customerID, productID);

            Shipping shipping = new Shipping();
            shipping.ShipItem(
                customerID, productID);
        }
    }
}
```

5. Open the `AssemblyInfo.cs` file in the project and add the following using directive:

```
using System.EnterpriseServices;
```

6. Add the following assembly-level attributes to the `AssemblyInfo.cs` file:

```
[assembly: ApplicationName("Ordering Application")]
[assembly: Description("Places an order")]
[assembly: ApplicationActivation(
    ActivationOption.Server)]
```

7. Change the `AssemblyVersion` and `AssemblyKeyFile` attribute in the `AssemblyInfo.cs` file as shown here:

```
[assembly: AssemblyVersion("1.0.0")]
[assembly: AssemblyKeyFile(@"..\..\..\70320.snk")]
```

8. Build the project. A `StepByStep7_17.dll` file is generated, and a strong name is assigned to the file based on the specified key file.

9. Launch the Visual Studio .NET command prompt and change the directory to the folder where the DLL file generated in step 8 resides. Issue the following command to install the assembly to the GAC:

```
gacutil /i StepByStep7_17.dll
```

10. At the command prompt, issue the following command to install the service component assembly to the COM+ Catalog:

```
regsvcs StepByStep7_17.dll
```

The Ordering component needs to work as a root object for a transaction. For this reason the Transaction attribute in Step-by-Step 7.17 uses the value TransactionOption.RequiresNew.

Now you have all the server-side components ready. In Step-by-Step 7.18, I create a client application that calls the Ordering component. I have created the client application as a Windows application; however, creating the client program as a Web application is not much different.

STEP BY STEP

7.18 Using Distributed Transactions: Creating a Client Order Form

1. Add a new Visual C# .NET Windows application named StepByStep7_18 to the solution.

2. In the Solution Explorer, right-click project StepByStep7_18 and select Add Reference from the context menu to add references to the System.EnterpriseServices and StepByStep7_17 components.

3. In the Solution Explorer, rename the default Form1.cs to OrderForm.cs. Open the form in code view and change all occurrences of Form1 to refer to OrderForm instead.

4. Add the following using directives:

```
using System.Data.SqlClient;
using StepByStep7_17;
```

5. Place one GroupBox control, two Label controls, two ComboBox controls (cboCustomers and cboProducts) and one Button control (btnPlaceOrder) on the form. Arrange the controls as shown in Figure 7.32.

6. Open Server Explorer and drag the Customers and Products table from the Northwind data connection node to the form. A SqlConnection object and two SqlDataAdapter objects are created on the form.

7. Right-click the first SqlDataAdapter object and select Generate DataSet from the context menu. In the Generate DataSet dialog box, choose the New radio button and

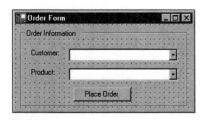

FIGURE 7.32
The design of a form that uses the Ordering serviced component.

name the new `DataSet` dsOrders. Select the Customers
table and click OK.

8. Right-click the second `SqlDataAdapter` object and select
Generate DataSet from the context menu. In the Generate
DataSet dialog box, choose the existing `DataSet` dsOrders.
Select the Products table and click OK.

9. Set the `DataSource` property to dsOrders1.`Customers`,
`DisplayMember` to `ContactName`, `ValueMember` to
`CustomerID`, and `DropDownStyle` to `DropDownList` for the
cboCustomers combo box. Set the `DataSource` property to
dsOrders1.`Product`, `DisplayMember` to `ProductName`,
`ValueMember` to `ProductID` and `DropDownStyle` to
`DropDownList` for the cboProduct combo box.

10. Double-click the form and add the following code in the
`Load` event handler:

```
private void OrderForm_Load(
    object sender, System.EventArgs e)
{
    sqlDataAdapter1.Fill(dsOrders1, "Customers");
    sqlDataAdapter2.Fill(dsOrders1, "Products");
}
```

11. Double-click the `Button` control and add the following
code to the `Click` event handler:

```
private void btnPlaceOrder_Click(
    object sender, System.EventArgs e)
{
    try
    {
        Ordering ordering = new Ordering();
        ordering.PlaceOrder(
            cboCustomers.SelectedValue.ToString(),
            (int) cboProducts.SelectedValue);
        MessageBox.Show("Order placed successfully");
    }
    catch(Exception ex)
    {
        MessageBox.Show(ex.Message);
    }
}
```

12. Build the project. Set the project `StepByStep7_18` as the
startup project.

continues

continued

13. Run the solution. Select a customer and a product from the Customers and Products combo boxes and click the Place Order button. You will see a message box confirming that the order is successfully placed. You can retrieve records from the `Billing` table and the Shipping table to find that one new record is added to each of them. This is the case when everything was as expected and the transaction was successfully committed.

14. Now consider a case where the `Billing` component is working fine but there is a problem with the `Shipping` component. To simulate this, open the Component Service administrative tool, right-click on the Shipping application, and select Delete from the context menu. COM+ 1.5 (Windows XP and Windows Server 2003) supports a less destructive way: You can select Disable from the context menu. Now run the client program. You get an error message showing that the `Shipping` component is not available. However, if you retrieve the data from the `Billing` and `Shipping` tables, neither the `Billing` nor `Shipping` table contains the record for sales that presented you with an error. Because there was an error, the transaction was automatically rolled back.

The client application created in Step-by-Step 7.18 does not itself take part in the transaction, but various server components that the client application uses do take part in a transaction. Automatic transaction processing increases the reliability of applications without putting lot of pain in programming.

In the last step of Step-by-Step 7.18, I simulated a scenario that an enterprise application should always be ready to deal with. This is a scenario where one or more of an application's components are unavailable. When the `Shipping` component was unavailable, you were not able to record orders in the system. For many applications, availability is the number one priority. Availability becomes a major challenge when applications are distributed because the points of failure are now increased and some of them are not even in your control.

I discuss how another COM+ service—Queued Components—solve the problem of availability in the next section.

Queued Components

From the perspective of a client, a q*ueued component* is a serviced component that can be invoked and executed asynchronously. The queued components are based on the Microsoft Message Queuing (MSMQ) technology, which is a part of the Windows operating system.

How Queued Components Work

Communication between a client and a queued component involves four basic components between the client and server, as shown in Figure 7.33. These components are

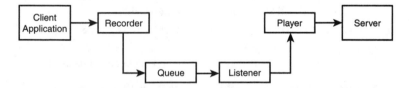

FIGURE 7.33
With queued components, messages are recorded in a message queue for later retrieval.

▶ Recorder—The Recorder kicks in when a client makes a call to the queued component. The recorder records the call, packages it as a message, and stores the message in the message queue.

▶ Queue—The Queue is a repository of messages. Each COM+ application has a set of queues assigned to it. There is one primary queue, five retry queues, and one dead-letter queue. When the message arrives from the recorder, the message waits in the primary queue to be picked up by the queued component. If there is an error in processing, the message is sent to the first retry queue. If the message processing fails in the first retry, the message is moved to the second retry queue, and so on. The retry queues differ from each other in the frequency with which they retry a message. The first retry queue retries messages most frequently, whereas the fifth one is the slowest. If there is an error in processing the message in the fifth queue, the message is finally moved to a dead-letter queue where no further retries are made. Occasionally, you may want to check the dead letter queue and custom process any failed messages.

▶ Listener—The Listener's role is to poll the queue for incoming messages and, when there is one, pass the message to the player.

▶ Player—The Player unpacks a message and calls the invoke methods that were recorded by the client on the queued component.

Creating a Queued Component

Creating a queued component is just like creating any other serviced component. To configure a component to work as a queued component you need to apply the following two attributes:

▶ ApplicationQueuing Attribute—You apply this attribute at the assembly level to enable queuing support for an application. If a client will call the queued component, then the QueueListenerEnabled property must be set to true.

```
[assembly: ApplicationQueuing(
          Enabled=true, QueueListenerEnabled=true)]
```

▶ InterfaceQueueing Attribute—You apply this attribute at the component level to specify the interface through which COM+ allows the calls on the component to be recorded and stored in the queue. For example:

```
[InterfaceQueuing(Enabled=true,
                  Interface="IOrdering")]
```

The execution lifetime of a queued component and the client application may be different. Therefore, when creating a queued component, you must follow these guidelines:

▶ Methods should not return any value or reference parameters.

▶ All calls made by the client should be self-sufficient. The queued component has no way to generate a callback to the client program if more information is needed.

▶ Methods should not throw any application-specific exceptions because the client may not be available to respond to the exceptions.

Step-by-Step 7.19 shows how to use a queued component that is capable of listening to a message queue. When a message arrives, the component receives orders and calls other components to process them.

STEP BY STEP

7.19 Using Queued Components: Creating an Ordering Component

1. Add a new Visual C# .NET Class library named StepByStep7_19 to the solution.

2. In the Solution Explorer, right-click project StepByStep7_19 and select Add Reference from the context menu to add references to the System.EnterpriseServices component and projects StepByStep7_15 and StepByStep7_16.

3. In the Solution Explorer, copy the Ordering.cs file from the StepByStep7_17 project to the current project. Open the file and change the namespace name to StepByStep7_19. Delete the default Class1.cs.

4. Apply the InterfaceQueuing attribute on the Ordering class and change the GUID in the Guid attribute:

```
[InterfaceQueuing(
    Enabled=true, Interface="IOrdering")]
[Transaction(TransactionOption.RequiresNew)]
[ClassInterface(ClassInterfaceType.None)]
[Guid("E02FF390-1E02-4a39-8C6D-DA8DDE2E9779")]
public class Ordering : ServicedComponent,
                        IOrdering
{
  ...
}
```

5. Open the AssemblyInfo.cs file in the project and add the following using directive:

```
using System.EnterpriseServices;
```

6. Add the following assembly-level attributes to the AssemblyInfo.cs file:

```
[assembly: ApplicationQueuing(
Enabled=true, QueueListenerEnabled=true)]
```

continues

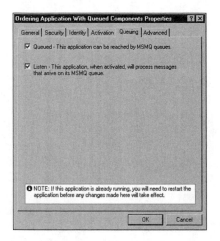

FIGURE 7.34
You can configure a COM+ application to support queuing through the Queuing tab of the Component Services administrative tool.

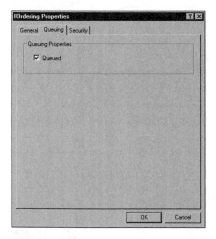

FIGURE 7.35
You can mark a component's interface to support queuing.

continued

```
[assembly: ApplicationName(
"Ordering Application With Queued Components")]
[assembly: Description("Places an order")]
[assembly: ApplicationActivation(
    ActivationOption.Server)]
```

Note that you have to add an `ApplicationQueuing` attribute to enable queuing for the application.

7. Change the `AssemblyVersion` and `AssemblyKeyFile` attribute in the `AssemblyInfo.cs` file as shown here:

```
[assembly: AssemblyVersion("1.0.0")]
[assembly: AssemblyKeyFile(@"..\..\..\70320.snk")]
```

8. Build the project. A `StepByStep7_19.dll` is generated, and a strong name is assigned to the file based on the specified key file.

9. Launch the Visual Studio .NET command prompt and change the directory to the folder where the DLL file generated in step 8 resides. Issue the following command to install the assembly to the GAC:

```
gacutil /i StepByStep7_19.dll
```

10. At the command prompt, issue the following command to install the service component assembly to the COM+ Catalog:

```
regsvcs StepByStep7_19.dll
```

After you have registered a serviced component in the COM+ Catalog, as you did in Step-by-Step 7.19, access the Properties window of the COM+ application via the Component Services administrative tool. In the Queuing tab, you will see that the options for queuing and listening are already configured as shown in Figure 7.34.

You can also configure an interface to support queuing through its Properties dialog box, as shown in Figure 7.35.

Creating a Client for a Queued Component

One of the ways you create an object in the client program is by using the new operator. However, you don't want to use that when working with a queue. With a queued component your objective is not to create an instance of an object but instead you need a way in which you can record a message for the client and store that in a queue so that the server object can read that message when possible.

Recording a message for a queued component is generally a three-step process:

1. Call the `Marshal.BindToMoniker()` method and pass it a moniker string that corresponds to the interface of the queued component. The moniker string is formed by preceding the full type name (qualified with namespace) with the string `"queue:/new:"`. For example:

   ```
   Marshal.BindToMoniker(@"queue:/new:StepByStep7_19.
   Ordering");
   ```

   The `Marshal.BindToMoniker()` method returns a reference to the interface identified by the given moniker string.

2. Use the interface reference obtained in step 1 to execute methods on the queued component. These methods are not executed immediately; instead, they are recorded and placed in the message queue.

3. When you've finished calling methods, call the `Marshal.ReleaseComObject()` method to release the reference to the interface reference obtained in step 1.

Step-by-Step 7.20 shows how to create a client program that uses the `Marshal.BindToMoniker()` method to record messages for a queued component.

STEP BY STEP

7.20 Using Queued Components: Creating a Client Order Form

1. Add a new Visual C# .NET Windows application named `StepByStep7_20` to the solution.

continues

continued

2. In the Solution Explorer, right-click project
StepByStep7_20 and select Add Reference from the context
menu to add references to the System.EnterpriseServices
and StepByStep7_19 components.

3. In the Solution Explorer, rename the default Form1.cs to
OrderForm.cs. Open the form in code view and change all
occurrences of Form1 to refer to OrderForm instead.

4. Add the following using directives:

```
using System.Data.SqlClient;
using StepByStep7_19;
using System.Runtime.InteropServices;
```

5. Place one GroupBox control, two Label controls, two
ComboBox controls (cboCustomers and cboProducts), and
one Button control (btnPlaceOrder) on the form. You can
use the design of the form in Figure 7.32.

6. Open Server Explorer and drag the Customers and
Products tables from the Northwind data connection node
to the form. A SqlConnection object and two
SqlDataAdapter objects are created on the form.

7. Right-click the first SqlDataAdapter object and select
Generate DataSet from the context menu. In the Generate
DataSet dialog box, choose the New radio button and
name the new DataSet dsOrders. Select the Customers
table and click OK.

8. Right-click the second SqlDataAdapter object and select
Generate DataSet from the context menu. In the Generate
DataSet dialog box, choose the existing DataSet dsOrders.
Select the Products table and click OK.

9. Set the DataSource property to dsOrders1.Customers,
DisplayMember to ContactName, ValueMember to CustomerID,
and DropDownStyle to DropDownList for the cboCustomers
combo box. Set the DataSource property to
dsOrders1.Product, DisplayMember to ProductName,
ValueMember to ProductID, and DropDownStyle to
DropDownList for the cboProduct combo box.

10. Double-click the form and add the following code in the
Load event handler:

```
private void OrderForm_Load(
    object sender, System.EventArgs e)
{
    sqlDataAdapter1.Fill(dsOrders1, "Customers");
    sqlDataAdapter2.Fill(dsOrders1, "Products");
}
```

11. Double-click the Button control and add the following
code to the Click event handler:

```
private void btnPlaceOrder_Click(
    object sender, System.EventArgs e)
{

    IOrdering ord = null;
    try
    {
        ord = (IOrdering) Marshal.BindToMoniker(
            @"queue:/new:StepByStep7_19.Ordering");
        ord.PlaceOrder(
            cboCustomers.SelectedValue.ToString(),
            (int) cboProducts.SelectedValue);
        MessageBox.Show("Order placed in the queue");
    }
    catch(Exception ex)
    {
        MessageBox.Show(ex.Message);
    }
    finally
    {
        Marshal.ReleaseComObject(ord);
    }
}
```

12. Build the project. Set the project StepByStep7_20 as the
startup project.

13. Run the solution. Select a customer and a product from
the Customers and Products combo boxes and click the
Place Order button. You will see that because both
Billing and Shipping components are available, the message is immediately processed.

14. Try disabling or uninstalling either the Billing or
Shipping component and run the client application again.
Note that the records for a sale are now not immediately
created in the database tables. Instead, this information is
now part of the message queue, waiting for the serviced

continues

continued

> component to be started. You can view the message queue
> for a computer via the Computer Management tool avail-
> able in the Administrative Tools section of the Windows
> Control Panel.

In Step-by-Step 7.20 you learned how to record messages in a queue
for a serviced component. You also experimented with making an
application available without regard to whether one or more components failed.

REVIEW BREAK

- ▶ A transaction is a series of operations performed as a single
  unit. A transaction is successful only when all the operations in
  that transaction succeed.

- ▶ The outcome of a transaction depends on the status of the
  abort bit that is maintained in the context of a transaction and
  the consistent and done bits, which are maintained in each
  context.

- ▶ You can use the methods of the ContextUtil class to change
  the status of the consistent and done bits programmatically.

- ▶ The AutoComplete attribute automatically calls the
  ContextUtil.SetComplete() method if a method completes
  successfully; otherwise, ContextUtil.SetAbort() is called to
  abort the transaction.

- ▶ A queued component is a serviced component that can be
  invoked and executed asynchronously. With the help of a
  queued component, you can make your application available
  even when some of its components are not.

CHAPTER SUMMARY

Enterprise applications have special needs for availability, reliability, scalability, and performance. COM+ provides an infrastructure that provides common services required for an enterprise application.

In this chapter, you learned how to use COM+ component services from your .NET programs. You created a serviced component and registered the component with the COM+ Catalog.

You also learned how to expose a .NET component to COM or COM+ programs. When a .NET component is visible to COM+, you can use the Component Services administrative tool to configure a component.

You also learned how to apply various attributes to your assemblies, classes, and methods to use the COM+ services. You used and appreciated the ease and power of attribute-based declarative programming for programming the component services.

You examined a bunch of COM+ services such as object construction, object pooling, just-in-time activation, automatic transactions, and queued components. You explored how these services work and how to use these services in your programs.

KEY TERMS

- ACID
- activation type
- COM+ application
- COM+ Catalog
- COM interface
- context
- DTC (Distributed Transaction Coordinator)
- just-in-time (JIT) activation
- object pooling
- queued component
- transaction

APPLY YOUR KNOWLEDGE

Exercises

7.1   Exposing Serviced Components via .NET Remoting

In an enterprise application, you may be required to expose business objects remotely. A general practice in that case is to add an extra tier that handles remote communication between the client and server. You can use your knowledge of .NET remoting and XML Web services for creating such a tier.

In this exercise, you learn how to expose a serviced component via a remoting server. You create three sets of programs: a serviced component that allows access to the Northwind database, a Singleton remoting server that exposes the serviced component, and a client program that connects to the remoting server to invoke methods on the serviced component.

Estimated Time: 30 minutes.

1. Launch Visual Studio .NET. Select File, New, Blank Solution, and name the new solution `320C07Exercises`. Click OK.

2. Add a new Visual C# .NET Class library project named `Exercise7_1SC` to the solution.

3. In the Solution Explorer, right-click project `Exercise7_1SC` and select Add Reference from the context menu to add a reference to the `System.EnterpriseServices` component.

4. In the Solution Explorer, rename the default `Class1.cs` to `NorthwindSC.cs`. Open the `NorthwindSC.cs` and replace the code with the following code (change the `Guid` attribute):

```
using System;
using System.Data;
using System.Data.SqlClient;
using System.EnterpriseServices;
using System.Runtime.InteropServices;
using System.Diagnostics;
```

```
namespace Exercise7_1SC
{
    public interface INorthwind
    {
        DataSet ExecuteQuery(
            string strQuery);
        int UpdateData(
            string strQuery, DataSet ds);
    }

    [EventTrackingEnabled(true)]
    [JustInTimeActivation(true)]
    [ObjectPooling(true, 2,4)]
    [Guid(
    "94AB3102-C44F-40de-A29F-309437D9EC86")]
    [ClassInterface(
        ClassInterfaceType.None)]
    public class NorthwindSC :
        ServicedComponent, INorthwind
    {
        private SqlConnection sqlcnn;
        private SqlDataAdapter sqlda;
        private DataSet ds;
        private EventLog eventLog;

        public NorthwindSC()
        {
            // Create a connection to the
            // Northwind SQL Server database
            sqlcnn = new SqlConnection(
                "data source=(local);" +
                "initial catalog=Northwind;" +
                "integrated security=SSPI");

            // Create an EventLog object
            // and assign its source
            eventLog = new EventLog();
            eventLog.Source = "Exercise7_1";
            // Write an entry to the event log
            eventLog.WriteEntry("A new " +
            "NorthwindSC object is created " +
            " and added to the object pool");
        }

        protected override void Activate()
        {
            eventLog.WriteEntry(
            "A NorthwindSC object is " +
            "activated from the object
➡pool");
        }
```

APPLY YOUR KNOWLEDGE

```
protected override void Deactivate()
{
    eventLog.WriteEntry(
    "A NorthwindSC object is " +
    " deactivated and is " +
    "returned to the object pool");
}

protected override bool
    CanBePooled()
{
    return true;
}

public DataSet ExecuteQuery(
    string strQuery)
{
    // Create a SqlDataAdapter object
    // to talk to the database
    sqlda = new SqlDataAdapter(
        strQuery, sqlcnn);

    // Create a DataSet object
    // to hold the results
    ds = new DataSet();

    // Fill the DataSet object
    sqlda.Fill(ds, "Results");
    // Deactivate the object
    // when the method returns
    ContextUtil.DeactivateOnReturn
        = true;
    return ds;
}

[AutoComplete]
public int UpdateData(
    string strQuery, DataSet ds)
{
    // Update the database
    sqlda = new SqlDataAdapter(
        strQuery, sqlcnn);
    SqlCommandBuilder sqlcb =
        new SqlCommandBuilder(sqlda);
    return sqlda.Update(
        ds.Tables["Results"]);
}
    }
}
```

5. Open the `AssemblyInfo.cs` file in the project and add the following using directive:

```
using System.EnterpriseServices;
```

6. Add the following assembly-level attributes in the `AssemblyInfo.cs` file:

```
[assembly: ApplicationName(
    "Northwind Data Application " +
    "exposed via Remoting")]
[assembly: Description(
    "Retrieve and Update data " +
    "from the Northwind database")]
[assembly: ApplicationActivation(
    ActivationOption.Server)]
```

7. Copy the `70320.snk` key pair file to the `320C07Exercises` folder. Change the `AssemblyVersion` and `AssemblyKeyFile` attributes in the `AssemblyInfo.cs` file as shown here:

```
[assembly: AssemblyVersion("1.0")]
[assembly:
AssemblyKeyFile(@"..\..\..\70320.snk")]
```

8. Build the project. An `Exercise7_1SC.dll` file is generated, and a strong name is assigned to the file based on the specified key file.

9. Launch the Visual Studio .NET command prompt and change the directory to the folder where the DLL file generated in step 8 resides. Issue the following command to install the assembly to the GAC:

```
gacutil /i Exercise7_1SC.dll
```

10. At the command prompt, issue the following command to install the service component assembly to the COM+ Catalog:

```
regsvcs Exercise7_1SC.dll
```

11. Add a new Visual C# .NET Console application named `Exercise7_1Server` to the solution.

APPLY YOUR KNOWLEDGE

12. In the Solution Explorer, right-click project `Exercise7_1Server` and select Add Reference from the context menu to add references to the `System.Runtime.Remoting`, `System.EnterpriseServices`, and `Exercise7_1SC` components.

13. In the Solution Explorer, rename the default `Class1.cs` to `NorthwindSCServer.cs`. Open the file and change the name of the class to `NorthwindSCServer` in the class declaration.

14. Add the following using directives:

```
using System.Runtime.Remoting;
using System.Runtime.Remoting.Channels;
using System.Runtime.Remoting.Channels.Tcp;
```

15. Add the following code in the `Main()` method:

```
[STAThread]
static void Main(string[] args)
{
    // Create and Register a TCP
    // server channel that
    // listens on port 1234
    TcpServerChannel channel =
        new TcpServerChannel(1234);
    ChannelServices.RegisterChannel(
        channel);

    // Register the service that
    // publishes NorthwindSC for
    // remote access in Singleton mode
    RemotingConfiguration.
        RegisterWellKnownServiceType
        (typeof(Exercise7_1SC.NorthwindSC),
        "NorthwindSC",
        WellKnownObjectMode.Singleton);
    Console.WriteLine(
        "Started server " +
        "in the Singleton mode");
    Console.WriteLine(
        "Press <ENTER> to  " +
        "terminate server...");
    Console.ReadLine();
}
```

16. Build the project. This step creates a remoting server that is capable of registering the `Exercise7_1SC.NorthwindSC` serviced component for remote invocation in the `Singleton` activation mode.

17. Add a new Visual C# .NET Windows application project (`Exercise7_1Client`) to the solution. Rename the default form `Form1.cs` to `NorthwindSCClient.cs`.

18. Add references to the .NET assemblies `System.Runtime.Remoting` and `System.EnterpriseServices` and the project `Exercise7_1SC` (the serviced component class assembly).

19. Add the following using directives:

```
using System.Runtime.Remoting;
using System.Runtime.Remoting.Channels;
using System.Runtime.Remoting.Channels.Tcp;
using Exercise7_1SC;
```

20. Place two `GroupBox` controls, a `TextBox` control (`txtQuery`), two `Button` controls (`btnExecute` and `btnUpdate`), and a `DataGrid` control (`dgResults`) on the form. Arrange the controls as shown in Figure 7.17.

21. Double-click the form and add the following code in the `Load` event handler:

```
private void NorthwindSCClient_Load(
    object sender, System.EventArgs e)
{
    // Register a TCP client channel
    TcpClientChannel channel =
        new TcpClientChannel();
    ChannelServices.RegisterChannel(
        channel);

    // Register the remote class as a valid
    // type in the client's
    // application domain
    RemotingConfiguration.
        RegisterWellKnownClientType(
        // Remote class
        typeof(NorthwindSC),
```

APPLY YOUR KNOWLEDGE

```
            // URL of the remote class
            "tcp://localhost:1234/NorthwindSC"
            );
    }
```

22. Double-click the Button controls and add the following code in their Click event handlers:

```
private void btnExecute_Click(
    object sender, System.EventArgs e)
{
    // Declare and instantiate
    // the remote serviced component
    NorthwindSC nsc= new NorthwindSC();

    try
    {
        // Call the ExecuteQuery() method
        dgResults.DataSource =
            nsc.ExecuteQuery(txtQuery.Text);
        dgResults.DataMember = "Results";
    }
    catch(Exception ex)
    {
        MessageBox.Show(ex.Message,
            "Invalid Query",
            MessageBoxButtons.OK,
            MessageBoxIcon.Error);
    }
}

private void btnUpdate_Click(
    object sender, System.EventArgs e)
{
    // Declare and instantiate
    // the remote serviced component
    NorthwindSC nsc= new NorthwindSC();
    try
    {
        // Call the UpdateData() method
        int intRows = nsc.UpdateData(
            txtQuery.Text,
            (DataSet) dgResults.DataSource);
        MessageBox.Show(String.Format(
            "{0} row(s) updated", intRows),
            "Row(s) Updated",
            MessageBoxButtons.OK,
            MessageBoxIcon.Information);

        // Load the updates and bind the
        // grid with the updates
        dgResults.DataSource =
            nsc.ExecuteQuery(txtQuery.Text);
```

```
        dgResults.DataMember = "Results";
    }
    catch(Exception ex)
    {
        MessageBox.Show(ex.Message,
            "Update Failed",
            MessageBoxButtons.OK,
            MessageBoxIcon.Error);
    }
}
```

23. Build the project. Start the remoting server and then start the client. Enter some queries to retrieve data from the Northwind database to test your programs.

7.2 Using Application Pooling and Recycling

Application pooling allows more than one instance of the COM+ server application to run at a time. By default, the size of the application pool is 1. If you set this size to a higher value, for example 4, then the first four activation requests to the application create four instances of dllhost.exe, each running this application. Later requests for applications are then routed through this pool of dllhost.exe processes. Application activation increases the scalability of the application and provides support for application failover.

Using the automatic application recycling service, you can configure an application to shut down and restart automatically when known problems occur. Some of the criteria for which you can configure recycling include lifetime limit, memory limit, call limit, and so on.

Both application pooling and recycling are features of COM+ 1.5. Currently the .NET Framework SDK does not provide any attribute to configure these services in your program. If you need to configure these services in a program, you must instead rely on the COM+ Administrative SDK.

APPLY YOUR KNOWLEDGE

However, you can also use the Component Services administrative tool to administratively configure these services. In this exercise, you learn how to configure application pooling and recycling on a machine running COM+ 1.5 (that is, Windows XP and Windows .NET Server computers).

Estimated Time: 10 minutes.

1. Open the Component services administrative tool.

2. Right-click the Ordering Application icon and select Properties from the shortcut menu. In the Ordering Application Properties dialog box, select the Pooling & Recycling tab, as shown in Figure 7.36.

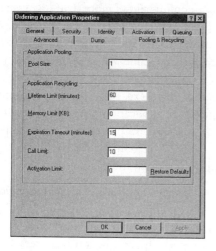

FIGURE 7.36
You can configure Application pooling and recycling properties for a COM+ application on computers running COM+ 1.5.

3. Set the Pool Size to 4, Lifetime limit to 5 minutes and the Call Limit to 10.

4. Apply the changes. Start the order form and place a few orders. In the list of the running processes, you will see that multiple instances of `dllhost.exe` are created for the Ordering Application, and if you wait for 5 minutes or place 10 orders, then a new `dllhost.exe` process is started.

Review Questions

1. What is the COM+ catalog and what is it used for?

2. What is the significance of using the `AutoComplete` attribute in a method declaration?

3. What is the use of the `CanBePooled()` method for a pooled object?

4. How does a client instantiate a queued component?

5. How can you use COM+ services to increase an application's throughput?

6. How would you specify the type of transaction available to a serviced component?

7. What is the use of the `ContextUtil` class?

8. What are some of the scenarios where you might want to use the COM+ object pooling service?

9. State a few guidelines for designing a queued component.

10. What is a COM Callable Wrapper (CCW)?

APPLY YOUR KNOWLEDGE

Exam Questions

1. You create a COM+ application named "Inventory Application." This application contains a single serviced component named InventoryStatus that is present in an assembly named inventorystatus.dll. The InventoryStatus component is used by many client applications to monitor the status of the inventory. The client applications access the serviced component on a frequent basis. Which of the following options should you choose to ensure that the methods on InventoryStatus are processed as quickly as possible?

   A. Configure Inventory Application to be a server application.

   B. Configure Inventory Application to be a library application.

   C. Configure the InventoryStatus component to use object pooling.

   D. Configure the InventoryStatus component to use just-in-time Activation.

2. You are creating a serviced component that will be called from both managed and unmanaged client applications. You use a class library project to write the business logic and then compile the project into a strongly named assembly. As a next step, you want to register the assembly in the COM+ Catalog. You want to detect and correct any registration errors before any client applications use the component. Which of the following tools should you use to register the assembly?

   A. Use the Assembly Registration tool (regasm.exe) to create entries in the Registry that describe the assembly.

   B. Use the Type Library Exporter (tlbexp.exe) to export the definition for the assembly.

   C. Use the Global Assembly Cache tool (gacutil.exe) to add the component to the global assembly cache.

   D. Use the .NET Services Installation tool (regsvcs.exe) to add the component to the COM+ Catalog.

3. You create a serviced component that allows users to connect to a homegrown ERP system that your company uses for various critical business operations. You register the component to the COM+ Catalog of the main application server. You enable the object pooling service for the component and set the Minimum Pool Size to 10 and Maximum Pool Size to 75. You monitor the statistics for the serviced component and find that 75 objects are already in use. What is the most likely result if one more request for an object is received?

   A. The request is queued until either a connection is available or the timeout limit has been exceeded.

   B. The request for the object is well received and a new object is created.

   C. The request generates an exception.

   D. The serviced component uses just-in-time activation to deactivate the objects that are not in use and then create an object for the new request.

APPLY YOUR KNOWLEDGE

4. You create a serviced component named
   `OrderProcess`. This component updates several
   SQL Server databases to complete a customer's
   order. The `OrderProcess` class includes the following code:

```
[Transaction(TransactionOption.Required)]
public class OrderProcess :
    ServicedComponent
{
    public void PlaceOrder(OrderInfo o)
    {
        // code to update various databases
    }
}
```

You must ensure the reliability of the
`PlaceOrder()` method. The `PlaceOrder()` method
should update either all or none of the databases.
What should you do?

   A. Add the following attribute to the
      `OrderProcess` class:

```
[JustInTimeActivation(false)]
```

   B. Add the following attribute to the
      `PlaceOrder()` method:

```
[AutoComplete()]
```

   C. Add the following line of code at the end of
      the `PlaceOrder()` method:

```
ContextUtil.EnableCommit();
```

   D. Add the following line of code at the end of
      the `PlaceOrder()` method:

```
ContextUtil.SetComplete();
```

5. You create a serviced component named
   `OrderProcess`. This component receives orders
   from the client applications in an asynchronous
   fashion. The `OrderProcess` class includes the following code:

```
namespace Exam70320
{
```

```
public interface IOrderProcess
{
    void PlaceOrder(OrderInfo o);
}
[Transaction(TransactionOption.Required)]
[InterfaceQueuing(Enabled=true,
        Interface="IOrdering")]
public class OrderProcess :
            ServicedComponent,
            IOrderProcess
{
    public void PlaceOrder(OrderInfo o)
    {
        // code to update various databases
    }
}
}
```

You need to write code for a client program that
uses the `OrderProcess` component to place an
order. Which code segment should you use?

   A.

```
IOrderProcess order = new IOrderProcess();
Order.PlaceOrder(orderInfo);
```

   B.

```
IOrderProcess order;
order = (IOrderProcess)
        Activator.GetObject
        (typeof(IOrderProcess),
      @"queued:/new:Exam70320.OrderProcess");
order.PlaceOrder(orderInfo);
```

   C.

```
IOrderProcess order;
order = (IOrderProcess)
        Marshal.BindToMoniker
      (@"queue:/new:Exam70320.OrderProcess");
order.PlaceOrder(orderInfo);
```

   D.

```
IOrderProcess order;
order = (IOrderProcess)
        Assembly.CreateInstance
      (@"queue:/new:Exam70320.OrderProcess");
order.PlaceOrder(orderInfo);
```

APPLY YOUR KNOWLEDGE

6. You create a queued component named `OrderProcess`. This component receives orders from the client applications in an asynchronous fashion. The `OrderProcess` class includes the following code:

```
namespace Exam70320
{
    public interface IOrderProcess
    {
        bool PlaceOrder(OrderInfo o);
    }
    [Transaction(TransactionOption.Required)]
    [InterfaceQueuing(Enabled=true,
            Interface="IOrderProcess")]
    public class OrderProcess :
                    ServicedComponent,
                    IOrderProcess
    {
        public bool PlaceOrder(OrderInfo o)
        {
            // code to update various databases
        }
    }
}
```

You get no compilation errors, but when you register this component using the .NET Services Installation Tool (`regsvcs.exe`), you get an error message: `Queuing not supported on interface 'IOrderProcess'`. What should you do to resolve this error?

A. Apply the following attribute on the class:

```
[ApplicationQueuing(
Enabled=true, QueueListenerEnabled=true)]
```

B. Apply the `InterfaceQueuing` attribute on the `IOrderProcess` interface rather than on the `OrderProcess` class.

C. Change the interface definition as follows and then change `OrderProcess` to implement this interface.

```
public interface IOrderProcess
{
    void PlaceOrder(OrderInfo o);
}
```

D. Apply the `AutoComplete` attribute on the `OrderProcess` class.

7. You are developing a serviced component that several client applications will use. Some client applications are COM based, whereas the other client applications run on the .NET Framework. In the future, you plan to release new versions of your serviced component but do not want to recompile the client applications. How should you design the interfaces for such a serviced component?

A. Define an interface and then use that interface to implement the serviced component. On the serviced component set the following attribute:

```
[ClassInterface(ClassInterfaceType.None)]
```

B. Set the following attribute on the serviced component:

```
[ClassInterface(
    ClassInterfaceType.AutoDual)]
```

C. Define an interface and then use that interface to implement the serviced component. Set the following attribute on the serviced component:

```
[ClassInterface(
    ClassInterfaceType.AutoDual)]
```

D. Set the following attribute on the serviced component:

```
[ClassInterface(
    ClassInterfaceType.AutoDispatch)]
```

APPLY YOUR KNOWLEDGE

8. You are writing a serviced component that will be used by users over the network. The number of users simultaneously supported by the component depends on the license agreement. Which of the following attributes would you use to restrict the number of simultaneous connections to the serviced component?

   A. The `JustInTimeActivation` attribute

   B. The `Transaction` attribute

   C. The `ObjectConstruction` attribute

   D. The `ObjectPooling` attribute

9. Your colleague is testing a queued component that she just developed. She can configure the serviced component with the Component Services administrative tool, but the client application cannot find the component. Which of the following options should you suggest to your colleague to resolve this problem?

   A. Use the Assembly Registration tool (`regasm.exe`) to install the component in Windows Registry.

   B. Use the Global Assembly Cache tool (`gacutil.exe`) to install the component in the global assembly cache.

   C. Copy the component to the directory of the client application.

   D. Copy the component to the Windows system directory.

10. You are creating a serviced component named `DataConnector`. After the component is deployed, the system administrators should be able to configure the component to connect to various data sources by specifying the connection string of the data source. The serviced component will be used by both COM and .NET applications. You want to retrieve the specified connection string in your component and change the behavior of the serviced component. Which of the following techniques should you use to achieve this?

   A. Override the `Activate()` method.

   B. Override the `Construct()` method.

   C. Override the `Deactivate()` method.

   D. Specify a constructor for the serviced component that receives a connection string as its parameter.

11. You have created a business object in Visual C# .NET. You want the business object to be used by COM clients as well as .NET clients. You want to deploy the business object on the client computers in such a way that the client can take advantage of late binding as well as early binding with the interfaces exposed by the business object. Which of the following methods would you use to accomplish this?

    A. Use Visual Studio .NET, open the project's property pages and change the Register for COM Interop option to `true`.

    B. Use the Assembly Registration tool (`regasm.exe`) with its `/tlb` option.

    C. Use the Type Library Exporter tool (`tlbexp.exe`) that ships as a part of the .NET Framework SDK.

    D. Use the `ConvertAssemblyToTypeLib()` method of the `TypeLibConverter` class in the `System.Runtime.InteropServices` namespace.

APPLY YOUR KNOWLEDGE

12. You have written the following code for a serviced component:

```
namespace Exam70320
{
    public interface IOrderProcess
    {
        bool PlaceOrder(OrderInfo o);
    }
    [JustInTimeActivation(true)]
    [Transaction(
        TransactionOption.Required)]
    public class OrderProcess :
                ServicedComponent,
                IOrderProcess
    {
        public bool PlaceOrder(OrderInfo o)
        {
            // code to update various databases
        }
    }
}
```

In the `PlaceOrder()` method you decide whether all the databases have been updated correctly. If yes then you commit the transaction and deactivate the current `OrderProcess` object. Which of the following methods should you use in the `PlaceOrder()` method to accomplish this requirement?

A. `DisableCommit()`

B. `EnableCommit()`

C. `SetAbort()`

D. `SetComplete()`

13. You create a serviced component that will be used by only the .NET client programs. You want to use the COM+ object creation service from the serviced component. Which of the following steps must you take for the programs to use the serviced component? (Select all that apply.)

A. Register the component in the Windows Registry.

B. Install the component in the global assembly cache.

C. Sign the component with a strong name.

D. Register the component in the COM+ Catalog.

14. You are developing a distributed order processing application for your company. The sales associates receive orders over the telephone. The orders are entered in the ordering system through a Windows form application. The Windows form application calls a set of serviced components to accomplish tasks. You must continue to receive orders even if one or more order processing components fail. Which of the following COM+ services should you use in the serviced components to ensure high availability of the system?

A. Queued components

B. Automatic transactions

C. Object pooling

D. Just-in-time activation

15. You have been given an assignment to develop the order processing application for your organization. The application needs to support a large number of users and should perform well even between 8:00 a.m. and 12:00 noon, which is the peak time for receiving and processing orders. Which of the following COM+ services would you use in your application? (Select all that apply.)

A. Queued components

B. Automatic transactions

C. Object pooling

D. Just-in-time activation

APPLY YOUR KNOWLEDGE

Answers to Review Questions

1. The COM+ Catalog is a repository that is used by COM+ to store the information about the serviced components and their runtime requirements.

2. Using the `AutoComplete` attribute in a method declaration is the equivalent of writing code to call `ContextUtil.SetComplete()` or `ContextUtil.SetAbort()`, respectively, when a method successfully completes or completes with an error.

3. When a pooled object is about to be deactivated, the `CanBePooled()` method is called to check whether the object should be returned to the object pool or instead destroyed. An object is returned to the object pool only when the `CanBePooled()` method returns `true`.

4. To instantiate a queued object, the client uses the `Marshal.BindToMoniker()` method. This method accepts a moniker name that identifies the target queued component. This method then instantiates a recorder for the queued component. The client can record all the calls on this recorder. When the queued component becomes available, the recorded calls are played back to the queued component.

5. You should use the COM+ just-in-time activation and object pooling services for the following reasons:

    • JIT activation enables clients to hold long-lived references on the server object (through a proxy) without consuming server resources.

    • JIT activation allows the server objects to be destroyed as soon as their work is finished to minimize the resource consumption on the server.

    • Object pooling caches the already-created objects and saves time by activating and deactivating the objects from the pool instead of re-creating them from scratch.

6. The `Transaction` attribute can be used to specify the type of transaction available to a component. This is done by setting its value to one of the `TransactionOption` values—`Disabled`, `NotSupported`, `Required`, `RequiresNew`, and `Supported`.

7. The `ContextUtil` class provides several methods and properties to obtain information about the COM+ object contexts.

8. Scenarios in which you might want to use the COM+ object pooling service include the following:

    • When the costs of creating an object are relatively high.

    • When usage costs are relatively low.

    • When an object will be reused often.

    • When you want to limit the number of object instances.

9. While designing a queued component you must consider the following guidelines:

    • Methods should not return any value or reference parameters.

    • All calls made by the client should be self-sufficient. The queued component has no way to generate a callback to the client program if more information is needed.

    • Methods should not throw any application-specific exceptions because the client may not be available to respond to the exceptions.

10. A CCW is a proxy object generated by the CLR so that existing COM applications can use .NET Framework components transparently.

Answers to Exam Questions

1. **B.** Method calls execute fastest when the application is configured as a library application. The library application executes in the client's process. For more information, see the section "COM+ Applications" in this chapter.

2. **D.** Among the given options, the only tool that actually registers a strongly named assembly with the COM+ Catalog is the .NET Services Installation tool (`regsvcs.exe`). For more information, see the section "Registering the Serviced Component into the COM+ Catalog" in this chapter.

3. **A.** If no object is available and no new object can be created because of the size restriction of the pool, the client requests are queued to receive the first available object from the pool. If an object cannot be made available within the time specified in the `CreationTimeOut` property, an exception is thrown. For more information, see the section "How Object Pooling Works" in this chapter.

4. **B.** When you use the `AutoComplete` attribute with a method, COM+ intercepts the method call to set the done bit and consistent bits after the method call returns. If there are no errors in the method call then the consistent bit is set to `True`; otherwise the consistent bit is set to False. This setting ensures that the changes to the database are committed or rolled backed reliably. For more information, see the section "How Automatic Transaction Works" in this chapter.

5. **C.** You use the `Marshal.BindToMoniker()` method to record messages for a queued component. For more information, see the section "Creating a Client for a Queued Component" in this chapter.

6. **C.** The interface that a queued component uses for queuing must have void methods having only pass-by-value parameters. Therefore, you need to change the return type of the `PlaceOrder()` method from `bool` to `void`. For more information, see the section "Creating a Queued Component" in this chapter.

7. **A.** The `ClassInterfaceType.None` is the recommended setting for the `ClassInterface` attribute. The `ClassInterfaceType.AutoDual` causes versioning problems, and `ClassInterfaceType.AutoDispatch` supports only late binding and does not allow configuration of methods through the Component Services administrative tool. For more information, see the section "Creating Interfaces That Are Visible to COM/COM+" in this chapter.

8. **D.** You can use the COM+ object pooling service to restrict the number of objects for a serviced component. Therefore, you use the `ObjectPooling` attribute. For more information, see the section "Object Pooling" in this chapter.

9. **B.** A queued component is activated as a server application. To ensure that the client is able to locate the component, you must install the component in the GAC. For more information, see the section "Installing the Component in the Global Assembly Cache" in this chapter.

10. **B.** You should override the `Construct()` method to receive the connection string specified by the administrator. For more information, see the section "Object Construction" in this chapter.

APPLY YOUR KNOWLEDGE

11. **B.** `Regasm.exe`, when used with the `/tlb` option, registers the assembly in the Registry (for late binding) and creates a CCW in a `tlb` file, which can be used by the client programs at the time of compilation (early binding). For more information, see the section "Exporting .NET Components Aas COM Type Libraries" in this chapter.

12. **D.** You should use the `SetComplete()` method because it sets the consistent bit as well as the done bit to true. Using the `EnableCommit()` method sets the consistent bit to true but also sets the done bit to false, which does not deactivate the object after the method call returns. For more information, see the section "Elements of Transaction Processing" in this chapter.

13. **C, D.** You must at least sign the component with a strong name and then register the component in the COM+ Catalog. Just registering the component with the Windows Registry is not sufficient, because the component must be available to COM+. In addition, installing the component in the global assembly cache is not required as long as you make sure that the process can locate the assembly. For more information, see the section "Creating and Consuming a Serviced Component" in this chapter.

14. **A.** To ensure high availability of the components, you should use the COM+ queued component service. For more information, see the section "Queued Components" in this chapter.

15. **C, D.** For achieving maximum performance, you can use COM+ object pooling and just-in-time activation services. For more information, see the section "Using Just-in-Time Activation with Object Pooling—A Recipe for High Throughput" in this chapter.

Suggested Readings and Resources

1. Visual Studio .NET Combined Help Collection

   • Writing Serviced Components

   • Serviced Components Programming Guidelines

   • COM+ Programming Overview

2. Building Distributed Applications with .NET, `msdn.microsoft.com/nhp/default.asp?contentid=28001271`.

3. The .NET Six-week series guide, `msdn.microsoft.com/net/guide`.

4. MSDN Index of How-To Articles, `msdn.microsoft.com/howto/howto_index.asp`.

5. .NET Architectural Sample Applications, `msdn.microsoft.com/library/en-us/dnbda/html/bdadotnetsamp0.asp`.

6. Enterprise Development Technology Map, `msdn.microsoft.com/library/en-us/Dndotnet/html/Techmap_enterprise1.asp`.

7. Derek Beyer. *C# COM+ Programming*. M&T Books, 2001.

8. Juval Lowy. *COM and .NET Component Services*. O'Reilly, 2001.

9. Roger Sessions. *COM+ and the Battle for the Middle Tier*. John Wiley & Sons, Inc. 2000.

This chapter covers the following Microsoft-specified objective for the "Creating and Managing Microsoft Windows Services, Serviced Components, .NET Remoting Objects, and XML Web Services" section of Exam 70-320, "Developing XML Web Services and Server Components with Microsoft Visual C# .NET and Microsoft .NET Framework":

Access unmanaged code from a Windows service, a serviced component, a .NET Remoting object, and an XML Web service.

▶ Although the .NET Framework can handle nearly all your application development needs, most organizations have already accumulated a large amount of useful code before they begin using the .NET Framework. It doesn't make sense to simply throw away this legacy code and rewrite everything from scratch. Fortunately, if you've followed recommendations to encapsulate your code into components over the years, you don't need to abandon old code to start getting the benefits of the .NET Framework. Instead, you can make use of the .NET Framework's interoperability features to use the following types of legacy code in Windows services, serviced components, .NET remoting objects, and XML Web services:

• Component Object Model (COM) components can be instantiated and invoked by .NET code.

• The .NET Platform Invoke capability (usually referred to as PInvoke) can be used to call the Windows application programming interface (API).

By using these interoperability features, you can ease your migration to .NET development. Making use of legacy components from .NET code means that you can migrate an application piece by piece rather than try to do it all at once.

CHAPTER 8

Calling Unmanaged Code

STUDY STRATEGIES

▶ If you have an existing COM object to work with, create a runtime callable wrapper (RCW) for the object to investigate the conversion process. If you don't have any existing objects, you can build one with an older version of Visual Basic or Visual C++.

▶ Experiment with PInvoke to invoke some common Windows API calls.

INTRODUCTION

Migrating to a new development platform can be a painful process. In extreme cases, you might have to throw away the results of years of work when you decide it's time for a new set of tools. This can make switching to a new platform a very difficult decision.

Fortunately, Microsoft recognized the need to provide easy migration paths from previous versions of its tools to the .NET world. In particular, if you heeded the advice to use COM for intercomponent communications and to design your applications as sets of COM servers and clients, you'll find the upgrade path to .NET smoother. That's because the .NET Framework includes good support for interoperating with existing COM-based code.

In Chapter 7, "Component Services," you learned how COM components are able to call the .NET code. The .NET Framework also allows the .NET components to instantiate and call COM components. Combine this with an existing modular architecture and you get an easy migration path: Move one module at a time from COM to .NET, and use the .NET interoperability features so that the components can continue to talk to one another.

In this chapter you'll learn about the facilities that the .NET Framework provides for using COM components and other legacy code. In particular, you'll learn about the tools and techniques that are necessary to call COM components and Windows API code from the .NET Framework.

You may want to use the unmanaged code from a variety of .NET applications such as a Windows service, a serviced component, a .NET remoting object, and an XML Web service. Basically the process of using unmanaged code from all of these applications is similar. I'll use Web services for most of the examples in this chapter; however, you can follow the same process for other .NET applications.

Using COM Components

Access unmanaged code from a Windows service, a serviced component, a .NET Remoting object, and an XML Web service.

You might already have a lot of development done in your organization that you would like to reuse with .NET development as you slowly migrate toward it. Fortunately, if your old programs use COM architecture, you don't have to do a "big bang" migration all at once. .NET components can call COM components, and COM components can call .NET components. This means that you can migrate one component (a control, a class library, and so on) at a time, and still keep all your code working together.

Why might you want to undertake such a gradual migration? There are four basic reasons for maintaining part of a system in COM components while moving other parts to .NET components:

▶ It takes time to learn enough about Visual C# .NET and the .NET Framework to be productive. While you're making your way up the learning curve, you may have to continue development of existing COM components.

▶ You may have components that can't be easily moved to .NET because they use language features that are no longer supported or because of other implementation quirks.

▶ It takes time to move code from one system to another. Unless you can afford extended downtime, a gradual move lets you write the converted code at a slower pace.

▶ Your application may depend on third-party controls or libraries for which you do not have the source code.

In the following sections you'll learn how to encapsulate COM components for use with .NET applications. There are both command-line and GUI tools for working with COM components. Before I talk about those tools, though, you should know a bit more about wrapper classes.

NOTE

ActiveX Controls   Prior to .NET, ActiveX was a major means of delivering encapsulated functionality such as controls to the Windows applications. I'll not be discussing ActiveX in this book because it is a client-side technology and has little use for creating server-side applications and components. For more information on using ActiveX from .NET applications, refer to my book, *MCAD/MCSD Training Guide: Exam 70-316, Developing and Implementing Windows-based Applications with Visual C# .NET and Visual Studio .NET.*

Understanding Runtime Callable Wrappers

As you probably already know, Visual C# .NET creates code that operates within the .NET CLR. Code that operates within the CLR is called *managed code*. Managed code benefits from the services that the CLR offers, including garbage collection, memory management, and support for versioning and security.

Code that does not operate within the CLR is called *unmanaged code*. Code that was created by tools that are older than the .NET Framework is by definition unmanaged code. COM components are unmanaged code because COM was designed before the CLR existed, and COM components don't make use of any of the services of the CLR.

Managed code expects that all the code with which it interacts will use the CLR. This is an obvious problem for COM components. How can you take a component that was developed before the advent of .NET and make it look like a .NET component to other .NET components? The answer is to use a proxy. In general terms, a *proxy* accepts commands and messages from one component, modifies them, and passes them to another component. The particular type of proxy that allows you to use COM components within a .NET application is called a *runtime callable wrapper* (RCW). That is, it's a proxy that can be called by the CLR.

Figure 8.1 shows schematically how the pieces fit together.

Building a COM DLL

To see how COM interoperability works, you need a COM library. Step-by-Step 8.1 shows how to build a simple one.

FIGURE 8.1
RCW allows you to use COM components within the .NET framework.

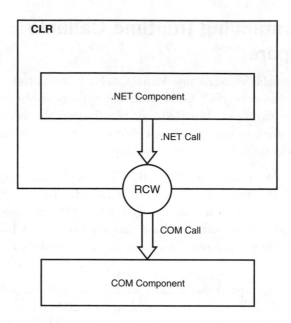

STEP BY STEP

8.1 Building a COM Dynamic Link Library (DLL)

1. Launch Visual Basic 6. Create a new ActiveX DLL project.

2. Select the Project1 node in the Project Explorer window and rename it `MyCustomer`.

3. Select the Class1 node in the Project Explorer window and rename it `Balances`.

4. Add this code to the `Balances` class:

```
Option Explicit

Private mintCustomerCount As Integer
Private macurBalances(1 To 10) As Currency

' Create a read-only CustomerCount property
Public Property Get CustomerCount() As Integer
    CustomerCount = mintCustomerCount
End Property

' Create a GetBalance method
Public Function GetBalance( _
   CustomerNumber As Integer) As Currency
```

```
        GetBalance = macurBalances(CustomerNumber)
    End Function

    ' Initialize the data
    Private Sub Class_Initialize()
        Dim intI As Integer
        mintCustomerCount = 10

        For intI = 1 To 10
            macurBalances(intI) = _
                Int(Rnd(1) * 100000) / 100
        Next intI
    End Sub
```

5. Save the Visual Basic project.

6. Select File, Make MyCustomer.dll to create the COM component.

> **NOTE**
>
> **If You Don't Have Visual Basic** Even if you don't have Visual Basic, you can still test COM interoperability by working with a COM library that's already installed on your computer. A variety of Microsoft components, including Office, SQL Server, and ADO, install COM libraries.

Registering a COM DLL

When you use Visual Basic 6 to build the MyCustomer.dll—as you did in Step-by-Step 8.1—the COM DLL is automatically registered in the Windows Registry.

If you are using the code files from the CD or if you have an unregistered COM DLL, you need to register the COM DLL in the Windows Registry before you can use it in .NET code. You can register by using regsvr32.exe in the command prompt as shown here:

```
regsvr32 MyCustomer.dll
```

Using the Type Library Importer Tool (tlbimp.exe)

The task of using COM components from the .NET Framework is substantially facilitated by the fact that COM components, like .NET components, have metadata that describe their interfaces. For .NET components, the metadata is embedded in the assembly manifest. For COM components, the metadata is stored in a type library. A type library can be a separate file, or (as with Visual Basic 6 class libraries) it can be embedded within another file.

The .NET Framework includes a tool, the Type Library Importer tool (`tlbimp.exe`), that can create an RCW from COM metadata contained in a type library, as seen in Step-by-Step 8.2.

STEP BY STEP

8.2 Using the Type Library Importer Tool

1. Launch a .NET command prompt by selecting Start, Programs, Microsoft Visual Studio .NET, Visual Studio .NET Tools, Visual Studio .NET Command Prompt.

2. Inside the command prompt window, navigate to the folder that contains the `MyCustomer.dll` COM library.

3. Enter this command line to run the Type Library Importer tool:

```
tlbimp MyCustomer.dll /out:NETMyCustomer.dll
```

4. Launch Visual Studio .NET. Create an ASP.NET Web service application named `320C08`.

5. Right-click the References node in Solution Explorer and select Add Reference.

6. Click the Browse button in the Add Reference dialog box. Browse to the `NETMyCustomer.dll` file that you created in step 3. Click OK to add the reference to the project.

7. Right-click the `Service1.asmx` file in Solution Explorer and rename it `StepByStep8_2.asmx`.

8. Click the hyperlink on the `StepByStep8_2.asmx` design view to switch to the code view. Change all the occurrences of `Service1` to refer to `StepByStep8_2`. Add the following `WebService` attribute before the `StepByStep8_2` class definition:

```
[WebService(Namespace="http://NetExam.org/Balance")]
public class StepByStep8_2 :
    System.Web.Services.WebService
```

9. Add the following Web method definition to the Web service:

```
[WebMethod]
public decimal RetrieveBalance(short custNumber)
```

```
    {
        NETMyCustomer.Balances b =
            new NETMyCustomer.Balances();
        return b.GetBalance(ref custNumber);
    }
```

10. Set the Web service as the start page for the project.

11. Run the project. You should see that a browser is launched showing the test page. Click on the RetrieveBalance method link. Enter a number between 1 and 10 for the custNumber parameter and click the Invoke button. A second browser window opens with that customer's balance.

In Step-by-Step 8.2, you use the Type Library Importer tool to create an RCW for the COM type library. This RCW is a library that you can add to your .NET project as a reference. After you do that, the classes in the COM component can be used just like native .NET classes. When you use a class from the COM component, .NET makes the call to the RCW, which in turn forwards the call to the original COM component and returns the results to your .NET managed code.

The Type Library Importer tool supports the command-line options listed in Table 8.1.

TABLE 8.1

COMMAND-LINE OPTIONS FOR THE TYPE LIBRARY IMPORTER TOOL

Option	Meaning
/asmversion:*versionNumber*	Specifies the version number for the created assembly
/delaysign	Prepares the assembly for delay signing
/help	Displays help for command-line options
/keycontainer:*containerName*	Signs the assembly with the strong name from the specified key container
/keyfile:*filename*	Specifies a file containing public/private key pairs that is used to sign the resulting file

continues

TABLE 8.1 *continued*

COMMAND-LINE OPTIONS FOR THE TYPE LIBRARY IMPORTER TOOL

Option	Meaning
/namespace:*namespace*	Specifies the namespace for the created assembly
/out:*filename*	Specifies the name of the created assembly
/primary	Produces a primary interop assembly
/publickey:*filename*	Specifies the file containing a public key that is used to sign the resulting file
/reference:*filename*	Specifies a file to be used to resolve references from the file being imported
/silent	Suppresses information that would otherwise be displayed on the command line during conversion
/strictref	Refuses to create the assembly if one or more references cannot be resolved
/sysarray	Imports COM SAFEARRAY as instances of the System.Array type
/unsafe	Creates interfaces without the .NET Framework security checks
/verbose	Displays additional information on the command line during conversion
/?	Displays help about command-line options

Using COM Components Directly

The Visual Studio .NET interface provides a streamlined way to use a COM component from your .NET code, as shown in Step-by-Step 8.3.

STEP BY STEP

8.3 Using a Direct Reference with a COM Library

1. Add a Web service page named StepByStep8_3.asmx to the project.

2. Right-click the References node in Solution Explorer and select Add Reference.

3. Select the COM tab in the Add Reference dialog box. Scroll down the list of COM components until you come to the MyCustomer library. Select the MyCustomer library, click Select, and then click OK.

4. Add the following Web method definition to the Web service:

```
[WebMethod]
public decimal RetrieveBalance(short custNumber)
{
    MyCustomer.Balances b =
        new MyCustomer.Balances();
    return b.GetBalance(ref custNumber);
}
```

5. Set the Web service as the start page for the project.

6. Run the project. You should see that a browser is launched showing the test page. Click on the RetrieveBalance method link. Enter a number between 1 and 10 for the custNumber parameter and click the Invoke button. A second browser window opens with that customer's balance.

NOTE

COM DLL Needs to Be Registered Before It Is Used MyCustomer.dll will not be in the COM tab of the Add Reference dialog box if it was not built in Step-by-Step 8.1. Refer to the section "Registering a COM DLL," earlier in this chapter, on how to register a COM DLL.

When you directly reference a COM library from the Visual Studio .NET Integrated Development Environment (IDE), the effect is almost the same as if you used the Type Library Importer tool to import the same library. Visual Studio .NET creates a new namespace with the name of the original library and then exposes the classes from the library within that namespace.

Although you can use either of the two methods described in this chapter to call a COM component from a .NET component, there are reasons to prefer one method over the other:

▶ For a COM component that will only be used in a single Visual C# .NET project and that you wrote yourself, use the easiest method: direct reference from the .NET project. This method is suitable only for a truly private component that does not need to be shared by the other projects.

▶ If a COM component is shared among multiple projects, use the Type Library Importer tool so that you can sign the resulting assembly and place it in the global assembly cache (GAC). Shared code must be signed with a strong name.

▶ If you need to control details of the created assembly—such as its name, namespace, or version number—you must use the Type Library Importer tool. The direct reference method gives you no control over the details of the created assembly.

GUIDED PRACTICE EXERCISE 8.1

The goal of this exercise is to compare the performance of two implementations of the same code, using a COM library for one implementation and a native .NET class for the other implementation. You should choose some code that takes a reasonably long time to run so that you can detect any differences between the two implementations.

How would you create such an application?

You should try working through this problem on your own first. If you get stuck, or if you'd like to see one possible solution, follow these steps:

1. Launch Visual Basic 6. Create a new ActiveX DLL project.

2. Select the Project1 node in the Project Explorer window and rename it `Numeric`.

3. Select the Class1 node in the Project Explorer window and rename it `Primes`.

4. Add this code to the `Primes` class:

```
Option Explicit

Public Function HighPrime(Max As Long) As Long
        Dim a() As Byte
        Dim lngI As Long
        Dim lngJ As Long

        ReDim a(Max)

        ' In the array, 1 indicates a prime,
        ' 0 indicates nonprime.
```

```
          ' Start by marking multiples
          ' of 2 as nonprime
          For lngI = 0 To Max
              If lngI Mod 2 = 0 And lngI <> 2 Then
                  a(lngI) = 0
              Else
                  a(lngI) = 1
              End If
          Next lngI
        ' Now execute the usual sieve
        ' of erasthones algorithm
          For lngI = 3 To Sqr(Max) Step 2
              If a(lngI) = 1 Then
                ' This is a prime,
                ' so eliminate its multiples
                For lngJ = lngI + lngI To Max _
                    Step lngI
                    a(lngJ) = 0
                Next lngJ
              End If
          Next lngI
          ' Find the largest prime by working backwards
          For lngI = Max To 1 Step -1
              If a(lngI) = 1 Then
                  HighPrime = lngI
                  Exit For
              End If
          Next lngI
    End Function
```

5. Save the Visual Basic project.

6. Select File, Build `Numeric.dll` to create the COM component.

7. In your Visual C# .NET project, right-click the References node of Solution Explorer and select Add Reference.

8. Select the COM tab in the Add Reference dialog box. Scroll down the list of COM components until you come to the Numeric library. Select the `Numeric` library, click Select, and then click OK.

9. Add a new class to your Visual C# .NET project. Name the class `Primes.cs`.

10. Add this code to the `Primes.cs` class:

```
using System;
public class Primes
{
    public int HighPrime(int max)
    {
```

continues

continued

```
                Byte[] a = new Byte[max];
                Int32 intI;
                Int32 intJ;

                // In the array, 1 indicates a prime,
                // 0 indicates nonprime. Start by marking
                // multiples of 2 as nonprime
                for(intI = 0;intI < max; intI++)
                {
                    if((intI % 2 == 0) && (intI != 2))
                        a[intI] = 0;
                    else
                        a[intI] = 1;
                }

                // Now execute the usual sieve
                // of erasthones algorithm
                for(intI = 3; intI <= System.Math.Sqrt(max);
                    intI=intI+2)
                {
                    if (a[intI] == 1)
                    {
                        // This is a prime,
                        // so eliminate its multiples
                        for(intJ = intI + intI; intJ < max;
                            intJ=intJ+intI)
                            a[intJ] = 0;
                    }
                }
                // Find the largest prime by working backward
                for(intI = max-1; intI > 0; intI--)
                {
                    if (a[intI] == 1)
                    {
                        break;
                    }
                }
                return intI;
        }
    }
```

11. Add a new Web service named
    `GuidedPracticeExercise8_1.asmx` to your Visual C# .NET
    project.

12. Switch to code view and add the following Web method defin-
    itions to the Web service definition:

```
[WebMethod]
public string CalculateCOMHighPrime(int maxNumber)
{
    Numeric.Primes COM_Primes = new Numeric.Primes();
    DateTime dt = DateTime.Now;
```

```
        Int32 intHighPrime =
            COM_Primes.HighPrime(ref maxNumber);
        TimeSpan ts = DateTime.Now.Subtract(dt);
        string COMResults = "High prime = " +
            intHighPrime.ToString() + " took " +
            ts.Ticks.ToString() + " ticks";
        return COMResults;
    }

    [WebMethod]
    public string CalculateNETHighPrime(int maxNumber)
    {
        Primes NET_Primes = new Primes();
        DateTime dt = DateTime.Now;
        Int32 intHighPrime =
            NET_Primes.HighPrime(maxNumber);
        TimeSpan ts = DateTime.Now.Subtract(dt);
        string NETResults = "High prime = " +
            intHighPrime.ToString() + " took " +
            ts.Ticks.ToString() + " ticks";

        return NETResults;
    }
```

13. Set the Web service as the start page for the project.

14. Run the project. You should see that a browser is launched showing the test page. Click on the CalculateCOMHighPrime method link. Enter a fairly large number in the maxNumber parameter and click the Invoke button. The code finds the largest prime number that is smaller than the number you entered by using the COM library, and it displays the results as shown in Figure 8.2.

15. Click the Back button in the main page and then click on the CalculateNETHighPrime method link. Enter the same large number that you previously entered for the COM implementation in the maxNumber parameter and click the Invoke button. The code finds the largest prime number that is smaller than the number you entered using the native .NET class and displays the results as shown in Figure 8.2.

If you have difficulty following this exercise, review the section "Using COM Components" earlier in this chapter. After doing that review, try this exercise again.

> **WARNING**
>
> **The Pitfalls of Performance** In Guided Practice Exercise 8.1, the .NET class was much faster than the COM class. But timing performance on Windows is notoriously difficult—for several reasons. First, although you can measure things down to the timer tick, the hardware does not provide precise-to-the-tick numbers. Second, because of caching and because other programs are in memory, timings tend not to be repeatable. Finally, it's hard to write exactly equivalent COM and .NET code. Nevertheless, repeated runs of a program such as this example can give you general information on which of two alternatives is faster.

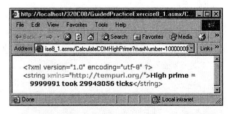

FIGURE 8.2
Running .NET code is much faster when compared to running COM code in the .NET framework.

R E V I E W   B R E A K

▶ Using COM components from .NET managed code requires the creation of an RCW.

▶ You can create an RCW for a COM component by using the Type Library Importer tool or by directly referencing the COM component from your .NET code.

▶ To use COM components that you did not create, you should obtain a PIA from the creator of the component.

▶ RCWs impose a performance penalty on COM code.

USING PLATFORM INVOKE

Access unmanaged code from a Windows service, a serviced component, a .NET Remoting object, and an XML Web service.

So far in this chapter, you've seen interoperability between managed code and unmanaged code by way of method calls to classes in COM libraries. There's a second way that the .NET Framework can interoperate with unmanaged code, though: by calling methods from unmanaged libraries. The *Platform Invoke* (often abbreviated as PInvoke) feature of .NET allows .NET code to call methods from unmanaged libraries such as the Windows API.

To call unmanaged methods from your .NET code, you need to provide the declarations of the method in your .NET code. Because the methods are implemented externally in unmanaged libraries, you should declare the methods in the .NET code with `extern` and `static` keywords.

Along with declaring the method, you should also apply a `DllImport` attribute of the `System.Runtime.InteropServices` namespace to the methods. The `DllImport` attribute tells the CLR where to find the implementation of the `extern` method by specifying the name of the unmanaged library. After the method is declared, you can use it in Visual C# .NET just like you use any other method. In addition to the name of the library, the `DllImport` attribute also accepts other parameters (see Table 8.2).

TABLE 8.2

PARAMETERS FOR THE DllImport ATTRIBUTE

Parameter	Description
CallingConvention	Defines the calling convention to use. The values are specified by the CallingConvention enumeration—Cdecl, FastCall, StdCall (default value), ThisCall, and Winapi.
CharSet	Specifies the character set to use. By default it uses CharSet.Ansi. The other possible values are CharSet.Auto, CharSet.Unicode, and CharSet.None (which is obsolete and behaves as CharSet.Ansi).
EntryPoint	Represents the name of the entry point in the DLL. If the EntryPoint field is not specified, the name of the method is used as the entry point. If the EntryPoint field is passed, then you can provide a custom name for the method.
ExactSpelling	Specifies whether the name of the entry point should exactly match the name of the method in the unmanaged DLL. By default the value is false.
PreserveSig	Indicates whether the method signature should be preserved or can be changed. By default the value is true.
SetLastError	Specifies whether the last error of the Win32 method should be preserved. By default the value is false.

Step-by-Step 8.4 shows you how to call the GetComputerName() method from the kernel32.dll library by using the DllImport attribute.

STEP BY STEP

8.4 Using Platform Invoke with the Windows API

1. Add a new Web service named StepByStep8_4.asmx to your Visual C# .NET application.

2. Switch to the code view. Enter the following using directives:

```
using System.Text;
using System.Runtime.InteropServices;
```

continues

continued

3. Add the following lines of code in the class definition,
which indicates that the GetComputerName() method is
implemented in kernel32.dll:

```
[DllImport("kernel32.dll", CharSet=CharSet.Auto)]
public static extern int GetComputerName(
    StringBuilder buffer, ref uint size);
```

4. Add the following Web method definition in the
StepByStep8_4.asmx file:

```
[WebMethod]
public string WebServerName()
{
    StringBuilder sbBuf = new StringBuilder(128);
    UInt32 intLen = (uint) sbBuf.Capacity;
    Int32 intRet=0;

    // Call the Win API method
    intRet = GetComputerName(sbBuf, ref intLen);

    return sbBuf.ToString();
}
```

5. Set the Web service as the start page for the project.

6. Run the project. You should see that a browser is launched
showing the test page. Click on the WebServerName
method link and click the Invoke button in the method
test page. The code displays the name of the Web server
where the Web service is run, as shown in Figure 8.3.

FIGURE 8.3
The PInvoke feature of .NET enables .NET code
to call methods from the Windows API.

In Step-by-Step 8.6, note the use of the CharSet.Auto parameter in
the DllImport attribute of the GetComputerName() method declaration. You may know that many Windows API calls come in two versions, depending on the character set that you're using. For example,
GetComputerName() really exists as GetComputerNameA() (for ANSI
characters) and GetComputerNameW() (for Unicode characters). The
Auto parameter instructs the .NET Framework to use the appropriate version of the API call for the platform where the code is
running.

Platform Invoke can also handle API calls that require structures as
parameters. For example, a call to the GetSystemTime() method fills
in a structure that consists of eight members that together indicate
the system time. Step-by-Step 8.5 shows how to represent this structure

in .NET code and pass the structure to the GetSystemTime() method to fill it with the Web server's time.

STEP BY STEP

8.5 Using Platform Invoke with a struct Parameter

1. Add a new Web service named StepByStep8_5.asmx to your Visual C# .NET application.

2. Switch to the code view. Enter the following using directives:

```
using System.Runtime.InteropServices;
```

3. Add the following lines of code in the class definition:

```
[StructLayout(LayoutKind.Sequential)]
public struct SystemTime
{
    public ushort year;
    public ushort month;
    public ushort dayOfWeek;
    public ushort day;
    public ushort hour;
    public ushort minute;
    public ushort second;
    public ushort millisecond;
}

[DllImport("Kernel32.dll")]
public static extern void GetSystemTime(
    out SystemTime time);
```

4. Add the following Web method definition to the Web service:

```
[WebMethod]
public SystemTime WebServerTime()
{
    SystemTime time;
    // call the Win32 API method
    GetSystemTime(out time);
    return time;
}
```

5. Set the Web service as the start page for the project.

6. Run the project. You should see that a browser is launched showing the test page. Click on the WebServerTime method link and click the Invoke button in the method test page. The method returns the time of the Web server in a structure as defined by the Web service, as shown in Figure 8.4.

continues

continued

FIGURE 8.4
Platform Invoke can also handle API calls that require structures as parameters.

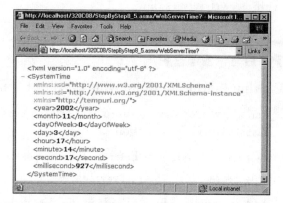

The tricky part of the code in Step-by-Step 8.5 lies in the declaration of the structure. In this case, the StructLayout attribute tells the Visual C# .NET compiler that the location of the individual fields is sequential within the structure. By using the StructLayout attribute, you can ensure that the .NET Framework constructs the same structure that the API method is expecting to receive.

Many API calls require a Rect structure, which consists of four members that are filled in with the coordinates of a rectangle. In Visual C# .NET, you can declare a structure with explicit byte offsets for each member, which lets you define any structure that the Windows API requires:

```
[StructLayout(LayoutKind.Explicit)]
public struct Rect
{
    [FieldOffset(0)] public Int32 left;
    [FieldOffset(4)] public Int32 top;
    [FieldOffset(8)] public Int32 right;
    [FieldOffset(12)] public Int32 bottom;
}
```

In this case, the StructLayout attribute tells the Visual C# .NET compiler that you'll explicitly specify the location of the individual fields within the structure. The FieldOffset attribute specifies the starting byte of each field within the structure.

▶ You can use the .NET Framework Platform Invoke facility to call methods from Windows libraries, including the Windows API.

▶ You should use the `StringBuilder` object for a Windows API call that expects a string buffer to be modified by the method.

CHAPTER SUMMARY

Although the .NET Framework is extensive, it is not all-encompassing. Many projects need to use a mixture of old (COM or Windows) components and new (.NET) components. Even if all the necessary facilities are available within the .NET Framework, it might not be feasible to migrate an entire existing application to .NET all at once.

The .NET Framework and Visual Studio .NET include a variety of features that are designed to make it easy to use legacy components. In this chapter, you learned about two of those features:

▶ The capability to instantiate and invoke objects from a COM component

▶ The capability to call methods from a Windows API or another DLL

COM components also depend on wrappers called RCWs to work with the .NET Framework. An RCW is a proxy that sends data back and forth between the COM component and .NET components. You can create RCWs with the Type Library Importer command-line tool or by adding the COM component to the references collection of a .NET project.

You might need to call methods from the Windows API or other DLLs. The .NET Platform Invoke functionality lets you do this. By using the `DllImport` attribute, you can tell the .NET Framework where to find the implementation of a method call.

KEY TERMS

- RCW
- managed code
- unmanaged code
- Platform Invoke

APPLY YOUR KNOWLEDGE

Exercises

8.1 Access COM Components from a Serviced Component

Accessing COM components from a serviced component is the same as accessing COM components from any .NET application. However, the RCWs referenced by serviced components should be strongly named. In this exercise you'll learn how to use the command-line options of the Type Library Importer tool to create a strongly named RCW and use it from a serviced component.

Estimated time: 20 minutes.

1. Launch a .NET command prompt by selecting Start, Programs, Microsoft Visual Studio .NET, Visual Studio .NET Tools, Visual Studio .NET Command Prompt.

2. Inside the command prompt window, navigate to the folder that contains the `MyCustomer.dll` COM library.

3. If you have already created the key file containing a public/private key pair in Step-by-Step 7.2 in Chapter 7, copy the key file `70320.snk` to this directory. If you haven't created one before, issue the following command to create a pair of public/private keys:

   `sn -k 70320.snk`

4. Enter this command line to run the Type Library Importer tool to create a strongly named RCW:

   ```
   tlbimp MyCustomer.dll
   ➥/keyfile:70320.snk /out:NETSMyCustomer.dll
   ```

5. Create a Blank Solution named `320C08Exercises` in the Visual Studio .NET IDE.

6. Add a Visual C# .NET Class library named `Exercise8_1` to the solution.

7. Right-click the References node in Solution Explorer and select Add Reference.

8. Click the Browse button in the Add Reference dialog box. Browse to the `NETSMyCustomer.dll` file that you created in step 4. Click OK to add the reference to the project.

9. Add a reference to the `System.EnterpriseServices` component in the current project.

10. In the Solution Explorer, rename the default `Class1.cs` to `BalanceSC.cs`.

11. Open the `BalanceSC.cs` and replace the code with the following code:

```csharp
using System;
using System.EnterpriseServices;
using NETSMyCustomer;

namespace Exercise8_1
{
    public interface IBalanceSC
    {
        decimal RetrieveBalance(
            short custNumber);
    }

    public class BalanceSC :
        ServicedComponent, IBalanceSC
    {
        public BalanceSC()
        {
        }

        public decimal RetrieveBalance(
            short custNumber)
        {
            Balances b = new Balances();
            return b.GetBalance(
                ref custNumber);
        }
    }
}
```

12. Open the `AssemblyInfo.cs` file in the project and add the following `using` directive:

    ```
    using System.EnterpriseServices;
    ```

13. Add assembly-level attributes `ApplicationName`, `Description`, and `ApplicationActivation` in the `AssemblyInfo.cs`, as follows:

    ```
    [assembly: ApplicationName(
    "Customer Balance Application")]
    [assembly: Description("Retrieves the " +
    "customer balance from a COM component")]
    [assembly: ApplicationActivation(
    ActivationOption.Library)]
    ```

14. Copy the `70320.snk` key pair file to the solution folder. Change the `AssemblyVersion` and `AssemblyKeyFile` attributes in the `AssemblyInfo.cs` file as shown here:

    ```
    [assembly: AssemblyVersion("1.0")]
    [assembly: AssemblyKeyFile(
        @"..\..\..\70320.snk")]
    ```

15. Build the project. An `Exercise8_1.dll` is generated, and a strong name is assigned to the file based on the specified key file.

16. Launch the Visual Studio .NET command prompt and change the directory to the folder where the DLL file generated in step 15 resides. Issue the following command to install the assembly to the GAC:

    ```
    gacutil /i Exercise8_1.dll
    ```

17. In the command prompt, issue the following command to install the service component assembly to the COM+ Catalog:

    ```
    regsvcs Exercise8_1.dll
    ```

18. Add a new Visual C# .NET Windows application named `Exercise8_1Test` to the solution.

19. Add references to the `System.EnterpriseServices` component and `Exercise8_1` project in the current project.

20. Rename the form `Form1` to `Balance`. Switch to code view and change all occurrences of `Form1` to refer to `Balance` instead.

21. Place two `Label` controls, two `TextBox` controls (`txtCustomerNumber` and `txtBalance`), and a `Button` control (`btnGetBalance`), on the form. Arrange the controls as shown in Figure 8.5.

FIGURE 8.5
Design of a form that calls the `BalanceSC` serviced component.

22. Switch to code view and add the following `using` directive:

    ```
    using Exercise8_1;
    ```

23. Double-click the `Button` control and add the following code to its `Click` event handler:

    ```
    private void btnGetBalance_Click(
        object sender, System.EventArgs e)
    {
        BalanceSC bsc = new BalanceSC();
        Int16 custNumber = Int16.Parse(
            txtCustomerNumber.Text);
        txtBalance.Text =
            bsc.RetrieveBalance(
            custNumber).ToString();
    }
    ```

24. Set `Exercise8_1Test` as the startup project.

APPLY YOUR KNOWLEDGE

25. Run the project. Enter a value between 1 and 10 in the first text box and click the Get Balance button to see that customer's balance. The balance is retrieved by a method call to the serviced component, which in turn retrieves the balance from a method call to a COM component.

Review Questions

1. Name some reasons to use COM components in a .NET project.

2. What is the purpose of an RCW?

3. How do you create an RCW?

4. What should you consider when choosing how to create an RCW?

5. What's the difference between COM interoperability and Platform Invoke?

6. What does the `CharSet.Auto` parameter in a `DllImport` attribute specify?

Exam Questions

1. Your application uses a COM component stored in a file named `ProcessOrders.dll`. You deploy the application via xcopy on the test server. Testers report that the orders are not being processed. The test server does have the .NET Framework installed. What could be the problem?

   A. The RCW for the COM component needs to be registered on the problem computers.

   B. `ProcessOrders.dll` is not stored in the Windows System directory.

   C. The problem computers are not connected to the Internet.

   D. Service Pack 1 for the .NET Framework is not installed on the problem computers.

2. Your colleague needs to make a call to a COM component named `TriState.dll` from a serviced component registered as a COM+ server application. You suggest to her that she use the Type Library Importer tool. What command-line option should you suggest so that the serviced component can access the methods of the COM component?

   A. Use the `/keyfile` option to assign a strong name to the COM component.

   B. Use the `/reference` option to set the reference to the serviced component.

   C. Use the `/primary` option to produce a primary interop assembly.

   D. Use the `/unsafe` option to disable the .NET Framework security checks.

3. You are responsible for migrating an existing COM application to Visual C# .NET. The existing application consists of eight COM server components and a single client user interface component that instantiates and invokes objects from the server components. You want to give the application's user interface an overhaul and migrate to Visual C# .NET with low risk and minimal downtime. How should you proceed?

   A. Completely rewrite the entire application, using Visual C# .NET.

   B. Bring only the user interface code into Visual C# .NET. Use COM interoperability to call the existing COM servers from the .NET

APPLY YOUR KNOWLEDGE

user interface code. Migrate the servers one by one.

C. Bring all the servers into Visual C# .NET. Use COM interoperability to call the migrated servers from the existing user interface code.

D. Cut and paste all the existing code into Visual C# .NET.

4. Your company supplies a COM component to provide advanced data analysis for your clients. Some of your clients are moving to the .NET Framework and require an RCW for your component. How should you proceed?

A. Use the ActiveX Library Importer tool to create and sign a PIA for your component.

B. Use the Type Library Importer tool to create and sign a PIA for your component.

C. Set a reference to your component from any Visual C# .NET project to create an RCW for your component.

D. Create a class that uses Platform Invoke to call methods from your component.

5. You wrote a COM component to supply random numbers in a specific distribution to a simple statistical client program. Now you're moving that client program to the .NET Framework. The COM component is used nowhere else, and you have not shipped copies to anyone else. You want to call the objects in the COM server from your new .NET client. How should you proceed?

A. Set a direct reference from your .NET client to the COM server.

B. Use the Type Library Importer tool to create an unsigned RCW for the COM component.

C. Use the Type Library Importer tool to create a signed RCW for the COM component.

D. Use Platform Invoke to instantiate classes from the COM component.

6. You have written several applications for your own use, all of which share classes from a COM component that you also wrote. You are moving the applications to .NET, but you intend to leave the COM component untouched. How should you proceed?

A. Set a direct reference from each application to the existing COM component.

B. Use the Type Library Importer tool to create an unsigned RCW for the COM component. Place a copy of this RCW in each application's directory.

C. Use Platform Invoke to call methods from the existing COM component in each application.

D. Use the Type Library Importer tool to create a signed RCW for the COM component. Place this RCW in the GAC.

APPLY YOUR KNOWLEDGE

7. Your .NET Remoting object needs to use a communications library from a third-party developer. This library is implemented as a COM component. What should you do to continue to use the classes and methods in the communications library?

   A. Obtain a PIA from the developer of the library. Install the PIA in the GAC.

   B. Use the Type Library Importer tool to create a signed RCW for the library. Install the RCW in the GAC.

   C. Use the Type Library Importer tool to create an unsigned RCW for the library. Install the RCW in the GAC.

   D. Create wrapper code that uses Platform Invoke to call methods from the library. Import this wrapper code into your application.

8. Your Visual C# ASP.NET Web service uses methods from a Visual Basic 6 COM library implemented as a DLL via an RCW. You built the RCW by directly referencing the COM DLL. Users are complaining of poor performance. Which of these changes is most likely to improve your application's performance?

   A. Recompile the Visual Basic 6 library as an EXE file.

   B. Switch your .NET application from Visual C# .NET to Visual Basic .NET.

   C. Use the Type Library Importer tool to create a new RCW.

   D. Rewrite the Visual Basic 6 library as a native .NET library.

9. Your project contains the following API declaration:

```
[DllImport("kernel32.dll",
    CharSet=CharSet.Auto)]
public static extern int GetComputerName(
    String buffer, ref uint size);
```

The project also contains code to use this API to display the computer name:

```
public static void ShowName()
{
        String buf = "";
        UInt32 intLen=128;
        Int32 intRet;

        // Call the Win API method
        intRet = GetComputerName(
            buf, ref intLen);

        Console.WriteLine(
            "This computer is named " +
            buf.ToString());
}
```

Users report that no computer name is displayed. What should you do?

   A. Use the `ref` keyword with the variable `buf` in the call to the `GetComputerName()` method.

   B. Tell the users that their computers have no names set in their network properties.

   C. Replace the use of a `String` object with a `StringBuilder` object in the code.

   D. Use the `out` keyword with the variable `buf` in the call to the `GetComputerName()` method.

10. You want to use an unmanaged DLL named `Balance.dll` in your Visual C# .NET application. `Balance.dll` does not provide any COM interfaces. How can you call the `RetrieveBalance()` method of this library in your .NET code?

APPLY YOUR KNOWLEDGE

A. Use the Type Library Importer tool.

B. Use the Windows Forms ActiveX Control Importer tool.

C. Use the `DllImport` attribute to declare the extern method `RetrieveBalance()` from `Balance.dll`.

D. Add a reference to the `Balance.dll` library in your Visual Studio .NET project.

11. You are using three classes from a COM component in your Visual C# .NET application. You'd like to give the RCW for the COM component the same version number as the rest of your components when you ship the application. What should you do?

A. Use Platform Invoke to call methods from the COM component, thus eliminating the RCW.

B. Directly import the COM component into the References list. Right-click the reference and select Properties to set the version number.

C. Recompile the existing COM library with the desired version number before creating the RCW.

D. Use the Type Library Importer tool with the `/asmversion` option to explicitly set the version of the RCW.

12. You are planning to use two classes from a COM component in your .NET application. You'd like to place these two classes into a namespace named `ComComponents`. What must you do?

A. Set a direct reference to the COM component. Create an empty class file in your .NET project. Specify the `ComComponents` namespace in that file and import the wrapper class.

B. Use the Type Library Importer tool with the `/namespace` option to set the namespace within the RCW.

C. Use the Type Library Importer tool with the `/out` option to create a file with the desired name.

D. Use Platform Invoke within a `namespace` declaration to import the classes.

13. Your application will use methods from a COM component that uses COM+ services such as object pooling and just-in-time activation. Which of these methods can you use to access the classes in the COM component? (Select the two best answers.)

A. Use Platform Invoke to declare the methods within the COM component.

B. Add the COM component directly to the Visual C# .NET toolbox.

C. Set a direct reference to the COM component in your Visual Studio .NET project.

D. Use the Type Library Importer tool to create an RCW for the COM component.

APPLY YOUR KNOWLEDGE

14. You have an existing COM component that contains shared classes. These classes encapsulate functionality that you want to use in your .NET application. How can you use these classes while maintaining the benefits of managed code, such as type safety and automatic garbage collection?

    A. Use the Type Library Importer tool with the `/strictref` option to create an RCW for the COM component.

    B. Call the methods from the COM component directly via Platform Invoke.

    C. Add a direct reference to the COM component.

    D. Rewrite the COM component as a .NET component.

15. Your application uses the `GetComputerName()` API method. This method exists in `kernel32.dll` in both the ANSI and Unicode versions. Your declaration is as follows:

    ```
    [DllImport("kernel32.dll")]
    public static extern int GetComputerName(
        StringBuilder buffer, ref uint size);
    ```

    Your code is failing with a `System.EntryPointNotFoundException` exception when you call this method. What should you do to fix this failure?

    A. Supply the full path for `kernel32.dll`.

    B. Add the `CharSet.Auto` parameter to the declaration.

    C. Declare the method as `GetComputerNameA()` instead of `GetComputerName()`.

    D. Declare the method as `GetComputerNameW()` instead of `GetComputerName()`.

Answers to Review Questions

1. You might use COM components in a .NET project because you need to migrate an existing application in small pieces or because the COM components contain unique functionality for which you do not have source code.

2. RCWs provide a proxy between .NET applications and COM components. The RCW translates .NET calls into COM calls and returns the COM results as .NET results.

3. You can create an RCW by using the Type Library Importer tool or by adding a direct reference to the COM component.

4. When deciding how to create an RCW, you should consider whether you own the source code for the COM component, whether the RCW needs to go into the GAC, and how many .NET applications will make use of the COM component.

5. COM interoperability enables you to instantiate COM classes within a .NET application and to invoke their members. Platform Invoke enables you to call methods from a DLL.

6. The `CharSet.Auto` parameter of the `DllImport` attribute tells the CLR to choose the correct version—ANSI or Unicode—of an API for the particular platform on which you are running the code.

Answers to Exam Questions

1. **A.** RCWs are installed by xcopy, just like any other .NET assemblies. .NET does not require the Internet to run, nor do RCWs depend on

APPLY YOUR KNOWLEDGE

Service Pack 1. When you add RCW to an application, you must make sure that that COM component is registered in the Windows Registry of the target computers. For more information, see the section "Using COM Components" in this chapter.

2. **A.** The RCW's referenced by serviced components should be strongly named. Therefore, with the given choices, you need to select the /keyfile command-line option of the tlbimp.exe tool. The /keyfile option is passed a filename that contains the public/private key pair to strongly sign an assembly. For more information, see the section "Using the Type Library Importer Tool (tlbimp.exe)" in this chapter.

3. **B.** Moving all the code takes longer than moving part of the code, and it introduces additional risk. Because you'd like to rewrite the user interface, you should move that component to .NET before moving the server components. For more information, see the section "Using COM Components" in this chapter.

4. **B.** As the vendor of the component, it's your responsibility to supply the PIA. For more information, see the section "Using COM Components" in this chapter.

5. **A.** For components that are used in a single project, and that you wrote, the simplest method of creating the RCW is best. For more information, see the section "Using COM Components Directly" in this chapter.

6. **D.** Shared libraries should be placed in the GAC. Code must be signed before it can be placed in the GAC, and only the Type Library Importer tool can sign an RCW. For more information, see the section "Using COM Components" in this chapter.

7. **A.** Because you did not write the code for the communications library, the proper way to proceed is to obtain a PIA from the original author. For more information, see the section "Using COM Components" in this chapter.

8. **D.** Changing from a DLL to an EXE file or from Visual C# .NET to Visual Basic .NET has no significant effect on performance. RCWs are the same no matter how they're created. But rewriting the library into .NET is likely to speed up performance because it eliminates the extra calls in the proxy layer. For more information, see the section "Using COM Components" in this chapter.

9. **C.** In the Platform Invoke calls, you should use a StringBuilder object instead of a String object to hold a string buffer that expects to be modified by the method. For more information, see the section "Using Platform Invoke" in this chapter.

10. **C.** Only the PInvoke feature of .NET allows you to call methods from unmanaged DLLs that do not provide any COM interfaces. Therefore, you need to use the DllImport attribute to tell the .NET Framework where to find the implementation of a method call. For more information, see the section "Using Platform Invoke" in this chapter.

11. **D.** Only the Type Library Importer tool can explicitly set the version number for an RCW. For more information, see the section "Using the Type Library Importer Tool (tlbimp.exe)" in this chapter.

APPLY YOUR KNOWLEDGE

12. **B.** Only the Type Library Importer tool can set the namespace for an RCW. For more information, see the section "Using the Type Library Importer Tool (`tlbimp.exe`)" in this chapter.

13. **C, D.** You can use COM components that use COM+ services by using the same techniques that you use with COM components. For more information, see the sections "Using COM Components" in this chapter.

14. **D.** Only managed code benefits from the features of the CLR. The only way to turn the component into managed code is to rewrite it in .NET. For more information, see the section "Using COM Components" in this chapter.

15. **B.** The `CharSet.Auto` parameter is necessary to tell the CLR to use the ANSI or Unicode versions of the method as appropriate to the operating system. For more information, see the section "Using Platform Invoke" in this chapter.

Suggested Readings and Resources

1. Visual Studio .NET Combined Help Collection, "Interoperating with Unmanaged Code."

2. Adam Nathan. *.NET and COM: The Complete Interoperability Guide.* Sams, 2002.

3. Andrew Troelsen. *COM and .NET Interoperability.* Apress, 2002.

This chapter covers the following Microsoft-specified objectives for the "Testing and Debugging" section of Exam 70-320, "Developing XML Web Services and Server Components with Microsoft Visual C# .NET and Microsoft .NET Framework":

Create a unit test plan.

▶ Before you release a product or component, the product needs to pass through different types of tests. This objective requires you to know the different types of tests that a product should undergo to verify its robustness, reliability, and correctness. These tests should be executed with a designed test plan that ensures that the product thoroughly meets its goals and requirements.

Implement tracing.

- **Configure and use trace listeners and trace switches.**

- **Display trace output.**

▶ Tracing helps in displaying informative messages during the application's runtime to give you a fair idea of how the application is progressing. This objective requires you to know how to use Debug and Trace class properties and methods, attach trace listeners, and apply trace switches. You should also know how to use ASP.NET tracing in a Web application.

Instrument and debug a Windows service, a serviced component, a .NET Remoting object, and an XML Web service.

- **Configure the debugging environment.**

- **Create and apply debugging code to components and applications.**

- **Provide multicultural test data to components and applications.**

- **Execute tests.**

- **Use interactive debugging.**

CHAPTER 9

Testing and Debugging

▶ The process of debugging helps you locate logical or runtime errors in an application. This objective requires you to know the various tools and windows that are available in Visual C# .NET to enable easy and effective debugging. This objective also requires you to know the various techniques for debugging a Windows service, a serviced component, a .NET remoting object, and an XML Web service.

Log test results.

- **Resolve errors and rework code.**

- **Control debugging in the Web.config file.**

- **Use SOAP extensions for debugging.**

▶ Logging is the technique for collecting execution information for a program. The execution information can greatly help you in determining the cause of problem with the code. In this chapter you'll learn different techniques to enable logging in your applications. You should also know how to resolve errors, enable and disable debugging through the web.config file, and how to use SOAP extensions for debugging a Web service.

STUDY STRATEGIES

▶ Review the "Introduction to Instrumentation and Tracing" and "Using the Debugger" sections of the Visual Studio .NET Combined Help Collection.

▶ Try calling different methods of the `Trace` and `Debug` classes. Note the differences in the output when you run a program using the `Debug` and `Release` configurations.

▶ Experiment with attaching predefined and custom-made listeners to `Trace` objects. Refer to Step-by-Step 9.2 and Guided Practice Exercise 9.1 for examples.

▶ Know how to implement trace switches and conditional compilation in applications. Refer to Step-by-Step 9.3 and Step-by-Step 9.4 for examples.

▶ Experiment with the different types of debugging windows that are available in Visual C# .NET. Understand their advantages and learn to use them effectively. They can be very helpful in resolving errors.

▶ Experiment with different debugging techniques such as local and remote debugging processes, debugging code in DLL files, and debugging SQL Server stored procedures.

▶ Experiment with debugging different types of applications such as a Windows application, Web application, Web service, serviced component, .NET remoting object, and Windows service.

INTRODUCTION

You need to test a distributed application to ensure its quality. Complex applications require multiple levels of testing, including unit testing, integration testing, and regression testing. An effective test plan can ensure that the application ships with the fewest possible defects. In this chapter you will learn what is involved in creating such a test plan.

Tracing is the process of monitoring an executing program. You trace a program by placing tracing code in the program with the help of the Trace and Debug classes. The tracing messages can be sent to a variety of destinations, including the Output window, a text file, an event log, or any other custom-defined trace listener, where they can be recorded to analyze the behavior of the program. Trace switches can be used to change the types of messages being generated without recompiling the application.

The process of testing may reveal various logical errors, or bugs, in a program. The process of finding the exact locations of these errors may be time-consuming. Visual C# .NET provides a rich set of debugging tools that make this process very convenient.

In this chapter I discuss techniques for testing and debugging different types of applications that make up an enterprise solution. I discuss how to test and debug a Windows application, Web application, Web service, serviced component, .NET remoting object, and Windows service.

I discuss two important techniques for monitoring an executing application. You'll learn how to log errors and other descriptive messages in an event log. You'll also learn how to publish the performance data for an application with the Windows performance counters.

TESTING

Create a unit test plan.

Instrument and debug a Windows service, a serviced component, a .NET Remoting object, and an XML Web service.

- **Provide multicultural test data to components and applications.**

- **Execute tests.**

Testing is the process of executing a program with the intention of finding errors (bugs). By *error* I mean any case in which a program's actual results fail to match the expected results. The criteria of the expected results may not include just the correctness of the program; they may also include other attributes, such as usability, reliability, and robustness. The process of testing may be manual, automated, or a mixture of both techniques.

In this increasingly competitive world, testing is more important than ever. A software company cannot afford to ignore the importance of testing. If a company releases buggy code, not only will it end up spending more time and money fixing and redistributing the corrected code, but it will also lose goodwill. In the Internet world, the competition is not even next door: It is just a click away!

Creating a Test Plan

Create a unit test plan.

A *test plan* is a document that guides the process of testing. A good test plan should typically include the following information:

▶ Which software components need to be tested

▶ What parts of a component's specification are to be tested

▶ What parts of a component's specification are not to be tested

▶ What approach needs to be followed for testing

▶ Who will be responsible for each task in the testing process

> **NOTE**
>
> **Correctness, Robustness, and Reliability** *Correctness* refers to a program's capability to produce expected results when the program is given a set of valid input data. *Robustness* is a program's capability to cope with invalid data or operations. *Reliability* is a program's capability to produce consistent results on every use.

▶ What the schedule is for testing

▶ What the criteria are for a test to fail or pass

▶ How the test results will be documented and used

Executing Tests

Incremental testing (sometimes also called *evolutionary testing*) is a modern approach to testing that has proven very useful for rapid application development (RAD). The idea of incremental testing is to test the system as you build it. Three levels of testing are involved in incremental testing:

▶ Unit testing—Unit testing involves testing elementary units of the application (usually classes).

▶ Integration testing—Integration testing tests the integration of two or more units or the integration between subsystems of those units.

▶ Regression testing—Regression testing usually involves the process of repeating the unit and integration tests whenever a bug is fixed, to ensure that the old bugs do not exist and that no new ones have been introduced.

Unit Testing

Units are the smallest building blocks of an application. In Visual C# .NET, these building blocks often refer to components or class definitions. Unit testing involves performing basic tests at the component level to ensure that each unique path in the component behaves exactly as documented in its specifications.

Usually, the same person who writes the component also does unit testing for it. Unit testing typically requires that you write special programs that use the component or class being tested. These programs are called *test drivers*; they are used throughout the testing process, but they are not part of the final product.

N O T E

NUnit   NUnit is a simple framework for writing repeatable tests in any .NET language. For more information, visit `http://nunit.sourceforge.net`.

The following are some of the major benefits of unit testing:

▶ It allows you to test parts of an application without waiting for the other parts to be available.

▶ It allows you to test exceptional conditions that are not easily reached by external inputs in a large, integrated system.

▶ It simplifies the debugging process by limiting the search for bugs to a small unit rather than to the complete application.

▶ It helps you avoid lengthy compile-build-debug cycles when debugging difficult problems.

▶ It enables you to detect and remove defects at a much lower cost than with other, later, stages of testing.

Integration Testing

Integration testing verifies that the major subsystems of an application work well with each other. The objective of integration testing is to uncover the errors that might result because of the way units integrate with each other.

Visualize the whole application as a hierarchy of components; integration testing can be performed in any of the following ways:

▶ Bottom-up approach—With this approach, the testing progresses from the smallest subsystem and then gradually progresses up in the hierarchy to cover the whole system. This approach may require you to write a number of test-driver programs that test the integration between subsystems.

▶ Top-down approach—This approach starts with the top-level system, to test the top-level interfaces, and gradually comes down and tests smaller subsystems. You might be required to write *stubs* (that is, dummy modules that mimic the interface of a module but have no functionality) for the modules that are not yet ready for testing.

▶ Umbrella approach—This approach focuses on testing the modules that have a high degree of user interaction. Normally, stubs are used in place of process-intensive modules. This approach enables you to release a graphical user interface (GUI)–based application early and gradually increase functionality. It is called the *umbrella approach* because the input/output modules are generally present on the edges, forming an umbrella shape. For example, think of an equipment rental company, whose component hierarchy resembles the hierarchy shown in Figure 9.1. Here the input/output modules are represented by solid lines because they are fully implemented, whereas the computational modules are represented by the dotted lines because a stub may be used in their place. In umbrella-approach integration testing, you test the input/output modules, which form the edge of an umbrella-like shape.

FIGURE 9.1

The umbrella approach of integration testing focuses on testing the modules that have a high degree of user interaction.

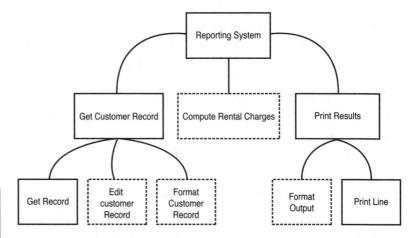

> **NOTE**
>
> **Limitations of Testing** Testing can show the presence of errors, but it can never confirm the absence of errors. Various factors such as the complexity of the software, requirements such as interoperability with various software and hardware, and globalization issues such as support for various languages and cultures, can create excessive input data and too many execution paths to be tested. Many companies do their best to capture most of the test cases by using automation (that is, using computer programs to find errors) and beta-testing (that is, involving product enthusiasts to find errors), but errors in final products are still a well-known and acknowledged fact.

Regression Testing

Regression testing should be performed any time a program is modified, either to fix a bug or to add a feature. The process of regression testing involves running all the tests mentioned in the preceding sections, as well as any newly added test cases to test the added functionality. Regression testing has two main goals:

▶ Verify that all known bugs are corrected.

▶ Verify that the program has no new bugs.

Testing International Applications

Testing an application designed for international usage involves checking the country and language dependencies of each locale for which the application has been designed. When testing international applications, you need to consider the following:

▶ You should test the application's data and user interface to make sure that they conform to the standards for date and time, numeric values, currency, list separators, and measurements for the locales and countries in which you plan to sell your product.

▶ You should test your application on as many language and culture variants as necessary to cover your entire market for the application. Operating systems such as Windows 2000 and Windows XP support the languages used in more than 120 cultures/locales.

▶ You should use Unicode for your applications. Applications that use Unicode run without requiring any changes on Windows 2000 and XP. If an application instead uses Windows code pages, you need to set the culture/locale of the operating system according to the localized version of the application that you are testing. Each such change requires you to reboot the computer.

▶ While testing a localized version of an application, you should make sure to use input data in the language that is supported by the localized version. This makes the testing scenario similar to the scenario in which the application actually will be used.

REVIEW BREAK

▶ Testing is the process of executing a program with the intention of finding errors. You should design an effective test plan to ensure that your application is free from all likely defects and errors.

▶ Unit testing ensures that each unit of an application functions precisely as desired. It is the lowest level of testing.

▶ Integration testing ensures that different units of an application function as expected by the test plan after they are integrated.

▶ Whenever code is modified or a new feature is added in an application, you should run all the existing test cases, along with a new set of test cases, to check the new feature. This helps you develop robust applications.

Tracing

Implement tracing.

- **Configure and use trace listeners and trace switches.**

- **Display trace output.**

Instrument and debug a Windows service, a serviced component, a .NET Remoting object and an XML Web service: Create and apply debugging code to components and applications.

The process of testing can reveal the presence of errors in a program, but to find the actual cause of a problem, you sometimes need the program to generate information about its own execution. Analysis of this information may help you understand why the program is behaving in a particular way and may lead to possible resolution of the error.

This process of collecting information about program execution is called *tracing*. You trace a program's execution in Visual C# .NET by generating messages about the program's execution with the use of the Debug and Trace classes.

The Trace and Debug classes have several things in common:

- ▶ They both belong to the System.Diagnostics namespace.

- ▶ They have members with the same names.

- ▶ All their members are static.

- ▶ They are conditionally compiled (that is, their statements are included in the object code only if a certain symbol is defined).

The only difference between the Debug and Trace classes is that the members of the Debug class are conditionally compiled, but only when the DEBUG symbol is defined. On the other hand, members of the Trace class are conditionally compiled, but only when the TRACE symbol is defined.

Visual C# .NET provides two basic configurations for a project: Debug and Release. Debug is the default configuration. When you compile a program by using the Debug configuration, both TRACE and

DEBUG symbols are defined, as shown in Figure 9.2. When you compile a program in the Release configuration, only the TRACE symbol is defined. You can switch between the Debug and Release configurations by using the Solution Configurations combo box on the standard toolbar (as shown in Figure 9.3) or by using the Configuration Manager dialog box (as shown in Figure 9.4) from the project's Property Pages dialog box.

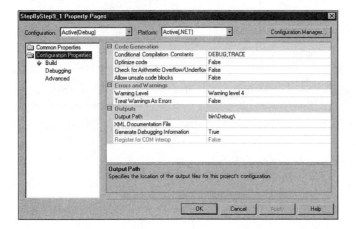

FIGURE 9.2◀
Both the TRACE and DEBUG symbols are defined in Debug configuration.

FIGURE 9.3▲
The standard toolbar for Visual Studio .NET contains a solutions configuration combo box to allow users to easily change solution configuration.

Later in this chapter, you will learn how to make these changes from within the program, through the command-line compilation options and through the configuration files.

When you compile a program by using the Debug configuration, the code that uses the Debug and the Trace classes is included in the compiled code. When you run such a program, both the Debug and Trace classes generate messages. On the other hand, when you compile a program by using the Release configuration, it does not include any calls to the Debug class. Thus, when such a program is executed, you get only the messages generated by the Trace class.

Table 9.1 summarizes the members of both the Trace and Debug classes.

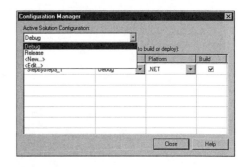

FIGURE 9.4▲
The Configuration Manager dialog box enables you to set configuration for projects in a solution.

NOTE

Tracing Helps in Resolving Hard-to-Reproduce Errors   When programs run in a production environment, they sometimes report errors (mostly related to performance or threading problems) that are difficult to reproduce in a simulated testing environment. Tracing a production application can help you get runtime statistics for the program; this might help you trap these hard-to-reproduce errors.

TABLE 9.1

MEMBERS OF Debug AND Trace CLASSES

Member	Type	Description
Assert()	Method	Checks for a condition and displays a message if the condition is false
AutoFlush	Property	Specifies whether the Flush() method should be called on the listeners after every write
Close()	Method	Flushes the output buffer and then closes the listeners
Fail()	Method	Displays an error message
Flush()	Method	Flushes the output buffer and causes the buffered data to be written to the listeners
Indent()	Method	Increases the current IndentLevel property by one
IndentLevel	Property	Specifies the indent level
IndentSize	Property	Specifies the number of spaces in an indent
Listeners	Property	Specifies the listeners that are monitoring the trace output
Unindent()	Method	Decreases the current IndentLevel property by one
Write()	Method	Writes the given information to the trace listeners in the Listeners collection
WriteIf()	Method	Writes the given information to the trace listeners in the Listeners collection only if a condition is true
WriteLine()	Method	Acts the same as the Write() method, but appends the information with a newline character
WriteLineIf()	Method	Acts the same as the WriteIf() method, but appends the information with a newline character

Using `Trace` and `Debug` to Display Information

Step-by-Step 9.1 demonstrates how to use some of the methods of the `Trace` and `Debug` classes.

STEP BY STEP

9.1 Using the `Trace` and `Debug` Classes to Display Debugging Information

1. Launch Visual Studio .NET. Select File, New, Blank Solution and name the new solution `320C09`.

2. Add a new Visual C# .NET Windows application named `StepByStep9_1` to the solution.

3. In the Solution Explorer, rename the default `Form1.cs` to `FactorialCalculator.cs`. Open the form in code view and change all occurrences of `Form1` to refer to `FactorialCalculator` instead.

4. Add four `Label` controls (with the heading label named `lblHeading`), two `TextBox` controls (`txtNumber` and `txtFactorial`), and a `Button` control (`btnCalculate`) to the form and arrange the controls as shown in Figure 9.5.

5. Switch to code view and add the following `using` directive:

```
using System.Diagnostics;
```

6. Double-click the `Button` control and add the following code to its `Click` event handler:

```
private void btnCalculate_Click(object sender,
    System.EventArgs e)
{
    // write a debug message
    Debug.WriteLine(
        "Inside Button Click event handler");
    // start indenting messages now
    Debug.Indent();
    int intNumber = Convert.ToInt32(txtNumber.Text);
    // make a debug assertion
    Debug.Assert(intNumber >= 0, "Invalid value",
```

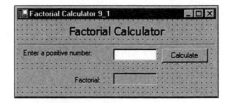

FIGURE 9.5
Design of a form that calculates the factorial of a given number.

continues

continued

```
        "negative value in debug mode");
    // write a trace assertion
    Trace.Assert(intNumber >= 0, "Invalid value",
        "negative value in trace mode");

    int intFac = 1;
    for (int i = 2; i <= intNumber; i++)
    {
        intFac = intFac * i;
        // write a debug message
        Debug.WriteLine(i,
            "Factorial Program Debug, Value of i");
    }
    // write a trace message if the condition is true
    Trace.WriteLineIf(intFac < 1,
        "There was an overflow",
        "Factorial Program Trace");
    // write a debug message if the condition is true
    Debug.WriteLineIf(intFac < 1,
        "There was an overflow",
        "Factorial Program Debug");

    txtFactorial.Text = intFac.ToString();
    // decrease the indent level
    Debug.Unindent();

    // write a debug message
    Debug.WriteLine(
        "Done with computations, returning...");
}
```

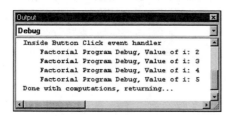

FIGURE 9.6
Debug and Trace messages are by default always displayed in the Output window.

7. Run the solution. Keep the program running and switch to the Visual Studio .NET Integrated Development Environment (IDE). Select View, Other Windows, Output. Push the pin on the title bar of the output window so that it does not hide automatically. Now switch to the running program; enter **5** in the text box and click the Calculate button. You should see tracing messages that are generated by the program (see Figure 9.6).

8. Now switch to the running program and enter the value **100** and click the Calculate button. Messages from both the Debug class and the Trace class (overflow message) are displayed in the output window. Note that the default configuration is the Debug configuration, where both the TRACE and DEBUG symbols are defined.

9. Enter a negative value, such as -1, and click the Calculate button. This causes the assertion to fail, and you see a dialog box that shows an Assertion Failed message, as shown in Figure 9.7. This message box is generated by the `Debug.Assert()` method in the code. The dialog box gives you three choices: Abort, to terminate the program; Retry, to break the program execution so that you can debug the program; and Ignore, to continue the execution as if nothing has happened. Click Ignore, and you see another Assertion Failed dialog box. This one was generated by the `Trace.Assert()` method in the code. Click the Abort button to terminate the program execution.

10. From the Solution Configurations combo box on the standard toolbar, select the `Release` configuration (`Release` configuration defines only the `TRACE` symbol). Run the program again. Enter the value **5** and click the Calculate button. The factorial is calculated, but no messages appear in the output window. Enter the value **100** and click the Calculate button. You should now see the overflow message generated by the `Trace` class in the output window. Finally, try calculating the factorial of -1. You should see just one dialog box, showing an Assertion Failed message. Click the Abort button to terminate the program.

FIGURE 9.7

The Assertion Failed dialog box is displayed when an assertion made in the `Assert()` method fails.

Note from Step-by-Step 9.1 that you can use the methods of the `Debug` and `Trace` classes (for example, the `WriteIf()` and `WriteLineIf()` methods) to display messages based on conditions. This can be a very useful technique if you are trying to understand a program's flow of logic. Step-by-Step 9.1 also demonstrates the use of the `Assert()` method. The `Assert()` method tests your assumption about a condition at a specific place in the program. When an assertion fails, the `Assert()` method pinpoints the code that is not behaving according to your assumptions. A related method is `Fail()`. The `Fail()` method displays a dialog box similar to the one that `Assert()` shows, but it does not work conditionally. The `Fail()` method signals unconditional failure in a branch of code execution.

Trace Listeners

Listeners are the classes that are responsible for forwarding, recording, and displaying the messages generated by the Trace and Debug classes. You can associate multiple listeners with the Trace and Debug classes by adding listener objects to their Listeners property. The Listeners property is a collection that is capable of holding any objects derived from the TraceListener class. Both the Debug and the Trace classes share their Listeners collection, so an object added to the Listeners collection of the Debug class is automatically available in the Trace class and vice-versa.

The TraceListener class is an abstract class that belongs to the System.Diagnostics namespace and has three implementations:

▶ DefaultTraceListener—An object of this class is automatically added to the Listeners collection. Its behavior is to write messages on the output window.

▶ TextWriterTraceListener—An object of this class writes messages to any class that derives from the Stream class that includes the console or a file.

▶ EventLogTraceListener—An object of this class writes messages to the Windows event log.

If you want a listener object to perform differently from these three listener classes, you can create your own class that inherits from the TraceListener class. When doing so, you must at least implement the Write() and WriteLine() methods.

Step-by-Step 9.2 shows how to create a custom listener class that implements the TraceListener class to send messages generated by the Debug and Trace class through email.

EXAM TIP

The Same Listeners for Debug and Trace   Messages sent through the Debug and Trace objects are directed through each listener object in the Listeners collection. Debug and Trace share the same Listeners collection, so any listener object that is added to the Trace.Listeners collection is also added to the Debug.Listeners collection.

STEP BY STEP

9.2 Creating a Custom TraceListener Object

1. Add a new Visual C# .NET Windows application named StepByStep9_2 to the solution.

2. Add a reference to System.Web.dll to the project.

3. Add a new class to the project named
`EmailTraceListener.cs`. Modify the class with the following code (changing the From address to an appropriate email address):

```csharp
using System;
using System.Diagnostics;
using System.Text;
using System.Web.Mail;

namespace StepByStep9_2
{
    public class EmailTraceListener : TraceListener
    {
        // Message log will be sent to this address
        private string mailto;
        // Store the message log
        private StringBuilder message;

        public EmailTraceListener(string mailto)
        {
            this.mailto = mailto;
        }

        // A custom listener must
        // override the Write() method
        public override void Write(string message)
        {
            if (this.message == null)
                this.message = new StringBuilder();
            this.message.Append(message);
        }

        // A custom listener must
        // override the WriteLine() method
        public override void WriteLine(string message)
        {
            if (this.message == null)
                this.message = new StringBuilder();
            this.message.Append(message);
            this.message.Append('\n');
        }

        // use the close method to send mail.
        public override void Close()
        {
            // ensure that the listener is flushed
            Flush();
            // MailMessage belongs to the
            // System.Web.Mail namespace
            // but can be used from
            // any managed application
            if (this.message != null)
            {
```

continues

continued

Sending Email Messages The types
in the `System.Web.Mail` namespace
can be used from any managed application, including both Web and
Windows applications. This functionality is supported only in the Windows
2000, Windows XP Professional, and
Windows Server 2003 operating systems. For other operating systems,
you can send email messages by
manually establishing Simple Mail
Transfer Protocol (SMTP) connections
through the `System.Net.Sockets.`
`TcpClient` class or by using an SMTP
component, which you might be able
to get from a component vendor for
free.

NOTE

```
    // Create a MailMessage object
    MailMessage mailMessage =
        new MailMessage();
    mailMessage.From =
        "tracelistener@youraddress.com";
    mailMessage.To = this.mailto;
    mailMessage.Subject =
    "Factorial Program Debug/Trace output";
    mailMessage.Body =
        this.message.ToString();
    //send the mail
    SmtpMail.Send(mailMessage);
    }
}

public override void Flush()
{
    // nothing much to do here
    // so call the base class's implementation
    base.Flush();
}
}
}
```

4. In Solution Explorer, copy the `FactorialCalculator.cs`
form from the `StepByStep9_1` project to the current project. Change the `Text` property of the form to `Factorial`
`Calculator 9_2`. Switch to the code view and change the
namespace of the form to `StepByStep9_2`. Delete the
default `Form1.cs` in the project.

5. Double-click the form and add the following code to the
`Load` event of the `FactorialCalculator` form, changing the
email address *Insert@youraddress.here* to a real address
that can receive email:

```
private void FactorialCalculator_Load(object sender,
    System.EventArgs e)
{
    // Add a custom listener to
    // the Listeners collection
    Trace.Listeners.Add(new EmailTraceListener(
        "Insert@youraddress.here"));
}
```

6. Attach an event handler to the `Closing` event of the
`FactorialCalculator` form and add the following code to
the event handler:

```
private void FactorialCalculator_Closing(
    object sender,
    System.ComponentModel.CancelEventArgs e)
{
    // Call the close methods for all listeners
    Trace.Close();
}
```

7. Set project `StepByStep9_2` as the startup project.

8. Run the solution, using the default `Debug` configuration. Enter a value and click the Calculate button. Close the form. Note that both `Debug` and `Trace` messages appear on the output window. A local SMTP server is used to email these messages to the specified addresses. Run the project again in the `Release` mode. Enter a large value, such as **100**, and click the Calculate button. The overflow message appears in the output window. Close the form. While you are closing the form, the messages generated by the `Trace` class are sent to the specified email address.

Trace Switches

So far in this chapter, you have learned that the `Trace` and `Debug` classes can be used to display valuable information related to program execution. You have also learned that it is possible to capture messages in a variety of formats. In this section, you will learn how to control the nature of messages that you want to get from a program.

You can use trace switches to set the parameters that control the level of tracing that needs to be done on a program. You set these switches via an Extensible Markup Language (XML)–based external configuration file. This is especially useful when the application you are working with is in production mode. You might initially want the application not to generate any trace messages. However, if the application later has problems or you just want to check on the application's health, you might want to instruct the application to emit a particular type of trace information by just changing the configuration file. You are not required to recompile the application; the application automatically picks up the changes from the configuration file when it restarts.

There are two predefined classes for creating trace switches: the BooleanSwitch class and the TraceSwitch class. Both of these classes derive from the abstract Switch class. You can also define your own trace switch classes by deriving classes from the Switch class.

You use the BooleanSwitch class to differentiate between two modes of tracing: trace-on and trace-off. Its default value is zero, which corresponds to the trace-off state. If it is set to any nonzero value, it corresponds to the trace-on state.

Unlike BooleanSwitch, the TraceSwitch class provides five different levels of tracing switches. These levels are defined by the TraceLevel enumeration and are listed in Table 9.2. The default value of TraceLevel for a TraceSwitch object is 0 (Off).

TABLE 9.2

THE TraceLevel ENUMERATION

Enumerated Value	Integer Value	Type of Tracing
Off	0	None
Error	1	Only error messages
Warning	2	Warning messages and error messages
Info	3	Informational messages, warning messages, and error messages
Verbose	4	Verbose messages, informational messages, warning messages, and error messages

Table 9.3 displays the important properties of the TraceSwitch class.

TABLE 9.3

IMPORTANT PROPERTIES OF THE TraceSwitch CLASS

Property	Description
Description	Describes the switch (inherited from Switch).
DisplayName	Specifies a name used to identify the switch (inherited from Switch).

Property	*Description*
Level	Specifies the trace level that helps select which trace and debug messages will be processed. Its value is one of the TraceLevel enumeration values (refer to Table 9.2).
TraceError	Returns true if Level is set to Error, Warning, Info, or Verbose; otherwise, it returns false.
TraceInfo	Returns true if Level is set to Info or Verbose; otherwise, it returns false.
TraceVerbose	Returns true if Level is set to Verbose; otherwise, it returns false.
TraceWarning	Returns true if Level is set to Warning, Info, or Verbose; otherwise, it returns false.

Step-by-Step 9.3 demonstrates how to use trace switches in an application.

STEP BY STEP

9.3 Using the TraceSwitch Class

1. Add a new Visual C# .NET Windows application named StepByStep9_3 to the solution.

2. In Solution Explorer, copy the FactorialCalculator.cs form from the StepByStep9_1 project to the current project. Change the Text property of the form to Factorial Calculator 9_3. Switch to the code view and change the namespace of the form to StepByStep9_3. Delete the default Form1.cs.

3. Declare the following static variable at the class level, just after the Main() method:

```
static TraceSwitch traceSwitch =
      new TraceSwitch("FactorialTrace",
      "Trace the factorial application");
```

4. Change the Click event handler of the Calculate button so that it has the following code:

```
private void btnCalculate_Click(object sender,
   System.EventArgs e)
{
```

continues

continued

```
    if (traceSwitch.TraceVerbose)
        // write a debug message
        Debug.WriteLine(
            "Inside the Button Click event handler");

    // start indenting messages now
    Debug.Indent();
    int intNumber = Convert.ToInt32(txtNumber.Text);

    if (traceSwitch.TraceError)
    {
        // make a debug assertion
        Debug.Assert(intNumber >= 0, "Invalid value",
            "negative value in debug mode");
    }

    int intFac = 1;
    for (int i = 2; i <= intNumber; i++)
    {
        intFac = intFac * i;
        // write a debug message
        if (traceSwitch.TraceInfo)
            Debug.WriteLine(i,
                "Factorial Program Debug, Value of i");
    }

    if (traceSwitch.TraceWarning)
        // write a debug message
        // if the condition is true
        Debug.WriteLineIf(intFac < 1,
            "There was an overflow",
            "Factorial Program Debug");

    txtFactorial.Text = intFac.ToString();
    // decrease the indent level
    Debug.Unindent();

    if (traceSwitch.TraceVerbose)
        // write a debug message
        Debug.WriteLine(
            "Done with computations, returning...");
}
```

5. Add an Application configuration file (`App.config`) to the project and modify it to contain the following code:

```
<?xml version="1.0" encoding="utf-8" ?>

<configuration>
    <system.diagnostics>
```

```
        <switches>
            <add name="FactorialTrace" value="4" />
        </switches>
    </system.diagnostics>
</configuration>
```

6. Set project StepByStep9_3 as the startup project.

7. Run the project, using the default Debug configuration.
   Enter the value 5; note that all messages appear in the output window. Enter a negative value and then a large value,
   and you see all the errors and warning messages. Close the
   form. Modify the XML file to change the value of
   FactorialTrace to 3. Run the project again; you should
   now see all messages except the one set with TraceLevel as
   Verbose. Repeat the process, with values of
   FactorialTrace in the configuration file changed to 2, 1,
   and 0.

8. Modify the program to change all Debug statements to
   Trace statements. Copy the XML configuration file to the
   bin\Release folder in the project and then repeat step 9,
   using the Release configuration.

> **EXAM TIP**
>
> **Switches in a Web Application or a
> Web Service** To enable trace
> switches in a Web application or a
> Web service, you need to add the
> `<system.diagnostics>` element to
> the application configuration file,
> web.config.

Conditional Compilation

The C# programming language provides a set of preprocessing directives. You can use these directives to skip sections of source files for
compilation, to report errors and warnings, or to mark distinct
regions of source code.

Table 9.4 summarizes the preprocessing directives that are available
in C#.

> **NOTE**
>
> **C# and the Preprocessor** There is
> no separate preprocessor in the C#
> compiler. The lexical analysis phase of
> the compiler processes all the prepro-
> cessing directives. C# uses the term
> *preprocessor* from a conventional
> point of view, in contrast to languages
> such as C and C++ that have sepa-
> rate preprocessors for taking care of
> conditional compilation.

TABLE 9.4

C# PREPROCESSING DIRECTIVES

Directives	Description
#if, #else, #elif, and #endif	These directives conditionally skip the sections of code. The skipped sections are not part of the compiled code.
#define and #undef	These directives define or undefine symbols in the code.
#warning and #error	These directives explicitly generate error or warning messages. The compiler reports errors and warnings in the same way it reports other compile-time errors and warnings.
#line	This directive alters the line numbers and source file filenames reported by the compiler in warning and error messages.
#region and #endregion	These directives mark sections of code. A common example of these directives is the code generated by Windows Forms Designer. Visual designers such as Visual Studio .NET can use these directives to show, hide, and format code.

In addition to providing preprocessing directives, the C# programming language also provides a ConditionalAttribute class.

You can mark a method as conditional by applying the Conditional attribute to it. The Conditional attribute takes one argument that specifies a symbol. The conditional method is either included or omitted from the compiled code, depending on the definition of the specified symbol at that point. If the symbol definition is available, the method's code is included; otherwise, the method's code is excluded from the compiled code.

The conditional compilation directives and methods with the Conditional attribute enable you to keep debugging-related code in the source code but exclude it from the compiled version. This removes the extraneous messages and the production programs do not encounter performance hits because of processing additional code. In this case, if you want to resolve some errors, you can easily activate the debugging code by defining a symbol and recompiling the program.

Step-by-Step 9.4 demonstrates the use of the `Conditional` attribute and the conditional compilation directives.

Conditional Methods A method must have its return type set to `void` to have the `Conditional` attribute applied to it.

STEP BY STEP

9.4 Using Conditional Compilation

1. Add a new Visual C# .NET Windows application named `StepByStep9_4` to the solution.

2. In Solution Explorer, copy the `FactorialCalculator.cs` form from the `StepByStep9_1` project to the current project. Change the `Text` property of the form to `Factorial Calculator 9_4`. Switch to the code view and change the namespace of the form to `StepByStep9_4`. Delete the default `Form1.cs`.

3. Add the following two conditional methods to the class definition:

```
[Conditional("DEBUG")]
public void InitializeDebugMode()
{
    lblHeading.Text =
        "Factorial Calculator: Debug Mode";
}
[Conditional("TRACE")]
public void InitializeReleaseMode()
{
    lblHeading.Text =
        "Factorial Calculator Version 1.0";
}
```

4. Attach an event handler to the form's `Load` event and add the following code:

```
private void FactorialCalculator_Load(
    object sender, System.EventArgs e)
{
    #if !DEBUG && !TRACE
    #error you should have either
➥DEBUG or TRACE defined
    #endif

    #if DEBUG
        Debug.WriteLine(
            "Program started in debug mode");
        InitializeDebugMode();
```

continues

continued

```
#else
    Trace.WriteLine(
        "Program started in release mode");
    InitializeReleaseMode();
#endif
}
```

5. Set project StepByStep9_4 as the startup project.

6. Run the solution, using the default Debug configuration. The heading of the form displays "Factorial Calculator: Debug Mode" (see Figure 9.8). The output window also displays a string: Program started in debug mode. Close the program and start it again in the Release mode. A different heading appears in the form (see Figure 9.9) and a different message appears in the output window.

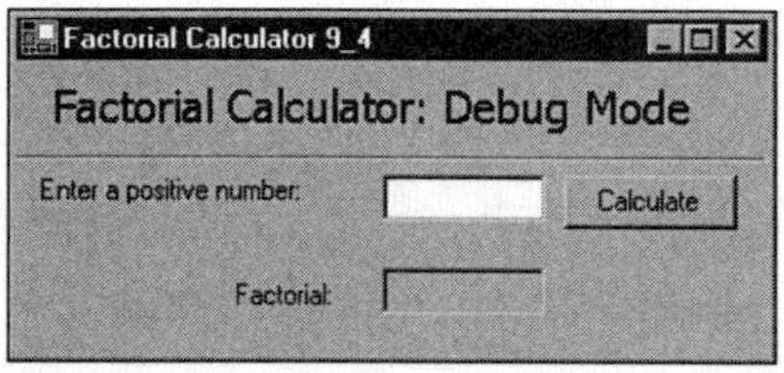

7. Add the following line as the very first line of the code:

#undef DEBUG

Run the program, using the Debug configuration. Note that the program is executed as if it were executed in the Trace configuration. The Debug configuration defines both the DEBUG and TRACE symbols, but the DEBUG symbol is undefined because of the #undef preprocessing directive. Therefore, the compiled code includes only the code specified in the #else part of the preprocessing directive.

8. Add the following line just after the directive placed in step 7:

#undef TRACE

Try running the program. Rather than run the program, the compiler throws an error message, complaining that both the DEBUG and TRACE symbols are undefined. This message is caused by the conditional logic in the Load event handler of the form.

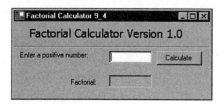

FIGURE 9.8
The Factorial Calculator is compiled conditionally via the Debug configuration.

FIGURE 9.9
The Factorial Calculator is compiled conditionally via the Release configuration.

You can define the DEBUG and TRACE symbols for the compiler in the following ways:

▶ By modifying the project's Property Pages dialog box.

▶ By using the `#define` directive at the beginning of the code file.

▶ By using the `/define` (`/d` for short) option with the command-line C# compiler.

Step-by-Step 9.4 demonstrated conditional compilation with the `DEBUG` and `TRACE` symbols. You can also use conditional compilation with any other custom-defined symbols to perform conditional compilation.

GUIDED PRACTICE EXERCISE 9.1

The goal of this exercise is to add an `EventLogTraceListener` object to the Factorial Calculator program so that it will write all `Trace` and `Debug` messages to the Windows event log.

This exercise will give you good practice on using trace listeners.

How would you create such a form?

You should try working through this problem on your own first. If you get stuck, or if you'd like to see one possible solution, follow these steps:

1. Add a new Visual C# .NET Windows application named `GuidedPracticeExercise9_1` to the solution.

2. In Solution Explorer, copy the `FactorialCalculator.cs` form from the `StepByStep9_1` project to the current project. Change the form's `Text` property to `Factorial Calculator GuidedPracticeExercise9_1`. Switch to the code view and change the form's namespace to `GuidedPracticeExercise9_1`. Delete the default `Form1.cs`.

3. Double-click the form to add an event handler for the `Load` event. Add the following code to the event handler:

```
private void FactorialCalculator_Load(
    object sender, System.EventArgs e)
{
```

continues

continued

```
//Add an event log listener to
//the Listeners collection
Trace.Listeners.Add(new EventLogTraceListener(
    "FactorialCalculator"));
}
```

4. Set project `GuidedPracticeExercise9_1` as the startup project.

5. Run the project. Enter a value for finding a factorial. Click the Calculate button. Close the program. Select View, Server Explorer. Navigate to your computer and expand the Event Logs node, the Application node, and the FactorialCalculator node. The messages generated by the `Trace` and `Debug` classes are added to the Application event log, as shown in Figure 9.10.

If you have difficulty following this exercise, review the sections "Trace Listeners" and "Using Trace and Debug Classes to Display Information," earlier in this chapter. After doing that review, try this exercise again.

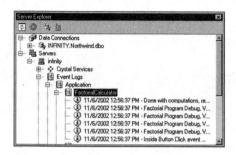

FIGURE 9.10
You can view the Windows Event Log from Server Explorer.

R E V I E W   B R E A K

▶ The `Trace` and `Debug` classes can be used to display informative messages in an application when the DEBUG and TRACE symbols are defined, respectively, at the time of compilation.

▶ By default, both TRACE and DEBUG symbols are defined in the `Debug` configuration for compilation, and only the TRACE symbol is defined for the `Release` configuration for compilation.

▶ Listeners are objects that receive trace and debug output. By default, both `Trace` and `Debug` classes have the `DefaultTraceListener` object in their `Listeners` collection. The `DefaultTraceListener` object displays messages in the output window.

▶ `Debug` and `Trace` objects share the same `Listeners` collection. Therefore, any listener object added to the `Trace.Listeners` collection is also added to the `Debug.Listeners` collection.

▶ Trace switches enable you to change the types of messages that are traced by a program, depending on the value stored in the XML configuration file. You need not recompile the application for this change to take effect; just restart it. You need to implement code to display the messages, depending on the value of the switch.

▶ C# preprocessing directives enable you to define and undefine symbols in an application, report errors or warnings, mark regions of code, and conditionally skip code for compilation.

▶ The Conditional attribute enables you to conditionally add or skip a method for compilation, depending on the value of the symbol that is passed as a parameter to the attribute.

ASP.NET Tracing

Implement tracing: Display trace output.

Log test results: Control debugging in the Web.config file.

In addition to the Trace and Debug classes, ASP.NET supports one more method for tracing, which is specially designed for Web applications and Web services. This method of tracing is called ASP.NET tracing.

With the help of ASP.NET tracing, you can view trace messages and diagnostics information of a Web request along with the page output or through a separate trace viewer utility (trace.axd). You can write custom trace messages by using the System.Web.TraceContext class. The TraceContext class is responsible for gathering execution details of a Web request. You can access the TraceContext object for the current request through the Trace property of the Page class. After you have the TraceContext object, you can invoke its member methods to write trace messages to the trace log. Table 9.5 lists some important members of the TraceContext class with which you should be familiar.

Tracing Beyond a Page The Page class exposes the Trace property to get access to the TraceContext object. If you want to write messages from outside the page (such as from the global.asax file or from the custom server controls) you can access the Trace property of the HttpContext object via the Control.Context or HttpContext.Current property.

IsEnabled Property The IsEnabled property can be dynamically assigned to turn tracing for a page on or off. It can also be used to include or exclude code based on the trace setting for a page.

TABLE 9.5

IMPORTANT MEMBERS OF TraceContext CLASS

Member	Type	Description
IsEnabled	Property	Specifies whether tracing is enabled for a request.
TraceMode	Property	Indicates the sort order in which the messages should be displayed. It can have one of three values—Default, SortByCategory, and SortByTime.
Warn()	Method	Writes the messages to the trace log in red, which indicates that they are warnings. It has three overloads—one with the message, one with the category and message, and the last one with the category, message, and exception object.
Write()	Method	Writes the messages in the trace log. It has three overloads, just like the Warn() method.

By default, tracing is not enabled. Thus, the trace messages and diagnostics information are not displayed. In the following sections I'll show you how to enable tracing at the page level as well as the application level.

ASP.NET Page-Level Tracing

You can enable tracing for a Page by using the Trace attribute of the Page directive. When the Trace attribute is set to true in the Page directive, the page appends the tracing information of the current Web request with its output. You can also enable tracing by setting the DOCUMENT object's Trace property to true. Step-by-Step 9.5 demonstrates how to enable tracing in a page and write trace messages in to the trace log.

STEP BY STEP

9.5 Using the TraceContext Class to Display Debugging Information in a Web application

1. Add a new Visual C# ASP.NET Web application named StepByStep9_5 to the solution.

2. Add a new Web form to the project. Name the Web form `FactorialCalculator.aspx`.

3. Place two `TextBox` controls (`txtNumber` and `txtFactorial`), three `Label` controls (one with the ID `lblHeading`), and a `Button` control (`btnCalculate`) on the Web form and arrange the controls as shown in Figure 9.11.

4. Switch to HTML view of the form in the designer. Add the `trace="true"` attribute to the `Page` directive:

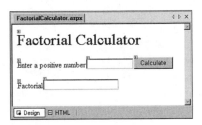

FIGURE 9.11
Design of a form that calculates the factorial of a given number.

```
<%@ Page language="c#"
        Codebehind="FactorialCalculator.aspx.cs"
        AutoEventWireup="false"
        Inherits="StepByStep9_5.FactorialCalculator"
        Trace="true"%>
```

5. Double-click the `Button` control and add the following code to the event handler to handle the `Click` event:

```
private void btnCalculate_Click(
    object sender, System.EventArgs e)
{
    // write a trace message
    Trace.Write("Factorial",
        "Inside Button Click event handler");
    int intNumber;
    try
    {
        intNumber = Convert.ToInt32(txtNumber.Text);
    }
    catch (Exception ex)
    {
        Trace.Warn("Factorial", "Invalid value", ex);
        return;
    }
    if(intNumber < 0)
    {
        Trace.Warn("Factorial",
            "Invalid negative value");
    }
    int intFac = 1;
    for (int i = 2; i <= intNumber; i++)
    {
        intFac = intFac * i;
        Trace.Write("Factorial", "Value of i: " + i);
    }
    if(intFac < 1)
        Trace.Warn("Factorial" ,
            "There was an overflow");
```

continues

continued

```
txtFactorial.Text = intFac.ToString();
Trace.Write("Factorial" ,
    "Done with computations, returning...");
}
```

6. Set project StepByStep9_5 as the startup project. Set the Web form as the start page for the project.

7. Run the project. Notice that the Web page displays a wide range of information after its general output. Enter a value into the number text box and click the Calculate button. You will see the factorial value displayed in the factorial text box, along with some trace messages in the Trace Information section of the trace log, as shown in Figure 9.12.

FIGURE 9.12
You can view the trace log along with a page's output by setting the `trace` attribute of the Page directive to `true`.

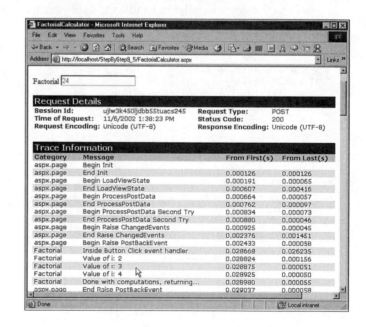

8. Try entering a negative value, or a larger value such as 100, and notice the trace messages displayed in the trace log. You should see that the warning messages are displayed in red.

As you can see, when tracing is enabled, ASP.NET displays a great amount of information related to the request, in addition to the trace messages written by you. The information is grouped in different tables:

▶ Request Details—Includes the session identifier, the time the request was made, the request character encoding, the type of HTTP request (GET or POST), the HTTP response status code, and the response character encoding.

▶ Trace Information—Includes the messages and warnings generated by the ASP.NET engine or generated by you making calls to the Write() or Warn() methods of the TraceContext class. It displays the information in four columns—the category of the message, the trace message, seconds since the first trace message was displayed, and seconds since the most recent trace message was displayed.

▶ Control Tree—Includes the entire collection of controls in the ASP.NET page hierarchically. The information is displayed in four columns—the control identifier, the fully qualified type of the control, the size (in bytes) of the rendered control including its child controls, and the size (in bytes) of the view state of the control excluding its child controls.

▶ Session State—Includes the session state only if any data is stored in the session. The table displays the session key, the fully qualified type of the session data stored, and the value of the session data.

▶ Cookies Collection—Includes the cookies associated with the application. The information displayed is the cookie's name, value, and size.

▶ Headers Collection—Includes the HTTP headers passed to the Web page. It displays the header's name and its value.

▶ Form Collection—Includes the form collection. It is displayed only if a Web form is defined in the page and the form is posting back from the server. It displays the name of the control that's in the form and its value.

▶ Querystring Collection—Includes the query string collection only if any query string parameters are passed during a request for the page. It displays the name of the query string parameter and its value.

▶ Server Variables—Includes all the server variables associated with the page. It displays the name of the server variable and its value.

As apparent from the preceding list, the trace log definitely helps a great deal with understanding the program's execution path. It provides information about state, performance, and the structure of page controls. This information can be of great help in debugging and improving the quality of the program.

ASP.NET Application-Level Tracing

You can enable tracing for an entire application by using the application configuration web.config file in the application's root directory. Enabling tracing through the web.config file allows you to view the trace information by using the trace viewer in a separate page instead of displaying it with the page output. The <trace> element is used to configure tracing for an application. The attributes of the <trace> element are element;attributes>

▶ enabled—Indicates whether tracing is enabled for an application. If enabled, you can use the trace viewer to view trace information.

▶ localOnly—Indicates whether the trace viewer can be viewed by only the local client (running on the Web server itself) or by any client.

▶ pageOutput—Indicates whether the trace information should be displayed along with the page output.

▶ requestLimit—Indicates the number of requests whose trace information should be stored on the server. Tracing gets disabled when the request limit is reached.

▶ traceMode—Indicates the order in which the trace messages should be displayed in the Trace Information section of the trace log. It can be either SortByCategory (sorted by the Category column) or SortByTime (sorted by the First(s) column).

Thus, when tracing is enabled for an application, you can use the trace viewer to view requests for each page (unless a page has its Page

EXAM TIP

Page-Level Tracing Overrides The page-level trace setting overrides the trace setting for the application. For example, if pageOutput is set to false in the web.config file and if the trace attribute is enabled at the page level, the trace information is still displayed along with the page output.

directive's `trace` attribute set to `false`). Trace viewer can be viewed by navigating to `trace.axd` from any directory in an application. You should notice that there is no `trace.axd` file in the application directory structure. Instead, this request is handled by the `TraceHandler` object defined in the `<httpHandlers>` element of the `machine.config` file. Trace viewer lists all the page requests in an application along with the time of request, the filename, HTTP status code, type of request, and a link to view the request's trace log. It also contains a link to clear the current trace information of all page requests.

Step-by-Step 9.6 demonstrates how to set application-level tracing.

STEP BY STEP

9.6 Setting Application-Level Tracing for a Web Application

1. Open the `web.config` file of the Web application `StepByStep9_5` from the Solution Explorer. Modify the `<trace>` element defined in the `<system.web>` element with the following code:

```
<trace
    enabled="true"
    requestLimit="10"
    pageOutput="false"
    traceMode="SortByTime"
    localOnly="true"
      />
```

2. Remove the `trace="true"` attribute from the `Page` directive of the form `FactorialCalculator.aspx`.

3. Run the project. Notice that there is no trace information along with the page display. Enter a value into the number text box and click the Calculate button. You will see the factorial value displayed in the factorial text box.

4. Now navigate to `trace.axd` under your application directory by typing **http://localhost/StepByStep9_5/Trace.axd** (substitute the name of your Web server to *localhost* if the Web server is not on your development computer). Notice the Application Trace page as shown in Figure 9.13.

continues

continued

FIGURE 9.13
Trace viewer displays all the page requests in the Application Trace page.

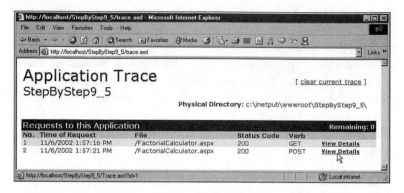

5. Click the View Details link in the second row (the one with the post request). The entire trace log for that page request is displayed as shown in Figure 9.14.

FIGURE 9.14
You can view the complete trace log of a page request by using the trace viewer utility (`trace.axd`).

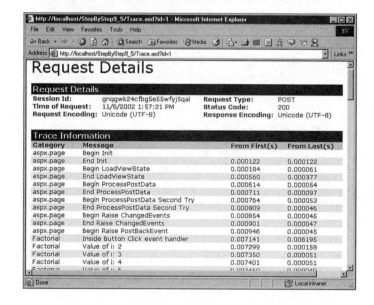

6. Now open the `web.config` file and change the `pageOutput` attribute to `true`. Run the project. Enter a value into the number text box and click the Calculate button. You should see the factorial value being displayed in the factorial text box, along with the entire trace log being appended to the trace output. You can also view the trace log with the help of the trace viewer, as shown in steps 4 and 5.

7. Now open the form in HTML view in the designer. Add the `trace="false"` attribute in the `Page` directive. Run the project. Enter a value into the number text box and click the Calculate button. You should see the factorial value being displayed in the factorial text box. Notice that neither the page output nor the trace viewer displays the trace information. The page level directive overrides the settings in the `web.config` file.

▶ The `System.Web.TraceContext` class can be used to display trace messages in a Web application. You can easily view these messages by using the trace viewer utility or at the end of the page output. ASP.NET displays various page request details, along with custom trace messages displayed by you.

▶ To enable ASP.NET tracing for each page, set the `trace` attribute of the `Page` directive to `true`.

▶ ASP.NET tracing also can be enabled at the application level by setting the `enabled` attribute of the `<trace>` element to `true` in the application-wide `web.config` file.

DEBUGGING

Instrument and debug a Windows service, a serviced component, a .NET Remoting object, and an XML Web service.

- **Configure the debugging environment.**
- **Use interactive debugging.**

Log test results.

- **Resolve errors and rework code.**
- **Control debugging in the Web.config file.**
- **Use SOAP extensions for debugging.**

Debugging is the process of finding the causes of errors in a program, locating the lines of code that are causing those errors, and fixing those errors.

N O T E

Runtime Errors and Compile-Time Errors   *Compile-time errors* are produced when a program does not comply with the syntax of the programming language. These errors are trivial and are generally pointed out by compilers themselves. *Runtime errors* occur in programs that are compiled successfully but do not behave as expected. The process of testing and debugging applies to runtime errors only. Testing reveals these errors, and debugging repairs them.

Without tools, the process of debugging can be very time-consuming and tedious. Thankfully, Visual Studio .NET comes loaded with a large set of tools and features to help you with various debugging tasks. Some of these features include

▶ Support for the cross-language debugging of Visual C# .NET, Visual Basic .NET, Visual C++ .NET, Managed Extensions for C++, script, and SQL.

▶ Support for debugging both managed and unmanaged applications.

▶ The ability to attach a debugger to a running program outside the Visual Studio .NET environment on a local machine or remote machine.

▶ Support for end-to-end debugging for distributed applications.

Configuring the Debugging Environment

When starting a program from Visual Studio .NET for debugging, you should ensure that the program is started in the Debug configuration. In addition to this, to enable debugging in the ASP.NET Web application or a Web service, make sure that the debug attribute of the `<compilation>` element in the `web.config` file is set to `true`.

```
<compilation
    defaultLanguage="c#"
    debug="true"/>
```

Also, in ASP.NET Web applications and Web services, ensure that the Enable ASP.NET Debugging option is set to `true`. The Enable ASP.NET Debugging option is found in the Configuration Properties, Debugging option in the project's Property Pages dialog box.

W A R N I N G

Applications Run Slowly in Debug Mode   When debugging is enabled for an application, the compiler includes extra debugging information in the page, creating a large output file that executes slowly.

N O T E

Debugging from Visual Studio .NET   When you run an application from Visual Studio .NET, it automatically attaches a debugger to the process in which your application is running. In the case of ASP.NET Web applications and Web services, the debugger is also attached to the ASP.NET worker process (`aspnet_wp.exe`), if the Enable ASP.NET Debugging option is set to `true` in the project's Property Pages dialog box.

Setting Breakpoints and Stepping Through Program Execution

A common technique for debugging is to execute a program step by step. This systematic execution allows you to track the flow of logic, to ensure that the program is following the same paths of execution that you expect it to follow. If it does not, you can immediately identify the location of the problem.

Using step-by-step execution of a program also gives you an opportunity to monitor the program's state before and after a statement is executed. For example, you can check the values of variables, the records in a database, and other changes in the environment. Visual Studio .NET provides tools to make these tasks convenient.

The Debug menu provides three options for step-by-step execution of a program (see Table 9.6). The keyboard shortcuts listed in Table 9.6 correspond to the default keyboard scheme of the Visual Studio .NET IDE. If you have personalized the keyboard scheme either through the Tools, Options, Environment, Keyboard menu, or through the Visual Studio .NET Start Page, you might have a different keyboard mapping. You can check out the keyboard mappings available for your customization through Visual Studio .NET's context-sensitive help.

TABLE 9.6

DEBUG OPTIONS FOR STEP-BY-STEP EXECUTION

Debug Menu Item	Keyboard Shortcut	Purpose
Step Into	F11	Use this option to execute code in step mode. If a method call is encountered, the program execution steps into the code of the method and executes the method in step mode.
Step Over	F10	Use this option when a method call is encountered and you do not want to step into the method code. When this option is selected, the debugger executes the entire method without any step-by-step execution (interruption), and then it steps to the next statement after the method call.
Step Out	Shift+F11	Use this option inside a method call to execute the rest of the method without stepping, and you resume step execution mode when control returns to the calling method.

Breakpoints are markers in code that signal the debugger to pause execution. When the debugger pauses at a breakpoint, you can take your time to analyze variables, data records, and other settings in the environment to determine the state of the program. You can also choose to execute the program in step mode from this point onward.

If you have placed a breakpoint in a button's `Click` event handler, the program pauses when you click the button and the execution reaches the breakpoint. You can then step through the execution for the rest of the event handler. When the execution of the event handler code finishes, the control is transferred back to the form. If you have another button on the form for which a breakpoint is not set in the event handler, then the program is no longer under step execution. You should mark breakpoints at all the places you would like execution to pause.

Step-by-Step 9.7 shows you how to set breakpoints and perform step-by-step execution using Visual Studio .NET.

STEP BY STEP

9.7 Setting Breakpoints and Performing Step-By-Step Execution

1. Add a new Visual C# Windows application named `StepByStep9_7` to the solution.

2. In Solution Explorer, copy the `FactorialCalculator.cs` form from the `StepByStep9_1` project to the current project. Change the form's `Text` property to `Factorial Calculator 9_7`. Switch to the code view and change the namespace of the form to `StepByStep9_7`. Delete the default `Form1.cs`.

3. Add the following method to the class:

```
private int Factorial(int intNumber)
{
    int intFac = 1;
    for (int i = 2; i <= intNumber; i++)
    {
        intFac = intFac * i;
    }
    return intFac;
}
```

4. Modify the `Click` event handler of `btnCalculate` so that it looks like this:

```csharp
private void btnCalculate_Click(object sender,
    System.EventArgs e)
{
    int intNumber, intFactorial;
    try
    {
        intNumber = Convert.ToInt32(txtNumber.Text);
        intFactorial = Factorial(intNumber);
        txtFactorial.Text = intFactorial.ToString();
    }
    catch(Exception ex)
    {
        Debug.WriteLine(ex.Message);
    }
}
```

5. In the event handler added in step 4, right-click the beginning of the line that makes a call to the `Factorial()` method and select Insert Breakpoint from the context menu. Note that the line of code is highlighted with red and also that a red dot appears on the left margin, as shown in Figure 9.15. You can alternatively create a breakpoint by clicking on the left margin adjacent to a line.

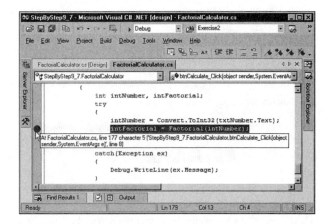

FIGURE 9.15
You can enter step-by-step execution mode by setting a breakpoint in a program.

6. Set project `StepByStep9_7` as the startup project.

7. Run the solution. Enter a value in the text box and click the Calculate button. Note that execution pauses at the location where you have marked the breakpoint. You should see an arrow on the left margin of the code as shown in Figure 9.16. This arrow indicates the next statement to be executed.

continues

continued

FIGURE 9.16
When the breakpoint is reached during execution, the execution of the program pauses at that point.

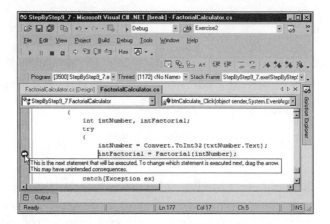

8. Press the F11 key to proceed to step into the code of the Factorial() method. Hover the cursor over the various variables in the Factorial() method to see the current values of these variables.

9. Select Debug, Windows, Breakpoints. The Breakpoints window appears, as shown in Figure 9.17. Right-click the breakpoint listed in the window and select Go To Disassembly. The Disassembly window appears, showing the program's object code along with the disassembled source code.

FIGURE 9.17
The Breakpoints window gives you convenient access to all breakpoint-related tasks in one place.

10. Close the Disassembly window. Select Debug, Step Out to automatically execute the rest of the Factorial() method and again start the step mode in the event handler at the next statement. Step through the execution until you see the form again.

11. Select Debug, Stop Debugging. The debugging session ends and the application is terminated.

12. In the code view, right-click the statement where you have set the breakpoint and select Disable Breakpoint from the context menu.

To set advanced options in a breakpoint, you can choose to create a new breakpoint by selecting New from the context menu of the code or from the toolbar in the Breakpoints window. The New Breakpoint dialog box (see Figure 9.18) has four tabs. You can use these tabs to set a breakpoint in a function, in a file, at an address in the object code, and when a data value (that is, the value of a variable) changes.

Clicking the Condition button opens the Breakpoint Condition dialog box, as shown in Figure 9.19. The Breakpoint Condition dialog box enables you to set a breakpoint based on the runtime value of an expression.

Clicking the Hit Count button opens the Breakpoint Hit Count dialog box, as shown in Figure 9.20. This dialog box enables you to break the program execution only if the specified breakpoint has been hit a given number of times. This can be especially helpful if you have a breakpoint inside a lengthy loop and you want to step-execute the program only near the end of the loop.

NOTE

The Disassembly Window Shows Native Code Instead of MSIL Although C# programs are compiled to Microsoft Intermediate Language (MSIL), they are just-in-time compiled to native code only at the time of their first execution. This means the executing code is never in IL; it is always in native code. Thus, you will always see native code instead of IL in the Disassembly window.

Disabling Versus Removing a Breakpoint When you remove a breakpoint, you loose all the information related to it. Instead of removing a breakpoint, you can choose to disable it. Disabling a breakpoint does not pause the program at the point of the breakpoint, but Visual C# .NET will remember the breakpoint settings. At any time, you can select Enable Breakpoint to reactivate the breakpoint.

FIGURE 9.18
The New Breakpoint dialog box enables you to create a new breakpoint.

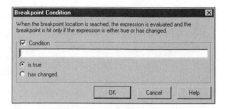

FIGURE 9.19
The Breakpoint Condition dialog box allows you to set a breakpoint that is based on the value of an expression at runtime.

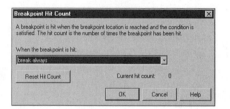

FIGURE 9.20
The Breakpoint Hit Count dialog box enables you to break the program execution only if the specified breakpoint has been hit a specified number of times.

Analyzing Program State to Resolve Errors

When you break the execution of a program, the program is at a particular state in its execution cycle. You can use various debugging tools to analyze the values of variables, the results of expressions, the path of execution, and so on, to help identify the cause of the error that you are debugging.

Step-by-Step 9.8 demonstrates various Visual C# .NET debugging tools, such as the Watch, Autos, Locals, This, Immediate, Output, and Call Stack windows.

STEP BY STEP

9.8 Analyzing Program State to Resolve Errors

1. Add a new Visual C# Windows application named `StepByStep9_8` to the solution.

2. In Solution Explorer, copy the `FactorialCalculator.cs` form from the `StepByStep9_7` project to the current project. Change the `Text` property of the form to `Factorial Calculator 9_8`. Switch to the code view and change the form's namespace to `StepByStep9_8`. Delete the default `Form1.cs`.

3. Change the code in the `Factorial()` method to the following:

```
private int Factorial(int intNumber)
{
    int intFac = 1;
    for (int i = 2; i < intNumber; i++)
    {
        intFac = intFac * i;
    }
    return intFac;
}
```

   Note in this code that I have introduced a logical error that I will later "discover" through debugging.

4. Set project `StepByStep9_8` as the startup project.

5. Run the program. Enter the value **5** in the text box and click the Calculate button. You should see that the result is not correct; this program needs to be debugged.

6. Set a breakpoint in the `Click` event handler of `btnCalculate` at the line where a call to the `Factorial()` method is being made. Execute the program. Enter the value **5** again, and click the Calculate button.

7. Press the F11 key to step into the `Factorial()` method. Select Debug, Windows, Watch, Watch1 to add a watch window. Similarly, select the Debug, Windows menu and add the Locals, Autos, This, Immediate, Output, and Call Stack windows. Pin down the windows so that they always remain in view and are easy to watch as you step through the program.

8. Look at the Call Stack window shown in Figure 9.21. It shows the method call stack, giving you information about the path taken by the code to reach its current point of execution. The currently executing method is at the top of the stack, as indicated by a yellow arrow. When this method is finished executing, the next entry in the stack will be the method receiving the control of execution.

FIGURE 9.21
The Call Stack window enables you to view the names of methods on the call stack, the parameter types, and their values.

9. Look at the This window, shown in Figure 9.22. In the This window you can examine the members associated with the current object (the Factorial form). You can scroll down to find the `txtNumber` object. You can change the values of these objects here. At this point, however, you don't need to change any values.

continues

continued

FIGURE 9.22
The This window enables you to examine the members associated with the current object.

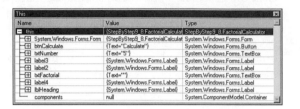

10. Activate the Autos window, which is shown in Figure 9.23. The Autos window displays the variables used in the current statement and the previous statement. The debugger determines this information for you automatically; that is why the name of this window is Autos.

FIGURE 9.23
The Autos window displays the variables used in the current statement and the previous statement.

11. Invoke the Locals window, which is shown in Figure 9.24. The Locals window displays the variables that are local to the current context (that is, the current method under execution) with their current values. Figure 9.24 shows the local variables in the Factorial() method.

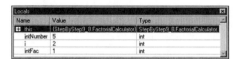

FIGURE 9.24
The Locals window displays the variables local to the current method under execution.

12. Invoke the Immediate window. Type **intNumber** in the Immediate window and press Enter. The Immediate window immediately evaluates and displays the current value of this variable in the next line. Now type the expression **Factorial(intNumber)**. The Immediate window calls the Factorial() method for a given value and prints the result. The Immediate window can therefore be used to print values of variables and expressions while you are debugging a program.

FIGURE 9.25
The Command window can appear in two modes: the command mode and the immediate mode.

13. Invoke the Watch 1 window. The Watch window enables you to evaluate variables and expressions. Select the variable `intFac` from the code and drag and drop it in the Watch 1 window. You can also double-click the next available row and add a variable to it. Add the variables `i` and `intNumber` to the Watch 1 window, as shown in Figure 9.26.

14. Step through the execution of the program by pressing the F11 key. Keep observing the way values change in the Watch 1 (or Autos or Locals) window. After a few steps, the method terminates. Note that the program executed only until the value of `i` was 4 and that the loop was not iterated back when the value of `i` was 5. This causes the incorrect output in the program.

15. Change the condition in the `for` loop to use the `<=` operator instead of `<` and press F11 to step through. The Unable to Apply Code Changes dialog box appears, as shown in Figure 9.27. This dialog box appears because after you have identified the problem and corrected the code, the source code is different from the compiled version of the program. If you choose to continue at this stage, your source code and program in execution are different, and that might mislead you. I recommend that you always restart execution in this case by clicking the Restart button. The code is then recompiled, and the program is started again.

continues

NOTE

Two Modes of the Command Window
The command window has two modes: the command mode and the immediate mode. When you select View, Other Windows, Command Window, the Command window is invoked in the command mode. You can distinctly identify the command mode because in this mode the Command window shows the > prompt (see Figure 9.25). You can use the command mode to evaluate expressions or to issue commands such as Edit to edit text in a file. You can also use regular expressions with the Edit command to make editing operations quick and effective.

On the other hand, when you invoke the Command window by selecting Debug, Window, Immediate, it opens in the immediate mode. You can use the immediate mode to evaluate expressions in the currently debugged program. The immediate mode does not show any prompt (see Figure 9.25). You can switch from immediate mode to command mode by typing **>cmd**, and you can switch from command mode to immediate mode by typing **immed** in the Command window.

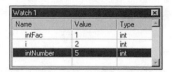

FIGURE 9.26
The Watch window enables you to evaluate variables and expressions.

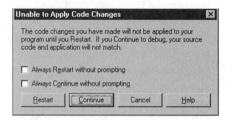

FIGURE 9.27
The Unable to Apply Code Changes dialog box appears if you edit code and then try to continue execution.

N O T E

Support for Cross-Language Debugging   Visual Studio .NET supports debugging of projects that contain managed code written in several languages. The debugger can transparently step into and out of languages, making the debugging process smooth for you as a developer. Visual Studio .NET also extends this support to unmanaged code, but with minor limitations.

---

continued

16. Enter the value **5** in the text box and click the Continue button. The program breaks into the debugger again because the breakpoint is still active. Step through the program and watch the values of the variables. The loop is executed the correct number of times, and you get the correct factorial value.

Debugging on Exceptions

You can control the way the debugger behaves when it encounters a line of code that throws an exception. You can control this behavior through the Exceptions dialog box, which is shown in Figure 9.28 and is invoked by selecting Debug, Exceptions. The Exceptions dialog box allows you to control the debugger's behavior for each type of exception defined on the system. In fact, if you have defined your own exceptions, you can also add them to this dialog box.

There are two levels at which you can control the behavior of the debugger when it encounters exceptions:

▶ When the exception is thrown—You can instruct the debugger to either continue or break the execution of the program when an exception is thrown. The default setting for Common Language Runtime (CLR) exceptions is to continue the execution, possibly in anticipation that there will be an exception handler.

▶ If the exception is not handled—If the program you are debugging fails to handle an exception, you can instruct the debugger to either ignore it and continue or to break the program's execution. The default setting for CLR exceptions is to break the execution, warning the programmer of the possibly problematic situation.

GUIDED PRACTICE EXERCISE 9.2

The Factorial Calculator program created in Step-by-Step 9.4 throws exceptions of type `System.FormatException` and `System.OverflowException` when users are not careful about the numbers they enter.

The later versions of this program (created in Step-by-Steps 9.7 and 9.8) catch the exception to prevent users from complaining about the annoying exception messages.

The goal of this exercise is to configure the debugger in Step-by-Step 9.8 so that when the reported exception occurs, you get an opportunity to analyze the program.

How would you configure the debugger?

In this exercise you will practice configuring the exception handling for the Visual Studio .NET debugger environment. You should try working through this problem on your own first. If you get stuck, or if you'd like to see one possible solution, follow these steps:

1. Open the Windows application project `StepByStep9_8`.

2. Activate the Exceptions dialog box by selecting Debug, Exceptions.

3. In the Exceptions dialog box, click the Find button. Enter `System.FormatException` and click the OK button. You are quickly taken to the desired exception in the exception tree view.

4. Select Break into the Debugger from the When the Exception Is Thrown group box.

5. Repeat steps 3 and 4 for `System.OverFlowException`.

6. Run the solution. Enter a nonnumeric value for which to find the factorial. This causes a `System.FormatException` error, and the debugger prompts you to either break or continue the execution. Select to break. You can see the values of various variables at this stage either by moving the mouse pointer over them or by adding the variables to the Watch window. On the

FIGURE 9.28
The Exceptions dialog box enables you to control the debugger's behavior for system and custom-defined exceptions.

continues

continued

next execution of the program, enter a very large value. This causes a `System.OverFlowException` error. Select to break when prompted by the debugger, and then analyze the values of the various variables.

If you have difficulty following this exercise, review the section "Debugging on Exceptions" and "Setting Breakpoints and Stepping Through Program Execution." After doing that review, try this exercise again.

REVIEW BREAK

▶ Debugging is the process of finding the causes of errors in a program, locating the lines of code that are causing the error, and fixing the errors.

▶ The three options available while performing step-by-step execution are Step Into, Step Over, and Step Out.

▶ Breakpoints enable you to mark code that signals the debugger to pause execution. After you encounter a breakpoint, you can choose to continue step-by-step execution or resume the normal execution by pressing F5 or by clicking the Resume button or the Continue button.

▶ The various tool windows, such as This, Locals, Immediate, Autos, Watch, and Call Stack, can be of great help in tracking the execution path and the status of variables in the process of debugging an application in Visual Studio .NET.

▶ When an application throws an exception, you can choose to either continue execution or break into the debugger (to start debugging operations such as step-by-step execution). You can customize this behavior for each exception object by using the Exceptions dialog box.

Debugging a Running Process

Until this point in the chapter, you have seen how to debug programs only by starting them from the Visual Studio .NET environment. However, Visual Studio .NET also allows you to debug processes that are running outside the Visual Studio .NET debugging environment. This feature can be quite helpful for debugging already-deployed applications.

To access external processes from Visual Studio .NET, you need to invoke the Processes dialog box, shown in Figure 9.29. You can do this in two ways:

▶ When you have a solution open in Visual Studio .NET, you can invoke the Processes dialog box by selecting Debug, Processes.

▶ When no solution is open in Visual Studio .NET, you don't see any Debug menu, but you can still invoke the Processes dialog box by selecting Tools, Debug Processes.

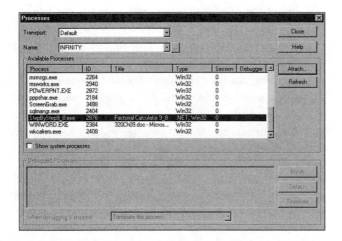

FIGURE 9.29

The Processes dialog box enables you to attach a debugger to a process that is under execution.

In the Processes dialog box, select the process that needs to be debugged in the Available Processes section and then click the Attach button to attach the process to the debugger. You can then open the source code files in Visual Studio .NET and place breakpoints in the code. Visual Studio .NET debugger breaks the execution of the process when the breakpoint is reached. You can invoke various debugging windows, such as the Watch, Locals, and Autos windows, to analyze variables and step through the program execution.

Step-by-Step 9.9 demonstrates how to attach the debugger to a process that is being executed.

STEP BY STEP

9.9 Attaching the Debugger to a Process That Is Being Executed

1. Using Windows Explorer, navigate to the bin\Debug folder inside the project folder for StepByStep9_8. Double-click the StepByStep9_8.exe file to launch the program.

2. Start a new instance of Visual Studio .NET and select Tools, Debug Processes. The Processes dialog box appears, as shown in Figure 9.29. You may have a different process list from what is shown in the figure.

3. Select the process named StepByStep9_8.exe in the Available Processes section and click the Attach button. This invokes an Attach to Process dialog box, as shown in Figure 9.30. Select the Common Language Runtime as the program type and keep all other options unchecked. Make sure you check the Show system processes option to view even the system processes on the machine. Click the OK button. You should now see the selected process in the Debugged Processes section of the Processes dialog box.

4. Click the Break button to break into the running process. Click the Close button to close the Processes dialog box for now.

5. Open the source code file in Visual Studio .NET. Set a breakpoint on the line of code that makes a call to the Factorial() method. Press F11 to step into the program.

6. Enter the value 5 in the form and click the Calculate button. The debugger breaks the execution when the breakpoint is reached.

FIGURE 9.30
The Attach to Process dialog box allows you to attach a debugger to a program that is running in a process outside of Visual Studio .NET.

7. Invoke Watch, Locals, Autos window to analyze variables and step through the program execution.

8. When the factorial result is displayed, invoke the Processes window again by selecting Debug, Processes. From the list of debugged processes, select StepByStep9_8 and click the Detach button.

9. Click the Close button to close the Processes dialog box. StepByStep9_8.exe is still executing, as it was when you initiated the debugging process.

However, to debug a deployed or running Web application, or a Web service, you need to attach the Visual Studio .NET debugger to the aspnet_wp.exe process running on the Web server. After this debugging setup is done, the Web programs can be debugged just like any other program.

Debugging a Remote Process

For remote debugging to work, the Machine Debug Manager (mdm.exe) should be running on the remote computer. mdm.exe is a Windows service that provides remote debugging support. If the remote computer has never been set up for remote debugging, you take one of the following steps to do a one-time configuration on the remote machine:

▶ Install Visual Studio .NET on the remote machine.

▶ Install Remote Components Setup on the remote machine. (You can start this from the Visual Studio .NET Setup Disc 1.)

You also must ensure that your user account is a member of the Debugger Users group on the remote machine. If you want to debug an ASP.NET worker process, you must also have administrative privileges (that is, you should be a member of the Administrators group) on the remote machine.

WARNING

Terminating aspnet_wp.exe The ASP.NET worker process (aspnet_wp.exe) processes requests from all ASP.NET applications. If, after debugging, you choose to terminate the aspnet_wp.exe process, it will affect all Web applications running on the server. You need to be especially careful when selecting this option on a production/shared server.

Don't Debug on a Production Server When you attach a debugger to the ASP.NET worker process aspnet_wp.exe, it freezes the execution of all other Web applications on that server. This might cause undesirable effects on a production server.

NOTE

Microsoft CLR Debugger (dbgclr.exe) The .NET Framework provides a tool called Microsoft CLR Debugger (dbgclr.exe). This tool is based on the Visual Studio .NET debugger and has most of the same features. This tool will be especially useful if you are not using Visual Studio .NET for developing your applications and still want all the powerful GUI-based debugging capabilities.

EXAM TIP

Debugging a Remote Process
The local computer and the remote computer must be members of a trusted domain for remote debugging to be possible.

DCOM Error While Debugging
Visual Studio .NET uses DCOM to enable remote debugging. If you get a DCOM configuration error while debugging, you didn't set up the remote machine to support remote debugging. To resolve the error make sure that you follow all the steps mentioned in this section.

If SQL Server is installed on the remote machine, the setup process just described also configures the machine for SQL Server stored procedures debugging, which is demonstrated at the end of this chapter, in Exercise 9.2.

In addition to the already-mentioned one-time setup of the remote machine, you also need to configure the Visual Studio .NET project on your local machine. To do this you take the following steps:

1. Set the Enable Remote Debugging option to true in the project's Property Pages dialog box as shown in Figure 9.31. The EXE file must be in a shareable directory on the remote machine.

2. Set the Remote Debug Machine option with the name of the machine on which the EXE file will run.

3. The EXE file must be in a shareable directory on the remote machine. The location of the EXE file on the remote machine must match the value of the Output Path property, which is on the Build property page in the Configuration Properties folder.

FIGURE 9.31
You must set the Enable Remote Debugging option to True to enable remote debugging.

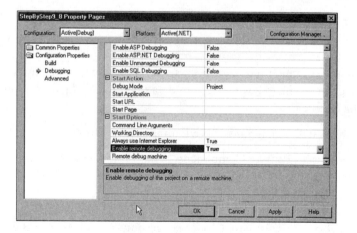

After you have completed the required setup, the process of debugging a remote process is almost the same as the process of debugging an already running process. The only difference is that prior to selecting a running process from the Processes dialog box, you need to select the remote machine name from the Processes dialog box (refer to Figure 9.29).

Debugging the Code in DLL Files

The process of debugging a DLL file is similar to the process of debugging an EXE file. There is one difference though: The code in the DLL file cannot be directly invoked, so you need to have a calling program that calls various methods/components of the DLL files.

You typically need to take the following steps to debug code in a DLL file:

1. Launch the program (such as an EXE file, a Web page, a Web service, and so on) that uses the components or methods in the DLL file.

2. Launch Visual Studio .NET and attach the debugger to the calling program. Set a breakpoint in the calling program where the method in the DLL file is called or in the source code of the DLL file. Continue with the execution.

3. The execution breaks when the breakpoint is reached. At this point, select Debug, Step Into to step into the DLL file's source code. Execute the code in step mode while you watch the value of its variables.

In addition, if the code files are executing on a remote machine, you need to make sure that the remote machine is set up with remote debugging support, as explained in the previous section.

Debugging Client-Side Scripts

Visual Studio .NET also allows you to debug client-side scripts. The process is similar to the process that I discussed earlier for Step-by-Step 9.9. However, you must note the following additional points for client-side scripting:

▶ Client-side debugging works only with Microsoft Internet Explorer.

▶ You have to enable script debugging in Internet Explorer. To do this, select Tools, Internet Options, select the Advanced tab, and uncheck the Disable Script Debugging option in the Browsing section.

▶ Attach the debugger to the `iexplore.exe` process displaying the Web form. This is required only if you are debugging an already running process. While attaching the process in the Attach to Process dialog box, make sure that you also select the Script option.

Debugging a Windows Service

In most aspects, debugging a Windows service is like debugging any other application. However, a Windows service runs within the context of the Service Control Manager. Therefore, to debug a Windows service, you must attach a debugger to the process in which the Windows service is running. If the Windows service is not already started, then you need to start the Windows service to perform debugging.

Step-by-Step 9.10 shows you how to debug the `OrderService` service created in Step-by-Step 6.1 in Chapter 6, "Windows Services." If you haven't already created this service, you should create it now to follow Step-by-Step 9.10.

> **WARNING**
>
> **Debugging Windows Service Processes**   When you attach a debugger to a Windows service, the service suspends its processing, but continues to be in the Started state. This may affect the execution of the Windows service. Therefore, you need to be especially careful when selecting this option on a production/shared server.

STEP BY STEP

9.10 Debugging Windows Services

1. Open the `320C06` solution in Visual Studio .NET.

2. Open the `OrderService.cs` file of the `StepByStep6_1` project that contains the code for the Windows service.

3. Place a breakpoint in the `fswOrders_Created()` method where the main task of the Windows service is performed.

4. Make sure that the `OrderService` is already installed. If not, then install the service by following the steps in Step-by-Step 6.3 in Chapter 6.

5. Open the Services administrative tool from the Administrative tool section of the Windows Control Panel. Browse through the services to locate the `OrderService` service. Ensure that the Windows service is running; if not, then start the Windows service.

6. Select Tools, Debug Processes. The Processes dialog box appears. Check the Show System Services checkbox. Select the process named `StepByStep6_1.exe` (`OrderService` Windows service) in the Available Processes section and click the Attach button. This invokes an Attach to Process dialog box. Select the Common Language Runtime option. Click the OK button. You should now see the selected process in the Debugged Processes section of the Processes dialog box. Click the Close button to close the Processes dialog box for now.

7. Create an XML file named `Orders.xml` and copy this file to the `c:\orders` directory. (Refer to Step-by-Step 6.3 for more details.)

8. You'll note that in a few moments the debugger breaks into the `fswOrders_Created()` method in the `OrderService.cs` file, where the breakpoint was placed. You can now step into the code of the Windows service and step through the program execution. Invoke the Watch, Locals, and Autos windows to analyze variables and step through the program execution.

9. When the `Orders.xml` file is moved from `c:\orders` to a new subdirectory `c:\orders\updated`, invoke the Processes dialog box again by selecting Debug, Processes. From the list of debugged processes, select `StepByStep6_1` and click the Detach button.

10. Click the Close button to close the Processes dialog box. Note that the `OrderService` Windows service (`StepByStep6_1.exe`) is still running, as it was when you initiated the debugging process.

In Step-by-Step 9.10, you could have placed breakpoints in the `OnStop()`, `OnPause()`, `OnContinue()` methods. You could have then used the Services administrative tool to stop, pause, or continue the Windows service to debug the code in these methods. However, it is not possible to debug the `OnStart()` method (that starts the service) or the `Main()` method (that creates the instance of the service) by the process explained in Step-by-Step 9.10 because a Windows service needs to be already started before you can attach a debugger.

To debug the constructor or the Main() method of a Windows service, you place a breakpoint in the Main() method and then run the application from Visual Studio .NET. Remember that this step just allows you to step into the Main() method but does not actually load the Windows service as the Service Control Manager does.

To debug the code in the OnStart() method, you can call the OnStart() method from the Main() method, as shown in the following code:

```
static void Main()
{
    System.ServiceProcess.ServiceBase[] ServicesToRun;

    // Place a breakpoint in the following line to
    // step into the OnStart() method
    // This line needs to be removed after the debug
    // process completes
    (new OrderService()).OnStart(null);

    ServicesToRun = new
        System.ServiceProcess.ServiceBase[]
        { new OrderService() };

    System.ServiceProcess.ServiceBase.Run(
        ServicesToRun);
}
```

In these lines of code, a call to the OnStart() method is added just to debug the code in the OnStart() method. After the debug process, you should remove the call to the OnStart() method.

If a Windows service is executing on a remote machine, you need to make sure that the remote machine is set up with remote debugging support, as explained in the section "Debugging a Remote Process."

NOTE

Debugging the OnStart() Method
When the Service Control Manager starts a Windows service by calling the OnStart() method, it waits just 30 seconds for the OnStart() method to return. If the method does not return in this time, the Service Control Manager shows an error that the service cannot be started.

Debugging a Serviced Component

A serviced component is stored in a DLL file. The code in the serviced component cannot be directly invoked, so you need to have a client (calling) program that creates the serviced component object and calls various methods of the serviced component.

Therefore to debug a serviced component, you need to take steps similar to those of debugging any DLL file. However, the debugging differs slightly depending on whether the serviced component application is a Library or Server application.

If the serviced component is a Library application, then the serviced component runs in the client application's process. In this case, you can set breakpoints in the serviced component or the client application and run the client application in debug mode. When the breakpoint is reached, you can step into the serviced component's code. In case of an already running client application, you can set breakpoints in the serviced component or the client application and attach a debugger to the client application's process.

On the other hand, if the serviced component is a Server application, then the serviced component runs in a separate process called dllhost.exe. Setting breakpoints in the client code and attaching a debugger to the client application debugs only the client application; it does not step into the code of the serviced component.

In this case, to debug the serviced component you should place breakpoints in the serviced component code and attach a debugger to the dllhost.exe process in which the desired serviced component is running. If multiple COM+ server applications are running on a machine, then multiple dllhost.exe processes will be running on the machine.

You can identify the unique process identifier (PID) of the dllhost.exe that is running your serviced component with the help of the Component Services administrative tool. Drill down to the COM+ Applications node and select View, Status View. You should now be able to view the PID for the dllhost.exe process that hosts the serviced component, as shown in Figure 9.32.

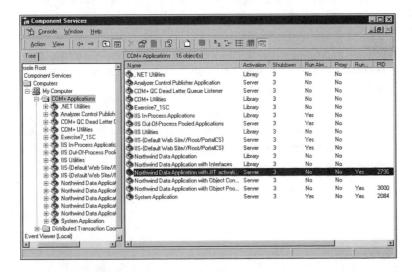

FIGURE 9.32

The Status View of the Component Services administrative tool gives detailed information on the status of the COM+ applications.

FIGURE 9.33

An Enterprise Services application that has Server activation mode runs in a separate process named dllhost.exe.

You can use the PID of the `dllhost.exe` process to attach a debugger to that process via the Processes dialog box, as shown in Figure 9.33.

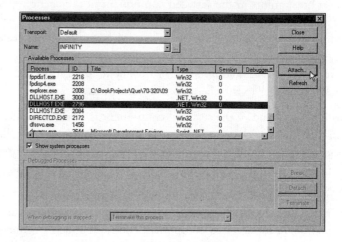

<table>
<tr><td>
WARNING

Setting the Computer Level Default Timeout When you increase the Transaction timeout value in the My Computer Properties dialog box, the setting affects all the transactions in the computer. Therefore, you should try to reset the default value as soon as possible, so that other applications using transactions are not affected in the computer.
</td></tr>
</table>

After attaching the process, you can place breakpoints to step into the code of the serviced component just like that of any other component. If you want to debug the client application as well, you should attach a debugger to the client application's process. So in this case, you attach debuggers to two processes: the serviced component's process and the client application's process.

However, note that while debugging, the serviced components involving transactions may raise `COMException` errors indicating transaction timeout problems. The default computer-level setting for transactions timeout is 60 seconds. While debugging, you may want to increase the transaction timeout value. You can do so by overriding the default settings for your serviced component: Select the Override global transaction timeout value option in the Transactions tab of the serviced component's Properties dialog box, as shown in Figure 9.34.

Note the default value for the timeout if overridden is 0, which means the transactions will never time out. However, you should set a value greater than 0, so that there are no chances of distributed deadlocks.

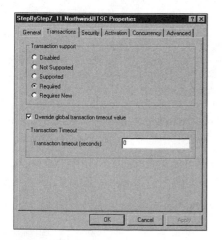

FIGURE 9.34

You can set the timeout value for the serviced component's transactions in the serviced component's Properties dialog box.

If you are debugging multiple serviced components that involve transactions, instead of increasing the timeout value for each serviced component, you can choose to increase the computer-level setting of the default timeout value. You can do this by changing the Transaction Timeout value in the Options tab of the My Computer Properties dialog box, as shown in Figure 9.35. You can open this dialog box by selecting Properties from the context menu of the My Computer node in the Component Services administrative tool.

If a serviced component is executing on a remote machine, you need to make sure that the remote machine is set up with remote debugging support, as explained in the section "Debugging a Remote Process."

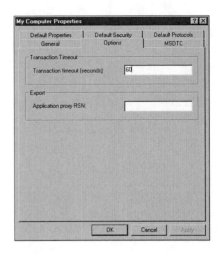

FIGURE 9.35
You can set the timeout value for all the distributed transactions in a computer in the My Computer Properties dialog box.

Debugging a .NET Remoting Object

A .NET remoting object is stored in a DLL file, such as a serviced component. A .NET remoting object executes in the process of the remoting server application, without respect to its activation mode.

Therefore, to debug a remoting object, you need to take the following steps:

1. If the remoting server is running in its own process, attach the debugger to that process.

2. If the remoting server is hosted in IIS, attach a debugger to the ASP.NET worker process (`aspnet_wp.exe`).

3. Set breakpoints in the remoting object class definition.

After taking these steps, the Visual Studio .NET debugger breaks the execution when it reaches the breakpoint in the code.

Attaching a debugger to the process in which the client application is running debugs only the client application and does not step into the code of the remoting object class definition. To debug both client and server applications, you can attach a debugger to both the applications and step seamlessly into the code of both the applications.

If a remoting object is executing on a remote machine, you need to make sure that the remote machine is set up with remote debugging support, as explained in the section "Debugging a Remote Process."

Debugging an XML Web Service

Debugging XML Web services is similar to debugging Web applications. They also run in the ASP.NET worker process (aspnet_wp.exe). The only difference is that, you need to take care of setting breakpoints in the Web methods, after which you can debug Web services in any of the following ways:

▶ You can run a Web service from Visual Studio .NET and then step into the code of the Web service by invoking the respective method through the Web service test page.

▶ You can also attach a debugger to the aspnet_wp.exe process to step into the code of the already-running Web service.

▶ You can create a client application for the Web service, which invokes its Web methods. You can then step into the Web service's code by running the client application from Visual Studio .NET.

▶ You can attach a debugger to an already-running client application and then step into the code of the Web service when the code reaches a breakpoint.

You should also make sure that the Web service application is configured for debugging. Please refer to the "Configuring the Debugging Environment" section, discussed earlier in the chapter, for more details. Also, if the Web service is executing on a remote machine, you need to make sure that the remote machine is set up with remote debugging support, as explained in the section "Debugging a Remote Process."

You can also use SOAP extensions of XML Web services for debugging. These SOAP extensions can be used to examine or modify the SOAP messages sent and received by the Web service or the client. Refer to the section "Creating and Using SOAP Extensions" in Chapter 5, "Advanced Web Services," for how to create and use SOAP extensions.

REVIEW BREAK

▶ You can attach the debugger to a running process (either local or remote) with the help of the Processes dialog box.

▶ When you attach a debugger to the ASP.NET worker process aspnet_wp.exe, it freezes the execution of all other Web applications on that server.

▶ You should have `mdm.exe` running on the remote machine to perform remote debugging.

▶ To debug a Windows service, you must attach a debugger to the process in which the Windows service is running.

▶ To debug COM+ library applications, you must attach a debugger to the process in which the client application is running.

▶ To debug COM+ server applications, you must attach a debugger to the `dllhost.exe` process in which the COM+ server application is running.

▶ To debug a .NET remoting object, you must attach a debugger to the process in which the remoting server application is running. If the object is hosted in IIS, you need to attach a debugger to the `aspnet_wp.exe` process.

▶ To debug an XML Web service, you need to attach a debugger to the `aspnet_wp.exe` or the client application that is calling Web methods of the Web service.

WORKING WITH EVENT LOGS

Instrument and debug a Windows service, a serviced component, a .NET Remoting object, and an XML Web service.

Event logging isthe standard way on the Windows platform for applications to log their events. You can easily monitor an application's behavior by using the Event Viewer utility to analyze its messages in the event log. In fact, you can also view events from the Visual Studio .NET environment, and you can access event logs through Server Explorer.

The Framework Class Library provides a set of classes especially designed to work with event logs. With the help of these classes, you can programmatically read from or write to event logs. Programmatic access might even allow you to automate some of the administrative tasks associated with an application.

By default, three event logs are available: Application, Security, and System. Other applications (including .NET applications) or operating system components, such as Active Directory, might add other event logs. Table 9.7 lists the important members of the EventLog class.

TABLE 9.7

IMPORTANT MEMBERS OF THE EventLog CLASS

Member	Type	Description
CreateEventSource()	Method	Opens an event source so that an application can write event information
Delete()	Method	Removes a log resource
DeleteEventSource()	Method	Removes an application's event source from the event log
Entries	Property	Gets the contents of the event log
Exists()	Method	Determines whether the specified log exists
Log	Property	Specifies the name of the log to read from or write to
LogDisplayName	Property	Represents a friendly name for the event log
LogNameFromSourceName()	Method	Gets the name of the log to which the specified source is registered
MachineName	Property	Specifies the name of the computer on which to read or write events
Source	Property	Specifies the source to register and use when writing to an event log
SourceExists()	Method	Finds whether a given event source exists
WriteEntry()	Method	Writes an entry in the event log

Each application interested in interacting with an event log must register an event source with the log. After an event source is registered, its information is stored in the system Registry and is available across application restarts.

EXAM TIP

Security Issues A program must have administrative privileges to create an event log. This is especially important in the case of ASP.NET because the ASP.NET worker process runs under a low-privilege account. The easiest way to ensure that the ASP.NET worker process has sufficient privilege is to configure ASP.NET to use the system account rather than the machine account. Alternatively, you can use the .NET Framework's security facilities to grant permissions on an assembly-by-assembly basis. For more details on these topics, see Chapter 11, "Security Issues."

NOTE

The Log Property Only the first eight characters of a Log name are significantly identified. So an event log with the name StepByStep9_11 is the same as StepByStep9_12.

The `CreateEventSource()` method allows you to register the application with an event log; if the event log does not already exist, this method creates it for you.

The `WriteEntry()` method of the `EventLog` object allows you to write messages to the event log specified by the event source. If the event source specified by the `Source` property of an `EventLog` object does not exist, the first call to the `WriteEntry()` method creates the event source before writing the entry to the event log. You can write different types of messages (information, error, warning, success audit, and failure audit) to an event log. These types are specified by the values in the `EventLogEntryType` enumeration.

The sample Windows form in Step-by-Step 9.11 demonstrates how to create an event log, register an application with the event log, unregister an application with an event log, write to an event log, and delete an event log.

STEP BY STEP

9.11 Creating and Writing to an Event Log

1. Add a Visual C# Windows application project to the solution. Name the project `StepByStep9_11`.

2. Rename the `Form1.cs` file `StepByStep9_11.cs` in the project. Switch to the form's code view and modify all references to `Form1` so that they refer to `StepByStep9_11` instead.

3. Place two `GroupBox` controls, three `Label` controls, one `TextBox` control (txtMessage, with `MultiLine` set to true), four `Button` controls (btnCreate, btnRemoveSource, btnRemoveLog, and btnWrite), one `ComboBox` control (cbEventLogs), and five `RadioButton` controls (rbError, rbInformation, rbFailureAudit, rbSuccessAudit, and rbWarning) on the form. Arrange the controls as shown in Figure 9.36.

4. Switch to the code view. Add the following using directive:

```
using System.Diagnostics;
```

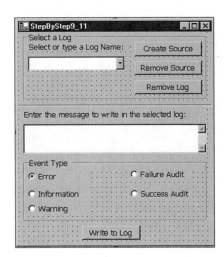

FIGURE 9.36
The `StepByStep9_11` form uses the `EventLog` class to create an event log and write entries to it.

continues

continued

5. Add the following code in the class definition:

```
// Create a member to hold EventLogEntryType
private EventLogEntryType eletEntryType =
    EventLogEntryType.Error;
```

6. Add a new method named `PopulateLogNames()` to the class definition and call it from the form's `Load` event handler:

```
private void StepByStep9_11_Load(
    object sender, System.EventArgs e)
{
    PopulateLogNames();
}
private void PopulateLogNames()
{
    cbEventLogs.Items.Clear();
    // Add eventlogs in to the combo box.
    foreach(EventLog el in
        EventLog.GetEventLogs())
        cbEventLogs.Items.Add(el.Log);
}
```

7. Attach a `Click` event handler to each `Button` control. Add the following code in the event handlers:

```
private void btnCreate_Click(
    object sender, System.EventArgs e)
{
    if (cbEventLogs.Text != "")
    {
        string strSourceName = "StepByStep9_11_"
                            + cbEventLogs.Text;
        // Check whether the source already exists
        if (!EventLog.SourceExists(strSourceName))
        {
            try
            {
                // Create event source and the
                // event log (if log doesn't exist)
                EventLog.CreateEventSource(
                    strSourceName,cbEventLogs.Text);
                PopulateLogNames();
                MessageBox.Show(
                    "Created EventSource " +
                    "for Selected EventLog");
            }
            catch(Exception ex)
            {
                MessageBox.Show(ex.Message);
            }
        }
}
```

```
        else
            MessageBox.Show("You already have an " +
            "EventSource attached to this EventLog",
            "Cannot Create EventSource");
    }
}

private void btnRemoveSource_Click(
    object sender, System.EventArgs e)
{
    if (cbEventLogs.Text != "")
    {
        string strSourceName = "StepByStep9_11_" +
                                cbEventLogs.Text;
        if (EventLog.SourceExists(strSourceName))
        {
            // Delete the Event Source
            EventLog.DeleteEventSource(strSourceName);
            MessageBox.Show("Deleted the EventSource "
                + "for Selected EventLog");
        }
        else
            MessageBox.Show("There is currently no " +
                "EventSource for selected EventLog");
    }
}

private void btnRemoveLog_Click(
    object sender, System.EventArgs e)
{

    string strLogName = cbEventLogs.Text.ToUpper();
    // Do not delete system created logs
    if (strLogName == "APPLICATION" ||
        strLogName == "SECURITY" ||
        strLogName == "SYSTEM")
    {
        string strMessage = "This program does not " +
            "allow the deletion of system " +
            "created EventLogs as this may " +
            "cause undesirable effects on " +
            "the working of your computer.";
        MessageBox.Show(
            strMessage, "Dangerous Operation");
        return;
    }
    // If the log exists
    if (EventLog.Exists(cbEventLogs.Text))
    {
        // Confirm deletion from user
        string strMessage = "This operation will " +
         "delete the selected EventLog and " +
         "its associated EventSources, Are you Sure?";
        if(MessageBox.Show(
```

continues

continued

```
                strMessage, "Confirm Deletion",
                MessageBoxButtons.YesNo) == DialogResult.Yes)
                  try
                  {
                      // Delete the Event Log
                      EventLog.Delete(cbEventLogs.Text);
                      PopulateLogNames();
                  }
                  catch(Exception ex)
                  {
                      MessageBox.Show(ex.Message,
                      "Error Deleting EventLog");
                  }
          }
          else
              MessageBox.Show("Selected EventLog does " +
                "not Exists", "Cannot Delete EventLog");
      }

      private void btnWrite_Click(object sender,
                     System.EventArgs e)
      {
          if (cbEventLogs.Text != "")
          {
              string strSourceName = "StepByStep9_11_" +
                  cbEventLogs.Text;

              // If Source exists
              if(EventLog.SourceExists(strSourceName))
                  try
                  {
                      // Write an entry into event log
                      EventLog.WriteEntry(strSourceName,
                               this.txtMessage.Text,
                         this.eletEntryType);
                      MessageBox.Show(
                          "Entry written to the " +
                          "log successfully");
                  }
                  catch(Exception ex)
                  {
                      MessageBox.Show(ex.Message,
                       "Cannot Write to selected EventLog");
                  }
              else
                  MessageBox.Show(
                      "There is no EventSource " +
                      "for selected EventLog",
                      "Event logging failed");
          }
          else
              MessageBox.Show("Please Select an EventLog " +
                      "to Write to.");
      }
```

8. Add the following event handler in the class definition. Attach this event handler to all the `RadioButton` controls on the form:

```
private void rbEventType_CheckedChanged(
    object sender, System.EventArgs e)
{
    // Set the eletEntryType member
    if (sender == rbWarning)
        eletEntryType = EventLogEntryType.Warning;
    else if (sender == rbInformation)
        eletEntryType = EventLogEntryType.Information;
    else if (sender == rbSuccessAudit)
        eletEntryType =
            EventLogEntryType.SuccessAudit;
    else if (sender == rbFailureAudit)
        eletEntryType =
            EventLogEntryType.FailureAudit;
    else
        eletEntryType = EventLogEntryType.Error;
}
```

9. Set the project `StepByStep9_11` as the startup project.

10. Run the project. Enter a name in the `ComboBox` control to create a source and log in to the System event log. Select from the combo box the log in which you want to write, enter the message in the message text box, select the type of the message from the radio button options, and click the Write button to write to the event log.

11. To view the logged messages, navigate to Server Explorer, expand the Servers node, and then select and expand the node that corresponds to your computer. Right-click the Events node and select Launch Event Viewer from the shortcut menu. This has the same effect as launching the Event Viewer from the Administrative Tools section of Windows Control Panel. Figure 9.37 shows the contents of a custom event log that was created by using the project `StepByStep9_11`.

WARNING

Deleting an Event Log You should use the `Delete()` method to delete an event log cautiously. When an event log is deleted, all event sources registered with it are also deleted, so no application can continue writing to that log. Do not attempt to delete an event log that was created by Windows or any other application that is important to you; if you do, those applications might crash or behave in unexpected ways.

NOTE

Security Log The Security log is read-only for all users.

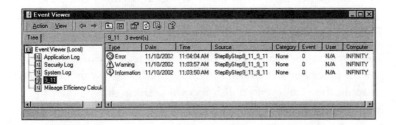

FIGURE 9.37
You can use the Windows Event Viewer to view the contents of the event logs.

WORKING WITH PERFORMANCE COUNTERS

Instrument and debug a Windows service, a serviced component, a .NET Remoting object, and an XML Web service.

Performance counters are Windows' way of collecting performance data from running processes. Microsoft Windows itself provides several hundred performance counters, each of which monitors a particular system parameter. In addition, various .NET server products, such as SQL Server, Exchange Server, and various .NET Framework applications, also publish their own custom performance counters.

Windows organizes performance counters into categories. Each category defines a specific set of performance counters. For example, there are categories such as Memory, Processor, and PhysicalDisk, and the Memory category has various counters such as Available Bytes, Cache Bytes, and Committed Bytes.

Some categories are further divided into instances. For example, the Process category is divided into several instances, each representing a running process on the computer. A new instance is added to the category whenever a new process is started, and the instance is removed when a process is killed. Each instance can have performance counters (such as I/O Read Bytes/sec) that specify the memory activity of a process. Usually all the instances in a category have the same list of performance counters. Of course each of the performance counters has unique performance data associated with it.

You can view existing performance counters in a navigable format in Visual Studio .NET Server Explorer, as shown in Figure 9.38.

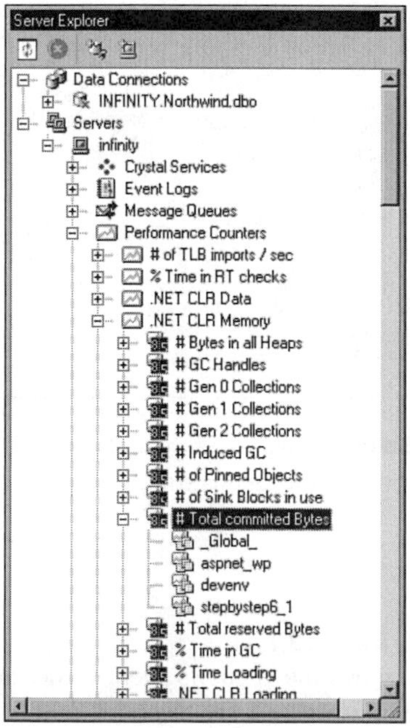

Note from Figure 9.38 that .NET CLR Data, .NET CLR Memory, and other nodes represent performance counter categories. Such nodes as # Total Committed Bytes and # Total Reserved Bytes are the performance counters in the .NET CLR Memory category. The _Global_, aspnet_wp, devenv, and others are the instances of the # Total Committed Bytes performance counter.

The PerformanceCounter class allows you to read performance samples for processes that are running on a machine. By using this class, an application can even publish its own performance counter to inform the world about its performance level.

FIGURE 9.38
Visual Studio .NET Server Explorer displays all the existing performance counters on a machine.

Table 9.8 lists some important members of the PerformanceCounter class.

TABLE 9.8

IMPORTANT MEMBERS OF THE PerformanceCounter CLASS

Member	Type	Description
CategoryName	Property	Specifies the performance counter category name.
Close()	Method	Closes the performance counter and frees all the resources.
CounterHelp	Property	Specifies the performance counter description.
CounterName	Property	Specifies the performance counter name.
CounterType	Property	Specifies the performance counter type.
Decrement()	Method	Decrements the performance counter value by one.
Increment()	Method	Increments the performance counter value by one.
IncrementBy()	Method	Increments or decrements the performance counter value by a specified amount.
InstanceName	Property	Specifies the instance name.
MachineName	Property	Specifies the computer name.
NextSample()	Method	Returns an object of type CounterSample that has properties such as RawValue, BaseValue, TimeStamp, and SystemFrequency. These properties provide you with detailed information on the performance data.
NextValue()	Method	Retrieves the current calculated value (a float type) for a performance counter.
RawValue	Property	Retrieves the raw, or uncalculated, value for a performance counter.
ReadOnly	Property	Indicates whether the PerformanceCounter object is in read-only mode.
RemoveInstance()	Method	Deletes an instance from the PerformanceCounter object.

The .NET Framework allows applications to create their own custom performance counters and publish their performance data. This performance data can then be monitored via the Performance Monitoring tool (perfmon.exe).

Visual Studio .NET makes it easy for you to create new performance categories and counters: It provides the Performance Counter Builder Wizard, which is available via Server Explorer. In Step-by-Step 9.12, you create a Windows application that publishes its performance and allows you to manually increase or decrease its performance.

STEP BY STEP

9.12 Publishing Performance Data

1. Add a Visual C# Windows application project to the solution. Name the project StepByStep9_12.

2. Rename the Form1.cs file StepByStep9_12.cs in the project. Switch to the code view of the form and modify all references to Form1 so that they refer to StepByStep9_12 instead.

3. Place five Label controls (of which one is named lblCurrentLevel and two represent lines), one TextBox control (txtLevel), and three Button controls (btnInc, btnDec, and btnSet) on the form. Arrange the controls as shown in Figure 9.39.

4. Open Server Explorer and select from the Servers node the server in which you want to create a performance counter. Right-click the Performance Counters node and select the Create New Category option. The Performance Counter Builder dialog box appears. Enter the values in the dialog box, as shown in Figure 9.40, and then click OK.

5. Select the StepByStep9_12 performance counter from the Performance Counters node in Server Explorer. Drag the performance counter that appears under the StepByStep9_12 node on the form. Set the Name of the counter to pc9_12 and the ReadOnly property to false.

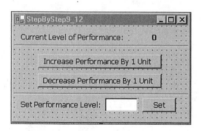

FIGURE 9.39
You can publish custom performance data for an application.

NOTE

Creating a Custom Performance Counter   When you create a new performance counter, you must specify a completely new category for your performance counter. It is not possible to add a new performance counter to an existing category; however, you can add several performance counters to a new custom category.

It is also possible to create performance counter categories programmatically by using the PerformanceCounterCategory.Create() method.

6. Switch to the code view. Add the following using directive:

```
using System.Diagnostics;
```

7. Attach `Click` event handlers to the button controls and add the following code in the event handlers:

```
private void btnSet_Click(
    object sender, System.EventArgs e)
{
    // Set the performance counter value
    pc9_12.RawValue = Int32.Parse(txtLevel.Text);
    lblCurrentLevel.Text =
        pc9_12.NextValue().ToString();
}

private void btnInc_Click(object sender,
                        System.EventArgs e)
{
    pc9_12.Increment();
    lblCurrentLevel.Text =
        pc9_12.NextValue().ToString();
}

private void btnDec_Click(object sender,
                        System.EventArgs e)
{
    pc9_12.Decrement();
    lblCurrentLevel.Text =
        pc9_12.NextValue().ToString();
}
```

8. Attach `Load` and `Closed` event handlers to the form and add the following code in the event handlers:

```
private void StepByStep9_12_Load(
    object sender, System.EventArgs e)
{
    lblCurrentLevel.Text =
        pc9_12.NextValue().ToString();
}

private void StepByStep9_12_Closed(
    object sender, System.EventArgs e)
{
    pc9_12.RawValue = 0;
}
```

9. Set the project `StepByStep9_12` as the startup project.

10. Run the project. Enter a number in the text box and click the Set button. The label immediately reflects the current value of the performance counter. Click the Increment and Decrement buttons and notice the value changing in the label.

FIGURE 9.40
The Performance Counter Builder dialog box enables you to create a new performance counter category and specify one or more counters to be placed within it.

REVIEW BREAK

▶ The System event log provides a central repository for various issues that an application may encounter while it is executing. Using an event log to record such messages not only makes the job of system administrator easy, but it allows other applications to take appropriate action when an entry is written to a log.

▶ Multiple event sources can write into an event log. However, an event source can be used to write into only one event log.

▶ Performance counters are organized in categories, and each category defines a specific set of performance counters.

▶ The process of reading a performance counter value is called sampling the performance counter. The process of updating a performance counter value is called publishing a performance counter.

CHAPTER SUMMARY

KEY TERMS

- debugging
- testing
- tracing

This chapter starts with a discussion on the importance of testing for an application. You learned that designing and executing a comprehensive test plan is desirable to ensure that an application is robust, accurate, and reliable.

The .NET Framework provides various classes and techniques that implement tracing in applications. You use tracing to display informative messages during a program's execution. The Trace and Debug classes provide different methods to generate messages at specific locations in the code. You have learned how trace switches can be applied to an application to give you control over the type of tracing information generated by an application without even requiring you to recompile the application.

You have also learned about the various C# preprocessing directives that are available in Visual C# .NET. You have seen how you can use the Conditional attribute to conditionally compile methods.

CHAPTER SUMMARY

The compiler pinpoints syntactical errors at compile time. The tough job is to find logical and runtime errors in an application. Visual C# .NET offers lots of tools for debugging. In this chapter, you learned about various tools available for debugging.

You also learned how to debug an already running process, debug a process running on a remote machine, and debug DLL files. You also applied these debugging concepts to debug a Windows service, a serviced component, a .NET remoting object, and an XML Web service.

Finally, you learned how to work with event logs and performance counters. As you continue to work with Visual C# .NET, you'll discover more benefits of the tools and techniques discussed in this chapter.

APPLY YOUR KNOWLEDGE

Exercises

9.1 Creating a Custom Trace Switch

The TraceSwitch and BooleanSwitch classes are two classes that provide trace switch functionality. If you need different trace levels or different implementations of the Switch class, you can inherit from the Switch class to implement your own custom trace switches.

In this exercise, you will learn how to create a custom switch. You will create a FactorialSwitch class that can be set with four values (Negative (-1), Off (0), Overflow (1), and Both (2)) for the Factorial Calculator form. The class will have two properties: Negative and Overflow.

Estimated time: 25 minutes.

1. Launch Visual Studio .NET. Select File, New, Blank Solution, and name the new project 320C09Exercises.

2. Add a new Windows application project to the solution. Name the project Exercise9_1.

3. Using the Add Class Wizard, add a new class to the project. Name the class FactorialSwitch and modify the class definition so that it has the following code:

```
using System;
using System.Diagnostics;

namespace Exercise9_1
{
    // The possible values for
    // the new switch
    public enum FactorialSwitchLevel
    {
        Negative   = -1,
        Off        = 0,
        Overflow   = 1,
        Both       = 2
    }
```

```
public class FactorialSwitch : Switch
{
    public FactorialSwitch(
        string displayName,
        string description)
        : base(displayName, description)
    {
    }
    public bool Negative
    {
        get
        {
            // return true if the
            // SwitchSetting is
            // Negative or Both
            if( (SwitchSetting == -1) ||
                (SwitchSetting == 2))
                return true;
            else
                return false;
        }
    }
    public bool Overflow
    {
        get
        {
            // return true if the
            // SwitchSetting is
            // Overflow or Both
            if ((SwitchSetting == 1) ||
                (SwitchSetting == 2))
                return true;
            else
                return false;
        }
    }
}
}
```

4. In Solution Explorer, right-click Form1.cs and rename it FactorialCalculator. Open the Properties window for this form and change its Name property to FactorialCalculator and Text property to Factorial Calculator Exercise 9_1. Switch to the code view of the form and modify the Main() method to launch FactorialCalculator rather than Form1.

APPLY YOUR KNOWLEDGE

5. Place two TextBox controls (txtNumber and txtFactorial), three Label controls and a Button control (btnCalculate) on the form and arrange the controls as shown earlier in Figure 9.5.

6. Open FactorialCalculator.cs in the code view. Add the following using directive:

```
using System.Diagnostics;
```

7. Add the following code in the class definition:

```
static FactorialSwitch facSwitch =
    new FactorialSwitch("FactorialTrace",
    "Trace the factorial application " +
    "using Factorial Switch");
```

8. Attach a Click event handler to the btnCalculate control with the following code:

```
private void btnCalculate_Click(
    object sender,
    System.EventArgs e)
{
    int intNumber = Convert.ToInt32(
        txtNumber.Text);

    if (facSwitch.Negative)
    {
        // make a debug assertion
        Debug.Assert(intNumber >= 0,
            "Invalid value",
            "negative value in debug mode");
    }

    int intFac = 1;
    for (int i = 2; i <= intNumber; i++)
    {
        intFac = intFac * i;
    }

    if (facSwitch.Overflow)
        // write a debug message
        // if the condition is true
        Debug.WriteLineIf(intFac < 1,
```

```
            "There was an overflow",
            "Factorial Program Debug");
    txtFactorial.Text = intFac.ToString();
}
```

9. Add an Application configuration file (App.config) to the project and modify it to contain the following code:

```
<?xml version="1.0" encoding="utf-8" ?>
<configuration>
    <system.diagnostics>
        <switches>
            <add name="FactorialTrace"
                value="2" />
        </switches>
    </system.diagnostics>
</configuration>
```

10. Set Exercise9_1 as the startup project.

11. Run the project, using the default Debug configuration. Notice that the assertion failed message is displayed only if the switch is set with the value –1 or 2. Similarly, the overflow message is displayed in the output window only if the switch value is set to 1 or 2.

12. Modify the program to change all Debug statements to Trace statements. Copy the XML configuration file to the bin\Release folder in the project and then repeat step 12, using the Release configuration.

The value set in the configuration file can be accessed through the SwitchSetting property of the Switch class. The Negative and Overflow properties of the FactorialSwitch class return true or false, depending on the value of the SwitchSetting property.

APPLY YOUR KNOWLEDGE

9.2   Using Visual C# .NET to Debug SQL Server Stored Procedures

You can perform step-by-step execution of SQL Server stored procedures in Visual C# .NET. This exercise shows you how.

Estimated time: 30 minutes.

1. Add a new Windows application project to the solution. Name the project Exercise9_2.

2. Rename the Form1.cs form MostExpensiveProdcuts.cs. Switch to code view and change all occurrences of Form1 to MostExpensiveProducts.

3. Select Project, Properties from the main menu. Select Debugging under the Configuration Properties node in the left pane of the Property Pages window. In the right pane, under the Debuggers node, choose true for Enable SQL Debugging, as shown in Figure 9.41.

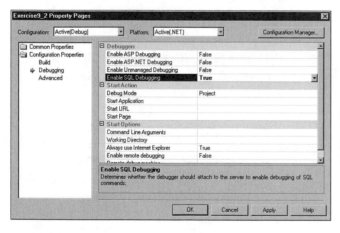

FIGURE 9.41
You should enable SQL debugging in the Property Pages dialog box to allow debugging of SQL Server stored procedures.

4. Drag a SqlDataAdapter component to the form. This activates the Data Adapter Configuration Wizard. Click Next. Select the Northwind database connection that you have already created in the earlier chapters or click the New Connection button to create a Northwind database connection. Click Next.

5. Choose the Use Existing Stored Procedures option in the Choose a Query Type page. Click Next. Select Ten Most Expensive Products from the Select combo box, as shown in Figure 9.42. Click Next and then click Finish. A SqlConnection component is created in the component tray.

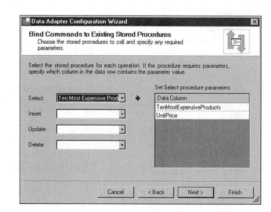

FIGURE 9.42
The Bind Commands to Existing Stored Procedures dialog box enables you to choose SQL stored procedures to bind to SqlCommand objects.

6. Select the sqlDataAdapter1 component, and then right-click and select Generate DataSet from the context menu. Select the New radio button and choose Ten Most Expensive Products from the check box list. Click OK to create a dataSet11 component in the component tray.

APPLY YOUR KNOWLEDGE

7. Place a `Button` control (`btnGetProducts`) and a `DataGrid` control (`dataGrid1`) on the form. Change the `DataGrid` control's `DataSource` property to `dataSet1` and `DataMember` property to `Ten Most Expensive Products`.

8. Add the following code in the `Click` event of the `Button` control:

```
private void btnGetProducts_Click(
  object sender, System.EventArgs e)
{
    sqlDataAdapter1.Fill(this.dataSet11);
}
```

9. Insert a breakpoint in the `Click` event handler, at the point of a call to the `Fill()` method of the `sqlDataAdapter1` object.

10. Open Server Explorer. Open the Data Connections node and select the stored procedure Ten Most Expensive Products. Right-click the stored procedure and select Edit Stored Procedure. Insert a breakpoint in the starting code line of the stored procedure, as shown in Figure 9.43.

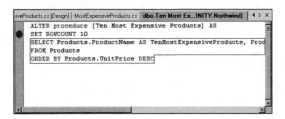

FIGURE 9.43
You can even insert a breakpoint in SQL Server stored procedures.

11. Run the project. Click the button. The program starts step-by-step execution as soon as it encounters the breakpoint in the `Fill()` method call line. Press F11. You are taken to the stored procedure code, where you can perform step-by-step execution.

This exercise teaches you how to debug SQL Server stored procedures by using step-by-step execution. In Figure 9.43, notice the SELECT statement enclosed in an outline (blue on your screen), which represents each step in the stored procedure (if the step occupies more than a line).

> **EXAM TIP**
>
> **Watching SQL Server Variables**
> You can use various tools, such as the Watch and Locals windows, to keep track of the values of the variables defined in the stored procedures during step-by-step execution. These tools are very helpful when you are debugging complex stored procedures.

9.3   Using Visual C# .NET to Set Conditional Breakpoints

This exercise shows you how to set conditional breakpoints. I'll set a breakpoint in the factorial calculation to break when the Factorial value overflows (that is, it becomes negative).

Estimated Time: 30 minutes.

1. Add a new Windows application project to the solution. Name the project `Exercise9_3`.

2. In Solution Explorer, right-click Form1.cs and rename it FactorialCalculator. Open the Properties window for this form and change its Name property to FactorialCalculator and Text property to Factorial Calculator Exercise 9_3. Switch to the form's code view and modify the Main() method to launch FactorialCalculator instead of Form1.

3. Place two TextBox controls (txtNumber and txtFactorial), three Label controls and a Button control (btnCalculate) to the form and arrange the controls as shown earlier in Figure 9.5.

4. Open FactorialCalculator.cs in the code view. Add the following using directive:

```
using System.Diagnostics;
```

5. Attach a Click event handler to the btnCalculate control and add the following code in the event handler:

```
private void btnCalculate_Click(
    object sender, System.EventArgs e)
{
    int intNumber =
        Convert.ToInt32(txtNumber.Text);

    int intFac = 1;
    for (int i = 2; i <= intNumber; i++)
    {
        intFac = intFac * i;
    }
    txtFactorial.Text = intFac.ToString();
}
```

6. Right-click the following line in the Click event handler for the Button control and select New Breakpoint from the context menu.

```
intFac = intFac * i;
```

This opens the New Breakpoint dialog box. Select the File tab. You will note that File, Line, and Character position are already marked correctly. Click the Condition button to open the Breakpoint Condition dialog box. Set the values in the dialog box as shown in Figure 9.44. Select the Condition check box. Enter **intFac < 1** in the Condition text box and select the Is True option. Click OK twice to dismiss the New Breakpoint dialog box.

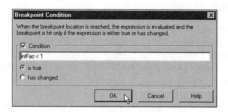

FIGURE 9.44
You can set conditional breakpoints in the Breakpoint Condition dialog box.

7. Run the project using the default Debug configuration. Enter a bigger number—say, 100—and click the Calculate button. You will notice that the running page breaks into the debugger when intFac has a negative value and the breakpoint is reached.

Review Questions

1. For what do you use a test plan?

2. What is the purpose of the Assert() method in the Debug and Trace classes?

3. What is the main purpose of the TraceListener class? What classes implement TraceListener in the Framework Class Library?

4. What are the two built-in trace switches in the .NET Framework Class Library?

5. What is the main advantage of trace switches?

APPLY YOUR KNOWLEDGE

6. What types of methods can be marked with the `Conditional` attribute?

7. What are the purposes of the `#error` and `#warning` preprocessing directives?

8. What are the three commands can you use to step through code while debugging?

9. What happens when you put a breakpoint in code?

10. What are some of the different windows that are available for debugging?

11. How can you attach the debugger to a running process in Visual C# .NET?

12. To verify that remote debugging is enabled on a system, what should you check?

13. How can you debug an already-running COM+ application?

Exam Questions

1. Which of the following activities correctly defines a typical unit test?

   A. Locate and fix errors.

   B. Run the application with carefully planned test data and determine whether it works according to its specification.

   C. Run a module with carefully planned test data and determine whether it works according to its specification.

   D. Verify that a program module integrates well with other modules in an application.

2. You are creating a .NET remoting object. You want to add code to the object to log error messages and warning messages. You want to log messages to both a log file and to the Windows application log, but do not want a message to be duplicated. Which of the following code segments should you use?

   A.

```
FileStream fileLog = new
    File.Create("RemObject.log");
EventLog eventLog = new
    EventLog("RemObject");
Trace.WriteLine(fileLog,
    "Sample Message");
Trace.WriteLine(eventLog,
    "Sample Message");
```

   B.

```
Trace.Listeners.Add(new
    EventLogListener("RemObject"));
Trace.Listeners.Add(new
  TextFileTraceListeners("RemObject.log"));
Trace.WriteLine("Sample Message");
Trace.WriteLine("Sample Message");
```

   C.

```
Trace.Listeners.Add(new
    EventLogListener("RemObject"));
Trace.Listeners.Add(
    new TextFileTraceListeners(
    "RemObject.log"));
Trace.WriteLine("Sample Message");
```

   D.

```
EventLogTraceListener eventLog =
    new EventLogTraceListener("RemObject");
TextFileTraceListeners fileLog =
new TextFileTraceListener("RemObject.log");
eventLog.WriteLine("Sample Message");
fileLog.WriteLine("Sample Message");
```

APPLY YOUR KNOWLEDGE

3. You are developing a Windows application that heavily uses SQL Server stored procedures. You are debugging a Windows form that calls the `YTDSales` stored procedure. The stored procedure uses a variable named `@Sales`. You want to see how the value of this variable changes as the code in the stored procedure executes. Which of the following options will allow you to do this?

   A. Use the SQL Server `PRINT` command to display the value of the `@Sales` variable at different places.

   B. Use the `Debug.Write` statement to print the value of the `@Sales` variable.

   C. Use the `Trace.Write` statement to print the value of the `@Sales` variable.

   D. Use the Locals window to monitor the value of `@Sales` as you step through the stored procedure.

4. In your C# program, you have the following lines of code:

```
TraceSwitch myTraceSwitch =
    new TraceSwitch(
    "SwitchOne", "The first switch");
myTraceSwitch.Level = TraceLevel.Info;
```

   Which of the following expressions in your program would evaluate to `false`?

   A. `myTraceSwitch.TraceInfo`

   B. `myTraceSwitch.TraceWarning`

   C. `myTraceSwitch.TraceError`

   D. `myTraceSwitch.TraceVerbose`

5. You are developing a retail Web site for selling readymade garments. Your application has a bunch of serviced components that execute the business logic. All the serviced components are marked with the `Transaction(TransactionOption.Required)` attribute. All the methods in the components are marked with the `AutoComplete` attribute. While testing the application you find that inventory is not being updated properly. When you attempt to debug the application, a `System.Runtime.InteropServices.COMException` is thrown. The exception includes the following message: `The root transaction wanted to commit, but transaction aborted`. You also find that this exception occurs only during the debugging session, and not when the components run outside of the debugger. You need to resolve this problem so that you can debug the application to find the problem with inventory updates. Which of the following options should you select to resolve this problem?

   A. Remove the `AutoComplete` attribute from each method. Within each method implementation, add calls to the `ContextUtil.SetComplete()` and `ContextUtil.SetAbort()` methods.

   B. Remove the `AutoComplete` attribute from each method. Within each method implementation add calls to the `ContextUtil.MyTransactionVote` and `ContextUtil.DeactivateOnReturn` properties.

   C. Use the Component Services administrative tool. Access the Properties dialog box for My Computer and increase the transaction time-out duration.

   D. Change the implementation of each method in the serviced component with the following code segment:

```
try
{
    // the business logic goes here
}
catch
{
    //log any error messages here
}
finally
{
    ContextUtil.SetComplete();
}
```

6. You are asked to implement tracing in an XML Web service so that the application displays both warning and error messages when the Debug configuration is used to run it and should display only error messages when the Release configuration of Visual C# .NET is used to run it. Which of the following code segments best meets this requirement?

A.

```
TraceSwitch traceSwitch =
    new TraceSwitch("MySwitch",
    "Error and Warning Switch");

#if DEBUG
    traceSwitch.Level = TraceLevel.Warning;
#else
    traceSwitch.Level = TraceLevel.Error;
#endif

Trace.WriteLineIf(traceSwitch.TraceWarning,
    "Warning Message");
Trace.WriteLineIf(traceSwitch.TraceError,
    "Error Message");
```

B.

```
TraceSwitch traceSwitch = new TraceSwitch(
    "MySwitch",
    "Error and Warning Switch");
#if DEBUG
    traceSwitch.Level = TraceLevel.Warning;
#else
    traceSwitch.Level = TraceLevel.Error;
#endif
```

```
Debug.WriteLineIf(traceSwitch.TraceWarning,
    "Warning Message");
Debug.WriteLineIf(traceSwitch.TraceError,
    "Error Message");
```

C.

```
TraceSwitch traceSwitch = new TraceSwitch(
    "MySwitch",
    "Error and Warning Switch");

#if TRACE
    traceSwitch.Level = TraceLevel.Warning;
#else
    traceSwitch.Level = TraceLevel.Error;
#endif

Trace.WriteLineIf(traceSwitch.TraceWarning,
    "Warning Message");
Trace.WriteLineIf(traceSwitch.TraceError,
    "Error Message");
```

D.

```
TraceSwitch traceSwitch = new TraceSwitch(
    "MySwitch",
    "Error and Warning Switch");

#if TRACE
    traceSwitch.Level = TraceLevel.Error;
#else
    traceSwitch.Level = TraceLevel.Warning;
#endif

Trace.WriteLineIf(traceSwitch.TraceWarning,
    "Warning Message");
Trace.WriteLineIf(traceSwitch.TraceError,
    "Error Message");
```

7. The configuration file of an XML Web service has the following contents:

```
<system.diagnostics>
    <switches>
        <add name="BooleanSwitch"
            value="-1" />
        <add name="TraceLevelSwitch"
            value="33" />
    </switches>
</system.diagnostics>
```

APPLY YOUR KNOWLEDGE

You are using the following statements to create switch objects in your code:

```
BooleanSwitch booleanSwitch =
    new BooleanSwitch(
    "BooleanSwitch", "Boolean Switch");
TraceSwitch traceSwitch = new TraceSwitch(
    "TraceLevelSwitch", "Trace Switch");
```

Which of the following options is correct regarding the values of these switch objects?

A. The `booleanSwitch.Enabled` property is set to false and `traceSwitch.Level` is set to `TraceLevel.Verbose`.

B. The `booleanSwitch.Enabled` property is set to true and `traceSwitch.Level` is set to `TraceLevel.Verbose`.

C. The `booleanSwitch.Enabled` property is set to false and `traceSwitch.Level` is set to `TraceLevel.Error`.

D. The `booleanSwitch.Enabled` property is set to false and `traceSwitch.Level` is set to `TraceLevel.Info`.

8. You are developing a Windows application. Your application's configuration files have the following code:

```
<system.diagnostics>
    <switches>
        <add name="TraceLevelSwitch"
            value="3" />
    </switches>
</system.diagnostics>
```

You have written the following tracing code in your program:

```
static TraceSwitch traceSwitch =
    new TraceSwitch(
    "TraceLevelSwitch",
    "Trace the application");

[Conditional("DEBUG")]
private void Method1()
```

```
{
    Trace.WriteLineIf(
        traceSwitch.TraceError,
        "Message 1", "Message 2");
}

[Conditional("TRACE")]
private void Method2()
{
    Trace.WriteLine("Message 3");
}

private void btnCalculate_Click(
    object sender, System.EventArgs e)
{
    if(traceSwitch.TraceWarning){
        Trace.WriteLine("Message 10");
        Method1();
    }
    else{
        Trace.WriteLineIf(
            traceSwitch.TraceInfo,
            "Message 20");
        Method2();
    }

    if (traceSwitch.TraceError)
        Trace.WriteLineIf(
            traceSwitch.TraceInfo,
            "Message 30");
    Trace.WriteLineIf(
            traceSwitch.TraceVerbose,
            "Message 40");
}
```

What tracing output would be generated if you ran your program in `Debug` mode and clicked the `btnCalculate` button?

A.

```
Message 10
Message 1
Message 2
Message 30
```

B.

```
Message 10
Message 2: Message 1
Message 30
```

C.

```
Message 10
Message 2
Message 30
Message 40
```

D.

```
Message 20
Message 3
Message 30
Message 40
```

9. You have the following segment of code in your program:

```
EventLogTraceListener traceListener =
    new EventLogTraceListener("TraceLog");

Trace.Listeners.Add(traceListener);
Debug.Listeners.Add(traceListener);

Trace.WriteLine("Sample Message");
Debug.WriteLine("Sample Message");
```

When you debug the program through Visual Studio .NET, how many times would the message "Sample Message" be written to the trace log?

A. 1

B. 2

C. 3

D. 4

10. Which of the following statements are true for remote debugging of processes? (Select two.)

A. Both the local and the remote machine should have Visual Studio .NET installed.

B. Only the local machine needs Visual Studio .NET.

C. Remote Components Setup is required on the local machine.

D. Remote Components Setup is required on the remote machine.

11. While you are debugging in Visual Studio .NET, you want to watch the value of only those variables that are in use in the current statement and the previous statement. Which of the following debugger windows is the easiest window to use to watch these variables?

A. Autos

B. Locals

C. This

D. Watch

12. You are debugging a Windows form. The form involves long calculations and iterations. You want to break into the code to watch the value of variables whenever the value of intValue changes in the following statement:

```
intValue = ProcessValue(intValue);
```

Which of the following options will quickly allow you to achieve this?

A. Run the application using step execution mode. Use the Step Out key to step out of execution from the ProcessValue function. Use the Immediate window to display the value of intValue before and after this line of code executes.

B. Set a breakpoint at the given statement. Set the Hit Count option "break when hitcount is equal to" to 1.

APPLY YOUR KNOWLEDGE

C. Set the breakpoint at the given statement. In the breakpoint condition dialog box enter `intValue != intValue` and check the Is True option.

D. Set the breakpoint at the given statement. In the breakpoint condition dialog box enter `intValue` and check the Has Changed option.

13. You want to debug a remote process. The remote machine does not have Visual Studio .NET installed on it. Which of the following options should you choose?

   A. Start the process on the remote machine first and then launch Visual Studio .NET on the local machine. Attach the debugger to the running process. Break into the execution of the remote process.

   B. Open the project of the remote process in Visual Studio .NET, set a breakpoint, and execute the process.

   C. Copy the remote application project to the local machine and debug it by using the Visual Studio .NET debugger.

   D. Open the project of the remote process in Visual Studio .NET on the remote machine and then set a breakpoint. Run Visual Studio .NET on the local machine and attach the debugger to the project.

14. You create a serviced component named `ConnectionDispenser`. This component is stored in the `DbUtils.dll` assembly and is registered in the COM+ catalog. The serviced component is configured to be activated as a library application. You discover that the `CreateNewConnection()` method is not working as expected. You want to debug any calls to this method. What should you do?

   A. Open the `ConnectionDispenser` solution. Set a breakpoint on the `CreateNewConnection()` method. Start the debugger.

   B. Open the solution for the client program. Set a breakpoint on the statement that calls the `ConnectionDispenser.CreateNewConnection()` method. Start debugging the client program.

   C. Attach the debugger to the `DbUtils.dll` process. Set a breakpoint on the `CreateNewConnection()` method.

   D. Attach the debugger to a `dllhost.exe` process. Set a breakpoint on the `CreateNewConnection()` method.

15. You want to debug a remote process that is running on a Windows 2000 Server computer that is not in your local computer's domain. The remote server has a full installation of Visual Studio .NET. The two domains do not have two-way trust established, but you do have a username and password on the remote Windows 2000 server. Which of the following would allow you to debug a process on that machine?

   A. Ask the administrator of the remote machine to start the Machine Debug Manager, and then launch Visual Studio .NET on your local machine and attach the debugger to the remote process.

   B. Ask the administrator of the remote machine to include your username and password in the Debugger Users group, and then launch Visual Studio .NET on your local machine and attach the debugger to the remote process.

   C. Use Terminal Server to log in to the remote machine. Launch Visual Studio on the remote machine and debug the process by attaching the debugger to it.

D. Use Terminal Server to log in to the remote machine. Launch Visual Studio .NET on the local machine and debug the process by attaching the debugger to it.

16. You are trying to debug a Windows application using Visual Studio .NET installed on your local machine. The Windows application is deployed on a remote server. When you attempt to debug the application, you get a DCOM configuration error. Which of the following steps should you take to resolve this problem?

A. Add your account to the Power Users group on the local computer.

B. Add your account to the Power Users group on the remote computer.

C. Add your account to the Debugger Users group on the local computer.

D. Add your account to the Debugger Users group on the remote computer.

Answers to Review Questions

1. A test plan is a document that guides the process of testing. This document should clearly specify the different approaches to testing, the test cases, the validation criteria of the tests, and so on.

2. The `Assert()` method takes a condition as its first parameter and then displays an Assertion Failed message if the condition evaluates to `false`.

3. `TraceListener` is an abstract class that provides functionality for receiving trace and debug messages. `DefaultTraceListener`, `TextWriterTraceListener`, and `EventLogTraceListener` are the three built-in classes that implement `TraceListener`.

4. The two built-in trace switches in the .NET Framework Class Library are `BooleanSwitch` and `TraceSwitch`.

5. The main advantage of trace switches is that you can easily change the value of trace switches by editing the application configuration (XML) file, using any text editor. To make these changes take effect, you need not recompile the application; you just need to restart it.

6. Before you can apply the `Conditional` attribute to a method, the method should have its return type set to `void`.

7. The `#error` and `#warning` preprocessing directives let you explicitly generate errors and warnings from code. The compiler reports errors and warnings in the same way it reports other compile-time errors and warnings.

8. The three commands that allow you to step through code are Step Into (steps into each statement of the method called), Step Over (performs the entire method call in one step), and Step Out (steps out of the method call).

9. When the debugger encounters a breakpoint in code, it pauses the execution of the application. The execution can be resumed via the stepping commands.

10. Visual Studio .NET provides a variety of windows to ease the debugging process. Some of these windows are This, Locals, Autos, Watch, Call Stack, and Breakpoints.

APPLY YOUR KNOWLEDGE

11. To attach the debugger to a running process, open Visual C# .NET, invoke the Processes dialog box, select the process from the list of processes, and click the Attach button.

12. You should verify that the remote machine has Machine Debug Manager (`mdm.exe`) running as a background process to enable debugging support. You should also verify that you are a member of the Debugger Users group so that you can remotely access the machine for debugging.

13. To debug a COM+ library application, you must attach a debugger to the process in which the client application is running. On the other hand, to debug a COM+ server application, you must attach a debugger to the `dllhost.exe` process in which the COM+ server application is running.

Answers to Exam Questions

1. **C.** A unit test involves running a module against carefully planned test data and checking whether it works according to its specification. Debugging is the process of locating and fixing errors. When you run a complete application against test data, you are performing system testing. Checking whether the modules integrate well is part of integration testing. For more information, see the section "Executing Tests" in this chapter.

2. **C.** To log messages to custom target locations, you need to add custom listeners to the `Trace.Listeners` collection. This eliminates choices A and D. In between B and C, C is correct because you want to log a message only once. For more information, see the section "Trace Listeners" in this chapter.

3. **D.** You can use the Locals window to keep track of the values of the variables defined in the stored procedure during its step-by-step execution. For more information, see the section "Analyzing Program State to Resolve Errors" and Exercise 9.2 in this chapter.

4. **D.** Setting the `Level` property of `TraceSwitch` to `TraceLevel.Info` allows it to capture all informational, warning, and error messages, but not the verbose messages. Thus, the `TraceInfo`, `TraceWarning`, and `TraceError` properties of the switch evaluate to `true`, but the `TraceVerbose` property evaluates to `false`. For more information, see the section "Trace Switches" in this chapter.

5. **C.** When you debug a program, the transaction may not complete in the set timeframe (the default is 60 seconds). In that case, the program throws the given exception. Because you have a bunch of components here, instead of setting the transaction timeout value for each of them individually, you can set the transaction timeout property for the applications running on the computer. For more information, see the section "Debugging a Serviced Component" in this chapter.

6. **A.** In answer A, for the `Debug` configuration where the `DEBUG` symbol is defined, the `Level` property of `traceSwitch` is set to `TraceLevel.Warning`. This causes both the `TraceWarning` and `TraceError` properties of this object to evaluate to `true` in the `Debug` configuration, causing both messages to be displayed. In the `Release` configuration, where only the `TRACE` symbol is defined, the `Level` property of `traceSwitch` is set to `TraceLevel.Error`. This causes the `TraceWarning` property to result in a

APPLY YOUR KNOWLEDGE

`false` value and the `TraceError` property to return a `true` value, causing only the error messages to be displayed. For more information, see the section "Trace Switches" in this chapter.

7. **B.** For `BooleanSwitch`, a value of `0` corresponds to `Off`, and any nonzero value corresponds to `On`. For `TraceSwitch` any number greater than `4` is treated as `Verbose`. From the given values in the configuration file, the `booleanSwitch` object should have its `Enabled` property set as `true` and the `traceSwitch` object should have its `Level` property set to `TraceLevel.Verbose`. For more information, see the section "Trace Switches" in this chapter.

8. **B.** The XML file has `3` as the value for `TraceLevelSwitch`, which causes the `Level` property to be set to `TraceLevel.Info`. This causes the `TraceError`, `TraceWarning`, and `TraceInfo` properties of the `traceSwitch` to be `true`; only the `TraceVerbose` property evaluates to `false`. Also, the third parameter of the `WriteLineIf()` method is used to categorize the output by specifying its value, followed by a colon (`:`) and then the trace message. For more information, see the section "Trace Switches" in this chapter.

9. **D.** The message `SampleMessage` will be written four times. Two instances of `EventLogTraceListeners` are added to the `Listeners` collection. Any message generated by the `Trace` and `Debug` classes will be listed twice. Because the program is running in the `Debug` mode, both the `Trace` and `Debug` statements will be executed. The net effect is that both the `Trace.WriteLine` and `Debug.WriteLine` messages will be written twice, making four entries in the trace log. For more information, see the section "Trace Listeners" in this chapter.

10. **B, D.** For remote debugging, Visual Studio .NET is not required on the remote machine. In this case, you need to run Remote Components Setup on the remote machine. You need to have Visual Studio .NET on the local machine to debug the remote processes. For more information, see the section "Debugging a Remote Process" in this chapter.

11. **A.** The Autos window gives you the most convenient access because it automatically displays names and values of all variables in the current statement and the previous statement at every step. For more information, see the section "Analyzing Program State to Resolve Errors" in this chapter.

12. **D.** When you want to break into the code when the value of a variable changes, the quickest approach is to set a conditional breakpoint where you specify the variable name and check the Has Changed option. For more information, see the section "Setting Breakpoints and Stepping Through Program Execution" and Exercise 9.3 in this chapter.

13. **A.** To debug a remote process, the process first needs to be started on the remote machine. You can then open Visual Studio .NET on the local machine and attach the debugger to the running process. After the debugger is attached, you can break into the code of the remote process and do step-by-step execution or set a breakpoint. For more information, see the section "Debugging a Remote Process" in this chapter.

14. **B.** A serviced component activated as a library application runs in the process of its caller. Therefore, to debug such an application you can set a breakpoint in the client application and then step into the serviced component code. For

APPLY YOUR KNOWLEDGE

more information, see the section "Debugging a Serviced Component" in this chapter.

15. **C.** If your local machine's domain does not have a two-way trust relationship with the remote computer's domain then you cannot debug a remote process. The only option you have is to log on to the remote machine by using Terminal Server, start Visual Studio .NET on the remote machine, and use Visual Studio .NET to attach the debugger to the process that is running on the same machine. You then debug as if you were debugging a process running on your local machine. For more information, see the section "Debugging a Remote Process" in this chapter.

16. **D.** If you get a DCOM configuration error while debugging, possibly you are not a member of the Debugger Users group on the remote machine. To resolve this, add your account on the remote machine to the Debugger Users group. For more information, see the section "Debugging a Remote Process" in this chapter.

Suggested Readings and Resources

1. Windows Forms QuickStart Tutorial:

   • Diagnostics topics in the "How Do I" section.

   • Debugging topics in the "How Do I" section.

2. Visual Studio .NET Combined Help Collection:

   • "Introduction to Instrumentation and Tracing."

   • "Using the Debugger."

3. Kevin Burton. *.NET Common Language Runtime Unleashed.* Sams, 2002.

4. Richard Grimes. *Developing Applications with Visual Studio .NET.* Addison-Wesley, 2002.

This chapter covers the following Microsoft-specified objective for the "Deploying Windows Services, Serviced Components, .NET Remoting Objects, and XML Web Services" section of Exam 70-320, "Developing XML Web Services and Server Components with Microsoft Visual C# .NET and Microsoft .NET Framework":

Plan the deployment of and deploy a Windows service, a serviced component, a .NET Remoting object, and an XML Web service.

Create a setup program that installs a Windows service, a serviced component, a .NET Remoting object, and an XML Web service.

• **Register components and assemblies.**

Configure client computers and servers to use a Windows service, a serviced component, a .NET Remoting object, and an XML Web service.

▶ An enterprise solution may involve different types of applications, such as Windows applications, Web applications, XML Web services, Windows services, serviced components, and .NET remoting objects. These applications may differ based on their look and feel and functionality, but they all work together to accomplish the goal of the enterprise.

After you have developed an application and ensured its quality, the next step is to distribute and install the application on the target computers. This process is called *deployment*. The planning for deployment and the process of deployment may vary depending on the type of a program and its targeted users. This exam objective requires you to know what's involved in the deployment of a Windows service, a serviced component, a .NET remoting object, and an XML Web service. The deployment of Web applications and Windows applications is of more interest to exams 70-315 and 70-316, respectively.

CHAPTER 10

Deployment

Implement versioning.

Plan, configure and deploy side-by-side deployments and applications.

▶ Applications created using the .NET Framework use two different types of assemblies: private assemblies and shared assemblies. Between the two assemblies, shared assemblies have support for versioning and side-by-side deployment (for different versions of an assembly). This exam objective requires you to know how to create shared assemblies, implement versioning, and use them for side-by-side deployment.

▶ Review the "Deployment Concepts" and "Deploying Applications" sections of the Visual Studio .NET Combined Help Collection.

▶ Understand the various ways to deploy an application and their benefits and shortcomings. Understand when to use XCOPY deployment versus Windows Installer deployment.

▶ Experiment with using setup projects and merge module projects to deploy .NET applications. Understand when you should choose to create a setup project versus a merge module project.

▶ Work with the different editors that are available in the Visual Studio .NET setup and deployment projects and thoroughly understand the purpose of each of these editors.

▶ Experiment with the Strong Name tool (sn.exe) to create a public/private key pair and then use the key pair to assign a strong name to an assembly. Work with the delay-signing feature and understand the scenarios in which it can be helpful.

▶ Understand the steps performed by the CLR to locate private and shared assemblies. Experiment with placing assemblies in the GAC.

INTRODUCTION

Assemblies are the smallest units of versioning and deployment in the .NET application. Assemblies are also the building blocks for programs such as Web services, Windows services, serviced components, and .NET remoting applications.

The .NET applications use two different types of assemblies: private assemblies and shared assemblies. Private assemblies are identified by their names and are deployed for the use of only a single application. Shared assemblies are identified by a strong name and are deployed for use by multiple applications. A strong name uses four attributes to identify an assembly: name of the assembly, version number, culture identity, and a public key token.

An assembly may also refer to the classes present in other assemblies. When an assembly is built, information about all other assemblies to which it refers is stored in the assembly manifest. The manifest, however, does not store the assembly's exact path because this path may differ on the computer where the assembly is deployed. At runtime when a class is referenced, the CLR reads the assembly manifest, retrieves the identification information for the referenced assembly, and then attempts to locate the referenced assembly. The mechanism used by the CLR to locate a private assembly is different from that of a shared assembly.

The set of rules that the CLR uses to locate an assembly is called *binding policy*. Binding policy is a deciding factor in how and where an application's assemblies should be deployed. In a successfully deployed application, the CLR should be able to bind to all the referenced assemblies. In other words, for a successful deployment you need to deploy your assemblies at a location where the CLR expects to find them. In the first part of this chapter, you will learn how to work with private and shared assemblies and how to deploy them successfully.

After you have identified the assemblies that need to be deployed, and identified where the assemblies need to be deployed, you need to find an effective way to package and distribute your application. That's what you'll study in the later part of this chapter. You will learn how to deploy a Web service, a Windows service, a serviced component, and a .NET remoting object.

The .NET Framework greatly simplifies various deployment tasks. In fact, just copying the files on the target computer can easily deploy some simple applications. For advanced deployment options and requirements, however, you may want to create a Windows Installer–based setup project. In this chapter, you'll also learn how to use Visual Studio .NET setup and deployment projects to create Windows Installer–based setup packages for deploying the given applications.

DEPLOYING PRIVATE ASSEMBLIES

Private assemblies are the simplest to deploy. All you need to do to deploy private assemblies is to copy them to the application's base directory or one of its subdirectories. In this section, you create a simple application that uses a private assembly. You then use this application to experiment with how the CLR locates private assemblies and how to configure the behavior of the CLR by using the application configuration file.

In Step-by-Step 10.1, you create two assemblies: One is a Windows application and the other is a library application, which is used by only the Windows application.

STEP BY STEP

10.1 Creating and Deploying an Application That Uses a Privately Deployed Assembly

1. Launch Visual Studio .NET. Select File, New, Blank Solution, and name the new solution 320C10.

2. Add a new Visual C# .NET Class library named MathLib to the solution.

3. In the Solution Explorer, rename the default Class1.cs to MathLib.cs.

4. Open the MathLib.cs and replace the code with the following code:

```
using System;
public class MathLib
{
```

```
   public static int Add(int n1, int n2)
   {
       return n1 + n2;
   }
}
```

5. Build the project.

6. Add a new Visual C# .NET Windows application named
   MathApp to the solution.

7. In the Solution Explorer, right-click project MathApp and
   select Add Reference from the context menu to add a reference to the MathLib component.

8. In the Solution Explorer, rename the default Form1.cs to
   MathApp.cs. Open the form in code view and change all
   occurrences of Form1 to refer to MathApp instead.

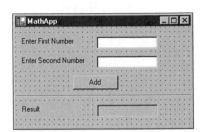

FIGURE 10.1
The MathApp.exe application calls methods
from the MathLib.dll to add two numbers.

9. Place four Label controls, three TextBox controls (txtN1,
   txtN2 and txtResult) and a Button control (btnAdd) on
   the form. Change one of the label's Size - Height property to 1 and BorderStyle property to Fixed3D, to represent
   it as a line. Arrange the controls as shown in Figure 10.1.

10. Double-click the Button control and add the following
    code in the Click event handler:

```
private void btnAdd_Click(
    object sender, System.EventArgs e)
{
    txtResult.Text =
        MathLib.Add(Convert.ToInt32(txtN1.Text),
            Convert.ToInt32(txtN2.Text)).ToString();
}
```

11. Run the project. Enter the two numbers in the text boxes
    and click the Add button. You should see the result of
    adding the two numbers in the third text box.

12. Change the solution configuration to Release mode and
    build the project. The project is now ready for deploy-
    ment.

13. Create a folder on your hard drive, named
    C:\MyPrograms\MathApplication. Copy the MathApp.exe
    and MathLib.dll files from the bin\Release folder of the
    MathApp project to this folder.

continues

continued

14. Run `MathApp.exe` from `C:\MyPrograms\MathApplication`.
Add two numbers. `MathApp.exe` successfully calls methods
from `MathLib.dll`.

In Step-by-Step 10.1, you can see that `MathApp.exe` can call methods
from `MathLib.dll`. This is possible because `MathApp.exe` stores information about the assemblies it needs to refer to. This information is
a part of the assembly manifest for `MathApp.exe`. You can check the
contents of an assembly manifest by using the MSIL Disassembler
(`ildasm.exe`). An alternative way to check this information is by
using the .NET Framework Configuration tool as shown in Step-by-
Step 10.2.

STEP BY STEP

10.2 Viewing Assembly Dependence Information for an Application

1. Open the Microsoft .NET Framework Configuration tool
from the Administrative Tools section of the Windows
Control Panel.

2. Click the Applications node in the tree view, as shown in
Figure 10.2.

FIGURE 10.2
The .NET Framework Configuration tool enables
you to configure an application.

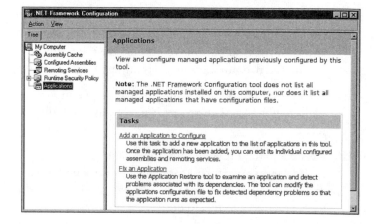

3. Click the Add an Application to Configure link.

4. In the Configure an Application dialog box, click the Other button and browse to the `C:\MyPrograms\MathApplication` folder to select `MathApp.exe`. Select this application and click OK.

5. Expand the new `MathApp` node in the tree view under the Applications node. Click the Assembly Dependencies child node to view all the `MathApp.exe` dependencies, as shown in Figure 10.3.

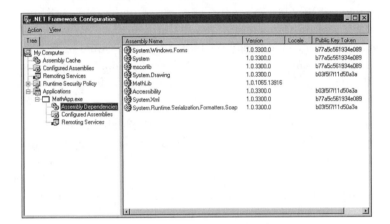

FIGURE 10.3
You can view an assembly's dependencies by using the .NET Framework Configuration tool.

In Figure 10.3, you see that unique public key tokens distinguish shared assemblies from private assemblies. If the public key token is not present, it means that the assembly is a private assembly. You also can see from Figure 10.3 that an application does not contain the complete file name and the location of the assembly file to which it needs to refer. The CLR instead uses a process called *probing* to locate the privately deployed assemblies. You can have a certain degree of control over the probing process if you modify the binding policy by using the application configuration file.

Binding Policy for Privately Deployed Assemblies

Binding policy for privately deployed assemblies is a set of rules that instructs the CLR to search for an assembly in specific locations. By default, the CLR uses a default binding policy, but you can use the application configuration file to specify binding rules that instruct the CLR to search for assemblies in additional locations.

For Windows applications, the application configuration file is application specific and is located in the application's base directory (where the EXE file is located). The name of application configuration file is of the format *ExecutableFileName*.config. For example, the application configuration file for MathApp.exe would be MathApp.exe.config. In the case of Web applications, the application configuration file is stored in the application's root directory and is named web.config.

The application configuration file is an XML file that may contain different elements for configuring various aspects of an application. The element in which you'll be most interested in this section is the <probing> element, which specifies additional search locations for an assembly. A stripped-down version of an application configuration file containing the <probing> element is as follows:

```
<?xml version="1.0"?>
<configuration>
  <runtime>
    <assemblyBinding
        xmlns="urn:schemas-microsoft-com:asm.v1">
      <probing privatePath="bin\retail;bin\debug" />
    </assemblyBinding>
  </runtime>
</configuration>
```

You can use the privatePath attribute of the <probing> element to specify the subdirectories of the application's base directory that might contain assemblies. Each of these subdirectories is delimited with a semicolon.

This application configuration file instructs the CLR to search assemblies in the application's bin\retail and bin\debug subdirectories, in addition to the search locations that are part of the default binding policy. You learn about the complete binding process for a privately deployed assembly in the following section.

How the CLR Binds to a Privately Deployed Assembly

The CLR takes the following steps to locate a privately deployed assembly:

1. The CLR determines the assembly's name from the manifest of the requesting assembly.

2. The CLR checks to see whether the requested assembly has already been loaded from the previous requests. If the assembly has already been loaded, the CLR binds to the assembly and stops searching any further.

3. The CLR reads the application configuration file to check whether any private path hints are available in the <probing> element. If there are hints, the CLR will use these directory locations to search the assembly.

4. If the referenced assembly has no culture information, the CLR uses the following locations in the given order to find the assembly:

   - *ApplicationBase**AssemblyName*.dll

   - *ApplicationBase**AssemblyName**AssemblyName*.dll

   - *ApplicationBase**PrivatePath1**AssemblyName*.dll

   - *ApplicationBase**PrivatePath1**AssemblyName*\
     AssemblyName.dll

   - *ApplicationBase**PrivatePath2**AssemblyName*.dll

   - *ApplicationBase**PrivatePath2**AssemblyName**Assembly
     Name*.dll

     .

     .

     .

   - *ApplicationBase**AssemblyName*.exe

   - *ApplicationBase**AssemblyName**AssemblyName*.exe

   - *ApplicationBase**PrivatePath1**AssemblyName*.exe

- *ApplicationBase*\PrivatePath1*AssemblyName*\
  AssemblyName.exe

- *ApplicationBase*\PrivatePath2*AssemblyName*.exe

- *ApplicationBase*\PrivatePath2*AssemblyName*\
  AssemblyName.exe

  .

  .

  .

Here `ApplicationBase` is the directory where the requesting application is installed; `AssemblyName` is the name of the assembly to search; and `PrivatePath1` and `PrivatePath2` are the hints provided in the `<probing>` element of the application configuration file. Note that the assembly name does not contain the extension; therefore the CLR searches for both DLL as well as EXE files. If the assembly is found in any of these locations, the CLR binds to the assembly and does not search any further.

5. If the referenced assembly has culture information, the following directories are searched:

- *ApplicationBase**Culture**AssemblyName*.dll

- *ApplicationBase**Culture**AssemblyName**AssemblyName*.dll

- *ApplicationBase*\PrivatePath1*Culture**AssemblyName*.dll

- *ApplicationBase*\PrivatePath1*Culture**AssemblyName*\
  AssemblyName.dll

- *ApplicationBase*\PrivatePath2*Culture**AssemblyName*.dll

- *ApplicationBase*\PrivatePath2*Culture**AssemblyName*\
  AssemblyName.dll

  .

  .

  .

- *ApplicationBase**Culture**AssemblyName*.exe

- *ApplicationBase**Culture**AssemblyName**AssemblyName*.exe

- *ApplicationBase*\PrivatePath1*Culture**AssemblyName*.exe

- *ApplicationBase*\PrivatePath1*Culture**AssemblyName*\
  AssemblyName.exe

- *ApplicationBase*\PrivatePath2*Culture**AssemblyName*.exe

- *ApplicationBase*\PrivatePath2*Culture**AssemblyName*\
  AssemblyName.exe

  .
  .
  .

> **NOTE**
>
> **Private Assembly's Version** Any version information contained in the private assembly is for informational purpose only. The CLR does not use the version information of a private assembly to bind to a specific version.

Here *Culture* is a culture code corresponding to the assembly. If the assembly is found in any of these locations, the CLR binds to the assembly and does not search any further.

6. If the CLR cannot locate the assembly after following the preceding steps, assembly binding fails.

Using the Assembly Binding Log Viewer Tool to Diagnose the Binding Process

The .NET Framework's Assembly Binding Log Viewer tool (fuslogvw.exe) displays the following information for failed assembly binds:

- ▶ A specific reason for the bind failure; for a privately deployed assembly the reason is usually "The system cannot find the file specified."

- ▶ Information about the calling assembly, including its name, the base directory, and a description of the private search paths.

- ▶ Identity of the requested assembly, including its name, version, culture, and public key token.

- ▶ A description of any Application, Publisher, or Administrator version policies that have been applied.

▶ Whether the assembly was found in the global assembly cache (GAC).

▶ A list of all probing URLs.

Some of the information from this list, such as version and version policies, applies to only the shared assemblies that you will learn later in this chapter. Still, the other pieces of information, such as the list of probing URLs, helps you diagnose why the CLR cannot locate a private assembly. You can use the output of the Assembly Binding Log Viewer tool to understand how the CLR locates assemblies, as shown in Step-by-Step 10.3.

STEP BY STEP

10.3 Using the Assembly Binding Log Viewer Tool to Understand How the CLR Locates Assemblies

1. Launch the Visual Studio .NET command prompt. Type **fuslogvw** to open the Assembly Binding Log Viewer tool.

2. Select the Log Failures check box, as shown in Figure 10.4.

3. Delete the `MathApp.dll` file from the `C:\MyPrograms\ MathApplication` folder. This enables the binding to fail when an application requests this assembly.

4. Run the `MathApp.exe` from the `C:\MyPrograms\ MathApplication` folder. You should see a dialog box showing the error message that the file or its dependencies are not found.

5. Now switch to Assembly Binding Log Viewer tool and click on the Refresh button. You should see an entry for the failed assembly bind, as shown in Figure 10.4.

6. Select the entry for `MathApp.exe` and click the View Log button. You should see a browser window displaying the following code:

```
*** Assembly Binder Log Entry
➥(12/1/2002 @ 10:30:08 AM) ***

The operation failed.
Bind result: hr = 0x80070002.
➥The system cannot find the file specified.
```

```
Assembly manager loaded from:  C:\WINNT\
➥Microsoft.NET\Framework\v1.0.3705\fusion.dll
Running under executable
➥C:\MyPrograms\MathApplication\MathApp.exe
--- A detailed error log follows.

=== Pre-bind state information ===
LOG: DisplayName = MathLib, Version=1.0.1065.18779,
➥Culture=neutral, PublicKeyToken=null
 (Fully-specified)
LOG: Appbase = C:\MyPrograms\MathApplication\
LOG: Initial PrivatePath = NULL
LOG: Dynamic Base = NULL
LOG: Cache Base = NULL
LOG: AppName = NULL
Calling assembly : MathApp, Version=1.0.1065.18782,
➥Culture=neutral, PublicKeyToken=null.
===

LOG: Processing DEVPATH.
LOG: DEVPATH is not set.
➥Falling through to regular bind.
LOG: Policy not being applied to reference at this
➥time (private, custom, partial,
➥or location-based assembly bind).
LOG: Post-policy reference: MathLib,
➥Version=1.0.1065.18779,
➥Culture=neutral, PublicKeyToken=null
LOG: Attempting download of new URL file:///C:/
➥MyPrograms/MathApplication/MathLib.DLL.
LOG: Attempting download of new URL file:///C:/
➥MyPrograms/MathApplication/MathLib/MathLib.DLL.
LOG: Attempting download of new URL
➥file:///C:/MyPrograms/MathApplication/MathLib.EXE.
LOG: Attempting download of new URL file:///C:/
➥ MyPrograms/MathApplication/MathLib/MathLib.EXE.
LOG: All probing URLs attempted and failed.
```

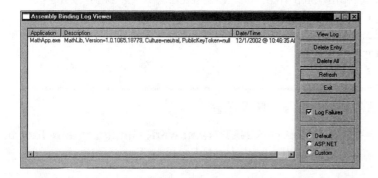

FIGURE 10.4
The Assembly Binding Log Viewer tool enables you to view the details of the failed assembly binds.

The binding log file displays valuable information about the binding process. The probing URLs at the end of the list show which directories the CLR searched for the assembly. If you had placed the assembly in any of these directories, the application would have executed successfully.

The MathLib assembly referenced in Step-by-Step 10.3 does not have any culture information in it. It would be a good exercise to specify the culture information for the MathLib assembly and then use the assembly binding log to analyze the behavior of the CLR. You can associate culture information with the MathLib assembly by changing the AssemblyCulture attribute of the assembly in the AssemblyInfo.cs file as shown here:

```
[assembly: AssemblyCulture("en-US")]
```

When you use such an assembly to build the MathApp.exe file and then follow the steps in Step-by-Step 10.3, you find that the CLR probes for assembly in only the following locations:

```
C:\MyPrograms\MathApplication\en-US\MathLib.DLL
C:\MyPrograms\MathApplication\en-US\MathLib\MathLib.DLL
C:\MyPrograms\MathApplication\en-US\MathLib.EXE
C:\MyPrograms\MathApplication\en-US\MathLib\MathLib.EXE
```

Using the .NET Framework Configuration Tool to Specify an Additional Probing Location

In Step-by-Step 10.3, the CLR used only its default binding policy to locate assemblies. Step-by-Step 10.4 shows how to use the .NET Framework Configuration tool to specify additional search locations for an assembly.

STEP BY STEP

10.4 Using the .NET Framework Configuration Tool to Specify Additional Probing Locations

1. Open the Microsoft .NET Framework Configuration Administrative tool from the Administrative Tools section of Windows Control Panel.

2. Right-click the `MathApp` application node (which was added in Step-by-Step 10.2) under the Applications node in the tree view and select Properties from the context menu.

3. In the Properties dialog box, enter additional probing locations in the Relative Search Path for Additional Assemblies text box, as shown in Figure 10.5. Click OK.

4. Open Windows Explorer, and navigate to the `C:\MyPrograms\MathApplication` folder. You should see an application configuration file named `MathApp.exe.config` containing the following code:

```xml
<?xml version="1.0"?>
<configuration>
  <runtime>
    <gcConcurrent enabled="true" />
    <assemblyBinding
      xmlns="urn:schemas-microsoft-com:asm.v1">
      <publisherPolicy apply="yes" />
      <probing privatePath="bin\debug;bin\retail" />
    </assemblyBinding>
  </runtime>
</configuration>
```

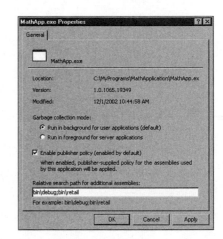

FIGURE 10.5
You can specify additional probing locations for an assembly by using the .NET Framework Configuration tool.

In Step-by-Step 10.4, you see that an easy way to specify additional probing locations for an assembly is to use the .NET Framework Configuration tool. This tool in fact stores this information in the application configuration file. You can also include probing information manually by using any editor to modify the application configuration file.

At this stage, you have a clear idea about how the CLR searches for privately deployed assemblies. You can use this knowledge to decide where you should deploy the assemblies while deploying an application that uses private assemblies.

REVIEW BREAK

▶ The set of rules that the CLR uses to locate an assembly is called a binding policy. Binding policy is a deciding factor in how and where an application's assemblies should be deployed.

▶ A private assembly is identified by its simple text name and is deployed for use by a single application.

continues

continued

> ▶ Use the application configuration file to modify binding policy for private assemblies. To do so, specify additional search locations for the assembly in the <probing> XML element.

DEPLOYING SHARED ASSEMBLIES

Implement versioning

Plan, configure and deploy side-by-side deployments and applications.

A shared assembly is shared among multiple applications on a machine. It is reasonable to store a shared assembly in a common place, which is well known to all the applications that use the assembly. However, if shared assemblies are identified by just their names—as the private assemblies are—then there is a problem because there might be a case when two software publishers might use the same name for an assembly, thereby overwriting files and causing applications using those assemblies to behave abnormally.

To resolve this problem, the .NET Framework requires all shared assemblies to have a strong name. A strong name uses four attributes to identify an assembly:

- ▶ Simple name
- ▶ Version number
- ▶ Culture identity (optional)
- ▶ Public key token

A regular Windows folder can differentiate files based on just their simple names and not their strong names. Therefore, to store strongly-named assemblies in a well-known shared location, you need a special type of storage. The .NET Framework provides this storage in the form of the global assembly cache (GAC). In addition to providing a shared location, the GAC also provides the following benefits for shared assemblies:

▶ **Integrity Check**—When assemblies are installed in the GAC, the GAC applies a strong integrity check on the assembly. This check guarantees that the contents of the assembly have not been changed since it was built.

▶ **Security**—The GAC allows only users with administrator privileges to modify its contents.

▶ **Side-by-side Versioning**—Multiple assemblies with the same name but different version number can be maintained in the global assembly cache.

In this section, you'll learn the following about shared assemblies:

▶ How to assign a strong name to an assembly

▶ How to add an assembly to the GAC

▶ How to reference an assembly from the GAC

▶ What the binding policy is for shared assemblies

▶ How the CLR binds to a shared assembly

▶ How to delay sign a shared assembly

Assigning a Strong Name to an Assembly

To create a strong name, you need an assembly's simple name, version number, an optional culture identity, and a key pair. The key pair consists of two related pieces of binary data: a public key and a private key.

The *public key* represents the identity of a software publisher. When you create a strongly named assembly, the public key is stored in the assembly manifest, along with other identification information, such as name, version number, and culture. This scheme does not look foolproof because the public key is easily available from the assembly manifest and one can easily fake an assembly identity with some other company's public key. To verify that only the legitimate owner of the public key has created the assembly, an assembly is signed with the publisher's *private key*. The private key is assumed to be known only to the assembly's publisher. The process of signing an assembly and verifying its signature works like this:

▶ **Signing an assembly**—When you sign an assembly, a cryptographic hash of the assembly's contents is computed. The hash is then encoded with the private key and is stored within the assembly. The public key is stored in the assembly manifest.

▶ **Verifying the signature**—When the CLR verifies an assembly's identity, it reads the public key from the assembly manifest and uses it to decrypt the cryptographic hash that is stored in the assembly. It then recalculates the hash for the current contents of the assembly. If the two hashes match, this ensures two things: The contents of the assembly were not tampered with after the assembly was signed and only the party that has a private key associated with the public key stored in the assembly has signed the assembly.

You can easily generate public/private key pairs by using the Strong Name tool (`sn.exe`), which is available in the .NET Framework SDK.

Step-by-Step 10.5 shows you how to create a public/private key pair by using the Strong Name tool (`sn.exe`).

STEP BY STEP

10.5 Creating a Public/Private Key Pair by Using the Strong Name Tool (`sn.exe`)

1. From the Visual Studio .NET program group in the Windows Start menu, launch the Visual Studio .NET command prompt.

2. Navigate to the `320C10` solution folder and issue the following command to create a pair of public/private keys:

```
sn -k 70320.snk
```

3. Both the public and private keys are created and stored in a file named `70320.snk`.

> **NOTE**
>
> **Signing a Multifile Assembly**   If an assembly consists of multiple files, just the file that contains the assembly manifest needs to be signed. The assembly manifest already contains file hashes for all the files that constitute the assembly implementation. The CLR can easily determine whether a file has been tampered with by matching its actual hash with what is stored in the assembly manifest.

Step-by-Step 10.6 shows you how to create a strongly-named assembly. You use the key file generated in Step-by-Step 10.5 to assign a strong name to an assembly.

STEP BY STEP

10.6 Assigning a Strong Name to an Assembly

1. Add a new Visual C# .NET Class Library project to the solution. Name the project RandomNumberGenerator.

2. Add a Component Class to the project and name it RandomNumberGenerator.cs. Delete Class1.cs.

3. Switch to the code view. Add the following lines of code just after the Component Designer–generated code section:

```
//stores minValue and maxValue
private int minValue=1, maxValue=100;

public int MinValue
{
    get
    {
        return minValue;
    }
    set
    {
        minValue = value;
    }
}

public int MaxValue
{
    get
    {
        return maxValue;
    }
    set
    {
        maxValue = value;
    }
}
public int GetRandomNumber()
{
    Random r = new Random();
    return r.Next(minValue, maxValue);
}
```

continues

continued

4. Open the `AssemblyInfo.cs` file of the
`RandomNumberGenerator` project. Scroll down in the file
and change the `AssemblyVersion` and `AssemblyKeyFile`
attributes as follows:

```
[assembly: AssemblyVersion("1.0")]
[assembly: AssemblyKeyFile(@"..\..\..\70320.snk")]
```

5. Build the project. `RandomNumberGenerator.dll` is generated, and a strong name is assigned to the file based on the
specified key file.

In Step-by-Step 10.6 you change the `AssemblyVersion` attribute of
the assembly from `1.0.*` to `1.0`. The assembly's version consists of
up to four parts:

```
<major>.<minor>.<build>.<revision>
```

If you want to use a fixed version value, you can hard-code it. The
default value of the version uses an asterisk in place of build and
revision numbers; this changes the build and revision each time you
modify and recompile the project. The build is calculated as the
number of days since January 1, 2000, and the revision is calculated
as the number of seconds since midnight divided by 2.

At runtime, the CLR uses version information to load a shared
assembly. In the next few examples, you may change and compile
your projects several times and as a result, you'll change the version
of the assembly if you use the default version property. This will
undesirably lead to multiple versions of the same assembly being
installed in the GAC when you wanted only the most recent one.

To have control over version numbers in the examples in this chapter, I'll hardcode the version number. Shortly you will also learn how
to install multiple versions of an assembly in the GAC and how to
manage their side-by-side execution.

In Step-by-Step 10.6 you used Visual Studio .NET to attach a
strong name to an assembly. If you want to do this by using a
command-line tool, you can use the Assembly Generation tool
(`al.exe`) with the `-keyfile` option.

Adding an Assembly to the GAC

After you have associated a strong name with an assembly, you can place the assembly in the GAC. There are several ways you can add an assembly to the GAC. Using the Windows Installer is the recommended approach, but there are some quick alternatives, too. However, you should use these quick approaches only for development purposes; they are not recommended for installing assemblies on the end user's computer.

Using Windows Installer to Add an Assembly to the GAC

Using Microsoft Windows Installer is the preferred way of adding assemblies to the GAC. Windows Installer maintains a reference count for assemblies in the GAC and provides uninstallation support. You will learn how to add assemblies using Windows Installer technology through the setup and deployment projects of Visual Studio .NET a little later in this chapter.

Using Windows Explorer to Add an Assembly to the GAC

The Assembly Cache Viewer Shell Extension (`shfusion.dll`) is installed as part of the .NET Framework. This extension allows you to view the complex structure of the GAC using Windows Explorer and allows administrators to install and uninstall assemblies using drag and drop and menu operations.

STEP BY STEP

10.7 Adding an Assembly to the GAC by Using Windows Explorer

1. Open Windows Explorer. Navigate to the assembly cache folder. It is usually `c:\WINNT\assembly` or `C:\Windows\assembly` (see Figure 10.6).

continues

FIGURE 10.6

The Assembly Cache Viewer Shell Extension enables you to view and manage the contents of the assembly cache by using Windows Explorer.

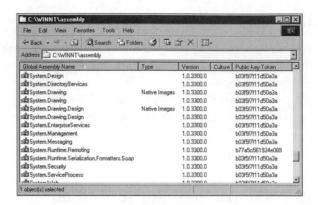

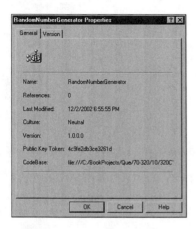

FIGURE 10.7

You can view the properties of the `RandomNumberGenerator` assembly that is installed in the GAC.

> **NOTE**
>
> **The Assembly Cache Folder** The assembly cache folder actually contains two caches: the GAC and the native image cache. When you view the assembly cache folder by using Windows Explorer, the Assembly Cache Viewer Shell Extension shows you a combined list of both caches. You can determine whether an assembly is from the GAC or from the native image cache by looking at the Type field in the list. When you add an assembly to the assembly cache folder by using Windows Explorer, it is added to the GAC. To add an assembly to the native image cache, you need to use the Native Image Generation tool (`ngen.exe`). The `ngen.exe` tool pre-compiles assemblies into processor-specific code.

2. Using Windows Explorer, drag the `RandomNumberGenerator.dll` file created in Step-by-Step 10.6 (in the `bin\Release` folder of the project) and drop it in the assembly cache folder.

3. In the assembly cache folder, right-click the `RandomNumberGenerator.dll` and select Properties from the shortcut menu. The Properties dialog box appears, as shown in Figure 10.7.

If you want to remove a file from the GAC, you just delete it from Windows Explorer by selecting File, Delete or by selecting Delete from the assembly's shortcut menu.

Using the .NET Framework Configuration Tool to Add an Assembly to the GAC

You can also use the .NET Framework Configuration tool (`mscorcfg.msc`) to manage an assembly in the GAC. Step-by-Step 10.8 guides you through the process of adding an assembly to the GAC by using the .NET Framework Configuration tool.

STEP BY STEP

10.8 Adding an Assembly to the GAC by Using the .NET Framework Configuration Tool

1. Open the Microsoft .NET Framework Configuration tool from the Administrative Tools section of Windows Control Panel. Select the assembly cache folder on the left pane under the My Computer node.

2. In the right pane, click the hyperlink Add an Assembly to the Assembly Cache. The Add an Assembly dialog box appears. Navigate to the `RandomNumberGenerator.dll` file in the `MathLib` project and click the OK button.

3. Click the other hyperlink, View List of Assemblies in the Assembly Cache. A list of installed assemblies appears. Ensure that the `RandomNumberGenerator` assembly is in this list, as shown in Figure 10.8.

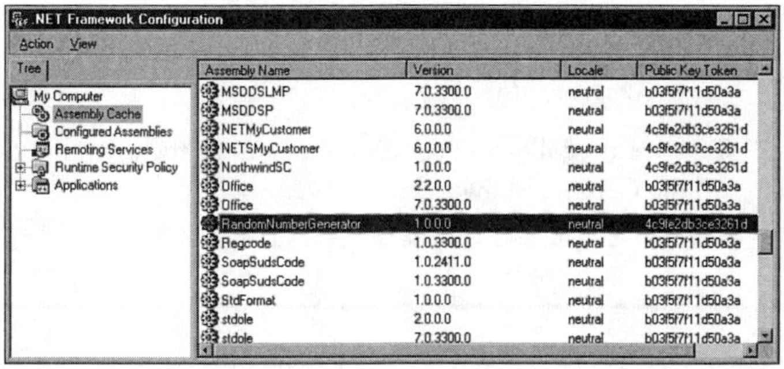

FIGURE 10.8
You can add assemblies in the GAC by using the .NET Framework Configuration Tool.

To uninstall an assembly by using the .NET Framework Configuration tool, you just select Action, Delete, or select Delete from the assembly's shortcut menu.

In addition to helping you add or remove assemblies, the .NET Framework Configuration tool helps you configure assemblies and manage their runtime security policies.

Using the Global Assembly Cache Tool (`gacutil.exe`) to Add an Assembly to the GAC

GacUtil.exe is a command-line tool that is especially useful for adding and removing assemblies from the GAC via a program script or a batch file. Step-by-Step 10.9 shows you how to add an assembly to the GAC by using `gacutil.exe`.

STEP BY STEP

10.9 Adding an Assembly to the GAC by Using the Global Assembly Cache Tool

1. From the Visual Studio .NET program group in the Windows Start menu, launch the Visual Studio .NET command prompt.

2. Change the directory to the folder where the `RandomNumberGenerator.dll` file resides in the RandomNumberGenerator project—in this case, the project's `bin\Release` directory.

3. Issue the following command to install the assembly to the GAC, as shown here:

```
gacutil /i RandomNumberGenerator.dll
```

You can list all the assemblies in the GAC by using the `gacutil.exe` tool with the `/l` option. You can use the `/u` option with the name of the assembly (without the file extension) to uninstall the assembly from the GAC:

```
gacutil /u RandomNumberGenerator
```

You can also choose to uninstall an assembly of a specific version and specific culture from the GAC by specifying its version, culture, and public key, along with the name of the assembly:

```
gacutil /u RandomNumberGenerator,Version=1.0.0.0,
➥Culture=neutral,PublicKeyToken=f26af4dbb33881b1
```

Referencing an Assembly from the GAC

Normally when you refer to an assembly in a Visual Studio .NET project, you can invoke the Add Reference dialog box and browse to the desired assembly. But after you have added an assembly to the GAC, this approach does not work because the GAC has a complex structure that cannot be directly enumerated by the Add Reference dialog box.

When you view the GAC by using the tools mentioned in the preceding section, you see an abstraction of its structure. If you instead switch to the command prompt and change the directory to the GAC folder, you see that the GAC is actually made up of various subdirectories, one for each assembly. Each of these directories further has subdirectories, whose names depend on the assemblies' versions and public keys. Each subdirectory stores the actual assembly file, along with some additional assembly information. Figure 10.9 shows how the GAC entry is made for the `RandomNumberGenerator` component on my computer.

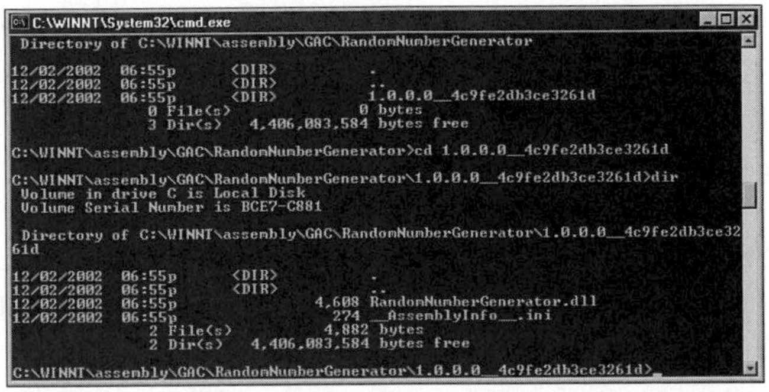

FIGURE 10.9
You can see how the assemblies are maintained in the GAC by exploring the GAC through the command window.

A good practice is to keep a copy of the assemblies installed in the GAC somewhere outside the GAC, where they are easily accessible via a pathname. You can then easily reference these assemblies through the Add Reference dialog box by browsing to the correct path. In fact, the .NET Framework uses the same techniques for all its own assemblies stored in the GAC. The .NET Framework also stores copies of those assemblies in the folder where the .NET Framework is installed.

Although you can add a reference to an assembly by browsing to the folder where it is stored, the convenient way is to have its name directly displayed in the Add Reference dialog box so that you can just check it to select it.

Step-by-Step 10.10 shows how to instruct Visual Studio .NET to add assemblies that are stored in a custom folder to the Add Reference dialog box.

STEP BY STEP

10.10 Displaying an Assembly in the Add Reference Dialog Box

1. Open the Registry Editor by launching `regedit.exe` from the Run dialog box, which you access by selecting Start, Run.

2. In the Registry Editor, browse to the key named `HKEY_LOCAL_MACHINE\SOFTWARE\Microsoft\.NETFramework\AssemblyFolders`.

3. At this level create a new key and name it `MyAssemblies`.

4. Double-click the (Default) value in the new key and change its value to the location of `RandomNumberGenerator.dll` in the `bin\Release` folder of the `RandomNumberGenerator` project, as shown in Figure 10.10.

5. Close the Registry Editor. Close all instances of Visual Studio .NET.

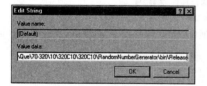

FIGURE 10.10
You can set the value of a Registry key in the Edit String dialog box.

In Step-by-Step 10.11 you create a small Windows application that, when executed, loads the components that are installed in the GAC. Before you begin Step-by-Step 10.11, make sure you have already installed the file `RandomNumberGenerator.dll` in the GAC.

STEP BY STEP

10.11 Creating a Windows Application That Uses the `RandomNumberGenerator` Component

1. Add a new Windows application project to the solution and name it `RandomNumberApp`.

2. In Solution Explorer, rename the `Form1.cs` file in the project to `RandomNumberApp.cs`. Switch to the code view of the form and modify all references to `Form1` so that they refer to `RandomNumberApp` instead.

3. Open the Add Reference dialog box. You should notice the `RandomNumberGenerator` component under the .NET tab. Add a reference to the `RandomNumberGenerator` component. Set the `Copy Local` property of the `RandomNumberGenerator` reference to `false`.

4. Activate the toolbox and then select the Components tab. Right-click an empty area on the tab and select Customize Toolbox from the shortcut menu. Click the .NET Framework Components tab and select `RandomNumberGenerator.dll`.

5. Drag the `RandomNumberGenerator` component from the toolbox and drop it on the form. Change its `MinValue` property to `500` and change `MaxValue` to `1000`.

6. Add a `Label` control (`lblResult`) and a `Button` control (`btnGenerate`) to the form. Empty the `Label` control's `Text` property. Set the `Button` control's `Text` property to `Generate a Random Number!`. Double-click the `Button` control to add an event handler for its `Click` event. Add the following code to the event handler:

```
private void btnGenerate_Click(object sender,
    System.EventArgs e)
{
    lblResult.Text = String.Format(
        "The next random number is: {0}",
        randomNumberGenerator1.GetRandomNumber());
}
```

7. Set the project `RandomNumberApp` as the startup project.

continues

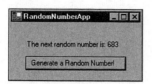

FIGURE 10.11
A form that generates a random number by using the RandomNumberGenerator component installed in the GAC.

continued

8. Run the solution. Click the button. A random number between 500 and 1,000 appears every time you press the button, as shown in Figure 10.11.

9. Copy the RandomNumberApp.exe from the bin\Release folder of the project to the C:\MyPrograms\ RandomNumberApplication folder. Run the file from the new location and verify that the application works as expected.

In Step-by-Step 10.11 you add a reference to the assembly stored in the bin\Release folder of the RandomNumberGenerator project. However, the application loads the assembly from the GAC, rather than its copy in the bin\Release folder. To understand this, you need to understand how the CLR locates shared assemblies; this is discussed in the following section.

Binding Policy for Shared Assemblies

For shared assemblies, the binding policy identifies a set of rules that specify:

▶ The directories in which the CLR should search for an assembly.

▶ The version of an assembly for which the CLR should search.

When the CLR searches a shared assembly, it goes through three stages of binding policy resolution, as shown in Figure 10.12.

At each of these stages, you can specify binding rules in XML-based configuration files. The three stages, in order, are as follows:

1. Application Policy Resolution—At this stage, the CLR looks for an application configuration file for the binding rules. This configuration file can be used to specify additional search paths for an assembly. In addition, you can also use this file to redirect the CLR to a specific version of an assembly. The application-specific binding rules are usually set either by the application developer or by an administrator.

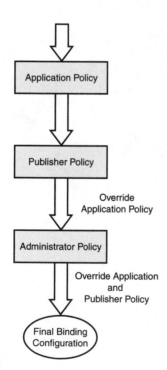

FIGURE 10.12
The CLR resolves the binding policy in three stages.

2. Publisher Policy Resolution—The next stage after the application policy resolution is the publisher policy resolution. The publisher of a shared assembly sets publisher policy to distribute service pack–like updates to customers. For example, take a scenario where a customer installs version 1.0. of an assembly from a vendor. Later, the vendor realizes that there are certain errors with this version and releases a service pack to fix those errors. In this case, the publisher distributes a new version 1.1 of the assembly, along with a publisher policy that redirects all previously installed applications to use the new version 1.1 of the assembly rather than the old version 1.0.

The publisher policy is specified in an XML file just as the application configuration file is. But unlike the application configuration file, the publisher policy is complied into an assembly. In addition, the publisher policy only contains information about redirecting the CLR to a different version of the assembly.

By default, the binding rules specified in the publisher policy override the application policy. If, however, you want an application to override the updates and continue using the existing versions, you can bypass the publisher policy file by specifying the `<publisherPolicy apply="no"/>` XML element in the application configuration file.

3. Administrator Policy Resolution—This stage is the final stage for applying the binding rules. The binding rules at this stage are specified by the administrator in the machinewide configuration file named `machine.config`. This file is stored in the `config` subdirectory under the .NET Framework installation directory on a machine.

The settings specified in the machine configuration file override any settings specified in the application policy and the publisher policy.

How the CLR Binds to a Shared Assembly

The CLR uses the following steps to locate a shared assembly:

1. Determine the correct version of the assembly by examining the application configuration file, publisher policy file, and machine configuration file in the order mentioned in the preceding section.

2. Check whether the assembly is already loaded. If the requested assembly has been loaded in one of the previous calls, then bind to the already loaded assembly and stop searching any further.

3. Check the GAC. If the assembly is in the GAC, then load the assembly from there, bind to it, and stop searching any further.

4. If a `<codebase>` element is specified in the configuration files, the CLR locates the assembly by using the paths specified in the `<codebase>` element. If the CLR finds the assembly, then the binding is successful; otherwise the binding request fails and the CLR stops searching any further.

5. The CLR reads the application configuration file to check whether any private path hints are available in the `<probing>` element. If there are hints, the CLR will use these directory locations to search the assembly.

6. If the referenced assembly has no culture information, the CLR uses the following locations in the given order to find the assembly:

   - *ApplicationBase**AssemblyName*.dll

   - *ApplicationBase**AssemblyName**AssemblyName*.dll

   - *ApplicationBase**PrivatePath1**AssemblyName*.dll

   - *ApplicationBase**PrivatePath1**AssemblyName*\\
     AssemblyName.dll

   - *ApplicationBase**PrivatePath2**AssemblyName*.dll

   - *ApplicationBase**PrivatePath2**AssemblyName*\\
     AssemblyName.dll

.
.
.

- *ApplicationBase\AssemblyName*.exe

- *ApplicationBase\AssemblyName\AssemblyName*.exe

- *ApplicationBase\PrivatePath1\AssemblyName*.exe

- *ApplicationBase\PrivatePath1\AssemblyName\
  AssemblyName*.exe

- *ApplicationBase\PrivatePath2\AssemblyName*.exe

- *ApplicationBase\PrivatePath2\AssemblyName\
  AssemblyName*.exe

.
.
.

Here *ApplicationBase* is the directory where the requesting application is installed; *AssemblyName* is the name of the assembly to search; and *PrivatePath1* and *PrivatePath2* are the hints provided in the *<probing>* element of the application configuration file. Note that the assembly name does not contain the extension; therefore the CLR searches for both DLL as well as EXE files. If the assembly is found in any of these locations, the CLR binds to the assembly and does not search any further.

7. If the referenced assembly has culture information, the following directories are searched:

   - *ApplicationBase\Culture\AssemblyName*.dll

   - *ApplicationBase\Culture\AssemblyName\AssemblyName*.dll

   - *ApplicationBase\PrivatePath1\Culture\AssemblyName*.dll

   - *ApplicationBase\PrivatePath1\Culture\
     AssemblyName\AssemblyName*.dll

   - *ApplicationBase\PrivatePath2\Culture\AssemblyName*.dll

- *ApplicationBase\PrivatePath2\Culture*
  AssemblyName\AssemblyName.dll

  .
  .
  .

- *ApplicationBase\Culture\AssemblyName*.exe

- *ApplicationBase\Culture\AssemblyName\AssemblyName*.exe

- *ApplicationBase\PrivatePath1\Culture\AssemblyName*.exe

- *ApplicationBase\PrivatePath1\Culture\AssemblyName*
  AssemblyName.exe

- *ApplicationBase\PrivatePath2\Culture*
  AssemblyName.exe

- *ApplicationBase\PrivatePath2\Culture\AssemblyName*
  AssemblyName.exe

  .
  .
  .

Here `Culture` is a culture code corresponding to the assembly. If the assembly is found in any of these locations, the CLR binds to the assembly and does not search any further.

8. If the CLR cannot locate the assembly after following the preceding steps, assembly binding fails.

Side-by-Side Execution of Shared Assemblies

From what you have learned, multiple versions of an assembly can exist in the GAC. The following are two common scenarios in which you might end up having multiple versions of an assembly:

▶ A feature upgrade of an assembly is released.

▶ A bug-fix service pack update of an assembly is released.

An application binds only to an assembly with the same identity with which the application was originally compiled. So if you release a new version of the assembly and remove the old one, existing applications will break because they still will be looking for an older version of the assembly.

Fortunately, the application, the machine, and the publisher configuration files give you a mechanism to redirect the binding requests to a different version of the assembly without any need to recompile already deployed applications.

Side-by-Side Execution in a Feature Upgrade Scenario

Consider a scenario where you have an application named RandomNumberApp that uses version 1.0 of a shared component named RandomNumberGenerator. When a new version 1.1 of the RandomNumberGenerator component is released, you install it in the GAC. Some of the applications on your server still use version 1.0 of the component. You want the already deployed RandomNumberApp to start using version 1.1 of the component. You do not want to recompile the RandomNumberApp and also do not want to affect the installation of other applications on the server.

The best policy in this scenario is to modify the application configuration file of RandomNumberApp to redirect any request for the version 1.0 of RandomNumberGenerator to the version 1.1 of that assembly. Modifying configuration files does not require the application to be recompiled, and if you modify the application configuration file, it affects only the application to which it belongs.

To demonstrate the scenario, Step-by-Step 10.12 installs version 1.1 of the RandomNumberGenerator assembly in the GAC.

STEP BY STEP

10.12 Installing Multiple Versions of an Assembly in the GAC

1. Open the RandomNumberGenerator.cs file in the RandomNumberGenerator project.

continues

continued

2. Modify the `GetRandomNumber()` method as follows:

```
public int GetRandomNumber()
{
    Random r = new Random();
    int rand = r.Next(minValue, maxValue);
    EventLog eventLog = new EventLog();
    eventLog.Source = "RandomNumberGenerator 1.1";
    eventLog.WriteEntry(
        "Random Number Generated:" + rand);
    return rand;
}
```

3. Open the `AssemblyInfo.cs` file. Scroll down in the file and change the `AssemblyVersion` as shown here:

```
[assembly: AssemblyVersion("1.1")]
```

4. Build the `RandomNumberGenerator` project. You should see the `RandomNumberGenerator.dll` file generated with version 1.1.

5. Copy the strongly-named assembly `RandomNumberGenerator.dll` to the GAC. You should be able to see that the GAC now has two versions of the `RandomNumberGenerator` assembly, as shown in Figure 10.13.

6. Run the `RandomNumberApp.exe` file from the `C:\MyPrograms` folder. You should notice that the file still uses the 1.0 version of the `RandomNumberGenerator` component (with which it was compiled) and does not create an entry in the event log.

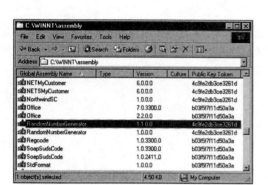

FIGURE 10.13
You can perform side-by-side versioning of shared assemblies in the GAC.

From Step-by-Step 10.12, note that the `RandomNumberApp` is still using the older version of the component because that's what is stored in its assembly manifest.

Step-by-Step 10.13 shows how to configure the application configuration file for `RandomNumberApp.exe` to use version 1.1 of the `RandomNumberGenerator` component.

STEP BY STEP

10.13 Using the .NET Framework Configuration Tool to Configure Application-Level Binding Policy for an Assembly

1. Open the Microsoft .NET Framework Configuration tool from the Administrative Tools section of the Windows Control Panel.

2. Click the Applications node in the tree view.

3. Click the Add an Application to Configure link.

4. In the Configure an Application dialog box, click the Other button and browse to the `C:\MyPrograms\RandomNumberApplication` folder to select `RandomNumberApp.exe`. Select this application and click OK.

5. Expand the new node in the tree view and click the Configured Assemblies child node.

6. Click the Configure an Assembly link.

7. In the Configure an Assembly dialog box, select the option button to choose an assembly from the list of assemblies that this application uses. Click the Choose Assembly button. Select the `RandomNumberGenerator` assembly, click Select, and then click Finish.

8. In the `RandomNumberGenerator` Properties dialog box, select the Binding Policy tab. Enter `1.0.0.0` as the requested version and `1.1.0.0` as the new version, as shown in Figure 10.14.

9. Click OK to save the configured assembly information.

10. View the `C:\MyPrograms\RandomNumberApplication` folder in Windows Explorer. You should find a `RandomNumberApp.exe.config` application configuration file added to the folder with the following contents:

```
<?xml version="1.0"?>
<configuration>
```

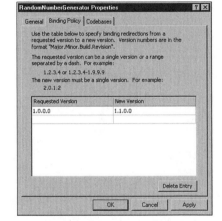

FIGURE 10.14
You can create a configured assembly and set its binding policy and other settings with the help of the Microsoft .NET Framework

> **WARNING**
>
> **No Validation** The .NET Framework Configuration tool performs no validation to determine whether the specified new version of the assembly even exists.

continues

continued

```
<runtime>
  <assemblyBinding
      xmlns="urn:schemas-microsoft-com:asm.v1">
    <dependentAssembly>
      <assemblyIdentity
          name="RandomNumberGenerator"
          publicKeyToken="4c9fe2db3ce3261d" />
      <bindingRedirect oldVersion="1.0.0.0"
          newVersion="1.1.0.0" />
    </dependentAssembly>
  </assemblyBinding>
</runtime>
</configuration>
```

11. Double-click the `RandomNumberApp.exe` file from the `C:\MyPrograms\RandomNumberApplication` folder in Windows Explorer. Click the button and check the entries in the Application event log to see that version `1.1.0.0` of the `RandomNumberGenerator` component is executed.

In Step-by-Step 10.13, you used the .NET Framework configuration tool to create an application configuration file. You can also create the application configuration file manually, although in that case you need to know that you have to use the `<assemblyBinding>` element and its sub-elements to redirect the version numbers.

Note that in the `<bindingRedirect>` element the values for the attribute `oldVersion` and `newVersion` need not be an old version and a new version respectively. You can, in fact, redirect an application using a newer version of an assembly to an older version also (provided, of course, that the changes are non-breaking).

When you use the application configuration file, you can configure only a single application, but what if you need to configure all the applications on a machine that uses the old version of `RandomNumberGenerator` to use its new version? In this case, it will be tedious to configure an assembly for each application. Further, you will also need to take care that the new applications installed also bind to the new version of the component. To ease this, you can add the `<assemblyBinding>` element in the `machine.config`, machine configuration file. However, you need Administrator privileges to edit the `machine.config` file. Step-by-Step 10.14 shows you how to configure an assembly for a machine using the .NET Framework Configuration tool.

STEP BY STEP

10.14 Using the .NET Framework Configuration Tool to Configure Machine-Level Binding Policy for an Assembly

1. Open the Microsoft .NET Framework Configuration tool from the Administrative Tools section of the Windows Control Panel.

2. Right-click the Configured Assemblies node in the tree view and select Add from its context menu.

3. In the Configure an Assembly dialog box, select the option button to choose an assembly from the assembly cache. Click the Choose Assembly button. Select the `RandomNumberGenerator` assembly version 1.0.0.0, click Select, and then click Finish.

4. In the `RandomNumberGenerator` Properties dialog box, select the Binding Policy tab. Enter **1.0.0.0** as the requested version and **1.1.0.0** as the new version.

5. Click OK to save the configured assembly information.

6. Open the `machine.config` file from the `config` folder of the Microsoft .NET Framework installation folder. Navigate to the `<assemblyBinding>` element and verify that binding policy for the `RandomNumberGenerator` component is added as shown here:

```
<configuration>
...
  <runtime>
    <assemblyBinding
        xmlns="urn:schemas-microsoft-com:asm.v1">
      ...
      <dependentAssembly>
        <assemblyIdentity name="RandomNumberGenerator"
          publicKeyToken="4c9fe2db3ce3261d" />
        <bindingRedirect oldVersion="1.0.0.0"
            newVersion="1.1.0.0" />
      </dependentAssembly>
    </assemblyBinding>
  </runtime>
</configuration>
```

continues

continued

7. Delete the `RandomNumberApp.exe.config` application configuration file from the `C:\MyPrograms\RandomNumberApplication` folder in Windows Explorer.

8. Double-click the `RandomNumberApp.exe` file from the `C:\MyPrograms\RandomNumberApplication` folder in Windows Explorer. Click the button and check the entries in the Application event log to see that version `1.1.0.0` of the `RandomNumberGenerator` component is executed.

Configuration performed in Step-by-Step 10.14 affects not only the `RandomNumberApp`, but in fact all applications that use the `RandomNumberGenerator` components on the given machine.

Side-by-Side Execution in a Service Pack Update Scenario

Consider another scenario in which you may end up having multiple versions of an assembly in the GAC. In this scenario, you are the company that publishes the `RandomNumberGenerator` component. You release version 1.0 of the component. Your customers develop applications, such as `RandomNumberApp`, that use the component. The customers report that there is a bug in the component that needs to be fixed at high priority. You plan to release a service pack of the component. The new version of the component is version 1.1. You want to deploy the component on the customers' computers in such a way that all existing applications that refer to version 1.0 of the `RandomNumberGenerator` component should now be redirected to version 1.1. You do not want extra configuration steps to have to be performed by customers' administrators.

The .NET Framework provides publisher policy for these very scenarios. To configure a publisher policy, use the publisher policy configuration file, which uses a format similar to that of the application configuration files. But unlike the application configuration file, a publisher policy file needs to be compiled into an assembly and placed in the GAC.

The steps involved in creating a publisher policy are as follows:

1. Create a publisher policy file.

2. Use the Assembly Generation tool (`al.exe`) to convert the publisher policy file into a strongly-named assembly. The name of the assembly should be of the format `policy.`*`majorNumber`*`.`*`minorNumber`*`.`*`AssemblyName`*`.dll`. Here, *`majorNumber`* and *`minorNumber`* are the major and minor version numbers of the existing assembly for which you want to redirect the binding requests. *`AssemblyName`* is the name of the assembly.

3. Install the publisher policy assembly to the GAC.

Step-by-Step 10.15 shows you how to create a publisher policy by using the .NET Framework Configuration tool.

STEP BY STEP

10.15 Configuring Publisher Policy for an Assembly

1. Create a new publisher configuration file named `policy.1.0.RandomNumberGenerator.config` in the folder where the original `RandomNumberGenerator.dll` assembly resides with the following code:

```
<configuration>
  <runtime>
    <assemblyBinding
      xmlns="urn:schemas-microsoft-com:asm.v1">
    <dependentAssembly>
      <assemblyIdentity
        name="RandomNumberGenerator"
        publicKeyToken="4c9fe2db3ce3261d"
                      />
      <bindingRedirect oldVersion="1.0.0.0"
        newVersion="1.1.0.0"/>
    </dependentAssembly>
    </assemblyBinding>
  </runtime>
</configuration>
```

You need to change the `publicKeyToken` attribute to the appropriate public key for your assembly (which you can locate in the configuration file that you built in Step-by-Step 10.14).

continues

continued

2. Launch the Visual Studio .NET prompt. Navigate to the folder where the publisher configuration file resides and run the following command:

```
al /link:policy.1.0.RandomNumberGenerator.config
➥/out:policy.1.0.RandomNumberGenerator.dll
➥/keyfile:..\..\..\70320.snk
```

You should see a publisher policy assembly named `policy.1.0.RandomNumberGenerator.dll` being generated.

3. Add the publisher policy assembly to the GAC.

4. Open the Microsoft .NET Framework Configuration tool from the Administrative Tools section of the Windows Control Panel.

5. Select the Configured Assemblies. In the pane on the right side, delete the `RandomNumberGenerator` assembly added in Step-by-Step 10.14. Now the assembly binding entries from the `machine.config` file are removed.

6. Double-click the `RandomNumberApp.exe` file from the `C:\MyPrograms\RandomNumberApplication` folder in Windows Explorer. Click the button and check the entries in the Application event log to see that version `1.1.0.0` of the `RandomNumberGenerator` component is executed. The version `1.1.0.0` assembly is selected due to the assembly bindings in the publisher policy assembly.

Binding redirections specified in the `machine.config` override those specified in the publisher policy. The publisher policy overrides the setting specified in the application configuration file. But an application can ignore the publisher policy altogether if you set the `apply` attribute of the `<publisherPolicy>` element to `"no"` in the `<assemblyBinding>` element of the application configuration file:

```
<publisherPolicy apply="no"/>
```

Delay Signing an Assembly

In Step-by-Step 10.6, when you signed an assembly, you used a key file that contained both the public key and a private key for a company. As discussed earlier in the chapter, the private key ensures that the assembly is signed only by its advertised publisher. Thus, in most companies, the private key is stored securely, and only a few people have access to it.

If the key is highly protected, it might be difficult to frequently access the key when multiple developers of a company are building assemblies several times a day. To solve this problem, the .NET Framework uses the delay signing technique for assemblies.

When you use delay signing, you use only the public key to build an assembly. Associating public keys with an assembly allows you to place the assembly in the GAC and complete most of the development and testing tasks with the assembly. Later, when you are ready to package the assembly, someone who is authorized signs the assembly with the private key. Signing with the private key ensures that the CLR will provide tamper protection for the assembly. The following list summarizes the steps involved with delay signing:

1. Extract a public key from the public/private key pair—To extract the public key from a file that is storing the public/ private key pair, you use the Strong Name tool as follows:

   ```
   sn.exe -p 70320.snk 70320PublicKey.snk
   ```

   At this stage, the `70320PublicKey.snk` file can be freely distributed to the development team, and the `70320.snk` file that contains both the private and public keys can be stored securely, possibly on a hardware device such as a smart card.

2. Use Visual Studio .NET to delay sign an assembly—To use delay signing in a Visual Studio .NET project, you need to modify the following two attributes of the project's `AssemblyInfo.cs` file and build the assembly:

   ```
   [assembly: AssemblyDelaySign(true)]
   [assembly: AssemblyKeyFile("70320PublicKey.snk")]
   ```

3. Turn off verification for an assembly in the GAC—By default, the GAC verifies the strong name of each assembly. If the private key is not used to sign the assembly, this verification fails. So for development and testing purposes, you can relax this

verification for an assembly by issuing the following command:

```
sn.exe -Vr RandomNumberGenerator.dll
```

If you execute this command, the GAC always skips the verification for this assembly in the future.

4. Sign a delay-signed assembly with the private key—When you are ready to deploy a delay-signed assembly, you need to sign it with the company's private key:

```
sn.exe -R RandomNumberGenerator.dll 70320.snk
```

5. Turn on verification for an assembly in the GAC—Finally, you can instruct the GAC to turn on verification for an assembly by issuing the following command:

```
sn.exe -Vu RandomNumberGenerator.dll
```

Using the Assembly Generation Tool for Delay Signing

The Assembly Generation tool (al.exe) generates an assembly with an assembly manifest from the given modules or resource files. A module is a Microsoft Intermediate Language (MSIL) file without an assembly manifest.

While generating an assembly, you can also instruct the Assembly Generation tool to sign or delay sign an assembly with the given public/private key file. When you use al.exe for delay signing, you also use the arguments listed in Table 10.1.

TABLE 10.1

ARGUMENTS PASSED TO al.exe FOR DELAY SIGNING

Argument	Description
`<sourcefiles>`	You replace `<sourcefiles>` with the names of one or more complied modules that will be the parts of the resulting assembly.
`/delay[sign][+¦-]`	You can use either the `delay` argument or the `delay[sign]` argument for delay signing. The option + is used to delay sign the assembly by storing just the public key manifest in the assembly manifest. The – option is used to fully sign an assembly with both public and private keys. If you do not use either + or –, the default value of – is assumed.
`/keyf[ile]:<filename>`	You can use either `keyf` or `keyfile` to specify the key file. You replace `<filename>` with the name of the file that stores the key(s).
`/out:<filename>`	You replace `<filename>` with the desired name of the output assembly file.

Assume that you want to create an assembly by linking two modules, `Sample1.netmodule` and `Sample2.netmodule`. The public key file is `SamplePublicKey.snk`, and the desired output assembly is `SignedSample.exe`. You would use the `al.exe` command as follows:

```
al.exe Sample1.netmodule,Sample2.netmodule
➥/delaysign+
➥/keyfile:SamplePublicKey.snk
➥/out:SignedSample.exe
```

REVIEW BREAK

▶ Shared assemblies are used by multiple applications on a machine. Shared assemblies are placed in the GAC and they enjoy special privileges such as file security, shared location, and side-by-side versioning.

▶ You generate a public/private key pair by using the Strong Name tool (`sn.exe`). This pair can be used to sign assemblies with a strong name.

▶ You can add a shared assembly to the GAC by using Windows Explorer, the .NET Framework Configuration tool, the Global Assembly Cache tool, and the Windows Installer.

continues

continued

▶ The best way to add an assembly in the GAC during deployment is to use Microsoft Windows Installer. The Windows Installer provides assembly reference-counting features and manages removal of assemblies at the time of uninstallation.

▶ When viewed in Windows Explorer, the assembly cache folder in the System folder displays assemblies from the GAC and native image cache.

▶ The CLR first searches the GAC to locate assemblies, and then it looks into the files and folders where the assembly is installed. Thus, loading shared assemblies from the GAC is efficient because the CLR does not engage itself in looking into the <codebase> and <probing> elements of the applicable configuration files.

▶ Different versions of an assembly can be deployed in the GAC for side-by-side execution. You can implement side-by-side execution of an assembly by configuring the binding policy in the application configuration file, the publisher policy file, or the machine configuration file.

▶ The publisher policy file can be used to deploy service packs, such as bug-fix updates, for the assemblies. The publisher policy file is an XML file that is converted into a strongly-named assembly and installed in the GAC.

▶ Delay signing allows you to place a shared assembly in the GAC by signing the assembly with just the public key. This allows the assembly to be signed with the private key at a later stage, when the development process is complete and the component or assembly is ready to be deployed. This process enables developers to work with shared assemblies as if they were strongly named, and it secures the private key of the signature from being accessed at different stages of development.

PACKAGING A .NET APPLICATION FOR DEPLOYMENT

Plan the deployment of and deploy a Windows service, a serviced component, a .NET Remoting object, and an XML Web service.

Packaging an application means identifying all the individual files and settings for an application and putting them together so that the application can be easily distributed and deployed on the target computers.

Different techniques are available to package an application for deployment. Choosing the correct packaging technique is important because it not only eases the process of deployment but also minimizes the total cost of ownership for the customers. The choice of packaging depends on the nature of the application and its users. For installing simple applications, sometimes a tool as simple as the XCOPY command can be used. For sophisticated requirements, you might want to use a tool that creates a Windows Installer–based setup package for the application.

Packaging an Application for Deployment by Copying the Files

Applications developed using the Microsoft .NET Framework do not generally use the Windows Registry for storing application-specific data and configuration settings. Instead, all settings are stored in XML-based configuration files.

It is possible to deploy such an application by copying all the build output and content files to a folder of your choice on the target computer. You can simply use the XCOPY command or use FTP if you are deploying across the Internet. When you need to uninstall an application, all you need to do is to delete the folder that contains the application's files. Because the deployment process is non-intrusive and causes minimal changes on the target computer, it is also sometimes called *zero-impact* installation.

NOTE

Deploying Multi-tier Applications Distributed applications are often designed as n-tier applications. In that case, different tiers of the application are often deployed on separate computers for the sake of modularity. To increase reliability and performance, a single tier may also sometimes be installed on multiple computers working together in a Web farm or cluster. Different tiers of an application are usually also different types of applications and have varied installation requirements.

For these reasons, it is hardly possible to devise a single mechanism for deploying the entire multi-tier application. The most common approach is to use a separate deployment mechanism for each tier of the application.

However, there are scenarios where copying the files is not sufficient for deploying an application. Some common installation tasks that are difficult to do just by copying the files include the following:

▶ For a Web service and a Web application, you also need to create a virtual directory on the Web server, set the virtual directory as an IIS application, and possibly configure security or other settings for the virtual directory.

▶ For a Windows Service, you need to register the service with the Windows Service Control Manager.

▶ For a serviced component, you need to register the component with the COM+ catalog.

▶ You may need to take extra steps to provide for the application's integration with the user's desktop, such as creating shortcuts and Start menu entries.

▶ You may need to add shared assemblies to the GAC.

▶ You may need to allow users to select features during installation.

▶ You may need to copy files to relative paths on the target machine that differ from the paths on the source machine.

▶ You may need to create or configure databases during the installation.

▶ You may need to add custom event logs and performance counters to the target machine.

▶ You may need to check whether the .NET Framework is installed on the target machine.

▶ You may need to present a user-friendly and branded user interface to the users.

▶ You may need to do license key management and user registration as part of the installation.

Because of these limitations, in general you use the XCOPY command only when the application is deployed by the system administrators or the application developers. This may be true for server-side applications because they are deployed on only a few servers and these servers are more likely to be closely administered.

On the other hand, if you are distributing your application commercially, in most cases you would like to package your application as a Windows Installer package.

Using Microsoft Windows Installer to Package an Application for Deployment

Microsoft Windows Installer is an installation and configuration service that is built into the Windows operating system. It gives you complete control over the installation of an application, a component, or an update.

Windows Installer includes many built-in actions for performing the installation process. In addition to performing the standard actions, such as installing files, creating shortcuts to files, making Start menu entries, and writing Registry entries, Windows Installer also offers several advanced features, some of which are listed here:

- ▶ It enables you to take custom actions during application installation. For example, you might want to run a SQL script to install an application database during application installation.

- ▶ It provides on-demand installation of features. This capability enables the user to install, at a later stage, a feature that was not installed during the application's initial installation. On-demand installation does not force the user to reinstall the entire installation package; the user can add just a single feature.

- ▶ It enables you to roll back an installation. Windows Installer maintains an undo operation for every operation that is performed during an application installation. If Windows Installer encounters any errors while installing an application, it can uninstall everything that was installed during the installation.

- ▶ It enables you to uninstall an application without breaking any other application that depends on it.

- ▶ It enables you to fix an application or one of its components if it becomes corrupted. This way, users spend less time uninstalling and reinstalling applications.

NOTE

Windows Installer Requirements
Windows Installer version 2.0 (the version used to install .NET applications) requires Windows NT 4.0 with Service Pack 6 or later, Windows XP, Windows .NET Server, Windows 2000, or Windows Me. Earlier Windows Installer versions require Windows NT 4.0 with Service Pack 3 or later, Windows XP, Windows 2000, or Windows Me. Windows Installer is also available as a redistributable file for Windows NT 4.0, Windows 95, and Windows 98, and it can be downloaded from www.microsoft.com/msdownload/platformsdk/sdkupdate/psdkredist.htm.

Updating Microsoft Windows Installer Although Windows Installer is built into Windows, you might need to install a redistributable file to get the latest version. Later in this chapter you will see how to create a Windows Installer bootstrapper to ensure that Windows Installer is updated (if necessary) on target machines.

Windows Installer manages all installed components on a system by keeping a database of information about every application that it installs, including files, Registry keys, and components.

When you create an installation program for Windows Installer, you create a Windows Installer (.msi) package. This package includes a number of database tables that describe the application to the Windows Installer. When this package is executed on the target machine, Windows Installer installs the program by reading the installation information stored in the Windows Installer package.

There are several ways to create a Windows Installer package. The most basic option is to manually create it by using the Windows Installer Software Development Kit (SDK), but for most practical requirements, you would instead use a visual tool that can help with the process. Visual Studio .NET provides a new category of projects called the Setup and Deployment projects that create setup packages by using Windows Installer. Many developers prefer installation tools from independent vendors, such as InstallShield and Wise Solutions. Specialized tools from these and other vendors provide a much higher level of customization and ease for creating Windows Installer–based setup programs.

Microsoft Visual Studio .NET through its Setup and Deployment projects offers four types of deployment project templates:

- ▶ Setup Project
- ▶ Web Setup Project
- ▶ Merge Module Project
- ▶ Cab Project

Visual Studio .NET also has a Setup Wizard that helps you interactively create these deployment templates. I'll briefly discuss the purpose of these deployment project templates in the following subsections. You'll use these templates later in this chapter.

Setup Project

The Setup Project template is used to create installation packages for deploying various types of applications such as Windows applications, Windows Services, console applications, and so on. The setup project creates an (.msi) installer package of the application. The setup project installs files into the specified directories in a target computer's file system.

Web Setup Project

You use this template to create installation packages for deploying Web-based applications such as an ASP.NET Web application or an XML Web service. Like the setup project template, the Web setup project also creates an (.msi) installer package, but this installer package installs files to a virtual directory on the target Web server.

Merge Module Project

Merge module projects enable you to package components that may be shared between multiple applications. A merge module is created as an .msm file. Merge modules are created for the use of the authors of applications that use the shared component.

Unlike the Windows Installer setup package (.msi file), merge modules are not installed directly; instead, merge modules are merged with the installer package of an application that uses the packaged component.

When an application containing a merge module is installed, the Windows installer maintains the component's reference count in the Windows database. When another application that uses the same version of the component is installed, instead of installing the component, Windows installer just increases the component's reference count. Later, when an application is uninstalled, Windows installer checks the reference count of shared components. A shared component is uninstalled only if the component is not being used by any other installed application.

Cab Project

CAB (short for "cabinet") files store a set of files in a compressed archive. A compressed archive may span over one or more files, each having a .cab extension. You can create CAB files by using the Visual Studio .NET Cab Project.

CAB files are often used when you need to reduce the size of your distribution. This may be necessary when you want to distribute the

N O T E **Use Authenticode Signing for Downloaded Code**   To ensure the credibility of code downloaded from the Internet, you should sign the code using Microsoft Authenticode technology. An Authenticode signature uses a digital certificate issued by a third-party certification authority (such as Verisign or Thawte) to assert a company's identity.

When users download an Authenticode-signed download package, they are presented with a digital certificate that shows the name of the software publisher as asserted by the certification authority. A user who trusts the certification authority and the software publisher can feel safe downloading and installing the software package.

You can use the File Signing tool (`signcode.exe`) to attach an Authenticode signature to the assembly.

programs over the Internet or on small-sized media such as floppy disks.

In an enterprise application, you normally use CAB files to package managed controls or the legacy ActiveX controls that will be hosted on the Web page. The controls are embedded in the Web page with the `<object>` element, and the path to the CAB files that contains the control is specified by the `CODEBASE` attribute. At runtime, such controls are downloaded to the user's computer and executed on demand.

Customizing Visual Studio .NET Setup and Deployment Projects

When you are creating a setup and deployment project, you might also want to provide custom features and perform custom actions while performing installation (for example, create Registry entries, provide a customized user interface for installation, perform custom actions, check for conditions to be satisfied for installation, create menu options and shortcuts, and so on).

Visual Studio .NET provides the following editors to customize various aspects of the installation process:

▶ File System Editor—The File System Editor provides a mapping of the file system on the target machine. Each folder is referred to with a special name that is converted to represent the folder on the target machine during the installation process. For example, at the time of installation, the special folder `User's Desktop` will be converted to the actual desktop path on the target machine.

   You can add files to various special folders, such as the `Application Folder`, `Common Files Folder`, `Program Files Folder`, `User's Desktop`, `System Folder`, `User's Startup Folder`, and many others—each of which represents a particular folder on the target machine.

▶ Registry Editor—The Registry Editor allows you to specify Registry keys, subkeys, and values that are added to the Registry on the target machine during the installation process. You can also import Registry files into the Registry Editor.

▶ File Types Editor—The File Types Editor enables you to associate file extensions and actions with applications. For example, files with an extension (.qry, .txt and so on) and actions (open, print, edit and so on) can be associated with the application. Later the application will get triggered whenever the associated actions are performed on the files with associated extensions.

▶ User Interface Editor—The User Interface Editor enables you to customize the user interface that is provided to the user during the installation process. The *user interface* is the various dialog boxes that appear during the installation process. The user interface provided to the user is divided into three stages: Start, Progress, and End. You can add different types of dialog boxes for each stage. Each stage allows only certain types of dialog boxes to be added.

The User Interface Editor displays the user interface that is applicable during both end user installation and administrative installation. You can customize the user interface for both of these types of installations. The administrative installation occurs when you run the msiexec command-line tool with the /a option.

▶ Custom Actions Editor—The Custom Actions Editor enables you to run compiled DLLs, EXEs, scripts, or assembly files at the end of an installation. These files can be used to perform custom actions that are vital but were not carried out during the installation. If the custom action fails, the entire installation process is rolled back. For example, you might have to install the database that your application requires during the installation process.

You can perform custom actions in four phases: Install, Commit, Rollback, and Uninstall.

▶ Launch Conditions Editor—The Launch Conditions Editor enables you to set conditions that are to be evaluated when an installation begins on a target machine. If the conditions are not met, the installation stops. For example, let's say you would like to install a Visual C# .NET application only if the .NET Framework is installed on the target machine. This condition is by default added by Visual Studio .NET. You might also need to perform other checks, such as whether a particular file exists on the target machine, or verify a particular Registry key value on the target machine.

EXAM TIP

The Strong Name and the Authenticode Signature   An assembly signed with a strong name does not automatically assert a company's identity, such as its name. For that purpose, you can use an Authenticode signature, in which case the company's identity is asserted.

An important thing to know is the order of commands when both the sn.exe and signcode.exe tools are used to sign an assembly. You must sign your assembly with the Strong Name tool (sn.exe) before you sign it with the File Signing tool (signcode.exe).

FIGURE 10.15
You can launch various editors for a setup project via Solution Explorer.

The Launch Conditions Editor enables you to perform searches on the target machine for a file, a Registry entry, or Windows Installer components. You can then add conditions to be evaluated for the search performed on the target machine.

The Setup and Web Setup project templates support all the editors provided by Visual Studio .NET. However, the Merge Module Project template does not provide support for the Launch Conditions Editor and User Interface Editor. This is understandable, as they are used to package components and not applications. The Cab Project template does not support any of these editors.

You can view an editor by either choosing its icon from Solution Explorer or right-clicking the project in Solution Explorer and choosing View and the respective editor option from the shortcut menu, as shown in Figure 10.15.

REVIEW BREAK

▶ Although the .NET Framework supports XCOPY deployment, XCOPY is not sufficient for advanced deployment requirements. For advanced requirements, you should instead use a Microsoft Windows Installer–based installation package to deploy applications.

▶ Microsoft Windows Installer is the built-in installation and configuration service of the Windows operating system. In addition to providing several advanced installation features, it provides features such as the capability to roll back an installation process, uninstall an application, and repair a component or an application.

▶ Visual Studio .NET provides four types of deployment templates: Setup Project (for Windows-based applications), Web Setup Project (for Web-based applications), Merge Module Project (for shared components and assemblies), and Cab Project (for managed and legacy ActiveX components to be downloaded over the Internet). Visual Studio .NET also provides the Setup Wizard, which helps in creating installation packages for any of these deployment projects.

DEPLOYING A WEB SERVICE

Create a setup program that installs a Windows service, a serviced component, a .NET Remoting object, and an XML Web service.

Configure client computers and servers to use a Windows service, a serviced component, a .NET Remoting object, and an XML Web service.

You can deploy a Web service on a Web server in a variety of ways:

- ▶ By manually copying the files

- ▶ By using the Copy Project command of Visual Studio .NET

- ▶ By using the Windows Installer package created with the Visual Studio .NET Web setup project

I'll present each of these techniques in the following subsections.

Deploying a Web Service by Manually Copying the Files

Deploying a Web service by manually copying the files is a four-step process:

1. Build the Web service—When you build a Web service application, all the code-behind files of the Web services are compiled into a DLL file and are stored in the bin subdirectory of the Web service application. This step enables you to deploy the compiled DLL files rather than the source files.

2. Select the files that need to be deployed—A Web service may need to deploy several additional files in addition to the DLL files created in step 1. Table 10.2 lists the various files that are created in a Visual C# .NET Web Service project and whether the file needs to be deployed. In addition to these files, you might also use some other files such as an .xml file or an .xsd file, which you may require on the production Web server.

TABLE 10.2

FILES IN A VISUAL C# .NET WEB SERVICE PROJECT

Web Service File	Description	Needs to be Deployed?
.asmx	This file contains the WebService processing directive and serves as the entry point for the XML Web service.	Yes
.asmx.cs	This file is a code-behind file that contains the source code for the XML Web Service. When you build the Web service, content of this file is compiled into a DLL file.	No
AssemblyInfo.cs	This file contains metadata about the assemblies in a project, such as name, version, and culture information. The contents of this file are also compiled into a DLL file.	No
web.config	An XML-based file that contains configuration information for the Web service.	Yes
global.asax	A file that contains information for handling application-level events.	Yes
global.asax.cs	The code-behind file that contains the source code for the global.asax. When the Web service is built, the contents of this file are compiled into a DLL file.	No
.csproj	This file contains settings for a Web service project for use by Visual C# .NET. This file is used only at the time of development.	No
.csproj.webinfo	Contains the path to the project on the development server.	No

Web Service File	Description	Needs to be Deployed?
.vsdisco	A file that provides dynamic discovery for all the Web services on a server. You should not usually deploy this file to the production server because in doing so, you will lose control over which Web services you want to make available to others.	No
.disco	A file that provides static discovery of Web services. This file includes only the Web services that you explicitly want to expose to others.	Yes
.dll	The assembly that contains the compiled output for the Web service project.	Yes
.pdb	A file that contains the debug symbols for the XML Web service and provides support for debugging of the XML Web service on the server. This file is created only when the project is compiled in the debug mode.	No
.sln	The file that stores the metadata of the Web service solution.	No

3. Copy the Files to the production server—After you have identified the files that are required for deployment, the next step
   is to deploy all these files to a folder on the production server.
   You can use any copy mechanism, such as XCOPY or FTP, to
   accomplish this.

4. Configure the Web service folder on the production server—
   Just copying the files to the production server is not enough;
   you also need to configure the target folder as a virtual directory, set access permissions for the virtual directory, and configure the virtual directory as an IIS application.

In addition to these steps, you may also need to perform additional steps, such as installing an assembly to the global assembly cache (GAC), or registering a serviced component with the COM+ catalog, setting up data access to SQL Server, and so on.

Deploying a Web Service by Using the Visual Studio .NET Copy Project Command

For Web applications, Visual Studio .NET provides a Copy Project command, which can help developers to quickly copy all the files in a project to a different location in the same machine or a different machine.

To use this tool, take the following steps:

1. Open the Web application that needs to be deployed in Visual Studio .NET.

2. Select Project, Copy Project. You see the dialog box as shown in Figure 10.16

3. Select the Web access method as FrontPage if you need the target project to be automatically set up as an IIS application.

4. Select the Copy Files Needed to Run This Application option if you want to deploy only the files necessary to run the Web application.

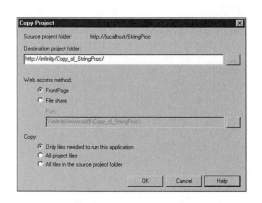

FIGURE 10.16
The Copy Project dialog box enables you to copy a Web project to the same server or to a different server.

Because the Copy Project command can also set the destination directory as an IIS application, it saves an extra step that would ordinarily be required when you use XCOPY or FTP to manually copy the files. As a Visual Studio .NET developer, this command is an easy way to transfer your application quickly to a different computer and test the results.

However, this technique may not be sufficient to deploy a Web service on the production Web server because the Copy Project command does not provide any options for configuring the settings of the virtual directory, such as an option for configuring directory security. In addition, the Copy Project command still shares many of the same limitations of the XCOPY command that were mentioned in the previous section.

Deploying a Web Service by Using a Windows Installer Package

Another option for deploying a Web service is by using the Visual Studio .NET Web setup project. You can use the various editors available in the Web setup project to automate most of the steps required for deploying a Web service to the target computer.

In Step-by-Step 10.16, you use the Web setup project to create a Windows Installer setup package for deploying the Northwind Web service that you created in Chapter 4, "Basic Web Services." You use the File System Editor to copy all the required files and use the Launch Conditions Editor to ensure that the Web service is installed on the target computer only if the target computer has support for Microsoft Data Access Components (MDAC) 2.7.

STEP BY STEP

10.16 Creating a Web Setup Project for the Northwind Web Service

1. Right-click the solution and select Add, Add Existing Project in Solution Explorer. Browse to the `C:\Inetpub\Northwind` directory and add the `Northwind` Web service project (created in Chapter 4) to the solution.

2. Add a new project to the solution. Select Setup and Deployment Projects from the Project Types tree and then select Web Setup Project from the list of templates on the right, as shown in Figure 10.17.

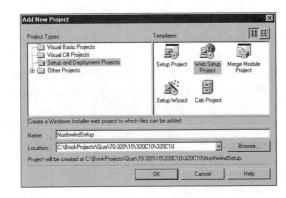

FIGURE 10.17
The Web Setup Project can be used to deploy a Web service application.

continues

continued

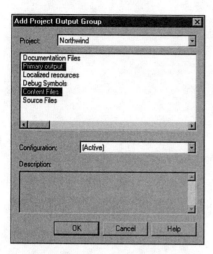

FIGURE 10.18
The Add Project Output Group dialog box enables you to add Web project resources to the Web Setup project.

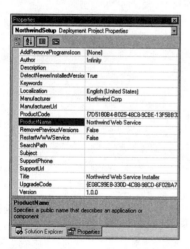

FIGURE 10.19
The Properties window enables you to set properties of the Web Setup project.

3. In Solution Explorer, right-click the project and select Add, Project Output from the context menu. This opens the Add Project Output Group dialog box, as shown in Figure 10.18. Select Northwind as the Project and select Primary Output and Content Files from the list box. Click OK.

4. Select the project in Solution Explorer. Activate the Properties window. Set the Manufacturer to Northwind Corp and the ProductName to Northwind Web Service and Title to Northwind Web Service Installer, as shown in Figure 10.19.

5. Open the File System Editor for the NorthwindSetup project by clicking the File System Editor icon in Solution Explorer. Select the Web Application Folder under the File System on the Target Machine node in the left pane of the editor.

6. Invoke the Properties window. Change the VirtualDirectory property to NorthwindApp, as shown in Figure 10.20.

7. Open the Launch Conditions Editor for the NorthwindSetup project by clicking the Launch Conditions Editor icon in Solution Explorer.

8. Select the Requirements on Target Machine node and select Action, Add Registry Launch Condition. This adds two nodes, one under the Search Target Machine node and another under the Launch Conditions node.

9. Select the newly created node under the Search Target Machine node and open the Properties window. Set the Name property to Search for MDAC Support, the Property property to MDACSUPPORT, the RegKey property to Software\Microsoft\DataAccess, the Root property to vsdrrHKLM, and the `Value` property to `FullInstallVer`, as shown in Figure 10.21.

FIGURE 10.20▲
You can configure some of the IIS settings through the properties of the Web Application Folder of the Web setup project.

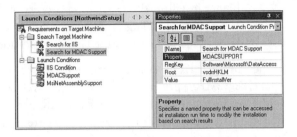

FIGURE 10.21▲
You can perform a search on Registry on the target Web server during the installation process via the Launch Conditions Editor.

10. Select the newly created node under the Launch Conditions Node and open the Properties window. Set the `Name` property to `MDACSupport`, the `Condition` property to `MDACSUPPORT >= "2.7"` and the `Message` property to `You must have MDAC version 2.7 or higher installed on this computer. Please contact the administrator for installation information.`, as shown in Figure 10.22.

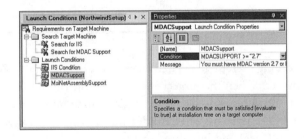

FIGURE 10.22◀
You can add launch conditions on the target Web server during the installation process via the Launch Conditions Editor.

11. Build the `NorthwindSetup` project. Open Windows Explorer and navigate to the `Release` folder inside the project folder. Run `setup.exe`. Alternatively, on the development machine, you can install by right-clicking the project in Solution Explorer and choosing the Install option from the context menu. This opens the Northwind Web Service Setup Wizard with a welcome screen. Click Next. The Select Installation Address screen appears, as shown in Figure 10.23. Select the default settings and click Next. Click Next again to start the installation. Click Close.

NOTE

Configuring IIS Settings In the case of Web applications and Web services, you may need to configure IIS settings as part of the deployment process. You can use the properties of the Web Application Folder in the Web setup project to accomplish this, as shown in Figure 10.20.

continues

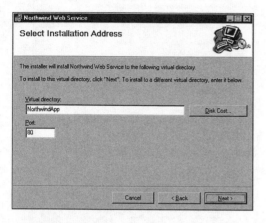

FIGURE 10.23
The Select Installation Address screen prompts the user to specify the virtual directory during the installation process.

> **WARNING**
>
> **Choosing a Virtual Directory** If you are testing your project and deploying the Web application on the same machine, make sure that you don't choose an existing virtual directory because you might lose the existing files in that directory.

continued

Note that if the target computer does not have MDAC 2.7 or higher installed, the installation process of the `NorthwindSetup` project fails and you get the error message set in the `Message` property of the launch condition.

12. Open Internet Explorer and navigate to `http://local-host/NorthwindApp/Customer.asmx`. (If the Web server is different from the local machine, substitute the server name for `localhost`.) Verify that the `GetCustomers()` Web method works as expected.

13. Select Settings, Control Panel, Add/Remove Programs from the Windows start menu to open the Add/Remove Programs dialog box. Select the Change or Remove Programs Icon from the left pane and select the Northwind Web Service application from the right pane. Click the Remove button to uninstall the Northwind Web Service application and click the Yes button. The Northwind Web Service application will be uninstalled from your application. Alternatively, on the development machine, you can also uninstall by right-clicking the setup project in Solution Explorer and choosing the Uninstall option from its context menu.

The preceding exercise illustrated the process of creating a Web setup project. When the project is compiled, the output files are placed in the `Release` or `Debug` folder, depending on the active configuration. The contents of the folder are an installer package (`.msi`), executables (`.exe`) and initialization (`.ini`) files. The `.msi` file is the installation package in the Microsoft Windows Installer format. If the Windows Installer Service is installed on your computer, you can directly start the installation by double-clicking this file. The executable files consist of `Setup.exe`, `InstMsiA.exe`, and `InstMsiW.exe`. `Setup.exe` (also called the Windows Installer Bootstrapper) bootstraps the installation process by first testing for the presence of the Windows Installer service on the target machine. If the Windows Installer service is not installed, the bootstrapper will first install it using either `InstMsiA.exe` (for Windows 9x and Me) or

InstMsiW.exe (for Windows NT/2000/XP/.NET), and then instruct the Windows Installer service to execute the installation based on the information stored in the installation package (.msi file). The setup.ini file stores the initialization settings, such as name of the installation database, for the bootstrap file setup.exe.

But there is one catch here. This setup project works only on computers where the .NET Framework runtime has been installed already. In fact, when you build the setup project, you will see the following message in the Output window of Visual Studio .NET:

> WARNING: This setup does not contain the .NET Framework which must be installed on the target machine by running dotnetfx.exe before this setup will install. You can find dotnetfx.exe on the Visual Studio .NET 'Windows Components Update' media. Dotnetfx.exe can be redistributed with your setup.

On the other hand, when you look at the Web setup project folder in the Solution Explorer window, you will see that it had created a Detected Dependencies folder and included a file named dotnetfxredist_x86_enu.msm in it. But the Exclude property of this file is set to true. This is just a placeholder module that stops Visual Studio .NET from automatically including the .NET Framework files from your installation of the .NET Framework into the project. If you try changing the Exclude property of the dotnetfxredist_x86_enu.msm file to false, Visual Studio .NET won't allow you and you will get an error at the time of building the project. The error message would say "ERROR: dotNETFXRedist_x86_enu.msm must not be used to redistribute the .NET Framework. Please exclude this merge module." Ideally, you should leave the Exclude property at its default value of true for the dotNETFXRedist_x86_enu.msm dependency.

Actually, the .NET Framework is a complex system, and installing the .NET Framework by just redistributing the files is not enough to get it to work successfully on the target machine. The merge module dotNETFXRedist_x86_enu.msm is included in the setup project as a proxy to prevent the dependency resolution system from detecting some of the .NET framework files and attempting to redistribute them as part of the setup package.

Ideally, the .NET Framework must be installed separately. There are several ways to accomplish this:

▶ Ask the user to run setup for .NET Framework from the Windows Component Upgrade CD that comes with Visual Studio .NET.

▶ Ask the user to download the .NET Framework from the Microsoft MSDN Download Center or from the Microsoft Windows Update Website, `http://windowsupdate.microsoft.com`.

▶ Use the .NET Framework bootstrapper (`Setup.exe`) that checks for the availability of the .NET Framework and installs it if it is not already installed.

Of course, for a professional setup program, you would not like to leave it to the users to perform a manual installation of the .NET Framework. Using the .NET Framework bootstrapper `Setup.exe` is a good idea. Microsoft provides a sample bootstrapper `Setup.exe` that you can readily use in your projects. I will tell you where to get and how to use this bootstrapper `Setup.exe` later in this chapter in Exercise 1. For now, I will assume that the .NET Framework is available on the machine where you will deploy your applications.

You can modify the configuration settings for a Web setup project by selecting the project in Solution Explorer and choosing Project, Properties from the main menu. This opens up the Project Property Pages dialog box as shown in Figure 10.24.

FIGURE 10.24

The Property Pages dialog box displays the configuration properties of the Web setup project.

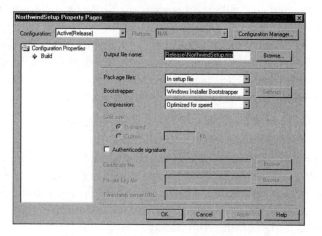

There are five main configuration properties:

▶ Output file name—Specifies the output filename of the installation package (.msi file).

▶ Package files—Specifies how to package the files. The options are, As Loose Uncompressed Files, In Setup File, and In Cabinet File(s). If the In Cabinet File(s) option is selected, then you can also specify the maximum size of the cab files.

▶ Bootstrapper—Specifies whether any bootstrap file needs to be created for launching the installation program. A bootstrap is required when the target machine does not have the Windows Installer service already installed. The None option generates only the installation package (.msi file). The Windows Installer Bootstrapper option creates a Setup.exe file capable of installing the Windows Installer service if that is not already installed.

▶ Compression—Specifies whether to optimize the installation files for size or speed or whether no optimization is required. The value Optimized for Speed uses a faster compression algorithm that unpacks the files quickly at install time. A faster compression algorithm usually results in a larger installation file. The value Optimized for Size uses a compression algorithm that runs more slowly but packs the files tightly. If None is selected then no optimization is performed.

▶ Authenticode signature—Enables you to specify the file containing the Authenticode certificate, Private key file, and the Timestamp server URL (provided by the certification authority).

The output files generated can be deployed (copied) to any target machine and then installed and later uninstalled. When an application is uninstalled, all the actions performed by the installer application during the installation on the target machine are undone, leaving the target machine to its original state. You can also choose to repair or re-install the application by clicking the Change button in the Add/Remove Programs dialog box.

> **NOTE**
>
> **Use Application Center to Deploy Web Applications and Windows Services to a Web Farm or a Cluster** Microsoft Application Center provides the synchronization capability to manage the deployment process across multiple servers in a Web farm or a clustered environment. For example, you can script Application Center to apply specific IIS settings on a Web server's virtual directory and the Application center will take care of applying that setting to all the Web servers involved. For more information on Application Center, see www. microsoft.com/applicationcenter.

Publishing Web Services

Before other developers can use a Web service, they must know about its location. You can provide a discovery mechanism on the Web server by deploying a discovery file (.disco) on your Web server or by registering the Web service in the UDDI Registry. For more information about how to publish Web service discovery information, refer to Chapter 4.

GUIDED PRACTICE EXERCISE 10.1

Visual Studio .NET provides a Setup Wizard template in the Setup and Deployment Project category. The Setup Wizard template simplifies the process of creating a setup package using a step-by-step approach.

In this exercise, you are required to create a Windows Installer–based setup package for the StringProc Web service that you created in Chapter 4.

How would you create a setup package using the setup wizard?

In this exercise, you will practice creating a setup package by using the setup wizard. You should try working through this problem on your own first. If you get stuck, or if you'd like to see one possible solution, follow these steps:

1. Right-click the solution and select Add, Add Existing Project in Solution Explorer. Browse to the C:\Inetpub\StringProc directory and add the StringProc Web service project (created in Chapter 4) to the solution.

2. Add a new project to the solution. Select Setup and Deployment Projects from the Project Types tree and then select Setup Wizard from the list of templates on the right.

3. Name the project StringProcSetup. Click OK. The Setup Wizard appears. The first screen of the wizard is the Welcome screen. Click Next.

4. The second screen of the wizard is the Choose a Project Type screen. Choose Create a Setup for a Web Application from the first group of options, as shown in Figure 10.25. Click Next.

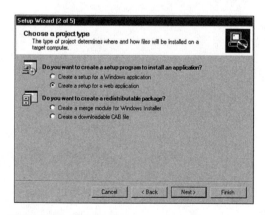

FIGURE 10.25
The Choose a Project Type screen in the setup wizard prompts the user to select the project type.

5. The third page of the wizard is the Choose Project Outputs to Include screen. Select Primary Output from StringProc and Content Files from StringProc, as shown in Figure 10.26. Click Next.

6. The fourth page of the wizard is the Choose Files to Include screen. Click Next.

7. The final page of the wizard is the Project Summary screen, as shown in Figure 10.27. Click Finish to create the project.

8. Select the new project StringProcSetup in Solution Explorer. Activate the Properties window. Set Manufacturer to StringProc Corp, ProductName to StringProc Web Service, and Title to StringProc Web Service Installer.

9. Open the File System Editor for the StringProcSetup project by clicking the File System Editor icon in Solution Explorer. Select the Web Application Folder under the File System on Target Machine node in the left pane of the editor. Invoke the Properties window. Change the VirtualDirectory property to StringProcApp.

10. Build the StringProcSetup project. Right-click the project in Solution Explorer and select the Install option. Install the project.

11. Open Internet Explorer and navigate to http://localhost/StringProcApp/Strings.asmx. (If the Web server is different from the local machine, substitute the server name for localhost.) Verify that the Web Service works as expected.

If you have difficulty following this exercise, review the sections "Deploying a Web Service" and "Using Visual Studio .NET to Create a Windows Installer Package" earlier in this chapter. After doing that review, try this exercise again.

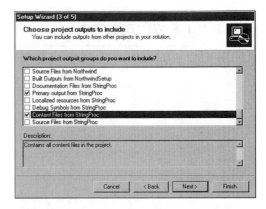

FIGURE 10.26
The Choose Project Outputs to Include screen in the setup wizard prompts the user to select the project output that the installer will deploy.

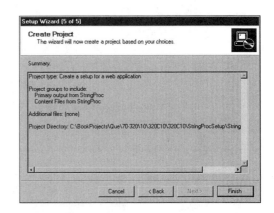

FIGURE 10.27
The Project Summary screen in the setup wizard shows the summary of the files to be included in the setup project.

▶ When you deploy a Web service by manually copying the files, you need to manually create the virtual directory and set the virtual directory as an IIS application. The Visual Studio .NET Copy Project command does this automatically for you. The Web setup project provides the maximum configuration options and total control over the installation process.

▶ Visual Studio .NET setup projects do not package the .NET Framework files for redistribution. You should ensure that the .NET Framework is already installed on the target machine, or better yet, you should use a bootstrapper program that installs the .NET Framework, if necessary, prior to installing the .NET application.

▶ If you want other developers to be able to locate and use your Web service, consider publishing your Web service to the UDDI registry.

CREATING INSTALLATION COMPONENTS

When you deploy an application, you may want to take certain customized actions during the installation process. Some examples of customized actions include registering a Windows service with the Service Control Manager, registering a serviced component with COM+ Explorer, creating a database, installing event logs, installing performance counters, and so on.

The .NET Framework provides you with an `Installer` class to help you perform customized installation actions such as those mentioned above. The `Installer` class is defined in the `System.Configuration.Install` namespace.

Understanding the `Installer` Class

The `System.Configuration.Install.Installer` class works as a base class for all the custom installers in the .NET Framework. Some of the important members of the `Installer` class that I will discuss in this chapter are listed in Table 10.3.

TABLE 10.3

IMPORTANT MEMBERS OF THE `Installer` CLASS

Member Name	Type	Description
Commit	Method	The code in the `Commit()` method is executed if the `Install()` method executes successfully.
Install	Method	Performs the specified actions during an application's installation.
Installers	Property	Collection of `Installer` objects that are needed for this `Installer` instance to successfully install a component.
Rollback	Method	If the `Install()` method fails for some reason, the code in the `Rollback()` method is called to undo any custom actions performed during the `Install` method.
Uninstall	Method	Performs the specified actions when a previously installed application is uninstalled.

You can derive a class from the `Installer` class and override the methods given in Table 10.3 to perform any custom actions.

If you want the derived installer class to execute when an assembly is installed, whether by using setup projects or by using the Installer Tool (`installutil.exe`), then you need to decorate the class with the `RunInstaller` attribute set to `true`:

```
[RunInstaller(true)]
```

The installer classes provide the infrastructure for making installation a transactional process. If an error is encountered during the `Install()` method, the `Rollback()` method tracks back all the changes and undoes them to leave the machine in the same clean state as it was before the process of installation started. The `Rollback()` method must know the order in which the installation steps were performed and exactly what changes were made so that it can undo those changes in the proper order.

Similarly, when an application is uninstalled, the `Uninstall()` method of the `Installer` class is called. The responsibility of the `Uninstall()` method is again to undo the changes done by the installation process so that the machine is left as clean as if the program had never been installed on it.

A question arises: How does the Install() method communicate its installation information to the Rollback() and Uninstall() methods? This question becomes even more interesting when you see that the Install() and Uninstall() methods are not called in the same process. Install() is called when the application is installed, whereas Uninstall() is called when the application is uninstalled. These two events might be separated by several days and computer restarts.

The Install() method communicates the installation state by persisting it in a file with the extension .InstallState. This file is placed in the installation directory of the application. The Installer class makes this file available to each of the Install(), Commit(), Rollback(), and Uninstall() methods by passing an IDictionary object to the contents of this file. Content in the .InstallState file is used by the Rollback() and Uninstall() methods to perform the required cleanup operation.

Predefined Installation Components

The .NET Framework provides five predefined installation components. Each of these installation components as listed in Table 10.4 is associated with a specific server component.

TABLE 10.4

PREDEFINED INSTALLATION COMPONENTS

Installer Name	Description
EventLogInstaller	Enables you to install and configure a custom event log. This class belongs to the System.Diagnostics namespace.
MessageQueueInstaller	Enables you to install and configure a message queue. This class belongs to the System.Messaging namespace.
PerformanceCounterInstaller	Enables you to install and configure a custom performance counter. This class belongs to the System.Diagnostics namespace.

Installer Name	Description
ServiceInstaller	Enables you to install a Windows service contained in a Windows service application. This class does work specific to the Windows service with which it is associated. The ServiceInstaller class belongs to the System.ServiceProcess namespace.
ServiceProcessInstaller	Enables you to install a Windows service application. This class does work common to all Windows services in an executable. The ServiceProcessInstaller class belongs to the System.ServiceProcess namespace.

Visual Studio .NET does not automatically add an installer for a server component, but it's easy to add one. For example, if you create a new Windows service project and access the Properties window for the project, you see a link as shown in Figure 10.28 to add predefined installer classes for the Windows service in the project.

Clicking on the Add Installer link adds an instance of the predefined installation component to a class named ProjectInstaller in your project. You can add as many instances of the installation components to the ProjectInstaller class as you need. Each instance of a predefined installation component is set with properties that help in re-creating that object on the production machine. All the installation components are added to the Installers collection of the ProjectInstaller class. When you compile the project to build an EXE or a DLL file, the ProjectInstaller class is now part of the output assembly. The ProjectInstaller class has the RunInstaller attribute set to true, so at the time of installation, the ProjectInstaller class takes the responsibility of installing all the predefined installation components in an assembly.

You'll learn how to use predefined installation components to install a Windows service in a forthcoming section, "Deploying a Windows Service."

FIGURE 10.28
You can add a predefined installer for a server component by clicking on the Add Installer hyperlink in the Properties window.

Custom Installation Components

You can also add a custom installer class to a project to perform custom actions during installation, such as compiling the code to a native image or creating a database on a target computer. These installer classes are compiled with your project and are then added to the deployment project as custom actions that are run at the end of the installation. You need to do the following to create a custom installer class:

1. Inherit a class from the `Installer` class.

2. Makes sure that the `RunInstaller` attribute is set to `true` in the derived class.

3. Override the `Install()`, `Commit()`, `Rollback()`, and `Uninstall()` methods to perform any custom actions.

4. In the setup project, use the Custom Actions Editor to invoke this derived class to do the required processing.

5. If needed, pass arguments from the Custom Actions Editor to the custom `Installer` class by using the `CustomActionData` property.

You'll learn how to use the preceding steps to create a custom installer class in a forthcoming section, "Deploying a Serviced Component."

Deploying an Assembly Containing the Installation Components

You can deploy an assembly containing installation components in one of the following two ways:

▶ By Using the Setup and Deployment Project Templates—To deploy an application that consists of installation components, you create a setup package by using the Setup and Deployment Project templates as you would do normally. But this time, you use the Custom Actions Editor to deploy the resources specified by the installer class. At the time of deployment, the setup program executes the `ProjectInstaller` class as a part of its custom installation action to create component resources. Step-by-Step 13.17 shows you how.

▶ By Using the Installer Tool (`installutil.exe`)—You can also use the command line Installer Tool (`installutil.exe`) to install the assemblies that contain additional component resources. To install the resources contained in an assembly named `Assembly1.dll`, you can use the following form of the `installutil.exe` command:

```
installutil.exe Assembly1.dll
```

You can also install resources contained in multiple assemblies together, like

```
installutil.exe Assembly1.dll
➥Assembly2.dll Assembly3.dll
```

If you instead want to launch the uninstaller for installation classes stored in an assembly, you use the `/u` or `/uninstall` option with the command, like

```
installutil.exe /u Assembly1.dll
```

I already discussed using the Installer tool (`installutil.exe`) in Chapter 6, "Windows Services." In the following section, I'll use Visual Studio .NET setup and deployment projects to install the installation components.

DEPLOYING A WINDOWS SERVICE

Create a setup program that installs a Windows service, a serviced component, a .NET Remoting object, and an XML Web service.

- **Register components and assemblies.**

Configure client computers and servers to use a Windows service, a serviced component, a .NET Remoting object, and an XML Web service.

Unlike a Web service, a Windows service application is installed in a directory on the file system of the target computer. You therefore use a Setup Project template rather than a Web Setup Project template to deploy a Windows service.

In addition, you also need to register a Windows service with the Windows Service Control Manager. The .NET Framework provides custom installation components to take care of this. You can install these components by configuring them as a custom action in the Custom Actions Editor of the setup projects.

I already discussed how to install a Windows service in Chapter 6. For background, I recommend you complete Step-by-Step 6.1 and Step-by-Step 6.2, if you have not already done so. In this section, I'll use the `OrderService` Windows service from Chapter 6 and discuss how to package it in a Windows installer package.

STEP BY STEP

10.17 Creating a Setup Project for the `OrderService` Windows Service

1. Add an existing Windows service project `StepByStep6_1` (`OrderService`, created in Chapter 6) to the solution.

2. Launch WordPad and create and add a file named `License.rtf` to the `StepByStep6_1` project folder with the following text:

```
OrderService End User License Agreement
You should carefully read the following terms and
conditions before using this software.
If you do not agree to any of the terms of this
License, then do not install, distribute, or use this
copy of OrderService. This software, and all
accompanying files, data, and materials, are
distributed AS IS and with no warranties
of any kind, whether express or implied. Good data
processing procedure dictates that any program be
thoroughly tested with non-critical data before
relying on it. The user must assume the entire risk
of using the program.
(c) All rights reserved.
```

3. Add a new project to the solution. In the Add Project dialog box, select Setup and Deployment projects from the Project Types tree and select Setup Project from the list of templates on the right. Name the project `OrderServiceSetup`.

4. In Solution Explorer, right-click the project and select Add, Project Output from the context menu. In the Add Project Output Group dialog box, select `StepByStep6_1` as the project and select Primary Output from the list box. Click OK.

5. In Solution Explorer, right-click the project and select Add, File from the context menu. In the Add Files dialog box, select the `License.rtf` added to the `StepByStep6_1` project in step 2. Click Open.

6. Select the `OrderServiceSetup` project in Solution Explorer. Open the User Interface Editor by clicking the User Interface Editor icon in Solution Explorer.

7. Right-click the Start node under the Install tree and select Add Dialog from the context menu. The Add Dialog dialog box appears. Select License Agreement, as shown in Figure 10.29. Click OK. Right-click License Agreement and choose Move Up twice to move the License Agreement dialog box to appear after the Welcome dialog box as shown in Figure 10.30. Select the `LicenseFile` property in the Properties window and select (Browse...) from the drop-down list. The Select Item in Project dialog box appears. Navigate to the Application Folder and select `License.rtf`.

8. Open the Custom Actions Editor by clicking the Custom Actions Editor icon in Solution Explorer.

9. Right-click the Custom Actions node in the editor and select Add Custom Action from the context menu. In the Select Item in the project dialog box, select Primary output from StepByStep6_1 (Active) under the Application Folder. Click OK.

10. Select the new project in Solution Explorer. Activate the Properties window. Set `Manufacturer` to `OrderService Corp`, set `ProductName` to `OrderService`, and `Title` to `OrderService Windows Service`.

11. Build the `OrderServiceSetup` project. Install the project. A License Agreement screen appears. Only when you select the I Agree option is the Next button enabled, as shown in Figure 10.31.

continues

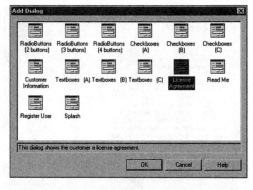

FIGURE 10.29
You can use the Add Dialog dialog box to add dialog boxes in the User Interface Editor.

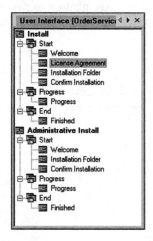

FIGURE 10.30
You can customize the user interface of the installation program via the User Interface Editor.

NOTE

The `LicenseFile` Property   The `LicenseFile` property of the License Agreement dialog box works only with Rich Text Format (RTF) files. If you specify a file of any other format, you don't get any error, but the contents of the file are not displayed in the license agreement.

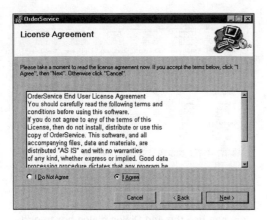

FIGURE 10.31
The customized License Agreement dialog box is added to the user interface to display the license agreement during the installation process.

continued

12. Click Next and you should see the Select Installation Folder screen, as shown in Figure 10.32. Change the installation folder if you want to and click Next and then click Close.

13. Open the Services administrative tool from the Administrative tools section of the Windows Control Panel. You should see the OrderService being added to the Services on the target machine.

In Step-by-Step 10.17, you learned how to use the Custom Actions Editor to install the predefined installation component. In addition, you also learned how to use the User Interface Editor to display custom screens, such as a License Agreement screen, during the setup process.

REVIEW BREAK

▶ Installation components enable you to take custom actions during the setup of an application. The .NET Framework provides a few predefined installer components for use with server components. You can also create custom installation components by deriving from the Installer class.

▶ The Windows Installer Service and the Installer tool (installutil.exe) perform installation in a transactional manner.

▶ If you want a custom installer class to execute when an assembly is installed—whether you use the setup projects or the Installer tool—then you need to apply the RunInstaller attribute to the class and set its value to true.

▶ You use the Setup Project template to create a setup program for a Windows Service.

DEPLOYING A SERVICED COMPONENT

Create a setup program that installs a Windows service, a serviced component, a .NET Remoting object, and an XML Web service.

- **Register components and assemblies.**

Configure client computers and servers to use a Windows service, a serviced component, a .NET Remoting object, and an XML Web service.

The two main steps to deploy a serviced component are as follows:

1. Register the serviced component with the COM+ catalog—There are three different ways for registration:

   - Lazy Registration—The .NET Framework automatically registers a serviced component with the COM+ catalog when the component is requested for the first time. The registration of a component requires administrative privileges and the component registration will fail if that application's first user does not have administrative privileges. This option may be used while developing or testing a component but is not a good idea for deployment.

   - Manual Registration—You can use the Component Services administrative tool (regsvcs.exe) to manually register a serviced component with the COM+ catalog. This technique of registration is useful in combination with XCOPY deployment of the serviced component.

   - Programmatic Registration—You can use the RegistrationHelper class to programmatically register a serviced component with the COM+ catalog. This registration technique is what you will use when creating a Windows Installer–based setup package for the deployment of a serviced component.

2. Install the serviced component assembly at a location where the CLR can locate it—Where the CLR locates an assembly also depends on the program that makes the request to an assembly. Therefore, the installation location may depend on how the component is registered with the COM+ catalog. There are two ways to register a serviced component in the COM+ catalog:

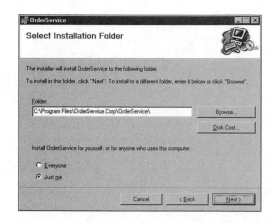

FIGURE 10.32
The Select Installation Folder screen enables the user to specify a custom installation folder during the installation process.

- Library Application—The serviced component, which is installed as a library application, is created in the process of the calling application. In this case, the serviced component may be deployed as a private application within the calling application directory structure. But if the serviced component is used by multiple calling applications, rather than introduce redundancy by copying the serviced component in the directory of each calling application, it is a better idea to install the serviced component in the GAC.

- Server Application—The serviced component, which is installed as a server application, is created in the process of dllhost.exe, which is located in the Windows System directory. Obviously, a better installation choice in this case also is the GAC.

From the preceding list, it is clear that in most cases you would install a serviced component assembly in the GAC. You would also either use the Component Services administrative tool for registration of a serviced component in the COM+ catalog, or you would use the RegistrationHelper class when programmatically registering a serviced component—for example, when registering through a setup program. I already covered the basics of COM+ catalog registration and discussed the use of the Component Services administrative tool in Chapter 7, "Component Services."

In this chapter, I'll cover the following two techniques to deploy a serviced component:

▶ Using a Visual Studio .NET setup and deployment project

▶ Using the Component Services administrative tool

Using a Visual Studio .NET Setup and Deployment Project to Deploy a Serviced Component

Step-by-Step 10.18 shows how to deploy a serviced component. In this exercise, you use a Visual Studio .NET setup project to deploy a serviced component. If the serviced component is deployed as a part of a Web application, you can also use a Web setup project for its deployment.

STEP BY STEP

10.18 Creating a Setup Project for the `NorthwindSC` Serviced Component

1. Add an existing Windows service project `StepByStep7_8` (`NorthwindSC`, created in Chapter 7) to the solution.

2. Right-click the project `StepByStep7_8` and choose Add, Add New Item from the context menu. The Add New Item dialog box appears. Select Installer Class from the right pane. Name the new class `NorthwindSCInstaller.cs`.

3. Add a reference to the `System.Windows.Forms.dll` to the `StepByStep7_8` project by using the Add Reference dialog box.

4. Open the `NorthwindSCInstaller.cs` file in the code view and add the following `using` directive:

```
using System.EnterpriseServices;
using System.Windows.Forms;
```

5. Add the following code after the Component Designer–generated code section in the class definition:

```
public override void Install(
    System.Collections.IDictionary stateSaver)
{
    try
    {
        string application = null;
        string tlbimp = null;

        // Get the location of the assembly
        string scassembly =
            GetType().Assembly.Location;

        // Install the assembly in the COM+ catalog
        RegistrationHelper rh =
            new RegistrationHelper();
        rh.InstallAssembly(scassembly,
            ref application, ref tlbimp,
            InstallationFlags.
            FindOrCreateTargetApplication);

        // Save the application name and assembly
        // location in the InstallState file
        stateSaver["application"] = application;
        stateSaver["scassembly"] = scassembly;
    }
```

continues

continued

```
            catch(Exception ex)
            {
                MessageBox.Show(
                    ex.Message, "Install Exception");
            }
        }

        public override void Uninstall(
            System.Collections.IDictionary savedState)
        {
            try
            {
                // Retrieve the application name and assembly
                // location from the InstallState file
                string application =
                    (string) savedState["application"];
                string scassembly =
                    (string) savedState["scassembly"];

                // Uninstall the assembly from the COM+ catalog
                RegistrationHelper rh =
                    new RegistrationHelper();
                rh.UninstallAssembly(scassembly, application);
            }
            catch(Exception ex)
            {
                MessageBox.Show(
                    ex.Message, "Uninstall Exception");
            }
        }
```

6. Build the `StepByStep7_8` project.

7. Add a new project to the solution. In the Add Project dialog box, select Setup and Deployment Projects from the Project Types tree and select Setup Project from the list of templates on the right. Name the project `NorthwindSCSetup`.

8. In Solution Explorer, right-click the project and select Add, Project Output from the context menu. In the Add Project Output Group dialog box, select `StepByStep7_8` as the project and select Primary Output from the list box. Click OK.

9. Open the Custom Actions Editor for the `NorthwindSCSetup` project. Right-click the Install node under the Custom Actions node and then select Add Custom Action from the shortcut menu. The Select Item

in Project dialog box appears. Look in the Application Folder and select Primary Output from StepByStep7_8 (Active). Click OK. The primary output is added to the Install node.

10. Now select the Uninstall node and select Add Custom Action from the context menu. The Select Item in Project dialog box appears. Look in the Application Folder and select Primary Output from StepByStep7_8 (Active). Click OK. The primary output is now also added to the Uninstall node, as shown in Figure 10.33.

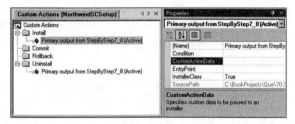

FIGURE 10.33
You can perform custom actions by using the Custom Actions Editor.

11. Open the File System Editor for the NorthwindSCSetup project. Select the File System on Target Machine node and choose Add Special Folder, Global Assembly Cache Folder from the context menu. Select the Global Assembly Cache Folder and select Add, Project Output from the context menu.

12. The Add Project Output Group dialog box appears. Select the StepByStep7_8 project and select Primary Output from the list of items to be added. Click OK. The File System Editor now appears as shown in Figure 10.34.

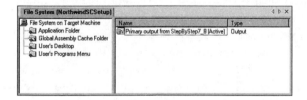

FIGURE 10.34
You can add files to special folders on the target machine by using the File System Editor.

continues

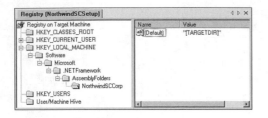

FIGURE 10.35
You can set the keys and values in the Registry with the help of the Registry Editor.

> ⚠ **WARNING**
>
> **Working with the Registry** Be extra careful when working with the Windows Registry. Take special care with the `DeleteAtUninstall` property of the Registry Settings Properties. Setting `DeleteAtUninstall` to true for a wrong key (such as `HKEY_LOCAL_MACHINE\SOFTWARE`) might have a very bad impact on the target computer.

continued

13. Open the Registry Editor for the `NorthwindSCSetup` project. Select the `HKEY_LOCAL_MACHINE` node and hierarchically add new keys to the node in the order `HKEY_LOCAL_MACHINE`, `Software`, `Microsoft`, `.NETFramework`, `AssemblyFolders`, and `NorthwindSCCorp`, as shown in Figure 10.35.

14. Add a new string value to the newly added `NorthwindSCCorp` key. Select the value and invoke the Properties window. Empty the `Name` property. When you do this, the `(Default)` name of the value is set (refer to Figure 10.35). Set the `Value` property to `[TARGETDIR]`. This is the folder where the assembly file copy is stored, along with the GAC.

15. Select the new project in Solution Explorer. Activate the Properties window. Set `Manufacturer` to `NorthwindSC Corp`, set `ProductName` to `NorthwindSC Serviced Component`, and set `Title` to `NorthwindSC Serviced Component Installer`.

16. Build the `NorthwindSCSetup` project. Install the project.

17. Open the Component Services administrative tool from the Administrative Tools section of the Windows Control Panel. You should see the `NorthwindSC` component in the `Northwind Data Application with Object Pooling` application is being added to the Component Services on the target machine.

In Step-by-Step 10.18, you used a custom installer component to register the serviced component with the help of the `RegistrationHelper` class. The Installer component is stored in the assembly of the serviced component itself. In the Custom Actions Editor, you add the output of this project to the `Install` and the `Uninstall` node. This instructs the setup program to activate the `Install()` and `Uninstall()` methods from the assembly at the time of deployment.

In Step-by-Step 10.18, you also learned how to place assemblies in the GAC. You learned how to make entries to the Windows

Registry. You added a Registry, which enables the serviced component assembly to be automatically displayed in the Visual Studio .NET Add Reference dialog box.

Using the Component Services Administrative Tool to Deploy a Serviced Component

The Component Services administrative tool provides a wizard to export a configured application as a Windows Installer package. This tool also provides a wizard to create a new COM+ application based on the information stored in a Windows Installer package. This deployment technique is most useful for transferring already configured COM+ applications from one computer to another. You can export the configured application as a Windows Installer package from one computer. Transfer the package to another computer and then use the COM+ Install wizard to create a new COM+ application based on it.

However, this COM+ Install wizard is of little use in installing new serviced components from a Windows Installer package that is created by Visual Studio .NET setup projects because COM+ can't recognize that.

Step-by-Step 10.19 shows how to export a COM+ application as a Windows Installer package.

STEP BY STEP

10.19 Using the Component Services Tool to Create an Installation Package for the `NorthwindSC` Serviced Component

1. Open the Component Services administrative tool from the Administrative Tools section of the Windows Control Panel.

continues

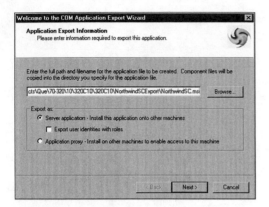

FIGURE 10.36
The Application Export Wizard screen of the wizard enables you to specify information required to export the COM+ application.

continued

   2. Right-click the Northwind Data Application with Object Pooling (created in StepByStep7_8) in the Component Services administrative tool and select Export from the context menu.

   3. The welcome screen of the COM Application Export Wizard appears. Click Next.

   4. The second screen of the wizard is the Application Export Wizard screen. Enter the full path and filename where the package file needs to be exported, as shown in Figure 10.36. Also, in the Export as Group box, select the Server Application option (see Figure 10.36). Click Next and then click Finish.

   5. Browse to the destination folder, where the package files are exported. You should see two files, NorthwindSC.msi and NorthwindSC.msi.cab, being created.

Now you have all the settings for the COM+ application, as well as the DLL files for the serviced component, in the MSI file. Step-by-Step 10.20 shows how to use the Component Services administrative tool to create a new COM+ application based on the information in the MSI file.

STEP BY STEP

10.20 Installing an Installation Package for the NorthwindSC Serviced Component Created with the COM+ Application Export Wizard

   1. Open the Component Services administrative tool from the Administrative Tools section of the Windows Control Panel.

2. Right-click the COM+ Application node and select New, Application from the context menu.

3. The welcome screen of the COM Application Install Wizard appears. Click Next.

4. The second screen of the wizard is the Install or Create a New Application screen. Click the Install Pre-built Application(s) button, as shown in Figure 10.37.

5. This opens the Install from Application File dialog box. Browse and select the NorthwindSC.msi package created in Step-by-Step 10.19. The Select Application Files screen of the wizard with the application file appears as shown in Figure 10.38. Click Next.

6. The Set Application Identity screen of the wizard appears. Select the Interactive user option, as shown in Figure 10.39. You can also provide user and password details if you want to install the application with a different identity. Click Next.

7. The Application Installation Options screen of the wizard appears. Select the Specific Directory option and specify a desired install directory for the component files, as shown in Figure 10.40. Click Next and then click Finish.

You should see the COM+ application Northwind Data Application with Object Pooling being added to the Component Services on the target machine.

continues

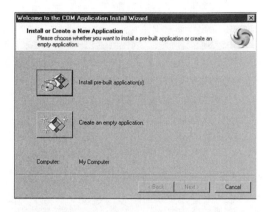

FIGURE 10.37
The Install or Create a New Application screen of the wizard enables you to install a pre-built application or create a new application.

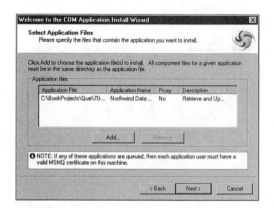

FIGURE 10.38
The Select Application Files screen of the wizard enables you to choose the files for the application you need to install.

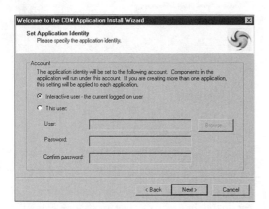

FIGURE 10.39
The Set Application Identity screen of the wizard enables you to specify the application identity.

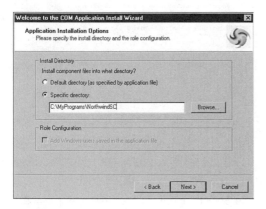

FIGURE 10.40
The Application Installation Options screen of the wizard enables you to specify the install directory and the role configuration.

continued

8. Browse to the install directory selected in step 7. You should see that two component files, `StepByStep7_8.dll` and `StepByStep7_8.tlb`, have been created.

Because the Component Services administrative tool was created before .NET, it does not allow you to install the assemblies in the GAC. If you want to use the COM+ Install wizard to install .NET applications, you must also take an extra step to register the serviced component in the GAC.

DEPLOYING A .NET REMOTING OBJECT

Create a setup program that installs a Windows service, a serviced component, a .NET Remoting object, and an XML Web service.

- **Register components and assemblies.**

Configure client computers and servers to use a Windows service, a serviced component, a .NET Remoting object, and an XML Web service.

A .NET remoting object is generally deployed with the server application that uses it. This server application may be created as a console application, a Windows application, a Windows service, or a Web application. Based on what you have studied so far, the process of deploying a .NET remoting object is very similar. I'll take most of the space in this section to demonstrate how to create and use a merge module.

Components such as serviced components and .NET remoting objects may be shared between multiple applications. You may want to distribute these components to be used by other developers as part of their applications. The process of packaging a component for reuse in other application is different from packaging a Windows application for deployment.

When you have a component that will be shared among multiple applications, you should package it as a merge module (.msm file). A merge module includes the actual component, such as a .dll file, along with any related setup logic, such as resources, Registry entries, custom actions, and launch conditions.

Merge modules cannot be installed directly. They need to be merged with the installation program of an application that uses the shared component and packaged into a merge module.

When you modify a component to release new versions, you create a new merge module for each of the new versions. A new merge module should be created for each successive version of a component to avoid version conflicts.

In this section, I'll package a remoting object created in Chapter 3, ".NET Remoting," as a merge module. Before proceeding further, you should complete all the Step-by-Step exercises of Chapter 3, if you have not completed them already.

STEP BY STEP

10.21 Creating a Merge Module Project for the DbConnect Remoting Object

1. Add existing remoting object projects StepByStep3_9 (the IDBConnect class created in Chapter 3) and StepByStep3_10 (the DbConnect class created in Chapter 3) to the solution.

2. Add a new project to the solution. In the Add Project dialog box, select Setup and Deployment Projects from the Project Types tree and select Merge Module Project from the list of templates on the right. Name the project DbConnectMergeModule.

3. In Solution Explorer, right-click the project and select Add, Project Output from the context menu. In the Add Project Output Group dialog box, select StepByStep3_10 as the project and select Primary Output from the list box. Click OK.

continues

continued

4. Build the `DbConnectMergeModule` project. Open Windows Explorer and navigate to the `Release` folder inside the project folder. Notice that the merge module `DbConnectMergeModule.msm` has been created.

In Step-by-Step 10.21, you create a simple Merge Module Project to package the `Dbconnect` remoting object. You can customize the merge module project just like any setup project discussed earlier in the chapter by using the File System Editor, Registry Editor, File Types Editor, and Custom Actions Editor.

If you later want to distribute the `DbConnect` remoting object with a remoting server application or any other application, you can just add the merge module created in Step-by-Step 10.21 to your application's setup project. Step-by-Step 10.22 shows you how to create a Web setup project that includes the merge module project for installing the `DbConnect` remoting component.

STEP BY STEP

10.22 Creating a Web Setup Project That Uses a Merge Module for Installing the DbConnect Remoting Object

1. Add existing remoting server project `StepByStep3_17` (provides hosting in IIS, created in Chapter 3) to the solution.

2. Add a new project to the solution. In the Add Project dialog box, select Setup and Deployment projects from the Project Types tree and select Setup Wizard from the list of templates on the right. Name the project `DbConnectServerSetup`.

3. In the wizard's welcome screen, click Next. In the wizard's Choose a Project Type screen choose Create a Setup for a Web Application from the first group of options. Click Next.

4. In the wizard's Choose Project Outputs to Include screen, select Primary Output from StepByStep3_17, Content Files from StepByStep3_17 and Merge Module from DbConnectMergeModule, as shown in Figure 10.41. Click Next, and then Next and then Finish.

5. Select the setup project `DbConnectServerSetup` in Solution Explorer. Activate the Properties window. Set `Manufacturer` to `DbConnect Corp`, `ProductName` to `DbConnect Server`, and `Title` to `DbConnect Remoting Server Installer`.

6. Open the File System Editor for the `DbConnectServerSetup` Project. Change the `VirtualDirectory` project of the `Web Application Folder` to `DbConenctServer`.

7. Build the `DbConnectServerSetup` project. Install the project. The remoting object is now available at `http://localhost/DbConnectServer/DbConnect.rem`.

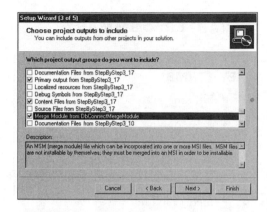

FIGURE 10.41
Merge module is added to a setup project for deployment.

You will of course need a .NET remoting client to access the URL in Step-by-Step 10.22. For more details on this, refer to Chapter 3.

R E V I E W   B R E A K

▶ To deploy a serviced component, you must register the component with the COM+ catalog and should install the component in the GAC.

▶ How you deploy a .NET remoting object depends mostly on the application that uses it. Remoting configuration is all stored in XML configuration files; therefore, no extra registration steps are required.

▶ When you have a component that will be shared among multiple applications, you should package it as a merge module (`.msm` file). Merge modules cannot be directly installed; instead they need to be merged with the installation program of an application, which uses the shared component.

Chapter Summary

KEY TERMS

- binding policy
- delay signing
- deployment
- GAC (global assembly cache)
- merge module
- native compilation
- native image cache
- private assembly
- publisher policy
- shared assembly
- side-by-side execution
- strong name

The chapter discussed how to deploy various .NET applications. I started the discussion with the deployment of assemblies. This discussion developed your understanding of how the CLR locates the shared assemblies and private assemblies. I also discussed how the side-by-side execution of assemblies works and how to configure binding policy in the application, publisher, and machine configuration files to control how the CLR locates assemblies.

You learned that some simple applications will be as easy to deploy as just copying the files from one location to another, whereas other applications may be complex and require reliance on the Microsoft Windows Installer Service.

I discussed how to create setup projects to deploy Web services, Windows services, serviced components, and .NET remoting objects. I also discussed how to use various types of editors provided in the setup and deployment projects to perform a specific type of task. Through these editors you can perform various tasks on the target server machine, such as placing files in multiple folders including the GAC, creating registry keys and values in the registry editor, associating file types with the application, checking on dependencies, performing custom actions at different phases (such as during Install, Commit, Rollback and Uninstall), customizing the user-interface of the installation process, and many more.

APPLY YOUR KNOWLEDGE

Exercises

10.1 Using Microsoft's Sample .NET Framework Bootstrapper

The setup projects created in this chapter assume that the .NET Framework is already installed on the target machine. You cannot use Visual Studio .NET setup and deployment projects to package the required .NET Framework along with a setup package. The .NET Framework has to be installed on the target machine by using a .NET Framework redistributable file (dotnetfx.exe) that is available through one of the following:

- The Windows Component Upgrade CD-ROM that comes with Visual Studio .NET

- The Microsoft MSDN Download Center (http://msdn.microsoft.com/downloads/ sample.asp?url=/MSDN-FILES/027/001/829/ msdncompositedoc.xml) or the Microsoft Windows Update Web site (http:// windowsupdate.microsoft.com)

Ideally, you would like a Windows application's installation program to perform a test for the availability of the .NET Framework on the target machine, and if the .NET Framework is not already installed, install it by using the .NET Framework redistributable file (dotnetfx.exe).

In this exercise you will learn how to use Microsoft's sample .NET Framework bootstrapper setup.exe file, along with a setup package generated through Visual Studio .NET, to check for the availability of the .NET Framework on the user's machine and install it by using the .NET Framework redistributable file, if it is not already installed.

Estimated time: 20 minutes.

1. Open the solution 320C10. In Solution Explorer, select the NorthwindSetup project.

2. Right-click the project and select Properties from the shortcut menu. In the NorthwindSetup project's Property Pages dialog box, change the Bootstrapper option to None. Click OK and build the project. Only the NorthwindSetup.msi file is created. It is created in the Release folder of the NorthwindSetup project.

3. Download the Setup.exe bootstrapper sample from http://msdn.microsoft.com/downloads/ sample.asp?url=/msdn-files/027/001/830/ msdncompositedoc.xml.

4. Install the downloaded sample. It installs two files on your computer: setup.exe and settings.ini. Copy both files to the Release folder of the NorthwindSetup project.

5. Open the settings.ini file in any text editor. Change its contents as follows:

```
[Bootstrap]
Msi=NorthwindSetup.msi
'LanguageDirectory=jpn
'ProductName=testproductname
'DialogText=
'CaptionText=
'ErrorCaptionText=
FxInstallerPath=d:\dotNetFramework
```

The value of *FxInstallerPath* is the path where you have stored the .NET Framework redistributable file, dotnetfx.exe. You can change the value to your actual path.

6. Open the setup.exe file. The installation is bootstrapped by the sample setup.exe file. It first tests for the availability of the .NET Framework. If the .NET Framework is not installed, it uses the path specified in FxInstallerPath to install the .NET Framework. Note that there are no

APPLY YOUR KNOWLEDGE

bootstrap files for installing the Microsoft Windows Installer. This check is a part of the .NET Framework installation and is automatically performed by `dotnetfx.exe`.

10.2 Creating a Database Script During Installation

In this chapter you have learned that the Custom Actions Editor enables you to perform custom actions during the installation process. In this exercise, you create a custom action to run the Northwind database installation script during installation of the `Northwind` Web service project. You will use `osql`, a command-line utility, to run the SQL script. This exercise assumes that you have Microsoft SQL Server installed on your machine.

Estimated time: 20 minutes.

1. Open the solution `320C10`. Add a Visual C# Class Library project to the solution. Name the project `InstallNorthwind`.

2. Add to the project the Northwind database installation script `instnwnd.sql` (which is usually available in the Microsoft SQL Server installation directory).

3. Right-click the project `InstallNorthwind` and choose Add, Add New Item from the context menu. The Add New Item dialog box appears. Add to the project an `Installer` class named `InstallNorthwind.cs`.

4. Open the `InstallNorthwind.cs` file in the code view. Add the following using directive:

   ```
   using System.Diagnostics;
   ```

5. Add the following code after the Component Designer–generated code section in the class definition:

```csharp
public override void Install(
   System.Collections.IDictionary
   savedState)
{
   // call the Install method
   // of the base class
   base.Install(savedState);
   string strSqlFilePath =
      this.Context.Parameters["Args"];

   // Run the osql process to run
   // the database script
   ProcessStartInfo psi =
      new ProcessStartInfo("osql.exe ",
      "-E -i " + "\"" +
      strSqlFilePath + "\"");
   psi.WindowStyle =
      ProcessWindowStyle.Hidden;
   try
   {
      Process p = Process.Start(psi);
      p.WaitForExit();
   }
   catch(Exception e)
   {
      // throw an InstallException with
      // the original exception message
      throw new InstallException(
         e.Message);
   }
}

public override void Commit(
   System.Collections.IDictionary
   savedState)
{
   // call the Commit method of
   // the base class
   base.Commit(savedState);
}
public override void Rollback(
   System.Collections.IDictionary
   savedState)
{
   // call the Rollback method
   // of the base class
   base.Rollback(savedState);
}
```

APPLY YOUR KNOWLEDGE

```
public override void Uninstall(
    System.Collections.IDictionary
    savedState)
{
    // call the Uninstall method
    // of the base class
    base.Uninstall(savedState);
}
```

6. Build the `InstallNorthwind` project.

7. Select the `NorthwindSetup` project in Solution Explorer. Open the File System Editor. Select the Web Application Folder node and add the `Primary Output from InstallNorthwind (Active)` file to the folder by selecting Action, Add, Project Output.

8. Select the Web Application Folder node and add the `instnwnd.sql` file from the `InstallNorthwind` project to the folder by selecting Action, Add, File.

9. Open the Custom Actions Editor for the `NorthwindSetup` project. Select the Custom Actions node and select Add Custom Action from the context menu. The Select Item in the Project dialog box appears. Select `Primary Output from InstallNorthwind (Active)` by navigating to the Application Folder. Click OK. The `Primary Output from InstallNorthwind (Active)` file is added to all four nodes under Custom Actions.

10. Select the newly added custom action under the Install node. Open the Properties window and set the `CustomActionData` property to `/Args="[TARGETDIR]instnwnd.sql"`.

11. Build the `NorthwindSetup` project. Install the project. This time, during installation, the Northwind database installation script is also executed.

Review Questions

1. What is the difference between deploying a private assembly and deploying a shared assembly?

2. What is a binding policy? How can you override the default binding policy of the CLR?

3. Describe the process by which the CLR binds to a shared assembly.

4. What is side-by-side execution?

5. What is the purpose of the File System Editor?

6. How can you customize the user interface of an installation process?

7. Where is the GAC located on a machine? How can you add items to the GAC?

8. What is meant by delay signing?

9. When should you use a merge module?

10. What is the purpose of the `CustomActionData` property in the Custom Actions Editor?

Exam Questions

1. You have created a database-driven Web service. Using Microsoft SQL Server, you have also generated an installation script for your database. This script is stored in a file named `InstData.sql`. When the clients deploy the Web service on their servers, the database should be created as part of the installation. You are creating a setup project by using Visual Studio .NET. Which of the following actions should you take to create the database as part of the installation process?

A. Create a component that derives from the `Installer` class. Override its `Install()` method to create the database. Add the component to the Install node of the Custom Actions Editor in the setup project.

B. Create a component that derives from the `Installer` class. Override its `Install()` method to create the database. Add the component to the Commit node of the Custom Actions Editor in the setup project.

C. Copy the `InstData.sql` file to the Application Folder on the File System on Target Machine by using the File System Editor. Add `InstData.sql` to the Install node of the Custom Actions Editor in the setup project.

D. Create a component that derives from the `Installer` class. Override its `Install()` method to create the database. Add the component to the Launch Conditions Editor in the setup project.

2. You are creating a setup project for a Windows service. In the Property Pages dialog box for the setup project, you have set the compression property to Optimized for Speed. Which of the following options will be true because of this configuration option? (Select the two best answers.)

A. All assemblies in the application will be pre-compiled to native code so that they run faster.

B. The resulting assemblies will be larger.

C. The setup package will be larger.

D. The setup project will run faster.

3. You have developed a database-intensive Web Service application. When the application is installed on the user's computer, the required database must also be installed. The execution of the program cannot continue without the database. Therefore, if setup of the database fails, you want to roll back the installation process. Which of the following editors would you use in the setup project to ensure that the database is properly installed on the target machine?

A. File System Editor

B. Custom Actions Editor

C. Launch Conditions Editor

D. Registry Editor

4. You have created a .NET remoting application that uses some components that are not shared by other applications. Each of these components creates its own assemblies, and all these assemblies have strong names associated with them. The application that uses these components is not required to load a specific version of these components. You do not want to store the assemblies directly under the application's installation folder. Which of the following options is the best approach for storing the assembly files for the application's components?

A. Store the components in the GAC.

B. Store the components anywhere you like and specify the path to them by using the `<codebase>` element in the application's configuration file.

APPLY YOUR KNOWLEDGE

C. Store the assemblies in one of the subdirectories under the application's installation directory and specify this subdirectory as part of the <probing> element in the application's configuration file.

D. Store the components in the Window's System directory.

5. You are responsible for maintaining the installation of a Windows service that listens for orders and updates the database. The Windows service uses a serviced component, OrderProcess.dll, which is signed with a strong name. You have installed version 1.0 of this serviced component in the root directory of the application. You later receive a version 2.0 of OrderProcess.dll, which you install in the global assembly cache, as well as the root directory of the application. You reconfigure the application configuration file of the Windows service to redirect version 1.0 calls to version 2.0. Now you receive version 3.0 of OrderService.dll, which you again install in the global assembly cache. You do not reconfigure the application configuration file. Now when you run the Windows service, which version of OrderService.dll is loaded and from which location?

A. Version 1.0 from the root directory of the application

B. Version 2.0 from the global assembly cache

C. Version 2.0 from the root directory of the application

D. Version 3.0 from the global assembly cache

6. When you install a Windows application on a target machine, you want to store the ReadMe.txt file in the installation directory selected by the user. You also want to create a shortcut for the ReadMe.txt file on the desktop of the target machine. While creating a setup project, which of the following actions would you take in the File System Editor to achieve this? (Select all that apply.)

A. Move the shortcut to the ReadMe.txt file from the Application Folder node to the User's Desktop node in the File System on Target Machine node.

B. Add the ReadMe.txt file to the Application Folder node of the File System on Target Machine node.

C. Create a shortcut to the ReadMe.txt file that is available in the Application Folder node of the File System on Target Machine node.

D. Add the ReadMe.txt file to the User's Desktop node in the File System on Target Machine node.

E. Move the shortcut to the ReadMe.txt file from the User's Desktop node to the Application Folder in the File System on Target Machine node.

7. You have written a component that will be shared among multiple applications. You want to install the component to the GAC. Which of the following tools will you use to achieve this? (Select the two best answers.)

A. sn.exe

B. gacutil.exe

C. ngen.exe

D. installutil.exe

APPLY YOUR KNOWLEDGE

8. You are a developer in a large manufacturing company. You are developing a complex inventory control application with a team of 15 developers. You have written two program modules, `inv1234.cs` and `inv5678.cs`, which are generic and will be used from several other applications within the company. You compiled both program modules by using a C# compiler to produce the `inv1234.netmodule` and `inv5678.netmodule` files. You now want to link both compiled modules into an assembly that you will install in the GAC to test some Windows forms that depend on this assembly. You have decided to keep the name of the assembly as `InvLib.dll`. You do not have access to the company's private key, but you have access to the company's public key. The public key is stored in a file named `BigCoPublic.snk`. When the testing is completed, your project manager will use the private key (stored in the `BigCoPrivate.snk` file) to fully sign all the assemblies in the accounting software application. Which of the following commands would you choose to successfully sign your assembly?

A.
```
al.exe inv1234.netmodule,inv5678.netmodule
➡/delaysign /keyfile:BigCoPublic.snk
➡/out:InvLib.dll
```

B.
```
al.exe inv1234.netmodule,inv5678.netmodule
➡/delaysign+ /keyfile:BigCoPublic.snk
➡/out:InvLib.dll
```

C.
```
al.exe inv1234.netmodule,inv5678.netmodule
➡/delaysign- /keyfile:BigCoPublic.snk
➡/out:InvLib.dll
```

D.
```
csc.exe inv1234.cs,inv5678.cs
➡/delaysign /keyfile:BigCoPublic.snk
➡/out:InvLib.dll
```

9. You are using the `Installer` tool (`installutil.exe`) to install server resources by executing the installer components in three assemblies. You issue the following command:
```
installutil Assembly1.exe
➡Assembly2.exe Assembly3.exe
```

During the execution of this command, the installation of `Assembly3.exe` fails. Which of the following will happen?

A. Only `Assembly1.exe` will be installed.

B. Only `Assembly2.exe` will be installed.

C. Both `Assembly1.exe` and `Assembly2.exe` will be installed.

D. None of the assemblies will be installed.

10. You work as a software developer in a large chemical manufacturing company. You create an XML Web Service that provides material safety information to its partners and customers. The Web service has been thoroughly tested with a test server. You now want to deploy the Web service on the company's production server. You do not want to manually configure any settings on the production machine. Which of the following methods of deployment should you choose?

A. FTP the files from the test server to the production server.

B. Use the XCOPY command to copy all your files to the production server.

C. Use the Visual Studio .NET Copy Project command to copy all the project files to the production server.

D. Create a Web setup project for your application and use the setup program to deploy the application on the production machine.

APPLY YOUR KNOWLEDGE

11. You want to create a customized setup program for a .NET application. One of the screens shown during installation should be available only from the administrative installation of Microsoft Windows Installer. Other setup options should be available for both regular and administrative installations. Which of the following editors would allow you to create such an installation program?

    A. File System Editor

    B. User Interface Editor

    C. Custom Actions Editor

    D. Launch Conditions Editor

12. Your application uses version `4.3.0.0` of the `FunChart` assembly. The producer of the assembly has issued version `4.3.1.0` of the assembly, together with a publisher policy file that dictates using `4.3.1.0` in place of `4.3.0.0` in all applications. You discover after testing that one of your applications, named `ChartApp`, which previously worked with `4.3.0.0`, fails with `4.3.1.0`. You want only this application to use the old version of the assembly, while letting all other applications use the new version. What should you do?

    A. Add the element `<publisherPolicy apply="no"/>` to the `ChartApp.exe.config` file.

    B. Add an administrator policy in the `machine.config` file that redirects requests for `4.3.1.0` to `4.3.0.0`.

    C. Delete the publisher policy from your computer.

    D. Copy version `4.3.0.0` of the assembly from the GAC to the folder containing `ChartApp.exe`.

13. You work as a software developer for a big pharmacy. You are writing some components that will be shared across several applications throughout the company. You want to place an assembly named `CommonComponents.dll` in the GAC for testing purposes. You do not have access to the company's private key, but you have stored the company's public key in the assembly manifest of `CommonComponents.dll`. Which of the following commands are you required to run to place your assembly in the GAC? (Select all that apply.)

    A.

    `sn.exe -Vr CommonComponents.dll`

    B.

    `sn.exe -Vu CommonComponents.dll`

    C.

    `gacutil.exe /i CommonComponents.dll`

    D.

    `gacutil.exe /u CommonComponents.dll`

14. Your Web service application is already deployed to your company's production Web server when you discover a logic error in one of Web methods. You have corrected the error and rebuilt the application on the test server. What is the easiest way to transfer the changes to the production server?

    A. Use FTP to move the changed files to the production server. Restart the WWW service on the production server.

    B. Build a Windows Installer project to install the entire application. Run the Installer project on the production server. Restart the WWW service on the production server.

C. Use FTP to move the changed files to the production server. Do not restart the WWW service on the production server.

D. Build a Windows Installer project to install the entire application. Run the Installer project on the production server. Do not restart the WWW service on the production server.

15. You are designing a Windows application that will be downloaded to a user's computer from your company's Web server. After it is installed on the user's computer, the application might request and download more components from the Web site, as needed for the user's requirements. The application uses several components that need to be installed in the GAC on the user's machine. You want to sign your components with a cryptographic digital signature, as well as with an Authenticode signature, so that your company's identity is certified through an independent certifying authority. Which of the following options would you use for signing the components before they are packaged for deployment?

A. Use `sn.exe` to sign the assemblies.

B. Use `signcode.exe` to sign the assemblies.

C. Use `sn.exe` followed by `signcode.exe` to sign the assemblies.

D. Use `signcode.exe` followed by `sn.exe` to sign the assemblies.

Answers to Review Questions

1. A private assembly is deployed for use by a single application and is deployed within the directory of the application that uses it. A shared assembly is deployed for use by multiple applications. Shared assemblies are signed with a strong name and are usually deployed in the GAC.

2. A binding policy is a set of rules that define how the CLR binds to an assembly. To modify the default binding policy of the CLR, use the policy configuration files—the application configuration file, publisher policy configuration file, and machine configuration file.

3. The CLR first determines the correct version of the assembly that needs to be located by analyzing the policy configuration files. The CLR then checks whether the assembly has been already loaded from one of the previous calls. If not, then the CLR searches the GAC for the correct assembly. Upon failure, the CLR checks for the presence of a <codebase> element in the policy configuration files. If there is one, the CLR uses the information in the <codebase> element to locate the assembly.

Otherwise, the CLR searches the assembly in the application's directory structure (in the base directory and in a subdirectory whose name is the same as the assembly itself). If the assembly has culture information, the CLR looks for the assembly in the culture subdirectory.

If all fails, the CLR checks the configuration files for the <probing> element and searches for the assembly in the subdirectories specified by the <probing> element.

APPLY YOUR KNOWLEDGE

4. Side-by-side execution is the capability to run multiple versions of the same assembly simultaneously. The CLR determines which assembly to load for a given application by using the assembly manifest of the calling application combined with the three policy configuration files—the application configuration file, publisher policy configuration file, and machine configuration file.

5. The File System Editor provides mapping of the file system on the target machine. The folders are referred to by special names that are converted during the installation process to represent the folders as per the file system on the target machine.

6. The User Interface Editor allows you to create your own user interface for the installation process. There are three stages of installation: Start, Progress, and End. This editor enables you to add different types of dialog boxes to each of the different stages. It provides special properties whose values can be evaluated to perform the installation according to the end user's choice.

7. The GAC is located in the assembly folder under the system folder on a machine. You can view shared assemblies in the GAC by navigating to the assembly folder in Windows Explorer. You can add shared assemblies to the GAC through Windows Explorer, the .NET Framework Configuration tool (mscorcfg.msc), the Global Assembly Cache tool (gacutil.exe), or the Windows Installer.

8. Delay signing is a process that allows you to place a shared assembly in the GAC by just signing the assembly with a public key. This allows the assembly to be signed with a private key at a later

stage, when the development process is complete and the component or assembly is ready to be deployed.

9. Merge modules should be used to package shared components with their related resources, Registry entries, custom actions, and launch conditions. Merge modules cannot be installed directly; rather, they are merged into setup projects.

10. The CustomActionData property is used to pass custom data from a setup program to the custom installer class.

Answers to Exam Questions

1. **A.** You can use the Custom Actions Editor to take custom actions such as database installations during application setup. If you have a component that derives from the Installer class and overrides the Install() method to create databases, it must be added to the Install node of the Custom Actions Editor. For more information, see the section "Creating Installation Components" in this chapter.

2. **C, D.** Modifying a setup project's Compression property to Optimized for Speed does not affect the size or the speed of the installed assemblies. Instead, the setup program compresses the assemblies by using a compression algorithm that is optimized for speed. As a result, you have a lower compression ratio, resulting in a large setup package that executes faster. For more information, see the section "Deploying a Web Service by Using a Windows Installer Package" in this chapter.

APPLY YOUR KNOWLEDGE

3. **B.** The Custom Actions Editor allows you to execute custom actions such as database installations while running the setup program. It also has provisions for performing an installation rollback if the installation operation fails. For more information, see the section "Creating Installation Components" in this chapter.

4. **C.** If the components are not shared between applications, it is not a good idea to store them in the GAC. You could use the <codebase> element in the application's configuration file, but in that case you must specify a version of the assembly. The applications in question are not specific about versions, so a good place to store the assemblies is in a folder inside the application's installation folder, with its location specified via the <probing> element in the application's configuration file. For more information, see the section "How the CLR Binds to a Privately Deployed Assembly" and "How the CLR Binds to a Shared Assembly" in this chapter.

5. **B.** As a first step, the CLR tries to determine the version of assembly by analyzing the configuration files. From application configuration files, the CLR knows that it should search for version 2.0 of the assembly instead of version 1.0. Therefore, as a next step when CLR queries the GAC, it can bind to version 2.0 of the assembly. For more information, see the section "How the CLR Binds to a Privately Deployed Assembly" and "How the CLR Binds to a Shared Assembly" in this chapter.

6. **A, B,** and **C.** To copy the ReadMe.txt file to the installation directory selected by the user at install time, you would add it to the Application Folder node in the File System on Target Machine node. To create a shortcut, you first create a shortcut to the ReadMe.txt file stored in the Application Folder node in the File System on Target Machine node. Then you move this shortcut from the Application Folder node to the User's Desktop in the File System on Target Machine node. For more information, see the section "Customizing Visual Studio .NET Setup and Deployment Projects" in this chapter.

7. **A, B.** When you want to install a component to the GAC, you first assign it a strong name. You do this by using the Strong Name tool (sn.exe). You can place a strongly named assembly in the GAC by using the Global Assembly Cache tool (gacutil.exe). For more information, see the section "Adding an Assembly to the GAC" in this chapter.

8. **B.** You can use the al.exe command to link already-compiled modules into an assembly. The process of including a public key in an assembly and signing it with a private key at a later stage is called delay signing. You can perform delay signing on an assembly by using al.exe with the /delay+ switch. For more information, see the section "Using the Assembly Generation Tool for Delay Signing" in this chapter.

9. **D.** installutil.exe performs installation in a transactional manner. If one of the assemblies fails to install, installutil.exe rolls back the installations of all other assemblies. So if the installation of Assembly3.exe fails, none of the assemblies will be installed. For more information, see the section "Deploying an Assembly containing the Installation Components" in this chapter.

10. **D.** When you copy the files for an XML Web service from one computer to another, you may have to manually configure a few things such as creation of the virtual directory. If you want all

APPLY YOUR KNOWLEDGE

these tasks to be automated, you should choose the Web setup projects to create a setup program. For more information, see the section "Packaging a .NET Application for Deployment" in this chapter.

11. **B.** You can customize the user interface of an installation program by using the User Interface Editor for both regular installation and administrative installation. For more information, see the section "Customizing Visual Studio .NET Setup and Deployment Projects" in this chapter.

12. **A.** The `<publisherPolicy>` element allows you to override publisher policy for a single application. Adding an administrator policy or deleting the publisher policy affects all applications on the computer, not just the one application. Copying the assembly has no effect on the binding, which is satisfied from the GAC. For more information, see the section "Side-by-Side Execution of Shared Assemblies" in this chapter.

13. **A, C.** You will have to first turn off the verification for partially signed assemblies. This can be done by using the `sn.exe` tool with the `-Vr` switch. Next the assembly can be installed to the GAC using the `/i` switch with the `gacutil.exe` command. For more information, see the section "Delay Signing an Assembly" in this chapter.

14. **C.** If a Web service is already installed on IIS, you can simply replace any updated files. ASP.NET will detect the changed files and automatically recompile the pages as clients request them. For more information, see the section "Deploying a Web Service" in this chapter.

15. **C.** `sn.exe` is used to sign an assembly with a cryptographic digital signature, whereas `signcode.exe` is used to sign an assembly with an Authenticode signature. When both are used together to sign an assembly, you should always use `sn.exe` before using `signcode.exe`. For more information, see the section "Cab Project" in this chapter.

Suggested Readings and Resources

1. The Visual Studio .NET Combined Help Collection:
   - "Deploying Applications and Components"
   - "Deployment Walkthroughs"
   - "Creating Installation Components"

2. Jeffery Ritcher. *Applied Microsoft .NET Framework Programming*. Microsoft Press, 2002.

3. Deploying .NET Applications: Lifecycle Guide. www.microsoft.com/downloads/release.asp?releaseid=40545.

4. Microsoft Support WebCast: Microsoft .NET: Deploying Applications with .NET. support.microsoft.com/servicedesks/webcasts/wc091902/wcblurb091902.asp.

This chapter covers the following Microsoft-specified objective for the "Creating and Managing Microsoft Windows Services, Serviced Components, .NET Remoting Objects, and XML Web Services" section of the "Developing XML Web Services and Server Components with Microsoft Visual C# .NET and the Microsoft .NET Framework" exam:

Implement security for a Windows service, a serviced component, a .NET Remoting object, and an XML Web service.

This chapter also covers the following Microsoft-specified objectives for the "Deploying Microsoft Windows Services, Serviced Components, .NET Remoting Objects, and XML Web Services" section of the "Developing XML Web Services and Server Components with Microsoft Visual C# .NET and the Microsoft .NET Framework" exam:

Configure security for a Windows service, a serviced component, a .NET Remoting object, and an XML Web service.

▶ Configure authentication type. Authentication types include Windows authentication, Microsoft .NET Passport, custom authentication, and none.

▶ Configure and control authorization. Authorization methods include file-based authorization and URL-based authorization.

▶ Configure and implement identity management.

C H A P T E R 11

Security Issues

▶ These days, it's not enough to write correct code. You must also write secure code if you want your applications to be widely useful. Thanks to the increasing connectivity of computers over LANs and the Internet, your applications will often be visible to thousands or millions of potential attackers. Thus, it's necessary to secure these applications so that only authorized users can work with them. These objectives test your understanding of the basic security features of the .NET Framework and the ways in which you can apply those features to particular applications.

STUDY STRATEGIES

▶ Use code access security to specify the permissions an assembly requires. Make sure you understand the differences between minimum and optional permission requests.

▶ Use the Microsoft .NET Framework Configuration tool to specify security policies for an assembly, and understand the effects of those policies on the assembly. Experiment with the interaction between multiple security policies for the same assembly.

▶ Use authentication to control who can access an ASP.NET application, and understand what happens when a user cannot be authenticated.

▶ Configure a Web service for secure access, and confirm that you cannot use the Web service without proper authentication and authorization.

INTRODUCTION

The .NET Framework includes a comprehensive set of security tools, including both low-level classes for managing security and an overall framework for applying these tools to particular applications. The tools for managing security include *code access security* and *role-based security*. Code access security enables you to control what code can execute on a particular computer, and what that code can do. Role-based security enables you to control the actions that particular users can take.

In this chapter, you'll learn about many aspects of .NET security. I'll start with the mechanics of code access security, and then discuss role-based security. The latter includes both authentication (determining who is trying to run code) and authorization (determining what this user can do). Finally, I'll give you some guidelines on applying these tools to Web services, remoting applications, Windows Services and Enterprise Services components.

CONFIGURING SECURITY

Implement security for a Windows service, a serviced component, a .NET Remoting object, and an XML Web service.

The .NET Framework offers a wide variety of security features. You can choose to run your machine in wide-open mode, with every user allowed to execute any .NET code, or you can lock down things selectively. You can control which programs have access to which resources, or which users have the right to execute which programs.

Broadly speaking, .NET security breaks down into two separate areas:

> ▶ Code access security—This type of security manages the security of .NET source code itself. You can tell the .NET Framework the resources your code needs to execute properly, and the .NET Framework will check for permission to access those resources on the machine at runtime. Code access security is very flexible and includes the capability to define your

own sets of necessary permissions. Code access security can also be used by administrators to ensure that undesired code never gets the chance to run on a system.

▶ Role-based security—This type of security manages the user rather than the code. Using role-based security allows you to provide (or deny) access to resources based on an identity provided by the user running the code. In practical terms, this means you can limit program execution to particular users or groups on the computer.

I'll cover both these types of security in this chapter, beginning with code access security. The .NET Framework also includes other security features, notably public key and private key encryption, which are not a part of the 70-320 exam.

Understanding Code Access Security

Code access security controls what code can do on your computer. Code access security is centered around permissions to use resources. The .NET Framework has an entire object-oriented system for managing code access security and the associated permissions. In the following sections, you'll learn about concepts involved in code access security:

▶ Permissions

▶ Code groups

▶ Permission sets

You'll also learn how to manage code access security. In particular, code can request permissions on a very fine-grained scale, and the administrator can choose to allow permissions on an equally fine-grained scale.

Understanding Permissions

Code access security is based on specific permissions that the Common Language Runtime (CLR) can grant to or deny from code. For example, the authorization to read or write information in the Windows Registry requires the `RegistryPermission` permission on that part of your code. As you'll see later in the chapter, code can make four different types of permission requests:

▶ It can request the minimum permissions that it requires to run.

▶ It can request optional permissions that it would like but does not require.

▶ It can refuse permissions to ensure that it does not have access to particular resources.

▶ It can demand permissions on the part of calling code.

The CLR decides, based on a variety of factors (including the origin of the code and the information in the machine and application configuration files), whether a particular permission should be granted. If a piece of code is unable to obtain the minimum permissions that it requires, that piece of code does not execute. The security settings of the computer determine the maximum permissions that code can be granted, but code is allowed to request (and receive) fewer permissions than the maximum.

The .NET Framework groups permissions into three types:

▶ *Code access permissions* represent access to a protected resource or the capability to perform a protected operation.

▶ *Identity permissions* represent access based on credentials that are a part of the code itself.

▶ *Role-based permissions* represent access based on the user who is running the code.

Each permission in the .NET Framework is represented by a particular class that derives from `System.Security.CodeAccessPermission`. Table 11.1 lists the permissions, which are the most important for controlling the actions that code can take on a particular computer.

TABLE 11.1

CODE ACCESS PERMISSIONS IN THE .NET FRAMEWORK

Permission	*Explanation*
DirectoryServicesPermission	Controls access to the System.DirectoryServices namespace.
DnsPermission	Controls access to domain name system (DNS) services.
EnvironmentPermission	Controls access to environment variables.
EventLogPermission	Controls access to the Windows event log.
FileDialogPermission	Controls access to files selected from the Open dialog box.
FileIOPermission	Controls access to reading and writing files and directories.
IsolatedStorageFilePermission	Controls access to private virtual file systems.
IsolatedStoragePermission	Controls access to generic isolated storage.
MessageQueuePermission	Controls access to message queuing via MSMQ.
OleDbPermission	Controls access to data via the System.Data.OleDb namespace.
PerformanceCounterPermission	Controls access to performance counters.
PrintingPermission	Controls access to printers.
ReflectionPermission	Controls access to the reflection features of .NET.
RegistryPermission	Controls access to the Windows Registry.
SecurityPermission	Controls access to unmanaged code.
ServiceControllerPermission	Controls access to starting and stopping services.
SocketPermission	Controls access to Windows sockets.
SqlClientPermission	Controls access to data via the System.Data.SqlClient namespace.
UIPermission	Controls access to the user interface.
WebPermission	Controls access to making Web connections.

> **NOTE**
>
> **Custom Permissions** If none of the code access permissions in Table 11.1 are quite right for your application, you can also define custom permissions. Custom permissions are discussed later in this chapter, in the section "Using Custom Security Attributes."

Requesting Minimum Permissions

To start working in the .NET security framework, your code can request the minimum permissions that it needs to function correctly. Step-by-Step 11.1 demonstrates the syntax for making such a request.

STEP BY STEP

11.1 Requesting Minimum Permissions

1. Launch Visual Studio .NET. Select File, New, Blank Solution and name the new solution 320C11.

2. Add a new Visual C# .NET Windows application named StepByStep11_1 to the solution.

3. In the Solution Explorer, rename the default Form1.cs to StepByStep11_1.cs. Open the form in code view and change all occurrences of Form1 to refer to StepByStep11_1 instead.

4. Place a Label control, a TextBox control (txtFileName), and a Button control (btnGetFile) on the form. Add an OpenFileDialog component (dlgOpen). Figure 11.1 shows a design for this form.

5. Switch to the code view and add the following code at the top after the using directives:

```
using System.Security.Permissions;
[assembly:FileDialogPermissionAttribute(
    SecurityAction.RequestMinimum, Unrestricted=true)]
```

6. Double-click the Button control and add the following code to handle the Click event of the Button control:

```
private void btnGetName_Click(object sender,
    System.EventArgs e)
{
    try
    {
        if(dlgOpen.ShowDialog() == DialogResult.OK)
            txtFileName.Text = dlgOpen.FileName;
    }
    catch (Exception ex)
    {
```

FIGURE 11.1
Design a form that requests the minimum permissions required to run this form.

```
            MessageBox.Show("Exception: " + ex.Message);
        }
    }
```

7. Compile the project. Launch the executable file from Windows Explorer (you'll find it in the project's `bin\Debug` directory) and verify that you can browse for a file.

The code in Step-by-Step 11.1 requests permissions by applying an attribute to an assembly. The `FileDialogPermissionAttribute` enables the assembly to request the `FileDialogPermission` permission, which in turn allows access to the system's file dialog boxes. In this particular case, the code runs without any problem, which means that it was granted the requested permission. By default you have full permissions to run any code that originates on your own computer. To see code access security in action, you need to learn how to manage the permissions granted to code on your computer. But first, you need to understand the concepts of code groups and permission sets.

Code Groups and Permission Sets

A *code group* is a set of assemblies that share a security context. You define a code group by specifying the membership condition for the group. Every assembly in a code group receives the same permissions from that group. However, because an assembly could be a member of multiple code groups, two assemblies in the same group might end up with different permissions.

The .NET Framework supports seven different membership conditions for code groups:

▶ Application directory—The application directory membership condition selects all the code in the installation directory of the running application.

▶ Cryptographic hash—The cryptographic hash membership condition selects all the code that matches a specified cryptographic hash. Practically speaking, this is a way to define a code group that consists of a single assembly.

N O T E

Cryptographic Hashing To calculate a cryptographic hash, the compiled code of an assembly is run through a cryptographic algorithm that generates a string of digits as a result. The string of digits is much shorter than the original assembly, and is therefore easier to evaluate. If you run the same assembly through the algorithm, you get the same hash out, but two different assemblies are extremely unlikely to generate an identical hash value.

▶ Software publisher—The software publisher membership condition selects all the code from a specified publisher, as verified by Authenticode signing.

▶ Site—The site membership condition selects all the code from a particular Internet domain.

▶ Strong name—The strong name membership condition selects all the code that has a specified strong name.

▶ URL—The URL membership condition selects all the code from a specified URL.

▶ Zone—The zone membership condition selects all the code from a specified security zone (Internet, local intranet, Trusted sites, My Computer, or Untrusted sites).

Permissions are granted in permission sets. A *permission set* is a set of one or more code access permissions that are granted as a unit. If you want to grant only a single permission, you must construct a permission set that contains only that single permission; you can't grant permissions directly. The .NET Framework supplies seven built-in permission sets:

▶ Nothing—The Nothing permission set grants no permissions.

▶ Execution—The Execution permission set grants permission to run but not to access protected resources.

▶ Internet—The Internet permission set grants limited permissions designed for code of unknown origin.

▶ LocalIntranet—The LocalIntranet permission set grants high permissions designed for code within an enterprise.

▶ Everything—The Everything permission set grants all permissions except for the permission to skip verification.

▶ SkipVerification—The SkipVerification permission set grants the permission to skip security checks.

▶ FullTrust—The FullTrust permission set grants full access to all resources. This permission set includes all permissions.

You can also create your own custom permission sets, as described in the "Granting Permission" section.

Granting Permission

The easiest way to grant or deny permissions in the .NET Framework is to use the Microsoft .NET Framework Configuration tool, as in Step-by-Step 11.2.

STEP BY STEP

11.2 Granting Permissions by Using the .NET Framework Configuration Tool

1. Open the Microsoft .NET Framework Configuration tool from the Administrative Tools section of the Windows Control Panel.

2. Expand the Runtime Security node, then the User node, and then the Permission Sets node to see the built-in .NET permission sets.

3. Right-click the `Everything` permission set and select Duplicate. A new permission set named `Copy of Everything` is created.

4. Right-click the `Copy of Everything` permission set and select Rename. Rename the permission set `No FileDialog`.

5. With the `No FileDialog` permission set selected, click the Change Permissions link in the right panel of the configuration tool. In the Create Permission Set dialog box, select File Dialog and click Remove. Click Finish to save your changes.

6. Expand the Code Groups node and click the default `All Code` code group. Click the Add a Child Code Group link in the right panel of the configuration tool.

7. In the Create Code Group dialog box, name the new group `StepByStep11_1`. Enter a description and click Next.

8. Choose the Hash condition. Click the Import button and browse to `StepByStep11_1.exe`. Click Open to calculate the hash for this file. Click Next.

9. Select the `No FileDialog` permission set and click Next. Click Finish to create the new code group.

continues

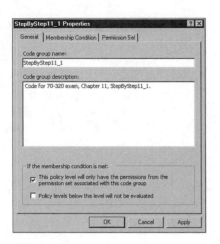

FIGURE 11.2
You can create a code group and grant or deny permissions in a GUI interface by using the Microsoft .NET Framework Configuration tool.

NOTE

Recalculate Hash If you create a code group with the cryptographic hash membership condition, you need to recalculate the hash whenever you make a change in the code. Compiling the project with changed code results in a different hash value than the one that you calculated previously (while creating a code group).

You can recalculate the hash by using the Microsoft .NET Framework Configuration tool. Locate the node for the code group and then right-click the code group and select Properties. On the Membership Condition tab, select Import. Browse to the project's executable file, click Open, and then click OK.

---

continued

10. Right-click the StepByStep11_1 code group and select Properties. Check the box to make this code group exclusive, as shown in Figure 11.2. Click OK.

11. Run the StepByStep11_1.exe application by double-clicking it in Windows Explorer. A policy exception error box appears, indicating that the code cannot be run. Click No to dismiss the error box.

In Step-by-Step 11.2, you first create a permission set (based on the built-in Everything permission set) that includes every permission except for the permission to use the file dialog boxes. You then create a code group that contains the executable file for the StepByStep11.1 example, and then you assign the No FileDialog permission set to this code group. The result is that the code cannot run because it requires at a minimum the one permission that the new security policy cannot grant to it.

Imperative Security

Requesting permissions through the use of attributes is known as *declarative security*. There's a second method to request permissions, known as *imperative security*. With imperative security, you create objects to represent the permissions that your code requires (see Step-by-Step 11.3). Guided Practice Exercise 11.1 will give you additional practice with imperative security.

STEP BY STEP

11.3 Imperative Security

1. Add a new Visual C# .NET Windows application named StepByStep11_3 to the solution.

2. In the Solution Explorer, rename the default Form1.cs to StepByStep11_3.cs. Open the form in code view and change all occurrences of Form1 to refer to StepByStep11_3 instead.

3. Place a Label control, a TextBox control (txtFileName), and a Button control (btnGetFile) on the form. Add an OpenFileDialog component (dlgOpen). You can reuse the design from Figure 11.1 for this form.

4. Switch to the code view and add the following using directive:

```
using System.Security.Permissions;
```

5. Add this code to allow the user to browse for a filename when he clicks the button:

```
private void btnGetName_Click(object sender,
    System.EventArgs e)
{
    try
    {
        FileDialogPermission fdp = new
        FileDialogPermission(
            PermissionState.Unrestricted);
        // Check to see whether the code
        // has the specified permission
        fdp.Demand();

        if(dlgOpen.ShowDialog() == DialogResult.OK)
            txtFileName.Text = dlgOpen.FileName;
    }
    catch(Exception ex)
    {
        MessageBox.Show("Exception: " + ex.Message);
    }
}
```

6. Compile the project. Launch the executable file from Windows Explorer and verify that you can browse for a file.

7. Run the Microsoft .NET Framework Configuration tool. Expand the Runtime Security node, then the User node, and then the Code Groups node and click the default All Code code group. Click the Add a Child Code Group link in the right panel of the configuration tool.

8. In the Create Code Group dialog box, name the new group StepByStep11_3. Enter a description and click Next.

9. Choose the Hash condition. Click the Import button and browse to StepByStep11_3.exe. Click Open to calculate the hash for this file. Click Next.

continues

> **EXAM TIP**
>
> **Command-line Permissions**   The .NET Framework SDK also includes the Code Access Security Policy tool, caspol.exe, that can manipulate code groups and permission sets from the command line. If you're trying to automate security operations, you can make good use of this tool from a batch file.

FIGURE 11.3
An exception is generated if the requested permission cannot be granted according to the security policy's current setting.

continued

10. Select the No FileDialog permission set (created in Step-by-Step 11.2) and click Next. Click Finish to create the new code group.

11. Right-click the StepByStep11_3 code group and select Properties. Check the first check box to make this code group exclusive. Click OK.

12. Launch the StepByStep11_3.exe file from Windows Explorer again. Click the Get File button. You'll see the security exception shown in Figure 11.3.

In Step-by-Step 11.3 you construct a FileDialogPermission object that represents unrestricted access to the file dialog boxes. It then calls the Demand() method of that object to demand the permission from the operating system. When the security policy is such that the permission cannot be granted, the code throws an exception.

Computing Permissions

Determining the actual permissions applied to any given piece of code is a complex process. To begin the process, you should think about permissions at the Enterprise level only. The CLR starts by examining the evidence that a particular piece of code presents to determine its membership in code groups at that level. *Evidence* is just an overall term for the various identity permissions (publisher, strong name, hash, and so on) that can go into code group membership.

Code groups are organized into a hierarchy; in Step-by-Step 11.2 you create the StepByStep11_1 code group as a child of the All Code code group. In general, the CLR examines all the code groups in the hierarchy to determine membership. However, any code group in the hierarchy may be marked as Exclusive (that's the effect of the check box that you select when creating the StepByStep11_1 code group). The CLR stops checking for group membership if code is found to be a member of an Exclusive code group. Either way, code is determined to be a member of zero or more code groups as a first step.

> **EXAM TIP**
>
> **Imperative Versus Declarative Security**   The only time you absolutely have to use imperative security is when you need to make security decisions based on factors that are known only at runtime, such as the name of a particular file. In many other cases declarative security is easier to use.

Next, the CLR retrieves the permission set for each code group that contains the code. If the code is a member of an `Exclusive` code group, only the permission set of that code group is taken into account. If the code is a member of more than one code group and none of them is an `Exclusive` code group, all the permission sets of those code groups are taken into account. The permission set for the code is the *union* of the permission sets of all relevant code groups. That is, if the code is a member of two code groups and one code group grants `FileDialog` permission but the other does not, the code has `FileDialog` permission from this step.

The process accounts for the permissions at one level (the `Enterprise` level). But there are actually four levels of permissions: `Enterprise`, `Machine`, `User`, and `Application Domain`. Only the first three of these levels can be managed within the .NET Framework Configuration tool. However, if you need specific security checking within an application domain (which, roughly speaking, is a session in which code runs), you can do this in code. An application domain can reduce the permissions granted to code within that application domain, but it cannot expand them.

The CLR determines which of the four levels are relevant by starting at the top (the `Enterprise` level) and working down. Any given code group can have the `LevelFinal` property, in which case the examination stops there. For example, if code is a member of a code group on the `Machine` level and that group has the `LevelFinal` property, only the `Enterprise` and `Machine` levels are considered when security is assigned. The CLR computes the permissions for each level separately and then assigns the code the intersection of the permissions of all relevant levels. That is, if code is granted `FileDialog` permission on the `Enterprise` and `Machine` levels but is not granted `FileDialog` permission on the `User` level, the code does not have `FileDialog` permission.

At this point, the CLR knows what permissions should be granted to the code in question, considered in isolation. But code does not run in isolation; it runs as part of an application. The final step of evaluating code access permissions is to perform a stack walk. In a *stack walk*, the CLR examines all code in the calling chain from the original application to the code being evaluated. The final permission set for the code is the *intersection* of the permission sets of all code in the calling chain. That is, if code is granted `FileDialog` permission but the code that called it was not granted `FileDialog` permission, the code is not granted `FileDialog` permission.

Requesting Other Types of Permissions

You might at times want to request a particular permission even though your application doesn't absolutely require that permission for a user to proceed. Optional permissions are used in such a case. If you refer to the code in Step-by-Step 11.1, you see that part of the permission attribute is the `SecurityAction.RequestMinimum` action. To request optional permissions, you use the `SecurityAction.RequestOptional` action.

To make use of optional permissions in Visual C# .NET, your code must have a `Main()` method with a `try-catch` block. If optional permissions for the assembly can't be granted, this block catches the exception. If minimum permissions can't be granted, the program is shut down, whether this block is present or not.

You can also tell the CLR about permissions that you do not want your code to have. This can be useful if the code is potentially available to untrusted callers (for example, users who invoke the code over the Internet) and you want to limit the potential harm that they can do. The action for this is `SecurityAction.RequestRefuse`.

Finally, you might want to ensure that all the code that calls your code has a particular permission. For example, you might want to raise an exception if any code in the calling stack doesn't have the `RegistryPermission` permission. You can do this by specifying `SecurityAction.Demand` in the declaration of the security attribute.

GUIDED PRACTICE EXERCISE 11.1

One reason you might choose to use imperative security rather than declarative security is to be able to easily catch security violations and respond to them automatically.

In this exercise, you are required to extend the "browse for file" example in Step-by-Step 11.1 and use imperative security to selectively disable part of a user interface that the user isn't able to activate under the current security policy.

How would you use imperative security in this form?

You should try working through this problem on your own first. If you get stuck, or if you'd like to see one possible solution, follow these steps:

1. Add a new Visual C# .NET Windows application named `GuidedPracticeExercise11_1` to the solution.

2. In the Solution Explorer, rename the default `Form1.cs` to `GuidedPracticeExercise11_1.cs`. Open the form in code view and change all occurrences of `Form1` to refer to `GuidedPracticeExercise11_1` instead.

3. Place two `Label` controls, one `TextBox` control (`txtFileName`), and one `Button` control (`btnGetFile`) on the form. Name one of the `Label` controls `lblMessage` and empty its `Text` property. Add an `OpenFileDialog` component (`dlgOpen`). Refer to Figure 11.4 for the design of this form.

4. Switch to the code view and add the following `using` directive:

```
using System.Security.Permissions;
```

5. Attach default event handlers to the form and the `Button` control. Add the following code to the event handlers to check security at load time and to enable the user to browse for a filename when he clicks the button:

```
private void GuidedPracticeExercise11_1_Load(
    object sender, System.EventArgs e)
{
    try
    {
        FileDialogPermission fdp = new
        FileDialogPermission(
            PermissionState.Unrestricted);
        // Check to see whether the code
        // has the specified permission
        fdp.Demand();
    }
    catch(Exception ex)
    {
        btnGetFile.Enabled = false;
        lblMessage.Text =
            "You do not have permission " +
            "to browse for file names";
    }
}
```

continues

continued

```
private void btnGetFile_Click(object sender,
    System.EventArgs e)
{
    try
    {
        if(dlgOpen.ShowDialog() == DialogResult.OK)
            txtFilename.Text = dlgOpen.FileName;
    }
    catch (Exception ex)
    {
        MessageBox.Show("Exception: " + ex.Message);
    }
}
```

6. Set the project as the startup project.

7. Compile the project. Run the compiled project from Windows Explorer. You should find it possible to browse for a file by clicking the button.

8. Select Start, Programs, Administrative Tools, Microsoft .NET Framework Configuration. Navigate to the User node beneath the Runtime Security Policy node.

9. Expand the Code Groups node under the User node and click the default All Code code group. Click the Add a Child Code Group link in the right panel of the Configuration tool.

10. In the Create Code Group dialog box, name the new group GuidedPracticeExercise11_1. Enter a description and click Next.

11. Choose the Hash condition. Click the Import button and browse to the executable file from this exercise. Click Open to calculate the hash for this file. Click Next.

12. Select the No FileDialog permission set (created in the Step by Step 11.2) and click Next. Click Finish to create the new code group.

13. Right-click the GuidedPracticeExercise11_1 code group and select Properties. Check the first check box to make this code group exclusive. Click OK.

14. Run the program from Windows Explorer again. The Button control should be disabled, and the message shown in Figure 11.4 should appear.

In Guided Practice Exercise 11.1, the imperative security object is used to check the permissions that the application has as soon as the form is loaded. If the call to the Demand() method fails, you know that the user is not able to invoke the File dialog box. In that case, the code disables the button that would otherwise launch the File dialog box and shows a warning message instead.

If you had difficulty following this exercise, you should review the sections "Code Groups and Permission Sets" and "Imperative Security," earlier in this chapter. After this review, you should try this exercise again.

FIGURE 11.4
Choosing imperative security allows you to easily check for permissions and respond to them by taking custom actions, such as customizing the user interface in the current instance.

Using Custom Security Attributes

In some cases, you might find that the built-in security permissions do not fit your needs. For example, say you have designed a custom class that retrieves confidential information from your company's database and you'd like to be able to restrict permission on it by a more specific means than by limiting SQL permissions.

In such cases, you can create your own custom permissions and add them to the .NET security framework. This requires quite a bit of code, and most developers never need to perform this task. But just in case you do, I outline the process here. You'll find more in-depth information, including all the code for a simple custom permission, in the "Securing Applications" section of the .NET Framework Developer's Guide.

To implement a custom permission, you must create a class that inherits from the CodeAccessPermission class. Your new class must override five key methods to provide its own interfaces to the security system:

▶ Copy()—This method creates an exact copy of the current instance.

▶ Intersect()—This method returns the intersection of permissions between the current instance and a passed-in instance of the class.

▶ `IsSubsetOf()`—This method returns `true` if a passed-in instance includes everything allowed by the current instance.

▶ `FromXml()`—This method decodes an XML representation of the permission.

▶ `ToXml()`—This method encodes the current instance as XML.

Your class must support a constructor that accepts an instance of the `PermissionState` enumeration (which has a value of `Unrestricted` or `None`). You might also want to implement custom constructors related to your particular business needs. For example, a database-related permission might require a constructor that accepts a server name, if permissions should be handled differently on test and development servers.

Although it's not strictly required, your code should also implement a method named `IsUnrestricted()`, which returns `true` if the particular instance represents unrestricted access to the resource. This makes your custom permission more compatible with the built-in permissions in the .NET Framework.

To support declarative security, you should also implement an attribute class for your permission. This attribute class should derive from `CodeAccessSecurityAttribute` (which in turn derives from `SecurityAttribute`). The class should override the `CreatePermission()` method of the `IPermission` interface. Within this function, you should create an instance of your base custom permission class and set its properties according to the parameters from the declarative security invocation. Any attribute class must be marked with the `Serializable` attribute so that it can be serialized into metadata, along with the class to which it is applied.

For your custom permission to actually protect the intended resource, you need to make changes to both the resource and to the .NET Framework on the computers where the permission is to be used. The changes to the resource are simple: Whenever an operation that is protected by the custom permission is about to be performed, the code should demand an instance of the permission. If the calling code can't deliver the permission, your class should refuse to perform the operation.

The changes you need to make to the .NET Framework are somewhat more complex than the changes that you make to the resource.

First, you need to create an XML representation of your custom permission in the format that is expected by the Code Access Security Policy tool (`caspol.exe`). You can create this XML representation by instantiating your permission and calling its `ToXml()` method. Given this XML representation, `caspol.exe` can add a permission set to the .NET Framework that contains your custom permission. It also adds the assembly that implements the custom permission to the list of trusted assemblies on the computer. You need to perform this step on every computer where your custom permission is to be used.

REVIEW BREAK

▶ Permissions control access to resources.

▶ Code can request the minimum permissions that it needs to run and optional permissions that it would like to have. It can also refuse permissions and demand permissions on behalf of calling code.

▶ Code access permissions represent access to resources, and identity permissions represent things that the .NET Framework knows about code.

▶ The .NET Framework supplies both attribute-based declarative security and class-based imperative security.

▶ A code group is a set of assemblies that share a security context.

▶ Permission sets are sets of permissions that can be granted as a unit.

▶ The CLR computes actual permissions at runtime based on code group membership and the calling chain of the code.

▶ Custom permissions enable you to create your own permissions to protect particular resources.

CONFIGURING AUTHENTICATION

Configure security for a Windows service, a serviced component, a .NET Remoting object, and an XML Web service: Configure authentication type. Authentication types include Windows authentication, Microsoft .NET Passport, custom authentication, and none.

To understand security in distributed applications, you must be knowledgeable about the closely intertwined subjects of authentication and authorization. *Authentication* refers to the process of obtaining credentials from a user and verifying her identity. After an identity has been authenticated, it can be authorized to use various resources. *Authorization* refers to granting rights based on that identity.

ASP.NET provides you with flexible alternatives for authentication. Some, but not all, of these authentication methods also make sense in regular Windows applications. You can perform authentication yourself in code, or delegate authentication to other authorities. Because it's the most comprehensive case, I'll consider authentication in the context of ASP.NET applications first, and discuss other types of distributed applications later in the chapter.

No Authentication

The simplest form of authentication is no authentication at all. To enable an application to execute without authentication, you add this element to its configuration file:

```
<authentication mode="None" />
```

Setting the mode to None tells ASP.NET that you don't care about user authentication. The natural consequence of this, of course, is that you can't base authorization on user identities because users are never authenticated.

IIS and ASP.NET Authentication

One thing that trips up some developers is that there are actually two separate authentication layers in an ASP.NET application. All requests flow through IIS before they're handed to ASP.NET, and IIS can decide to deny access before the ASP.NET process even knows about the request. Here's a rundown on how the process works:

1. IIS first checks to make sure that the incoming request comes from an IP address that is allowed access to the domain. If not, the request is denied.

NOTE

Configuration Files   Each ASP.NET application has its own configuration file named web.config. In addition, there is a computerwide configuration file named machine.config. Sub-webs can have their own independent web.config file as well. Configuration files are XML files that can be dynamically updated at runtime. For more details on the ASP.NET configuration mechanism, refer to *MCAD/MCSD Developing and Implementing Web Applications with Visual C# .NET and Visual Studio .NET Training Guide, Exam 70-315* (ISBN 0-7897-2822-2).

2. Next, IIS performs its own user authentication, if it's configured to do so. I talk more about IIS authentication later in the chapter. By default, IIS allows anonymous access, so requests are automatically authenticated.

3. If the request is passed to ASP.NET with an authenticated user, ASP.NET checks to see whether impersonation is enabled. If impersonation is enabled, ASP.NET acts as though it were the authenticated user. If not, ASP.NET acts with its own configured account.

4. Finally, the identity from step 3 is used to request resources from the operating system. If all the necessary resources can be obtained, the user's request is granted; otherwise, it is denied.

As you can see, several security authorities interact when the user requests a resource or a Web page. If things aren't behaving the way you think they should, it can be helpful to review this list and make sure that you've considered all the factors involved.

Authentication Providers

So what happens when a request gets to ASP.NET? The answer depends on the site's configuration. The ASP.NET architecture delegates authentication to an authentication provider—a module whose job it is to verify credentials and provide authentication. ASP.NET ships with three authentication providers:

▶ The Windows authentication provider enables you to authenticate users based on their Windows accounts. This provider uses IIS to perform the actual authentication and then passes the authenticated identity to your code.

▶ The Passport authentication provider uses Microsoft's Passport service to authenticate users.

▶ The Forms authentication provider uses custom HTML forms to collect authentication information and allows you to use your own logic to authenticate users. Credentials are then stored in a cookie.

To select an authentication provider, you make an entry in the `<system.web>` element in the `web.config` file for the application. You can use one of these entries to select the corresponding built-in authentication provider:

```
<authentication mode="Windows" />

<authentication mode="Passport" />

<authentication mode="Forms" />
```

You can also create your own custom authentication provider. This doesn't mean that you plug a new module in place of the supplied provider; it means that you write custom code to perform authentication, and set the authentication mode for the application to `None`. For example, you might depend on an ISAPI filter to authenticate users at the level of incoming requests. In that case, you wouldn't want to use any of the .NET authentication providers.

Configuring IIS Authentication

If you decide to use Windows authentication within your applications, you need to consider how to configure IIS authentication because the Windows identities are actually provided by IIS. IIS offers four different authentication methods:

▶ If you select anonymous authentication, IIS does not perform any authentication. Anyone is allowed access to the ASP.NET application.

▶ If you select basic authentication, users must provide a Windows username and password to connect. However, this information is sent across the network in clear text, making basic authentication dangerously insecure on the Internet.

▶ If you select digest authentication, users must still provide a Windows username and password to connect. However, the password is hashed (scrambled) before being sent across the network. Digest authentication requires that all users be running Internet Explorer 5 or later and that Windows accounts be stored in Active Directory.

▶ If you select Windows integrated authentication, passwords never cross the network. Users must still have a Windows username and password, but either the Kerberos or challenge/response protocols are used to authenticate the user. Windows integrated authentication requires that all users be running Internet Explorer 3.01 or later.

Step-by-Step 11.4 gives you practice in setting authentication at the IIS level.

STEP BY STEP

11.4 Configuring IIS Authentication

1. Add a new Visual C# ASP.NET application named StepByStep11_4 to the solution. Add some text to the default Web Form so that you can later verify that it displays properly.

2. Open the web.config file for the application and verify that the authentication mode is set to Windows.

3. In Windows, select Start, Programs, Administrative Tools, Internet Services Manager.

4. In Internet Services Manager, drill down into the tree view until you find the node that corresponds to your Visual C# ASP.NET application. This node has the same name as the application, and it is located beneath the Default Web Site node. Right-click the application node and select Properties.

5. In the Properties dialog box, click the Directory Security tab. Click the Edit button in the Anonymous Access and Authentication Methods section to open the Authentication Methods dialog box, shown in Figure 11.5.

6. Uncheck the Anonymous Access check box and the Integrated Windows Authentication check box.

7. Set the project as the startup project.

8. Check the Basic Authentication check box. Click Yes and then click OK twice to save your changes.

FIGURE 11.5
IIS offers four different authentication methods.

continues

FIGURE 11.6
The Windows authentication provider allows you to authenticate users based on their Windows accounts.

continued

9. In Visual Studio .NET, select Debug, Run Without Debugging to run the project. You should see the Enter Network Password dialog box shown in Figure 11.6. Enter your username and password to see the start page for the application. To log on to a domain account, enter the username as DOMAIN\User.

Passport Authentication

The Microsoft .NET Passport is an online service (www.passport.net) that enables users to use a single email address and a password to sign in to any .NET Passport-participating Web site or service. Users can create a free Passport account by registering at any .NET Passport participating Web site or by using the Windows XP .NET Passport Registration Wizard.

ASP.NET has built-in connections to Microsoft's Passport authentication service. If your users have signed up with Passport and you configure the authentication mode of the application to be Passport authentication, all authentication duties are offloaded to the Passport servers.

Passport uses an encrypted cookie mechanism to indicate authenticated users. If users have already signed in to Passport when they visit your site, they'll be considered authenticated by ASP.NET. Otherwise, they'll be redirected to the Passport servers to log in.

To use Passport authentication, you need to download the Passport *Software Development Kit (SDK)* and install it on your server. The SDK can be found at msdn.microsoft.com/downloads/ default.asp?URL=/downloads/sample.asp?url=/msdn-files/027/001/ 885/msdncompositedoc.xml.

You also need to license Passport authentication. Currently, the license fees are $10,000 per year, plus a periodic $1,500 testing fee. You can get details on licensing Passport at www.microsoft.com/ netservices/passport/.

Forms Authentication

Forms authentication provides you with a way to handle authentication using your own custom logic within an ASP.NET application. (Note that this is different from custom authentication using an ISAPI filter, which takes place before the request ever gets to ASP.NET.) With forms authentication, the logic of the application goes like this:

1. When a user requests a page from the application, ASP.NET checks for the presence of a special cookie. If the cookie is present, the request is processed.

2. If the cookie is not present, ASP.NET redirects the user to a Web form that you provide.

3. You can carry out whatever authentication checks you like in your form. When the user is authenticated, you indicate this to ASP.NET, which creates the special cookie to handle subsequent requests.

Step-by-Step 11.5 demonstrates the use of forms authentication.

STEP BY STEP

11.5 Implementing Forms Authentication

1. Add a new Visual C# ASP.NET application named StepByStep11_5 to the solution. Add some text to the default Web form so that you can later verify that it displays properly.

2. In Windows, select Start, Programs, Administrative Tools, Internet Services Manager.

3. In Internet Services Manager, drill down into the tree view until you find the node that corresponds to your Visual C# ASP.NET application. This node has the same name as the application, and is located beneath the Default Web Site node. Right-click the application node and select Properties.

continues

continued

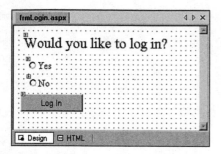

FIGURE 11.7
Forms authentication provides a way to handle
authentication by using your own custom logic.

4. In the Properties dialog box, click the Directory Security
tab. Click the Edit button in the Anonymous Access and
Authentication Methods section to open the
Authentication Methods dialog box.

5. Check the Anonymous Access check box. This causes IIS
to pass all requests directly to ASP.NET for processing.

6. If you receive a security warning, Click Yes and then click
OK twice to save your changes.

7. Add a new Web form to the Visual C# ASP.NET application. Name the new form `frmLogin.aspx`.

8. Place a `Label` control, two `RadioButton` controls (`rbYes`
and `rbNo` with GroupName `LogIn`), and a `Button` control
(`btnLogin`) on the form. Figure 11.7 shows a design for
this form.

9. Switch to code view and add the following using directive:

```
using System.Web.Security;
```

10. Add this code to handle the `Button` control's `Click` event:

```
private void btnLogin_Click(
    object sender, System.EventArgs e)
{
    if(rbYes.Checked)
        FormsAuthentication.RedirectFromLoginPage(
            "Admin", false);
}
```

11. Edit the `web.config` file to replace both the
`<authentication>` and `<authorization>` elements as
follows:

```
<authentication mode="Forms">
    <forms loginUrl="frmLogin.aspx"
     name="StepByStep11_5"
     timeout="1" />
</authentication>

<authorization>
    <deny users="?" />
</authorization>
```

12. Set the project as the startup project.

13. Run the solution. Instead of the start page of the application, your browser displays the custom login form. To proceed further, you need to select the Yes radio button and click the Login button.

Of course, in a real application you'd likely implement a more sophisticated authentication scheme than just making users select a radio button! But in forms-based authentication, you can use any login scheme you can code. You might, for example, store usernames and IP addresses in a database, and allow only users who connect from their registered IP address. Or you might develop a Web service that allows authenticating users over the Internet.

Note the change to the `<authorization>` element of the configuration file in this example. By default, the `<authorization>` element contains an `<allow>` element:

```
<allow users="*" />
```

With that authorization setting, ASP.NET allows all users—even unauthenticated users—access to application resources. The * wildcard matches any user. For Step-by-Step 11.5, I changed this to a `<deny>` element:

```
<deny users="?" />
```

The ? wildcard matches only unauthenticated users. The net effect is to allow authenticated users access to all resources, while denying unauthenticated users access to any resources.

The `<forms>` element contains the name of the URL of the form to use for login authentication, the name of the cookie to use, and a `timeout` attribute. The `timeout` attribute controls the period a user can work with the application before being directed back to the login page. (Step-by-Step 11.5 sets to the very low value of 1 minute for testing.)

When the user is authenticated, the form calls the `RedirectFromLoginPage()` method of the `FormsAuthentication` object. The two parameters to this method are the name of the authenticated user and a Boolean value that controls whether to save a permanent (cross-session) cookie. In Step-by-Step 11.5, the second parameter is `false`, so the cookie is stored in memory, and only for the length of the browser session.

Note that the login form doesn't contain any reference to the page where the user will go after authenticating. The forms authentication provider automatically keeps track of the name of the page that the user was trying to access and sends him there when you call the `RedirectFromLoginPage()` method.

CONFIGURING AUTHORIZATION

Configure security for a Windows service, a serviced component, a .NET Remoting object, and an XML Web service: Configure and control authorization. Authorization methods include file-based authorization and URL-based authorization.

After your application has authenticated users, you can proceed to authorize their access to resources. But there's a question to answer first: Just who is the user who you are granting access to? It turns out that there are different answers to that question, depending on whether you implement impersonation. With impersonation, the ASP.NET process can actually take on the identity of the authenticated user.

Impersonation applies only to applications that use ASP.NET to communicate with the server. For other server applications (such as services and serviced components), impersonation doesn't come into the picture.

After a user has been authenticated and you've decided whether to use impersonation, you can proceed to grant access to resources. ASP.NET uses the role-based authorization features of the .NET Framework for this purpose.

In this section I discuss both impersonation and role-based authorization.

Implementing Impersonation

Configure security for a Windows service, a serviced component, a .NET Remoting object, and an XML Web service: Configure and implement Identity management.

ASP.NET impersonation is controlled by entries in the applicable `web.config` file. The default setting is no impersonation. You can also explicitly specify this setting by including this element in the file:

```
<identity impersonate="false"/>
```

With this setting, ASP.NET does not perform user impersonation. What does that mean? It means that ASP.NET will always run with its own privileges. By default, ASP.NET runs as an unprivileged account named `ASPNET`. You can change this by making a setting in the `<processModel>` element of the `machine.config`. This setting can only be changed in `machine.config`, so any change automatically applies to every site on the server (and no site can have a setting different from that of the server) when the ASP.NET worker process is restarted. To use a high-privilege system account rather than a low-privilege account, set the `userName` attribute of the `<processModel>` element to `"SYSTEM"`.

So when impersonation is disabled, all requests will run in the context of the account running ASP.NET—either the `ASPNET` account or the `SYSTEM` account. This is true whether you're using anonymous access or authenticating users in some fashion.

The second possible setting is to turn on impersonation:

```
<identity impersonate="true"/>
```

In this case, ASP.NET takes on the identity passed to it by IIS. If you're allowing anonymous access in IIS, it means that ASP.NET impersonates the `IUSR_ComputerName` account that IIS itself uses. If you're not allowing anonymous access, ASP.NET will take on the credentials of the authenticated user and make requests for resources as if it were that user.

Finally, you can specify a particular identity to use for all authenticated requests:

```
<identity impersonate="true"
    name="DOMAIN\username"
    password="password"/>
```

With this setting, all requests are made as the specified user (assuming that the password is correct in the configuration file).

Step-by-Step 11.6 will give you some practice in configuring impersonation.

> **WARNING**
>
> **SYSTEM Account Is High-privileged** Don't run ASP.NET under the SYSTEM account unless you absolutely need to. Because this is a high-privilege account, it opens your server to disastrous changes should a security hole in ASP.NET ever be discovered and exploited.

STEP BY STEP

11.6 Using Impersonation

1. Add a new Visual C# ASP.NET application named StepByStep11_6 to the solution. Add some text to the default Web form so that you can later verify that it displays properly.

2. In Windows, select Start, Programs, Administrative Tools, Internet Services Manager.

3. In Internet Services Manager, drill down into the tree view until you find the node that corresponds to your Visual C# ASP.NET application. This node will have the same name as the application and will be located beneath the Default Web Site node. Right-click the application node and select Properties.

4. In the Properties dialog box, click the Directory Security tab. Click the Edit button in the Anonymous Access And Authentication Methods section to open the Authentication Methods dialog box.

5. Uncheck the Anonymous Access check box. Check the Basic authentication check box.

6. Click Yes if you receive a security warning, and then click OK twice to save your changes.

7. Add a new Web form to your Visual C# ASP.NET application. Name the new form StepByStep11_6.aspx.

8. Place a TextBox control (txtAuthenticatedUser) on the form.

9. Switch to code view and add the following using directive:

```
using System.Security.Principal;
```

10. Add the following code to the Page_Load() event handler (you'll learn about the Identity and Principal objects in the next section of the chapter):

```
private void Page_Load(
    object sender, System.EventArgs e)
{
    WindowsIdentity wi = WindowsIdentity.GetCurrent();
    txtAuthenticatedUser.Text = wi.Name;
}
```

11. Edit the `web.config` file to replace both the
`<authentication>` and `<authorization>` elements as
follows:

```
<authentication mode="Windows">
</authentication>

<authorization>
    <allow users="*" />
</authorization>
```

12. Set the new Web form as the start page for the project. Set
the project as the startup project.

13. Run the solution. Log in using a Windows username and
password. (Depending on your network configuration,
you may not receive a login prompt at this point.) The
form will display the name of the ASP.NET user (which
will be something like DOMAIN\ASPNET) because you don't
have impersonation turned on at this point.

14. Stop the project. Edit the `web.config` file to include
impersonation:

```
<authentication mode="Windows">
</authentication>
<identity impersonate="true" />

<authorization>
    <allow users="*" />
</authorization>
```

15. Run the solution again. Log in using a Windows username and password. The form will display the username
and domain that you supplied for authentication, indicating that the ASP.NET process has taken on the identity of
the authenticated user.

> **Custom Authorization** If for some reason you want to develop a custom authorization scheme, you can implement `IIdentity` and `IPrincipal` in your own classes. In use, these classes function very much like the Windows-based classes that are demonstrated in the remainder of this chapter.

Identity and Principal Objects

Within a Visual C# .NET Windows application, authorization is handled by the role-based security system. Role-based security revolves around two interfaces: `IIdentity` and `IPrincipal`. For applications that use Windows accounts in role-based security, these interfaces are implemented by the `WindowsIdentity` and `WindowsPrincipal` objects, respectively.

The `WindowsIdentity` object represents the Windows user who is running the current code. The properties of this object allow you to retrieve information such as the username and his authentication method.

The `WindowsPrincipal` object adds functionality to the `WindowsIdentity` object. The `WindowsPrincipal` object represents the entire security context of the user who is running the current code, including any roles to which he belongs. When the CLR decides which role-based permissions to assign to your code, it inspects the `WindowsPrincipal` object.

Step-by-Step 11.7 demonstrates the use of the `WindowsIdentity` and `WindowsPrincipal` objects.

STEP BY STEP

11.7 Using the `WindowsIdentity` and `WindowsPrincipal` Objects

1. Add a new Visual C# .NET Windows application named `StepByStep11_7` to the solution.

2. In the Solution Explorer, rename the default `Form1.cs` to `StepByStep11_7.cs`. Open the form in code view and change all occurrences of `Form1` to refer to `StepByStep11_7` instead.

3. Place a `ListBox` control named `lbProperties` and a `Button` control named `btnGetProperties` on the form.

4. Switch to the code view and add the following using directive:

```
using System.Security.Principal;
```

5. Double-click the `Button` control and add the following code to retrieve properties when the `Button` control is clicked:

```
private void btnGetProperties_Click(object sender,
    System.EventArgs e)
{
    // Tell the CLR which principal policy is in use
    AppDomain.CurrentDomain.SetPrincipalPolicy(
        PrincipalPolicy.WindowsPrincipal);
    lbProperties.Items.Clear();

    // Get the current identity
    WindowsIdentity wi = WindowsIdentity.GetCurrent();
    // Dump its properties to the listbox
    lbProperties.Items.Add("WindowsIdentity:");
    lbProperties.Items.Add("  Authentication type: " +
        wi.AuthenticationType);
    lbProperties.Items.Add("  Is Anonymous: " +
        wi.IsAnonymous);
    lbProperties.Items.Add("  Is Authenticated: " +
        wi.IsAuthenticated);
    lbProperties.Items.Add(
        "  Is Guest: " + wi.IsGuest);
    lbProperties.Items.Add(
        "  Is System: " + wi.IsSystem);
    lbProperties.Items.Add("  Name: " + wi.Name);
    lbProperties.Items.Add("  Token: " +
        wi.Token.ToString());

    // Get the current principal
    WindowsPrincipal prin = new WindowsPrincipal(wi);
    // Dump its properties to the listbox
    lbProperties.Items.Add("WindowsPrincipal:");
    lbProperties.Items.Add("  Authentication Type: " +
        prin.Identity.AuthenticationType);
    lbProperties.Items.Add("  Is Authenticated: " +
        prin.Identity.IsAuthenticated);
    lbProperties.Items.Add("  Name: " +
        prin.Identity.Name);
    lbProperties.Items.Add("  Member of Users: " +
        prin.IsInRole(@"INFINITY\Users"));
}
```

6. Set the project as the startup project.

7. Run the project and click the Get Properties button. You should see output similar to that in Figure 11.8.

The code in Step-by-Step 11.7 first tells the CLR that you're using the standard Windows authentication method, by calling the

WARNING

Modifying the Domain Name This code contains a reference to a specific domain named `INFINITY` in its call to the `IsInRole()` method. You should change that to the name of your own domain to test this code.

'FIGURE 11.8
`WindowsIdentity` and `WindowsPrincipal` classes enable you to retrieve current user information and also let you evaluate role membership for the current user.

`SetPrincipalPolicy()` method of the current application domain. It then retrieves the `WindowsIdentity` object of the current user by using the static `GetCurrent()` method of the `WindowsIdentity` object. After it displays some of the properties of the `WindowsIdentity` object, it gets the corresponding `WindowsPrincipal` object by passing the `WindowsIdentity` object to the constructor of the `WindowsPrincipal` class.

Note that the properties of the `WindowsIdentity` object are somewhat richer than those of the `WindowsPrincipal` object, but that the `WindowsPrincipal` object lets you evaluate role membership for the current user. If you want to work with only the `WindowsPrincipal` object, you can retrieve it from the `Thread.CurrentPrincipal()` static method.

Verifying Role Membership

One way to manage role-based security is to use the `IsInRole()` method of the `WindowsPrincipal` object to determine whether the current user is in a specific Windows group (see Step-by-Step 11.8). The results of this method call can be used to modify your application's user interface or to perform other tasks.

STEP BY STEP

11.8 Verifying Role Membership

1. Add a new Visual C# .NET Windows application named `StepByStep11_8` to the solution.

2. In the Solution Explorer, rename the default `Form1.cs` to `StepByStep11_8.cs`. Open the form in code view and change all occurrences of `Form1` to refer to `StepByStep11_8` instead.

3. Place a `Label` control (`lblMembership`) on the form.

4. Switch to the code view and add the following using directives:

```
using System.Security.Principal;
using System.Threading;
```

5. Double-click the form and add the following code to handle the Load event of the form:

```
private void StepByStep11_8_Load(object sender,
    System.EventArgs e)
{
    // Tell the CLR to use Windows security
    AppDomain.CurrentDomain.SetPrincipalPolicy(
        PrincipalPolicy.WindowsPrincipal);
    // Get the current principal object
    WindowsPrincipal prin =
        (WindowsPrincipal) Thread.CurrentPrincipal;
    // Determine whether the user is an admin
    Boolean fAdmin = prin.IsInRole(
        WindowsBuiltInRole.Administrator);
    // Display the results on the UI
    if(fAdmin)
        lblMembership.Text =
            "You are in the Administrators group";
    else
        lblMembership.Text =
            "You are not in the Administrators group";
}
```

6. Set the project as the startup project.

7. Run the project. The form will tell you whether or not you're in the Administrators group.

There are three available overloaded forms of the `IsInRole()` method:

▶ `IsInRole(WindowsBuiltInRole)`—This form uses one of the `WindowsBuiltInRole` constants to check for membership in the standard Windows groups.

▶ `IsInRole(String)`—This form checks for membership in a group with the specified name.

▶ `IsInRole(Integer)`—This form checks for membership in a group by using the specified role identifier (RID). RIDs are assigned by the operating system and provide a language-independent way to identify groups.

Using the `PrincipalPermission` Class

In the previous section I discussed the use of the `IsInRole()` method of the `WindowsPrincipal` object in managing role-based security. An alternative way to manage identities is to perform imperative or declarative security checking with role-based security by using the `PrincipalPermission` class, as in Step-by-Step 11.9, or the `PrincipalPermissionAttribute` attribute.

STEP BY STEP

11.9 Using the `PrincipalPermission` Class

1. Add a new Visual C# .NET Windows application named `StepByStep11_9` to the solution.

2. In the Solution Explorer, rename the default `Form1.cs` to `StepByStep11_9.cs`. Open the form in code view and change all occurrences of `Form1` to refer to `StepByStep11_9` instead.

3. Switch to the code view and add the following using directives:

```
using System.Security.Permissions;
using System.Security.Principal;
```

4. Double-click the form and add the following code, which should run when the form is loaded:

```
private void StepByStep11_9_Load(object sender,
    System.EventArgs e)
{
    // Tell the CLR to use Windows security
    AppDomain.CurrentDomain.SetPrincipalPolicy(
      PrincipalPolicy.WindowsPrincipal);
    // Create a new PrincipalPermission object
    // This object matches any user
    // in a group named Developers
    PrincipalPermission pp = new PrincipalPermission(
        null, "Developers");
    // See whether the user is in the group
    try
    {
        pp.Demand();
        MessageBox.Show(
            "You are in the Developers group");
    }
    catch (Exception ex)
```

```
    {
        MessageBox.Show("Exception: " + ex.Message);
    }
}
```

5. Set the project as the startup project.

6. Run the project. If you're a member of a group named Developers, you see a message box that tells you so. If you are not a member of that group, you see a security exception message from the `PrincipalPermission` class, telling you that the requested permission could not be granted.

Checking permissions by using role-based security is very similar to checking permissions by using code access security. The difference lies in what you are checking. The constructor for the `PrincipalPermission` class accepts both a name and a group name, so you can also use it to check whether a specific user is running the code.

▶ The .NET Framework supports both authentication and authorization. Authentication refers to verifying a user's identity. Authorization refers to granting rights based on that identity.

▶ Users must satisfy any IIS authentication requirements before ASP.NET authentication takes over.

▶ ASP.NET authentication uses interchangeable authentication providers. You can choose Windows authentication, Passport authentication, or forms-based authentication.

▶ Identity impersonation lets the ASP.NET process act as the authenticated user.

▶ The `WindowsPrincipal` and `WindowsIdentity` classes let you check the authentication status of the current user.

▶ You can use the `IsInRole()` method of the `WindowsPrincipal` object to check for membership in Windows groups.

▶ The `PrincipalPermission` class enables you to perform declarative and imperative role-based security operations.

SECURITY FOR WINDOWS SERVICES

In most aspects, a Windows service is an application like any other. You can use code access security to specify the permissions that this application needs, and control whether those permissions are available by using the .NET Framework configuration tool.

But because Windows services are launched at bootup time, and run for the entire time that the operating system is loaded, you need to pay special attention to the security context in which they run. The security context for a service is initially specified by the Account property of the ServiceProcessInstaller object that was used to place the service on the system (although the user can later change this context by using the Services administrative tool). The .NET Framework lets you choose one of the four values of the ServiceAccount enumeration for this property:

> **Some Accounts Are XP-Only**   The LocalService and NetworkService accounts are available only on Windows XP and Windows Server 2003. These accounts do not exist on Windows 2000 or older operating systems.

- ▶ LocalService—This account is a built-in account that has few privileges on the local computer. When accessing resources from a remote computer, the LocalService account presents anonymous credentials.

- ▶ NetworkService—This account is a built-in account that has few privileges on the local computer. When accessing resources from a remote computer, the NetworkService account presents the computer's credentials.

- ▶ LocalSystem—This account is a built-in account that has high privileges on the local computer. When accessing resources from a remote computer, the LocalSystem account presents the computer's credentials.

- ▶ User—This account is a built-in account for a specific user on the network. When you select the User value for the Account property, you must also supply a valid Windows username and password. The service runs with the privileges of the specified user, and presents that user's credentials when requesting network resources.

The LocalSystem account is used for most of the built-in services in Windows, such as the Computer Browser, Event Log, and Indexing services. These are services which require extensive access to resources on your computer to do their work. It may be tempting to install your own services by using this account as well, but you should consider carefully whether your services need such sweeping privileges. Remember that ease of use is balanced by danger in this case. If you've made an error in your code, an attacker could potentially exploit your service to gain the privileges of the account under which it runs. If that account is the LocalSystem account, a successful attacker could take over the entire computer.

SECURITY FOR WEB SERVICES

Because they are applications layered on top of ASP.NET, Web services offer you many opportunities for configuring and implementing security. You can choose to secure things at the level of IIS itself, or in the ASP.NET layer, or in the application itself. Depending on the choices you make, nearly any type of security can be applied to a Web service.

In this section of the chapter, I'll first trace through the layers involved in a Web service, showing you where and how you can apply security. Then I'll give you some general advice on securing Web services. Finally, you'll learn a little about the new WS-Security specification, which will bring additional security tools to Web services.

Platform and Application Security

Because SOAP messages come in via HTTP on port 80, IIS handles them on Windows servers. This means that you can use the full spectrum of IIS authentication modes for a Web service: anonymous, basic, digest, integrated (Windows), and so on. You can also configure IIS to accept requests from only a specified range of IP addresses. If the incoming SOAP request fails to authenticate (assuming that you have disabled anonymous authentication) or the IP address is not allowed access to the server, that's it; the Web service will not be called.

Assuming that the SOAP request properly authenticates, the next question is which identity will be passed to ASP.NET and then to the Web service. This depends on the type of authentication you've

> **NOTE**
>
> **No Forms or Passport** Forms authentication and Passport authentication are not supported for Web services applications.

performed, and on whether impersonation is enabled; you can make settings in the web.config file for a Web service to control impersonation, just as you can for any other ASP.NET application (see the section "Implementing Impersonation" earlier in the chapter for details). In particular:

▶ If impersonation is disabled, then requests will run in the security context of either the ASPNET account or the SYSTEM account, depending on the <processModel> element setting in the machine.config file.

▶ If impersonation is enabled and you allow anonymous access in IIS, requests will run in the security context of the IUSR_*ComputerName* account.

▶ If impersonation is enabled, you do not allow anonymous access, and you do not specify a user identity in the identity tag, requests run in the security context of the authenticated Windows user.

▶ If impersonation is enabled, you do not allow anonymous access, and you do specify a user identity in the identity tag, requests run in the security context of the specified Windows user.

After the user has been authenticated and the identity for ASP.NET requests has been determined, the next line of defense is the ASMX file that implements the Web service itself. You can protect this file with either URL authorization or file authorization.

URL authorization is specified within the web.config file as part of the <authorization> element. You saw an example of this earlier in the chapter:

```
<authorization>
    <deny users = "?" />
</authorization>
```

URL authorization allows you to deny access to a resource (in this case, any resource in the Web service application) to unauthenticated users, or to grant access to only specified users. If you're using Windows authentication in IIS, you can also protect the file by using file authorization. For file authorization, right-click on the ASMX file in Windows Explorer and select Properties. The Security tab of the Properties dialog box, shown in Figure 11.9, lets you control which Windows users can open the file.

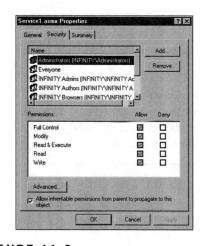

FIGURE 11.9
You can set file authorization properties for a Web service via its Properties dialog box.

Assuming that the authenticated user can read the ASMX file, the final line of defense is code within the file. You can use imperative or declarative code access security or role-based security within an ASMX file, just as you can inside of any other assembly.

Configuring Web Services for Security

Here are some guidelines for securing your Web services:

▶ If you need to be able to authorize access to resources based on the caller's identity, you should set up your server to perform Windows authentication with impersonation. For example, if only some of the authorized users should be able to read access from a particular database table, or via a particular COM+ serviced component, you'll need to take this approach so that the caller's security context is available to other components.

▶ If all users of your Web service should be able to access the same resources after they're authenticated, you should set up your server to perform Windows authentication without impersonation. Then you can use declarative or imperative security to provide resource access to the account under which ASP.NET is running.

▶ You should generally avoid using Windows authentication with a fixed identity (established by the `<identity>` element in the `web.config` file). This strategy requires storing the password for the fixed identity account in clear text in the configuration file, which is an inherently insecure situation.

▶ On production servers, you should disable HTTP-GET and HTTP-POST access to Web services, limiting them to SOAP access. This is most important when the Web service should be available only to clients on your intranet, and those same clients are allowed to browse to the Internet. Under those circumstances, a malicious Web page on the Internet could contain a carefully-crafted link that would cause the client to invoke the internal-only Web service. This is only possible through the HTTP-GET and HTTP-POST protocols, because Web pages can't create a SOAP message as part of a link. To disable such access, modify the `<webServices>` section of the `machine.config` or `web.config` file as follows:

WARNING

Impersonation and Scalability Windows authentication with impersonation can limit the scalability of applications that depend on database connections. Connection pooling happens only for connections with identical security contexts. If you use impersonation, connections won't pool between different users. In this situation you may want to consider Windows authentication without impersonation instead.

```
<webServices>
  <protocols>
    <add name="HttpSoap"/>
    <!-- <add name="HttpPost"/> -->
    <!-- <add name="HttpGet"/> -->
    <add name="Documentation"/>
  </protocols>
</webServices>
```

Remember, the chief challenge in Web services security is to decide how to authenticate users. You'll see some sample code for interacting with a secured Web service in Exercise 11.1. After a user has been authenticated, a Web service is a Windows application like any other, and you can use the same declarative and imperative security tools that you use with other applications.

WS-Security

The final topic you should be aware of in Web services security is a new standard called WS-Security. You can be relatively certain that this material will not be on the 70-320 exam, for the simple reason that it was not formalized until after the exam was written. But it's such a crucial piece of the Web services puzzle that I'd be remiss in not at least mentioning it.

WS-Security is part of a new set of Microsoft standards, GXA, introduced in late 2002. GXA, the Global XML Web Services Architecture, is Microsoft's latest idea about how to make Web Services more reliable and functional. GXA isn't a single protocol; it's a scheme for building a whole family of protocols that can be used in many Web Services applications. Some of the design principles for the GXA protocols include the following:

▶ XML-Based Data Models—The good news is that you already know XML. The bad news is that you probably don't know about XML Information Sets, otherwise known as Infosets, so there's still something to learn here. msdn.microsoft.com/library/en-us/dnxml/html/ xmlinfoset.asp will get you started with the basics.

▶ Transport Neutrality—In theory, at least, GXA does not depend on HTTP. Of course in theory SOAP doesn't depend on HTTP, either.

▶ Application Domain Neutrality—The GXA protocols are designed to be broadly useful, but extensible for specific application domains. That's good for the developer, because it means more general-purpose (and hence saleable) skills.

▶ Decentralization and Federation—GXA does not depend on central authorities to manage things. You can view this as a good move from the standpoint of scalability. You can also view this as Microsoft trying to avoid extending its "Big Brother" image if you're so inclined.

▶ Modularity—GXA is designed to be modular, so you need to learn only the pieces that you want to use.

The goal of WS-Security is to add security features directly to the SOAP messages passed to and from a Web service, rather than use external services (such as IIS) to manage security. WS-Security does this by defining a set of namespaces and tags that can be used within the SOAP Header to perform three functions:

▶ Authentication

▶ Encryption

▶ Signing

When WS-Security is fully implemented, SOAP messages will be able to contain user credentials, contain digital signatures to verify those credentials, and be encrypted to protect those credentials from eavesdroppers. You can learn more about WS-Security in the GXA section of the MSDN web site. A good starting point is Scott Seely's white paper "Understanding WS-Security," available at `msdn.microsoft.com/library/en-us/dnglobspec/html/wssecurspecindex.asp`.

REMOTING SECURITY

As with Windows services and Web services, .NET Remoting applications are like any other .NET application, and can use the same imperative and declarative security techniques to protect resources. The major difference is that remoting introduces additional "plumbing" to allow your object to be called from client applications on other computers. The objects themselves can still be protected with .NET security, just like any other objects.

With remoting applications, the major security-related decision that you need to make is which application will host the remoting server. You have three choices here:

▶ Host in a console application

▶ Host in a Windows service

▶ Host in ASP.NET

Hosting your remoting server in a console application is convenient, but that's about the only thing you can say in favor of this approach. You may want to use a console application, as I did in Chapter 3, ".NET Remoting," when you're developing a new remoting server. Console applications are easier to make changes to and to debug than either Windows services or ASP.NET applications. The problem, from a security standpoint, is that console applications don't have any built-in authentication or authorization mechanisms. You can write your own custom authentication and authorization code, of course, but such schemes are notoriously difficult to actually make secure.

When you host your remoting server in a Windows service, you're limited to using the TCP channel. This means that you must write custom code to handle authentication and authorization, with the attendant danger of writing code that doesn't quite work. However, you can use the security of the underlying TCP channel to provide secure communication by making use of the IPSec standard.

With a Windows service as your remoting host, it's easy to limit the damage that a security breach can do by choosing an appropriate account to run the service. You can also use permission refusals to make sure that the service cannot perform dangerous actions beyond the scope of its regular operations.

For secure communications—for instance, when your remoting server must make objects available to authenticated clients over the Internet—your best bet is to host the server in ASP.NET. That's because hosting in ASP.NET automatically makes all of the authentication, authorization, and security features of IIS available to your server, just as they are available to a Web service. Clients must use the HTTP channel to communicate with the server, which is slower than the TCP channel but more secure. You can also use the logging features of IIS to track requests to the remoting server.

When the remote object is hosted in ASP.NET, you must specify the credentials to be used for authentication via the credentials property of the channel. This code must exist in the remoting client proxy class. If you neglect to do this, then credentials won't be passed to the remoting server, even if you successfully authenticate with ASP.NET. Fortunately, the code is simple, because you can extract the default cached credentials that were used to authenticate in the first place:

```
IDictionary cp =
ChannelServices.GetChannelSinkProperties( _
RemoteObjectProxy);
cp["credentials"] = _
CredentialCache.DefaultCredentials;
```

Reviewing these choices, you can see that ASP.NET is generally the best hosting solution for a remoting server that must provide secure access for authenticated clients. For a remoting server that has no authentication requirements, you'll probably find that hosting in a Windows service requires fewer resources and is easier to deploy.

ENTERPRISE SERVICES SECURITY

Serviced components benefit from a set of authentication and authorization services that are included in the Enterprise Services (COM+) infrastructure. Authentication is provided over the RPC channel between client and server, so clients will automatically present to the server with their Windows identities. Authorization is provided by COM+ security roles, which rely on Windows accounts. An Enterprise Services role can contain Windows users and Windows groups. You can limit access to applications, components, interfaces, and methods within a serviced component to members of specific roles.

In general, you can manage security for serviced components through a combination of attributes within your .NET project, and the Component Services tool, as shown in Step-by-Step 11.10.

STEP BY STEP

11.10 Implementing Security for a Serviced Component

1. Add a new Visual C# Class library project to the solution, named `InventoryService`.

2. Right-click the `Class1.cs` file and rename it to `Inventory.cs`.

3. Right-click the References folder and select Add Reference. Select the `System.EnterpriseServices` reference from the .NET tab of the Add Reference dialog box and click OK.

4. Add code to create the `Inventory` class as a serviced component:

```
using System;
using System.EnterpriseServices;
namespace InventoryService
{
    public interface ISell
    {
        void Sell(int intAmount);
    }

    [ComponentAccessControl(),
    SecureMethod(),
    SecurityRole("InventoryUsers")]
    public class Inventory
        : ServicedComponent, ISell
    {
        public Inventory() {}

        [AutoComplete(),
        SecurityRole("InventoryUsers")]
        public void Sell(int intAmount)
        {
            // Work of the component
            // would go here
        }
    }
}
```

5. Open a Visual Studio .NET command prompt. Navigate to the directory containing the `InventoryService` project and create a key file by entering this command:

```
sn -k InventoryService.snk
```

6. Open the `AssemblyInfo.cs` file. Add the following using directive:

```
using System.EnterpriseServices;
```

7. Add assembly-level attributes `ApplicationName`, `Description`, and `ApplicationActivation` in the `AssemblyInfo.cs` as follows:

```
[assembly: ApplicationName("InventoryComponent")]
[assembly: ApplicationAccessControl(
    AccessChecksLevel=
    AccessChecksLevelOption.ApplicationComponent)]
[assembly: SecurityRole("InventoryUsers")]
```

8. Change the `AssemblyVersion` and `AssemblyKeyFile` attribute in the `AssemblyInfo.cs` file as shown here:

```
[assembly: AssemblyVersion("1.0.0")]
[assembly: AssemblyKeyFile(
    @"..\..\InventoryService.snk")]
```

9. Build the project to create `InventoryService.dll`.

10. Switch to the Visual Studio .NET command prompt and navigate to the project's `bin\Debug` directory. Enter this command to register the assembly with COM+:

```
regsvcs InventoryService.dll
```

11. Add a new Visual C# .NET Windows application project to the solution. Name the new project `InventoryClient`. Set the new project as the startup project for the solution.

12. Right-click the References folder and select Add Reference. Add references to the `System.EnterpriseServices` component and `InventoryService` project.

13. In the Solution Explorer, rename the default `Form1.cs` to `InventoryClient.cs`. Open the form in code view and change all occurrences of `Form1` to refer to `InventoryClient` instead.

14. Place a `Label` control, a `TextBox` control (`txtAmount`), and a `Button` control (`btnSell`) on the default form in the project.

continues

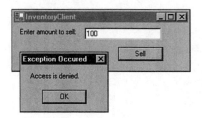

FIGURE 11.10
The Inventory component is available only to the users in the InventoryUsers COM+ role.

continued

15. Switch to the code view and add the following using directive:

```
using InventoryService;
```

16. Double-click the Button control and add code to handle the button's Click event:

```
private void btnSell_Click(
    object sender, System.EventArgs e)
{
    try
    {
        Inventory inv = new Inventory();
        MessageBox.Show("Sale succeded");
    }
    catch(Exception ex)
    {
        MessageBox.Show(ex.Message,
            "Exception Occured");
    }
}
```

17. Run the solution, enter a number in the textbox, and click the button. You'll receive an exception message as shown in Figure 11.10, because you're not a member of the InventoryUsers COM+ role. Close the form.

18. Launch the Component Services tool from the Administrative Tools section of the Windows Control Panel.

19. In the Component Services tool, expand the tree to locate the Users node for the InventoryUsers role, as shown in Figure 11.11. Right-click the node and select New, User. In the Select Users or Groups dialog box, locate your own user account and click Add, and then click OK.

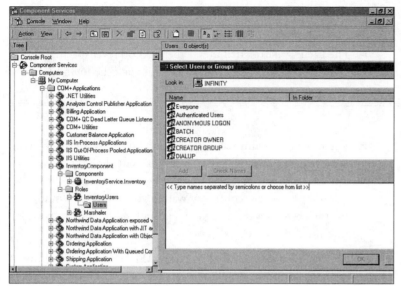

FIGURE 11.11
The Component Services administrative tool
enables you to configure roles and users for a
serviced component.

20. Run the solution again, enter a number in the text box,
and click the button again. This time the call will succeed
because your account is a member of the proper COM+
role.

Step-by-Step 11.10 shows the essential attributes that you can use to
configure security for a serviced component:

▶ The `ApplicationAccessControl` attribute at the assembly level
  enables access checking at the process and component level.

▶ The `SecurityRole` attribute at the assembly level specifies the
  COM+ roles that will be able to use any of the classes from
  the assembly.

▶ The `ComponentAccessControl` attribute at the class level enables
  component-level access checking.

▶ The `SecurityRole` attribute at the class level specifies the
  COM+ roles that will be allowed to create instances of the
  class.

▶ The SecureMethod attribute at the class level allows you to use the Component Services tool to configure roles for the class.

▶ The SecurityRole attribute at the method level specifies the COM+ roles that will be allowed to invoke the method.

REVIEW BREAK

▶ The most important security decision you must make with a Windows service is which security account should be used to run the service. You can choose between the LocalSystem account or a user account on Windows 2000. On Windows XP, the LocalService and NetworkService accounts provide additional flexibility.

▶ Because Web services are hosted by ASP.NET, they have the entire spectrum of IIS authentication, authorization, and security features available to them.

▶ You can use IIS to control access to a Web service, and then use declarative or imperative security to control the Web service's access to resources.

▶ WS-Security is a new specification for a set of SOAP headers to handle authentication, encryption, and signing directly in SOAP messages.

▶ Remoting servers that require secure hosting are best run in the ASP.NET process. Remoting servers that require additional speed but less security can be run in a Windows service host instead.

▶ You can configure security for serviced components by applying attributes within the code for the components and then specifying COM+ roles with the Component Services tool.

CHAPTER SUMMARY

In this chapter you learned about some of the security features that you can apply to server-side and distributed applications.

The .NET Framework also includes two complete security systems configurable by administrators. Code access security controls the access of code to sensitive resources. Code can determine exactly which resources it requires or would like, and administrators can determine exactly which resources to make available. The CLR checks to see whether the requested resources are available before it lets your code run.

Role-based security enables you to make decisions in your code based on the user who is currently logged on. You can check for a particular username or for membership in a built-in or custom Windows group, and make decisions accordingly.

Security in ASP.NET revolves around authentication and authorization. You can choose from several authentication providers, including Windows, forms, and Passport authentication. After you've authenticated a user, you can authorize his access to resources.

Windows services, Web services, Remoting, and Enterprise Services each share in the overall .NET security framework, but they each have their own particular security issues. With Windows services, you need to consider carefully the account under which the service will run. With Web services, you must decide how much authentication you need, and configure IIS to provide that authentication. With a remoting server, you must balance the security and performance needs of your application in choosing a host process. With a serviced component, you may choose to use COM+ roles to manage all your security.

KEY TERMS

- authentication
- authorization
- code access security
- code group
- configured assembly
- declarative security
- imperative security
- impersonation
- permission
- permission set
- role-based security

APPLY YOUR KNOWLEDGE

Exercises

11.1 Building a Client for a Secure Web Service

In the chapter, you saw how to configure a Web Service to require authentication. But how do you build a client that can supply credentials? In this exercise, you'll learn how to alter the proxy class in a Web service client project to pass the current user's credentials to a Web service, using the StringProc Web service that you constructed in Chapter 4.

Estimated Time: 15 minutes.

1. Launch Visual Studio .NET. Select File, New, Blank Solution and name the new solution 320C11Exercises.

2. Add a new Visual C# .NET Windows application named Exercise11_1 to the solution.

3. In the Solution Explorer, rename the default Form1.cs to Exercise11_1.cs. Open the form in code view and change all occurrences of Form1 to refer to Exercise11_1 instead.

4. Right-click the References node in Solution Explorer and select Add Web Reference. Enter **http://*localhost*/StringProc/Strings.asmx** as the Address and hit Enter, changing the server name to match that of your own Web server. Click Add Reference to add the Web reference.

5. Add two TextBox controls (txtInput and txtOutput) and a Button control (btnUpperCase) to the form.

6. Click the Show All Files button on the Solution Explorer toolbar.

7. Drill into the Web References node until you locate the Reference.cs file. Double-click the file to open it.

8. Locate the constructor for the class, and modify its code as follows:

```
public Strings(): base()
{
    base.PreAuthenticate = true;
    base.Credentials =
        System.Net.CredentialCache.
        DefaultCredentials;
    this.Url =
"http://localhost/StringProc/Strings.asmx";
}
```

9. Double-click the Button control and add this code to handle the Click event (changing *localhost* to the name of your own server, if the Web server is not a local server):

```
private void btnUpperCase_Click(
    object sender, System.EventArgs e)
{
    localhost.Strings s =
        new localhost.Strings();
    txtOutput.Text = s.ToUpper(
        txtInput.Text);
}
```

10. Set the project as the startup project.

11. Run the project. Enter a string in the input textbox and click the button. After a pause while the Web service is invoked, you'll see the string in uppercase in the output textbox.

The proxy classes that are built by wsdl.exe (which, you'll recall, is invoked when you add a Web reference from within the Visual Studio .NET IDE) are based on the System.Web.Services.Protocols. SoapHttpClientProtocol class. This class exposes two properties that you can use to create authenticated Web services clients.

APPLY YOUR KNOWLEDGE

The most important of these properties is the `Credentials` property. You can use this property to specify the security credentials that the proxy will use to contact the Web services server. In Exercise 11.1, the code passes the credentials of the current user:

```
base.Credentials = _
  System.Net.CredentialCache.
  DefaultCredentials;
```

You can also use this property to pass the credentials of a specific user in a specific domain, provided you know that user's password:

```
base.Credentials = _
  new NetworkCredential("username",
  "password", "domain");
```

This second form is convenient for testing, but you should be wary of it in actual development, because it results in a password being embedded in the MSIL for your project in plain text.

The second property used in Exercise 11.1 is the `PreAuthenticate` property. When you set this property to `true`, the client will pass the credentials with the initial SOAP request. If it's set to `false`, then the client will send the credentials only if it receives a 401 Access Denied response from the server, which results in an extra round trip across the network.

11.2 Declarative Role-Based Security

Just like code access security, role-based security can be declarative or imperative. This exercise shows how to use declarative role-based security to cause an exception if the user is not in a specified group.

Estimated Time: 15 minutes.

1. Add a new Visual C# .NET Windows application named `Exercise11_2` to the solution.

2. In the Solution Explorer, rename the default `Form1.cs` to `Exercise11_2.cs`. Open the form in code view and change all occurrences of `Form1` to refer to `Exercise11_2` instead.

3. Add the following using directive:

```
using System.Security.Permissions;
using System.Security.Principal;
```

4. Modify the class declaration for the form to include a declarative security line with the `PrincipalPermissionAttribute`:

```
[PrincipalPermissionAttribute(
    SecurityAction.Demand,
    Role="Administrators")]
public class Exercise11_2 :
    System.Windows.Forms.Form
```

5. Double-click the form and add code to run when you open the form:

```
private void Exercise11_2_Load(
    object sender, System.EventArgs e)
{
    MessageBox.Show("You are a member " +
        "of the Administrators group");
}
```

6. Set the project as the startup project.

7. Run the project. If you're not in the local Administrators group, you should see a security exception. Otherwise, the form should load and the display the message box.

Review Questions

1. What types of permission requests can an application make?

2. What are the three types of permission objects?

3. What is the difference between declarative and imperative security?

APPLY YOUR KNOWLEDGE

4. What do the `WindowsIdentity` and `WindowsPrincipal` objects represent?

5. What are authentication and authorization?

6. What are the default accounts for the ASP.NET process?

7. Name four types of authentication that you can specify in an ASP.NET configuration file.

8. What is meant by impersonation in ASP.NET?

9. What should you consider when deciding whether to host a remoting server in ASP.NET or in a Windows service?

10. How can you configure a Web service to require users to log in with their Windows credentials?

Exam Questions

1. Your application requires permission to read environment variables and to prompt users with the Open File dialog box to function properly. Which .NET security features should you use to ensure that your code has these capabilities?

   A. Code access security

   B. Role-based security

   C. Encryption

   D. Type safety

2. Your application requires the user to be in the Developers group to activate certain functions. Which .NET security feature should you use to ensure that the user is in this group?

   A. Code access security

   B. Role-based security

   C. Encryption

   D. Type safety

3. You are using code access security to verify that your application has permission to access databases via OLE DB. As part of your testing procedure, you created a permission set that denies OLE DB permissions. You also created a code group that uses a hash code membership condition to select your application's executable assembly, and you assigned the permission set to this code group. You set this code group to be an exclusive code group and verified that your program is unable to obtain OLE DB permissions.

   To continue development, you change the code group to use the `FullTrust` permission set and continue adding new code to your application. When you're ready to test the security features, you change back to the permission set without OLE DB permissions. However, you find that your application can access files via OLE DB, even though you have not changed the declarative security within the application.

   Why is your code able to use OLE DB even though the code group denies OLE DB permissions?

APPLY YOUR KNOWLEDGE

A. Changing code within your application changes its hash code, so the compiled assembly is no longer a member of the code group.

B. After you've assigned the `FullTrust` permission set to a code group, the code group ignores attempts to set more restrictive permissions.

C. The `Exclusive` property on a code group applies only when the code group is first created.

D. You must reboot your development computer to update the membership records of the code group.

4. Assembly A is a member of the following code groups (and only the following code groups):

Level	Code Group	Permission Set	Exclusive
Enterprise	All Code	Everything	No
Enterprise	Company Code	LocalIntranet	No
Enterprise	Restricted Code	Internet	No
Enterprise	Restricted Components	Nothing	No

What permission does the CLR assign to Assembly A?

A. Everything

B. LocalIntranet

C. Internet

D. Nothing

5. Assembly B is a member of the following code groups (and only the following code groups):

Level	Code Group	Permission Set	Exclusive	Level-Final
Enterprise	All Code	Everything	No	No
Enterprise	Company Code	LocalIntranet	No	No
Machine	Restricted Code	Internet	No	No
User	Restricted Components	Nothing	No	No

What permission does the CLR assign to Assembly B?

A. Everything

B. LocalIntranet

C. Internet

D. Nothing

6. Assembly C is a member of the following code groups (and only the following code groups):

Level	Code Group	Permission Set	Exclusive	Level-Final
Enterprise	All Code	Everything	No	No
Enterprise	Company Code	LocalIntranet	Yes	No
Machine	Restricted Code	Internet	No	No
User	Restricted Components	Nothing	No	No

APPLY YOUR KNOWLEDGE

What permission does the CLR assign to Assembly C?

A. Everything

B. LocalIntranet

C. Internet

D. Nothing

7. Assembly D is a member of the following code groups (and only the following code groups):

Level	Code Group	Permission Set	Exclusive	Level-Final
Enterprise	All Code	Everything	No	No
Enterprise	Company Code	LocalIntranet	No	No
Machine	Restricted Code	Internet	No	Yes
User	Restricted Components	Nothing	No	No

What permission does the Common Language Runtime assign to Assembly D?

A. Everything

B. LocalIntranet

C. Internet

D. Nothing

8. Your code will be called from the Internet and you want to minimize the chance that it can do unintentional damage to the local computer. As a result, you want to ensure that your code is not granted Registry permissions. Which `SecurityAction` action should you use with the `FileIOPermissionAttribute` declaration?

A. `SecurityAction.RequestMinimum`

B. `SecurityAction.RequestOptional`

C. `SecurityAction.Demand`

D. `SecurityAction.RequestRefuse`

9. Your code wants to ensure that all code in the calling chain has File I/O permissions. Which `SecurityAction` action should you use with the `RegistryPermission` object?

A. `SecurityAction.RequestMinimum`

B. `SecurityAction.RequestOptional`

C. `SecurityAction.Demand`

D. `SecurityAction.RequestRefuse`

10. Which of these tasks requires you to use imperative security rather than declarative security?

A. Ensuring that your application has access to a specific key in the Windows Registry

B. Ensuring that your application can open a particular file whose name is specified by a configuration file that can be edited at runtime

C. Ensuring that your application has access to a specific environment variable whose name is known at design time

D. Ensuring that your application has access to SQL Server databases

11. You have implemented forms-based authentication for your ASP.NET application. Some users report that they cannot access any resources on the site, even though you have verified that these users are entering correct authentication information. What could be the problem?

APPLY YOUR KNOWLEDGE

A. These users are using a version 4 browser.

B. These users have disabled cookies for your Web site.

C. These users do not have a Microsoft Passport.

D. These users are connecting from the Internet rather than a local intranet.

12. You want to allow any authenticated user access to your ASP.NET application, but refuse access to all unauthenticated users. Which setting should you place in the application's `web.config` file?

A.
```
<deny users="?" />
```

B.
```
<deny users="*" />
```

C
```
<allow users="?" />
```

D.
```
<allow users="*" />
```

13. You are allowing anonymous or Windows-integrated authentication on your IIS server. ASP.NET is running with machine-level privileges. Your ASP.NET application uses Windows authentication with impersonation enabled. What account will ASP.NET use when a user attempts to retrieve a page from the application?

A. The user's own Windows account

B. The `ASPNET` account

C. The `IUSR_ComputerName` account

D. An account in the local Administrators group

14. Your ASP.NET application contains this setting in the `web.config` file:

```
<identity impersonate="true"
  name="MAIN\Charles"
  password="CharlesPassword"/>
```

You are allowing only digest or Windows integrated authentication in IIS. What identity will ASP.NET use to authorize resources if a user with the Windows account Fred in the `MAIN` domain logs in?

A. `MAIN\Fred`

B. `ASPNET`

C. `MAIN\Charles`

D. `IUSR_ComputerName`

15. You have created a Windows service that collects event log information from various computers around the network and then consolidates this information into a local disk file. The service does not need system-level privileges on the local computer, but it must be able to authenticate to the remote computers. You run the Windows service on a Windows XP Professional machine. Which security context should you use for this service?

A. `LocalService`

B. `NetworkService`

C. `LocalSystem`

D. `User`

APPLY YOUR KNOWLEDGE

Answers to Review Questions

1. An application can request minimum or optional permissions, refuse permissions, or demand permissions of its callers.

2. Code-based, identity, and role-based.

3. Declarative security works by assigning attributes to assemblies; imperative security works by instantiating the various security classes and using them directly.

4. The `WindowsIdentity` object represents a logged-on user; the `WindowsPrincipal` object represents the entire security context of the logged-on user.

5. Authentication refers to verifying credentials to determine the identity of a user. Authorization refers to granting access to resources to an authenticated user.

6. By default ASP.NET runs as a low-privilege user named `ASPNET`. You can also configure ASP.NET to run as a high-privilege `SYSTEM` account.

7. You can specify None, Windows, Passport, or Forms authentication in an ASP.NET configuration file.

8. If you enable ASP.NET impersonation, the ASP.NET user acts as the authenticated user when requesting access to resources.

9. Generally speaking, ASP.NET offers higher security and more flexible authentication options for a remoting server, whereas a Windows service offers better performance.

10. You can configure authentication for a Web service by selecting properties for the IIS server that hosts the service. If you disable anonymous access, users will be required to supply a username and password to access the Web service.

Answers to Exam Questions

1. **A.** Checking whether code has a particular privilege is the function of code access security. For more information, see the section "Understanding Code Access Security" in this chapter.

2. **B.** Role-based security enables you to check whether a user is in a particular group. For more information, see the section "Verifying Role Membership" in this chapter.

3. **A.** Hash codes are calculated from the MSIL code of an assembly, so changing the assembly's contents changes its hash code. For more information, see the section "Code Groups and Permission Sets" in this chapter.

4. **A.** Within a level, the permission set granted to an assembly is the union of all the permission sets of code groups on that level to which the assembly belongs. For more information, see the section "Computing Permissions" in this chapter.

5. **D.** Across levels, the permission set granted to an assembly is the intersection of all the permission sets of the levels. Because the user level grants no permissions to Assembly B, Assembly B gets no permissions from the Common Language Runtime. For more information, see the section "Computing Permissions" in this chapter.

6. **B.** The `Company Code` code group is marked as an exclusive code group, so only its permission set is taken into account when determining the permission set for the assembly. For more information, see the section "Computing Permissions" in this chapter.

APPLY YOUR KNOWLEDGE

7. **C.** Because the code group on the Machine level is marked with the `LevelFinal` property, the code group on the user level is not taken into account when determining the permission set for this assembly. For more information, see the section "Computing Permissions" in this chapter.

8. **D.** `SecurityAction.RequestRefuse` tells the CLR that your assembly does not want to be granted the specified permission. For more information, see the section "Requesting Other Types of Permissions" in this chapter.

9. **C.** `SecurityAction.Demand` demands the specified permission of the calling code. For more information, see the section "Requesting Other Types of Permissions" in this chapter.

10. **B.** You must use imperative security to check access to resources whose names are not known until runtime. For more information, see the section "Imperative Security" in this chapter.

11. **B.** Forms authentication depends on cookies to indicate that a browser session has been authenticated. For more information, see the section "Configuring Authentication" in this chapter.

12. **A.** The question mark (?) wildcard matches unauthenticated users, whereas the asterisk (*) wildcard matches all users (authorized or not). If you deny access to all unauthenticated users, only authenticated users will be able to use the application. For more information, see the section "Configuring Authentication" and "Configuring Authorization" in this chapter.

13 **C.** If you allow anonymous authentication in IIS, users will never be prompted for their Windows credentials. ASP.NET will impersonate the identity of IIS itself, the `IUSR_ComputerName` account. For more information, see the section "Implementing Impersonation" in this chapter.

14 **C.** If you specify an account name in the identity element, that account is used to impersonate all authenticated users. For more information, see the section "Implementing Impersonation" in this chapter.

15. **B.** The `NetworkService` account has few privileges on the local computer, but presents the computer's credentials when accessing network resources. The `LocalService` account, by contrast, uses anonymous credentials with network resources, and the `LocalSystem` account has high privileges on the local computer. A properly configured user account could work in this scenario, but there's no need to create a user account when one of the built-in accounts will work fine. For more information, see the section "Security for Windows Services" in this chapter.

APPLY YOUR KNOWLEDGE

Suggested Readings and Resources

1. Visual Studio .NET Combined Help Collection

   • Securing Applications

2. Brian A. LaMacchia, et al. *.NET Framework Security.* Addison-Wesley, 2002.

3. *Building Secure ASP.NET Applications,* msdn.microsoft.com/library/en-us/ dnnetsec/html/secnetlpMSDN.asp.

FINAL REVIEW

Fast Facts

Practice Exam

Now that you've read this book, worked through the exercises, Guided Practice Exercises, and Step-by-Steps, and acquired as much hands-on experience using Visual C# .NET with the XML, server-side, and distributed aspects of .NET as you could, you are ready for the exam. This chapter is designed to be the "final cram in the parking lot" before you walk into the testing center. You can't reread the whole book in an hour, but you will be able to read this section in that time.

This chapter is organized by objective category, giving you not just a summary, but a review of the most important points from the book. Remember, this is just a review, not a replacement for the actual study material! It's meant to be a review of concepts and a trigger for you to remember useful bits of information you will need when taking the exam. If you know the information in here and the concepts that stand behind it, chances are good that the exam will be a snap.

CREATING AND MANAGING MICROSOFT WINDOWS SERVICES, SERVICED COMPONENTS, .NET REMOTING OBJECTS, AND XML WEB SERVICES

Fast Facts

Create and manipulate a Windows service.

- Windows services are applications that conform to the interface of the Windows Service Control Manager (SCM). ACM is the part of Windows

EXAM 70-320

that is responsible for managing Windows services.

▶ Windows services are quite distinct from regular Windows applications. One of most apparent distinctions is that Windows applications usually lack a GUI. In addition, a Windows service typically runs in the background and runs in its own process with a specific user identity.

▶ Windows services must be installed in the Windows services database before they can be used. The Windows services database is a part of Windows Registry. It is recommended, however, that you should not directly modify the database, but rather modify the database through the SCM.

▶ You can easily create Windows services by using the functionality provided by the `System.ServiceProcess.ServiceBase` class.

▶ The `System.ServiceProcess.ServiceProcessInstaller` and the `System.ServiceProcess.ServiceInstaller` classes provide the functionality for custom installation of Windows service applications.

▶ For installation tools such as `installutil.exe` to install an assembly, the assembly must have a class derived from `System.Configuration.Install.Installer`. If any custom installers (such as Windows service installers) need to be installed, they are added to the `Installers` collection of the `Installer` class.

▶ Several tools are available for monitoring and controlling Windows services. Some notable tools are the Services MMC snap-in, Visual Studio .NET Server Explorer, the `net.exe` command-line utility and the Service Control command-line utility (`sc.exe`).

▶ Some programs may also need to monitor Windows services programmatically. The FCL provides the `System.ServiceProcess.ServiceController` class to programmatically control the Windows services.

▶ The `ServiceController.GetServices()` method is used to enumerate installed services on a computer. You can use the `Start()`, `Stop()`, `Pause()`, and `Continue()` methods to change the status of a Windows service. The `WaitforStatus()` synchronous method is useful when you would like the current thread to pause execution and wait for the Windows service to enter in the specified state.

Write code that is executed when a Windows service is started or stopped.

▶ When the SCM sends a start message to a Windows service, first the `Main()` method of the Windows service application is executed. This method creates one or more instances of the Windows service and passes them to the `Run()` method of the `ServiceBase` class. This method provides the references of the Windows service objects to the SCM. The SCM uses these references to communicate with the Windows service.

▶ The Service Control utility (`sc.exe`) is distributed as a part of Windows XP and later operating systems and as a part of the Win32 SDK and the .NET Framework SDK. This utility is the most powerful tool for controlling and configuring Windows services.

Create and consume a serviced component.

▶ Rather than provide a new version of component services, the Microsoft .NET Framework relies on the COM+ component services that ship as a part of Windows 2000, Windows XP, and the Windows Server 2003.

▶ COM+ component services provide several features for increasing the security, reliability, availability, efficiency, and scalability of an enterprise application as part of the operating system infrastructure.

▶ A distributed application may use different types of applications, such as a Windows application, Windows service, Web application, Web service, remoting server, and so on, to consume a serviced component.

Implement a serviced component.

▶ Classes that want to use COM+ component services must derive from the `System.EnterpriseServices.ServicedComponent` class.

▶ To use COM+ services in your program, you need not write a lot of code. Instead, you use declarative attributes to specify whether a class should receive particular services.

▶ The declarative attributes applied to a class are stored in the COM+ Catalog as part of the assembly registration process. At runtime, COM+ can read the COM+ Catalog to determine what services a component should receive and provide those services.

▶ COM+ uses interception to provide various runtime services. Interception is a mechanism that enables COM+ to capture calls to any object and execute its own code before passing the call to the object.

▶ COM+ creates different contexts for objects that have different runtime requirements. A proxy is used to provide interception services between the objects in different contexts.

▶ The COM+ object pooling service enables you to maintain already created instances of a component that are ready to be used by any client that requests the component.

▶ To use the object pooling service, a class must override the `CanBePooled()` method of the `ServicedComponent` class. In addition, you need to apply the `ObjectPooling` attribute on the class or configure the component via the Component Services administrative tool to use object pooling.

▶ The COM+ just-in-time activation service allows you to minimize the period of time an object lives and consumes resources on the server.

▶ You can enable the just-in-time activation service declaratively in your programs by using the `JustInTimeActivation` attribute or administratively via the Component Services administrative tool. You must, however, indicate to COM+ whether an object should be deactivated after a method call by setting the done bit to True.

▶ The COM+ object construction service enables you to specify initialization information for a serviced component. It is possible to use the Component Services administrative tool to configure the initialization information for a component to change the way a component behaves.

▶ A transaction is a series of operations performed as a single unit. A transaction is successful only when all the operations in that transaction succeed.

▶ The outcome of a transaction depends on the status of the abort bit that is maintained in the context of a transaction and the consistent and done bits that are maintained in each context.

▶ You can use the methods of the `ContextUtil` class to change the status of the consistent and done bits programmatically.

▶ The `AutoComplete` attribute automatically calls the `ContextUtil.SetComplete()` method if a method completes successfully. Otherwise, `ContextUtil.SetAbort()` is called to abort the transaction.

▶ A queued component is a serviced component that can be invoked and executed asynchronously. With the help of a queued component, you can make your application available even when some of its components are not.

Create interfaces that are visible to COM.

▶ COM+ does not understand .NET and therefore cannot directly provide services to the .NET component. Instead, an assembly registration process must be used to expose a .NET component as a COM component.

▶ To enable communication between COM and .NET components, the .NET Framework generates a COM Callable Wrapper (CCW). The CCW enables communication between the calling COM code and the managed code and handles conversion between the data types, as well as other messages between the COM types and the .NET types.

▶ A class must implement an interface with those methods on which method-level configuration is required.

▶ Depending on the `ClassInterface` attribute to automatically generate class interfaces is not recommended because it leads to versioning problems. You should set the `ClassInterface` attribute for a class to the `ClassInterfaceType.None` value and create your own interface explicitly.

Create a strongly named assembly.

▶ An assembly must be signed with a strong name before the assembly can be registered into the COM+ Catalog.

Register the component in the global assembly cache.

▶ A serviced component is generally shared by several client applications. Therefore, the most recommended place to install a serviced component assembly is the Global Assembly Cache (GAC) because it ensures that the CLR can always locate an assembly.

Manage the component by using the Component Services tool.

▶ Administrators can use the Component Services administrative tool to configure COM+ applications at runtime. Using this tool, they can change certain behavior of a COM+ application without recompiling the application.

Create and consume a .NET remoting object.

▶ An Application domain, or `AppDomain`, is the smallest execution unit for a .NET application. The CLR allows several application domains to run within a single Windows process.

▶ Distributed Applications enable communication between objects that run in different application domains and processes.

▶ The `System.Net`, `System.Runtime.Remoting`, and `System.Web.Services` namespaces enable the .NET Framework to support distributed application development.

▶ .NET remoting enables objects in different application domains to talk to each other even when they are separated by applications, computers, or the network.

▶ The process of packaging and sending method calls among objects across the application boundaries via serialization and deserialization is called marshaling.

▶ Marshal-by-value (MBV) and Marshal-by-reference (MBR) are the two types of remotable objects. MBV objects are copied to the client application domain from the server application domain, whereas only a reference to the MBR objects is maintained in the client application domain. A proxy object is created at the client side to interact with the MBR objects.

Implement server-activated components.

▶ MBR remotable objects can be activated in two modes: server-activated mode and client-activated mode.

▶ Server-activated objects (SAO) are those remote objects whose lifetime is directly controlled by the server.

▶ You can activate SAOs in two ways: `SingleCall` (object is created for each client request) and `Singleton` (object is created once on the server and is shared by all clients).

▶ The `SingleCall` activation mode provides the maximum scalability because it does not maintain any state and the object lives for the shortest duration possible.

Implement client-activated components.

▶ Client-activated objects (CAOs) are created for each client when the client requests that a remote object be created. These objects maintain state for each client with which they are associated.

▶ The lease-based lifetime process determines how long the Singleton SAO and CAO should exist.

Select a channel protocol and a formatter. Channel protocols include TCP and HTTP. Formatters include SOAP and binary.

▶ A channel is an object that transports messages across remoting boundaries such as application domains, processes, and computers. The .NET Framework provides implementations for HTTP and TCP channels to allow communication of messages over the HTTP and TCP protocols, respectively.

▶ A channel has two end points. A channel at the receiving end—the server—listens for messages at a specified port number from a specific protocol. A channel object at the sending end—the client—sends messages through the specified protocol at the specified port number.

▶ Formatters are the objects that are used to serialize and deserialize data into messages before they are transmitted over a channel. You can format messages in SOAP or the binary format with the help of the `SoapFormatter` and `BinaryFormatter` classes in the FCL.

▶ The default formatter to transport messages to and from the remote objects for the HTTP channel is the SOAP formatter; for TCP channel it is the binary formatter.

▶ You should create a server channel that listens on a given port number and register the channel with the remoting framework before you register the remotable class.

▶ The type of channel registered by the client must be compatible with the type of channel the server uses for receiving messages.

▶ You do not specify a port number when you register the client channel. The port number is instead specified at the time of registering the remote class in the client's domain.

▶ To register SAO objects, you call the `RemotingConfiguration.RegisterWellKnownServiceType()` method on the server side, and the `RemotingConfiguration.RegisterWellKnownClientType()` method on the client side.

▶ To register CAO objects, you call the `RemotingConfiguration.RegisterActivatedServiceType()` method on the server side and the `RemotingConfiguration.RegisterActivatedClientType()` method on the client side.

▶ You can use only the object's default constructor to instantiate SAO at the client side, whereas you can use any of the object's constructors to instantiate CAO.

Create client configuration files and server configuration files.

▶ The .NET Framework enables you to store remoting configuration details in an XML-based configuration file rather than the code file. This causes any changes in the configuration file to be automatically picked up without any need to recompile the code files.

▶ To configure remoting configuration details from configuration files, you should call the `RemotingConfiguration.Configure()` method and pass the name of the configuration file.

▶ You can distribute the interface assembly to the client instead of the implementation assembly by creating an interface that defines the contract and exposes the member definitions to the client. The remotable class should implement this interface.

▶ You can use the soapsuds tool to automatically generate the interface class for the remotable object rather than manually define the interface. However, the soapsuds tool works only when the HTTP channel is used for communication.

▶ To create an interface that allows client-activated remote objects to be created, you should create an additional interface that declares as many different methods as there are constructors in the remotable class. Each of these methods should be able to create the remote object in a way defined by its corresponding constructor.

Implement an asynchronous method.

▶ You can invoke a method asynchronously by calling the `BeginInvoke()` method on the delegate of that method.

▶ You can be notified automatically when an asynchronous method ends. However, you must first create another delegate object (of `AsyncCallback` type) that refers to the callback method that you need to execute when the remote method ends. And then you should pass the delegate to the callback method as an argument to the `BeginInvoke()` method.

Create the listener service.

▶ You can choose to run the remoting host as a console application, as a Windows service, or as an IIS application.

▶ You can use IIS as an activation agent only when the underlying communication is an HTTP channel. Using IIS as an activation agent eliminates the need to write a separate server program that listens on a unique port number (IIS uses port 80).

▶ When creating IIS-hosted remote objects, you cannot specify constructor parameters; therefore using IIS to activate CAO is not possible.

Instantiate and invoke a .NET Remoting object.

▶ To create a remotable class, inherit the remotable class from the `MarshalByRefObject` class.

▶ A remotable class is usually connected with the remoting framework through a separate server program. The server program listens to the client request on a specified channel and instantiates the remote object or invokes calls on it as required.

Create and consume an XML Web service.

▶ Web services provide you with the means to create objects and invoke their methods even though your only connection to the server is via the Internet.

▶ Communication with Web services is via XML messages transported by the HTTP protocol.

▶ Because they communicate over HTTP, Web services are typically not blocked by firewalls.

▶ The Simple Object Access Protocol (SOAP) encapsulates object-oriented messages between Web service clients and servers.

▶ The Universal Description, Discovery, and Integration protocol (UDDI) allows you to find Web services by connecting to a directory.

▶ The Web Services Description Language (WSDL) lets you retrieve information on the classes and methods that are supported by a particular Web service.

Control characteristics of Web methods by using attributes.

▶ Properties of the `WebMethod` attribute enable you to control such things as the cache duration, session state, and transactions of the Web method.

▶ You should be cautious about using session state in a Web service. Session state can tie up server resources for an extended time. If you use session state in a popular Web service, you will apply heavy demands to RAM on your Web server.

Create and use SOAP extensions.

▶ A SOAP extension enables you to intercept SOAP messages at all stages of processing: before and after serialization, and before and after deserialization.

▶ SOAP extensions are classes that are derived from the base `SoapExtension` class.

▶ SOAP extensions can run on a Web services client, server, or both.

▶ The `GetInitializer()` method is called once when the SOAP extension is first loaded.

▶ The `Initialize()` method is called once for each call to a Web method being monitored by the SOAP extension.

▶ The `ChainStream()` method allows you to intercept the actual SOAP message stream.

▶ The `ProcessMessage()` method is called with the actual SOAP requests and responses.

Create asynchronous Web methods.

▶ By default, calls to a Web method are synchronous, and block the client program until the SOAP response is returned.

▶ Proxies generated by `wsdl.exe` also enable you to make asynchronous calls to a Web service.

▶ One way to make an asynchronous Web method call is to supply a delegate function that the .NET Framework will call back when the SOAP response is ready.

▶ Another way to make an asynchronous Web method call is to use a `WaitHandle` object to wait for one or more calls to complete.

▶ The `Abort()` method of an appropriate `WebClientAsyncResult` object can be called to abort asynchronous Web method calls.

Control XML wire format for an XML Web service.

▶ SOAP messages can be formatted in a variety of ways. You can use literal or encoded parameter formatting, document or RPC-style body formatting, and wrapped or bare parameters.

▶ The .NET Framework enables you to dictate the format of SOAP messages through applying attributes to the Web service or Web method at both the server and the proxy class.

▶ The `XmlElement` attribute enables you to specify the name and other details of a parameter in a SOAP message.

▶ The `XmlAttribute` attribute enables you to specify that the `XmlSerializer` should serialize the class member as an XML attribute.

Instantiate and invoke an XML Web service.

▶ Visual Studio .NET includes an ASP.NET Web Service template that you can use to build your own Web services.

▶ To make a class available via a Web service, you mark the class with the `WebService` attribute.

▶ To make a method available via a Web service, you mark the method with the `WebMethod` attribute.

▶ To test a Web service, run the project in the Visual Studio .NET IDE.

▶ You can generate proxy classes for a Web service manually by using the Web Services Description Language tool.

▶ You can generate proxy classes for a Web service automatically by setting a Web reference to point to the Web service.

▶ You can test and debug a Web service without a client application by using one of several SOAP proxy tools.

Implement security for a Windows service, a serviced component, a .NET Remoting object, and an XML Web service.

▶ The most important security decision you must make with a Windows service is which security account should be used to run the service. You can choose between the `LocalSystem` account or a user account on Windows 2000. On Windows XP, the `LocalService` and `NetworkService` accounts provide additional flexibility.

▶ Because Web services are hosted by ASP.NET, they have the entire spectrum of IIS authentication, authorization, and security features available to them.

▶ You can use IIS to control access to a Web service, and then use declarative or imperative security to control the access of the Web service to resources.

▶ WS-Security is a new specification for a set of SOAP headers to handle authentication, encryption, and signing directly in SOAP messages.

▶ Remoting servers that require secure hosting are best run in the ASP.NET process. Remoting servers that require additional speed but less security can be run in a Windows service host instead.

▶ You can configure security for serviced components by applying attributes within the code for the components and then specifying COM+ roles with the Component Services tool.

Access unmanaged code from a Windows service, a serviced component, a .NET Remoting object, and an XML Web service.

▶ Using COM components from .NET managed code requires the creation of an RCW.

▶ You can create an RCW for a COM component by using the Type Library Importer tool or by directly referencing the COM component from your .NET code.

▶ To use COM components that you did not create, you should obtain a PIA from the component's creator.

▶ RCWs impose a performance penalty on COM code.

▶ You can use the .NET Framework platform invoke facility to call functions from Windows libraries, including the Windows API.

▶ You should use a `StringBuilder` object for a Windows API call that expects a string buffer to be modified by the method.

CONSUMING AND MANIPULATING DATA

Access and manipulate data from a Microsoft SQL Server database by creating and using ad hoc queries and stored procedures.

▶ Transact-SQL is the Microsoft SQL Server dialect of the ANSI SQL-92 standard query language.

▶ You can execute T-SQL statements from a variety of interfaces, including the Visual Studio .NET IDE, OSQL, SQL Query Analyzer, or custom applications.

▶ SELECT statements retrieve data from tables in a database.

▶ INSERT statements add new data to tables in a database.

▶ UPDATE statements modify existing data in tables in a database.

▶ DELETE statements remove data from tables in a database.

▶ Stored procedures provide a way to keep compiled SQL statements on the database server.

▶ The ADO.NET SqlCommand object enables you to execute stored procedures.

▶ Stored procedures can have both input and output parameters. Input parameters are variables that are used by the stored procedure. Output parameters let the stored procedure return results to the caller.

▶ The @@IDENTITY variable returns the most recent identity value from the connection.

Create and manipulate DataSets.

Manipulate a DataSet schema.

▶ DataSet schema files represent the metadata that describes the allowable content of a DataSet.

▶ You can create a DataSet schema file from scratch by dragging and dropping elements and attributes within the DataSet schema designer.

▶ Simple types allow you to apply constraints to the data that will be allowed in a DataSet.

▶ You can quickly create a DataSet schema to represent an existing table by dragging and dropping the table from Server Explorer to the DataSet schema designer.

Manipulate DataSet relationships.

▶ To create a primary key or a unique key in a DataSet schema, drag and drop the key tool from the Toolbox to an XML element.

▶ To create a one-to-many relationship, drag and drop the relation tool from the Toolbox to the child table of the relationship.

▶ To create a nested relationship, drag and drop the child table to the parent table.

Create a strongly typed DataSet.

▶ A strongly typed DataSet brings the benefits of early binding to your data access code. Early binding reduces the time required to invoke an object's properties, methods, and events because the references to the object's properties, methods, and events are resolved at compile time instead of runtime.

▶ You can create a strongly typed DataSet by using the component designer with components dragged from Server Explorer, or by building a DataSet schema file.

▶ When you're working with a strongly typed DataSet in code, IntelliSense will show you the names of the tables and columns contained within the DataSet.

Access and manipulate XML data.

Access an XML file by using the Document Object Model (DOM) and an XmlReader.

▶ The Document Object Model (DOM) is a W3C standard for representing the information contained in an HTML or XML document as a tree of nodes.

▶ The XmlReader class defines an interface for reading XML documents. The XmlTextReader class inherits from the XmlReader class to read XML documents from streams.

▶ The XmlNode object can be used to represent a single node in the DOM.

▶ The XmlDocument object represents an entire XML document.

Transform DataSet data into XML data.

▶ The XmlDataDocument class is a subclass of the XmlDocument class that can be synchronized with a DataSet.

▶ You can start the synchronization process with the XmlDataDocument or with the DataSet, or you can use a schema file to construct both objects.

▶ Changes to one synchronized object are automatically reflected in the other.

▶ You can use an XmlTextWriter object to persist an XmlDocument object back to disk.

Use XPath to query XML data.

▶ XPath is a language for specifying or selecting parts of an XML document. XPath is a query language for XML.

▶ An XPath expression returns a set of zero or more nodes from the DOM representation of an XML document.

▶ The SelectNodes() method of the XmlDocument object returns a set of nodes selected by an XPath expression.

▶ The XPathDocument and XPathNavigator objects are optimized for fast execution of XPath queries.

▶ The XPathNavigator object allows random-access navigation of an XML document's structure.

Generate and use an XSD schema.

▶ You can extract an inline schema from an XML file by using the ReadXmlSchema() method of the DataSet class.

▶ You can infer a schema from the structure of an XML file by using the InferXmlSchema() method of the DataSet class.

Write a SQL statement that retrieves XML data from a SQL Server database.

▶ The FOR XML clause in the SQL Server SELECT statement lets you generate XML documents directly from SQL Server data.

▶ By choosing appropriate options in FOR XML, you can map SQL Server columns as either attributes or elements in the generated XML. You can also choose whether to Base64-encode binary columns, and whether to embed schema information.

▶ You can use the ExecuteXmlReader() method of the SqlCommand object to retrieve XML from a SQL Server database and assign it to classes within the .NET Framework.

Update a SQL Server database by using XML.

▶ The SQLXML package contains XML-related updates for SQL Server 2000.

▶ You can use DiffGrams to package updates to SQL Server tables as XML files. The SqlXmlCommand object can apply DiffGrams to a SQL Server database.

Validate an XML document.

▶ You can validate an XML document for conformance with an inline schema, an external schema, a DTD, or an XDR file by using the XmlValidatingReader class.

TESTING AND DEBUGGING

Create a unit test plan.

▶ Testing is the process of executing a program with the intention of finding errors. You should design an effective test plan to ensure that your application is free from all likely defects and errors.

▶ Unit testing ensures that each unit of an application functions precisely as desired. It is the lowest level of testing.

▶ Integration testing ensures that different units of an application function as expected by the test plan after they are integrated.

▶ Whenever code is modified or a new feature is added in an application, you should run all the existing test cases, along with a new set of test cases, to check the new feature. This helps you develop robust applications.

Implement tracing.

Configure and use trace listeners and trace switches.

▶ Listeners are objects that receive trace and debug output. By default, there is one listener, DefaultTraceListener, attached to the Trace and Debug classes. This listener displays the messages in the Output window.

▶ The Debug and Trace objects share the same Listeners collection. Therefore, any Listener object added to the Trace.Listeners collection is also added to the Debug.Listeners collection.

▶ Trace switches enable you to change the type of messages traced by a program, depending on a value stored in the XML configuration file. You need not recompile the application for this change to take effect; you just restart it. You need to implement code to display the messages, depending on the value of the switch.

▶ Visual C# .NET preprocessor directives allow you to define symbols in an application, mark regions of code, and conditionally skip code for compilation.

Display trace output.

▶ The Trace and Debug classes can be used to display informative messages in an application when the DEBUG and TRACE symbols are defined, respectively, at the time of compilation.

▶ By default, both the TRACE and DEBUG symbols are defined in the Debug configuration of a project, whereas only the TRACE symbol is defined for the Release configuration.

Instrument and debug a Windows service, a serviced component, a .NET Remoting object, and an XML Web service.

Configure the debugging environment.

▶ The Conditional attribute enables you to conditionally add or skip a method for compilation, depending on the value of the symbol passed as a parameter to the attribute.

Create and apply debugging code to components and applications.

▶ You can attach the debugger to a running process (either local or remote) with the help of the Processes dialog box.

▶ When you attach a debugger to the ASP.NET worker process aspnet_wp.exe, it freezes the execution of all other Web applications on that server.

▶ You should have mdm.exe running on the remote machine to perform remote debugging.

▶ To debug a Windows service, you must attach a debugger to the process in which the Windows service is running.

▶ To debug COM+ library applications, you must attach a debugger to the process in which the client application is running.

▶ To debug COM+ server applications, you must attach a debugger to the dllhost.exe process in which the COM+ server application is running.

▶ To debug a .NET remoting object, you must attach a debugger to the process in which the remoting server application is running. In case the object is hosted in IIS, you need to attach a debugger to the aspnet_wp.exe process.

▶ To debug a Web service, you need to attach a debugger to aspnet_wp.exe or the client application that is calling Web methods of the Web service.

▶ The System.Web.TraceContext class can be used to display trace messages in a Web application. You can easily view these messages by using the trace viewer utility or at the end of the page output. ASP.NET displays various page request details, along with any custom trace messages from the code.

▶ To enable ASP.NET tracing for a single page, set the `trace` attribute of the `Page` directive to True.

Provide multicultural test data to components and applications.

▶ Test the application's data and user interface to make sure that they conform to the locale's standards for date and time, numeric values, currency, list separators, and measurements.

▶ If you are developing for Windows 2000 or Windows XP, test your application on as many language and culture variants as necessary to cover your entire market for the application. These operating systems support the languages used in more than 120 cultures/locales.

▶ You should use Unicode for your application. Applications using Unicode do not require you to make any changes on Windows 2000 and XP. If your application uses Windows code pages instead, you need to set the culture/locale of the operating system according to the localized version of the application that you are testing, and reboot after each change.

▶ While testing a localized version of an application, make sure that you use input data in the language supported by the localized version. This will make the testing scenario most like the scenario in which the application will be actually used.

Execute tests.

▶ Debugging is the process of finding the causes of errors in a program, locating the lines of code that are causing the errors, and fixing the errors.

▶ When an application throws an exception, you can choose either to continue execution or to break into the debugger (to start debugging operations such as step-by-step execution). You can customize this behavior for each exception object by using the Exceptions dialog box.

Use interactive debugging.

▶ The three options available while performing step-by-step execution are Step Into, Step Over, and Step Out.

▶ Breakpoints enable you to mark code that signals the debugger to pause execution. After you encounter a breakpoint, you can choose to continue step-by-step execution or resume the normal execution by pressing F5 or by clicking either the Resume button or the Continue button.

▶ The various tool windows, such as This, Locals, Immediate, Autos, Watch, and Call Stack, can be of great help in tracking the execution path and the status of variables in the process of debugging an application in Visual Studio .NET.

Log test results.

▶ The System event log provides a central repository for various issues that an application may encounter while it is executing. Using an event log to record such messages not only makes the job of system administrator easy, but it enables other applications to take appropriate action when an entry is written to a log.

▶ Multiple event sources can write into an event log. However, an event source can be used to write into only one event log.

- Performance counters are organized in categories, and each category defines a specific set of performance counters.

- The process of reading a performance counter value is called sampling the performance counter. The process of updating a performance counter value is called publishing a performance counter.

Resolve errors and rework code.

- The most important thing about resolving errors is to be systematic. Use the ASP.NET debugging tools to verify the location of the error in your code. Then correct the code to remove the error.

- After reworking the code, it is crucial to run the same test that identified the error in the first place. The reworked code should pass the test without error.

Control debugging in the Web.config file.

- You can also enable ASP.NET tracing at the application level by setting the enabled attribute of the <trace> element to True in the application-wide web.config file.

Use SOAP extensions for debugging.

- Because SOAP extensions have full access to the SOAP message stream (both requests and responses, before and after serialization), they're useful whenever you suspect a protocol-level error in your code. You can use a SOAP extension to inspect and modify messages between Web services, clients, and servers.

DEPLOYING WINDOWS SERVICES, SERVICED COMPONENTS, .NET REMOTING OBJECTS, AND XML WEB SERVICES

Plan the deployment of and deploy a Windows service, a serviced component, a .NET Remoting object, and an XML Web service.

- Although the .NET Framework supports XCOPY deployment, XCOPY is not sufficient for advanced deployment requirements. For advanced requirements, you should instead use a Microsoft Windows Installer[nd]based installation package to deploy applications.

- The Microsoft Windows Installer is the built-in installation and configuration service of the Windows operating system. In addition to providing several advanced installation features, it provides features such as the capability to roll back an installation process, uninstall an application, and repair a component or an application.

- Visual Studio .NET provides four types of deployment templates: Setup Project (for Windows-based applications), Web Setup Project (for Web-based applications), Merge Module Project (for shared components and assemblies), and Cab Project (for Managed and legacy ActiveX components to be downloaded over the Internet). Visual Studio .NET also provides the

Setup Wizard, which helps in creating installation packages for any of these deployment projects.

Create a setup program that installs a Windows service, a serviced component, a .NET Remoting object, and an XML Web service.

▶ When you deploy a Web service by manually copying the files, you need to manually create the virtual directory and set the virtual directory as an IIS application. The Visual Studio .NET Copy Project command does this automatically for you. The Web Setup project provides the maximum configuration options and total control over the installation process.

▶ A Visual Studio .NET Setup Project does not package the .NET Framework files for redistribution. You should ensure that the .NET Framework is already installed on the Web server, or better yet, you should use a bootstrapper program that installs the .NET Framework prior to installing the Web service.

▶ The Windows Installer Service and the Installer tool (installutil.exe) perform installation in a transactional manner.

▶ If you want a custom installer class to execute when a Web Setup project or the Installer tool is used to install an assembly, you need to apply the RunInstallerAttribute to the class and set its value to true.

▶ You use the Setup Project template to create a setup program for a Windows Service.

▶ How you deploy a .NET remoting object depends mostly on the application that uses it. The configuration settings for a .NET remoting object are stored in an XML configuration file, so no extra registration steps, such as those involving modifications to the Windows Registry, are required to deploy a .NET remoting object.

▶ When you have a component that will be shared among multiple applications, you should package it as a merge module (.msm file). Merge modules cannot be installed directly. They need to be packaged into a merge module and merged with the installation program of an application that uses the shared component.

Register components and assemblies.

▶ Installation components enable you to take custom actions application setup. The .NET Framework provides a few predefined installer components for use with server components. You can also create custom installation components by deriving from the Installer class.

▶ To deploy a serviced component, you must register the component with the COM+ Catalog and should install the component in the GAC.

▶ If you want other developers to be able to locate and use your Web service, consider publishing your Web service to a UDDI registry.

Publish an XML Web service.

Enable static discovery.

▶ Disco is Microsoft's standard format for discovery documents, which contain information on Web services.

- The Web Services Discovery Tool, `disco.exe`, can retrieve discovery information from a server that exposes a Web service.

Publish XML Web service definitions in the UDDI.

- UDDI, the Universal Description, Discovery, and Integration protocol, is a multi-vendor standard for discovering online resources, including Web services.

- You can publish your Web Service in the UDDI by filling out the submission forms at an online UDDI site.

Configure client computers and servers to use a Windows service, a serviced component, a .NET Remoting object, and an XML Web service.

- Shared assemblies are used by multiple applications on a machine. Shared assemblies are placed in the GAC and they enjoy special privileges such as file security, shared location, and side-by-side versioning.

- You generate a public/private key pair by using the Strong Name tool (`sn.exe`). This pair can be used to sign assemblies with a strong name.

- You can add a shared assembly to the GAC by using Windows Explorer, the .NET Framework Configuration tool, the Global Assembly Cache tool, and the Windows Installer.

- The best way to add an assembly in the GAC during deployment is to use Microsoft Windows

Installer. The Windows Installer provides assembly reference-counting features and manages removal of assemblies at the time of un-installation.

- When viewed in Windows Explorer, the assembly cache folder in the `System` folder displays assemblies from the GAC and native image cache.

- The CLR first searches the GAC to locate assemblies, and then it looks into the files and folders where the assembly is installed. Thus, loading shared assemblies from the GAC is efficient because the CLR does not engage itself in looking into the `<codebase>` and `<probing>` elements of the applicable configuration files.

- Delay signing enables you to place a shared assembly in the GAC by signing the assembly with just the public key. This allows the assembly to be signed with the private key at a later stage, when the development process is complete and the component or assembly is ready to be deployed. This process enables developers to work with shared assemblies as if they were strongly named, and it protects the private key of the signature from being accessed at different stages of development.

Implement versioning.

- The set of rules that the CLR uses to locate an assembly is called binding policy. Binding policy is a deciding factor in how and where an application's assemblies should be deployed.

- A private assembly's simple text name identifies it, and it is deployed for use by a single application.

▶ The application configuration file is used to modify binding policy for private assemblies. To do so, specify additional search locations for the assembly in the <probing> XML element.

Plan, configure, and deploy side-by-side deployments and applications.

▶ Different versions of an assembly can be deployed in the GAC for side-by-side execution. You can implement side-by-side execution of an assembly by configuring the binding policy in the application configuration, the publisher policy file, or the machine configuration file.

▶ The publisher policy file can be used to deploy service packs, such as bug-fix updates, for the assemblies. The publisher policy file is an XML file which is converted into a strong named assembly and installed in the GAC.

Configure security for a Windows service, a serviced component, a .NET Remoting object, and an XML Web service.

▶ Permissions control access to resources.

▶ Code can request the minimum permissions that it needs to run and optional permissions that it would like to have. It can also refuse permissions and demand permissions on the part of calling code.

▶ Code access permissions represent access to resources, whereas identity permissions represent things that the .NET Framework knows about code.

▶ The .NET Framework supplies both attribute-based declarative security and class-based imperative security.

▶ Code groups are sets of assemblies that share a security context.

▶ Permission sets are sets of permissions that can be granted as a unit.

▶ The CLR computes actual permissions at run-time based on code group membership and the calling chain of the code.

▶ Custom permissions enable you to create your own permissions to protect particular resources.

▶ The most important security decision you must make with a Windows service is which security account should be used to run the service. You can choose between the LocalSystem account or a user account on Windows 2000. On Windows XP, the LocalService and NetworkService accounts provide additional flexibility.

▶ Because Web services are hosted by ASP.NET, they have the entire spectrum of IIS authentication, authorization, and security features available to them.

▶ You can use IIS to control access to a Web service, and then use declarative or imperative security to control the Web service's access to resources.

▶ WS-Security is a new specification for a set of SOAP headers to handle authentication, encryption, and signing directly in SOAP messages.

▶ Remoting servers that require secure hosting are best run in the ASP.NET process. Remoting servers that require additional speed but less security can be run in a Windows service host instead.

▶ You can configure security for serviced components by applying attributes within the code for the components and then specifying COM+ roles with the Component Services tool.

Configure authentication type. Authentication types include Windows authentication, Microsoft .NET Passport, custom authentication, and none.

▶ The .NET Framework supports both authentication and authorization. Authentication refers to verifying a user's identity. Authorization refers to granting rights based on that identity.

▶ Users must satisfy any IIS authentication requirements before ASP.NET authentication takes over.

▶ ASP.NET authentication uses interchangeable authentication providers. You can choose Windows authentication, Passport authentication, or forms-based authentication.

Configure and control authorization. Authorization methods include file-based authorization and URL-based authorization.

▶ After you have authenticated a user, you can use authorization to control the user's access to resources.

▶ File-based authorization uses operating system security to allow or deny resources to files such as .aspx files and .asmx files.

▶ URL-based authorization uses the <authorization> section in the web.config file to control access to an application.

Configure and implement identity management.

▶ Identity impersonation enables the ASP.NET process to act as the authenticated user.

▶ The WindowsPrincipal and WindowsIdentity classes enable you to check the current user's authentication status.

▶ You can use the IsInRole() method of the WindowsPrincipal object to check for membership in Windows groups.

▶ The PrincipalPermission class enables you to perform declarative or imperative role-based security operations.

This practice exam contains 77 questions that are representative of what you should expect on the actual exam "Developing XML Web Services and Server Components with Microsoft Visual C# .NET and the Microsoft .NET Framework" (exam 70-320). The answers appear at the end of this practice exam. I strongly suggest that when you take this practice exam, you treat it just as you would the actual exam at the test center. Time yourself, read carefully, don't use any reference materials, and answer all the questions as best you can.

Some of the questions may be vague and require you to make deductions to come up with the best possible answer from the possibilities given. Others may be verbose, requiring you to read and process a lot of information before you reach the actual question. These are skills that you should acquire before attempting to take the actual exam. Take this practice exam, and if you miss more than 19 questions, try rereading the chapters that contain information on the subjects in which you were weak. You can use the index to find keywords to point you to the appropriate locations.

Practice Exam

1. You are working with this XML file:

```xml
<?xml version="1.0" encoding="UTF-8"?>
<Orders>
  <Order OrderNumber="142">
    <Part PartNumber="12"/>
    <Part PartNumber="14"/>
    <Part PartNumber="22"/>
  </Order>
  <Order OrderNumber="143">
    <Part PartNumber="22"/>
    <Part PartNumber="18"/>
  </Order>
</Orders>
```

Which XPath expressions can you use to return the second `<Part>` element from the first `<Order>` element? (Select two.)

A. `/Orders/Order[1]/Part[2]`

B. `/Orders/Order[0]/Part[1]`

C. `(/Orders/Order/Part)[2]`

D. `(/Orders/Order/Part)[1]`

2. You are building a class for a component that will be registered with COM+. So far you have designed the class as follows:

```
public interface ICustomer
{
    int64 GetBalance(string CustID);
}

public class Customer
    : ServicedComponent, ICustomer
{
}
```

You want to ensure that only the interface you have designed explicitly is registered with COM+. How should you specify the `ClassInterface` attribute?

A. Accept the default `ClassInterface`

B. Use `ClassInterface.None`

C. Use `ClassInterface.AutoDispatch`

D. Use `ClassInterface.AutoDual`

3. You have been using version 1.1 of SpiffyLib, a .NET class library, in your applications for some time. SpiffyLib comes from SpiffyWare, an external vendor. You have developed multiple in-house applications that reference and use SpiffyLib 1.1, which is installed in the GAC on your computers.

Now SpiffyWare has released SpiffyLib 2.0, which is not 100% backward compatible with SpiffyLib 1.1. You would like to start using SpiffyLib 2.0 in new applications, but you want existing applications to continue to use SpiffyLib 1.1. What should you do?

A. Remove SpiffyLib 1.1 from the GAC. Install SpiffyLib 1.1 in the folder of each application that uses it. Install SpiffyLib 2.0 in the GAC.

B. Install SpiffyLib 2.0 in the GAC. Add a `.config` file to each existing application, telling it to use SpiffyLib 1.1.

C. Install SpiffyLib 2.0 in the GAC. Make no other changes to the existing configuration.

D. Install SpiffyLib 2.0 in the folder of each new application. Do not install SpiffyLib 2.0 in the GAC until you have retired or rewritten all the existing applications.

4. You have been developing a serviced component in Visual C# .NET. To develop the component, you have been writing code, registering the component with COM+, testing, and repeating the cycle. After a day of development, you notice that the component appears in the COM+ Catalog multiple times. How can you prevent the component from appearing in COM+ more than once as you rebuild versions of the component?

A. Use the `Guid` Attribute to assign a constant GUID to the class.

B. Use the `ClassInterface.None` attribute so that you can hard-code the component's interfaces.

C. Install the component in the Global Assembly Cache.

D. Build the component in release mode instead of in debug mode.

5. You are working with a SQL Server database that contains a table named Patients and a table named Visits. The Patients table contains columns PatientID (a unique identifier for the patient and the primary key of the table) and PatientName (the name of the patient). The Visits table contains the columns VisitID (a unique identifier for the visit and the primary key of the table), PatientID (a foreign key that points to the PatientID column in the Patients table), VisitCost (the bill for the visit), and VisitDate (the date of the visit).

You want to write a query that returns the number of visits that each patient has made, together with the patient's name, provided that the total cost of the visits is at least $100. Which SQL statement should you use?

A.

```
SELECT Patients.PatientName,
Count(Visits.VisitID)
FROM Patients INNER JOIN Visits
 ON Patients.PatientID = Visits.PatientID
GROUP BY Patients.PatientName
WHERE Sum(Visits.VisitCost)>=100
```

B.

```
SELECT Patients.PatientName,
Count(Visits.VisitID)
FROM Patients INNER JOIN Visits
 ON Patients.PatientID = Visits.PatientID
GROUP BY Patients.PatientName
WHERE Visits.VisitCost >=100
```

C.

```
SELECT Patients.PatientName,
Count(Visits.VisitID)
FROM Patients INNER JOIN Visits
 ON Patients.PatientID = Visits.PatientID
GROUP BY Patients.PatientName
HAVING Sum(Visits.VisitCost)>=100
```

D.

```
SELECT Patients.PatientName,
Count(Visits.VisitID)
FROM Patients INNER JOIN Visits
 ON Patients.PatientID = Visits.PatientID
GROUP BY Patients.PatientName
HAVING Visits.VisitCost >=100
```

6. Your application needs to load the contents of an XML file into memory. You don't need rich navigation through the XML file; a single pass to locate the data of interest is sufficient for the application. Which class should you use to implement this requirement?

A. `XPathNavigator`

B. `XmlReader`

C. `XmlTextReader`

D. `XPathExpression`

7. Your code is making asynchronous calls to two different Web methods. You then execute other code until you arrive at a point where you require results from one or the other of the asynchronous calls. You can proceed with further processing as soon as either result is available. How should your code wait for the results of the asynchronous calls?

A. Use a pair of delegate callbacks, one for each Web method.

B. Use a `WaitHandle.WaitAny()` method call, specifying both Web methods.

C. Use a `WaitHandle.WaitAll()` method call, specifying both Web methods.

D. Use two `WaitHandle.WaitOne()` method calls, one for each Web method.

8. Your application monitors IIS activities under Windows 2000. To perform its work, this application needs administrative access to the computer. You've chosen to build this application as a Windows service. Which security context should you use as the startup account for the service?

   A. `LocalSystem`

   B. `LocalService`

   C. `NetworkService`

   D. `User`

9. Your company supplies a COM component to provide advanced communications capabilities to applications. Some of your clients are moving to Visual C# .NET and require an RCW for your component. How should you proceed?

   A. Use the Type Library Importer tool to create and sign a PIA for your component.

   B. Set a reference to your component from any Visual C# .NET project to create an RCW for your component.

   C. Create a class that uses platform invoke to call functions from your component.

   D. Use the ActiveX Library Importer tool to create and sign a PIA for your component.

10. Your application contains this code:

```
[Conditional("DEBUG")] _
void PrintDebugText()
{
   Debug.WriteLine("In debug mode");
}

private void Button2_Click(
   Object sender, System.EventArgs e)
{
   PrintDebugText();
   Trace.WriteLine("In Button Click");
}
```

You run the application in release mode and click the `Button2` control. What is the result?

   A. A compile time error occurs

   B. A runtime error occurs

   C. The Output window prints

```
In debug mode
In Button Click
```

   D. The Output window prints

```
In Button Click
```

11. You are designing a distributed application for a major hosting service of online journals. The application will be heavily used by thousands of eager journal writers every hour. For greater scalability, you need to make sure that the application can be deployed in a load-balanced configuration. How should you host the remotable object in this scenario?

   A. As a server-activated object in `Singleton` activation mode.

   B. As a server-activated object in `SingleCall` activation mode.

   C. As a client-activated object that uses the HTTP channel.

   D. As a client-activated object that uses the TCP channel.

12. You have developed a .NET Remoting server that is used by employees in your organization to place vacation time requests. The server makes a `Singleton` SAO named `VacationRequest` available. Clients send their employee IDs when they create the object, and then later post it with their vacation requests. The server then records the information in a Jet database.

    You discover that at peak times vacation requests are getting confused—for example, the vacation request from Employee 3285 is getting saved as a request from Employee 4288. What can you do to fix this issue?

A. Switch from using a `Singleton` SAO to using a CAO

B. Switch from using a `Singleton` SAO to using a SingleCall SAO

C. Switch the database from Jet to SQL Server

D. Issue a confirmation number with each call to the object that the employee can later refer to

13. You have used the Web Services Discovery Tool to retrieve information about a Web service named `CustomerBalance`. Which file will contain the URL for any documentation of the `CustomerBalance` Web service?

A. `results.discomap`

B. `CustomerBalance.disco`

C. `Reference.cs`

D. `CustomerBalance.wsdl`

14. The ASMX file in your Web Service contains the following code:

```
using System.Web.Services;

[WebService(Namespace="http://my.org")]
public class Customers
    : System.Web.Services.WebService
{
    public int32 Balance(string CustNumber)
    {
        // Stub to test function
        return 5;
    }
}
```

You compile the Web Service and set a Web reference to it from a client application. However, you are unable to call the `Balance()` method from the client application. What must you do?

A. Add the `[WebMethod()]` attribute to the `Balance()` method.

B. Rewrite the `Balance()` method to have its return type set to void and the return value passed through an output parameter.

C. Add the `Balance()` method to the WSDL file for the Web Service.

D. Register the Web Service with a UDDI Registry.

15. Your application contains the following code to update a SQL Server database via an XML DiffGram:

```
private void btnUpdate_Click(
    object sender, System.EventArgs e)
{
    // Connect to the SQL Server database
    SqlXmlCommand sxc =
     new SqlXmlCommand(
     "Provider=SQLOLEDB;" +
     "Server=(local);database=Northwind;" +
     "Integrated Security=SSPI");

    // Set up the DiffGram
    sxc.CommandType =
        SqlXmlCommandType.DiffGram;
    sxc.SchemaPath = "..\diffgram.xsd"
    FileStream fs =
     new FileStream(@"..\..\diffgram.xml",
        FileMode.Open);
    sxc.CommandStream = fs;
    // And execute it
    sxc.ExecuteNonQuery();
    MessageBox.Show(
        "Database was updated!");
}
```

The code executes and the data specified in the `diffgram.xml` file is properly updated when you run the application on your own computer. However, when you deploy the application to a production computer you receive a `System.IO.FileNotFoundException`. What should you do to fix this problem?

A. Move the DiffGram files to the root directory on the production computer.

B. Install the .NET Framework SP2 on the production computer.

C. Install the SQLXML package on the production computer.

D. Modify the connection string to explicitly use the name of the production computer.

16. You have written a Windows forms application that allows the user to input a new value for an environment variable through a form. If the code does not have environment permissions, you want it to fail gracefully. You've placed a demand for Environment permissions at the assembly level, with the `SecurityAction.RequestOptional` flag. However, when you test the application, the form will not load. What could be the problem?

A. Environment permissions can be requested only at the class level.

B. You must also request Registry permissions to manipulate the environment.

C. In addition to requesting Environment permissions, your code must also demand the same permission of its callers.

D. When requesting optional permissions, you must request all permissions that your assembly needs, including user interface permissions.

17. In which of these situations should you use `tlbimp`, the Type Library Importer tool? (Select two.)

A. You must call a COM component that you wrote from Visual C# .NET code.

B. You must produce a strong-named assembly that calls methods from one of your company's COM components.

C. You require objects from Microsoft Word in your .NET application.

D. You need to be able to call Windows API functions in `kernel.dll` from your .NET code.

18. Which of these tasks requires you to use imperative security rather than declarative security?

A. Refusing dangerous permissions such as registry permission.

B. Ensuring that your application has access to an environment variable whose name is not known until runtime.

C. Ensuring that your application has access to a specific file whose name is known at design time.

D. Ensuring that your application has access to an Oracle database as a specific user.

19. Your application uses version 2.3.0.0 of the `FunGraph` assembly. The producer of the assembly has issued version 2.3.1.0 of the assembly, together with a publisher policy file that dictates using `2.3.1.0` in place of `2.3.0.0` in all applications. You discover after testing that one of your applications, named `DiskGraph`, which previously worked with `2.3.0.0`, fails with `2.3.1.0`. You want only this application to use the old version of the assembly, while letting all other applications use the new version. What should you do?

A. Add the element `<publisherPolicy apply="no"/>` to the `DiskGraph.exe.config` file.

B. Add an administrator policy specifying that requests for `2.3.0.0` should be satisfied with `2.3.0.0`.

C. Delete the publisher policy from your computer.

D. Copy version 2.3.0.0 of the assembly from the GAC to the folder containing `DiskGraph.exe`.

20. You have designed a Windows service that includes a peer-to-peer layer to network with other instances of the same service on different computers. The service will need to present the computer's credentials to remote servers, but it does not need extensive permissions on the local computer. The service will run on a mix of Windows 2000 and Windows XP hosts. Which security context should you use for this service?

    A. `LocalService`

    B. `NetworkService`

    C. `LocalSystem`

    D. `User`

21. You are building a .NET Remoting server to deliver `Class1` as a server-activated object. The interface of `Class1` is defined as follows:

```
public class Class1 : MarshalByRefObject
{
    public int Property1;

    private DateTime p_property2;

    public DateTime Property2
    {
        get
        {
            return p_property2;
        }
        set
        {
            p_property2 = value;
        }
    }

    private double p_method3;

    public double Method3()
    {
```

```
        return p_method3;
    }

    public static string Property4;
}
```

Which member of `Class1` will **NOT** be available remotely?

    A. `Property1`

    B. `Property2`

    C. `Method3`

    D. `Property4`

22. You want to host a remotable class via the .NET Remoting framework so that remote clients can instantiate the class and invoke methods on it. Your business standards require you to use Integrated Windows authentication to authenticate users of the object. Which of the following techniques should you use to host the remotable class?

    A. Use Internet Information Services (IIS) as a Remoting host.

    B. Use a console application as a Remoting host.

    C. Create a Windows service and use that to host the remotable class.

    D. Use a Web Service application to host the remotable class.

23. Your application calls a Web service that delivers detailed demographic information. This information takes some time to generate, and your application is unresponsive while you're waiting for the results. What can you do to fix this problem?

    A. Use asynchronous calls to invoke the Web service.

    B. Install a faster link to the Internet.

    C. Install more memory in the client computer.

    D. Generate a proxy with the `wsdl.exe` tool.

24. You are creating a schema file to represent the Customers table in your database. You need to represent a field named CustomerContact in this schema. Data entered in the CustomerContact field is a string with up to 25 characters. What should you use to represent this field in the XML schema?

    A. Attribute

    B. Simple type

    C. Element

    D. Complex Type

25. You are building a .NET Remoting server that will make an object named `Account` available to client applications. The client applications are built in .NET, and they include the class file for the `Account` object. Unfortunately, some of the processing information in the class file is confidential.

    How should you remove this confidential information from the client applications without breaking their functionality?

    A. Rewrite the client applications in C++ so that they do not contain managed code.

    B. Define an interface, `IAccount`, which contains all the public members of the `Account` class. Implement the interface in the `Account` class. Ship only the interface with the client application.

    C. Remove the implementation code from the client's copy of the `Account` class.

    D. Rewrite the application as a Web Service application instead of a Remoting application.

26. Your application contains the following XML file:

    ```
    <?xml version="1.0" encoding="utf-8" ?>
    <Trials>
      <Trial TrialID="1">
    ```

```
      <Courtroom>1</Courtroom>
    </Trial>
    <Trial TrialID="2">
      <Courtroom>4</Courtroom>
    </Trial>
    <Trial TrialID="3">
      <Courtroom>3</Courtroom>
    </Trial>
</Trials>
```

Your application uses the `ReadXmlSchema()` method of the `DataSet` object to create a `DataSet` object with an appropriate schema for this XML file. Which of the following mappings between XML entities and `DataSet` object entities will this method create?

A. `Trials` and `Trial` will become `DataTable` objects. `Courtroom` will become a `DataColumn` object. `TrialID` will not be mapped.

B. `Trials` and `Trial` will become `DataTable` objects. `TrialID` will become a `DataColumn` object. `Courtroom` will not be mapped.

C. `Trials` and `Trial` will become `DataTable` objects. `TrialID` and `Courtroom` will become `DataColumn` objects.

D. `Trials` will become a `DataTable` object. `Trial` and `Courtroom` will become `DataColumn` objects. `TrialID` will not be mapped.

27. You are designing a .NET Remoting server that will be hosted by IIS and ASP.NET. This server will make a `Singleton` class named `ReportWriter` available to clients. Clients will be deployed on several different operating systems and platforms. Which channel and formatter should you use to implement this server?

    A. `TcpChannel` and `SoapFormatter`

    B. `TcpChannel` and `BinaryFormatter`

    C. `HttpChannel` and `SoapFormatter`

    D. `HttpChannel` and `BinaryFormatter`

28. You have called a Web method asynchronously in your code. Your application has a backlog of other processing to do at this point, so you want to continue working on other tasks until the Web method return value is available. How should you manage the asynchronous call?

    A. Call the `End` method immediately after calling the `Begin` method.

    B. Use the `WaitHandle.WaitOne()` method to wait for the result of the call.

    C. Supply a callback delegate to be executed when the results are ready.

    D. Poll the value of the `IAsyncResult.IsCompleted` property until it returns `true`.

29. You are designing a SOAP extension that will run within a variety of Web service clients. This extension will monitor messages for confidential information, and delete such information if it is found. In which message state should you invoke this SOAP extension?

    A. `BeforeDeserialize`

    B. `AfterDeserialize`

    C. `BeforeSerialize`

    D. `AfterSerialize`

30. You are going to use classes from three different COM components in your .NET application via COM interop. You'd like to place all these components into a uniform namespace. What should you do?

    A. Use the Type Library Importer tool with the `/out` option to create a file with the desired name.

    B. Use the Type Library Importer tool with the `/namespace` option to set the namespace within each RCW.

    C. Set a direct reference to each COM component. Declare a namespace for the entire project. Refer to that project from your actual project.

    D. Use PInvoke within a namespace to invoke methods from each component.

31. You are developing a .NET Remoting application that allows client programs to instantiate a class named `Account`. You want the remote object to be created on the server so that it can access the corporate financial information, which is stored on an intranet. However, you want client programs to control the creation and the lifetime of the remote objects. Which of the following methods of the `RemotingConfiguration` class would you choose to register the remotable class with the Remoting system on the server?

    A. `RegisterWellKnownServiceType()`

    B. `RegisterActivatedServiceType()`

    C. `RegisterWellKnownClientType()`

    D. `RegisterActivatedClientType()`

32. Your Visual C# .NET project contains the following code:

```
DefaultTraceListener t1 =
   new DefaultTraceListener();
Debug.Listeners.Add(t1);
Debug.WriteLine("Debug Message");
Trace.WriteLine("Trace Message");
```

You run the application in Debug mode. What output does this section of code produce?

A.

```
Debug Message
```

B.

```
Debug Message
Debug Message
```

C.

```
Debug Message
Trace Message
```

D.

```
Debug Message
Debug Message
Trace Message
Trace Message
```

33. You are using the DataSet schema designer within Visual Studio .NET to design a schema for part of an inventory application. This part of the application includes a Warehouse table and a Room table. Each warehouse contains multiple rooms. You've created an element to represent the Warehouse table. Which XML schema component should you add to this element to represent the Room table?

A. Attribute

B. Group

C. Facet

D. Element

34. You are using code access security in your application. The application absolutely requires permission to access the Windows Registry. Which type of `RegistryPermission` permission request should your code make?

A. `SecurityAction.Demand`

B. `SecurityAction.RequestRefuse`

C. `SecurityAction.RequestOptional`

D. `SecurityAction.RequestMinimum`

35. Your assembly is a member of five code groups, as follows:

EnterpriseA, at the enterprise level, grants Registry, Environment, FileDialog, and FileIO permissions to the code.

EnterpriseB, at the enterprise level, grants FileDialog permissions to the code.

MachineA, at the machine level, grants Registry, Environment, and FileIO permissions to the code.

MachineB, at the machine level, grants Environment and FileIO permissions to the code. This code group has its LevelFinal bit set.

UserA, at the user level, grants FileIO permissions to the code.

Which of these permissions will the code be granted as a result of its membership in these code groups?

A. FileIO

B. Registry, Environment, FileIO

C. Registry, Environment, FileIO, FileDialog

D. FileDialog, Environment, FileIO

36. Your Visual C# .NET project contains the following code:

```
DefaultTraceListener t1 =
    new DefaultTraceListener();
Debug.WriteLine("Debug Message");
Trace.WriteLine("Trace Message");
```

You run the application in Debug mode. What output does this section of code produce?

A.

```
Debug Message
```

B.

```
Debug Message
Debug Message
```

C.

```
Debug Message
Trace Message
```

D.

```
Debug Message
Debug Message
Trace Message
Trace Message
```

37. You want to use a Web service that supplies address verification services from your application. You know the URL of the `.asmx` file published by the Web service. What step should you take first?

    A. Run the Web Services Discovery tool.

    B. Open the `.asmx` file in a Web browser.

    C. Run the XML Schema Definition tool.

    D. Copy the `.asmx` file to your client project.

38. You are performing a final QA pass on a Web Service client, and you discover that the name of one of the parameters on the Web Service server has changed. All the documentation for the client has been printed, so you do not want to change the name of the client parameter. What should you do to fix this mismatch?

    A. Use the `SoapDocumentMethod` attribute to specify the `Bare` parameter style for this method.

    B. Use a SOAP extension on the client to detect the old parameter name and change it to the new parameter name before the message is sent.

C. Use the `SoapDocumentMethod` attribute with `Use=SoapBindingUse.Literal` to specify literal encoding for this method.

D. Use the `XmlElement` attribute to rename the parameter in the SOAP messages.

39. You are implementing a SOAP Extension to write usage statistics to a disk file. In which method should you open the disk file?

    A. `Initialize()`

    B. `GetInitializer()`

    C. `ChainStream()`

    D. `ProcessMessage()`

40. You have written a serviced component and now need to debug it when it's being used by a client process. The serviced component is stored in a file named `sc.dll`, and is a Server application. The client process is named `cp.exe`. To which process should you attach the debugger to trace calls within the serviced component?

    A. `sc.dll`

    B. `cp.exe`

    C. `aspnet.exe`

    D. `dllhost.exe`

41. You have created a class that uses COM+ with object pooling via the `System.EnterpriseServices` namespace. You're ready to install your component on a production server and would like to monitor the object pool to see whether it is properly sized. How should you do this?

A. Activate component events and statistics within the Component Services administrative tool.

B. Add code to the class to write messages to the event log whenever an instance of the class is created or destroyed.

C. Add code to the class to maintain a custom performance monitor with object pool statistics.

D. Use a performance monitor to track the committed RAM on the server to deduce the number of instances of the object created.

42. Your application uses the `GetComputerName` API function, which exists in `kernel32.dll` in both ANSI and Unicode versions. Your declaration is as follows:

```
[DllImport("kernel32.dll")]
public static extern int GetComputerName(
    StringBuilder buffer, ref uint size);
```

Your code is failing, with a `System.EntryPointNotFoundException` exception, whenever you call this function. What should you do to fix the failure?

A. Add the `CharSet.Auto` parameter to the declaration.

B. Supply the full path for `kernel32.dll`.

C. Declare the function as `GetComputerNameA` instead of `GetComputerName`.

D. Declare the function as `GetComputerNameW` instead of `GetComputerName`.

43. You are designing an application to monitor your network and log SOAP messages. This application should run full time, as long as the monitoring computer is booted, whether or not there is a user logged on. Which sort of application should you design?

A. Web Service

B. Serviced Component

C. ASP.NET application

D. Windows Service

44. Your application's database includes a table of orders that contains three million rows of data. Each row includes the order date as well as other information. Your application allows the user to enter a date, and then will display all the orders placed on that date. Which strategy should you use to retrieve the orders?

A. Create a parameterized stored procedure that accepts the order date as a parameter.

B. Retrieve the orders table to a `DataSet` object and build a `DataView` object to contain only the required orders.

C. Create an ad hoc SQL statement that includes the date entered by the user as part of the SQL statement.

D. Create a view on the server that includes only the required orders.

45. You are working programmatically with an XML document. You don't know anything about the structure of this document, other than it is valid XML. Which of these methods can you use to retrieve the root element of the document?

A. Load the document into an `XmlDocument` object and retrieve its `DocumentElement` property.

B. Load the document into an `XmlNode` object and retrieve its `DocumentElement` property.

C. Load the document into an `XmlDocument` object and retrieve its `DocumentType` property.

D. Load the document into an `XmlNode` object and retrieve its `DocumentType` property.

46. You have used Visual C# .NET to build a Windows service to implement a custom networking protocol. Which tool can you use to install the Windows service for testing your program?

    A. xcopy

    B. Services MMC snap-in

    C. gacutil

    D. installutil

47. You are designing a Web Service that will return roughly 250K of database information to clients on your intranet. How should you declare the Web method?

    A.

    ```
    [WebMethod(BufferResponse=false)]
    public Object GetData() { … }
    ```

    B.

    ```
    [WebMethod(CacheDuration=0)]
    public Object GetData() { … }
    ```

    C.

    ```
    [WebMethod(CacheDuration=7200)]
    public Object GetData() { … }
    ```

    D.

    ```
    [WebMethod(EnableSession=true)]
    public Object GetData() { … }
    ```

48. You have purchased a commercial SOAP extension for use with your Web Service. This extension encrypts some attributes in the AfterSerialize event on the client and decrypts the attributes in the BeforeDeserialize event on the server. Now you want to add your own SOAP extension to track some statistics on the incoming XML data. This SOAP extension will need access to the decrypted attributes from the other SOAP extension. How should you implement the new SOAP extension?

A. Add the new SOAP extension in the BeforeDeserialize event with a higher priority than the existing SOAP extension.

B. Add the new SOAP extension in the BeforeDeserialize event with a lower priority than the existing SOAP extension.

C. Add the new SOAP extension in the AfterDeserialize event with a higher priority than the existing SOAP extension.

D. Add the new SOAP extension in the AfterDeserialize event with a lower priority than the existing SOAP extension.

49. Your application contains this code:

```
EventLog el = new EventLog();
el.Source = "MyLog";
el.WriteEntry("MyLog",
 "A message",
 EventLogEntryType.Error);
```

You have not called EventLog.CreateEventSource("MyLog") anywhere in your application, and the MyLog event log does not already exist. What happens when you execute this code?

A. A runtime error occurs.

B. The message is displayed in a message box.

C. The message is written to the MyLog event log.

D. The message is written to the Application event log.

50. Your project contains the following API declaration:

```
[DllImport("kernel32.dll", CharSet=CharSet.Auto)]
public static extern int GetComputerName(
    String buffer, ref uint size);
```

The project also contains code to use this API to display the computer name:

```
public static void ShowName()
{
    String buf = "";
    UInt32 intLen=128;
    Int32 intRet;

    // Call the Win API method
    intRet = GetComputerName(
      buf, ref intLen);

    Console.WriteLine(
      "This computer is named " +
      buf.ToString());
}
```

Users report that no computer name is displayed. What should you do?

A. Use ref with the variable buf in the call to the GetComputerName() function.

B. Replace the use of String with StringBuilder in the code.

C. Tell the users that their computers have no names set in their network properties.

D. Use out with the variable buf in the call to the GetComputerName() function.

51. You wrote a COM component to store webcam data for future use. Now you want to use that component from .NET. The COM component is used nowhere else, and you have not shipped copies of it to anyone else. You want to call the objects in the COM server from your new .NET client. How should you proceed?

A. Use the Type Library Importer tool to create an unsigned RCW for the COM component.

B. Use the Type Library Importer tool to create a signed RCW for the COM component.

C. Set a direct reference from your .NET client to the COM server.

D. Use PInvoke to instantiate classes from the COM component.

52. Your Visual C# .NET project contains the following code:

```
DefaultTraceListener t1 =
  new DefaultTraceListener();
Debug.Listeners.Add(t1);
Debug.WriteLine("Debug Message");
Trace.WriteLine("Trace Message");
```

You run the application in Release mode. What output does this section of code produce?

A.

```
Trace Message
```

B.

```
Debug Message
Debug Message
```

C.

```
Trace Message
Trace Message
```

D.

```
Debug Message
Debug Message
Trace Message
Trace Message
```

53. You are designing a network application that depends on several Windows services. You want to allow users to list all the services on the computer and select the ones that they want to monitor. Which class can you use to enumerate the running services?

A. ServiceBase

B. ServiceInstaller

C. ServiceController

D. ServiceProcessInstaller

54. You are using a SQL INSERT statement to insert records in a table named Customers. The Customers table has the following structure:

CustomerID—integer, identity, no default value, cannot be null

CustomerName—varchar(75), no default value, cannot be null

CustomerCountry—varchar(30), default value 'USA', cannot be null

Employees—int, no default value, can be null

Which column must you explicitly specify in the INSERT statement?

A. CustomerID

B. CustomerName

C. CustomerCountry

D. Employees

55. You are attempting to retrieve all orders placed on July 19, 1996 from a SQL Server database. You have written the following SQL statement:

```
SELECT * FROM Orders
WHERE OrderDate = 7/19/1996
```

The statement executes without error, but does not return any rows. You are certain that the database contains orders from the date. How should you correct the SQL statement?

A.

```
SELECT * FROM Orders
WHERE OrderDate = #7/19/1996#
```

B.

```
SELECT * FROM Orders
WHERE OrderDate = July 19, 1996
```

C.

```
SELECT * FROM Orders
WHERE OrderDate = '7/19/1996'
```

D.

```
SELECT * FROM Orders
WHERE OrderDate = "7/19/1996"
```

56. You have developed a translation component that allows you to turn XML files with specific formatting into WAP files. You plan to use this component in multiple ASP.NET applications. You are now ready to use the Visual Studio .NET interface to build a setup project for your component. Which type of project should you build?

A. Setup project

B. Web setup project

C. Merge module project

D. CAB project

57. You have created a class that makes use of COM+ transactions through the System.EnterpriseServices namespace. During the course of its activities, the class calls various methods of the ContextUtil class. Which of these methods can the class use to indicate that its work is finished and that it approves of committing the transaction? (Select the two best answers.)

A. DisableCommit()

B. EnableCommit()

C. SetAbort()

D. SetComplete()

58. You are using IIS to authenticate users of an ASP.NET application. Part of your corporate security guidelines states that passwords must never cross the Internet in clear text. Which authentication methods can you use? (Select two.)

A. Anonymous

B. Digest

C. Windows Integrated

D. Basic

59. You use a `SqlDataAdapter` object to fill a `DataSet` object with the contents of the Parts table in your database. The PartName of the first part is "widget." You synchronize an `XmlDataDocument` object with the `DataSet` object. In the `DataSet` object, you change the PartName of the first customer to "thingamabob." After that, in the `XmlDataDocument` object, you change the Value of the corresponding Node to "thingummy." When you call the `Update()` method of the `SqlDataAdapter` object, what is the effect?

    A. The PartName in the table remains "widget."

    B. The PartName in the table is updated to "thingummy."

    C. The PartName in the table is updated to "thingamabob."

    D. The CLR prompts you as to whether the name should be "thingummy" or "thingamabob."

60. You have built and tested a Web service named `PerfMonService`. The service uses some application-wide event handling that is contained in the `Global.asax` file. Now you are ready to deploy the Web service to a production server. Which of these files should you deploy to the production server? (Choose two.)

    A. `PerfMonService.asmx`

    B. `AssemblyInfo.cs`

    C. `Global.asax.cs`

    D. `Web.config`

61. You are using XPath to retrieve information from an XML file of electronic components. Some of the components are grouped into assemblies and subassemblies, and this grouping is represented in the hierarchy of the XML file. You wish to write an XPath expression to select every occurrence of the `Volts` attribute in the XML file, regardless of the level where this attribute appears. Which XPath expression can you use for this purpose?

    A. `./@Volts`

    B. `./Volts`

    C. `//@Volts`

    D. `//Volts`

62. You are developing a SOAP extension to run in a Web Service client application. Your SOAP extension includes a class named `MyExtensionAttribute` to flag methods to which the extension applies. The client project contains this code:

```
private btnGetData_Click(
 System.Object sender,
 System.EventArgs e) _
{
    // Call a Web method on the object
    InvWebService.Inventory I = _
     new InvWebService.Inv();
    objWarehouse.Inv = I.GetLatest();
}
```

    Where should you apply the `MyExtensionAttribute` attribute so that it interacts with the SOAP requests generated by this procedure?

    A. To the `btnGetData_Click` event handler

    B. To the `GetInitializer()` method in your SOAP extension

    C. To the `GetLatest()` method in the Web Service proxy class

    D. To the `Load` event of the form containing this button

63. You have built a Windows Service application that will monitor network activity on a specified TCP/IP port. You intend to allow the user to specify the port as a parameter from the Services MMC snap-in. Where should you process the user's selection?

A. In the `Main()` method of the service

B. In the `OnStart()` method of the service

C. In the `Run()` method of the service

D. In the `OnContinue()` method of the service

64. Your ASP.NET application contains this setting in the `web.config` file:

```
<identity impersonate="true"
    name="CORP\Bill"
    password="BillPassword"/>
```

You are allowing only Windows integrated authentication in IIS. What identity will ASP.NET use to authorize resources if a user with the Windows account Bob in the CORP domain logs in?

A. `ASPNET`

B. `CORP\Bob`

C. `CORP\Bill`

D. `IUSR_ComputerName`

65. You have created a serviced component named `LicenseManager`. The `LicenseManager` component reads software licensing details from an XML configuration file. You want the system administrator to be able to enter the name of the configuration file, which should then be used when the component is instantiated. The system administrator will enter this name through the Component Services administration tool. How should you retrieve this entry?

A. Override the `Construct()` method of your component.

B. Override the `Activate()` method of your component.

C. Create a constructor for your component that uses the data.

D. Create an interface for your component that uses the data.

66. `ChartLib` is a COM component that was developed internally and is used in most of your company's applications. You are now migrating those applications to .NET, and want to continue to use the `ChartLib` component. How should you proceed to reuse the component with the least work?

A. Use Platform Invoke to declare the functions within the COM component.

B. Use `tlbimp` to create an unsigned RCW, and place the RCW in each application's folder.

C. Use `tlbimp` to create an unsigned PIA, and place the unsigned PIA in the GAC.

D. Use `tlbimp` to create a signed PIA, and place the signed PIA in the GAC.

67. You have developed a Remoting application and are now building a setup package to install this application on your company's production servers. The setup package installs several SQL scripts that must be executed on the target machine. If the SQL scripts fail, then the installation should be aborted. Which setup editor should you use to manage the installation logic for these scripts?

A. File System Editor

B. Registry Editor

C. Launch Conditions Editor

D. Custom Actions Editor

68. You have created a serviced component that accepts vacation requests from employees for processing by the payroll system. You register the component in the COM+ catalog of the company's main application server. You enable object pooling services for the component and set Minimum Pool Size to 5 and Maximum Pool Size to 10. However, you have underestimated

the demand for vacations, and 12 users attempt to use the application simultaneously. What is the result?

A. The first ten requests for the object are satisfied with new instances. The last two requests are queued until an instance is available, or until the specified timeout period elapses.

B. The first ten requests for the object are satisfied with new instances. The last two requests fail with an `object not found` exception.

C. The first ten requests for the object are satisfied with new instances. The last two requests are satisfied by recycling the first two objects, thus disconnecting the first two requests.

D. Component Services increases the pool size to 12 so as to be able to satisfy all the requests.

69. You have written a .NET class library that will be shared by multiple applications on your computer. You wish to manage this component by providing a single file that can be shared by all assemblies. What should you do? (Select the two best answers.)

A. Generate a native image using the `ngen.exe` tool.

B. Install the library in the GAC using the `gacutil.exe` tool.

C. Create a strong name for the component using the `sn.exe` tool.

D. Register the component using the `regsvcs.exe` tool.

70. You have written the following code for a serviced component:

```
public interface Iorder
{
    bool ConfirmOrder(OrderInfo o);
}
```

```
[JustInTimeActivation(true), _
 Transaction(TransactionOption.Required)]
public class OrderConfirm
    : ServicedComponent, IOrder
{
    public bool ConfirmOrder(OrderInfo o)
    {
        // Code to check database for order
        // Code to check credit rating
        // Code to decrease available credit
        // Code to place order
    }
}
```

At the end of the `ConfirmOrder()` method you decide whether all the databases involved have been updated correctly. If yes then you commit the transaction and deactivate the current `OrderConfirm` object. Which of the following methods should you use in the `PlaceOrder()` method to accomplish this requirement?

A. `SetComplete()`

B. `DisableCommit()`

C. `EnableCommit()`

D. `SetAbort()`

71. You are invoking a Web service that returns a `DataTable` object. Your client application is written in Visual C# .NET, whereas the Web service itself is written in Visual C# .NET. The Web service is outside your corporate firewall. You receive an `object not found` error when you call the method that returns the `DataTable`. What could be the problem?

A. The client project and the server project are not written in the same language.

B. The firewall is blocking all SOAP calls.

C. The client project does not contain a reference to the `System.Data` namespace.

D. The `DataTable` object cannot be serialized.

72. You have installed a Web Service on an IIS computer named SHINBONE that allows anonymous access. Impersonation is enabled in the ASP.NET Web.config file for the Web Service, but no user identity is specified for the impersonation. You have ASP.NET installed to use the ASPNET account. Bob, who is a member of the CORP domain on the server, submits a SOAP request to the Web Service. Under which security context does this request execute?

    A. IUSR_SHINBONE

    B. CORP\Bob

    C. ASPNET

    D. CORP\Guest

73. You have developed a graphing component that will be made available to your customers via download from the Internet. To ensure your customers of the safety of the component, you wish to sign it in such a fashion as to guarantee both the integrity of the code and the identity of the code. What should you do?

    A. Sign the code using sn.exe.

    B. Sign the code using signcode.exe.

    C. Sign the code first with sn.exe, then with signcode.exe.

    D. Sign the code first with signcode.exe, then with sn.exe.

74. You are using the Web Services Description Language tool to create a proxy class for a Web service. The Web service exposes a class named Supplier. You already have a Supplier class in your application. What should you do to allow both classes to coexist in the same application?

    A. Rename the existing class.

    B. Manually edit the generated proxy class to change the classname that it contains.

    C. Use the /namespace option of the Web Services Description Language tool to specify a unique namespace for the new class.

    D. Use the /out option of the Web Services Description Language tool to specify a unique output filename for the new class.

75. You have defined a stored procedure in your database as follows:

```
CREATE PROC GetCustomers
  @Country varchar(25)
AS
  SELECT * FROM Customers
  WHERE Country = @Country
```

The stored procedure executes without error from SQL Query Analyzer. Now you are using code behind a form with this stored procedure. The form includes a SqlConnection object named cnn, and a DataGrid control named dgCustomers:

```
SqlCommand cmd = new SqlCommand();
DataSet ds = new DataSet();
SqlDataAdapter da = _
 new SqlDataAdapter();
cmd.Connection = cnn;
cmd.CommandText = "GetCustomers";
cmd.Parameters.Add(new SqlParameter(
 "@Country", SqlDbType.VarChar, 25));
cmd.Parameters["@Country"].Value =
   "France";
da.SelectCommand = cmd;
da.Fill(ds, "Customers");
dgCustomers.DataSource = ds;
dgCustomers.DataMember = "Customers";
```

When you run the code, you receive an unhandled exception of type System.Data.SqlClient. SqlException on the line that calls the Fill() method. What should you do to fix this error?

A. Explicitly set the `CommandType` object of the `SqlCommand` object to `CommandType.StoredProcedure`.

B. Replace the stored procedure with an ad hoc SQL statement containing the actual country string.

C. Use a `SqlDataReader` object instead of a `DataSet` object to retrieve the data.

D. Call the `Open()` method of the `SqlConnection` object before calling the `Fill()` method of the `DataAdapter`.

76. You are developing a Windows Service by inheriting from the `System.ServiceProcess.ServiceBase` class. Which handler are you required to implement in your service?

A. `OnStop`

B. `OnStart`

C. `OnPause`

D. `OnContinue`

77. Your Windows application contains the following code:

```
Boolean bContinue = true;
Debug.Assert(bContinue, "Debug Message");
bContinue = false;
Trace.Assert(bContinue, "Trace Message");
```

You run the application in Release mode. What will be the result of running this code segment?

A. `Trace Message` will appear in a dialog box.

B. `Debug Message` will appear in a dialog box.

C. `Trace Message` will appear in the Output window.

D. `Debug Message` will appear in the Output window.

ANSWERS TO EXAM QUESTIONS

1. **A, C.** XPath node numbering is 1-based. The expression /Orders/Order[1]/Part[2] explicitly selects the second <Part> element under the first <Order> element. The expression (/Orders/Order/Part)[2] selects the second <Part> element in the entire file, which happens to be under the first <Order> element in this case. The parentheses are necessary because the square bracket operator normally takes precedence over the path operators.

2. **B.** Both AutoDispatch and AutoDual generate interfaces for you when registering a class with COM+. The default value is AutoDispatch, which generates a late-bound interface (whereas AutoDual generates both early- and late-bound interfaces). To define your own interfaces, you must explicitly set the ClassInterface attribute to None.

3. **C.** Multiple versions of the same assembly can exist side by side in the GAC. In the absence of a policy to the contrary, .NET applications use only the version of an assembly with which they were originally compiled.

4. **A.** By providing a hard-coded GUID for the component, you prevent the registration process from generating a new GUID each time the component is registered with COM+.

5. **C.** You're interested in the total cost of visits, so you must use the Sum() operator on the VisitCost column. To filter after the sum is taken, you must use a HAVING clause. Using WHERE does not help because it filters the data to include only individual rows where the cost is at least $100.

6. **C.** The `XmlTextReader` is optimized for forward-only, read-only processing of an XML file. You can't use the `XmlReader` class directly in an actual implementation because the `XmlReader` class is an abstract class.

7. **B.** You can't use delegates, because they won't pause the code at this point. To coordinate two or more methods and proceed when any one of them completes, you use `WaitHandle.WaitAny()` method.

8. **A.** The `LocalSystem` value defines a highly privileged account. As compared to this, the `LocalService` and `NetworkService` values provide a lower privilege level for the security context. Privileges for `User` depend on the specified username and password.

9. **A.** Because you developed the component, the proper course of action is to produce a PIA for it. You can use the Type Library Importer tool to do this.

10. **D.** In Release mode, the `DEBUG` symbol is not defined. Therefore, the compiler simply ignores the call to `PrintDebugText()` method, without throwing an error. The `Trace.WriteLine()` method executes normally and prints its string to the Output window.

11. **B.** `SingleCall` SAOs have no state, so they're easy to load-balance just by adding new servers. For a heavily loaded application, SAOs are preferable to CAOs because they do not transmit as much data across the network for each call.

12. **A.** With a `Singleton` SAO, state is persisted, but all clients of the object share the same state. With a `SingleCall` SAO, state is not persisted. With a CAO, each client can persist its own state, which avoids the problem with clients sharing state.

13. **B.** The Disco (`.disco`) file is the only one that contains pointers to non-XML resources.

14. **A.** The Web methods exposed by a Web Service are only those methods that are declared public and are decorated with the `WebMethod` attribute. You are not required to use either UDDI or WSDL with a Web Service.

15. **C.** The `SqlXmlCommand` object is supplied as part of the SQLXML download package. It is not installed with the base .NET Framework.

16. **D.** When you use the `SecurityAction.RequestOptional` flag, the CLR does not grant you any permissions that you did not explicitly request. This contrasts with `SecurityAction.RequestMinimum`, which allows the CLR to grant extra permissions.

17. **A, B.** You should not use `tlbimp` on code from another vendor. Rather, you should go to that vendor to get the Primary Interop Assembly (PIA) for the COM library that you wish to call. Also, `tlbimp` is not necessary for calling Windows API functions.

18. **B.** Declarative code access security can handle only scenarios where you know the details at design time. If the security requirements are finalized at runtime, you must use imperative security.

19. **A.** The `<publisherPolicy>` element allows you to override publisher policy for a single application. Adding an administrator policy or deleting the publisher policy affects all applications on the computer, not just the one application. Copying the assembly will have no effect on the binding, which is satisfied from the GAC.

20. **C.** The `NetworkService` and `LocalSystem` accounts both present the computer's network credentials to any remote server. However, the `NetworkService` account is not available on Windows 2000.

21. **D.** Static members (defined by the `static` keyword in Visual C# .NET) are not available remotely.

22. **A.** When you use IIS to host a remotable class, the full spectrum of IIS authentication and authorization methods are available to the Remoting infrastructure.

23. **A.** Using an asynchronous call to invoke a Web Service allows other code in your application to execute while you're waiting for the Web service to return results. When the results are ready, the asynchronous call can invoke a callback method to make them available.

24. **B.** A simple type can be modified by facets, which enable you to specify data restrictions such as minimum, maximum, or exact length.

25. **B.** By using an interface to define the contract between the Remoting server and the client, you can keep the two synchronized without leaking any implementation details to the client.

26. **C.** The `ReadXmlSchema()` method maps nested elements in the XML file to related `DataTable` objects in the `DataSet` object. At the leaf level of the DOM tree, both elements and attributes are mapped to `DataColumn` objects.

27. **C.** To make efficient use of the features of IIS and ASP.NET from a Remoting server, you should use the `HttpChannel`. For maximum interoperability with clients across platforms and languages, you should use the `SoapFormatter`.

28. **C.** To wait for the result of an asynchronous Web method call with minimum overhead, you should supply a callback delegate. If you call the `End` method or use the `WaitHandle.WaitOne()` method, you effectively convert the asynchronous call back to a synchronous call. If you use a polling loop, you'll adversely affect performance.

29. **D.** This SOAP extension needs to monitor and alter the XML messages that are sent from client to server. These messages are available on the client only in the `AfterSerialize` stage.

30. **B.** You can specify the namespace for an RCW by using the `/namespace` switch with the Type Library Importer tool.

31. **B.** In this scenario, you need to register a client-activated remote object, which you can do using the `RegisterActivatedServiceType()` method. The `RegisterActivatedClientType()` method is used to register the CAO with the Remoting system in the client's application domain. The other two options are for creating the server-activated objects.

32. **D.** In Debug mode, both debug and trace messages are active. Creating a new `DefaultTraceListener` object and adding it to the `Listeners` collection results in each message being output twice (through the built-in `DefaultTraceListener` and through the newly-added `DefaultTraceListener`). The `Debug` and `Trace` messages share the same `Listeners` collection, so adding an object to one adds it to the other.

33. **D.** To represent a child table in a hierarchy in an XML schema, you must use an element. This element will contain the complex element representing the child table.

34. **D.** With `SecurityAction.RequestMinimum`, your code will throw an exception if it cannot obtain the requested permission. `SecurityAction.Demand` requires callers to have the permission, but that does not mean the current assembly will have the permission. `SecurityAction.RequestOptional` does not guarantee that the permission will be granted, and `SecurityAction.RequestRefuse` guarantees that your code will not receive the specified permission.

35. **B.** At each level, the permissions are the union of all permissions granted at that level. So this gives you Registry, Environment, FileDialog, and FileIO permissions at the enterprise level; Registry, Environment, and FileIO permissions at the machine level; and FileIO permissions at the user level. The total permissions are the intersection of the level permissions. However, because the MachineB code group has the LevelFinal bit set, the user level permissions are not considered by this assembly. So the final effective permissions are the intersection of the machine and enterprise permissions.

36. **C.** In Debug mode, both debug and trace messages are active. But creating a new `DefaultTraceListener` object, without adding it to the `Listeners` collection, has no effect on the output. Only the built-in `DefaultTraceListener` is used in this example.

37. **A.** The Web Services Discovery tool retrieves copies of the files that you need to proceed with this project.

38. **D.** The `XmlElement` attribute lets you alter the SOAP requests sent to the server without changing any of your code.

39. **B.** The `GetInitializer()` method is called once when the SOAP extension is first invoked, and is the appropriate event for one-time resource setup. The `Initialize()` method is called every time the SOAP extension is invoked.

40. **D.** Component Services launches Server components in a separate instance of the `dllhost.exe` process. You can determine which of several `dllhost` processes corresponds to a particular serviced component by using the Status View within the Component Services administrative tool.

41. **A.** When you check the Activate Component Events and Statistics option within the Component Services administrative tool, you can monitor a variety of statistics on pooled components, including the number of objects in the pool, the number currently activated, and the number of objects currently executing a client request.

42. **A.** When an API call exists in both ANSI and Unicode versions, you can use the `CharSet.Auto` parameter to tell the .NET Framework to automatically choose the correct version based on the current platform.

43. **D.** A Windows Service can be set to start whenever the operating system starts, and it continues to run when users log on or off the machine.

44. **A.** Parameterized stored procedures are faster and more secure than ad hoc SQL statements. A view cannot contain parameters, so you'd need to build a new view for every request. The `DataSet` object approach would result in all rows of the table being transferred to the client, which would perform very poorly.

45. **A.** The `DocumentElement` property of an `XmlDocument` object returns an `XmlNode` object that represents the root node in the underlying XML document.

46. **D.** Installing a Windows Service requires communicating with the Service Control Manager (SCM). Of the listed tools, only `installutil` can communicate with the SCM to install a new service.

47. **A.** Setting the `BufferResponse` property to `false` sends back the data in chunks, so that the client process won't time out while waiting for it. `CacheDuration` specifies how long the response will be cached for succeeding calls, and doesn't have any effect on a single call to the method. Session state doesn't need to be enabled unless you require the Web Service to be stateful.

48. **A.** SOAP extensions execute in order from lowest priority to highest priority. Because your SOAP extension needs to work with the XML data, it must be invoked in the `BeforeDeserialize` event rather than in the `AfterDeserialize` event (when the XML has been converted back to native objects).

49. **C.** If you attempt to write an event log entry to a log that you have not yet created, the .NET framework automatically creates the appropriate source. Calling the `CreateEventSource()` method is optional.

50. **B.** In the calls via PInvoke, you should use `StringBuilder` rather than `String` to hold a string buffer that expects to be modified by the function.

51. **C.** In this situation, where you wrote the component and there's no question of it being used elsewhere, the easiest way to bring it into .NET is to just set a direct reference.

52. **C.** In Release mode, only trace messages are active. Creating a new `DefaultTraceListener` and adding it to the `Listeners` collection results in each message being output twice (through the built-in `DefaultTraceListener` and through the newly added `DefaultTraceListener`). The `Debug` and `Trace` messages share the same `Listeners` collection, so adding an object to one adds it to the other.

53. **C.** The `ServiceController.GetServices()` method returns a list of the Windows services installed on the computer.

54. **B.** An `INSERT` statement must specify values for non-nullable, non-identity columns that do not have a default value.

55. **C.** SQL Server uses single quotes to delimit date values. The reason the original SQL did not return an error was that SQL Server treated the date as a mathematical operation involving two divisions, and silently converted the result into a date.

56. **C.** A merge module project provides a way to include a component in more than one setup project. The merge module cannot be installed on its own, but it is the ideal way to deliver a shared component.

57. **B, D.** The `SetComplete()` method call sets both the consistent bit and the done bit to True, so the transaction can be committed. The `EnableCommit()` method call sets the consistent bit to true but leaves the done bit set to False, which also allows committing the transaction but does not deactivate the object.

58. **B, C.** Anonymous authentication does not actually authenticate users at all, and Basic authentication transmits passwords in plain text. Digest authentication encrypts the password before it crosses the Internet, and Windows Integrated authentication uses either Kerberos or challenge/response to keep passwords off the wire entirely.

59. **B.** The `DataSet` object and the `XmlDataDocument` object are two views of the same data in memory. The last change you make to this data will be saved, regardless of which object you used to make the change.

60. **A, D.** The `.asmx` and `.config` files are required on the Web server at runtime. The `.cs` files are compiled into the code-behind DLL for the Web service, and so do not need to be deployed to the production server.

61. **C.** Because `Volts` is an attribute rather than an element, you must refer to it as `@Volts` in an XPath expression. To select this attribute wherever it appears in the XML file, you should use `//` as the current context to cause the search to start at the root of the file.

62. **C.** SOAP extensions are activated by applying the corresponding attribute to the Web method proxy that you want to intercept.

63. **B.** When a Windows service is started, any start-up parameters are passed to the `OnStart()` method.

64. **C.** If you turn on impersonation and specify a username in the identity tag, then that identity will be used for any user who successfully authenticates to the IIS server.

65. **A.** The `Construct()` method of a serviced component enables you to retrieve data entered in the Component Services administration tool. Serviced components cannot have non-default constructors.

66. **D.** Placing an RCW or PIA in the GAC makes it available to all .NET applications on the computer. But you can't put an unsigned assembly in the GAC.

67. **D.** The Custom Actions Editor enables you to add logic to a setup project that encompasses rollback in case of difficulty.

68. **A.** After the pool of objects is exhausted, further requests are queued until an object is available or until the specified timeout period elapses.

69. **B, C.** To share the class library among multiple applications, you should place it in the GAC. As a prerequisite to this, you must assign a strong name to the component. Components can be shared whether or not they are native images. The `regsvcs.exe` tool is used only for serviced components, not for regular class libraries.

70. **A.** The `SetComplete()` method both commits the transaction and deactivates the current object at the end of the method call.

71. **C.** NET Web services can serialize complex objects and pass SOAP messages containing these objects across firewalls and across language boundaries. However, the client application must contain information about how to reconstitute the object, including a reference to the object's definition.

72. **A.** Because the IIS server allows anonymous access, any user will run as `IUSR_SHINBONE` in the IIS process. With impersonation enabled but no user identity specified, ASP.NET assumes the identity of the user within the IIS process. Even though the user has credentials on the domain, those credentials are never used in this example.

73. **C.** Signing the code with `sn.exe` provides proof that the code has not been altered, but does not provide any evidence of the code's origin. Signing the code with `signcode.exe` applies a digital certificate to indicate the code's origin, but does not provide protection against tampering. You must sign the code with both tools to guarantee both integrity and identity. When you use both tools, you must always use `sn.exe` first.

74. **C.** Specifying a unique namespace for the new object removes the chance that it can clash with a pre-existing object name, and does not require you to change any existing code.

75. **A.** If you do not specify the command type of a `SqlCommand` object, it defaults to `CommandType.Text`, which will not work with a stored procedure. You could also make the code work by using an ad hoc SQL statement, but this is an undesirable solution because the code will run more slowly and be less secure.

76. **B.** The `CanShutdown`, `CanStop`, and `CanPauseAndContinue` properties let you specify which service events a Windows service can handle. However, there is no `CanStart` property; you must always handle start requests from the SCM by implementing an `OnStart()` event handler.

77. **A.** In release mode, calls of any sort to the Debug class have no effect. Assertion failures appear in a dialog box, not in the Output window in Windows applications.

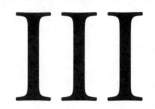

PART

III

APPENDIXES

Though there are no objectives on the exam that directly test your knowledge of ADO.NET, you'll find that ADO.NET knowledge is assumed by many of the objectives. In this appendix, you'll learn the basics of ADO.NET, its architecture, and its most useful objects.

APPENDIX A

ADO.NET Basics

INTRODUCTION

ADO.NET is one of the core .NET technologies that Microsoft expects every .NET developer to understand. While there are many books on the market that cover ADO.NET in depth, this appendix will give you the basics just in case you need a quick refresher. You'll learn about the overall architecture of ADO.NET, the specific objects in ADO.NET and its constituent namespaces, and some of the common data access tasks that you can perform with those objects.

ADO.NET ARCHITECTURE

ADO.NET is the overall name for the set of classes (spread across a number of namespaces, including `System.Data`, `System.Data.Common`, `System.Data.SqlTypes`, `System.Data.SqlClient`, and `System.Data.OleDb`) that the .NET Framework provides for working with data in relational databases. One of the strengths of ADO.NET is that you can equally well use the same objects to work with data that isn't stored relationally. For example, you could use XML files, or even plain text files, to hold the data that ADO.NET uses. Regardless of the original source, the high-level abstract ADO.NET objects are the same.

The ADO.NET object model is broken up into two distinct sets of objects—data provider objects and `DataSet` objects—because the .NET Framework separates the task of using data from the task of storing data. A `DataSet` object provides a memory-resident, disconnected set of objects that you can load with data. A data provider object handles the task of working directly with data sources. One of the provider objects, the `DataAdapter` object, serves as a conduit between the two sets of objects. By using a `DataAdapter` object, you can load data from a database into a `DataSet` object and later save changes back to the original data source.

Figure A.1 shows schematically how these two sets of objects fit together in the overall ADO.NET architecture.

FIGURE A.1
ADO.NET architecture.

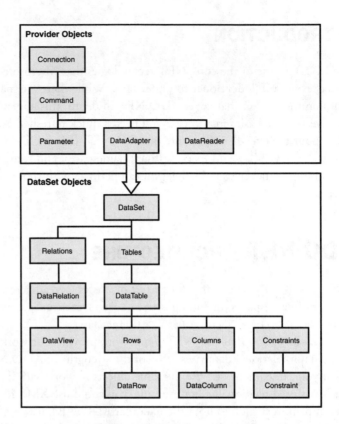

THE ADO.NET OBJECT MODEL

In generic terms, the data provider objects manage the database for your application, and the DataSet objects manage the data model for the application. In this section, I drill into these objects in turn, starting with the data provider objects. I use the SQL Server data provider objects for examples, but keep in mind that the basic ADO.NET syntax is the same no matter what data source you're using.

Data Providers and Their Objects

You should know about five main data provider objects:

▶ Connection

▶ Command

- ► Parameter

- ► DataReader

- ► DataAdapter

These are the generic names for the classes defined in `System.Data.Common` namespace. In fact, you'll seldom (if ever) write code that uses these generic objects. Each data provider has implementations of these objects with specific names.

A data provider is a namespace that implements these five classes (and some other classes and enumerations) for use with a particular database. For example, you can work with data stored in a SQL Server database by using the SQL Server data provider, which is implemented in the `System.Data.SqlClient` namespace. In this namespace, the object names are as follows:

- ► SqlConnection

- ► SqlCommand

- ► SqlParameter

- ► SqlDataReader

- ► SqlDataAdapter

But the SQL Server data provider is not the only alternative for retrieving data in ADO.NET. The .NET Framework also ships with the OLE DB data provider, implemented in the `System.Data.OleDb` namespace. In this namespace, the corresponding object names are as follows:

- ► OleDbConnection

- ► OleDbCommand

- ► OleDbParameter

- ► OleDbDataReader

- ► OleDbDataAdapter

Although the .NET Framework 1.0 includes only two data providers, there are other alternatives. For example, Microsoft released both an Open Database Connectivity (ODBC) data provider and an Oracle data provider as add-ons to the .NET

> **EXAM TIP**
>
> **Not All OLE DB Is Equal**   Though from the name it seems that the OLE DB data provider should work with any existing OLE DB provider, that's not the case. It's designed to work with only the SQL Server, Jet 4.0, and Oracle OLE DB providers. Other providers might work but are not supported.

Managed Provider for Oracle The Oracle managed provider, an add-on to the .NET Framework 1.0, can be downloaded from www.microsoft.com/downloads/release.asp?releaseid=40032.

Framework 1.0, and included them in the .NET Framework 1.1. Third parties are also planning to release other providers. You should expect to see many more data providers in the coming months, just as there were many ODBC and OLE DB drivers in earlier data access models.

I'll use the SQL Server data provider objects in all my examples, but you should keep in mind that the techniques you learn to work with objects from this namespace will also work with objects from other data provider namespaces.

The `SqlConnection` Object

The `SqlConnection` object represents a single persistent connection to a SQL Server data source. ADO.NET automatically handles connection pooling, which contributes to better application performance by eliminating the overhead involved in constantly creating and destroying connections. When you call the `Close()` method of a `SqlConnection` object, the connection is returned to a connection pool. ADO.NET does not immediately destroy connections in a pool. Instead, they're available for reuse if another part of an application requests a `SqlConnection` object that matches with the same connection details of a previously closed `SqlConnection` object.

Table A.1 shows the most important members of the `SqlConnection` object.

TABLE A.1

IMPORTANT MEMBERS OF THE SqlConnection CLASS

Member	Type	Description
BeginTransaction()	Method	Starts a new transaction on this `SqlConnection` object
ChangeDatabase()	Method	Changes the current database for the `SqlConnection` object
Close()	Method	Returns the `SqlConnection` object to the connection pool
ConnectionString	Property	Specifies the server to be used by this `SqlConnection` object
CreateCommand()	Method	Returns a new `SqlCommand` object that executes via this `SqlConnection` object
Open()	Method	Opens the `SqlConnection` object

There are several ways to create `SqlConnection` objects in Visual Studio .NET applications. Step-by-Step A.1 shows how you can use drag-and-drop to build a `SqlConnection` object.

STEP BY STEP

A.1 Creating a `SqlConnection` Object from Server Explorer

1. Create a new Visual C# .NET Windows application named `320AppA`.

2. Hover your mouse over the Server Explorer tab until Server Explorer opens. Right-click on the Data Connections node and select Add Connection.

3. Fill in the Data Link Properties dialog box as shown in Figure A.2. You may need to supply a server name, username, and password, depending on your network configuration. Click OK.

4. Drag the newly-created server node from Server Explorer and drop it on the default form. This creates an object named `sqlConnection1` in the component tray.

5. Place a `Button` control (`btnConnect`) and a `TextBox` control (`txtConnectionString`) on the form.

6. Switch to the code view and add the following `using` directive:

```
using System.Data.SqlClient;
```

7. Double-click the `Button` control and enter this code to handle the `Click` event of the `Button` control:

```
private void btnConnect_Click(
    object sender, System.EventArgs e)
{
    sqlConnection1.Open();
    txtConnectionString.Text =
        sqlConnection1.ConnectionString;
    sqlConnection1.Close();
}
```

8. Run the project and click the button. The code connects to the SQL Server database on the local computer and echoes the connection string to the `TextBox` control.

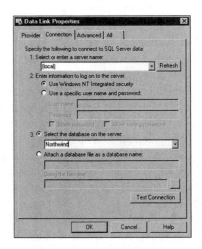

FIGURE A.2
You can create a new data connection using the Data Link Properties dialog box.

You can also create a `SqlConnection` directly in code. Step-by-Step A.2 demonstrates this technique.

STEP BY STEP

A.2. Creating a `SqlConnection` Object in Code

1. Add a new form to your Visual C# .NET project.

2. Place a `Button` control (`btnConnect`) and a `TextBox` control (`txtConnectionString`) on the form.

3. Switch to the code view and add the following using directive:

```
using System.Data.SqlClient;
```

4. Double-click the `Button` control and enter this code to handle the `Click` event of the `Button` control:

```
private void btnConnect_Click(object sender,
    System.EventArgs e)
{
    SqlConnection cnn = new SqlConnection();
    cnn.ConnectionString = "Data Source=(local);" +
    "Initial Catalog=Northwind;" +
    "Integrated Security=SSPI";
    cnn.Open();
    txtConnectionString.Text = cnn.ConnectionString;
    cnn.Close();
}
```

5. Insert the `Main()` method to launch the form. Set the form as the startup object for the project.

6. Run the project and click the button. The code connects to the SQL Server database on the local computer and echoes the connection string to the `TextBox` control.

> **EXAM TIP**
>
> **The Parts of a Connection String**
> A connection string has three parts. First is the *Data Source*, which is the name of the server to which you'd like to connect. You can use `(local)` as a shortcut name for the SQL Server instance running on the same computer as this code. Second is the *Initial Catalog*, which is the name of the database on the server to use. Third is authentication information; it can be either `Integrated Security=SSPI` to use Windows authentication or `User ID=username;Password=password` to use SQL Server authentication. There are other optional parameters, but these three are the most important.

The `SqlCommand` and `SqlParameter` Objects

The `SqlCommand` and `SqlParameter` objects work together to retrieve data from a data source after you've made a connection. The `SqlCommand` object represents something that can be executed, such as an ad hoc query string or a stored procedure name. The `SqlParameter` object represents a single parameter to a stored procedure.

Table A.2 shows the most important members of the `SqlCommand` object.

IMPORTANT MEMBERS OF THE SqlCommand CLASS

Member	Type	Description
CommandText	Property	Specifies the statement to be executed by the `SqlCommand` object
CommandType	Property	Indicates what type of command this `SqlCommand` object represents
Connection	Property	Represents the `SqlConnection` object through which this `SqlCommand` object executes
CreateParameter()	Method	Creates a new `SqlParameter` object for this `SqlCommand` object
ExecuteNonQuery()	Method	Executes a `SqlCommand` object that does not return a resultset
ExecuteReader()	Method	Executes a `SqlCommand` object and places the results in a `SqlDataReader` object
ExecuteScalar()	Method	Executes a `SqlCommand` object and returns the first column of the first row of the resultset
ExecuteXmlReader()	Method	Executes a `SqlCommand` object and places the results in an `XmlReader` object
Parameters	Property	Contains a collection of `SqlParameter` objects for this `SqlCommand` object

Step-by-Step A.3 gives an example of using the `ExecuteScalar()` method, which provides you with an easy way to retrieve a single value (such as an aggregation) from a database.

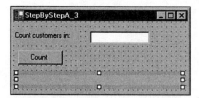

FIGURE A.3
This form uses the `ExecuteScalar()` method to retrieve a single value from a database.

STEP BY STEP

A.3 Using the `ExecuteScalar()` Method

1. Add a new form to your Visual C# .NET project.

2. Place a `Button` control (`btnCount`), a `TextBox` control (`txtCountry`), and a `Label` control (`lblResults`) on the form. Figure A.3 shows the design of this form.

3. Switch to the code view and add the following using directives:

```
using System.Data;
using System.Data.SqlClient;
```

4. Double-click the `Button` control and enter this code to handle the `Click` event of the `Button` control:

```
private void btnCount_Click(object sender,
    System.EventArgs e)
{
    // Connect to the database
    SqlConnection cnn = new SqlConnection();
    cnn.ConnectionString = "Data Source=(local);" +
    "Initial Catalog=Northwind;" +
    "Integrated Security=SSPI";
    // Create a new ad hoc query
    // To count customers in the selected country
    SqlCommand cmd = cnn.CreateCommand();
    cmd.CommandType = CommandType.Text;
    cmd.CommandText =
     "SELECT COUNT(*) FROM Customers " +
     " WHERE Country = '" + txtCountry.Text + "'";
    // Use ExecuteScalar to return results
    cnn.Open();
    lblResults.Text =
    "There are " + cmd.ExecuteScalar() +
    " customers in " + txtCountry.Text;
    cnn.Close();
}
```

5. Insert the `Main()` method to launch the form. Set the form as the startup object for the project.

6. Run the project. Enter a country name such as France and click the button. The code connects to the SQL Server database on the local computer and fills in the `Label` control's text with a string that includes the results of the ad hoc query.

The `SqlDataReader` Object

The `SqlDataReader` object is designed to be the fastest possible way to retrieve a resultset from a database. A `SqlDataReader` object can be constructed only by calling the `ExecuteReader()` method of a `SqlCommand` object (see Step-by-Step A.4). The resultset contained in a `SqlDataReader` object is forward-only, read-only. That is, you can only read the rows in the resultset sequentially from start to finish, and you can't modify any of the data. This behavior of simply delivering data as quickly as possible results in the `SqlDataReader` object being called a "firehose" data connection.

STEP BY STEP

A.4 Using a `SqlDataReader` Object

1. Add a new form to your Visual C# .NET project.

2. Place a `Button` control (`btnGetCustomers`) and a `ListBox` control (`lbCustomers`) on the form.

3. Switch to the code view and add the following `using` directives:

```
using System.Data;
using System.Data.SqlClient;
```

4. Double-click the `Button` control and enter this code to handle the `Click` event of the `Button` control:

```
private void btnGetCustomers_Click(object sender,
    System.EventArgs e)
{
    // Connect to the database
    SqlConnection cnn = new SqlConnection();
    cnn.ConnectionString = "Data Source=(local);" +
    "Initial Catalog=Northwind;" +
    "Integrated Security=SSPI";
    // Create a new ad hoc query
    // to retrieve customer names
    SqlCommand cmd = cnn.CreateCommand();
    cmd.CommandType = CommandType.Text;
    cmd.CommandText =
        "SELECT CompanyName FROM Customers "
    + " ORDER BY CompanyName";
    // Dump the data to the user interface
    cnn.Open();
```

continues

continued

```
SqlDataReader dr = cmd.ExecuteReader();
while (dr.Read())
{
    lbCustomers.Items.Add(dr.GetString(0));
}
// Clean up
dr.Close();
cnn.Close();
}
```

5. Insert the `Main()` method to launch the form. Set the form as the startup object for the project.

6. Run the project and click the button. The code connects to the SQL Server database on the local computer and fills the `ListBox` control with a list of customers from the database.

You can think of the `SqlDataReader` object as a data structure that can contain one row of data at a time. Each call to the `SqlDataReader.Read()` method loads the next row of data into this structure. When there are no more rows to load, the `Read()` method returns `false`, which tells you that you've reached the end of the data. To retrieve individual columns of data from the current row, the `SqlDataReader` object provides a series of methods (such as the `GetString()` method used in Step-by-Step A.4) that take a column number and return the data from that column. There's also a `GetValue()` method that you can use with any column, but the typed methods are faster than the `GetValue()` method.

Table A.3 shows the most important members of the SqlDataReader object. You don't need to memorize all the data methods (others aren't even shown in this table), but you should understand the pattern that they represent.

TABLE A.3

IMPORTANT MEMBERS OF THE SqlDataReader CLASS

Member	Type	Description
Close()	Method	Closes the SqlDataReader object
GetBoolean()	Method	Gets a Boolean value from the specified column
GetByte()	Method	Gets a byte value from the specified column
GetChar()	Method	Gets a character value from the specified column
GetDateTime()	Method	Gets a date/time value from the specified column
GetDecimal()	Method	Gets a decimal value from the specified column
GetDouble()	Method	Gets a double value from the specified column
GetFloat()	Method	Gets a float value from the specified column
GetGuid()	Method	Gets a Global Unique Identifier (GUID) value from the specified column
GetInt16()	Method	Gets a 16-bit integer value from the specified column
GetInt32()	Method	Gets a 32-bit integer value from the specified column
GetInt64()	Method	Gets a 64-bit integer value from the specified column
GetString()	Method	Gets a string value from the specified column
GetValue()	Method	Gets a value from the specified column
GetValues()	Method	Gets an entire row of data and places it in an array of objects
IsDbNull()	Method	Indicates whether a specified column contains a null value
Read()	Method	Loads the next row of data into the SqlDataReader object

> **WARNING**
>
> **Close Your SqlDataReader Objects!**
> The SqlDataReader object makes exclusive use of its SqlConnection object as long as it is open. You are not able to execute any other SqlCommand objects on that connection as long as the SqlDataReader object is open. Therefore, you should always call the SqlDataReader.Close() method as soon as you finish retrieving data.

The SqlDataAdapter Object

The final data provider object I'll consider, the SqlDataAdapter object, provides a bridge between the data provider objects and the DataSet objects that you'll learn about in the next section. You can think of the `SqlDataAdapter` object as a two-way pipeline between the data in its native storage format and the data in a more abstract representation (the `DataSet` object) that's designed for manipulation in an application.

Table A.4 shows the most important members of the `SqlDataAdapter` object.

TABLE A.4

IMPORTANT MEMBERS OF THE SQLDATAADAPTER CLASS

Member	Type	Description
DeleteCommand	Property	Specifies the `SqlCommand` object used to delete rows from the data source
Fill()	Method	Transfers data from the data source to a `DataSet` object
InsertCommand	Property	Specifies the `SqlCommand` object used to insert rows from the data source
SelectCommand	Property	Specifies the `SqlCommand` object used to select rows from the data source
Update()	Method	Transfers data from a `DataSet` object to the data source
UpdateCommand	Property	Specifies the `SqlCommand` object used to update rows from the data source

Later in this chapter (in the "Using `Dataset` Objects" section) you'll learn more about using the `SqlDataAdapter` object in conjunction with the `DataSet` object to manipulate data.

The DataSet Objects

Unlike the data provider objects, there's only one set of `DataSet` objects. The `DataSet` objects are all contained in the `System.Data` namespace. The `DataSet` objects represent data in an abstract form that is not tied to any particular database implementation. In this section, I'll introduce you to the `DataSet` object and the other objects that it contains:

- ▶ DataSet

- ▶ DataTable

- ▶ DataRelation

- ▶ DataRow

- ▶ DataColumn

- ▶ DataView

The DataSet Object

The DataSet object itself is a self-contained memory-resident representation of relational data. A DataSet object contains other objects, such as DataTable and DataRelation objects, that hold the actual data and information about the design of the data. The DataSet object is designed to be easy to move between components. In particular, specific methods convert a DataSet object to an XML file and vice versa. Because they're easily serialized, DataSet objects can also be passed between remoted components or Web service servers and clients.

WARNING **Microsoft-specific Technology** As a part of the .NET Framework, DataSet objects are currently Microsoft-only objects. Returning a DataSet from a Web service may make it more difficult for clients written in non-.NET platforms to use that service.

Table A.5 shows the most important members of the DataSet object.

TABLE A.5

IMPORTANT MEMBERS OF THE DATASET CLASS

Member	Type	Description
AcceptChanges()	Method	Marks all changes in the DataSet object as having been accepted
Clear()	Method	Removes all data from the DataSet object
GetChanges()	Method	Gets a DataSet object that contains only the changed data in this DataSet object
GetXml()	Method	Gets an XML representation of the DataSet object
GetXmlSchema()	Method	Gets an XML Schema Definition (XSD) representation of the DataSet object's schema
Merge()	Method	Merges two DataSet objects

continues

TABLE A.5   *continued*

IMPORTANT MEMBERS OF THE DATASET CLASS

Member	Type	Description
ReadXml()	Method	Loads the DataSet object from an XML file
ReadXmlSchema()	Method	Loads the DataSet object's schema from an XSD file
Relations	Property	Specifies a collection of DataRelation objects
Tables	Property	Specifies a collection of DataTable objects
WriteXml()	Method	Writes the DataSet object to an XML file
WriteXmlSchema()	Method	Writes the DataSet object's schema to an XSD file

The DataTable Object

The DataTable object represents a single table within the DataSet object. A single DataSet object can contain many DataTable objects. Table A.6 shows the most important members of the DataTable object.

TABLE A.6

IMPORTANT MEMBERS OF THE DATATABLE CLASS

Member	Type	Description
ChildRelations	Property	Specifies a collection of DataRelation objects that refer to children of this DataTable object
Clear()	Method	Removes all data from the DataTable object
ColumnChanged()	Event	Occurs when the data in any row of a specified column has been changed
ColumnChanging()	Event	Occurs when the data in any row of a specified column is about to be changed
Columns	Property	Specifies a collection of DataColumn objects
Constraints	Property	Specifies a collection of Constraint objects
NewRow()	Method	Creates a new, blank row in the DataTable object

Member	*Type*	*Description*
ParentRelations	Property	Specifies a collection of DataRelation objects that refer to parents of this DataTable object
PrimaryKey	Property	Specifies an array of DataColumn objects that provide the primary key for this DataTable object
RowChanged()	Event	Fires when any data in a DataRow object has been changed
RowChanging()	Event	Fires when any data in a DataRow object is about to be changed
RowDeleted()	Event	Occurs when a row has been deleted
RowDeleting()	Event	Occurs when a row is about to be deleted
Rows	Property	Specifies a collection of DataRow objects
Select()	Method	Selects an array of DataRow objects that meet specified criteria
TableName	Property	Specifies the name of this DataTable object

As you can see, you can manipulate a DataTable object as either a collection of DataColumn objects or a collection of DataRow objects. The DataTable object also provides events that you can use to monitor data changes. For example, you might bind a DataTable object to a DataGrid control and use these events to track the user's operations on the data within the DataGrid control.

The DataRelation Object

As I mentioned earlier, the DataSet object can represent the structure and data of an entire relational database. The DataRelation object stores information on the relations between DataTable objects within a DataSet object. Table A.7 shows the most important members of the DataRelation object.

TABLE A.7

IMPORTANT MEMBERS OF THE DATARELATION CLASS

Member	Type	Description
ChildColumns	Property	Specifies a collection of DataColumn objects that define the foreign key side of the relationship
ChildKeyConstraint	Property	Returns a ForeignKeyConstraint object for the relationship
ChildTable	Property	Specifies a DataTable object from the foreign key side of the relationship
ParentColumns	Property	Specifies a collection of DataColumn objects that define the primary key side of the relationship
ParentKeyConstraint	Property	Returns a PrimaryKeyConstraint object for the relationship
ParentTable	Property	Specifies a DataTable object from the primary key side of the relationship
RelationName	Property	Specifies the name of the DataRelation object

The DataRow Object

Continuing down the object hierarchy from the DataSet object past the DataTable object, you come to the DataRow object. As you can guess by now, the DataRow object represents a single row of data. When you're selecting, inserting, updating, or deleting data in a DataSet object, you normally work with DataRow objects.

Table A.8 shows the most important members of the DataRow object.

TABLE A.8

IMPORTANT MEMBERS OF THE DATAROW CLASS

Member	Type	Description
BeginEdit()	Method	Starts editing the DataRow object
CancelEdit()	Method	Discards an edit in progress
Delete()	Method	Deletes the DataRow object from its parent DataTable object

Member	Type	Description
EndEdit()	Method	Ends an edit in progress and saves the changes
IsNull()	Method	Returns true if a specified column contains a null value
RowState	Property	Returns information on the current state of a DataRow object (for example, whether it has been changed since it was last saved to the database)

The DataColumn Object

The DataTable object also contains a collection of DataColumn objects. A DataColumn object represents a single column in the DataTable object. By manipulating the DataColumn objects, you can determine and even change the structure of the DataTable object.

Table A.9 shows the most important members of the DataColumn object.

TABLE A.9

IMPORTANT MEMBERS OF THE DATACOLUMN CLASS

Member	Type	Description
AllowDbNull	Property	Indicates whether the DataColumn object can contain null values
AutoIncrement	Property	Indicates whether the DataColumn object is an identity column
ColumnName	Property	Specifies the name of the DataColumn object
DataType	Property	Specifies the data type of the DataColumn object
DefaultValue	Property	Specifies the default value of this DataColumn object for new rows of data
MaxLength	Property	Specifies the maximum length of a text DataColumn object
Unique	Property	Indicates whether values in the DataColumn object must be unique across all rows in the DataTable object

The `DataView` Object

The `DataView` object represents a view of the data contained in a `DataTable` object. A `DataView` object might contain every `DataRow` object from the `DataTable` object, or it might be filtered to contain only specific rows. Filtering can be done by SQL expressions (returning, for example, only rows for customers in France) or by row state (returning, for example, only rows that have been modified).

Table A.10 shows the most important members of the `DataView` object.

TABLE A.10

IMPORTANT MEMBERS OF THE DATAVIEW CLASS

Member	Type	Description
AddNew()	Method	Adds a new row to the `DataView` object
AllowDelete	Property	Indicates whether deletions can be performed through this `DataView` object
AllowEdit	Property	Indicates whether updates can be performed through this `DataView` object
AllowNew	Property	Indicates whether insertions can be performed through this `DataView` object
Count	Property	Specifies the number of rows in this `DataView` object
Delete()	Method	Deletes a row from this `DataView` object
Find()	Method	Searches for a row that matches the specified sort key value
FindRows()	Method	Returns an array of rows that match the specified sort key value
Sort()	Method	Sorts the data in a `DataView` object

REVIEW BREAK

- ▶ The ADO.NET object model includes both database-specific data provider classes and database-independent `DataSet` classes.
- ▶ Data providers contain implementations of the `Connection`, `Command`, `Parameter`, `DataReader`, and `DataAdapter` objects optimized for a particular database product.

▶ The `SqlConnection` object represents a connection to a data-base.

▶ The `SqlCommand` object represents a command that can be executed.

▶ The `SqlParameter` object represents a parameter of a stored procedure.

▶ The `SqlDataReader` object provides a fast way to retrieve a resultset from a command.

▶ The `SqlDataAdapter` object implements a two-way pipeline between the database and the data model.

▶ The `DataSet` object represents the structure and data of an entire relational database in memory. It's composed of `DataTable`, `DataRelation`, `DataRow`, and `DataColumn` objects.

▶ The `DataView` object provides a filtered row of the data from a `DataTable` object.

USING DataSet OBJECTS

Now that you've seen the ADO.NET objects, it's time to see what you can do with them. In particular, I'm going to concentrate on some of the basic operations, including the following:

▶ Populating a `DataSet` object from a database

▶ Navigating `DataSet` objects and retrieving data

▶ Using strongly typed `DataSet` objects

▶ Using `DataSet` objects with multiple tables

▶ Finding and sorting data in `DataSet` objects

Mastering these skills will enable you to work with ADO.NET in the context of applications such as Web services and remoted servers. If you're interested in exploring ADO.NET in more depth, you'll find a list of references at the end of the appendix.

Populating a `DataSet` Object from a Database

Before you can do anything with data in a `DataSet` object, you must get the data into the `DataSet` object (see Step-by-Step A.5). In general, you can follow a four-step pattern to move data from the database to a DataSet object:

1. Create a `SqlConnection` object to connect to the database.

2. Create a `SqlCommand` object to retrieve the desired data.

3. Assign the `SqlCommand` object to the `SelectCommand` property of a `SqlDataAdapter` object.

4. Call the `Fill()` method of the `SqlDataAdapter` object.

STEP BY STEP

A.5 Filling a DataSet Object

1. Add a new form to your Visual C# .NET project.

2. Place a `Button` control (`btnLoad`) and a `DataGrid` control (`dgProducts`) on the form. Set the `Caption` property of the `DataGrid` control to `Products`.

3. Switch to the code view and add the following `using` directives:

```
using System.Data;
using System.Data.SqlClient;
```

4. Double-click the `Button` control and enter this code to handle the `Click` event of the `Button` control:

```
private void btnLoad_Click(object sender,
    System.EventArgs e)
{
    // Create a SqlConnection
    SqlConnection cnn = new SqlConnection(
    "Data Source=(local); Initial Catalog=Northwind;"+
    " Integrated Security=SSPI");
    // Create a SqlCommand
    SqlCommand cmd = cnn.CreateCommand();
    cmd.CommandType = CommandType.Text;
    cmd.CommandText = "SELECT * FROM Products " +
      " ORDER BY ProductName";
```

```
    // Set up the DataAdapter and fill the DataSet
    SqlDataAdapter da = new SqlDataAdapter();
    da.SelectCommand = cmd;
    DataSet ds = new DataSet();
    da.Fill(ds, "Products");
    // Display the data on the user interface
    dgProducts.DataSource = ds;
    dgProducts.DataMember = "Products";
}
```

5. Insert the `Main()` method to launch the form. Set the form as the startup object for the project.

6. Run the project and click the button. The code connects to the SQL Server database on the local computer and fills the `DataGrid` control with the result of executing the SQL statement, as shown in Figure A.4.

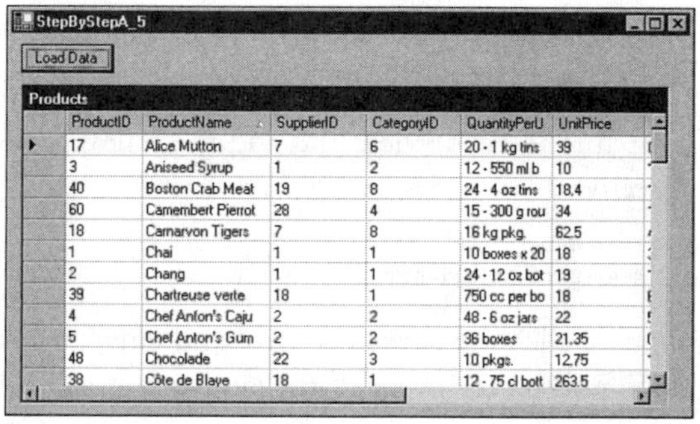

FIGURE A.4
You can bind a `DataGrid` control to data stored in a `DataSet` object.

Step-by-Step A.5 demonstrates a couple of shortcuts that you can use in your ADO.NET code. First, the constructor for the `SqlConnection` object has an overloaded form that lets you supply the connection string when you create the object. Second, this code doesn't explicitly call the `Open()` and `Close()` methods of the `SqlConnection` object. Instead, it lets the `SqlDataAdapter` object make those calls when it needs the data. Doing this not only cuts down on the amount of code you need to write, but it also improves the scalability of your application by keeping the `SqlConnection` object open for the shortest possible period of time.

EXAM TIP

Choose a Table Name   The second parameter to the `DataAdapter.Fill()` method is the name of the `DataTable` object to create from the data supplied by the `SelectCommand` property. The `DataTable` object name does not have to match the table name in the underlying database. The example in Step-by-Step A.5 would work just as well if you placed data from the Products table into a `DataTable` object named Starship (although that would be a pretty poor idea from the standpoint of code maintainability).

Navigating DataSet Objects and Retrieving Data

If you're familiar with classic ADO, you're used to recordsets: collections of records that have a pointer to the current record. DataSet objects have no concept of a current record pointer. Instead, you navigate a DataSet object by working with the collections that the DataSet object contains (see Step-by-Step A.6).

STEP BY STEP

A.6 Navigating a DataSet Object

1. Add a new form to your Visual C# .NET project.

2. Place a Button control (btnLoadData) and a ListBox control (lbData) on the form.

3. Switch to the code view and add the following using directives:

```
using System.Data;
using System.Data.SqlClient;
```

4. Double-click the Button control and enter this code to handle the Click event of the Button control:

```
private void btnLoadData_Click(object sender,
    System.EventArgs e)
{
    // Create a SqlConnection
    SqlConnection cnn = new SqlConnection(
  "Data Source=(local); Initial Catalog=Northwind;" +
  " Integrated Security=SSPI");
    // Create a SqlCommand
    SqlCommand cmd = cnn.CreateCommand();
    cmd.CommandType = CommandType.Text;
    cmd.CommandText = "SELECT * FROM Customers " +
        " WHERE Country = 'France'";
    // Set up the DataAdapter and fill the DataSet
    SqlDataAdapter da = new SqlDataAdapter();
    da.SelectCommand = cmd;
    DataSet ds = new DataSet();
    da.Fill(ds, "Customers");
    // Dump the contents of the DataSet
    lbData.Items.Add("DataSet: " + ds.DataSetName);
    foreach (DataTable dt in ds.Tables)
    {
```

```
        lbData.Items.Add("  DataTable: " +
            dt.TableName);
        foreach (DataRow dr in dt.Rows)
        {
            lbData.Items.Add("    DataRow");
            foreach (DataColumn dc in dt.Columns)
            {
                lbData.Items.Add("        " + dr[dc]);
            }
        }
    }
}
```

5. Insert the Main() method to launch the form. Set the
   form as the startup object for the project.

6. Run the project and click the button. The code dumps
   the contents of the DataSet object to the ListBox control,
   as shown in Figure A.5.

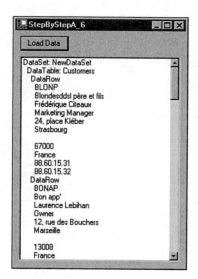

FIGURE A.5
You can move through the contents of a
DataSet object by iterating its collection
objects.

Step-by-Step A.6 shows how you can visit every piece of data in a
DataSet object by properly selecting nested foreach loops. It also
shows a general syntax for retrieving data: Locate the DataRow and
DataColumn objects whose intersection contains the data that you're
interested in, and use the dr[dc] indexer syntax to retrieve the actual
data value. You can use a variety of other syntaxes to retrieve data.
Given a DataTable variable named dt that refers to the data from the
Customers table, for example, either of these statements would
retrieve the value in the first column of the first row of data in the
DataTable object:

```
dt.Rows[0][0]
dt.Rows[0]["CustomerID"]
```

Using Strongly Typed DataSet Objects

All the syntaxes shown in the previous section for retrieving data
have one thing in common: They're all *late-bound*. That is, the
.NET Framework doesn't know until runtime that CustomerID is a
valid column name. One of the innovations of ADO.NET is a pro-
vision to create strongly typed DataSet objects. In a strongly typed
DataSet object, columns actually become properties of the row. This

allows you to write an early-bound version of the data-retrieval expression:

```
dt.Rows[0].CustomerID
```

In addition to being faster than the late-bound syntaxes, the early-bound syntax has the advantage of making column names show up in IntelliSense tips as you type code.

Any time when you use the Generate DataSet link in the Properties window for a `SqlDataAdapter` object on a form, Visual Studio .NET builds a strongly typed `DataSet` object. You can also build strongly typed `DataSet` objects by using the XSD designer, as in Step-by-Step A.7.

STEP BY STEP

A.7 Designing a Strongly Typed `DataSet` Object

1. Select Project, Add New Item in your Visual C# .NET project.

2. In the Add New Item dialog box, select the DataSet template. Give the name `dsSuppliers.xsd` to the new DataSet. Click Open to create the XSD file, and open it in the Designer.

3. Open Server Explorer.

4. Expand the tree under Data Connections to show a SQL Server data connection that points to the Northwind sample database, and then the Tables node of the SQL Server. Drag the Suppliers table from Server Explorer and drop it on the design surface for the DataSet. Figure A.6 shows the resulting XSD Design view. The *E* icons for each column of the database table indicate that those columns have been rendered as XML elements.

5. Save the DataSet. At this point, your project will contain a new class named `dsSuppliers`, which is a strongly typed `DataSet` object that you can use in code.

6. Add a new form to your Visual C# .NET project.

7. Place a `Button` control (`btnLoadData`) and a `ListBox` control (`lbData`) on the form.

FIGURE A.6
You can create a strongly typed `DataSet` object in the XSD designer of Visual Studio .NET.

8. Switch to the code view and add the following using directives:

```
using System.Data;
using System.Data.SqlClient;
```

9. Double-click the Button control and enter this code to handle the Click event of the Button control:

```
private void btnLoadData_Click(object sender,
    System.EventArgs e)
{
    // Create a SqlConnection object
    SqlConnection cnn = new SqlConnection(
    "Data Source=(local); Initial Catalog=Northwind;" +
    " Integrated Security=SSPI");
    // Create a SqlCommand object
    SqlCommand cmd = cnn.CreateCommand();
    cmd.CommandType = CommandType.Text;
    cmd.CommandText = "SELECT * FROM Suppliers";
    // Set up the DataAdapter and fill the DataSet
    SqlDataAdapter da = new SqlDataAdapter();
    da.SelectCommand = cmd;
    dsSuppliers ds = new dsSuppliers();
    da.Fill(ds, "Suppliers");
    // Dump the contents of the DataSet
    foreach (dsSuppliers.SuppliersRow suppRow
      in ds.Suppliers)
    {
      lbData.Items.Add(suppRow.SupplierID +
        " " + suppRow.CompanyName);
    }
}
```

10. Insert the Main() method to launch the form. Set the form as the startup object for the project.

11. Run the project and click the button. The code displays two columns from the DataSet object in the ListBox control, as shown in Figure A.7.

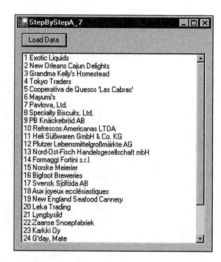

FIGURE A.7
A strongly typed DataSet object allows you to create early-bound data retrieval expressions.

Using the dsSuppliers class to define the DataSet object in this case gives you several syntactical benefits. You can refer to the Suppliers DataTable object as a property of the DataSet object. You can also refer to the columns in the DataRow objects in this DataTable object as properties of the DataRow object. The strongly typed DataSet object automatically defines a class named SuppliersRow to represent one DataRow object with strong typing.

Using `DataSet` Objects with Multiple Tables

The `DataSet` objects you've seen so far in this appendix have contained a single `DataTable` object. But a `DataSet` object is not limited to a single `DataTable` object; in fact, there's no practical limit on the number of `DataTable` objects that a `DataSet` object can contain. By using `DataAdapter` objects, you can connect a single `DataSet` object to more than one table in the SQL Server database. You can also define `DataRelation` objects to represent the relationship between the `DataTable` objects in the `DataSet` object as shown in Step-by-Step A.8.

STEP BY STEP

A.8 Building a `DataSet` Object Containing Multiple `DataTable` Objects

1. Add a new form to your Visual C# .NET project.

2. Place a `Button` control (btnLoadData) and a `DataGrid` control (dgMain) on the form.

3. Switch to the code view and add the following using directives:

```
using System.Data;
using System.Data.SqlClient;
```

4. Double-click the `Button` control and enter this code to handle the `Click` event of the `Button` control:

```
private void btnLoadData_Click(object sender,
    System.EventArgs e)
{
    // Create a SqlConnection and a DataSet
    SqlConnection cnn = new SqlConnection(
  "Data Source=(local); Initial Catalog=Northwind;" +
    " Integrated Security=SSPI");
    DataSet ds = new DataSet();
```

```
// Add the customers data to the DataSet
SqlCommand cmdCustomers= cnn.CreateCommand();
cmdCustomers.CommandType = CommandType.Text;
cmdCustomers.CommandText =
    "SELECT * FROM Customers";
SqlDataAdapter daCustomers = new SqlDataAdapter();
daCustomers.SelectCommand = cmdCustomers;
daCustomers.Fill(ds, "Customers");

// Add the Orders data to the DataSet
SqlCommand cmdOrders = cnn.CreateCommand();
cmdOrders.CommandType = CommandType.Text;
cmdOrders.CommandText = "SELECT * FROM Orders";
SqlDataAdapter daOrders = new SqlDataAdapter();
daOrders.SelectCommand = cmdOrders;
daOrders.Fill(ds, "Orders");

// Add the Order Details data to the DataSet
SqlCommand cmdOrderDetails = cnn.CreateCommand();
cmdOrderDetails.CommandType = CommandType.Text;
cmdOrderDetails.CommandText =
    "SELECT * FROM [Order Details]";
SqlDataAdapter daOrderDetails =
    new SqlDataAdapter();
daOrderDetails.SelectCommand = cmdOrderDetails;
daOrderDetails.Fill(ds, "OrderDetails");

// Add Relations
DataRelation relCustOrder = ds.Relations.Add(
"CustOrder",
ds.Tables["Customers"].Columns["CustomerID"],
ds.Tables["Orders"].Columns["CustomerID"]);

DataRelation relOrderOrderDetails =
    ds.Relations.Add(
    "OrderOrderDetails",
    ds.Tables["Orders"].Columns["OrderID"],
    ds.Tables["OrderDetails"].Columns["OrderID"]);

// And show the data on the user interface
dgMain.DataSource = ds;
dgMain.DataMember = "Customers";
}
```

5. Insert the `Main()` method to launch the form. Set the form as the startup object for the project.

6. Run the project and click the button. The code loads all three database tables into the `DataSet` object, and then it displays the customers' information on the data grid, as shown in Figure A.8.

continues

continued

FIGURE A.8
A Windows Forms `DataGrid` control can be bound to multiple tables of a `DataSet` object.

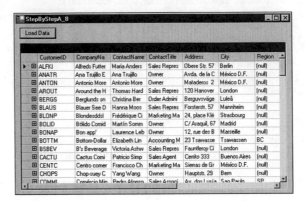

The code in Step-by-Step A.8 uses three different `SqlDataAdapter` objects to move data from three different database tables into a single `DataSet` object. The data from each `SqlDataAdapter` object is stored in a separate `DataTable` object. You could also use a single `SqlDataAdapter` object for the same purpose, by changing its `SelectCommand` property each time you want to load a separate table. The code then adds `DataRelation` objects to specify the relationships between these `DataTable` objects. The `Add()` method of the `DataSet.Relations` collection takes three parameters:

▶ A name for the `DataRelation` object to be created

▶ A `DataColumn` object that represents the primary key side of the relationship

▶ A `DataColumn` object that represents the foreign key side of the relationship

Although the `DataGrid` control in Step-by-Step A.8 initially displays only the customers' data, all the data is available. The `DataGrid` control contains built-in logic to help you navigate between related `DataTable` objects in a `DataSet` object. If you click the + sign to the left of a row of customer data, the `DataGrid` control shows a list of the relationships that involve that row, as shown in Figure A.9.

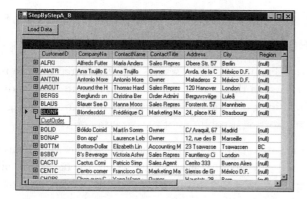

FIGURE A.9

When the `DataGrid` control is bound to a `DataSet` object that contains multiple related tables, it displays the relationship when a row node is clicked.

The relationship is called a *hotlink*. Clicking the link loads all the related rows on the other side of that relationship into the `DataGrid` control, as shown in Figure A.10. Note that the parent rows area of the `DataGrid` control contains information on the customer row where the navigation started.

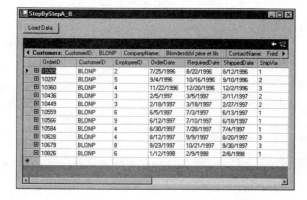

FIGURE A.10

You can view the child table's data in a `DataGrid` control when the relationship link is clicked.

Because this `DataSet` object has another level of detail, you can repeat the process. Click the + sign next to an order to see the relationships in which that order is involved. Finally, clicking the hotlink beneath an order reveals all the order detail rows for that order. The parent rows area contains details on both the customer and the order that were used to get to this point.

Finding and Sorting Data in DataSet Objects

The .NET Framework offers several object-oriented ways to find and sort data. In this section, I'll show you how to use two of these ways: by using the `DataTable.Select()` method and by using the filtering and sorting capabilities of the `DataView` object.

Using the `Select()` method of the `DataTable` object is a convenient way to find particular `DataRow` objects within the `DataTable` object (see Step-by-Step A.9). This method extracts an array of `DataRow` objects that you can work with.

STEP BY STEP

A.9 Using the `DataTable.Select()` Method

1. Add a new form to your Visual C# .NET project.

2. Place a `Button` control (btnSelect), a `TextBox` control (txtCountry), and a `ListBox` control (lbSelected) on the form.

3. Switch to the code view and add the following `using` directives:

```
using System.Data;
using System.Data.SqlClient;
```

4. Double-click the `Button` control and enter this code to handle the `Click` event of the `Button` control:

```
private void btnSelect_Click(object sender,
    System.EventArgs e)
{
    // Create a SqlConnection
    SqlConnection cnn = new SqlConnection(
    "Data Source=(local); Initial Catalog=Northwind;" +
    " Integrated Security=SSPI");
    // Create a SqlCommand
    SqlCommand cmd = cnn.CreateCommand();
    cmd.CommandType = CommandType.Text;
    cmd.CommandText = "SELECT * FROM Customers";
    // Set up the DataAdapter and fill the DataSet
    SqlDataAdapter da = new SqlDataAdapter();
    da.SelectCommand = cmd;
    DataSet ds = new DataSet();
```

```
da.Fill(ds, "Customers");
// Use the Select method
 // To get a sorted array of DataRow objects
DataRow[] adr = ds.Tables["Customers"].Select(
"Country = '" + txtCountry.Text + "'",
"ContactName ASC");
// Dump the result to the user interface
lbSelected.Items.Clear();
foreach(DataRow dr in adr)
{
    lbSelected.Items.Add(dr[0] + " " + dr[1] +
    " " + dr[2]);
}
}
```

5. Insert the `Main()` method to launch the form. Set the form as the startup object for the project.

6. Run the project. Enter a country name and click the button. You see the first three columns from the `DataRow` objects for customers in that country, as shown in Figure A.11.

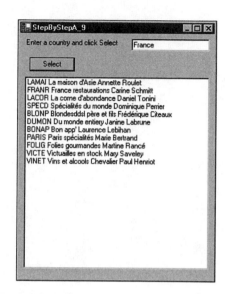

FIGURE A.11

The `DataTable.Select()` method allows you to select a collection of rows that are sorted by a given sort expression and that match a given filter expression.

The `Select()` method of the `DataTable` object constructs an array of `DataRow` objects, based on up to three factors: a filter expression, a sort expression, and a state constant.

Filter expressions are essentially SQL WHERE clauses that are constructed according to these rules:

▶ Column names containing special characters should be enclosed in square brackets.

▶ String constants should be enclosed in single quotes.

▶ Date constants should be enclosed in pound signs.

▶ Numeric expressions can be specified in decimal or scientific notation.

▶ Expressions can be created by using AND, OR, NOT, parentheses, IN, LIKE, comparison operators, and arithmetic operators.

▶ The + operator is used to concatenate strings.

▶ Either * or % can be used as a wildcard to match any number of characters. A wildcard can be used only at the start or end of a string.

▶ Columns in a child table can be referenced with the expression *Child.Column*. If the table has more than one child table, you use the expression *Child(RelationName).Column* to choose a particular child table.

▶ The `Sum`, `Avg`, `Min`, `Max`, `Count`, `StDev`, and `Var` aggregates can be used with child tables.

▶ Supported functions include `CONVERT`, `LEN`, `ISNULL`, `IIF`, and `SUBSTRING`.

In the code in Step-by-Step A.9, the filter expression is built by concatenating the text from the `txtCountry` control with a column comparison.

If you don't specify a sort order in the `Select()` method, the rows are returned in primary key order or in the order of addition, if the table doesn't have a primary key. You can also specify a sort expression that consists of one or more column names and the keywords `ASC` or `DESC` to specify ascending or descending sorts. For example, this is a valid sort expression:

```
Country ASC, CompanyName DESC
```

This expression sorts first by country, in ascending order, and then by company name within each country, in descending order.

Finally, you can also select `DataRow` objects according to their current state by supplying one of the `DataViewRowState` constants. Table A.11 shows these constants.

TABLE A.11

DataViewRowState Constants

Constant	Meaning
Added	Specifies new rows that have not yet been committed
CurrentRows	Specifies all current rows, whether they are unchanged, modified, or new
Deleted	Specifies deleted rows
ModifiedCurrent	Specifies modified rows
ModifiedOriginal	Specifies original data from modified rows

Constant	Meaning
None	Specifies no rows
OriginalRows	Specifies original data, including rows that have been modified or deleted
Unchanged	Specifies rows that have not been changed

You can also sort and filter data by using a DataView object (see Step-by-Step A.10). The DataView object has the same structure of rows and columns as a DataTable object, but it also lets you specify sorting and filtering options as properties of the DataView object. Typically you create a DataView object by starting with a DataTable object and specifying options to include a subset of the rows in the DataTable object.

> **NOTE**
> **From a DataTable Object to an Array** You can quickly create an array that holds all the contents of a DataTable object by calling the Select() method with no parameters:
>
> ```
> DataRow[] adr = dt.Select();
> ```

STEP BY STEP

A.10 Using a DataView Object to Sort and Filter Data

1. Add a new form to your Visual C# .NET project.

2. Place a Button control (btnLoad) and a DataGrid control (dgCustomers) on the form.

3. Switch to the code view and add the following using directives:

```
using System.Data;
using System.Data.SqlClient;
```

4. Double-click the Button control and enter this code to handle the Click event of the Button control:

```
private void btnLoad_Click(object sender,
    System.EventArgs e)
{
    // Create a SqlConnection
    SqlConnection cnn = new SqlConnection(
  "Data Source=(local); Initial Catalog=Northwind;" +
  " Integrated Security=SSPI");
    // Create a SqlCommand
    SqlCommand cmd = cnn.CreateCommand();
    cmd.CommandType = CommandType.Text;
    cmd.CommandText = "SELECT * FROM Customers";
```

continues

continued

```
        // Set up the DataAdapter and fill the DataSet
        SqlDataAdapter da = new SqlDataAdapter();
        da.SelectCommand = cmd;
        DataSet ds = new DataSet();
        da.Fill(ds, "Customers");
        // Create a DataView based on
        // the Customers DataTable
        DataView dv = new
            DataView(ds.Tables["Customers"]);
        dv.RowFilter = "Country = 'France'";
        dv.Sort = "CompanyName ASC";
        dgCustomers.DataSource = dv;
}
```

5. Insert the `Main()` method to launch the form. Set the form as the startup object for the project.

6. Run the project and click the button. The `DataGrid` control displays only the customers from France, sorted in ascending order by column `CompanyName`.

The constructor for the `DataView` object in Step-by-Step A.10 specifies the `DataTable` object that includes the data from which the `DataView` object can draw. By setting the `RowFilter`, `Sort`, and `RowStateFilter` properties of the `DataView` object, you can control which rows are available in the `DataView` object, as well as the order in which they are presented. I don't use the `RowStateFilter` property in Step-by-Step A.10; `RowStateFilter` allows you to select, for example, only rows that have been changed since the `DataTable` object was loaded. The `RowStateFilter` property can be set to any one of the `DataViewRowState` constants listed in Table A.11.

EDITING DATA WITH ADO.NET

Now that you know how to retrieve data with ADO.NET, there's one other important database-related topic to cover: editing data. ADO.NET supports all the normal database operations of updating existing data, adding new data, and deleting existing data.

As you read the following sections, you need to keep in mind the distinction between the data model and the database. As you work with data in the DataSet object and its subsidiary objects, you alter the data in the data model. These changes are not reflected in the underlying database until and unless you call the Update() method of the SqlDataAdapter object. So far I've only been using the SqlDataAdapter object to move data from the database to the data model; in the following sections, you'll see how to move data back from the data model to the database.

Updating Data

Updating data is easy: You simply assign a new value to the item in the DataRow object that you want to change. But there's more to finishing the job. For the Update() method of the SqlDataAdapter object to write changes back to the database, you need to set its UpdateCommand property to an appropriate SqlCommand object. Step-by-Step A.11 shows you how.

STEP BY STEP

A.11 Using a SqlDataAdapter Object to Update Data in a Database

1. Add a new form to your Visual C# .NET project.

2. Place two Label controls, one ComboBox control (cboCustomerID), one TextBox control (txtContactName), and a Button control (btnAdd) on the form. Figure A.12 shows the design for the form.

3. Switch to the code view and add the following using directives:

```
using System.Data;
using System.Data.SqlClient;
```

4. Add the following code in the class definition:

```
// Create SwlConnection, DataSet, SqlDataAdapter
// And DataRow[] ADO.NET objects
SqlConnection cnn = new SqlConnection(
    "Data Source=(local); Initial Catalog=Northwind;" +
    " Integrated Security=SSPI");
```

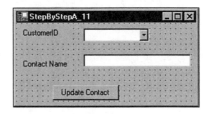

FIGURE A.12
You can update the data in a database by using a SqlDataAdapter object.

continues

continued

```
DataSet ds = new DataSet();
SqlDataAdapter da = new SqlDataAdapter();
DataRow[] adrEdit;
```

5. Double-click the form and enter this code to load data
when the form is opened:

```
private void StepByStepA_11_Load(
    object sender, System.EventArgs e)
{
    // Create a SqlCommand to select data
    SqlCommand cmdSelect = cnn.CreateCommand();
    cmdSelect.CommandType = CommandType.Text;
    cmdSelect.CommandText =
      "SELECT CustomerID, ContactName FROM Customers";
    // Create a SqlCommand to update data
    SqlCommand cmdUpdate = cnn.CreateCommand();
    cmdUpdate.CommandType = CommandType.Text;
    cmdUpdate.CommandText = "UPDATE Customers SET " +
        "ContactName = @ContactName " +
        " WHERE CustomerID = @CustomerID";
    cmdUpdate.Parameters.Add("@ContactName",
        SqlDbType.NVarChar,30, "ContactName");
    cmdUpdate.Parameters.Add("@CustomerID",
        SqlDbType.NChar,5, "CustomerID");
    cmdUpdate.Parameters["@CustomerID"].SourceVersion
        = DataRowVersion.Original;
    // Set up the DataAdapter and fill the DataSet
    da.UpdateCommand = cmdUpdate;
    da.SelectCommand = cmdSelect;
    da.Fill(ds, "Customers");
    // Fill the data in the ComboBox
    cboCustomerID.DisplayMember = "CustomerID";
    cboCustomerID.ValueMember = "CustomerID";
    cboCustomerID.DataSource = ds.Tables["Customers"];
}
```

6. Double-click the ComboBox control and enter this code to
handle the SelectedIndexChanged event:

```
private void cboCustomerID_SelectedIndexChanged(
        object sender, System.EventArgs e)
{
    // Get just that customer's DataRow
    adrEdit = ds.Tables["Customers"].Select(
        "CustomerID = '" +
        cboCustomerID.SelectedValue + "'");
    // Make sure there's some data
    if (adrEdit != null)
    {
        txtContactName.Text =
          adrEdit[0]["ContactName"].ToString();
    }
}
```

7. Double-click the `Button` control and enter this code to handle the `Click` event of the `Button` control:

```
private void btnUpdate_Click(object sender,
    System.EventArgs e)
{
    // Make sure there's some data
    if (adrEdit != null)
    {
        // Prompt for new data and
        // put it in the DataRow object
        adrEdit[0]["ContactName"] =
            txtContactName.Text;
        // And save the changes
        da.Update(ds, "Customers");
        MessageBox.Show("Contact Name Updated!");
    }
}
```

8. Insert the `Main()` method to launch the form. Set the form as the startup object for the project.

9. Run the project. The code displays all the Customer ID values in the `ComboBox` control, with the corresponding contact name value from the database in the text box. Select a customer ID (such as `ALFKI`) from the combo box and update the text box with a new contact name. Click the button. The change is written back to the database, and the update message is displayed in a message box.

The `Update()` method of the `SqlDataAdapter` object is syntactically similar to the `Fill()` method. It takes as its parameters the `DataSet` object to be reconciled with the database and the name of the `DataTable` object to be saved. You don't have to worry about which rows or columns of data are changed. The `SqlDataAdapter` object automatically locates the changed rows. It executes the `SqlCommand` object specified in its `UpdateCommand` property for each of those rows.

In Step-by-Step A.11, the `UpdateCommand` property has two parameters. The `SqlParameter` objects are created by a version of the constructor that takes four parameters rather than the three that you saw earlier in this appendix. The fourth parameter is the name of a `DataColumn` that contains the data to be used in this particular parameter. Note also that you can specify whether a parameter should be filled in from the current data in the `DataSet` object (the default) or the original version of the data, before any edits were made. In this case, the @CustomerID parameter is being used to locate the row to edit in the database, so the code uses the original value of the column as the value for the parameter.

Adding Data

To add data to the database, you must supply a SqlCommand object for the InsertCommand property of the SqlDataAdapter object, as in Step-by-Step A.12.

STEP BY STEP

A.12 Adding Data with a SqlDataAdapter Object

1. Add a new form to your Visual C# .NET project.

2. Place four Label controls, three TextBox controls (txtCustomerID, txtCompanyName, and txtContactName) and a Button control (btnAdd) on the form. Figure A.13 shows a design for the form.

3. Switch to the code view and add the following using directives:

```
using System.Data;
using System.Data.SqlClient;
```

4. Double-click the form and enter this code to load data when the form is opened:

```
// Create some ADO.NET objects
SqlConnection cnn = new SqlConnection(
    "Data Source=(local); Initial Catalog=Northwind;" +
    " Integrated Security=SSPI");
DataSet ds = new DataSet();
SqlDataAdapter da = new SqlDataAdapter();

private void StepByStepA_12_Load(
    object sender, System.EventArgs e)
{
    // Create a SqlCommand to select data
    SqlCommand cmdSelect = cnn.CreateCommand();
    cmdSelect.CommandType = CommandType.Text;
    cmdSelect.CommandText =
        "SELECT CustomerID, CompanyName, " +
        "ContactName FROM Customers";
```

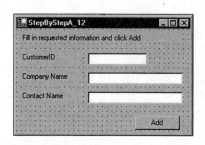

FIGURE A.13
You can use the InsertCommand property of the SqlDataAdapter object to insert new customers into a database.

```
    // Create a SqlCommand to insert data
    SqlCommand cmdInsert = cnn.CreateCommand();
    cmdInsert.CommandType = CommandType.Text;
    cmdInsert.CommandText = "INSERT INTO Customers " +
        "(CustomerID, CompanyName, ContactName) " +
        "VALUES(@CustomerID, @CompanyName, " +
        "@ContactName)";
    cmdInsert.Parameters.Add("@CustomerID",
        SqlDbType.NChar,5, "CustomerID");
    cmdInsert.Parameters.Add("@CompanyName",
        SqlDbType.NVarChar,40, "CompanyName");
    cmdInsert.Parameters.Add("@ContactName",
        SqlDbType.NVarChar,30, "ContactName");
    cmdInsert.Parameters["@CustomerID"].SourceVersion
        = DataRowVersion.Original;
    // Set up the DataAdapter and fill the DataSet
    da.SelectCommand = cmdSelect;
    da.InsertCommand = cmdInsert;
    da.Fill(ds, "Customers");
}
```

5. Double-click the Button control and enter this code to handle the Click event of the Button control:

```
private void btnAdd_Click(object sender,
    System.EventArgs e)
{
    // Create a new DataRow
    DataRow dr = ds.Tables["Customers"].NewRow();
    // Set values
    dr[0] = txtCustomerID.Text;
    dr[1] = txtCompanyName.Text;
    dr[2] = txtContactName.Text;
    // And append the new row to the DataTable
    ds.Tables["Customers"].Rows.Add(dr);
    // Now save back to the database
    da.Update(ds, "Customers");
    MessageBox.Show("Row added!");
}
```

6. Insert the Main() method to launch the form and set the form as the startup object for the project.

7. Run the project. Enter data in the TextBox controls and click the button. The code adds the new row to the database.

As you can see from Step-by-Step A.12, the process of adding a new DataRow object to a DataTable object has several steps. First you call the NewRow() method of the DataTable object. This returns a DataRow object that has the proper schema for that particular DataTable object. Then you can set the values of the individual items in the DataRow object. Finally, you call the Add() method of the DataTable object to actually append this DataRow object to the DataTable object.

Of course, appending the DataRow object to the DataTable object doesn't make any changes to the database. For that, you need to call the Update() method of the SqlDataAdapter object once again. If the SqlDataAdapter object finds any new rows in its scan of the database, it calls the SqlCommand object specified by its InsertCommand property once for each new row. This SqlCommand object does the actual work of permanently saving the data.

Deleting Data

The DataRow object contains a Delete() method that deletes an entire DataRow object from the DataTable object. To cause the changes to the database to persist, you need to call the Update() method of the SqlDataAdapter object, as in Step-by-Step A.13.

STEP BY STEP

A.13 Deleting Data with a SqlDataAdapter Object

1. Add a new form to your Visual C# .NET project.

2. Place a Label control, a ComboBox control (cboCustomerID) and a Button control (btnDelete) on the form.

3. Switch to the code view and add the following using directives:

```
using System.Data;
using System.Data.SqlClient;
```

4. Double-click the form and enter this code to load data when the form is opened:

```
// Create some ADO.NET objects
SqlConnection cnn = new SqlConnection(
    "Data Source=(local); Initial Catalog=Northwind;" +
    " Integrated Security=SSPI");
DataSet ds = new DataSet();
SqlDataAdapter da = new SqlDataAdapter();
```

```csharp
private void StepByStepA_13_Load(
    object sender, System.EventArgs e)
{
    // Create a SqlCommand to select data
    SqlCommand cmdSelect = cnn.CreateCommand();
    cmdSelect.CommandType = CommandType.Text;
    cmdSelect.CommandText =
        "SELECT CustomerID, ContactName FROM Customers";
    // Create a SqlCommand to delete data
    SqlCommand cmdDelete = cnn.CreateCommand();
    cmdDelete.CommandType = CommandType.Text;
    cmdDelete.CommandText = "DELETE FROM Customers " +
        " WHERE CustomerID = @CustomerID";
    cmdDelete.Parameters.Add("@CustomerID",
        SqlDbType.NChar,5, "CustomerID");
    cmdDelete.Parameters["@CustomerID"].SourceVersion =
        DataRowVersion.Original;
    // Set up the DataAdapter and fill the DataSet
    da.SelectCommand = cmdSelect;
    da.DeleteCommand = cmdDelete;
    da.Fill(ds, "Customers");
    // Fill the data in the ComboBox
    cboCustomerID.DisplayMember = "CustomerID";
    cboCustomerID.ValueMember = "CustomerID";
    cboCustomerID.DataSource = ds.Tables["Customers"];
}
```

5. Double-click the Button control and enter this code to handle the Click event of the Button control:

```csharp
private void btnDelete_Click(object sender,
    System.EventArgs e)
{
    // Find the specified row and delete it
    foreach( DataRow dr in ds.Tables["Customers"].Rows)
    {
        if(dr[0] == cboCustomerID.SelectedValue)
        {
            dr.Delete();
            break;
        }
    }
    // Save the changes
    da.Update(ds, "Customers");
    MessageBox.Show("Row deleted!");
}
```

6. Insert the Main() method to launch the form. Set the form as the startup object for the project.

7. Run the project. The form pops up with a ComboBox control that contains all the customer IDs and a Button control. Select a customer ID and click the button. The selected customer is deleted from the DataSet object and from the database.

Note in Step-by-Step A.13 that the deletion command uses the original value of the CustomerID column to locate the correct row to delete from the database.

REVIEW BREAK

▶ You can change data in a DataSet object just by treating the items in the DataSet object like any other variables.

▶ To move data to a DataSet object, create an appropriate DataAdapter object and call its Fill() method.

▶ To move through a DataSet object, you can use nested foreach loops, or you can simply specify which DataRow object and DataColumn object contain the data that you're interested in.

▶ Strongly typed DataSet objects enable you to use early-bound syntax with your data access code.

▶ You can use DataRelation objects to specify the relationships between multiple tables in a DataSet object.

▶ The DataTable.Select() method and the DataView object offer two different ways to find and sort data.

▶ To cause changes from the data model to persist to the underlying database, you must call the Update() method of the SqlDataAdapter object.

▶ The UpdateCommand property of the SqlDataAdapter object specifies a SqlCommand object to be executed for all changed rows.

▶ The InsertCommand property of the SqlDataAdapter object specifies a SqlCommand object to be executed for all new rows.

▶ The DeleteCommand property of the SqlDataAdapter object specifies a SqlCommand object to be executed for all deleted rows.

SUMMARY

The .NET Framework offers an incredible amount of flexibility for consuming and manipulating data. A major part of this flexibility is implemented in the ADO.NET objects, which span multiple namespaces. ADO.NET includes both data provider objects, which are tied to specific data sources, and `DataSet` objects, which provide a purely abstract view of relational data. After seeing the object model, you learned how to apply it to a number of problems, including loading and saving data, finding and sorting data, and editing data.

APPLY YOUR KNOWLEDGE

Suggested Readings and Resources

1. Kalen Delaney. *Inside SQL Server 2000.* Microsoft Press, 2000.

2. Mike Gunderloy. *ADO and ADO.NET Programming.* Sybex, 2002.

3. .NET Framework SDK Documentation:

   • Accessing Data with ADO.NET

4. SQL Server Books Online

   • Transact-SQL Reference

5. Bill Vaughn. *ADO.NET and ADO Examples and Best Practices for VB Programmers.* Apress, 2002.

6. Bob Beauchemin. *Essential ADO.NET.* Addison-Wesley, 2002.

XML Standards and Syntax

The exam objectives of 70-320 have a wide coverage of XML-related topics. To prepare for most of the exam objectives, you need to have a basic understanding of XML. In this appendix, you'll learn the basics of XML, its syntax, and its standards.

INTRODUCTION

XML (Extensible Markup Language) is a simple, flexible, powerful, and portable markup language developed by the World Wide Web Consortium (W3C). XML contains human-readable data combined with human-readable metadata. That is, XML files contain regular text, so you can read them. And they contain both data and descriptions of that data.

XML provides a simple format for describing data. XML does not contain any pre-defined tags, unlike HTML (Hypertext Markup Language). You can create your own tags in XML. Therefore, depending on your application's needs, you can create specialized tags. For example, for a publishing business, you can create tags such as Author, Title, ISBN, and so on. Because the structure of XML is simple and extensible, it is useful in applications such as exchange of information between organizations, Web site publishing, object serialization, remote procedure calls, and so on.

SYNTAX OF AN XML DOCUMENT

An XML document contains only text data. Therefore, an XML document can be easily created or edited with any simple text editor. An XML document does not contain any pre-defined tags, but XML adopts a strict syntax for defining data in the XML document. This section discusses various rules one should follow while creating an XML document.

> **NOTE**
>
> **Well-Formed XML Document** If an XML document conforms to the XML syntax, it is known as a `well-formed` XML document.

Here's a concrete example to start with. This XML file represents data for two customers:

```
<?xml version="1.0" encoding="UTF-8"?>
<!-- Customer list for Bob's Tractor Parts -->
<Customers>
    <Customer CustomerNumber="1">
        <CustomerName>Lambert Tractor Works
        </CustomerName>
        <CustomerCity>Millbank</CustomerCity>
        <CustomerState>WA</CustomerState>
    </Customer>
    <Customer CustomerNumber="2">
```

```
        <CustomerName><![CDATA[Joe's Garage]]>
        </CustomerName>
        <CustomerCity>Doppel</CustomerCity>
        <CustomerState>OR</CustomerState>
    </Customer>
</Customers>
```

XML Declaration

The first thing that you find in an XML file is the *XML declaration*:

```
<?xml version="1.0" encoding="UTF-8"?>
```

The declaration tells you three things about this document:

- ▶ It's an XML document.
- ▶ It conforms to the XML 1.0 specification of W3C.
- ▶ It uses the UTF-8 character set (a standard set of characters for the Western alphabet).

The XML declaration is optional. However, the W3C XML recommendation suggests you include the XML declaration. The XML declaration can help in identifying the XML version and the character encoding used in an XML document. The lines that begin with the <? string and end with the ?> string are called processing instructions (PIs). Processing instructions are used to provide information to the application processing an XML document on how to process the XML document.

XML Comments

An XML document can contain comments. Comments are set off by the opening string <!-- and the closing string -->. Here's an example:

```
<!-- Customer list for Bob's Tractor Parts -->
```

XML Elements

Even without knowing anything about XML, you can see some things just by looking at the sample document. In particular, XML consists of tags (that is, markup, which is contained within angle brackets) and character data. The character data is the information stored in the XML files and the tags (markup) record the structure of the XML file. XML tags usually describe the data contained by them rather than describing the format and layout information.

Tags appear in pairs, with each opening tag matched by a closing tag. The closing tag has the same text as the opening tag, prefixed with a forward slash. For example, if <CustomerCity> is the opening tag, </CustomerCity> is the closing tag.

An opening tag together with a closing tag and the content between them define an *element*. Tags in an XML document contain the name of the element. For example, here's a single element from the sample document:

```
<CustomerState>OR</CustomerState>
```

This defines an element whose name is CustomerState and whose data is OR.

Elements can sometimes contain no content. In that case, you can create an *empty element* to maintain the structure of the XML document. For example, here's an element with no content:

```
<Citizen></Citizen>
```

This defines an element whose name is Citizen.

Empty elements can also be defined with a shorter syntax; for example:

```
<Citizen/>
```

In this case, you do not provide the closing tag, but you end the opening tag with />.

Elements can be nested, but they cannot overlap. So the following is legal XML, defining an element named `Customer` that has three child elements:

```
<Customer CustomerNumber="1">
    <CustomerName>Lambert Tractor Works</CustomerName>
    <CustomerCity>Millbank</CustomerCity>
    <CustomerState>WA</CustomerState>
</Customer>
```

But the following is not legal XML because the `CustomerCity` and `CustomerState` elements overlap:

```
<Customer CustomerNumber="1">
    <CustomerName>Lambert Tractor Works</CustomerName>
    <CustomerCity>Millbank<CustomerState>
    </CustomerCity>WA</CustomerState>
</Customer>
```

Nested elements have a parent-child relationship. So in the preceding example, the `Customer` element is the parent of the `CustomerName` element. A parent element can contain any number of child elements, but a child element belongs to only one parent element. Every element in an XML document is a child element except one element. This is the root element in the XML document that contains all the other child elements. The root element in the sample document is named `Customers`.

The effect of these rules—that nesting is okay, overlapping is not okay, and there is a single root element—is that any XML document can be represented as a tree of nodes. Figure B.1 illustrates the tree-like structure of the sample document.

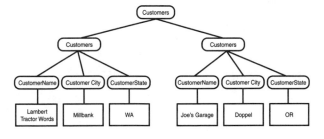

FIGURE B.1
An XML document can be represented as a tree of nodes.

XML Attributes

Elements can contain attributes. An *attribute* is a piece of data that further describes an element. Attributes appear in name-value pairs in an element's opening tag. For example, the sample document includes this opening tag for an element:

```
<Customer CustomerNumber="1">
```

This declares an element named `Customer`. The `Customer` element includes an attribute whose name is `CustomerNumber` and whose value is 1.

The value of the attribute should always be enclosed in either single or double quotation marks.

XML Naming Convention

If you're familiar with HTML, you know that in HTML, some elements have names dictated by the HTML specification. For example, the `<H1>` tag specifies a first-level heading. XML takes a different approach. You can make up any name you like for an XML element or attribute, subject to some simple naming rules:

▶ A name can contain any alphanumeric character.

▶ A name can contain underscores, hyphens, and periods.

▶ A name must not contain any whitespace.

▶ A name must start with a letter or an underscore.

The names of the XML elements and attributes can be in uppercase, lowercase, or both, but are case-sensitive. For example, the following is not legal XML because the opening tag and closing tag of the element do not match:

```
<CustomerState>OR</customerState>
```

Handling Special Characters in XML Data

Some characters have special meaning for the programs that process XML. For example, the opening angle bracket indicates the beginning of a tag. The quotation marks enclose the attributes, and so on. But sometime you may also like to use these characters as part of the XML data.

XML offers two ways to deal with special characters in data. First, for individual characters you can use entity references. Five entity references are defined in the XML standard:

- ▶ `&lt`—Translates to < (opening angle bracket).

- ▶ `&gt`—Translates to > (closing angle bracket).

- ▶ `&amp`—Translates to & (ampersand).

- ▶ `&apos`—Translates to ' (apostrophe).

- ▶ `&quot`—Translates to " (quotation mark).

You can also use a `CDATA` section to hold any arbitrary data, whether the data contains special characters or not. The sample document uses this approach to store a customer name containing an apostrophe, as follows:

```
<CustomerName><![CDATA[Joe's Garage]]></CustomerName>
```

XML Namespaces

An XML document can contain one or more *namespace* declarations. The sample document does not declare a namespace. Here's the example for a namespace declaration:

```
<Customers xmlns:tr="urn:schemas-tractor-repair">
```

The namespace is declared as part of the root tag for the document. In this particular case, the namespace (introduced with the special `xmlns` characters) defines the prefix `tr` for tags within the namespace. `urn` (uniform resource name) is an arbitrary string whose purpose is to distinguish this namespace from other namespaces.

XML namespaces serve the same purpose as .NET namespaces: They help cut down on naming collisions. After declaring the `tr` namespace, an XML document could use a tag such as this:

```
<tr:CustomerState>OR</tr:CustomerState>
```

This example indicates that the `CustomerState` tag is from the `tr` namespace and should not be confused with any other `CustomerState` tag.

SUMMARY

A great deal of complexity is available in XML that is not discussed in this section. But these basics give you a head start in understanding most of the XML that you're likely to run across until you start working with XML in depth.

XML is ubiquitous in the .NET Framework. The .NET Framework uses XML for the following benefits:

- ▶ Compliance with the W3C standards.

- ▶ Extensibility.

- ▶ Pluggable architecture.

- ▶ Performance.

- ▶ Tight integration with ADO.NET.

Suggested Readings and Resources

1. Benoît Marchal. *XML by Example*. QUE, 1999.

2. W3C XML Home Page, `www.w3.org/xml`.

3. XML Tutorial, `www.w3schools.com/xml`.

Glossary

A

ACID   An acronym coined for the atomic, consistent, isolated, and durable properties of a transaction.

activation type   An activation category for a serviced component application that indicates whether the application runs in or out of its client's process space (a library or a server application).

ad hoc query   A set of SQL statements that are executed immediately.

application domain   Application domains provide a secure and versatile unit of processing that the common language runtime (CLR) can use to provide isolation between applications.

asynchronous call   A call to a method that does not block the calling code while waiting for results.

authentication   The process of determining the identity of a user from the supplied credentials.

authorization   The process of determining what types of access rights are available to an authenticated user or a process.

B

binding policy   The rules that specify how the CLR locates and binds to the assemblies that make up an application. The default binding policy of the CLR can be configured by using the configuration files.

C

channel   The channel has responsibility for transmitting all messages between client and object across the process boundary. The channel has been designed to work transparently with different channel types, is compatible with OSF DCE standard RPC, and supports single and multithreaded applications.

code access security   Security based on permission requests made by running code.

code group   A group of zero or more modules that share a common security policy.

COM+ application   A primary unit of administration and security for COM+ Component Services. A COM+ application is a group of components that, generally speaking, perform related functions. These components further consist of interfaces and methods.

COM+ catalog   A COM+ repository that maintains the configuration information for the components.

COM interface   A collection of related public methods that provide access to a COM object. The set of interfaces on a COM object composes a contract that specifies how programs and other objects can interact with the COM object.

context   A set of runtime properties that define the environment associated with a COM+ object.

D

DataSet   An in-memory relational store that abstracts away many of the differences between database implementations.

DataSet schema   The schema of a DataSet describes the types of data that the DataSet contains; it is the metadata for the Dataset.

debugging   The process of locating logical or runtime errors in an application. Debugging involves finding the causes of the errors and fixing them.

declarative security   Security based on attributes that declare the desired permissions.

delay signing   A technique that enables you to place a shared assembly in the GAC by just signing the assembly with the public key. This allows the assembly to be signed with the private key at a later stage, when the development process is complete and the component or assembly is ready to be deployed. This process enables developers to work with shared assemblies as if they were strongly named and yet also secure the private key of the signature from being accessed at different stages of development.

deployment   A process by which an application or component is distributed in the form of installation package files to be installed on the other computers.

deserialization   The process of converting an XML message to one or more objects.

DiffGram   An XML message that contains information for updating the information in a DataSet object or a SQL Server database.

Disco   A Microsoft standard for Web Services Discovery. Also known as "Discovery of Web Services."

DOM (Document Object Model)   A W3C standard for representing the content of an XML document as a set of nodes arranged in a hierarchy.

DTC (Distributed Transaction Coordinator)   A Windows service that manages transactions and transaction-related communications that are distributed across two or more resource managers on one or more systems to ensure ACID properties.

DTD (Document Type Definition)   A standard for describing the information that can be contained in an HTML or XML document.

E - F - G

GAC (global assembly cache)   A machine-wide code cache that stores shared assemblies.

H - I

Identity column   An identity column is one whose value is automatically assigned by the server when a new row is entered.

imperative security   Security based on instantiated classes.

impersonation   Specifying the credentials that a process should present in place of the authenticated user's credentials.

J

just-in-time (JIT) activation   The capability of a COM+ object to be activated only as needed for executing requests from its client. Objects can be deactivated even while clients hold references to them, allowing otherwise idle server resources to be used more productively.

K

key   A unique identifier for a piece of information.

L - M

managed code   Code that is written in one of the .NET languages and is executed by the CLR.

marshaling   Packaging and sending interface method calls across thread or process boundaries via serialization and deserialization.

merge module   A type of project that enables you to create reusable setup components that help in deploying shared components. Merge modules cannot be directly installed; instead they need to be merged with installers of applications that use the shared component packaged as a merge module.

metadata   Metadata is data about data. For example, a DataSet schema is data that describes the structure of a DataSet object.

N

native compilation   The process of precompiling assemblies in processor-specific machine code. Native compilation can be done with the help of the Native Image Generator tool (ngen.exe).

native image cache   A cache that contains precompiled assemblies.

nested Relationship   A relationship in an XML file in which one element contains another element. For example, `<pets><dog name="unix"/></pets>`.

O

object pooling   A performance optimization based on using collections of already created objects. Pooling results in more efficient resource allocation.

ODBC(Open Database Connectivity)   A specification for an API that defines a standard set of routines with which an application can access data in a data source.

OLE DB   A set of COM interfaces that provide applications with uniform access to data stored in diverse information sources, regardless of their location or type.

one-to-many relationship   A relationship in an XML file that ties together two separate elements.

OSQL   A SQL Server command-line tool for executing queries.

P

parameter   A piece of information passed to a stored procedure at runtime.

permission   A permission in .NET controls access to a resource.

permission set   A set of one or more permissions that can be granted or denied as a unit.

Platform Invoke   The feature of the .NET Framework that enables you to call the Windows API and other DLL procedures from managed code.

private assembly   An assembly that is deployed for use by only a single application. A private assembly is stored in the same directory structure as the application that uses it.

proxy   An interface-specific object that packages parameters for that interface in preparation for a remote method call. A proxy runs in the sender's address space and communicates with a corresponding stub in the receiver's address space.

publisher policy   A set of rules that enables vendors to redirect assembly references from one version to another. The publisher policy is used to deploy service packs, such as updates of an assembly. The publisher policy is stored inside an XML configuration file, which is compiled into an assembly and placed in the GAC.

Q

queued components   A COM+ service that provides an easy way to invoke and execute components asynchronously. Message processing can occur without regard to the availability of either the sender or the receiver.

R

RCW (runtime callable wrapper)   A proxy that enables .NET code to make use of COM classes and members.

remoting   The .NET remoting system is an architecture designed to simplify communication between objects living in different application domains, whether on the same computer or not.

role-based security   Security based on the identity of the current user.

runtime host   The environment in which CLR is started and managed. When you install the .NET Framework, you get three runtime hosts that are already configured—the Windows shell, ASP.NET, and Internet Explorer. The Runtime hosts create application domains, which run the managed code on behalf of the user.

S

SCM (Service Control Manager)   A part of the Windows operating system that manages Windows services. SCM also manages the Windows service database (which is stored in the Windows Registry) and provides a mechanism through which other programs can interact with the Windows service database and the Windows service in execution.

serialization   The process of converting objects to their XML representations.

side-by-side execution   The ability to run multiple versions of the same assembly simultaneously.

simple type   An XML schema description of a piece of information together with restrictions on the content of that information.

shared assembly   An assembly that can be referenced by more than one application. A shared assembly must have an associated strong name.

SOAP (Simple Object Access Protocol)   A standard for transmitting objects as XML over HTTP.

SOAP Extension   A class that is invoked during the serialization or deserialization of SOAP messages.

SOAP Request   A SOAP message sent from client to server to invoke a Web method.

SOAP Response A SOAP message sent from server to client with the results of a Web method.

SQL-92 The official ANSI specification for Structured Query Language.

SQL Query Analyzer A SQL Server graphical tool for executing queries.

stored procedure A set of SQL statements stored on the server for later execution.

strong name A name that identifies an assembly by its simple text name, version number, culture information (if provided), and a public key token.

strongly typed DataSet A DataSet based on an XML Schema file, which enables table and column names to be used with an early-bound syntax.

synchronous call A method call that does not allow further instructions in the calling process to be executed until the method returns.

T

testing The process of executing programs and determining whether they worked as expected. Testing is the process of revealing errors by executing programs with various test cases and test data.

tracing The process of displaying informative messages in an application at the time of execution. Tracing messages can be helpful for checking the health of a program or finding errors even though the program is already in production.

Transact-SQL Also called T-SQL, the SQL-92 dialect used in Microsoft SQL Server.

transaction A unit of work that is done as an atomic operation—that is, the operation succeeds or fails as a whole.

U

UDDI (Universal Description, Discovery, and Integration) A standard for discovering details of Web services and other business services available via the Internet.

unmanaged code Code written in a non-.NET environment that does not benefit from the services of the CLR.

V

Valid XML document An XML document is valid if it conforms to the schema in a DTD or XSD file.

W

W3C (World Wide Web Consortium) The standards body that maintains the standards for HTML and XML.

Web method A method of a Web service that can be invoked by client applications.

Web reference Information in a Visual Studio .NET project that enables you to use objects that are supplied by a Web service. A Web reference is essentially a Web service proxy. *See also* Web service proxy.

Web service A Web service enables you to instantiate and invoke methods on objects over the Internet.

Web service proxy A component that hides the internal details for invoking a Web service from the Web service client.

well-formed XML document An XML document is well-formed if it conforms to the syntactic rules for XML.

Windows service A long-running process that runs in the background, usually without any user interaction. A Windows service must conform to the interface provided by the Windows Service Control Manager (SCM).

WSDL (Web Services Description Language) An XML language that describes the interface of a Web service.

X - Y - Z

XPath A language for retrieving sets of nodes from an XML document.

XML attribute A piece of information describing an XML element.

XML element Information delimited by a start and end tag in an XML document; for example, `<LastName>Gates</LastName>`.

XML wire format The structure of the actual XML messages passed between Web services servers and clients.

Overview of the Certification Process

You must pass rigorous certification exams to become a Microsoft Certified Professional. These closed-book exams provide a valid and reliable measure of your technical proficiency and expertise. Developed in consultation with computer industry professionals who have experience with Microsoft products in the workplace, the exams are conducted by two independent organizations. Prometric offers the exams at more than 3,500 authorized Prometric testing centers around the world. Virtual University Enterprises (VUE) testing centers offer exams at more than 3,000 locations.

To schedule an exam, contact Prometric Testing Centers (800-755-EXAM or www.2test.com) or VUE (800-TEST-REG or www.vue.com/ms).

TYPES OF CERTIFICATION

Currently Microsoft offers seven types of certification, based on specific areas of expertise:

- ▶ **Microsoft Certified Professional (MCP).** An MCP is qualified to implement a Microsoft product or technology as part of a business solution in an organization. Candidates can take elective exams to develop areas of specialization. MCP is the base level of expertise.

- ▶ **Microsoft Certified Systems Administrator (MCSA).** An MCSA is qualified to implement, manage, and troubleshoot existing network and system environments based on the Microsoft Windows 2000 and Windows .NET Server platforms.

- ▶ **Microsoft Certified Systems Engineer (MCSE).** An MCSE is qualified to analyze business requirements and design and implement the infrastructure for business solutions based on the Microsoft Windows 2000 platform and Microsoft server software. The MCSE credential is the next step up from the MCSA.

- ▶ **Microsoft Certified Application Developer (MCAD).** An MCAD is qualified to use Microsoft technologies to develop and maintain department-level applications, components, Web or desktop clients, and back-end data services. This is the entry-level developer certification.

- ▶ **Microsoft Certified Solution Developer (MCSD).** An MCSD is qualified to design and develop leading-edge business solutions by using Microsoft development tools, technologies, and platforms, including Microsoft Office and Microsoft BackOffice. MCSD is the highest level of expertise that has a focus on software development.

▶ **Microsoft Certified Database Administrator (MCDBA).** An MCDBA is qualified to implement and administer Microsoft SQL Server databases.

▶ **Microsoft Certified Trainer (MCT).** An MCT is instructionally and technically qualified to deliver Microsoft Official Curriculum (MOC) and MSDN training courses.

> **NOTE** **Keep Yourself Updated** Microsoft's certifications and the exams that lead to them are under constant revision. For up-to-date information about each type of certification, visit the Microsoft Training & Certification Web site, at www.microsoft.com/traincert. You also can contact the following sources:
>
> • Microsoft Regional Education Service Center for North America: 800-635-7544
>
> • mcphelp@microsoft.com

CERTIFICATION REQUIREMENTS

The following sections describe the certification requirements for the various types of Microsoft certification.

> **NOTE** **Discontinued Exams** An asterisk following an exam in any of the following lists means that it is slated for retirement.

How to Become an MCP

Passing any Microsoft exam (with the exception of exam 70-058, "Networking Essentials") is all you need to do to become certified as an MCP.

How to Become an MCSA

You must pass three core exams and one elective exam to become an MCSA. The following sections show both the core requirements and the electives you can take to earn this certification.

MCSA Core Exams

You must pass three core exams from the following list to earn credit toward the MCSA certification:

▶ 70-210, "Installing, Configuring, and Administering Microsoft Windows 2000 Professional"

OR

70-270, "Installing, Configuring, and Administering Microsoft Windows XP Professional"

▶ 70-215, "Installing, Configuring, and Administering Microsoft Windows 2000 Server"

OR

70-275, "Installing, Configuring, and Administering Microsoft Windows .NET Server"

▶ 70-218, "Managing a Microsoft Windows 2000 Network Environment"

OR

70-278, "Managing a Microsoft Windows .NET Server Network Environment"

MCSA Elective Exams

You must pass any one of the exams from the following list of electives exams to earn credit toward the MCSA certification:

- ▶ 70-028, "Administering Microsoft SQL Server 7.0"

- ▶ 70-081, "Implementing and Supporting Microsoft Exchange Server 5.5"*

- ▶ 70-086, "Implementing and Supporting Microsoft Systems Management Server 2.0"

- ▶ 70-088, "Implementing and Supporting Microsoft Proxy Server 2.0"*

- ▶ 70-214, "Implementing and Administering Security in a Microsoft Windows 2000 Network"

- ▶ 70-216, "Implementing and Administering a Microsoft Windows 2000 Network Infrastructure"

- ▶ 70-224, "Installing, Configuring, and Administering Microsoft Exchange 2000 Server"

- ▶ 70-227, "Installing, Configuring, and Administering Microsoft Internet Security and Acceleration (ISA) Server 2000 Enterprise Edition"

- ▶ 70-228, "Installing, Configuring, and Administering Microsoft SQL Server 2000 Enterprise Edition"

- ▶ 70-244, "Supporting and Maintaining a Microsoft Windows NT Server 4.0 Network"

- ▶ The CompTIA exam "A+" and "Network+"

- ▶ The CompTIA exams "A+" and "Server+"

The MCSA is the first Microsoft certification to recognize some third-party certification exams as electives. Two particular combinations of exams from CompTIA qualify as MCSA elective exams.

How to Become an MCSE

You must pass five core exams (four operating system exams and one design exam) and two elective exams to become an MCSE.

The following sections show the core requirements and the electives that you can take to earn MCSE certification.

MCSE Operating System Exams

You must pass these four core requirements to earn credit toward the MCSE certification:

- ▶ 70-210, "Installing, Configuring, and Administering Microsoft Windows 2000 Professional"

  OR

  70-270, "Installing, Configuring, and Administering Microsoft Windows XP Professional"

- ▶ 70-215, "Installing, Configuring, and Administering Microsoft Windows 2000 Server"

  OR

  70-275, "Installing, Configuring, and Administering Microsoft Windows .NET Server"

- ▶ 70-216, "Implementing and Administering a Microsoft Windows 2000 Network Infrastructure"

  OR

  70-276, "Implementing and Administering a Microsoft Windows .NET Server Network Infrastructure"

- ▶ 70-217, "Implementing and Administering a Microsoft Windows 2000 Directory Services Infrastructure"

  OR

70-277, "Implementing and Administering a Microsoft Windows .NET Server Directory Services Infrastructure"

MCSE Design Exams

You must pass one of the design electives on this list to earn credit toward the MCSE certification:

▶ 70-219, "Designing a Microsoft Windows 2000 Directory Services Infrastructure"

▶ 70-220, "Designing Security for a Microsoft Windows 2000 Network"

▶ 70-221, "Designing a Microsoft Windows 2000 Network Infrastructure"

▶ 70-226, "Designing Highly Available Web Solutions with Microsoft Windows 2000 Server Technologies"

MCSE Elective Exams

You must pass two of the following elective exams to earn credit toward the MCSE certification:

▶ 70-019, "Designing and Implementing Data Warehouses with Microsoft SQL Server 7.0"

▶ 70-028, "Administering Microsoft SQL Server 7.0"

▶ 70-029, "Designing and Implementing Databases with Microsoft SQL Server 7.0"

▶ 70-056, "Implementing and Supporting Web Sites Using Microsoft Site Server 3.0"*

▶ 70-080, "Implementing and Supporting Microsoft Internet Explorer 5.0 by Using the Microsoft Internet Explorer Administration Kit"*

▶ 70-081, "Implementing and Supporting Microsoft Exchange Server 5.5"*

▶ 70-085, "Implementing and Supporting Microsoft SNA Server 4.0"*

▶ 70-086, "Implementing and Supporting Microsoft Systems Management Server 2.0"

▶ 70-088, "Implementing and Supporting Microsoft Proxy Server 2.0"*

▶ 70-214, "Implementing and Administering Security in a Microsoft Windows 2000 Network"

▶ 70-218, "Managing a Microsoft Windows 2000 Network Environment"

▶ 70-219, "Designing a Microsoft Windows 2000 Directory Services Infrastructure"

▶ 70-220, "Designing Security for a Microsoft Windows 2000 Network"

▶ 70-221, "Designing a Microsoft Windows 2000 Network Infrastructure"

▶ 70-222, "Migrating from Microsoft Windows NT 4.0 to Microsoft Windows 2000"

▶ 70-223, "Installing, Configuring, and Administering Microsoft Clustering Services by Using Microsoft Windows 2000 Advanced Server"

▶ 70-224, "Installing, Configuring, and Administering Microsoft Exchange 2000 Server"

▶ 70-225, "Designing and Deploying a Messaging Infrastructure with Microsoft Exchange 2000 Server"

▶ 70-226, "Designing Highly Available Web Solutions with Microsoft Windows 2000 Server Technologies"

▶ 70-227, "Installing, Configuring, and Administering Microsoft Internet Security and Acceleration (ISA) Server 2000 Enterprise Edition"

- ▶ 70-228, "Installing, Configuring, and Administering Microsoft SQL Server 2000 Enterprise Edition"

- ▶ 70-229, "Designing and Implementing Databases with Microsoft SQL Server 2000 Enterprise Edition"

- ▶ 70-230, "Designing and Implementing Solutions with Microsoft BizTalk Server 2000 Enterprise Edition"

- ▶ 70-232, "Implementing and Maintaining Highly Available Web Solutions with Microsoft Windows 2000 Server Technologies and Microsoft Application Center 2000"

- ▶ 70-234, "Designing and Implementing Solutions with Microsoft Commerce Server 2000"

- ▶ 70-244, "Supporting and Maintaining a Microsoft Windows NT Server 4.0 Network"

You cannot count the same exam as both a core exam and an elective exam to obtain MCSE certification.

How to Become an MCAD

You must pass two core exams and one elective exam to earn MCAD certification.

The following sections show the core requirements and the electives that you can take to earn MCAD certification.

MCAD Core Exams

You must pass two of the following core exams to earn credit toward the MCAD certification:

- ▶ 70-305, "Developing and Implementing Web Applications with Microsoft Visual Basic .NET and Microsoft Visual Studio .NET"

OR

70-306, "Developing and Implementing Windows-Based Applications with Microsoft Visual Basic .NET and Microsoft Visual Studio .NET"

OR

70-315, "Developing and Implementing Web Applications with Microsoft Visual C# .NET and Microsoft Visual Studio .NET"

OR

70-316, "Developing and Implementing Windows-based Applications with Microsoft Visual C# .NET and Microsoft Visual Studio .NET"

- ▶ 70-310, "Designing XML Web Services and Server Components with Microsoft Visual Basic .NET and the Microsoft .NET Framework"

OR

70-320, "Designing XML Web Services and Server Components with Microsoft Visual C# .NET and the Microsoft .NET Framework"

MCAD Elective Exams

You must pass one of the following elective exams to earn credit toward the MCAD certification:

- ▶ 70-229, "Designing and Implementing Databases with Microsoft SQL Server 2000 Enterprise Edition"

- ▶ 70-230, "Designing and Implementing Solutions with Microsoft BizTalk Server 2000 Enterprise Edition"

- ▶ 70-234, "Designing and Implementing Solutions with Microsoft Commerce Server 2000"

You may also count as an elective one of the four core exams 70-305, 70-306, 70-315, and 70-316. The elective exam must be from the opposite technology as the exam that you counted as core. For example, if you take the exam "Developing and Implementing Windows-based Applications With Visual C# .NET and Visual Studio .NET" (Exam 70-316) as a core exam, you can take either the "Developing and Implementing Web Applications With Visual C# .NET and Visual Studio .NET" (Exam 70-315) or the "Developing and Implementing Web Applications With Visual Basic .NET and Visual Studio .NET" (Exam 70-305) as an elective.

How to Become an MCSD

There are two different tracks for the MCSD certification. The new track is for the MCSD for Microsoft .NET certification, and the old track covers the previous versions of Microsoft technologies. The requirements for both tracks are listed in the following sections.

The MCSD for Microsoft .NET Track

For the MCSD for Microsoft .NET certification, you must pass four core exams and one elective exam. Both the core and elective exams are listed in the following sections.

MCSD for Microsoft .NET Track Core Exams

You must pass four of the following core exams to earn credit toward the MCSD for Microsoft .NET certification:

▶ 70-305, "Developing and Implementing Web Applications with Microsoft Visual Basic .NET and Microsoft Visual Studio .NET"

    OR

70-315, "Developing and Implementing Web Applications with Microsoft Visual C# .NET and Microsoft Visual Studio .NET"

▶ 70-306, "Developing and Implementing Windows-Based Applications with Microsoft Visual Basic .NET and Microsoft Visual Studio .NET"

    OR

70-316, "Developing and Implementing Windows-Based Applications with Microsoft Visual C# .NET and Microsoft Visual Studio .NET"

▶ 70-310, "Designing XML Web Services and Server Components with Microsoft Visual Basic .NET and the Microsoft .NET Framework"

    OR

70-320, "Designing XML Web Services and Server Components with Microsoft Visual C# .NET and the Microsoft .NET Framework"

▶ 70-300, "Analyzing Requirements and Defining .NET Solution Architectures"

MCSD for Microsoft .NET Track Elective Exams

You must pass one of the following elective exams to earn credit toward the MCSD for Microsoft .NET certification:

▶ 70-229, "Designing and Implementing Databases with Microsoft SQL Server 2000 Enterprise Edition"

▶ 70-230, "Designing and Implementing Solutions with Microsoft BizTalk Server 2000 Enterprise Edition"

▶ 70-234, "Designing and Implementing Solutions with Microsoft Commerce Server 2000"

The MCSD Old Track

For the old track for MCSD certification, you must pass three core exams and one elective exam. Both the core and elective exams are listed in the following sections.

MCSD Old Track Core Exams

You must pass three of the following core exams to earn credit toward the MCSD certification:

► 70-016, "Designing and Implementing Desktop Applications with Microsoft Visual C++ 6.0"

OR

70-156, "Designing and Implementing Desktop Applications with Microsoft Visual FoxPro 6.0"

OR

70-176, "Designing and Implementing Desktop Applications with Microsoft Visual Basic 6.0"

► 70-015, "Designing and Implementing Distributed Applications with Microsoft Visual C++ 6.0"

OR

70-155, "Designing and Implementing Distributed Applications with Microsoft Visual FoxPro 6.0"

OR

70-175, "Designing and Implementing Distributed Applications with Microsoft Visual Basic 6.0"

► 70-100, "Analyzing Requirements and Defining Solution Architectures"

MCSD Old Track Elective Exams

You must pass one of the following elective exams to earn credit toward the MCSD certification:

► 70-015, "Designing and Implementing Distributed Applications with Microsoft Visual C++ 6.0"

► 70-016, "Designing and Implementing Desktop Applications with Microsoft Visual C++ 6.0"

► 70-019, "Designing and Implementing Data Warehouses with Microsoft SQL Server 7.0"

► 70-029, "Implementing a Database Design on Microsoft SQL Server 7.0"

► 70-057, "Designing and Implementing Commerce Solutions with Microsoft Site Server 3.0, Commerce Edition"*

► 70-091, "Designing and Implementing Solutions with Microsoft Office 2000 and Microsoft Visual Basic for Applications"*

► 70-105, "Designing and Implementing Collaborative Solutions with Microsoft Outlook 2000 and Microsoft Exchange Server 5.5"

► 70-152, "Designing and Implementing Web Solutions with Microsoft Visual InterDev 6.0"

► 70-155, "Designing and Implementing Distributed Applications with Microsoft Visual FoxPro 6.0"

► 70-156, "Designing and Implementing Desktop Applications with Microsoft Visual FoxPro 6.0"

► 70-175, "Designing and Implementing Distributed Applications with Microsoft Visual Basic 6.0"

► 70-176, "Designing and Implementing Desktop Applications with Microsoft Visual Basic 6.0"

▶ 70-229, "Designing and Implementing Databases with Microsoft SQL Server 2000 Enterprise Edition"

▶ 70-230, "Designing and Implementing Solutions with Microsoft BizTalk Server 2000 Enterprise Edition"

▶ 70-234, "Designing and Implementing Solutions with Microsoft Commerce Server 2000"

To obtain MCSD certification, you cannot count the same exam as both a core exam and an elective exam.

How to Become an MCDBA

You must pass three core exams and one elective exam to earn MCDBA certification.

The following lists show the core requirements and the electives that you can take to earn MCDBA certification.

MCDBA Core Exams

You must pass the following three core exams to earn credit toward the MCDBA certification:

▶ 70-028, "Administering SQL Server 7.0"

OR

70-228, "Installing, Configuring, and Administering Microsoft SQL Server 2000 Enterprise Edition"

▶ 70-029, "Designing and Implementing Databases with Microsoft SQL Server 7.0"

OR

70-229, "Designing and Implementing Databases with Microsoft SQL Server 2000 Enterprise Edition"

▶ 70-215, "Installing, Configuring, and Administering Microsoft Windows 2000 Server"

OR

70-275, "Installing, Configuring, and Administering Microsoft Windows .NET Enterprise Server"

MCDBA Elective Exams

You must pass one of these elective exams to earn credit toward the MCDBA certification:

▶ 70-015, "Designing and Implementing Distributed Applications with Microsoft Visual C++ 6.0"

▶ 70-019, "Designing and Implementing Data Warehouses with Microsoft SQL Server 7.0"

▶ 70-155, "Designing and Implementing Distributed Applications with Microsoft Visual FoxPro 6.0"

▶ 70-175, "Designing and Implementing Distributed Applications with Microsoft Visual Basic 6.0"

▶ 70-216, "Implementing and Administering a Microsoft Windows 2000 Network Infrastructure"

▶ 70-276, "Implementing and Administering a Microsoft .NET Server Network Infrastructure"

▶ 70-305, "Developing and Implementing Web Applications with Microsoft Visual Basic .NET and Microsoft Visual Studio .NET"

▶ 70-306, "Developing and Implementing Windows-Based Applications with Microsoft Visual Basic .NET and Microsoft Visual Studio .NET"

- ▶ 70-310, "Designing XML Web Services and Server Components with Microsoft Visual Basic .NET and the Microsoft .NET Framework"

- ▶ 70-315, "Developing and Implementing Web Applications with Microsoft Visual C# .NET and Microsoft Visual Studio .NET"

- ▶ 70-316, "Developing and Implementing Windows-based Applications with Microsoft Visual C# .NET and Microsoft Visual Studio .NET"

- ▶ 70-320, "Designing XML Web Services and Server Components with Microsoft Visual C# .NET and the Microsoft .NET Framework"

How to Become an MCT

To understand the requirements and process for becoming an MCT, you need to obtain the MCT Program Guide document from the following Web site:

www.microsoft.com/traincert/mcp/mct/guide

The MCT Program Guide explains the four-step process of becoming a MCT. The general steps for the MCT certification are as follows:

1. Obtain one of the Microsoft premier certifications: MCSE, MCSD, or MCDBA.

2. Attend a classroom presentation of a Microsoft course taught by a Microsoft Certified Trainer at a Microsoft Certified Technical Education Center (CTEC).

3. Demonstrate instructional presentation skills by attending a Train-the-Trainer course or by providing proof of experience in technical training.

4. Complete the MCT application, which you can fill out on the MCT Web site.

What's on the
CD-ROM

This appendix provides a brief summary of what you'll find on the CD-ROM that accompanies this book. For a more detailed description of the PrepLogic Practice Tests, Preview Edition, exam simulation software, see Appendix F, "Using the PrepLogic, Preview Edition, Software." In addition to the PrepLogic Practice Tests, Preview Edition, software, the CD-ROM includes an electronic version of the book, in Portable Document Format (PDF), and the source code used in the book.

THE *PREPLOGIC PRACTICE TESTS, PREVIEW EDITION*

PrepLogic is a leading provider of certification training tools. Trusted by certification students worldwide, PrepLogic is the best practice exam software available. In addition to providing a means of evaluating your knowledge of this book's material, PrepLogic Practice Tests, Preview Edition, features several innovations that help you improve your mastery of the subject matter.

For example, the practice tests enable you to check your score by exam area or domain, to determine which topics you need to study more. Another feature allows you to obtain immediate feedback on your responses, in the form of explanations for the correct and incorrect answers.

PrepLogic Practice Tests, Preview Edition, exhibits most of the full functionality of the Premium Edition but offers only a fraction of the total questions. To get the complete set of practice questions and exam functionality, visit www.preplogic.com and order the Premium Edition for this and other challenging exam training guides.

For a more detailed description of the features of the PrepLogic Practice Tests, Preview Edition, see Appendix F.

AN EXCLUSIVE ELECTRONIC VERSION OF THE TEXT

The CD-ROM also contains an electronic PDF version of this book. This electronic version comes complete with all figures as they appear in the book. You will find that the search capability of the reader is handy for study and review purposes.

COMPLETE CODE SAMPLES

You'll find the complete source code for every Step-by-Step, Guided Practice Exercise, and Exercise for the book on the CD. Just open any of the solution files in your copy of Visual Studio .NET and you'll be ready to follow along with the text.

Using the *PrepLogic, Preview Edition* Software

This book includes a special version of the PrepLogic Practice Tests software, which is a revolutionary test engine designed to give you the best in certification exam preparation. PrepLogic offers sample and practice exams for many of today's most in-demand and challenging technical certifications. A special Preview Edition of the PrepLogic Practice Tests software is included with this book as a tool to use in assessing your knowledge of the training guide material while also providing you with the experience of taking an electronic exam.

This appendix describes in detail what PrepLogic Practice Tests, Preview Edition, is, how it works, and what it can do to help you prepare for the exam. Note that although the Preview Edition includes all the test simulation functions of the complete, retail version, it contains only a single practice test. The Premium Edition, available at www.preplogic.com, contains the complete set of challenging practice exams designed to optimize your learning experience.

THE EXAM SIMULATION

One of the main functions of PrepLogic Practice Tests, Preview Edition, is exam simulation. To prepare you to take the actual vendor certification exam, PrepLogic is designed to offer the most effective exam simulation available.

QUESTION QUALITY

The questions provided in the PrepLogic Practice Tests, Preview Edition, are written to the highest standards of technical accuracy. The questions tap the content of this book's chapters and help you review and assess your knowledge before you take the actual exam.

THE INTERFACE DESIGN

The PrepLogic Practice Tests, Preview Edition, exam simulation interface provides you with the experience of taking an electronic exam. This enables you to effectively prepare to take the actual exam by making the test experience familiar. Using this test simulation can help eliminate the sense of surprise or anxiety you might experience in the testing center because you will already be acquainted with computerized testing.

THE EFFECTIVE LEARNING ENVIRONMENT

The PrepLogic Practice Tests, Preview Edition, interface provides a learning environment that not only tests you through the computer but also teaches the material you need to know to pass the certification exam. Each question includes a detailed explanation of the correct answer, and most of these explanations provide reasons as to why the other answers are incorrect. This information helps to reinforce the knowledge you already have and also provides practical information you can use on the job.

SOFTWARE REQUIREMENTS

PrepLogic Practice Tests requires a computer with the following:

- ▶ Microsoft Windows 98, Windows ME, Windows NT 4.0, Windows 2000, or Windows XP

- ▶ A 166MHz or faster processor

- ▶ A minimum of 32MB of RAM

> **NOTE** As with any Windows application, the more memory, the better the performance.

- ▶ 10MB of hard drive space

INSTALLING *PREPLOGIC PRACTICE TESTS, PREVIEW EDITION*

You can install PrepLogic Practice Tests, Preview Edition, by following these steps:

1. Insert the PrepLogic Practice Tests, Preview Edition, CD into your CD-ROM drive. The Autorun feature of Windows should launch the software. If you have Autorun disabled, select Start, Run. Go to the root directory of the CD and select setup.exe. Click Open, and then click OK.

2. The Installation Wizard copies the PrepLogic Practice Tests, Preview Edition, files to your hard drive. It then adds PrepLogic Practice Tests, Preview Edition, to your Desktop and the Program menu. Finally, it installs test engine components to the appropriate system folders.

REMOVING *PREPLOGIC PRACTICE TESTS, PREVIEW EDITION* FROM YOUR COMPUTER

If you elect to remove the PrepLogic Practice Tests, Preview Edition, you can use the included uninstall process to ensure that it is removed from your system safely and completely. Follow these instructions to remove PrepLogic Practice Tests, Preview Edition, from your computer:

1. Select Start, Settings, Control Panel.

2. Double-click the Add/Remove Programs icon. You are presented with a list of software installed on your computer.

3. Select the PrepLogic Practice Tests, Preview Edition, title you want to remove. Click the Add/Remove button. The software is removed from you computer.

USING *PREPLOGIC PRACTICE TESTS, PREVIEW EDITION*

PrepLogic is designed to be user friendly and intuitive. Because the software has a smooth learning curve, your time is maximized because you start practicing with it almost immediately. PrepLogic Practice Tests, Preview Edition, has two major modes of study: Practice Test and Flash Review.

Using Practice Test mode, you can develop your test-taking abilities as well as your knowledge through the use of the Show Answer option. While you are taking the test, you can expose the answers along with a detailed explanation of why the given answers are right or wrong. This enables you to better understand the material presented.

Flash Review mode is designed to reinforce exam topics rather than quiz you. In this mode, you are shown a series of questions but no answer choices. Instead, you can click a button that reveals the correct answer to the question and a full explanation for that answer.

Starting a Practice Test Mode Session

Practice Test mode enables you to control the exam experience in ways that actual certification exams do not allow. To begin studying in Practice Test mode, click the Practice Test radio button from the main exam customization screen. This enables the following options:

▶ **The Enable Show Answer button.** Clicking this button activates the Show Answer button, which allows you to view the correct answer(s) and full explanation for each question during the exam. When this option is not enabled, you must wait until after your exam has been graded to view the correct answer(s) and explanation.

▶ **The Enable Item Review button.** Clicking this button activates the Item Review button, which allows you to view your answer choices. This option also facilitates navigation between questions.

▶ **The Randomize Choices option.** You can randomize answer choices from one exam session to the next. This makes memorizing question choices more difficult, thereby keeping questions fresh and challenging longer.

To your left, you are presented with the option of selecting the preconfigured practice test or creating your own custom test. The preconfigured test has a fixed time limit and number of questions. Custom tests enable you to configure the time limit and the number of questions on your exam.

The Preview Edition on this book's CD includes a single preconfigured practice test. You can get the compete set of challenging PrepLogic Practice Tests at www. preplogic.com to make certain you're ready for the big exam.

Click the Begin Exam button to begin your exam.

Starting a Flash Review Mode Session

Flash Review mode provides an easy way to reinforce topics covered in the practice questions. To begin studying in Flash Review mode, click the Flash Review radio button from the main exam customization screen. Select either the preconfigured practice test or create your own custom test.

Click the Best Exam button to begin your Flash Review mode session with the exam questions.

Standard *PrepLogic Practice Tests, Preview Edition* Options

The following list describes the function of each of the buttons you see:

> NOTE
>
> Depending on the options, some of the buttons are grayed out and inaccessible—or they might be missing completely. Buttons that are appropriate are active.

- ▶ **Exhibit.** This button is visible if an exhibit is provided to support the question. An *exhibit* is an image that provides supplemental information that is necessary to answer the question.

- ▶ **Item Review.** This button leaves the question window and opens the Item Review screen. From this screen you can see all questions, your answers, and your marked items. You can also see correct answers listed here, when appropriate.

- ▶ **Show Answer.** This option displays the correct answer, with an explanation about why it is correct. If you select this option, the current question is not scored.

- ▶ **Mark Item.** You can check this box to flag a question that you need to review further. You can view and navigate your marked items by clicking the Item Review button (if it is enabled). When grading your exam, you are notified if you have marked items remaining.

- ▶ **Previous Item.** You can use this option to view the previous question.

- ▶ **Next Item.** You can use this option to view the next question.

- ▶ **Grade Exam.** When you have completed your exam, you can click to end your exam and view your detailed score report. If you have unanswered or marked items remaining, you are asked whether you would like to continue taking your exam or view the exam report.

Seeing Time Remaining

If the test is timed, the time remaining is displayed on the upper-right corner of the application screen. It counts down minutes and seconds remaining to complete the test. If you run out of time, you are asked whether you want to continue taking the test or end your exam.

Getting Your Examination Score Report

The Examination Score Report screen appears when the Practice Test mode ends—as a result of time expiration, completion of all questions, or your decision to terminate early.

This screen provides a graphical display of your test score, with a breakdown of scores by topic. The graphical display at the top of the screen compares your overall score with the PrepLogic Exam Competency Score. The PrepLogic Exam Competency Score reflects the level of subject competency required to pass the particular vendor's exam. Although this score does not directly translate to a passing score, consistently matching or exceeding this score does suggest that you possess the knowledge needed to pass the actual vendor exam.

Reviewing Your Exam

From the Your Score Report screen, you can review the exam that you just completed by clicking on the View Items button. Navigate through the items, viewing the questions, your answers, the correct answers, and the explanations for those questions. You can return to your score report by clicking the View Items button.

CONTACTING PREPLOGIC

If you would like to contact PrepLogic for any reason, including to get information about its extensive line of certification practice tests, please contact PrepLogic online at `www.preplogic.com`.

Customer Service

If you have a damaged product and need service, please call the following phone number:

   800-858-7674

Product Suggestions and Comments

We value your input! Please email your suggestions and comments to the following address:

`feedback@preplogic.com`

LICENSE AGREEMENT

YOU MUST AGREE TO THE TERMS AND CONDITIONS OUTLINED IN THE END USER LICENSE AGREEMENT ("EULA") PRESENTED TO YOU DURING THE INSTALLATION PROCESS. IF YOU DO NOT AGREE TO THESE TERMS DO NOT INSTALL THE SOFTWARE.

Suggested Readings and Resources

.NET USER ASSISTANCE

Your first source for help with any aspect of Visual Studio .NET should be the user assistance resources that Microsoft ships with their .NET products. These include:

► **.NET Framework Documentation**—All the classes, methods, properties, and other members of the .NET Framework Base Class Library are documented in this help file. This file is installed by the .NET Software Development Kit (SDK), and is also integrated into the Visual Studio .NET help file.

► **Visual Studio .NET Documentation**—This file includes help on all aspects of the Visual Studio interface, as well as a series of walkthroughs and samples that you can refer to for examples of using particular pieces of code.

► **Samples and QuickStart Tutorials**—These are installed by the .NET Framework SDK and are available through Start, Programs, Microsoft .NET Framework SDK, Samples, QuickStart Tutorials. This set of HTML pages shows examples of many aspects of the .NET Framework in both Visual C# .NET and Visual Basic .NET, and includes links to both working copies and source code for each example.

BOOKS

Adam Nathan. *.NET AND COM: The Complete Interoperability Guide.* Sams, 2002.

Andrew Troelsen. *COM and .NET Interoperability.* Apress, 2002.

Andrew Troelsen. *C# and the .NET Platform.* Apress, 2001.

Ben Albahari, Peter Drayton, & Brad Merrill. *C# Essentials.* O'Reilly, 2002

Bob Beauchemin. *Essential ADO.NET.* Addison Wesley, 2002.

Brian A. LaMacchia, et al. *.NET Framework Security.* Addison-Wesley, 2002.

Dan Wahlin. *XML For ASP.NET Developers.* Sams, 2002.

David Chappell. *Understanding .NET.* Addison Wesley, 2001.

David Sceppa. *Microsoft ADO.NET (Core Reference).* Microsoft Press, 2002.

Dietel. *C# How to Program.* Prentice Hall, 2001.

Derek Beyer. *C# COM+ Programming.* M&T Books, 2001.

Don Box. *Essential .NET Vol.1: The Common Language Runtime.* Addison Wesley, 2002.

Eric Newcomer. *Understanding Web Services: XML, WSDL, SOAP, and UDDI.* Addison Wesley, 2002.

Ingo Rammer. *Advanced .NET Remoting.* Apress, 2002.

Jeffery Ritcher. *Applied Microsoft .NET Framework Programming.* Microsoft Press, 2001.

John E. Simpson. *XPath and XPointer.* O'Reilly, 2002.

John Griffin. *XML and SQL Server.* New Riders, 2001.

Juval Lowy. *COM and .NET Component Services.* O'Reilly, 2001.

Kalen Delaney. *Inside SQL Server 2000.* Microsoft Press, 2000.

Kenn Scribner and Mark C. Stiver. *Applied SOAP: Implementing .NET XML Web Services.* Sams, 2001.

Kevin Burton. *.NET Common Language Runtime Unleashed.* Sams, 2002.

Mike Gunderloy. *ADO and ADO.NET Programming.* Sybex, 2002.

Richard Grimes. *Developing Applications with Visual Studio .NET.* Addison Wesley, 2002.

Roger Jennings. *Visual C# .NET XML Web Services Developer's Guide.* McGraw-Hill/Osborne, 2002.

Roger Sessions. *COM+ and the Battle for the Middle Tier.* John Wiley & Sons, Inc. 2000.

Scott Short. *Building XML Web Services for the Microsoft .NET Platform.* Microsoft Press, 2002.

William Oellerman. *Architecting Web Services.* Apress, 2002.

WEB SITES

`msdn.microsoft.com/net`   The MSDN Web site contains extensive technical documentation on all aspects of .NET development.

`msdn.microsoft.com/vs/techinfo`   The Visual Studio .NET Developer Center will keep you up to date on the latest headlines, code samples, and information related to using Visual Studio .NET to develop applications.

`msdn.microsoft.com/architecture`   The .NET Architecture Center contains a wealth of information on best practices for designing distributed .NET applications.

`msdn.microsoft.com/theshow`   The .NET Show keeps you up to date on the cutting-edge technologies for Windows and Web applications.

`support.microsoft.com/webcasts`   Microsoft Support WebCasts is a free Internet broadcast service that often presents live technical presentations on .NET- and ASP.NET- related topics. Each presentation is followed by a live Q&A session. Through this URL you can access archives of the past presentations and register for future presentations.

`www.windowsforms.net`   WindowsForms.Net is a Microsoft-sponsored community Web site that includes downloads and tools, samples, and user-contributed code for developing Windows forms applications.

`www.asp.net`   The ASP.NET site is a Microsoft-sponsored community Web site that focuses specifically on ASP.NET. You can find ASP.NET-related discussions, samples, and user-contributed code for developing ASP.NET applications.

`www.gotdotnet.com`   The GotDotNet site is a Microsoft-sponsored community Web site that includes downloads and tools, samples, and user-contributed code.

`www.syncfusion.com/FAQ/winforms`   The Windows Forms FAQ site is an excellent compilation of frequently asked questions and answers from various Windows forms–related newsgroups and mailing lists.

`discuss.develop.com`   DevelopMentor' discussion Web site hosts a number of mailing lists for .NET related discussions.

`msdn.microsoft.com/net/ecma`   The `MSDN` ECMA page contains ECMA C# and Common Language Infrastructure Standards specification documents.

`groups.google.com`   Google Groups contains the entire archive of Usenet discussion groups. Many of these discussion groups are for Microsoft .NET and related topics. You can use this Web site to get troubleshooting help either by reading the archives or by posting messages to the relevant discussion groups.

Index

SYMBOLS

A

C

C#, 615-616
CAB (cabinet) files, 733
CAB (cabinet) Project template (Setup and Deployment projects), 733
CacheDuration property (WebMethod attribute), 304
Call Stack window (Visual C# .NET), 637
callback delegates, asynchronous Web methods, 350-352
CAO (client-activated objects), 196-197
  Abstract Factories, 252-255
  creating, 218
  instantiating, 220-223
  interface assemblies, 248-249
  invoking, 221-223
  lifetime leases, 198-199
  registering remotable classes as CAO, 218-219
  soapsuds.exe, 248
  versus SAO (server-activated objects), 197-198
CCW (COM Callable Wrappers), 451
  .NET component interfaces, 475
  type libraries, 452-453
channels
  http channels, 190-193
  IChannelReceiver interface, 189
  port numbers, 189
  remoting client channels, 207, 220
  server channels, 203
  TCP channels, 190-193
class interfaces, creating, 479
classes
  BooleanSwitch classes, 612
  ConditionalAttribute classes, 616
  ContextUtil class (System.EnterpriseServices namespace), 463-464
  Debug classes
    displaying debugging information, 605-607
    properties/methods, 604
    trace listeners, 608-611
    tracing, 602-603
  EventLog class, 656-657
  FileSystemWatcher component, methods, 403-404
  http channel classes, 190
  Installer class
    installing Windows services, 405-409
    properties/methods, 750-752
  Page class, 622

PerformanceCounter class, 663
PrincipalPermission class, 822-823
ProjectInstaller class, 407, 753
proxy classes, 358
RegistrationHelper class (FCL), 471
remotable classes
  creating, 201-202, 263-264
  hosting via IIS, 264-265
  IIS, 256
  registering, 203, 207
  registering as CAO (client-activated objects), 218-219
  registering as SAO (server-activated objects), 204-206, 212-214
ServiceBase classes, 395-399
ServiceController class, 395, 419-426
ServicedComponent Class, 455
ServiceInstaller class, 395, 405-407
ServiceProcessInstaller class, 395, 405-406
TCP channel classes, 190-191
trace classes, 602-603
  displaying debugging information, 605-607
  properties/methods, 604
  trace listeners, 608-611
TraceContext class, 621-622
TraceSwitch classes, 612-615
versus components, 455
XmlDataDocument class, 110, 113, 116-118
XmlDocument class, 105-109
XmlNode class, 103-107
XmlReader class, 96-97
XmlTextReader class, 97-101
XmlValidatingReader class, 139-141, 145
XPathNavigator class, 127-132
ClassInterface attribute (System.Runtime.InteropServices namespace), 476-481
clauses, 52, 147-152
client order forms, 538-540, 545-547
client-side scripts, debugging, 647-648
client-side SOAP extensions, writing, 343-348
closing tags, XML documents, 944
CLR (Common Language Runtime), 181, 449
  application domains
    boundaries, 181
    creating, 182
    .NET remoting, 185-214, 218-223, 226-232, 237-244, 248-249, 252-255
  assemblies, 687, 692-695, 712-716
  permissions, 789

binding log files, 698
CAB (cabinet) files, 733
copying
   deploying Web services, 737-739
   packaging applications, 729-730
DLL files, COM+ (Component Object Model+), 459
GAC (global assembly cache) files, deleting, 706
mscoree.dll files, assembly registration process, 451
publisher policy configuration files, 722-723
XML files, 94-109
FileSystemWatcher components, 403-404
filling DataSet objects (ADO.NET), 918-919
filtering data via DataView Object (ADO.NET DataSet objects), 931-932
filtering functions (XPath), 124
finding
   DataSet object data (ADO.NET), 928-931
   .NET components via COM+ (Component Object Model+), 450-452
fine tuning applications, 507
FOR XML clause, 147-152
formatting
   bare parameters, 366-368
   binary formatters, 192-193
   encoded parameter formatting, 362-364
   literal parameter formatting
      versus encoded parameter formatting, 364
      Web services, 359-362
   RPC-style body formatting, 364-366
   SOAP formatters, 192-193
   SQL (Structured Query Language) statements, 46
   wrapped parameters, 366-368
   XML in Query Analyzer, 147
   XmlElement attribute, Web services, 368-370
Forms (Windows), DataGrid control, 926-927
Forms authentication, 811-813

G

GAC (global assembly cache), 440, 451, 700, 705-709
generating
   interface assemblies, soapsuds.exe, 244-247
   XSD (XML Schema Definition) schemas, 133, 136-139
GetInitializer() method, SOAP extensions, 338
Global Assembly Cache Tool, 708
granting permissions, .NET Framework Configuration Tool, 795

GUID
   assembly registration process, 450
   COM+ (Component Object Model+) applications, identifying, 482-483

H

hosting remotable classes via IIS, 264-265
HTTP channels
   classes, 190
   SOAP formatters, 193
   versus TCP channels, 191
http server channels, creating/registering, 203

I

IasyncResult.IsCompleted property, asynchronous Web methods, 353
IChannelReceiver interface (channels), 189
IDbConnect Object Abstract Factories, interface assemblies, 249-250
identifying
   COM+ (Component Object Model+) applications, 482-483
   serviced components, 482-483
   XPath attributes, 123
   XPath elements, 122
identity columns, SQL (Structured Query Language) servers, 71
identity permissions, 790
IIdentity, 818
IIS
   .NET remoting, 256-257
   authentication, 806-810
   IIS-hosted remote objects, instantiating/invoking, 258-260
   remotable classes, 256, 264-265
   settings, configuring, 743
ILease interface, 198-199
Immediate window (Visual C# .NET), 638
imperative security, 796-798
impersonation
   implementing, 814-817
   scalability, 827
   Web service security, 826
incremental testing, 598-600
inferring XML schemas, 138

J – K

unit testing, 598-599
unmanaged code
    COM components, 567
    PInvoke (Platform Invoke), 578-580
UPDATE statements (T-SQL), 44, 61-62
updating
    data via ADO.NET, 933-935
    SQL servers via XML (Extensible Markup Language),
        154-159
    Windows Installer, 732
URL authorization, Web services, 826
URL membership conditions (code groups), 794
User accounts (ServiceAccount enumerations), 824
User Interface Editor (Visual Studio .NET), customizing
    Setup and Deployment projects, 735
user interfaces, Windows services, 390

V

validating XML documents, 139
    against DTD (Document Type Definition), 144-146
    against external schemas, 141-144
    against inline schemas, 140-141
    XmlValidatingReader class, 141, 145
variables, 71-76
verifying role membership, 820-821
versioning
    ClassInterface attribute (System.Runtime.InteropServices
        namespace), 480-481
    components, AssemblyVersion attribute, 485
    private assemblies, 695
    shared assemblies, 704, 716-722
viewing failed assembly binds, Assembly Binding Log Viewer
    tool (.NET Framework), 696-698
Visual C# .NET
    Autos window, 638
    Call Stack window, 637
    Command window, 639
    Debug configuration, 602-603
    declarative tags, 455
    Immediate window, 638
    Locals window, 638
    Release configuration, tracing, 603
    This window, 637
    Trace configuration, compiling programs, 603

T-SQL (Transact-Structured Query Language) queries,
    running, 50-51
Watch window, 639
Visual Studio .NET
    client-side scripts, debugging, 647-648
    COM components, 572-574
    Copy Project command, deploying Web services, 740
    cross-language debugging, 640
    Custom Actions Editor, customizing Setup and Deployment
        projects, 735
    Debug menu, 631
    Debugging, 630
    File System Editor, customizing Setup and Deployment
        projects, 734
    File Types Editor, customizing Setup and Deployment
        projects, 735
    Launch Conditions Editor, customizing Setup and
        Deployment projects, 735
    Registry Editor, customizing Setup and Deployment projects,
        734
    Setup and Deployment projects, 732
        CAB (cabinet) Project template, 733
        customizing, 734-735
        deploying serviced components, 760-765
        launching editors, 736
        Merge Module Project template, 733
        Merge Module Projects, creating, 769-770
        Setup Project template, 732
        Web Setup Project template, 733, 741-747
        Web Setup Projects, creating, 770
    Setup Wizard, 732
    User Interface Editor, customizing Setup and Deployment
        projects, 735
    Windows service applications, creating, 407-409
    Windows services
        creating applications, 407-409
        debugging, 648-650
Visual Studio .NET IDE, 45-46
Visual Studio .NET Server Explorer
    performance counters, 662
    Windows services, controlling, 416-417
.vsdisco (dynamic discovery) files, 312

W

X

informIT